Between Figure and Ground:
Seeing in Premodernity

Between Figure and Ground: Seeing in Premodernity

Edited by Saskia C. Quené

Deutscher
Kunstverlag

The Open Access version and the pre-press of this publication were supported by the Swiss National Science Foundation for the promotion of scientific research.

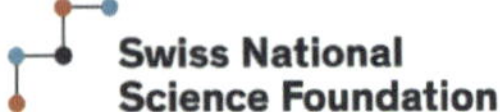

The printed version of this publication was supported by the Geschwister Boehringer Ingelheim Stiftung für Geisteswissenschaften, the Tübinger Kunstgeschichtliche Gesellschaft e.V., the Universitätsbund Tübingen, and the Karl-Jaberg-Stiftung Bern.

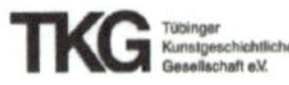

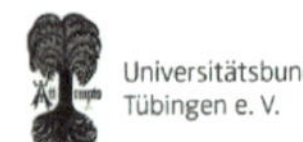

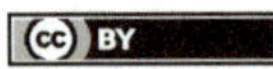

Library of Congress Control Number:
2024936916

Bibliographic information published by the Deutsche Nationalbibliothek
The Deutsche Nationalbibliothek lists this publication in the Deutsche Nationalbibliografie; detailed bibliographic data are available on the internet at http://dnb.dnb.de.

Graphic design and typesetting:
Dorothee Dähler, Kaj Lehmann

Printing and binding:
Beltz Grafische Betriebe, Bad Langensalza

ISBN: 978-3-422-80121-9
e-ISBN (PDF): 978-3-422-80122-6
DOI: https://doi.org/10.1515/9783422801226

www.deutscherkunstverlag.de
www.degruyter.com

Questions about General Product Safety Regulation productsafety@degruyterbrill.com

Table of Contents

Part 1
Staging Figures

Part 3
Beyond the Surface

Part 4
Navigating Dichotomies

Part 5
Transgressing Depth

Sharing Ground: An Introduction in Conversation with David Young Kim

Saskia C. Quené

11

During the final dinner of our conference *Between Figure and Ground: Seeing in Premodernity* in June 2022 at eikones – Center for the Theory and History of the Image in Basel, Switzerland, we moved aside our plates and glasses and started drawing charts on the paper placemats in front of us. In the left column, we collected terms for "figure" in different languages, like "figure" and "*imago*," "image," "*Bild*," "*Abbild*," "*figura*," and "*Figur*." In the right, we added "*Grund*" and "*campo*," "*Feld*" and "field," "plane" and "*piano*." In the middle column, references to phenomena, artifacts, and concepts that subversively undermined the stated dichotomy soon covered surfaces. Lines and arrows started to connect terms and ideas across languages, delineating an interdisciplinary network of backgrounds, heritages, and presumptions. After three days of challenging paper presentations and intense discussions, we stared puzzled at the dense diagrams in our midst. Because only moments before, we had thought that we could solve the riddle once and for all and provide the next generation with a clear display of how to employ these terms in their historical, phenomenological, and philosophical settings. Instead, we realized, as so often, that the conference had shed light on a barren field of land that was deeper and more complex than we could have envisioned three days prior.

In the following months, however, I still aimed at writing an introduction in which I would explain what the terms "figure" and "ground" in their different configurations and historical contexts mean, what they refer to, how they were used, and why they became fundamental to art critique, art-historical scholarship, and academic writing over the course of the twentieth century. Then, I would argue to what extent the figure/ground dichotomy is unsuited to describe premodern art, referring to articles in this volume that exemplify, critique, and expand vocabularies used to describe, analyze, and interpret artifacts. In that way, I would have laid the ground to productively revise anachronistic attachments to paradigms, drawing attention to what can be seen and described between picture planes and pictorial spaces and thus *between* figure and ground. But then I did not write that introduction.

First of all, my introduction would have awkwardly questioned the very purpose of this volume. It would have contradicted everything I had discovered about figures and grounds. Edgar

Rubin's famous vase can be perceived as two profiles facing each other and relies on its sharp black-and-white contrasts [fig. 380]. But this contrast between figure and ground does not map neatly onto any premodern artifact within my scope. My undertaking to find a blueprint with more shades of gray, which would have merely replaced Rubin's gestalt, would have defeated our efforts. The clarity I aimed to gain by emphasizing differences and contrasts became as appealing as it unveiled itself as dangerously simplifying and void.

So why not get rid of "figure" and "ground" altogether? Why not leave it all behind to go *beyond* figure and ground? Why still look for what can be explored in that narrow place *between* figures and grounds? Why still try to detangle that web of lines and arrows on that placemat in front of us? Why *do* we have to talk about "figure and ground," despite all good reasons not to? When David Young Kim and I started tackling this question in our post-conference online conversations in January 2023, we sourced answers to questions that had been hiding under the surface of our visible scholarly interests. Why were *we* looking at that narrow place *between* figures and grounds?

Around the same time, the articles for this volume started arriving in my email inbox, and they felt more relevant than ever before. Focusing on singular images and examples, every close reading or material analysis coping with figure and ground proved that there were plenty of alternatives to simply erasing these terms. Artifacts shifted their power and meaning dramatically because we had started looking more consciously and had resisted being fooled by language's implications, tackling modern *Begriffs-geschichten*. These texts didn't address a mere art-historiographical or methodological problem: Simply by asking what could be seen and described "between figure and ground," they revised anach-ronisms as much as they solved theoretical problems lying at the heart of medieval, (early) modern, and contemporary discourses.

Along those lines and apart from "figure and ground," two more pairs of terms pushed to the forefront during the prepara-tion of this volume: "*Fläche und Raum*," and "space and plane." In reading through first drafts of papers, I noticed how figures started to shift from being described as shapes or forms on surfaces to elements within pictorial, virtual, or real spaces, and back again.

Walking through the Getty Museum in Los Angeles a few months earlier, I was struck by a painting by Gerolamo Savoldo depicting Mary Magdalene [fig. 15]. She was looking at me from the opposite wall, curious and startled, self-consciously mourning her loss while hiding in a most precious golden silk fabric. I was stunned, not in the first place by the so-called aesthetic experience but by the idea that this figure that had taken off the gilded cloth of honor from behind her and had wrapped herself into a gold ground. When I walked closer, I observed that even the squares of gold leaf that can be seen in panel paintings had become neat, squared creases in the depicted silk [fig. 16]. Excited because this painting would be a nice addition to the very problematic narrative that tries to tell the story of the disappearance of the gold ground in the fifteenth and sixteenth centuries, merely treating it as a static ground in the most modern sense of the word, I was even more stunned by the fact that, most literally, the ground had become the figure.

The question of what can be seen between figure and ground challenges the distinction between the modernist picture plane and pictorial space. Medieval theories of the image since at least Athanasius of Alexandria's Third Discourse against the Arians written in the fourth century discuss the status of the image as, for example, being identical, similar, or different to or from the depicted subject, precisely because the image appears to be an artifact. Accordingly, artifacts had to negotiate their relationship toward experience as well as toward the imaginative throughout the centuries. Considering premodern space as neither infinite nor empty, geometrical exercises on surfaces (which can be perspectival) visualize distances between marks or figures. The place of ground is, therefore, necessarily ambivalent and relates to spatial configurations as well as to the surface on which marks are placed. However, the premodern ground can never be equivalent to the picture plane or *Bildfläche*, nor to space in the modern sense of the word, neither within the depicted pictorial space or the *Bildraum*. The premodern image is, at last, present *and* represented between figure and ground.

Gerolamo Savoldo painted at least three more versions of his Mary Magdalene, which are now in Berlin, Florence, and London [fig. 18–21]. Making use of the possibility to compare

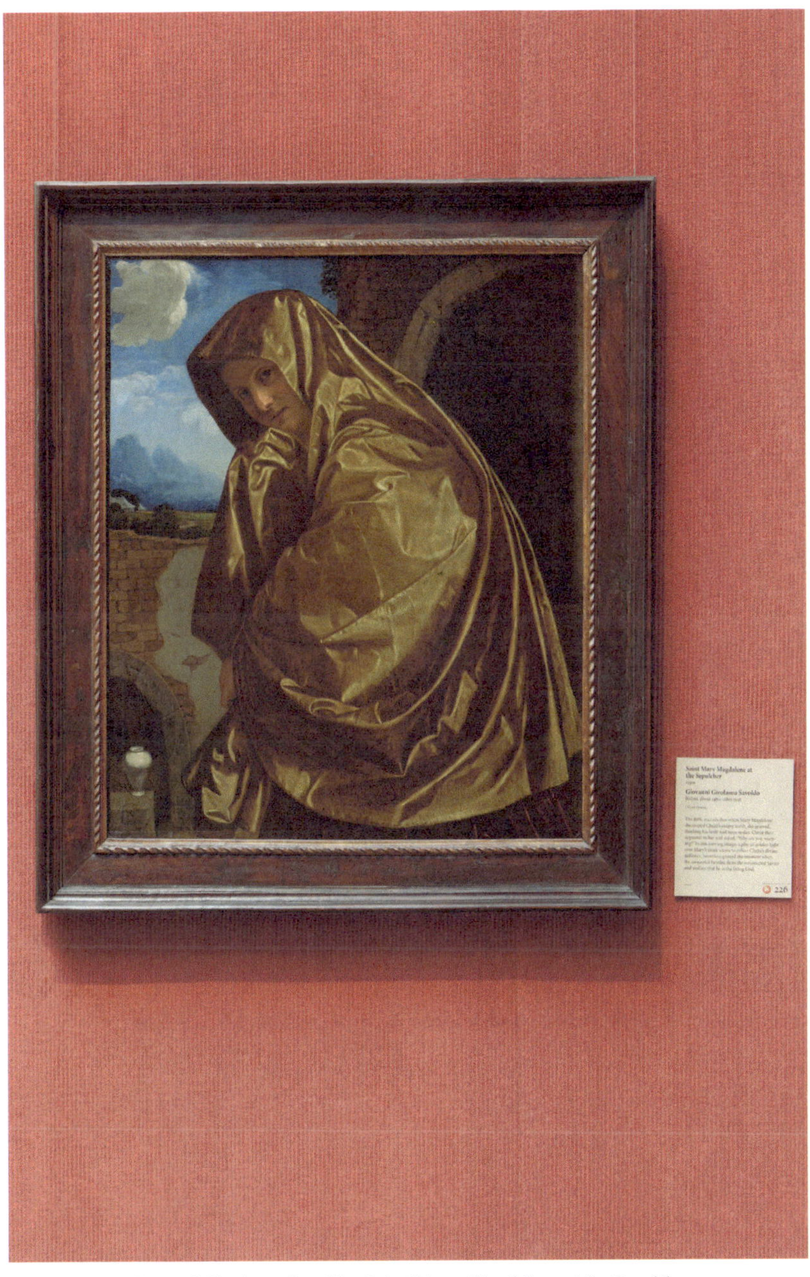

Giovanni Girolamo Savoldo, *Saint Mary Magdalene at the Sepulchre*,
ca. 1530–1540, oil on canvas, 92.7 × 79.4 cm.
J. Paul Getty Museum, inv. 97.PA.55, Los Angeles.

Fig. 15

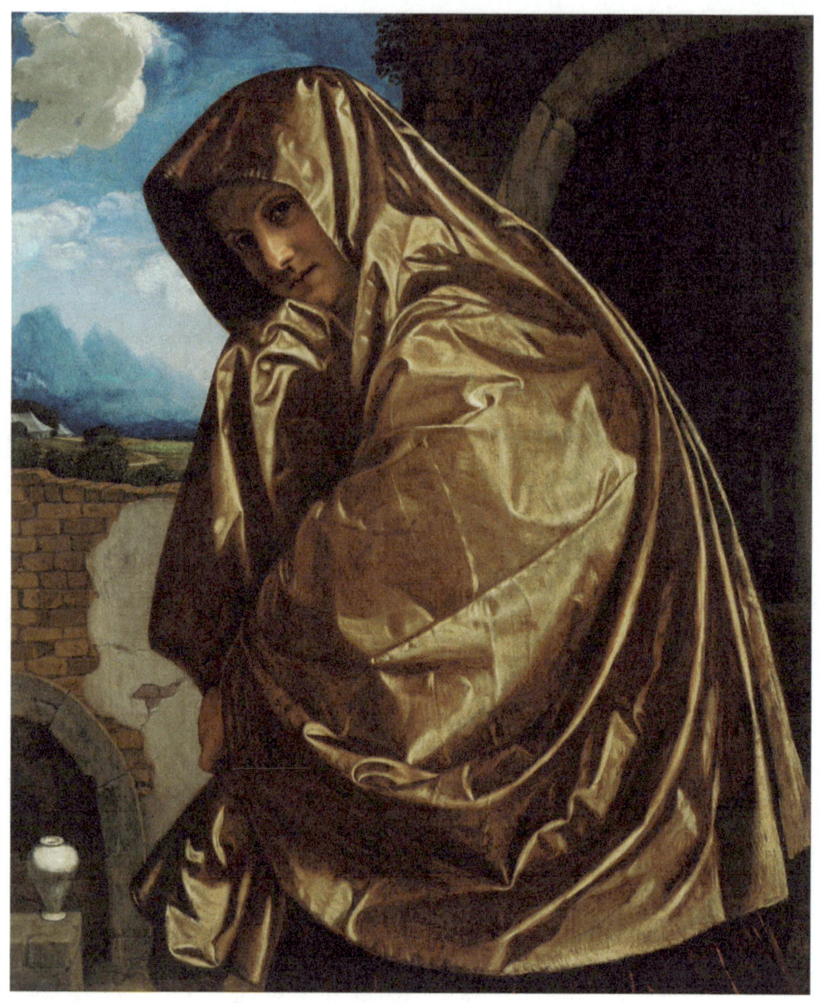

Giovanni Girolamo Savoldo, *Saint Mary Magdalene at the Sepulchre*, ca. 1530–1540, oil on canvas, 92.7 × 79.4 cm. J. Paul Getty Museum, Los Angeles.

Fig. 16

digital reproductions of all four versions in one publication, the most significant difference between the paintings lies in Savoldo's depiction of light and shade. The Los Angeles version shows a green meadow with a picturesque trail toward a church in front of a steep mountain reaching into an almost Californian-blue sky [fig. 16]. With sweeping brush strokes, a white swirling cloud presents itself like a peony, a *Pfingstrose* or a rose-of-Pentecost. In the Berlin version, the figure of Magdalene is placed within a decaying architectural setting [fig. 18]. Standing in front of bricked-up arches, her dimly lit shawl casts a shadow over her daunted face. Savoldo captures the metamorphosing moment of Magdalene's disbelief, while she turns toward the risen man himself, as Mary Pardo argues in her 1989 essay.[1] This moment in time is emphasized in the painting preserved today in Florence, in which the rising morning sun lights up the sky, turning it into a fiery field of bold hues of color [fig. 19]. That is, if you catch her in the right moment and in the right angle [fig. 20]. In the London version, the sun still hides behind the horizon line, illuminating the lower edges of the slim clouds above the reflective surface of a lake. Mirroring the cold colors of early dawn, Savoldo has replaced Magdalene's gold shawl by a silver one [fig. 21]. Here, more than in any other version, the "reflective envelope," as Pardo calls it, "is both a magnet to the viewer's eye and a shield blocking direct access to the image's interior."[2] And further: "The viewer is effectively caught up in a triangular relationship with two fictive entities—the painted figure returning his glance and the imagined figure ensnaring it in a net of reflections."[3]

These reflections are, nevertheless, dependent on the fact that Savoldo depicted either gold or silver fabrics, that, most exclusively, absorb, reflect, and refract light being cast from a source in front of the picture plane. As Michael Fried observed in more general terms: "The painting itself, the painting as artefact, emerges as a kind of transactional field belonging at once to both the virtual, depicted world situated 'beyond' the picture surface and the actual, physical world grounded 'this' side of that

1
Mary Pardo, "The Subject of Savoldo's Magdalene," *The Art Bulletin* 17, no. 1 (1989): 67–91.

2
Ibid., 69.

3
Ibid., 74.

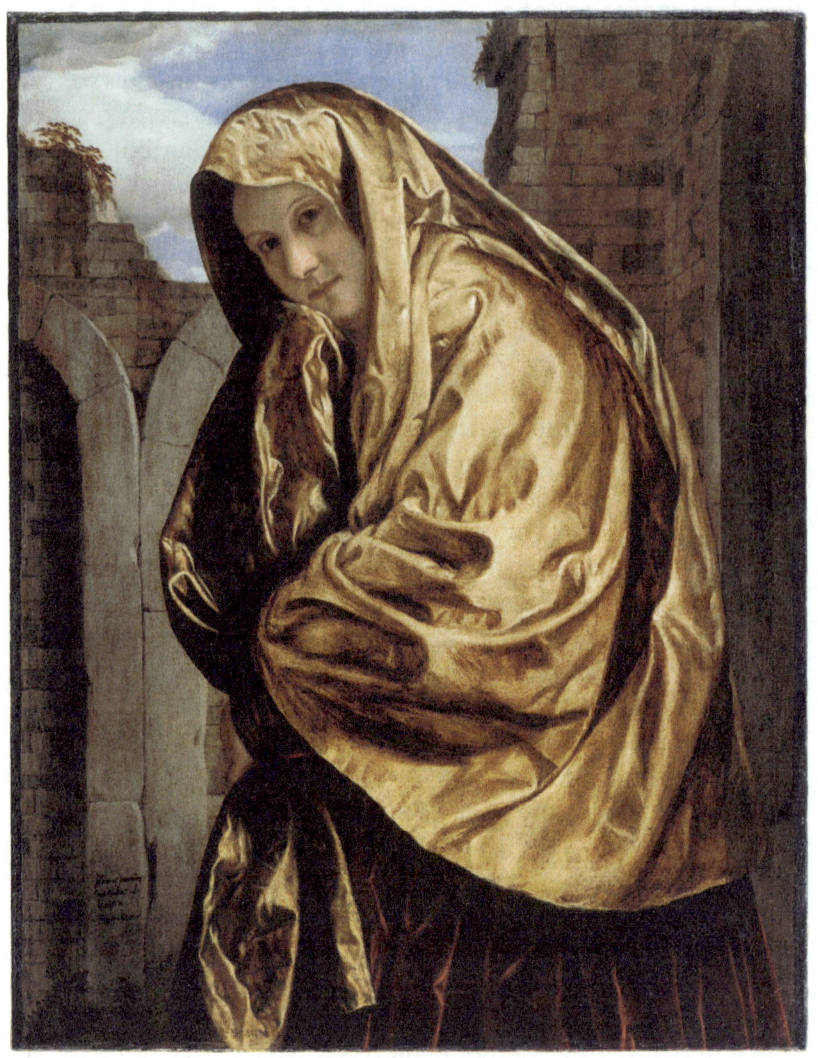

Giovanni Girolamo Savoldo, *Die Venezianierin (heilige Maria Magdalena)*, ca. 1530–1540, oil on canvas, ca. 92 × 73 cm. Gemäldegalerie, Ident-Nr. 307, Berlin.

Fig. 18

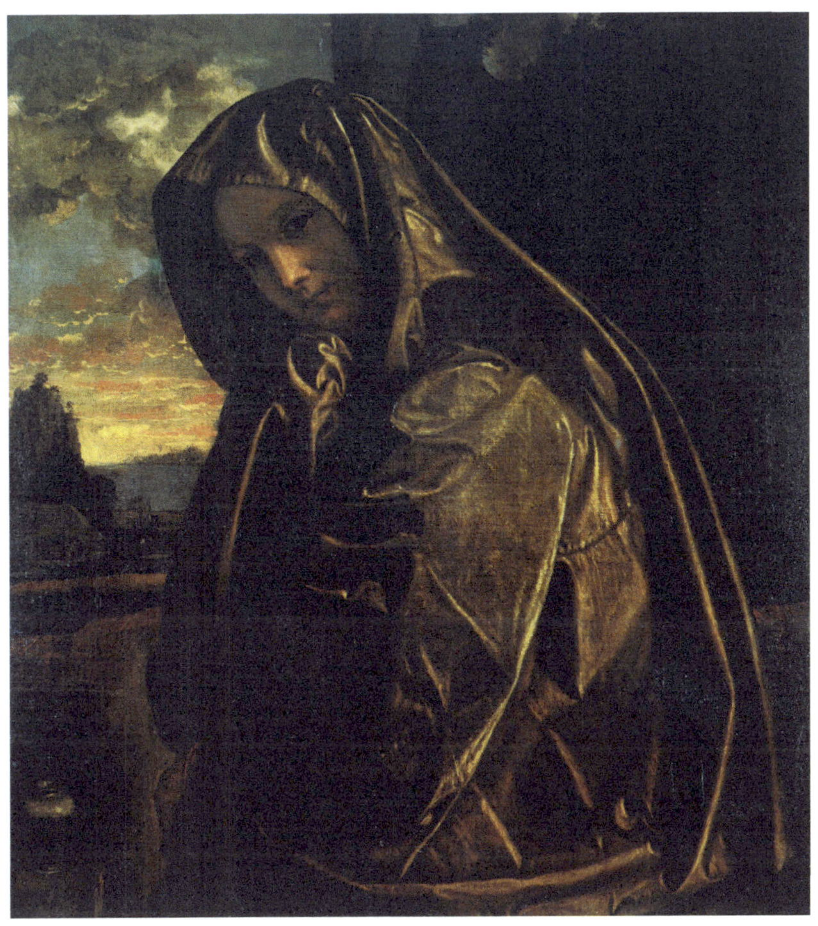

Giovanni Girolamo Savoldo, *Santa Maria Maddalena*,
ca. 1530–1540, oil on canvas, 84 × 77.5 cm.
Gallerie degli Uffizi, collezione Contini Bonacossi, Florence.

Fig. 19

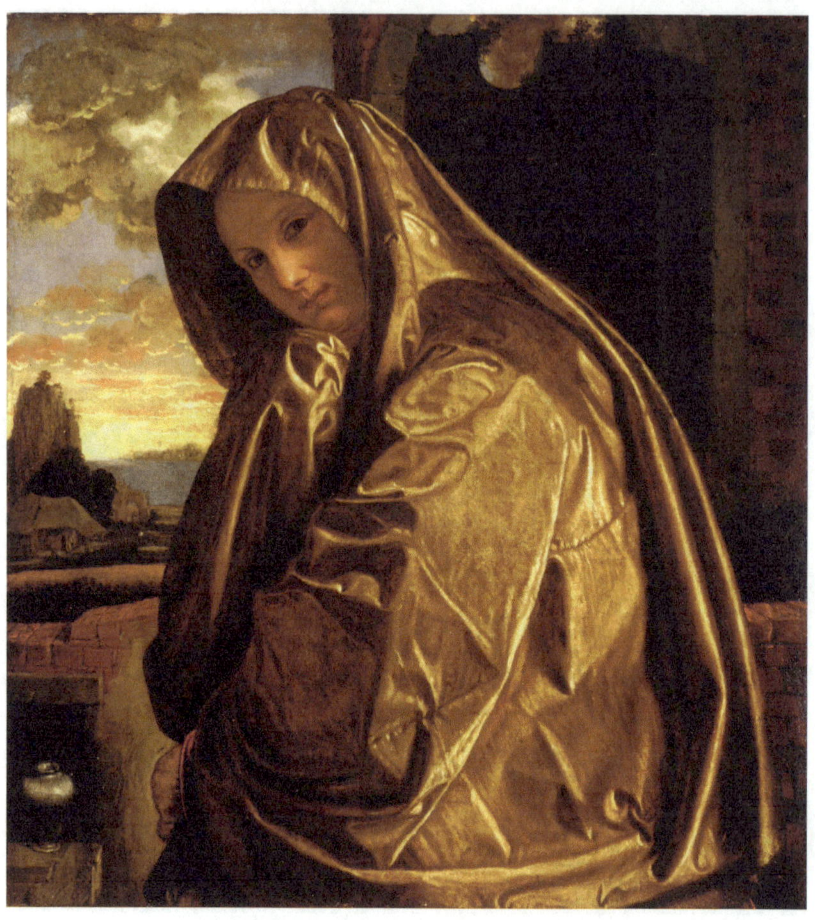

Giovanni Girolamo Savoldo, *Santa Maria Maddalena*, ca. 1530–1540, oil on canvas, 84 × 77.5 cm. Gallerie degli Uffizi, collezione Contini Bonacossi, Florence.

Fig. 20

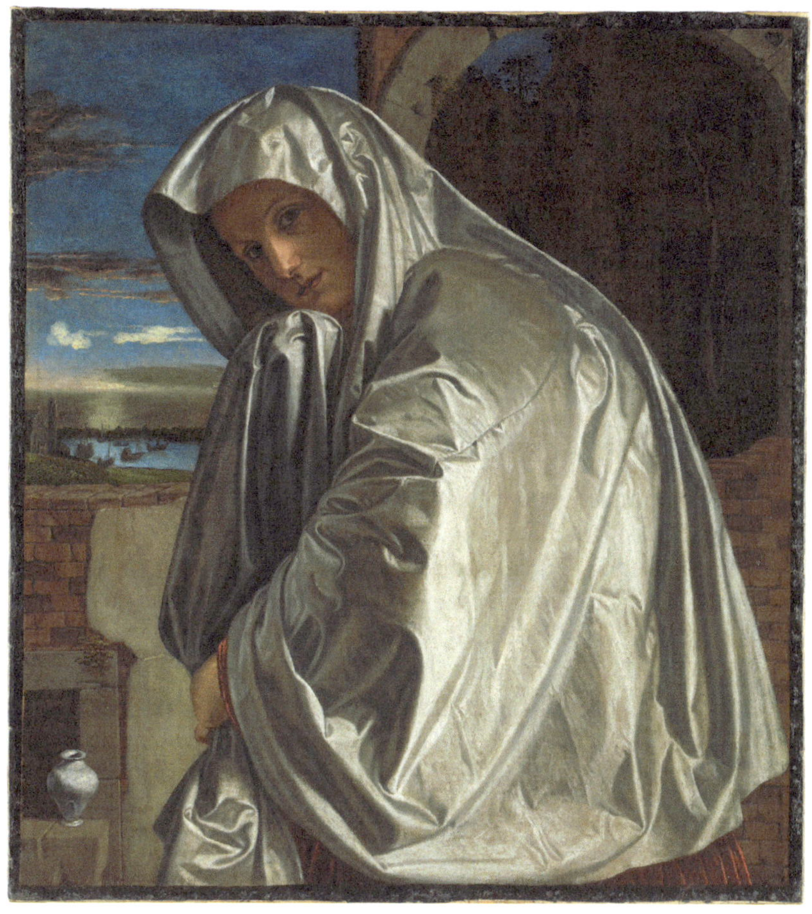

Giovanni Girolamo Savoldo, *Mary Magdalene*, ca. 1530–1540, oil on canvas, 89.1 × 82.4 cm. The National Gallery, inv. NG1031, London.

Fig. 21

surface, in the latter which, in intimate proximity to the canvas, the painter, paintbrush in his right hand and (traditionally) palette in his left, actively pursued his enterprise."[4] While the painter emerges to the foreground in Fried's argument, Magdalene's figure, her body, hair, and hands remain hidden within the illuminated ground. Her cloth becomes a playground for faces and masks Fried discovers in the folds of her garment. Fulfilling multiple pictorial functions, she meanders between figure and ground as much as between planes and spaces.

In Basel toward the end of the conference, we became more and more aware of the fact that space and *Raum* reference different entities, just like plane and *Fläche*. While *Raum* seemed to incorporate the possibility of endless expansion stronger, space remained undetermined regarding its attachment to or detachment from phenomenological, philosophical, or scientific contexts. Dipping into these differences felt, at times, unsettling, destabilizing the ground we believed to stand on. Still, it's through the cracks the light comes in, so we opened a Pandora's box of new questions: Can *Grund*, *Fläche*, *Raum*, ground, space, or plane have borders? Can figures, images, and pictures have frames? Are they two-, three-, or four-dimensional? Spatial or geometrical, (non-) Euclidian or perspectival? And how do we answer these questions specifically within certain medial, temporal, and historical contexts? Is that even possible?

David Young Kim: It's worth trying! Even though most contributions are in English, this volume is deliberately multilinguistic. Many authors self-translated their texts from German to English. Then, there is your labor as an editor who is moving between languages to intervene while looking for common ground. As an art historian who is a native Dutch speaker but moves easily and fluently between multiple languages, I would first like to ask you a question about multilingualism and method. What demarcates your role as editor between linguistic "correction" (if that is the right term) and conceptual intervention? The Sapir-Whorf thesis,

4
Michael Fried, *Painting with Demons: The Art of Gerolamo Savoldo* (London: Reaktion, 2021), p. 141.

an idea that has been discredited yet has recently received reevaluation, argues that language can shape our perception and stance toward the world. Put simply, does your multilingual disposition feed into your thinking about the ground as a concept? How have the connotations of the terms "*Grund*," "ground," "*fond*," "*campo*" in different languages shaped your thinking?

Saskia C. Quené: I wouldn't have come across the question of what can be seen or described between figure and ground if I hadn't been able to think it through in multiple languages. Musing on these shifts in meaning led to the question of whether all these terms aren't inevitably failing what they imply to describe. As a first-year student in Berlin, I remember presenting in front of a painting at the Gemäldegalerie. When I started pointing toward an ambiguous detail with my finger, my professor immediately interrupted and told me that this wouldn't be the right class or discipline for me if I didn't find the *words* to elucidate what I saw. At that moment, I understood excitedly that "looking" at art would not be enough. Perhaps even Heinrich Wölfflin was motivating himself when he sighed: "*Hier rächt sich die Armut der Sprache. Man müßte tausend Worte haben, um alle Übergänge bezeichnen zu können*" ("This is where the poverty of language takes its revenge. You would have to have a thousand words to describe all the transitions"). Or, as Ocean Vuong puts it in *On Earth We're Briefly Gorgeous*: "I am writing to reach you—even if each word I put down is one word further from where you are." Working across borders is, to be honest, what really fuels and excites me.

So yes, I do indeed think that language can shape our perception and determine what and how we see, even if it remains imperfect, *per speculum in aenigmate*. In German, this means that if we talk and write more often about *Feuerwehrfrauen* und *Expertinnen*, we impact reality and eventually become a more inclusive society where firefighters can be female as much as they can be male. However, this still doesn't tackle the problem that most languages are fond of dualisms or oppositions, just like "figure" and "ground," arguably more than paintings. In your recent book *Groundwork*, you undo "the hierarchical binary of figure/ground by showing how each passes into and imparts characteristics to the other." Are you, David, with that, tapping into a new, critically informed idea of what language can do to shape our views and minds toward a more benevolent and creative employment of concepts like ambiguity, fluidity, graduation, range, scale, and spectrum? What can language learn from art?

DK: Your suggestion that language can move beyond binaries and embrace fluidity and ambiguity is enabling and significant for so many reasons: categories of identity that depend on language can manifest themselves in their translation from text to the political realm as containers that generate and sustain violent systems of power: the incarceration system, the nation-state, the museum. By the term and practice of *groundwork,* I am proposing that language, in embracing figuration beyond the figural, can prompt observation of what is hiding in plain sight, even as we acknowledge that latent presence is often bound and has yet to come into view. "Figure and ground" isn't simply a dynamic that catalyzes formalist thinking. There are ethical possibilities and, indeed, ethical consequences to calling attention to the tensions implicit within a binary such as figure and ground. Before we investigate those stakes, a basic question for you: Does "ground" in Dutch have certain resonances that don't exist in German and English? And how do you, as a scholar, make use of this productive linguistic static?

SQ: You're right, language is so personal. For me, *Grund* has always had a philosophical-phenomenological undertone. It felt very distinct from *Boden*, which describes the ground beneath our feet, the floor, or plane. I like the German word "*Grund*" because it transports a rich *Begriffsgeschichte*, it is equipped with ambiguity. In contrast, the Dutch *grond* describes a place more than a space, it might be closer to *campo*, or even *campus*. The Dutch ground is flat and doesn't translate to "reason," as the German term "*Grund*" does. In that regard, the Dutch term is, therefore, similar to the English "ground." On the other hand, the Italian *campo* is very rich in a different direction. It refers to "field" more than to "plane," which derives from *piano*. The German *Feld*, again, in contrast, doesn't have that particular dimension of depth while the Dutch *bodem* translates to "bottom" but only partially to the German *Boden*.

In my writing, I aim to look for productive ways to employ ambiguity to make my writing more precise. Within one language,

I like to embrace the *Begriffsgeschichten* or multiple meanings of terms, because I think they can do justice to different forms of experience one might have had. I can't change my queerness or my complexion, but I can switch languages and I can try to acknowledge multivalence. A German verb I love very dearly is *aufheben*, or *aufgehoben sein*, because it means "to resolve" and "to preserve" or "to be resolved" and "to be preserved" at the same time. This makes a lot of sense when it comes to the relationship between figure and ground, in which one can partake in the other in multiple ways. As human figures, we shape and create or destroy and neglect our planet and its surroundings all at once, but at the same time, the world creates us. It shapes our identities and determines, at least to some extent, what we are and become. Language reflects this reciprocity as much as image-making.

DK: The climate catastrophe and ongoing war in Ukraine are surely feeding into my current interest in the concept of figure and ground. Martha Nussbaum observed in her philosophical thinking on fragility that work often comes from a deep psychic place. The political is personal. Scholarship is intimate. I'm often asked why the mutuality of the figure with its surroundings appears as a red thread in my work. The immediate answer is personal history. Like many Korean Americans, my parents were originally Northern Korean refugees who escaped to Seoul just before the Korean War. Tragically, an aunt of mine was caught by Communist border guards as the family was attempting to cross with their belongings to the south. She and her children haven't been heard from since the ceasefire in 1953. The motif of such family trauma frequently gets overlooked in the model minority myth that characterizes the perception of Asians in Western countries. Then my parents emigrated to Brazil, as visas to South America were more readily available for applicants of Asian descent. This "background" of refugee and seemingly interminable immigrant displacement impressed on me that the idea or ideal of belonging to any territory or nation-state was contingent. Meanwhile, this unstable sense of "ground" contrasted with an attitude toward land I encountered in school, that of American "manifest destiny," the idea that the United States was ordained to expand across the continent. So, for me, the question that I pose to any material isn't "*que sais-je?*" (what do I know?) as Montaigne put it. It's more "where am I?" That is, how do I orient myself toward this material as a physical being who feels perpetually adrift in the world? Some may question that uncovering this is terribly sentimental and "American," but I think it's important to reveal how one has forged a personal relationship to scholarly subject matter. One's position to scholarship is personal *and* political. What about you, Saskia? How does your personal history relate to your choice of "ground" as a topic of contemplation?

SQ: I think that sentimentality is underrated, and apart from that I think there is incredible strength in displaying character, especially in professional environments. Along those lines, I do notice that your question is making me uncomfortable. I grew up in Amsterdam but moved out of my family home as a young teenager. Nevertheless, I never really questioned if I was entitled to carve out space for myself. You may call it *polderarrogantie*, a Dutch arrogance fostered by the necessity and ability to create earth out of water, to create one's own ground to stand on. However, at this point, I am a bit afraid to drift off into a conversation backed up by "*psychologie van de koude grond*," so "psychology from the cold soil," which means dilettante psychology flourishing on untended land. Would you mind returning to language and sharing some Korean words and contexts for "ground"? Is there something the Korean language has helped you see? I'm still grappling with the fact that this volume only covers Western perspectives and Western premodern art. Do you think I've missed an opportunity?

DK: Korean has several words for ground: 땅 (*ttang*, which refers to land or property); 바닥 (*badak*, which refers to ground understood as floor); or 토양 (*toyang*, which denotes ground as soil). For me, this understanding of ground in terms of languages relates to the "lost" ground of Northern Korea, which my family fled before the Korean War. In that view, "ground" is not only a physical space. It is an affective dimension that is imbued with nostalgia. That ground as "land" is accessible only through memory for my parents' generation, and for me, through imagination and storytelling—so embedded within the philological terms is emotion. I am always struck by the notion that the English word "terms" delimits a concept (hence the connection with the word "terminal" or endings) and I think what the volume is trying to do is the opposite. With works of art, we can see how ground is a fundamental and foundational concept for thinking in general. At the same time, the volume shows how those very notions of "fundament" and "foundation" can be fugitive too, that is to say difficult to grasp despite the solidity of the depiction of ground.

As for the concern that the volume focuses on "premodern" and "Western" works of art (and I use the quotation marks intentionally): while we use words like "comprehensive" and "thorough" to describe "good" scholarship, another way to think about our writing is focusing on what thought can unfold and open up. I recently encountered the book by Crystal Mun-hye Baik titled *Reencounters*, a work on the Korean War and the role of memory in the diaspora: she "ends" her work not with the term "Conclusion" but with "An Opening" composed of poetry and photography which meditates on the 'opacity' of North Korea as both political and conceptual ground. What is more, as the work of Bakirathi Mani and others have argued, the very desire for thoroughness in terms of a "global art history" is in and of itself tied to a neo-imperialist enterprise. Remarking on the ideological ties between art history and politics, a scholar once remarked: "first comes the conqueror, and then comes the art historian." In a volume on the relationship between figure and ground, it is good to be mindful of the aspiration to "cover ground." Can we, therefore, explore the metaphor of "research field" (*Forschungsfeld* or *Forschungsgebiet*) and assumptions thereof? Who gets to say that they are a "native" or a stranger to a certain field of study, and on what grounds?

SQ: Yes, defining a field of research also means to claim ground for oneself, to control borders, and to keep others out. It's a counterproductive gesture toward collaboration and, therefore, toward knowledge and its distribution. It's arguably nothing less than an inherited colonial gesture that is shaping academia until this day. By ensuring that our field is more fertile than others, we foster power dynamics: not everyone can or should (dare to) enter certain areas of research, and the most productive grounds are "cultivated" by the biggest figures. It can be hard to know where you are allowed to investigate and look for new paths, especially as a younger scholar.

In terms of teaching, German *Grundkurse* often focus on equipping students with art-historical methods and terminologies they can apply independently in other courses on more specific subject matters. In contrast, art history departments across the United States are grappling with the idea of the survey, itself a term that connects to the idea of "surveying" and, therefore, to the act of dominating ground. In comparison, academic systems encourage and preserve the "Western" art-historical canon in different ways. In Europe, most departments are structured around medieval, early modern, modern, and contemporary art, which leads to the fact that a lot of students start their art-historical journey looking at medieval art. This has huge disadvantages: I strongly believe that it would be helpful to discuss Agnes Martin and Marina Abramovič before turning to complex illumination techniques or medieval portal sculpture. Rachel Dressler and Benjamin Tilghman hinted at a "neo formalist turn" in art-historical scholarship in their introduction to issue nine of *Different Visions* from 2023, "On Unstable Ground," and I do think that "digging in the ground" fosters new ways of formal and material analysis that can be non-elitist, inclusive, and democratic rather than superficial or socially indifferent. There is no formalism without language, and I am excited about these new approaches to premodern art, to which this book aims to contribute.

The first section of this volume, Staging Figures, unpacks the dynamic between the categories of figure and ground by acknowledging the beholder as much as the gazes from within the image itself. Three extended case studies by Noa Turel, Claudia Blümle, and Beate Fricke unfold the webs of entanglement constituted by curtains, stages, architectural models, liturgical vessels, and inscriptions. Noa Turel reminds us: "Layers, neatly divided, are indeed everywhere in modernity—from theatrical scenery, through Georges Méliès early cinematic special effects, to Disney's multipane camera. Perception, always operating through culturally established patterns, directs us to read fifteenth-century art as, similarly, a set of illusory overlays." She reminds us further: "This conception of the medium did not yet exist in the 1400s. Rather, in that visual culture, a multitude of three-dimensional objects, ranging from sculpture, through architecture, to theatrical props were habitually polychromed, and what we nowadays classify as *a* painting (namely one with a flat, often rectangular support) was but one subcategory of the broader category of 'paintworks,' which encompassed essentially everything that painters created (or finished), including polychromed sculpture and live pageants." She then proceeds to "explore the question of figure and ground in fifteenth-century art by drawing on a rare resource: three figureless images." In doing so, Turel concludes that Master WA, the artist of the figureless images under investigation, "was incentivized to promote a certain ambiguity and fluidity between two-, three-, and four-dimensional imagery that characterizes much of the professional endeavor of many fifteenth-century painters. [They] invariably thought about painted settings neither as 'space' in the modern sense of the word, nor as flat grounds or planes."

Likewise, Claudia Blümle draws our attention to *tableau vivant* curtains as mediators between still life and presence, play and representation: "Open curtains present the figures behind them in front of opaque grounds. On the other hand, they frame the figure by emphasizing the surface of a wall or textile as parallel to the picture plane, the picture frame, and the image itself. By positioning the figure in front of a background instead of in space, they transform the scene into a picture." In drawing from these analyses, Blümle offers a new interpretation of Petrus Christus's *Man of Sorrows* , the Salzburg Master's *Christ as the Man of Sorrows*, and Jean Fouquet's *Portrait of King Charles VII*.

Focusing on the iconography of the annunciation to Mary and the Incarnation, Beate Fricke investigates how painting bears the potential to mediate between form, idea, and spirit. In Pedro da Córdoba's panel from the *mezquita* in Córdoba, Fricke's contribution shows "how art historians ... can address and reveal pictorial challenges and artistic solutions without using established terms and paradigms such as perspective, figure, and ground." In acknowledging "the historical baggage these terms carry," Fricke challenges us to go beyond figure and ground to uncover new pathways.

The second section of this volume brings together three contrasting approaches toward the question of how we can describe and, therefore, translate figure-ground configurations. Gottfried Boehm's short and dense article "*Ikonische Differenz*" was first published in 2011 in the journal *Rheinsprung 11*, named after the address of eikones – Center for the Theory and History of the Image in Basel, where our conference took place. While his contribution can be read as a condensation of a lifelong examination of the relationship between modern figures and grounds, it is included in this volume as a point of departure, a "ground" to draw on that is neither blank nor determined. Moreover, the article's translation by Anthony Mahler can be seen as a contribution toward a multilinguistic and transnational *Bildwissenschaft* that encourages the examination of the multiplicity of the meanings "terms" have to offer.

Along those lines, Bruno Haas presents a new and consequential reading of the premodern "ground" (*campus*) as *locus* (place). At the core of his argument lies the fundamental warning that the description of pictorial effects presupposes the constitution of an adequate terminology: "Descriptive categories are never neutral, they are part of a *Sprachspiel* (Wittgenstein) that predetermines what can be seen and said."

Veronica Peselmann then traces the emergence of "figure-and-ground" as a paradigm in encyclopedic sources. Perusing French and German dictionary lemmata and entries in encyclopedia from between 1780 and 1890, she follows the conceptual lineage and formation from "figure" and "ground" to "figure-and-ground:" "The terms 'figure' and 'ground' were listed separately until the beginning of the nineteenth century. While 'figure' was largely described as a precise formal and spatial unit, the term 'ground' included aspects of material, technique, composition, and pictorial space. ...Throughout the nineteenth century, the ground becomes less concerned with material matters. Instead, compositional aspects of ground come to the fore, paving the way for the introduction of the lemma 'background.'"

The third section of this volume, Beyond the Surface, highlights three artistic techniques relying on complex entanglements between figure and ground: stained glass, gold leaf, and semi-transparent paper. Marion Gartenmeister discusses color, grisaille, and transparency in stained glass: "it is crucial to remember that glass painting does not rely on an opaque support that needs to be covered up or concealed, but that instead the material is intended to be visible in the completed work of art.... They oscillate between figure and pictorial ground, but they also remain material support." Focusing on examples of later medieval and early modern stained glass from Switzerland, the aim of her contribution is "to describe various relations of figure and ground, while taking into account the technical processing of the material ground."

This oscillation between figure and ground emerges as a critical issue in Ambrogio Lorenzetti's *Annunciation*, in which the Incarnation takes place within the gold ground between Mary and the Angel. The article points out how gold was used as a mechanism to envelope the viewer into the work's realm. Gold as a spectral material has the potential to transform a painting into a phenomenological experience based on theological accounts of optics, vision, and metaphysics; and, most importantly, the experience of their observers. Acting as neither figure, nor ground, sheets of gold leaf appear first and foremost in-between.

Manipulating the seemingly opaque flatness of the white paper, Nicola Suthor reveals in her article how Leonardo da Vinci traced his figures through semi-transparent paper grounds: "The idea that the draftsman develops a pictorial idea *ex nihilo* on a sheet ignores the multi-layered network of references that unfolds between line progressions and latent grounds." Moreover, in this case, tracing must be understood as a strategy to help materialize the fluidity of memory. Through repetition, the line becomes an engram, a new figure and foundation. With the 'inartistic' process of tracing, Leonardo introduced a barrier between figure and ground that, at the same time, blurs this difference and allowed him to create freely from memory.

In the section Navigating Dichotomies, Tom Steinert reconstructs the intricate "*Ideen- und Begriffsgeschichte*" of "figure and ground" as a concept in *Gestaltpsychologie* (gestalt psychology) and *Kunstwissenschaft* (art studies) between 1750 and 1950. Presenting *puzzle portraits* as forerunners of Edgar Rubin's famous ambiguous images, he zooms in on Rudolf Arnheim and the Psychologisches Institut at the Berlin University as much as on the contingent dissemination of ideas across Europe and the United States in the twentieth century. In his extensive historical account, supporting cast members become protagonists and vice versa, shaping the prehistory for this very volume.

Christoph Poetsch considers the relationship between figure and ground in premodernity as a decisive factor for the perception of images as pictures. In discussing depictions of meta-physical and transcendental realms, his article investigates how the handling of different materials bearing pictures reflect artist's approaches toward pictures as representations: "My thesis is that image theories and their metaphysics relate to pictorial space and figure/ground constellations by means of specific transpositions." These specific transpositions mediate as much between the physical and the metaphysical realm as they specify how pictures are composites of an image or representation, a medium or material carrying the image, and the referent the image is referring to.

The experiment then described in Raphael Rosenbergs's contribution acknowledges these different modes of perception images encourage. He asks whether either the figures, the geometrical configuration of surfaces, or the depicted spaces guide the viewer's eyes. Participants were asked to draw "compositional lines" on the surface of tablets showing different depictions of the Last Supper that were then mapped onto the participants' recorded rapid eye movements. Rosenberg observes: "Even when foreshortening was seen as decisive for the composition, as in Tintoretto's *Last Supper* in San Giorgio Maggiore, it did not trigger gaze movements." Concluding that "participants were not exploring the three-dimensional spaces depicted through one-point perspectival methods," one could ask accordingly, on what grounds we still distinguish perspectival from geometrical or other modes of planar configuration.

The last section of this volume, titled Transgressing Depth, navigates realms between figures and grounds in four pioneering contributions by Aden Kumler, Karin Leonhard, Péter Bokody, and Jürgen Müller focusing respectively on medieval shadows, hidden faces, embedded spaces, and ephemeral figures. Revising the art-historical dictum that cast shadows cannot be found in medieval paintings, Aden Kumler makes an impressive case "for the necessity and the rewards of examining the meeting of figure, ground, and light in medieval painting from perceptual and conceptual angles other than those that have long framed our perspective upon European medieval painting." She considers the interaction of figure and ground in painted cast shadows as a "hermeneutic device in medieval painting, whose presence invites the beholder to question and reflect upon what painting gives them to see and to understand."

In her contribution on a multilayered painting by David Bailly, Karin Leonhard traces the reception of these visible and invisible layers from the seventeenth through the twentieth century through close pictorial analysis: "If we take these observations seriously, then there would be not only one pictorial ground from which the figures stand out clearly, but several grounds or rather a bottomless '*fond*,' into which they have sunk and which now allows them to stay in the picture on different levels of time and (in)visibility. And indeed, even now, despite the added clarity that recent technical analysis has provided, only contradictory impressions and statements can be recorded." On the other hand: "the chimera ... reveals itself precisely only when the duality of figure and ground dissolves in our perception."

Péter Bokody focuses on images-within-images that are more clearly separable. In Andrea Mantegna's *Picture-Bearers*, pictures appear as three-dimensional objects within the primary pictorial space. These "images-within-images introduce a plurality to the prevailing system of foreshortening. Images-within-images have been interpreted as an afterthought to composite medieval image-fields, but in this case, they have a bearing on the construction of virtual space itself. Viewers are once again invited to abandon their prescribed point of view and explore the multiplicity of virtual spaces. In this process, the painting's ground becomes destabilized."

In Pieter Bruegel the Elder's *Magpie on the Gallows*, the instability of the ground as a proleptic ground becomes the prerequisite for the instability of the figure. The magpie on the gallows as an ambiguous image mediates between the picture plane and pictorial spaces and evolves and transforms in time, becoming memory as much as it hints toward the future. As Jürgen Müller formulates: "Those who seek to determine the relationship between figure and ground in early modern painting think about spatial relationships and those of the surface at the same time: what is above or below, what is left or right within the picture? But also, what is in the foreground, middle ground or background? The problem of figure and ground, therefore, demarcates a double interest. Both are concerned with orientation ..., we presuppose the spatial orientation of the recipient. In doing so, we are self-assuring us as spatial beings. We recognize and experience space as for-me, as accessible and reachable."

In the broadest sense, the contributions in this volume aim to destabilize the notion of premodern space as a phenomenological entity in which figures move as beings surrounded by endless grounds while acknowledging the impossibility of reaching beyond our own time and place. The multifaceted flexibility in which space as ground, *campus*, *locus*, or *topos* appears in images and written sources throughout the centuries is reflected in the diverse methodologies employed by this volume's authors. In presenting a kaleidoscope of possibilities to approach "figure" and "ground," I hope this book will be an opening more than a conclusion indeed.

Selected Bibliography

The following selected bibliography offers a curated list of sources drawn from the chapters of this volume, as well as additional titles relevant to the study of figure-ground-relationships in premodern art and beyond. These works encompass foundational texts that have shaped discourses as well as contemporary critical analyses. However, it is not intended to be exhaustive or conclusive. Readers are therefore encouraged to use this bibliography as a guide to survey new fields of inquiry.

A

Adama van Scheltema, Frederik. "Das Problem des Grundes in der Geschichte der Kunst." *Geistige Welt: Vierteljahresschrift für Kultur- und Geisteswissenschaften* 1 (1946): 16–27.

Ahmed, Sara. *Queer Phenomenology: Orientations, Objects, Others*. Durham: Duke University Press, 2006.

Alloa, Emmanuel. "Bildwissenschaft in Byzanz: Ein Iconic Turn Avant la Lettre?" *Studia Philosophica* 69 (2010): 11–35.

Alloa, Emmanuel. "Seeing-as, Seeing-in, Seeing with: Looking Through Pictures." *The Palgrave Handbook of Image Studies*, ed. by Krešimir Pungar, 483–499. Basingstoke: Palgrave Macmillan, 2021.

Arasse, Daniel. *L'Annonciation Italienne: Une Histoire de Perspective*. Paris: Hazan, 1999.

Arasse, Daniel. *Histoire de Peintures*. Paris: Gallimard, 2006.

Arnheim, Rudolf. *Art and Visual Perception: A Psychology of the Creative Eye*. Berkeley/Los Angeles/London: University of California Press/Cambridge University Press, 1954.

Arnheim, Rudolf. *Toward a Psychology of Art*. Berkeley, CA: University of California Press, 1966.

Arnheim, Rudolf. "Perception of Perspective Pictorial Space from Different Viewing Points." *Leonardo* 10 (1977): 283–88.

Arnheim, Rudolf. *New Essays on the Psychology of Art*. Berkeley, CA: University of California Press, 1986.

Auerbach, Erich. "Figura." *Scenes From the Drama of European Literature, Theory and History of Literature* 9, 11–76. Minneapolis, MN: University of Minnesota Press, 1984.

B

Bachelard, Gaston. *La Poétique de l'Espace*. Paris: Presses Universitaires de France, 1957.

Bachelard, Gaston. *The Poetics of Space*. Translated by Maria Jolas. Boston, MA: Beacon Press, 1994.

Bailey, Douglass W. *Breaking the Surface: An Art/Archaeology of Prehistoric Architecture*. Oxford: Oxford University Press, 2018.

Baker-Bates, Piers, and Elena M. Calvillo. *Almost Eternal: Painting on Stone and Material Innovation in Early Modern Europe* (vol. 10). Leiden: Brill, 2018.

Balke, Friedrich, and Hanna Engelmeier. *Mimesis und Figura: Mit einer Neuausgabe des „Figura"-Aufsatzes von Erich Auerbach* (Medien und Mimesis, vol. 1). Paderborn: Fink, 2016.

Bałus, Wojciech. "Diaphanum: Bildwissenschaftliche Überlegungen zur Glasmalerei," In *Licht(t)räume: Festschrift für Brigitte Kurmann-Schwarz zum 65. Geburtstag*, ed. by Barbara von Orelli-Messerli, Eva-Maria Scheiwiller-Lorber, Angela Schiffhauer, and Katharina Georgi, 11–17. Petersberg: Michael Imhof, 2016.

Bałus, Wojciech. "A Matter of Matter: Transparent – Translucent – Diaphanum in the Medium of Stained Glass." In *Investigations in Medieval Stained Glass: Materials, Methods, and Expressions*, ed. by Brigitte Kurmann-Schwarz and Elizabeth Carson Pastan, 109–188. Leiden: Brill, 2019.

Barry, Fabio. "Walking on Water: Cosmic Floors in Antiquity and the Middle Ages." *The Art Bulletin* 89, no. 4 (20 iversity Press, 2020.

Bawden, Tina. *Die Schwelle im Mittelalter: Bildmotiv und Bildort*. Köln: Böhlau, 2014.

Bawden, Tina. "Shifting Grounds and Shifting Perspectives: The Crucifixion Sequence in the Sacramentary of Robert of Jumièges (Rouen, Bibliothèque municipale MS Y 6 [274])." On Unstable Ground, ed. by Rachel Dressler and Benjamin C. Tilghman, special issue, *Different Visions: New Perspectives on Medieval Art* 9 (2023). https://doi.org/10.61302/BBMD8532.

Baxandall, Michael. *Painting and Experience in Fifteenth-Century Italy: A Primer in the Social History of Pictorial Style*. Oxford: Oxford University Press, 1988.

Belting, Hans, *An Anthropology of Images: Picture, Medium, Body*. Translated by Thomas Dunlap. Princeton, NJ: Princeton University Press, 2011.

Benjamin, Walter: "Über die Malerei oder Zeichen und Mal." *Gesammelte Schriften* 2 (1977), ed. by Rolf Tiedemann and Hermann Schweppenhäuser, 603–607. Frankfurt am Main: Suhrkamp, 1989.

Blumenberg, Hans. *Die Sorge Geht Über den Fluss*. Frankfurt am Main: Suhrkamp, 1987.

Blumenberg, Hans. *Höhlenausgänge*. Frankfurt am Main: Suhrkamp, 1989.

Blumenberg, Hans. *Die Ontologische Distanz: Eine Untersuchung zur Krisis der Philosophischen Grundlagen der Neuzeit*. Berlin: Suhrkamp, 2022.

Blümle, Claudia. "Glitzernde Falten: Goldgrund und Vorhang in der Frühneuzeitlichen Malerei." In *Szenen des Vorhangs: Schnittflächen der Künste*, ed. by Gabriele Brandstetter and Sibylle Peters, 45–66. Freiburg im Breisgau: Rombach, 2008.

Boehm, Gottfried, "Augenmaß: Zur Genese der Ikonischen Evidenz." In *Movens Bild: Zwischen Evidenz und Affekt*, ed. by Gottfried Boehm, Birgit Mersmann, and Christian Spies, 15–43. Munich: Fink, 2008.

Boehm, Gottfried and Matteo Burioni, eds., *Der Grund: Das Feld des Sichtbaren*. Munich: Fink, 2012.

Boehm, Gottfried. "Der Grund. Über das Ikonische Kontinuum." In *Der Grund. Das Feld des Sichtbaren*, ed. by Gottfried Boehm and Matteo Burioni, 28–92. Munich: Fink, 2012.

Boehm, Gottfried. "Ikonische Differenz", *Rheinsprung 11 – Zeitschrift für Bildkritik* 1 (2011): 170–176.

Bohde, Daniela. "Gestalt," *kritische berichte* 35, no. 3 (2007): 67–72.

Bokody, Péter, *Images-within-Images in Italian Painting: Reality and Reflexivity*. Burlington, VT: Ashgate, 2015.

Bokody, Péter and Alexander Nagel. *Renaissance Metapainting*. London: Harvey Miller, 2020.

Bouman, Jan C.: *The Figure-Ground Phenomenon in Experimental and Phenomenological Psychology* (= Diss. phil., Stockholms universitet), Stockholm 1968.

Bredekamp, Horst. *Der Bildakt*. Berlin: Klaus Wagenbach, 2015.

Bredekamp, Horst. *Image Acts: A Systematic Approach to Visual Agency*. Berlin: De Gruyter, 2018.

Bruno, Giuliana. *Surface: Matters of Aesthetics, Materiality, and Media*. Chicago, IL: University of Chicago Press, 2014.

Bryson, Norman. *Looking at the Overlooked: Four Essays on Still Life Painting*. Cambridge, MA: Harvard University Press, 1990.

Bunim, Miriam Schild. *Space in Medieval Painting and the Forerunners of Perspective.* New York: Columbia University Press, 1940.

Burioni, Matteo. "Der Künstler als *Champion*: Kunsttheoretische Figuren des Grundes in der Frühen Neuzeit." In *Departure for Modern Europe: A Handbook of Early Modern Philosophy (1400–1700)*, ed. by Hubertus Busche, 954–968. Munich: Felix Meiner, 2011.

Burioni, Matteo. "Grund und *campo*: Die Metaphorik des Bildgrundes in der Frühen Neuzeit oder: Paolo Uccellos *Schlacht von San Romano*." In *Der Grund: Das Feld des Sichtbaren*, ed. by Gottfried Boehm and Matteo Burioni, 94–149. Munich: Fink, 2012.

Butt, Amy. "Made up Ground: Architecture, Science Fiction, and the Surface of Imagined Worlds." *Architecture and Culture* (2023): 1–23. https://doi.org/10.1080/20507828.2023.2169822.

C

Camille, Michael. *Image on the Edge: The Margins of Medieval Art*. Cambridge, MA: Harvard University Press, 1992.

Camille, Michael. "Before the Gaze: The Internal Senses and Late Medieval Practices of Seeing." In *Visuality Before and Beyond the Renaissance: Seeing as others saw*, ed. by Robert S. Nelson, 197–223. Cambridge: Cambridge University Press, 2000.

Caplan, Jane, ed. *Written on the Body: The Tattoo in European and American History.* Princeton, NJ: Princeton University Press, 2000.

Carman, Charles H. *Leon Battista Alberti and Nicholas Cusanus: Towards an Epistemology of Vision for Italian Renaissance Art and Culture*, Burlington, VT: Ashgate, 2014.

Carruthers, Mary J. "Moving Images in the Mind's Eye." In *The Mind's Eye. Art and Theological Argument in the Middle Ages*, ed. by Jeffrey F. Hamburger and Anne-Marie Bouché, 287–305. Princeton, NJ: Princeton University Press, 2006.

Casey, Edward S. *The Fate of Place: A Philosophical History*. Berkeley, CA: University of California Press, 1997.

Cassegrain, Guillaume. "Le Miracle de la Surface: Véronèse, Tintoret et l'Espace Visionnaire." *Bulletin de l'Association des Historiens de l'Art Italien* 6 (1999–2000): 15–22.

Cassin, Barbara, ed. *Dictionary of Untranslatables: A Philosophical Lexicon*. Translated by Seven Rendall, Christian Hubert, Jeffrey Mehlman, Nathaniel Stein, and Michael Syrotinski. Princeton, NJ: Princeton University Press, 2014.

Chastel, André. "Le Tableau dans le Tableau." In *Fables, Formes, Figures*, ed. by André Chastel, 75–98. Paris: Flammarion, 1978.

Clark, T. J. "Painting at Ground Level." Tanner Lectures on Human Values, Princeton University, 17–19 April 2002.

Colie, Rosalie Littell. *Paradoxia Epidemica: The Renaissance Tradition of Paradox.* Princeton, NJ: Princeton University Press, 1966.

Colish, Marcia Lillian. "The Carolingian Debates over 'Nihil' and 'Tenebrae': A Study in Theological Method." *Speculum* 59 (1984): 757–795.

Cranston, Jodi. *The Muddied Mirror: Materiality and Figuration in Titian's Later Paintings*. University Park, PA: Pennsylvania State University Press, 2010.

D

Delarue, Dominic, Thomas Kaffenberger, and Christian Nille, eds. *Raumbilder / Bildräume: Studien aus dem Grenzbereich von Raum und Bild*. Regensburg: Schnell & Steiner, 2017.

Deleuze, Gilles and Félix Guattari. *A Thousand Plateaus*. Translated by Brian Massumi. Minneapolis, MN: University of Minnesota Press, 1987.

Denery, Dallas G. *Seeing and Being Seen in the Later Medieval World: Optics, Theology and Religious Life*. Cambridge: Cambridge University Press, 2005.

Denery, Dallas G. "Vision and Visual Error in Later Middle Ages." In *Arabic and Latin Theory of Perspective* (Micrologus 29), ed. by Agostino Paravicini Bagliani, 203–218. Florence: SISMEL, 2021.

Dünne, Jörg and Stephan Günzel, eds. *Raumtheorie: Grundlagentexte aus Philosophie und Kulturwissenschaften*. Frankfurt am Main: Suhrkamp, 2006.

Dressler, Rachel. "Standing on Rocky Ground: Terrain in the Bayeux Embroidery." On Unstable Ground, ed. by Rachel Dressler and Benjamin C. Tilghman, special issue, *Different Visions: New Perspectives on Medieval Art* 9 (2023). https://doi.org/10.61302/XPQW7156.

Dupré, Sven, ed. *Perspective as Practice: Renaissance Cultures of Optics*. Turnhout: Brepols, 2015.

E

Endres, Johannes, Barbara Wittmann, and Gerhard Wolf, eds. *Ikonologie des Zwischenraums: Der Schleier als Medium und Metapher*. Paderborn: Fink, 2005.

Ellis, Willis D. *Gestalt Psychology and Meaning*. Berkeley, CA: The Sather Gate Book Shop, 1930.

Ellis, Willis D., ed. *A Source Book of Gestalt Psychology*, London: Kegan Paul, Trench, Trubner & Co., 1938.

F

Fiedler, Konrad. "Vom Ursprung der Künstlerischen Tätigkeit [1887]." In *Konrad Fiedler. Schriften zur Kunst* (Bild und Text, vol. 1), ed. by Gottfried Boehm, 111–220. Munich: Fink, 1991.

Fricke, Beate. "Presence Through Absence: Thresholds and Mimesis in Painting." *Representations* 130 (2015): 1–27.

Fricke, Beate and Lucas Burkart, eds. *Shifting Horizons: A Line and its Movement in Art, History and Philosophy*. Basel: Schwabe, 2022.

Friedberg, Anne. *The Virtual Window: From Alberti to Microsoft*. Cambridge, MA: MIT Press, 2006.

Frodl-Kraft, Eva. "Farbendualitäten, Gegenfarben, Grundfarben in der Gotischen Malerei." In *Von Farbe und Farben: Albert Knoepfli zum 70. Geburtstag*, ed. by Albert Knoepfli and Hans Joachim Albrecht, 293–302. Zurich: Manesse, 1980.

G

Gamboni, Dario. *Potential Images: Ambiguity and Indeterminacy in Modern Art*. London: Reaktion Books, 2002.

Ganz, David and Thomas Lentes, eds. *Sehen und Sakralität in der Vormoderne* (KultBild vol. 4), Berlin: Reimer, 2011.

Ganz, David and Stefan Neuner, eds. *Mobile Eyes: Peripatetisches Sehen in den Bildkulturen der Vormoderne*. Paderborn: Fink, 2013.

Gertsman, Elina. "Phantoms of Emptiness: The Space of the Imaginary in Late Medieval Art." *Art History* 41, no. 5 (2018): 801–837.

Gertsman, Elina, ed. *Abstraction in Medieval Art: Beyond the Ornament*. Amsterdam: Amsterdam University Press, 2021. https://doi.org/10.2307/j.ctv1g13jk5

Gombrich, Ernst H. *Art and Illusion: A Study in the Psychology of Pictorial Representation*. New York: Pantheon Books, 1960.

Gombrich, Ernst H. *Kunst und Illusion: Zur Psychologie der Bildlichen Darstellung*. Cologne: Phaidon, 1967.

Gombrich, Ernst H. *Shadows: The Depiction of Cast Shadows in Western Art*. New Haven, CT: National Gallery Publications and Yale University Press, 1995.

Greenberg, Clement. "Modernist Painting." *Art and Literature* 4 (1965): 193–201.

Greenberg, Clement. "Collage [1948]." In *Die Essenz der Moderne: Ausgewählte Essays und Kritiken*, ed. by Karlheinz Lüdeking, 157–162. Hamburg: Philo Fine Arts, 2009.

H

Haas, Bruno. *Die Ikonischen Situationen*. Paderborn: Fink, 2015.

Hahn, Cynthia J. "Visio Dei: Changes in Medieval Visuality." In *Visuality Before and Beyond the Renaissance: Seeing as Others Saw*, ed. by Robert S. Nelson, 169–196. Cambridge: Cambridge University Press, 2000.

Hamburger, Jeffrey F. and Anne-Marie Bouché, eds. *The Mind's Eye: Art and Theological Argument in the Middle Ages*. Princeton, NJ: Princeton University Press, 2006.

Hartmann, George W. *Gestalt Psychology: A Survey of Facts and Principles*, New York: The Ronald Press Company, 1935.

Hediger, Christine and Angela Schiffhauer. "Werkstoff Glas: Überlegungen zur Materialität von Glasmalerei in Moderne und Mittelalter," *Kunst und Architektur in der Schweiz* 58, no. 4 (2007): 15–23.

Heidegger, Martin. *Der Satz vom Grund*. Pfullingen: Neske, 1957.

Heidegger, Martin. *Identität und Differenz* (Gesamtausgabe, vol. 11). Frankfurt am Main: Vittorio Klostermann, 1976.

Heidegger, Martin. "On the Essence of Ground." Translated by William McNeill. In *Pathmarks*, ed. by William McNeill, 97–135. Cambridge: Cambridge University Press, 1998.

Heidegger, Martin. *Identity and Difference*. Translated by Joan Stambaugh. Chicago, IL: University of Chicago Press, 2002.

Husserl, Edmund. *Experience and Judgment: Investigations in a Genealogy of Logic*. Translated by James S. Churchill and Karl Ameriks, ed. by Ludwig Landgrebe. Evanston, IL: Northwestern University Press, 1973.

I

Imdahl, Max. *Giotto, Arenafresken: Ikonographie, Ikonologie, Ikonik*. Munich: Fink, 1988.

J

Jollet, Étienne. "Introduction." In *Le Fond de l'Œuvre*, ed. by Émilie Chedeville, Étienne Jollet, and Claire Sourdin, 13–26. Paris: Édition Sorbonne, 2020.

Jonas, Hans. "Homo Pictor und die Differentia des Menschen." *Zeitschrift für Philosophische Forschung* 15 (1961): 161–176.

K

Katz, David. *Gestaltpsychologie*. Basel: Schwabe, 1944.

Kay, Sarah. "Legible Skins: Animals and the Ethics of Medieval Reading." *Postmedieval: A Journal of Medieval Cultural Studies* 2 (2011): 13–32.

Kemp, Martin. *The Science of Art: Optical Themes in Western Art from Brunelleschi to Seurat*. New Haven, CT: Yale University Press, 1990.

Kemp, Wolfgang. *Rembrandt: Die Heilige Familie mit dem Vorhang*. Frankfurt am Main: Fischer, 1992.

Kemp, Wolfgang. *Die Räume der Maler: Zur Bilderzählung seit Giotto*. Munich: C. H. Beck, 1996.

Kenaan, Hagi. "Tracing Shadows: Reflections on the Origins of Painting." In *Pictorial Languages and Their Meanings: Liber Amicorum in Honor of Nurith Kenaan-Kedar*, ed. by Christine B. Verzar and Gil Fishhof, 17–28. Tel Aviv: Tel Aviv University Press, 2006.

Kenaan, Hagi. "The Ground's Hidden Surface." *Wolkenkuckucksheim: International Journal of Architectural Theory* 12 (2007): 17–28.

Kendrick, Laura. *Animating the Letter: The Figurative Embodiment of Writing from Late Antiquity to the Renaissance*. Columbus, OH: Ohio State University Press, 1999.

Kepes, Gyorgy. *Language of Vision*. Chicago, IL: P. Theobald, 1944.

Kernodle, Georges. *From Art to Theatre: Form and Convention in the Renaissance*. Chicago, IL: University of Chicago Press, 1943.

Kessler, Herbert L. *Spiritual Seeing: Picturing God's Invisibility in Medieval Art*. Philadelphia, PA: University of Pennsylvania Press, 2000.

Kessler, Herbert L. "Sacred Light from Shadowy Things." *Codex Aquilarensis* 32 (2016): 237–270.

Kim, David Young. "Why Weight? The Heaviness of Art and Narrative Force." In *Matters of Weight: Force, Gravity, and Aesthetics in the Early Modern Period*, ed. by David Young Kim, 9-34. Emsdetten: Edition Imorde, 2013.

Kim, David Young. "Points on a Field: Gentile da Fabriano and Gold Ground." *Journal of Early Modern History* 23, no. 2–3 (2019): 191–226. https://doi.org/10.1163/15700658-12342636.

Kim, David Young. *Groundwork: A History of the Renaissance Picture*. Princeton, NJ: Princeton University Press, 2022.

Kim, Susan and Asa Simon Mittman. "The Skin We Stand On: Landscape-Skinscape in the Tiberius B.v *Marvels of the East*." On Unstable Ground, ed. by Rachel Dressler and Benjamin C. Tilghman, special issue, *Different Visions: New Perspectives on Medieval Art* 9 (2023). https://doi.org/10.61302/NQTB9141.

Klemm, Tanja. *Bildphysiologie: Wahrnehmung und Körper in Mittelalter und Renaissance*. Berlin: Akademie Verlag, 2019.

Koffka, Kurt. *Principles of Gestalt Psychology*. New York: Harcourt, 1935.

Köhler, Wolfgang. *Gestalt Psychology*. New York: Horace Liveright, 1929.

Krüger, Klaus. *Giottos Figuren: Mimesis und Imagination*. Göttingen: Wallstein, 2023.

Krüger, Klaus. *Figura als Bild*. Göttingen: Wallstein, 2024.

Kuhn, Rudolf. *Komposition und Rhythmus*. Berlin: De Gruyter, 1980.

Kuhn, Rudolf. *On Composition as Method and Topic*. Frankfurt am Main: Lang, 2000.

Kumler, Aden. "Abstractions Gothic Grounds." In *Abstraction in Medieval Art: Beyond the Ornament*, ed. by Elina Gertsman, 55–87. Amsterdam: Amsterdam University Press, 2021. https://doi.org/10.2307/j.ctv1g13jk5.6.

Kumler, Aden. "'All Form is a Process of Notation'. Hrabanus Maurus's 'Exemplativist' Art." In *L'Art Medieval Est-il Contemporain? / Is Medieval Art Contemporary?*, ed. by Charlotte Denoël, Larisa Dryansky, Isabelle Marchesin, and Erik Verhagen, 91–111. Turnhout: Brepols, 2023.

Kurbjuhn, Charlotte. *Kontur: Geschichte einer Ästhetischen Denkfigur* (Quellen und Forschungen zur Literatur- und Kulturgeschichte, vol. 81). Berlin: De Gruyter, 2014.

Kurmann-Schwarz, Brigitte. "'Fenestre vitree [...] Significant Sacram Scripturam': Zur Medialität Mittelalterlicher Glasmalerei des 12. und 13. Jahrhunderts." In *Glasmalerei im Kontext: Bildprogramme und Raumfunktionen*, ed. by Rüdiger Becksmann, 61–73. Nuremberg: Germanisches Nationalmuseum, 2005.

Kurmann-Schwarz, Brigitte. "The Role of Ornament in the Conception and Significance of Medieval Figurative Stained Glass." In *The Concept and Fabrication of Stained Glass from the Middle Ages to Art Nouveau*, ed. by International Colloquium Corpus Vitrearum, 13–21. Barcelona: Corpus Vitrearum Catalunya, 2022.

L

Lakey, Christopher. "The Materiality of Light in Medieval Italian Painting." In *Medieval Materiality*, ed. by Anne E. Lester and Katherine C. Little, 119–136. Boulder, CO: University of Colorado, 2015.

Lakey, Christopher. *Sculptural Seeing: Relief, Optics, and the Rise of Perspective in Medieval Italy*. New Haven, CT: Yale University Press, 2018.

Leonhard, Karin. *The Fertile Ground of Painting: Seventheenth-Century Still Lifes & Nature Pieces*. London: Harvey Miller, 2020.

Levine, Caroline. *Forms: Whole, Rhythm, Hierarchy, Network*. Princeton, NJ: Princeton University Press, 2015.

Lewis, Sarah Elizabeth. "Groundwork: Race and Aesthetics in the Era of Stand Your Ground Law." *Art Journal* 79 (2020): 92–113.

Lička, Lukáš. "Shadows in Medieval Optics, Practical Geometry, and Astronomy: On a *Perspectiva* Ascribed to Thomas Bradwardine." *Early Science and Medicine* 27 (2022): 179–223.

M

Mach, Ernst. *Beiträge zur Analyse der Empfindungen*, Jena: G. Fischer, 1886.

Marin, Louis. "Mimésis et Description." *Word & Image: A Journal of Verbal/Visual Enquiry* 4, no. 1 (1988): 25–36.

Marin, Louis. *Opacité de la Peinture: Essais sur la Représentation au Quattrocento*. Paris: Usher, 1989.

Marin, Louis. "The Order of Words and the Order of Things in Painting." *Visible Language* 23 (1989): 188–203.

Marin, Louis. *To Destroy Painting*. Translated by Mette Hjort. Chicago, IL: University of Chicago Press, 1995.

Marin, Louis. "The Frame of Representation and Some of Its Figures." In *On Representation*, translated by Catherine Porter, 352–372. Stanford, CA: Stanford University Press, 2001.

Marx, Karl. *Grundrisse: Foundations of the Critique of Political Economy (Rough Draft)*. Translated by Martin Nicolaus. New York: Vintage Books, 1973.

McNamee, Megan. "Picturing as Practice: Placing a Square on a Square in the Central Middle Ages." In *Canonical Texts and Scholarly Practices: A Global Comparative Approach*, ed. by Anthony Grafton, and Glenn W. Most, 200–223. Cambridge: Cambridge University Press, 2016.

McNamee, Megan. "Imaging and Imagining Solidity." In *After the Carolingians: Re-Defining Manuscript Illumination in the 10th and 11th Centuries*, ed. by Beatrice Kitzinger and Joshua O'Driscoll, 86–117. Boston, MA: De Gruyter, 2019.

McNamee, Megan. "Early Romanesque Abstraction and the 'Unconditionally Two-dimensional Surface.'" In *Abstraction in Medieval Art: Beyond the Ornament*, ed. by Elina Gertsman, 267–284. Amsterdam: Amsterdam University Press, 2021.

Merleau-Ponty, Maurice. *Phénoménologie de la Perception*. Paris: Gallimard, 1945.

Merleau-Ponty, Maurice. "Eye and Mind." Translated by Carleton Dallery. In *The Primacy of Perception and Other Essays on Phenomenological Psychology, the Philosophy of Art, History and Politics*, ed. by James M. Edie, 159–190. Evanston, IL: Northwestern University Press, 1964.

Merleau-Ponty, Maurice. *The Visible and the Invisible*. Translated by Alphonso Lingis, ed. by Claude Lefort. Evanston, IL: Northwestern University Press, 1968.

Metzger, Wolfgang. *Laws of Seeing*. Cambridge, MA/London: MIT Press, 2006.

Milner, Max. *L'Envers du Visible: Essai sur l'Ombre*. Paris: Seuil, 2005.

Mitchell, W. J. T. *Picture Theory: Essays on Verbal and Visual Representation*. Chicago, IL: University of Chicago Press, 1994.

Mitchell, W. J. T. "Vier Grundbegriffe der Bildwissenschaft." In *Bildtheorien: Anthropologische und Kulturelle Grundlagen des Visualistic Turn*, ed. by Klaus Sachs-Hombach, 319–327. Frankfurt am Main: Suhrkamp, 2009.

Mocan, Mira. "'Lucem Demonstrat Umbra': Ombra e Immagine fra Letteratura e Arte nel Medioevo." In *Manipolare la Luce in Epoca Premoderna*, ed. by Daniela Mondini and Vladimir Ivanovici, 185–199. Mendrisio: Mendrisio Academy Press/Silvana Editorale, 2014.

Morison, Benjamin. *On Location: Aristotle's Concept of Place*. Oxford: Oxford Aristotle Studies, 2002.

Müller, Jürgen. *Das Paradox als Bildform: Studien zur Ikonologie Pieter Bruegels d. Ä.* Munich: Fink, 1999.

N

Nancy, Jean-Luc. *The Ground of the Image*. Translated by Jeff Fort. New York: Fordham University Press, 2005.

Neuner, Stefan. "Figur und Grund." In *Lexikon Kunstwissenschaft: Hundert Grundbegriffe*, ed. by Stefan Jordan and Jürgen Müller, 112–116. Stuttgart: Reclam, 2012.

O

O'Driscoll, Joshua. "Visual Vortex: An Epigraphic Image from an Ottonian Gospel Book" *Word and Image* 27, no. 3 (2011): 309–321.

Ohly, Friedrich. *Schriften zur Mittelalterlichen Bedeutungsforschung*. Darmstadt: Wissenschaftliche Buchgesellschaft, 1977.

P

Panofsky, Erwin. "'Imago Pietatis': Ein Beitrag zur Typengeschichte des 'Schmerzensmanns' und der 'Maria Mediatrix.'" In *Festschrift für Max J. Friedländer zum 60. Geburtstage*, 261–308. Leipzig: E. A. Seemann, 1927.

Panofsky, Erwin. *Early Netherlandish Painting: Its Origins and Character*. Cambridge, MA: Harvard University Press, 1953.

Panofksky, Erwin. "Die Perspektive als 'Symbolische Form' (1924/1925)." In *Erwin Panofsky. Deutschsprachige Aufsätze* (vol. 2), ed. by Karen Michels und Martin Warnke, 664–757. Berlin: Akademie Verlag, 1998.

Panofsky, Erwin. *Perspective as Symbolic Form*. Translated by Christopher S. Wood. New York: Zone Books, 1991.

Partridge, Joy. "Elements of Uncertainty: Visualizing the 'Spheres' of Water and Earth in the Late Middle Ages." On Unstable Ground, ed. by Rachel Dressler and Benjamin C. Tilghman, special issue, *Different Visions: New Perspectives on Medieval Art* 9 (2023) https://doi.org/10.61302/NAQJ5747.

Pastoureau, Michel. *Figures et Couleurs: Étude sur la Symbolique et la Sensibilité Médiévale*. Paris: Léopard d'Or, 1987.

Perler, Dominik. "Can We Trust our Senses? Fourteenth-Century Debates on Sensory Illusions." In *Uncertain Knowledge: Scepticism, Relativism, and Doubt in the Middle Ages*, ed. by Dallas G. Denery, Kantik Ghosh, and Nicolette Zeeman, 63–90. Turnhout: Brepols, 2014.

Peselmann, Veronica. *Der Grund der Malerei: Materialität im Prozess bei Corot und Courbet*. Berlin: Reimer, 2020.

Pichler, Wolfram. "Zur Kunstgeschichte des Bildfeldes." In *Der Grund: Das Feld des Sichtbaren*, ed. by Gottfried Boehm and Matteo Burioni, 441–472. Munich: Fink, 2012.

Pichler, Wolfram and Ralph Ubl. *Bildtheorie zur Einführung*. Hamburg: Junius, 2014.

Pind, Jörgen L. "Figure and Ground at 100." *The Psychologist* 25, no. 1 (2012): 90–91.

Pind, Jörgen L. *Edgar Rubin and Psychology in Denmark: Figure and Ground*. Cham: Springer, 2014.

Poetsch, Christoph. *Platons Philosophie des Bildes: Systematische Untersuchungen zur Platonischen Metaphysik*. Frankfurt am Main: Klostermann, 2019.

Popova, Maria. *Figuring*. Edinburgh: Canongate Books, 2019.

Pratschke, Margarete. *Gestaltexperimente unterm Bilderhimmel: Das Psychologische Institut im Berliner Stadtschloss und die Avantgarde*. Paderborn: Fink, 2016.

Prevost, Bertrand. *Peindre sous la Lumière: Leon Battista Alberti et le Moment Humaniste de l'Évidence*. Rennes: Presses Universitaires de Rennes, 2013.

Puttfarken, Thomas. *The Discovery of Pictorial Composition: Theories of Visual Order in Painting, 1400–1800*. New Haven, CT: Yale University Press, 2000.

Q

Quené, Saskia C. *Goldgrund und Perspektive: Fra Angelico im Glanz des Quattrocento*. Berlin/Boston: Deutscher Kunstverlag, 2022. https://doi.org/10.1515/9783422800533.

Quené, Saskia C. "Figures, Grounds, and Gold: Relocating the Madonna of Humility." On Unstable Ground, ed. by Rachel Dressler and Benjamin C. Tilghman, special issue, *Different Visions: New Perspectives on Medieval Art* 9 (2023). https./doi.org/10.61302/YAGI7299.

R

Randall, Lilian M. C. *Images in the Margins of Gothic Manuscripts*. Berkeley, CA: University of California Press, 1966.

Raphael, Max. *Die Farbe Schwarz: Zur materiellen Konstituierung der Form*. Frankfurt am Main: Qumran, 1984.

Raynaud, Dominique. *Optics and the Rise of Perspective: A Study in Network Knowledge Diffusion*. Oxford: The Bardwell, 2014.

Raynaud, Dominique. "A Hitherto Unknown Treatise on Shadows Referred to by Leonardo da Vinci." In *Perspective as Practice. Renaissance Cultures of Optics*, ed. by Sven Dupré, 259–277. Turnhout: Brepols, 2019.

Rosenberg, Raphael. "Vom Technischen Fortschritt zur Geschichte des Sehens: Entwicklung als Paradigma der Kunsthistoriografie." In *Umgang mit der Temporalität in den Sozial- und Geisteswissenschaften*, ed. by Thomas Maissen et al., 175–196. Bochum: Winkler, 2019.

Rubin, Edgar. *Synsoplevede Figurer: Studier i psykologisk Analyse: Første Del*. Diss. phil., Københavns Universitet. Copenhagen/Kristiania, 1915.

Rubin, Edgar. *Visuell Wahrgenommene Figuren: Studien in Psychologischer Analyse*. Copenhagen: Gyldendal, 1921.

Russo, Daniel. "Plans, Fonds, Surfaces: Présence Visuelle et Politique de l'Objet à l'Époque Carolingienne." In *Charlemagne et les Objets: Des Thésaurisations Carolingiennes aux Constructions Mémorielles*, ed. by Philippe Cordez, 3–27. Bern: Peter Lang, 2012.

S

Sandler, Lucy Freeman. "The Study of Marginal Imagery: Past, Present, Future." *Studies in Iconography* 18 (1997): 1–49.

Schapiro, Meyer. "On Some Problems in the Semiotics of Visual Art: Field and Vehicle in Image-Signs." *Simiolus: Netherlands Quarterly for the History of Art* 6, no. 1 (1972–1973): 9–19.

Schellewald, Barbara. "Gold, Licht und das Potenzial des Mosaiks." *Zeitschrift für Kunstgeschichte* 79, no. 4 (2016): 461–480.

Schirra, Jörg and Zsuzsanna Kondor. "Das bildphilosophische Stichwort 24: Figur/Grund-Differenzierung." *IMAGE: Zeitschrift für Interdisziplinäre Bildwissenschaft* 14, no. 2 (2018): 181–193. http://dx.doi.org/10.25969/mediarep/16401.

Schneider, Wolfgang C. et al., eds. *"Videre et Videri Coincidunt": Theorien des Sehens in der Ersten Hälfte des 15. Jahrhunderts* (Texte und Studien zur Europäischen Geistesgeschichte). Münster: Aschendorff, 2011.

Scholz, Oliver. *Bild, Darstellung, Zeichen: Philosophische Theorien Bildlicher Darstellung*. Frankfurt am Main: Klostermann, 2004.

Seel, Martin. *Ästhetik des Erscheinens*. Frankfurt am Main: Suhrkamp, 2003.

Seidel, Linda. "Formalism." In *A Companion to Medieval Art: Romanesque and Gothic in Northern Europe*, ed. by Conrad Rudolph, 171–194. Hoboken: Blackwell, 2019.

Shartrand, Emily. "'I Have The High Ground!': The Snail and Knight Motif in the Margins of Manuscripts." On Unstable Ground, ed. by Rachel Dressler and Benjamin C. Tilghman, special issue, *Different Visions: New Perspectives on Medieval Art* 9 (2023). https://doi.org/10.61302/UVKB8713.

Silva, José Filipe and Juhana Toivanen. "Perceptual Errors in Late Medieval Philosophy." In *The Senses and the History of Philosophy: Rewriting the History of Philosophy*, ed. by Brian Glenney and José Filipe Silva, 106–130. New York: Routledge, 2019.

Skaug, Erling S. "Not Just Panel and Gound." In *Preparation for Painting: The Artist's Choice and its Consequences*, ed. by Joyce H. Townsend, Tiarna Doherty, Gunnar Heydenreich, and Jacqueline Ridge, 22–29. London: Archetype, 2008.

Steinert, Tom. *Komplexe Wahrnehmung und moderner Städtebau*. Zürich: Park Books, 2014.

Steinert, Tom. "Regaining Complex Perception. Gestalt Thinking in 20th Century Architectural Theory." *gestalt theory: An International Multidisciplinary Journal* 4 (2014): 325–337.

Stoichiță, Victor. *The Self-Aware Image: An Insight into Early Modern Metapainting*. Translated by Lorenzo Pericolo. Chicago, IL: Harvey Miller, 2015.

Stoichiță, Victor. *A Short History of the Shadow.* London: Reaktion Books, 1999.

Stols–Witlox, Maartje. *A Perfect Ground: Preparatory Layers for Oil Paintings 1550–1900*. London: Archetype, 2018.

Stumpel, Jeroen. "On Grounds and Backgrounds: Some Remarks about Composition in Renaissance Painting." *Simiolus* 18 (1988): 219–243.

Stumpel, Jeroen. "'Here is the Thing': On Object, Ground and Background in the History of Art and Images." *Art & Perception* 12, no. 2 (2024): 144–169.

Suthor, Nicola. „Vertiefte Einblicke: Zur Sichtbarkeit des Malgrundes." In *Rembrandts Rauheit*, 81–111. Paderborn: Fink, 2014.

T

Tachau, Katherine H. *Vision and Certitude in the Age of Ockham: Optics, Epistemology, and the Foundations of Semantics, 1250–1345* (Studien und Texte zur Geistesgeschichte des Mittelalters 22). Leiden: Brill, 1988.

Thebaut, Nancy. "The Double-Sided Image: Abstraction and Figuration in Early Medieval Painting." In *Abstraction in Medieval Art: Beyond the Ornament*, ed. by Elina Gertsman, 213–244. Amsterdam: Amsterdam University Press, 2021.

Thebaut, Nancy. "Zones, Stripes, and Strata: The Banded Grounds of Early Medieval Paintings." On Unstable Ground, ed. by Rachel Dressler and Benjamin C. Tilghman, special issue, *Different Visions: New Perspectives on Medieval Art* 9 (2023) https://doi.org/10.61302/PTAF6811.

Toivanen, Juhana. "Perceptual Experience: Assembling a Medieval Puzzle." In *Philosophy of Mind in the Early and High Middle Ages* (The History of the Philosophy of Mind 2), ed. by Margaret Cameron, 134–156. New York: Routledge, 2018.

Treharne, Elaine. *Perceptions of Medieval Manuscripts: The Phenomenal Book*. Oxford: Oxford University Press, 2021. https://doi.org/10.1093/oso/9780192843814.001.0001.

Turel, Noa. *Living Pictures: Jan van Eyck and Painting's First Century*. New Haven, CT: Yale University Press, 2020.

V

Verstegen, Ian. "Between Presence and Perspective: The Portrait-in-a-Picture in Early Modern Painting." *Zeitschrift für Kunstgeschichte* 71 (2008): 513–526.

W

Wagemans, Johan, James H. Elder, Michael Kubovy, Stephen E. Palmer, Mary A. Peterson, Manish Singh, and Rüdiger von der Heydt. "A Century of Gestalt Psychology in Visual Perception 1: Perceptual Grouping and Figure–Ground Organization." *Psychological Bulletin* 138, no. 6 (2012): 1172–1217.

Weigel, Sigrid. "Die Richtung des Bildes: Zum Links-Rechts von Bilderzählungen und Bildbeschreibungen in Kultur- und Mediengeschichtlicher Perspektive." *Zeitschrift für Kunstgeschichte* 64 (2001): 449–474.

Westerby, Matthew J. "Restabilizing a Locus Designatus: Capitals as Gnomons on the Cloister Ground at Santa Maria de Ripol." On Unstable Ground, ed. by Rachel Dressler and Benjamin C. Tilghman, special issue, *Different Visions: New Perspectives on Medieval Art* 9 (2023). https://doi.org/10.61302/GMPM4874.

Wharton, Edith. *Italian Backgrounds*. New York: Charles Scribner's Sons, 1905.

White, John. *The Birth and Rebirth of Pictorial Space*. London: Farber and Farber, 1957.

White, Richard. *The Middle Ground. Indians, Empires, and Republics in the Great Lakes Region, 1650–1815*. Cambridge: Cambridge University Press, 1991.

Whittington, Karl. "Diagramming Triumph in Trecento Painting: Augustine and Thomas from Page to Wall." In *New Horizons in Trecento Italian Art*, ed. by Karl Whittington and Bryan Keene, 231–244. Turnhout: Brepols, 2020.

Wiesing, Lambert: *Artifizielle Präsenz: Studien zur Philosophie des Bildes*, Frankfurt am Main: Suhrkamp, 2005.

Wiesing Lambert. *Artificial Presence: Philosophical Studies in Image Theory*. Translated by Nils F. Schott. Stanford, CA: Stanford University Press, 2009.

Wirth, Jean. "Soll man Bilder Anbeten? Theorien zum Bilderkult bis zum Konzil von Trient." In *Bildersturm: Wahnsinn oder Gottes Wille?*, ed. by Cécile Dupeux, Peter Jezler, and Jean Wirth, 28–37. Munich: Fink, 2000.

Wölfflin, Heinrich. *Die Klassische Kunst: Eine Einführung in die Italienische Renaissance*. Munich: Bruckmann, 1899.

Wölfflin, Heinrich. *Kunstgeschichtliche Grundbegriffe: Das Problem der Stilentwickelung in der Neueren Kunst* (Quellen zur Geschichte der Kunstgeschichte). Munich: Bruckmann, 1915.

Wollheim, Richard. "Seeing-as, Seeing-in, and Pictorial Representation." In: *Art and Its Objects: With Six Supplementary Essays*, 137–151. Cambridge: Cambridge University Press, 1980.

Wollheim, Richard. "On Pictorial Representation." *The Journal of Aesthetics and Art Criticism* 56, no. 3 (1998): 217–226.

Wood, Christopher S. "Introduction." In *Perspective as Symbolic Form*. Translated by Christopher S. Wood, 7–24. New York: Zone Books, 1991.

Wright, Alison. *Frame Work: Honour and Ornament in Italian Renaissance Art*. New Haven, CT: Yale University Press, 2019.

Z

Zorach, Rebecca. *The Passionate Triangle*. Chicago, IL: University of Chicago Press, 2011.

Acknowledgements

Between Figure and Ground: Seeing in Premodernity would not have existed without Matteo Burioni, with whom I developed the idea to realize a conference in Basel, Switzerland, when I was still a graduate student at eikones – Center for the Theory and History of the Image. Despite the disruptions caused by the COVID-19 pandemic, which forced us to postpone the conference twice from June 2020 to June 2022, our generous financial supporters—the Swiss National Science Foundation, the University of Basel, the Ellen J. Beer Stiftung, the University of Bern, and the Humboldt University of Berlin—remained patient and supportive. Their commitment sustained my anticipation as I transferred to Berkeley, California in early 2022.

My heartfelt thanks go to Gina Ketterer, the organizational powerhouse behind our final event. Her proactive approach and perceptiveness made it possible to enjoy three days of buoyant exchange and thought-provoking conversations. Nadia Wipfli from the University of Bern and Daniela Steinebrunner from the University of Basel also deserve special recognition for their administrative support, which made even the post-conference tasks seamless. Thank you.

Throughout the following months, conversations with conference participants, colleagues, and students continued. The idea to create a book that would foreground experiencing complex premodern figure-and-ground relationships through written as much as visual arguments evolved at Dorothee Dähler's and Kaj Lehmann's Zürich design studio. They shared my excitement to challenge formal dichotomies and became the most excellent partners in crime. Readers may have already noticed how figure- and page numbers create a dynamic space between figure and ground throughout the book. It was an honor to witness their creativity and learn from their approaches.

Pablo Schneider from the Deutsche Kunstverlag was brave enough not to be scared off by our imagination and excitedly took on the project. Arielle Thürmel and Stefanie Kruszyk were as supportive as they were patient to wait for the best result and I am thankful for their help and insight. I am indebted to the Swiss National Science Foundation for generously supporting the development and Open Access publication of this extensive volume. Without the SNSF, both the conference and the publication would not have come to life. The Geschwister Boehringer Ingelheim Stiftung für Geisteswissenschaften, the Tübinger Kunstgeschichtliche Gesellschaft e.V., the Universitätsbund Tübingen, and the Karl-Jaberg-Stiftung Bern contributed to subsidize the ambitious hardcover print edition. I appreciate their trust and patronage.

Aaron Bogart and Moritz Bensch contributed tremendously through their canny and accurate editing in multiple languages, and I am grateful for their guidance and ability to catch what I had missed. Four anonymous reviewers shared their time and expertise to productively join us in the process, for which I am grateful. However, nothing would have appeared on paper without the commitment, perseverance, and expertise of the authors in this volume. I am grateful for their enthusiasm, effort, and reliability and it was an honor to pursue this project with you. Last but not least, I am deeply indebted to Gregor von Kerssenbrock-von Krosigk, who was responsible for obtaining most of the image rights while keeping track of what had to be done next. His farsighted and versatile assistance lets me keep my cool and makes me look forward to every deadline.

Part 1
Staging Figures

Rogier van der Weyden's *Seven Sacraments Altarpiece*, self-reflexive like much of his oeuvre, combines ideas about mimesis, mediation, and the sacred [fig. 51].[1] Tasked (we assume) with iterating the relatively new iconography of the Seven Sacraments as a conceptual whole, Rogier takes an almost shockingly literal approach. The side chapels of a Gothic church are populated by figures in contemporaneous garb enacting Baptism, Confirmation, and Reconciliation (left) and Ordination, Marriage, and Extreme Unction (right). The seventh sacrament to complete the set, the Eucharist, famously (and appropriately) occurs at the high altar near the center of the painting. The very center is dedicated to an oversized Crucifixion scene in the fore.

So familiar is the visual analogy between the Passion and the contemporaneous rite, that the sheer oddness of the Crucifixion motif is often overlooked. The painting features what Panofsky termed a "diaphragm" composition, namely a sliced-open interior scene pressing up against the picture plane, its pictorial space thus melding with that of the viewers.[2] In this work, the melding is accentuated by the presumed function of this very artifact as a high altarpiece within a space not unlike the one depicted in it. Why, then, did Rogier choose to blur the divide between actual and pictorial space but block the latter's main doorway? I propose that he does so to compel us to walk around. The foregrounding of two rites bracketing a good Christian life—Baptism and Extreme Unction—leaves little room for misinterpretation; the viewer is indeed expected to "walk" (metaphorically, live) clockwise from left to right, or, more accurately, from the center foreground, around and back again to God, incarnate on the cross. The circular structure of this painting, coupled with the deliberate vacillation between space and surface (with the Eucharist in the back rhyming with Christ's body in the fore), are both common pictorial strategies in Early Netherlandish

1
On this painting see Dirk de Vos, *Rogier van Der Weyden: The Complete Works* (New York: Harry N. Abrams, 1999), pp. 217–225, n. 11, among many others. On the iconography of the Seven Sacraments see Ann Eljenholm Nichols, *Seeable Signs: The Iconography of the Seven Sacraments, 1350–1544* (Woodbridge, UK: Boydell Press, 1994).

2
Erwin Panofsky, *Early Netherlandish Painting, Its Origins and Character* (Cambridge, MA: Harvard University Press, 1953), p. 58.

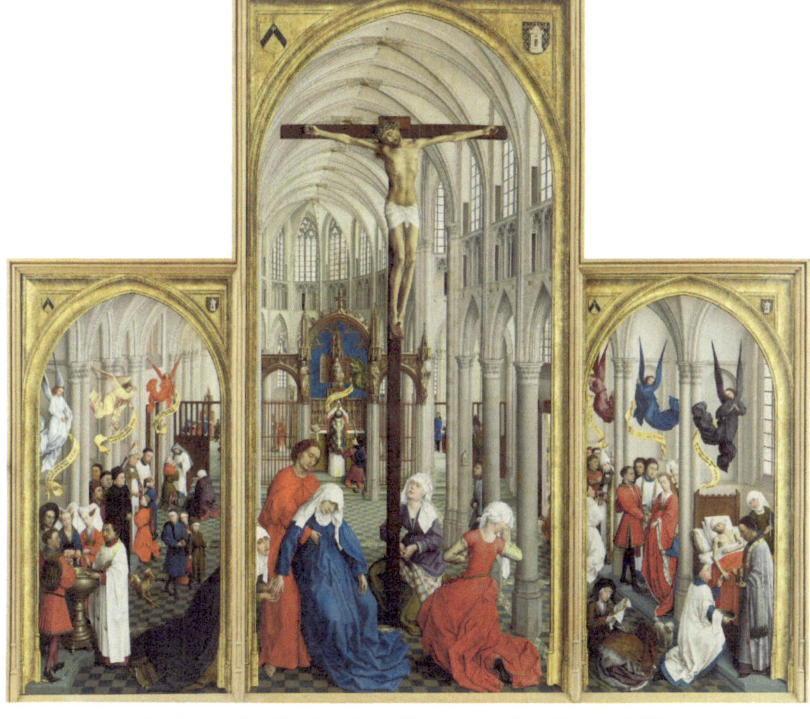

Rogier van der Weyden, *Seven Sacraments Altarpiece*, ca. 1450, oil on oak, central panel 200 × 97 cm, each side 119 × 63 cm. Koninklijk Museum voor Schone Kunsten, inv. nr. 393-395, Antwerp.

Fig. 51

painting.[3] Each also seems to upend any clearcut division between figures and ground; closely entwined, both the pictorial space and the bodies populating it play an essential role in the production of meaning.

Paintings such as Rogier's *Seven Sacraments* speak directly to the question underlying the present volume: given that the dichotomy "figure and ground" is a creature of modern art criticism, how did painters active earlier conceptualize pictorial structure? Many scholars have grappled with this question, though the debate curiously impacted the overall scholarly conversation far less than other types of questions, ranging from connoisseurship to iconography.[4] Thomas Puttfarken focused the fourth chapter of his *The Discovery of Pictorial Composition*, aptly titled "Figure and Ground (Or, the Human Body vs the Rest of the World)," on the perceived dichotomy, arguing that conceptualizing the pictorial ground as part of a "meaningless system of planimetric commensuration" would undercut its highest perceived value to a Renaissance viewer, namely its illusionism.[5] I would nuance that point by arguing that the viewing contract of most Early Netherlandish paintings was predicated not so much on the actual illusion of reality as on the convention of perceived accessibility. Rogier's *Seven Sacraments*, specifically, tapped an even more concrete viewing experience related to its novel iconography (a point I return to at the end of this paper), but its circular, immersive structure is premised on a conception of painting as essentially a spatial intervention.[6] And while Puttfarken's point that the Renaissance picture "has no ontological status apart from its figures and objects" may be debated, the visual evidence strongly suggests that, in the 1400s, pictorial spaces were meant to be experienced in the

3
Another famous example is the patron at the fore "holding up" the Autun church in the background of Jan van Eyck's *Virgin and Child with Chancellor Nicolas Rolin* (Louvre, Paris).

4
Panofsky's *Early Netherlandish Painting*, for instance is rarely remembered for its extensive forays into comparative late-medieval theories of representation, derived from his 1924 essay "Perspective as Symbolic Form" (English edition 1997).

5
Thomas Puttfarken, *The Discovery of Pictorial Composition* (New Haven, CT: Yale University Press, 2000), pp. 97–98.

6
See Noa Turel, *Living Pictures: Jan van Eyck and Painting's First Century* (New Haven, CT: Yale University Press, 2020), pp. 97–121.

round, as if from within. Within those spaces, viewers were invited to exercise what I elsewhere termed "somatic spectatorship."[7]

To fully understand this term, it is crucial to first undo a tenet of modern art criticism, one very much related to the figure-ground dichotomy, namely the idea that painting is somehow an essentially flat, two-dimensional medium. Modern thinkers such as Maurice Denis and Clement Greenberg treated painting's presumed flatness as a premise. This presumed flatness is what prompts us, I believe, to think of painting in terms of layers not merely of paint (a material fact), but also of elements—such as, indeed, the figures *over* the ground. Layers, neatly divided, are indeed everywhere in modernity—from theatrical scenery, through Georges Méliès' early cinematic special effects, to Disney's multipane camera. Perception, always operating through culturally established patterns, directs us to read fifteenth-century art as, similarly, a set of illusory overlays.

This conception of the medium did not yet exist in the 1400s. Rather, in that visual culture, a multitude of three-dimensional objects, ranging from sculpture, through architecture, to theatrical props, were habitually polychromed, and what we nowadays classify as *a* painting (namely one with a flat, often rectangular support) was but one subcategory of the broader category of "paintworks," which encompassed essentially everything that painters created (or finished), including polychromed sculpture and live pageants. In my article, I would like to further explore the question of figure and ground in fifteenth-century art by drawing on a rare resource: three figureless images.

Master WA's Prints

The engravings reproduced in figures 54–56 form part of the enigmatic oeuvre of the unidentified (though attempts have been made) monogrammist Master WA, also known as Master W with Key.[8]

7
Ibid., pp. 116–121.

8
The WA prints are reproduced in volume VII of *The New Hollstein Dutch & Flemish Etchings Engravings and Woodcuts 1450–1700*, ed. Ilja M. Veldman, Ger Luijten, and Friedrich Wilhelm Heinrich Hollstein (Roosendaal: Koninklijke Van Poll / Rijksprentenkabinet, Rijksmuseum Amsterdam, 1993). For the scholarly literature on Master WA / W with Key, see below.

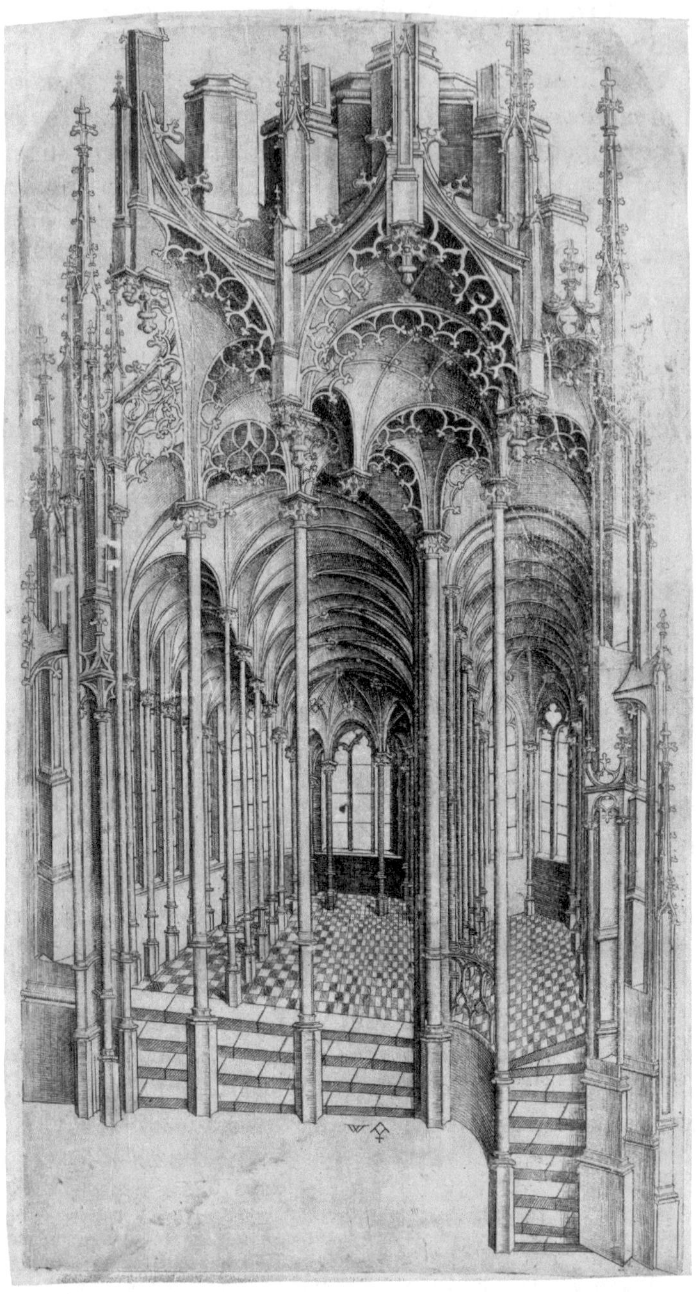

Master WA, A Gothic Hall, ca. 1465–1590, engraving, 34.9 × 19 cm.
Kupferstichkabinett, inv. nr. 181-1881, Berlin.

Fig. 54

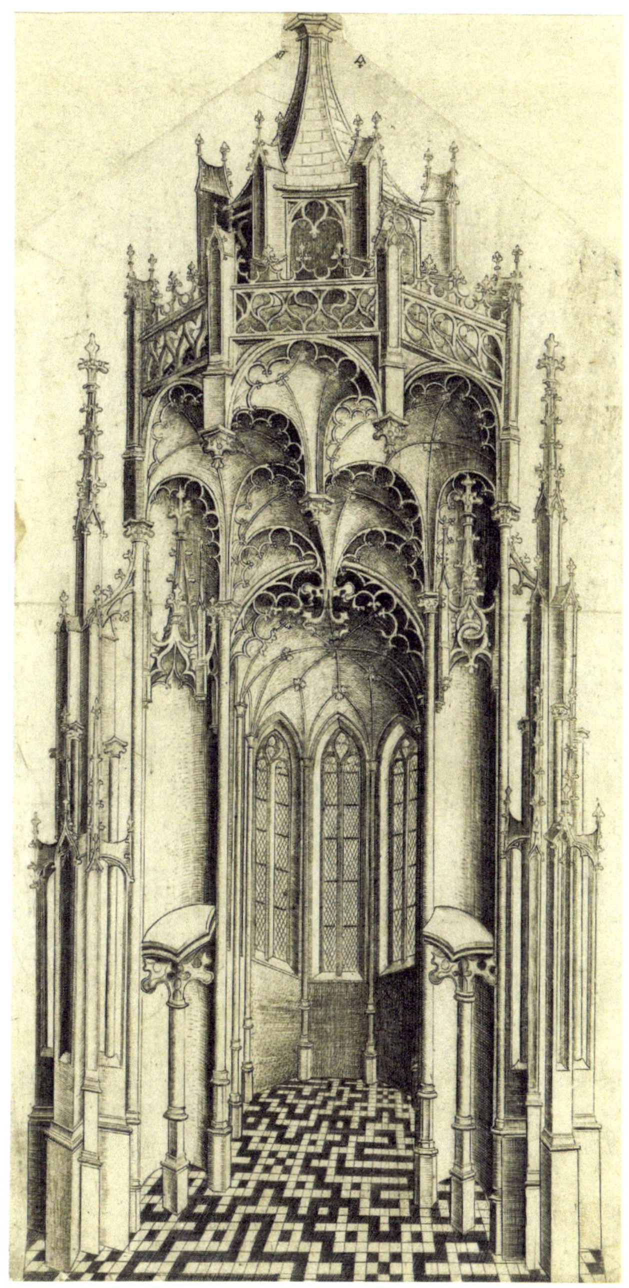

Master WA, Interior of a Gothic Chapel, ca. 1465–1590, engraving, 39.5 × 18.5 cm.
British Museum, inv. nr. E,1.193, London.

Fig. 55

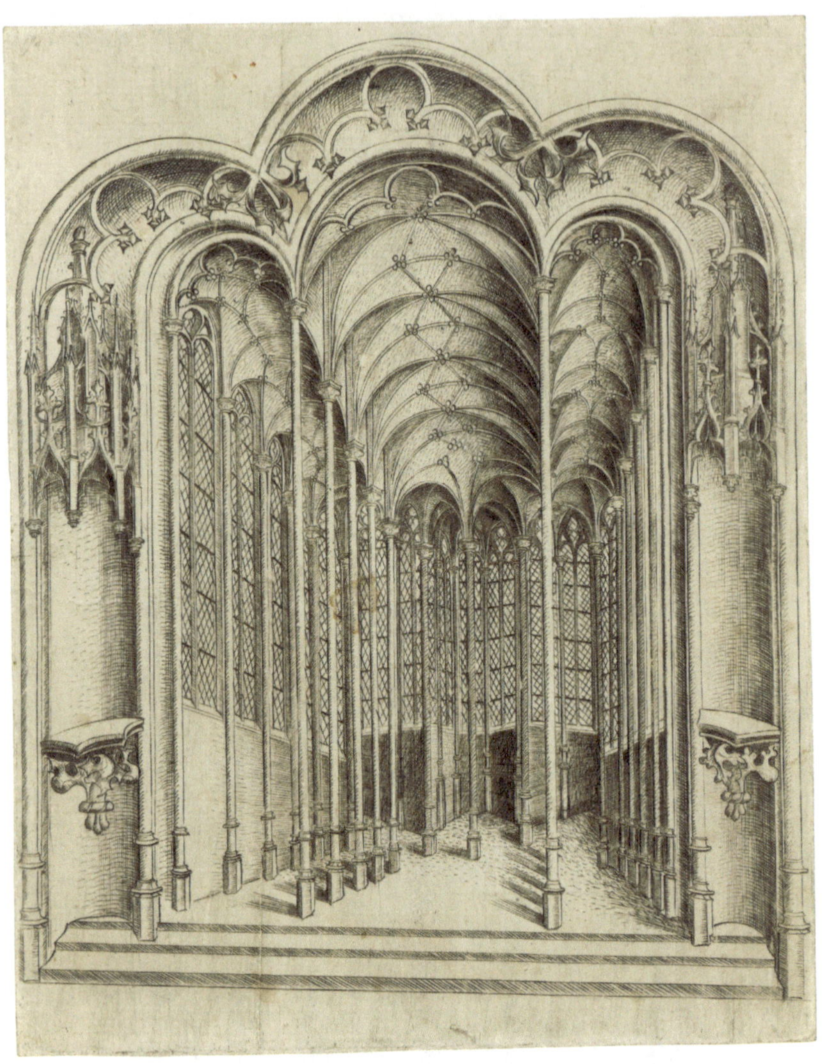

Master WA, Interior of a Gothic Church, ca. 1465–1590, engraving, 16.5 × 13.4 cm.
Rijksmuseum, inv. nr. RP-P-1986-42, Amsterdam.

Fig. 56

Drawing on these three engravings, I will trace the intrinsic and extrinsic evidence that ties them to spatial modes of art-making and viewing, to show how the conception of pictorial space in paintings and engravings was still deeply rooted in the practices, possibilities, and limitations of spatially immersive art like sculpture, architecture, and live spectacle.

Attempts to unpack the conception of pictorial composition in early Renaissance art, and especially in Early Netherlandish painting, face the dual challenge of seemingly sparse ekphrastic texts and, more crucially, a dearth of a certain type of visual evidence. Preparatory drawings, especially the kind used to design whole compositions, are rarely preserved from the 1400s north of the Alps. So, the WA group of engravings, likely produced in Bruges in the third quarter of the fifteenth century, provide rare insight into artistic processes. As many art historians have noted, these processes were greatly affected by the parallel creation of numerous artifacts that do not currently survive, most notably the production, on a very large scale, of ephemeral props, costumes, and stages for theatrical and pageantry productions.[9]

Since mechanically reproduced, illustrated festival books were only introduced in the sixteenth century, leading ephemeral forms of art before 1500 are preserved almost exclusively in texts.[10] One such text, from an accounting report for a 1468 Burgundian ducal wedding, describes a panel ("tabernacle") that was set, on that occasion, atop the court's gate:

> Item, a great relief-panel [tabernacle] was made to be put on and attached to the wall above the large gate of the court, in which were carved two lions holding the helmet, shield, and crest of my aforementioned master, surrounded

9
See, among many others, Georges Kernodle, *From Art to Theatre: Form and Convention in the Renaissance* (Chicago: University of Chicago Press, 1943); Mark Trowbridge, *Art and Ommegangen: Paintings, Processions, and Dramas in the Late-Medieval Low Countries*, PhD diss. (Institute of Fine Arts, New York University, 2000); and Jacob Wisse, *Official City Painters in Brabant, 1400–1500: A Documentary and Interpretive Approach*, PhD diss. (Institute of Fine Arts, New York University, 1999).

10
On the dearth of fifteenth-century visual records see Wim Blockmans and Esther Donckers, "Self-Representation of Court and City in Brabant and Flanders in the Fifteenth and Early Sixteenth Centuries," in *Showing Status: Representation of Social Positions in the Late Middle Ages*, Wim Blockmans and Antheun Janse, eds. (Turnhout: Brepols, 1999), pp. 81–111, esp. p. 94.

> by the coats of arms of the duchy, county, domain, and title of this [master]. Richly painted and decorated. And on top of that crest, on one side is carved the statue of St. Andrew, and on the other side the statue of St. George.[11]

This description unmistakably corresponds with the object depicted in one of Master WA's prints [fig. 59]; two lions, exhibiting (and surrounded by) Charles the Bold's insignia within a quasi-architectural framework ("tabernacle"), flanked by carved representations of St. Andrew and St. George. The court official Olivier de la Marche, who was directly involved in the production of the festivities, supplements this description by noting that Charles's device, "*Je l'ay emprins*," was inscribed at the bottom of this panel.[12]

Based on the unequivocal connection between the description and the print, Max Lehrs argued that Master WA was a goldsmith active in Bruges and associated with the court of Duke Charles the Bold.[13] This hypothesis seems quite plausible because Bruges was

11
"Item a este fait ung grant tabernacle pour metre et atachier ou mur dessus la grant porte de lentree de la court / ou quel lon a entretaillie deux lyons tenant les heaulme escu et tymbre de mondits[eigneu]r / auiron[n]e de blasons des armes des duche / comte seigneurte et tiltre dicelui s[eigneu]r. Richement paints et aornez et en hault dudit tymbre / a lun des costez est lymage de saint andrieu entretaillie / et a lautre cost est lymage de saint george." Archives générales du Royaume in Brussels (AGR), N 1795, fols. 80r–80v.

12
Olivier de La Marche, *Mémoires d'Olivier de La Marche: maître d'hôtel et capitaine des gardes de Charles le Téméraire,* 4 vols., Jules d'Arbaumont, ed. (Paris: Librairie Renouard, H. Loones, 1883–1888), vol. 3, p. 115.

13
Max Lehrs, *Der Meister W A [Gable symbol]: Ein Kupferstecher der Zeit Karls des Kühnen* (Leipzig: K. W. Hiersemann, 1895). Lehr reiterated the findings of his monograph on the Master in volume 5 of his monumental *Katalog* in 1930 (Max Lehrs, *Geschichte Und Kritischer Katalog Des Deutschen, Niederländischen Und Französischen Kupferstichs Im XV. Jahrhundert*. 18 vols. [Vienna: Gesellschaft für vervielfältigende Kunst, 1908–1934], vol. 5, pp. 1–24). That volume is still the most useful text on Master WA, as all the preceding publications, including Wolfgang Boerner's 1927 dissertation on the engraver (Bonn, Rheinischen Friedrich-Wilhelms-Universität), are summarized therein. It is clear from the inscription "Kraeck" on the print reproduced in figure 6 that this artist operated in the Netherlands. In addition to the print, the argument for Bruges is based on a technical detail: Lehr, quoting Passavant, thought that some of the papers' watermarks are typical of Bruges (Lehrs, *Geschichte*, vol. 5, p. 2). According to Ursula Mayr-Harting, monogram signing is a phenomenon that developed in the Netherlands in the final quarter of the fifteenth century (*Early Netherlandish Engraving, c. 1440–1540* [Oxford: Ashmolean Museum, 1997], p. 8). On the coat-of-arms print and two others in Master WA's oeuvre see, most recently, the catalogue essays on objects nos. 50, 51, 52 by Barbara Welzel in Till-Holger Borchert and Gabriele Keck, eds., *Charles le Téméraire, 1433–1477 splendeurs de la cour de Bourgogne*, trans. Susan Marti (Brussels: Mercatorfonds, 2009), pp. 222–223. Note that some of Welzel's assertions do not withstand close scrutiny. For instance, her claim that the tabernacle engraving's provenance is traceable to the Burgundian court library (p. 222) is incorrect. Based on both the card catalogue and the

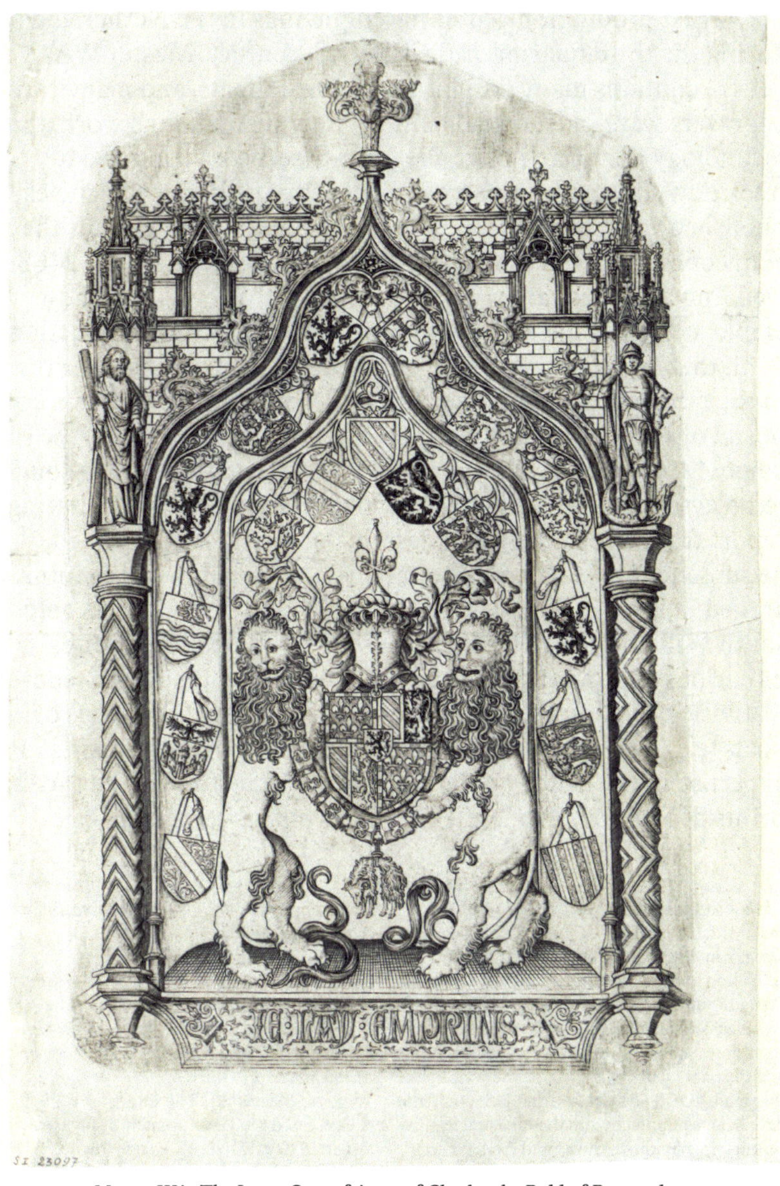

Master WA, The Large Coat of Arms of Charles the Bold of Burgundy,
ca. 1470–1475, engraving, 33.5 × 20.3 cm. KBR, inv. nr. S.I 23097, Brussels.

Fig. 59

the largest production center for engravings in the Netherlands during the third quarter of the fifteenth century, Master WA's oeuvre contains many designs for metal artifacts, and many early engravers were indeed goldsmiths.[14] Relying on Lehr's work, the technology historian André Wegener-Sleeswyk purported to track down the engraver's precise identity in a series of articles published from 1989–1995.[15] Wegener-Sleeswyk interprets the connection between the panel print and documents of the 1468 wedding festivities as evidence that Master WA was somehow employed by the ducal court in connection with that production. With that as his premise, he hypothesizes that the sign after the W in the monogram denotes neither an A nor a key, but rather a composite of the letter A and a cross, and thus a clever play on the surname *A Cruce* (a Latinized form of *vanden Cruce*). He then sought, to no avail, a name fitting the monogram in the same accounting report from which the panel description derives. Undeterred, he subsequently scanned other archival documents and eventually argued in favor of identifying Master WA with the Bruges goldsmith Willem vanden Cruce. He also tried to tie more groups of curious engravings in the Master's oeuvre to the 1468 wedding festivities, including eight of the earliest known engravings of boats [e.g., figs. 61 and 62]. Wegener-Sleeswyk drew on his expertise in the history of technology to argue that Master WA's prints depict not actual, full-size boats but rather small-scale

manuscripts' internal stamps, MS 15960-62, from which the print was purportedly taken, was not an integral part of the Burgundian collection but was subsumed into the Belgian Royal Library (KBR) from the Varia Family archives. This manuscript is a compilation of all sorts of graphic renditions of heraldic insignia, and the pages still extant in it bear a watermark that reads "DL & Cie 1840"—that is, it could not have been compiled before the mid-nineteenth century. It is unknown how (and from where) the panel print [fig. 59], which is undoubtedly an authentic fifteenth-century engraving, made its way into the Varia collection.

14
Metal-plate *intaglio* printing was a relatively new technology, developed in the 1430s in workshops of south-German goldsmiths. See Mayr-Harting, *Early Netherlandish Engraving*, pp. 5–15.

15
André Wegener-Sleeswyk, "The Engraver Willem A Cruce and the Development of the Chain Wale," in *Tractrix: Yearbook for the History of Science, Medicine, Technology and Mathematics* 1 (1989): pp. 21–44; André Wegener-Sleeswyk, "The Engraver Willem A Cruce and the Development of the Chain Wale," in *The Mariner's Mirror* 76, no. 4 (1990): pp. 345–361; André Wegener-Sleeswyk, "De Graveur WA: Een Speeurtocht," in *Gens Nostra* XLIX (1994): pp. 1–13; and André Wegener-Sleeswyk, "De graveur WA: Speurtocht naar een Vlaamse monogrammist," in *Spiegel-historiael* 30 (1995): pp. 7–8, 280–287.

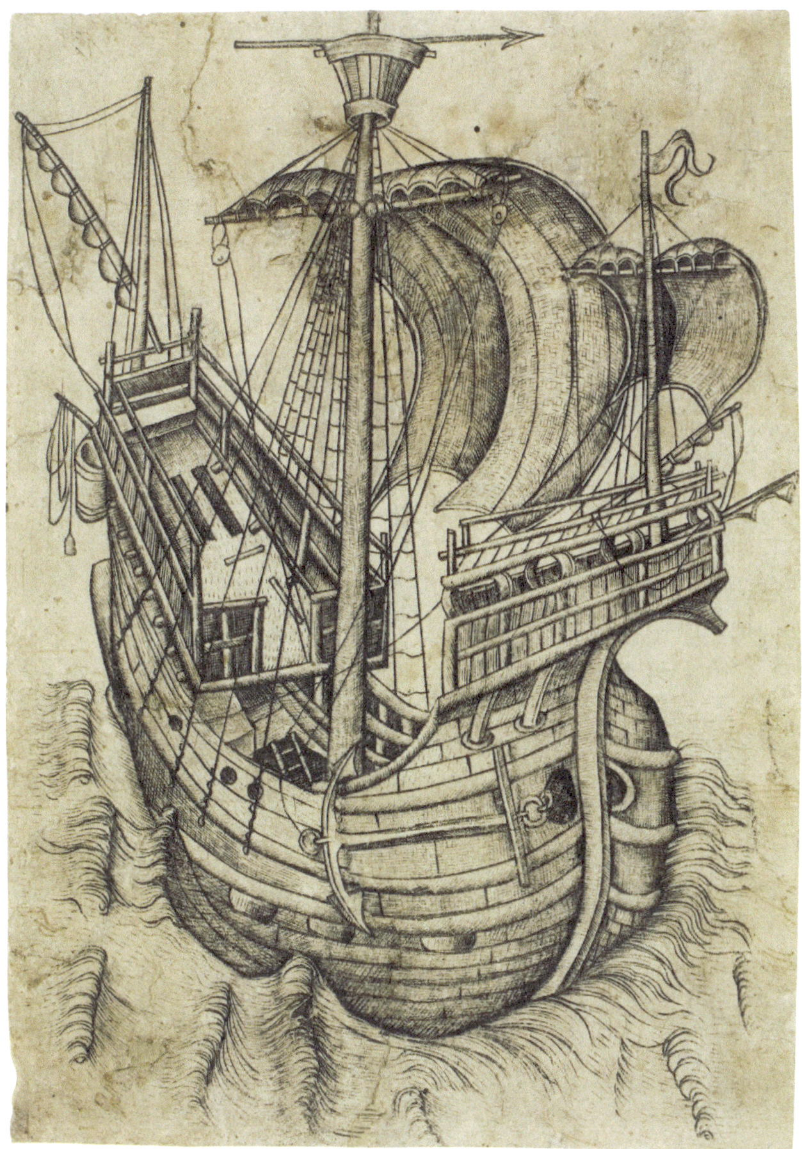

Master WA, Three-Masted Ship Steering to the Right, ca. 1460–1480, engraving, 21.5 × 16 cm. The Art Institute of Chicago, Gift of Mrs. Potter Palmer, Jr., inv. nr. 1955.1231, Chicago.

Fig. 61

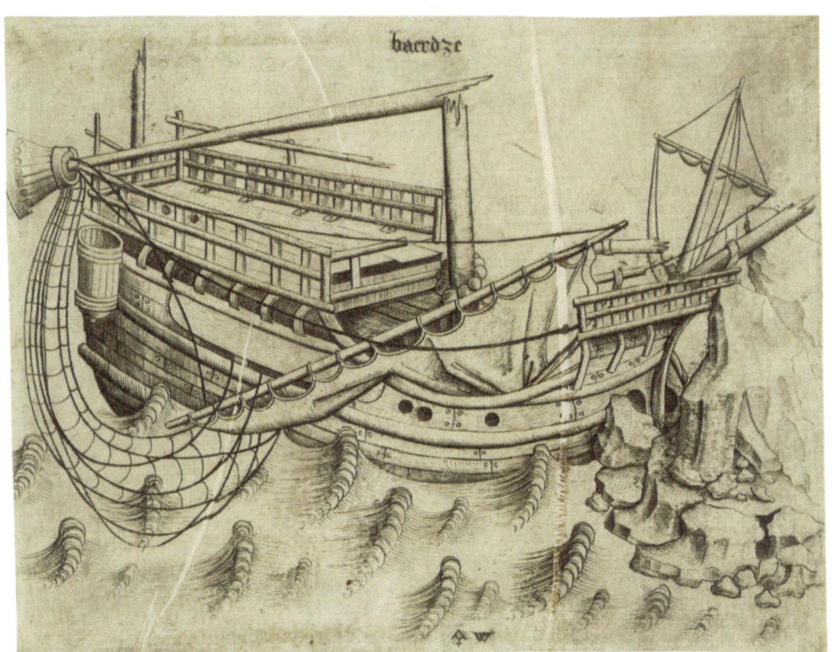

Master WA, A Wrecked Ship "baerdze," ca. 1465–1490, engraving, 13.4 × 17.7 cm. Kupferstichkabinett, inv. nr. 101-1891, Berlin.

Fig. 62

models, and so he suggested they relate to boat-shaped platters (*nefs*) featured in the ducal wedding-night banquet.[16]

The detailed accounts book and chronicle descriptions of the boats, however, reveal elements not depicted in the print, most notably, the duke's elaborate insignia. This relates to a more foundational question: If many of Master WA's engravings were indeed related to the wedding festivities production, what was their function in that context? The lack of insignia rules out the possibility that these prints were direct, court-sanctioned illustrations of the festivities; they were not, in other words, illustrations for something like a lost early festival book. Further ruling out any propaganda use are similar boat prints in which a mast is broken—certainly not the image of might and success the duke sought to project with this motif [fig. 62]. A glance at the subsequent part of the accounts' description reveals that even the portal panel print, which of course does feature Charles's insignia, lacks an important element mentioned in all descriptions of that artifact: the elaborate wine fountains that flanked the gate during the first two days of the festivities, a costly and unusually generous gift from the duke to his subjects, which would surely be emphasized in any propaganda context:[17]

> and lower on the two sides, on each side a figure, one made and carved in the manner of a Turkish archer dispensing red wine from Beaune from the tip of his

16
Wegener-Sleeswyk, "De graveur WA," p. 281. La Marche described the boats as: "trante nefz, chascune d'icelles portant le nom de l'une des seigneuries de mondit seigneur de Bourgoingne ... toutes painctes d'or et d'asur, armoyées chascune des armes de la seigneurie dont elle se nommoit.... et au plus hault avoit ung grant estendard de soye noir et violet, semé de fusilz d'or, et de grans lettres où estoit le mot de monseigneur: Je l'ay emprins.... et tout au plus près du vif que on pouvoit faire la semblance d'une caracque ou d'ung grant navire." La Marche, *Mémoires* 3, pp. 133–134. De Roovere in his Dutch description also refers to these as *craken*; see A. J. Enschedé, "Huwelijksplechtigheden van Karel van Bourgondië en Margaretha van York," *Kronijk van het Historisch Gezelschap te Utrecht* XXII (1866): pp. 17–71, esp. p. 40. On Master WA and boats see, most recently, Achim Timmermann, "The Ship in the Shop: An Art History of Late Medieval Ship Models," in *International Journal of Maritime History* 33, no. 2 (2021): pp. 257–288.

17
Jesse Hurlbut has established that it was customarily the hosting town and not the court that bore the cost of such fountains (*Ceremonial Entries in Burgundy: Philip the Good and Charles the Bold [1419–1477]*, PhD diss. [University of Indiana, 1990], p. 179). As the court paid for these fountains, they surely would have wanted this unusual display of largesse, much stressed in La Marche's chronicle, to form an important part of any visual propaganda effort.

> arrow, and on the other side a [figure] made like a German cross-bowman shooting and dispensing white Rhine wine from the tip of his bow. Those Beaune and Rhine wines were each falling into a large stone basin [which] had been placed there in the middle of the street for this, so that everyone who wished to drink there could come. The whole panel is attached and affixed to the wall over the said portal, all gilded in precious gold and richly painted, so that it could be there for as long as it can last.[18]

La Marche affirms that the panel was to be affixed above the ducal residence's gate "in perpetuity."[19] Since this panel was visible from the street well into the Habsburg reign, any artisan active in Bruges in the final quarter of the fifteenth century could have made the drawing after which the panel print by Master WA was produced.

It is equally unlikely that Master WA's prints were produced for use in the preparatory, production stage of the 1468 festivities. Wegener-Sleeswyk suggests the boat print could have served as a design for those who crafted the banquet boats.[20] While a version of the drawings behind these engravings may have been produced by the group of painters who designed the banquets, it seems improbable that those drawings were reproduced to serve as patterns. The engravings are far too general to serve as actual woodwork work-patterns. More importantly, why would, say,

18
"[E]t aux deux costez plus bas / a ch[ac]un lez ung p[ar]sonnage / lun fait et taillie a facon dun archier turquois gettant uin de beaune p[ar] le bout de sa flesche / et a lautre lez ung fait co[m]me ung cre[n]nokinier alleman tirant et gettant par le bout de son uireton uin de rin. lesquelz uin de beaunne et de rin / cheoient chu[c]un en ung grant barq de pierre p[ou]r ce mis jlecques en my la rue afin que tous ceulx qui y uouldroient broire y peuissent auenir / tout le quel tabernacle ou tableau est atachie et mis ferme ou mur dessus lad[icte] porte tout dore de fin or et richement paint / afin quil y puist estre tant quil pourra durer." AGR N 1795 fols. 80r–80v.

19
"[À] perpetual." *Mémoires* 4, p. 103.

20
One of his suggestions was that this was used much in the way a team of workers today would use a photocopier (Wegener-Sleeswyk, "De graveur WA," p. 282). Even if this would have been in any way necessary—which is unlikely, because it does not resonate with the organized and centralized operation emerging from AGR N 1795, and nothing comparable survives from the practice of building *actual* boats, so the specialized carpenters could certainly do without models—the relatively costly technology of reproduction and the level of detail of the print turn this into an improbability.

Cornilles de Zwarte, a master shipbuilder (*maistre charpontier de naves*) and his team from Sluis (Bruges's North Sea outlet), whose payments are recorded in the same accounting book, even require visual pointers from a goldsmith? There is no mention of printing in the detailed lists of materials in the accounts, nor is there a particular reason to think that reproductions were even necessary—all the pageantry props were executed in one building where everyone had access to the original drawings (*patrons*) and the artists who conceived the designs in the first place. And of course, lacking the insignia, none of these engravings fully corresponds to the ephemeral artifacts that were actually produced (based on their descriptions), so could not in practice have served as effective execution patterns for them.

At the same time, however, Lehr was very much correct to deduce a connection between Master WA and the Burgundian court based on the panel print—for whoever commissioned this engraving must have had at least sympathy for (if not outright affiliation with) that court. Furthermore, the curious correlation between the artifacts produced in 1468 and the highly unusual motifs in Master WA's enigmatic oeuvre ought not be dismissed. Precisely those engravings that have few, if any, parallels in the oeuvres of other period printmakers—the boats, the tents, other military scenes, as well as the three figureless images at focus here—align with the 1468 wedding banquets production. For instance, it has been suggested that the prints featuring whimsical military scenes may be tied to Charles's military operations, but it is not clear that the duke would have appreciated such a light depiction of one of his actual campaigns and, again, with no proper insignia.[21] Those images seem far more resonant with the figurines (*marmousets*) of militiamen (*gens d'armes*) that were

21
Hollstein, *Dutch and Flemish Etchings, Engravings and Woodcuts* 12, pp. 218–219. This large group of military prints (too numerous to reproduce here, see ibid., pp. 24–33) are especially puzzling. They feature odd rectangular traces around them, perhaps some sort of crop marks. They also hold subtle clues to the depiction of different, distinct armies, some perhaps more organized than others (perhaps an allusion to town militias?), which implies a greater narrative context, maybe one that also included captions. They may therefore have been intended to serve as glue-in illustrations in books printed in Bruges's incipient publishing industry. In fact, a curious possibility never entertained in the literature that I have come across is that Master WA was not a goldsmith but rather a manuscript illuminator—one of the only classes of artisans required to identify with a monogram in late fifteenth-century Bruges.

incorporated into comical performances, as specified in the accounts.[22] Master WA's prints are thus likely connected, somehow, both to the ducal court in general and to the 1468 wedding production in particular. However, they are neither part of the after-the-fact propaganda efforts, nor an aid in the preparation of the artifacts.

I propose that that the question of the nature of those connections may be best approached from a pragmatic angle: What was the marketable use of these engravings? They must have had one because artists in the fifteenth century created little that they did not expect to sell, either on commission or on the open market. That is ever more so the case for early products of such a costly novel reproduction medium as intaglio printing was in the 1460s and 1470s Netherlands. Master WA expected either several people to pay for one of these, or one patron to pay for several of them.[23] The context of the engraver's own oeuvre suggests that the former scenario is the likelier one. Most of the more enigmatic prints—including the three figureless spaces—were likely created as design patterns marketed to fellow craftsmen on the open market.

Surface and Space

Master WA's extant oeuvre comprises about eighty engravings, few of which can be understood as a finished, independent work of art.[24] For instance, the large foliage design from the Metropolitan Museum of Art is clearly a pattern for a single motif to be incorporated into a larger object [fig. 67].[25] Even this simple

22
The term *marmouset,* while generally denoting "figurine," was also frequently used to connote something comical or grotesque; see Guy de Poerck, "Marmouset. Histoire d'un mot," in *Revue belge de philologie et d'histoire* 37, no. 3 (1959): pp. 615–644.

23
Not too many people, however; even though a plate could potentially yield several thousand prints (Mayr-Harting, *Early Netherlandish Engraving*, p. 5), a relatively small number of this Master's impressions—mostly about one or two of each—survive, which suggests they were issued in particularly small editions.

24
Those include, for instance, several small-scale images of saints reproduced in F. W. H. Hollstein, *Hollstein's Dutch and Flemish Etchings, Engravings and Woodcuts* 12, pp. 212–216.

25
On this print, see Nadine Orenstein, "Master W. with Key," *Metropolitan Museum of Art Bulletin* 54, no. 4 (1997), p. 15.

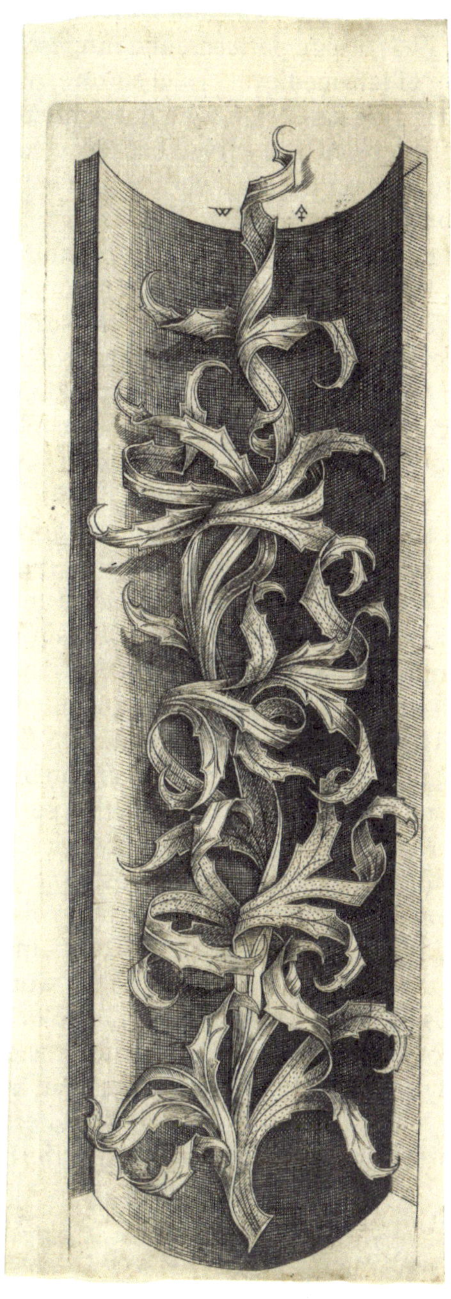

Master WA, Furrow with Gothic Leaves, ca. 1465–1490, engraving, 29.2 × 10.6 cm.
The Metropolitan Museum of Art, Harris Brisbane Dick Fund, inv. nr. 1929, 29.16.1, New York.

Fig. 67

print, however, already features an ambiguity that characterizes many of Master WA's design patterns, and interestingly echoes a broader alterity of late medieval visual culture: namely, it is not clear whether the print is a design for a flat painted (or printed) image or a sculpted object. The curved backdrop could give an idea of volume to a carver or metalworker, or it could record the pattern of shadows for a painter.[26]

This ambiguity becomes particularly pronounced in Master WA's prints that feature empty interiors, compounded by an ambiguity of scale. While in certain prints the scale is clear (e.g., a design for a crosier printed in several parts specifically so it can serve as a model on a one-to-one scale), in other engravings the scale is so ambiguous that it obscures the nature of the connection between model and design.[27] For instance, what is the function of the landscape in the St. Bartholomew print [fig. 69]? Initially, this motif seems to suggest that the whole composition was meant to serve as a design for a painting, but why then is it packed, as so many of Master WA's engravings, with intricate and fanciful tracery and architectural details? And if this is a design for sculpture, what does the landscape stand for? Master WA's three prints of figureless images are perhaps the most perplexing in that regard [figs. 54–56]. As instantiated by Rogier's *Seven Sacraments*, these sort of "diaphragm" Gothic spaces were ubiquitous in paintings, illuminations, and other flat media in this period, and so on its face it seems Master WA's settings could have served as models.

However, all three images seem almost excessively rich in tracery and detail, more so than most extant paintings (where such florid designs, that may detract from the main scenes, were less common in the fifteenth century than they would become later in the 1500s). Yet, the prints are also not so evidently effective as designs for carved objects; for instance, the elaborate ceilings they portray rest on columns so slender that, in reality, could never bear their loads. The representation of materials is confusing; the frame of one space is formulated at the bottom edge as

26
The curve does make the former scenario likelier, in my opinion, as a flat background would have been more useful for two-dimensional images and thus have a greater commercial appeal.

27
Hollstein, *Dutch and Flemish Etchings, Engravings and Woodcuts* 12, p. 226.

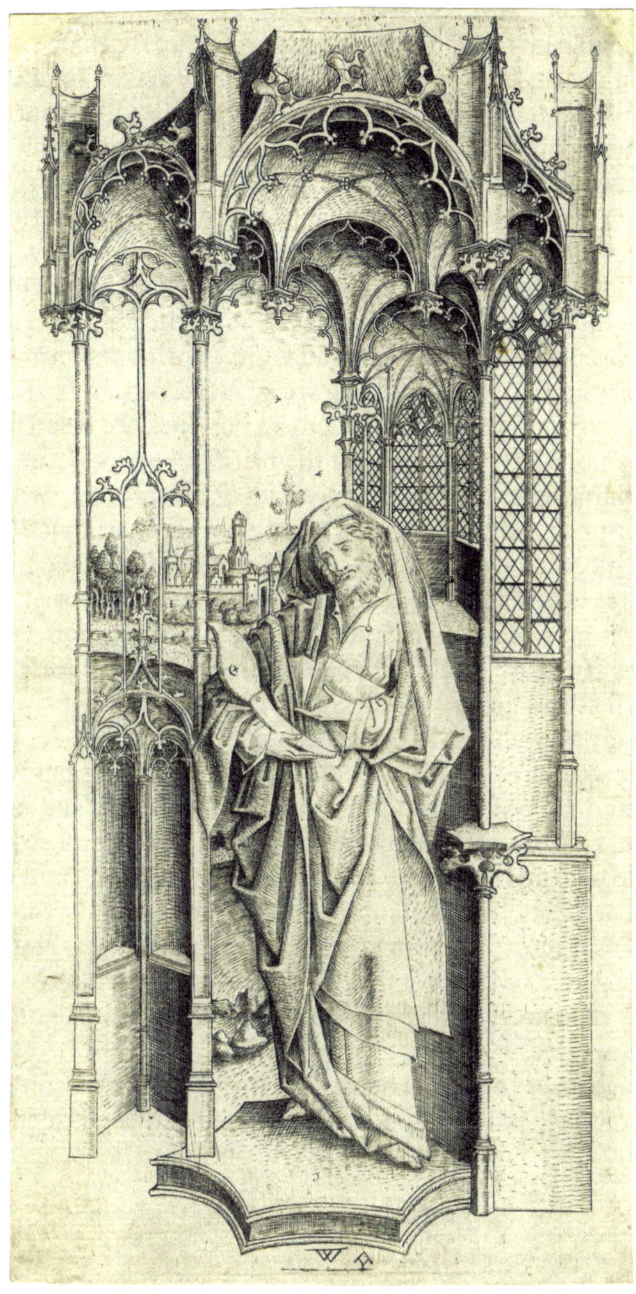

Master WA, St. Bartholomew, ca. 1465–1490, engraving, 22.5 × 11.1 cm.
British Museum, inv. nr. 1845,0809.208, London.

Fig. 69

a stone pilaster but if constructed it would have had to be crafted from a pliable material because it curves on top (with no seam marks on the shaft). These are no accidents of incompetence; Master WA engraved actual architectural details with clear articulation of materials and structure.[28] Compilations of fifteenth-century prints feature few parallels to the Master's odd subjects. There are almost no extant prints of empty interiors, and certainly none of odd ones such as these, and very few boats.

Understanding the purpose and use of these engravings requires, therefore, a closer unpacking of intrinsic clues. The fact that the St. Bartholomew print and another print depicting a figureless pavilion [fig. 71] both feature a landscape that is visible through the windows of the structures but does not bleed beyond their open borders, suggests that the prints were not patterns for full painting compositions. With no figures, action, or theme, the latter print especially can be nothing other than a model, and one most likely for a large-scale three-dimensional object. The sparse landscape, not particularly useful as a pictorial model in itself, is probably a mere indicator of scale. Even more telling, while the structure effuses the late-Gothic taste for florid ornament, it features no curved surfaces. Highly labor-intensive, those would only be viable in small permanent fixtures. The depicted structure, on the other hand, could be built by joining flat wood planks, and its roof likely comprises stretched fabric and papier-mâché moldings. The knowledge Master WA is marketing here is how to deceptively imbue a large pavilion with the opulence of small artifacts. The design, like the one in the St. Bartholomew print, is thus most likely for the kind of temporary pavilions and backdrops used to frame stages along the path of processions. It strikes the modern viewer as odd partly because none of these objects survives.

Such stages of single saints and prophets were a common motif in French and Burgundian processional theater, such as

28
See, for some examples, Hollstein, *Dutch and Flemish Etchings, Engravings and Woodcuts* 12, pp. 247–249. It is worth mentioning that at least one engraver of the period is known to have been trained not as a goldsmith but as an architect: the 's-Hertogenbosch-based Alart du Hameel (active ca. 1478–1506; see Jane Campbell Hutchison, ed., *The Illustrated Bartsch 9: Early German Artists, Israel van Meckenem, Wenzel von Olmütz and Monogrammists* (New York: Abaris books, 1981), p. 231.

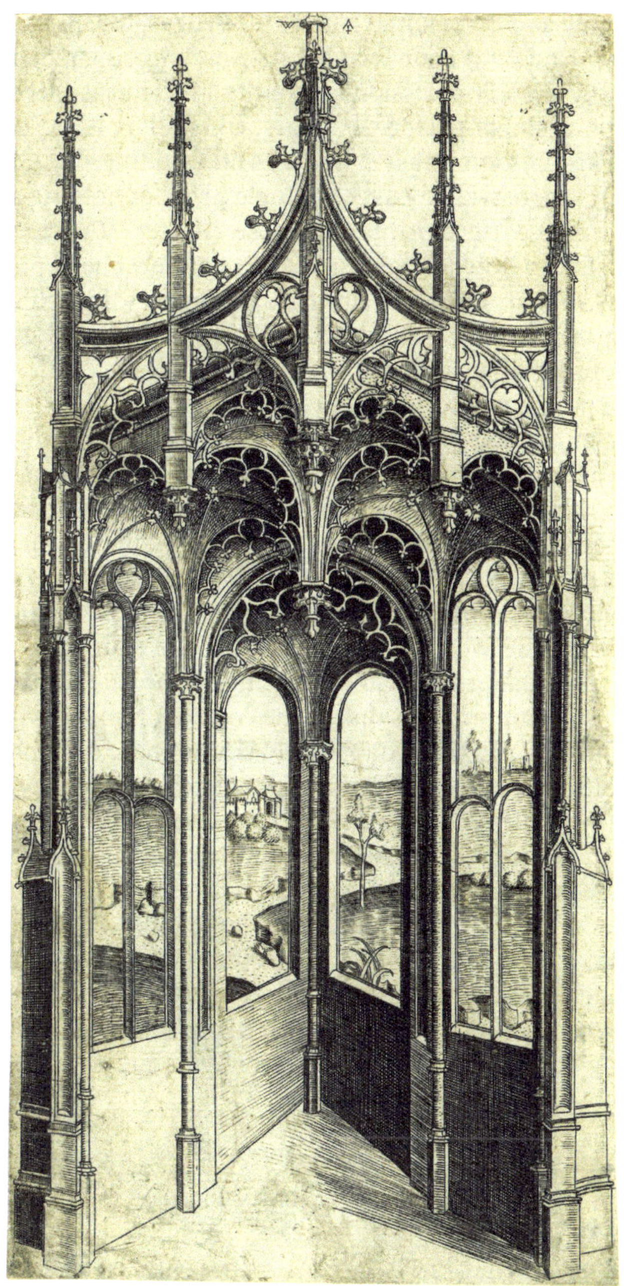

Master WA, Vista Through a Structure, ca. 1465–1490, engraving, 22.5 × 11.1 cm.
British Museum, inv. nr. E,1.194, London.

Fig. 71

ommegangen and ceremonial entries. In Bruges, for instance, the Twelve Apostles and Four Evangelists were ongoing motifs in the annual Holy Blood procession and in the 1440 ducal entry there were six such single-performer stages, which Bart Ramakers dubs "'statue-like' presentations."[29] In the 1468 wedding-day entry into Bruges there was at least one single prophet holding a banderole.[30] In the pattern prints, I propose, Master WA is teaching other craftsmen how to craft large and relatively cheap polyhedral structures so that they seem curved and opulent—indeed so that, like many artifacts of various media in this period, they could loosely reference the aesthetic of goldwork.

His pavilion designs seem very much in line with the lists of materials purchased for the 1468 production (e.g., wood, metal, cloth, and, above all, papier-mâché), and along with the intersection of motifs they pose an interesting third possibility for the connection between the prints and the wedding festivities. Master WA may have been a clever opportunist who somehow gained access to the concept *patrons* and other drawings from the planning phase of the 1468 wedding celebration (on the court and city side alike), intellectual property that, judging by the rate of payments to the master painters, was one of the costliest remnants from that production. He then adapted and edited these designs into marketable patterns for different types of paintworks—polychromed pageantry props and sets, wax and papier-mâché figurines, permanent sculptures, or paintings. Rather than serving as models for the workers in 1468, these images, which curiously correlate with the banquet motifs but agree on few of the actual details, are indeed more a set of visual ideas than the sort of detailed execution drawings continuously created during the production effort. They are thus most likely adapted from the designs by the well-remunerated, celebrity painters involved

29
Bart A. M. Ramakers, "Multifaceted and Ambiguous: The *Tableaux Vivants* in the Bruges Entry of 1440," in *The Mediation of Symbol in Late Medieval and Early Modern Times = Medien der Symbolik in Spätmittelalter und Früher Neuzeit*, Rudolf Suntrup, Jan Veenstra, and Anne Bollmann, eds. (Frankfurt: Peter Lang, 2005), pp. 163–194, here pp. 177–179. On the Holy Blood see Andrew Brown, "Civic Ritual: Bruges and the Counts of Flanders in the Later Middle Ages," in *The English Historical Review* 112 (1997): pp. 277–299, 284.

30
See Enschedé, "Huwelijksplechtigheden van Karel van Bourgondië en Margaretha van York," p. 27.

in the production, which Master WA somehow obtained through his connections and re-monetized.[31]

Master WA's general yet intricate ideas, for which engraving was indeed a much more suitable medium than woodblock prints, could be put to all sorts of uses. The tracery patterns could serve as models for painters as well as sculptors and joiners. There was indeed an entire category of woodworkers in the Netherlands dedicated to producing intricate architectural forms for objects such as the *caisses*, or frame-boxes of carved retables.[32] The boat prints could have been used to craft an object such as the late fifteenth-century St. Ursula reliquary [fig. 74], or could potentially have served as models for details in pictures, e.g. the carrack in the background of the 1558 *Fall of Icarus* [fig. 75]. It could also, interestingly, have been used as a model in another pageantry production; a similar large ship model is depicted, for instance, in the first illustrated festival book printed in the Netherlands, describing Charles V's 1515 entry into Bruges [fig. 76]. The resemblance of this sixteenth-century ship to the one in Master WA's print, both echoing public festivities in the same city but forty-eight years apart, one at (and by) the court and one for the court, almost materializes the iterative visual dialogue, through paintworks, that came to define the Burgundian state's visual culture.

Commercial reasoning, namely the ubiquity of civic spectacles by the late fifteenth century, warranted that the prints be geared more toward usage in street pageants, rather than banquets. This, I suggest, is the key to the function of the three figureless prints. Rather than designs for paintings *or* larger actual objects, they are likely designs for a combination of the two. There are notable differences between the foreground and the background in all three. While the foregrounds, or outer frames, offer executable formulations of tracery, materials and structural details, the

31
Master WA's oeuvre does contain other groups of prints that are closer to an execution pattern. The design for a monstrance reproduced in Hollstein, *Dutch and Flemish Etchings, Engravings and Woodcuts* 12, p. 232, echo (and probable copy) contemporaneous early German engravings (e.g., by Wenzel von Olmutz, reproduced in Hutchison, *The Illustrated Bartsch* 9 pt. 2, p. 186, no. 083).

32
See Lynn Jacobs, *Early Netherlandish Carved Altarpieces, 1380–1550: Medieval Tastes and Mass Marketing* (Cambridge, UK: Cambridge University Press, 1998), pp. 210–211.

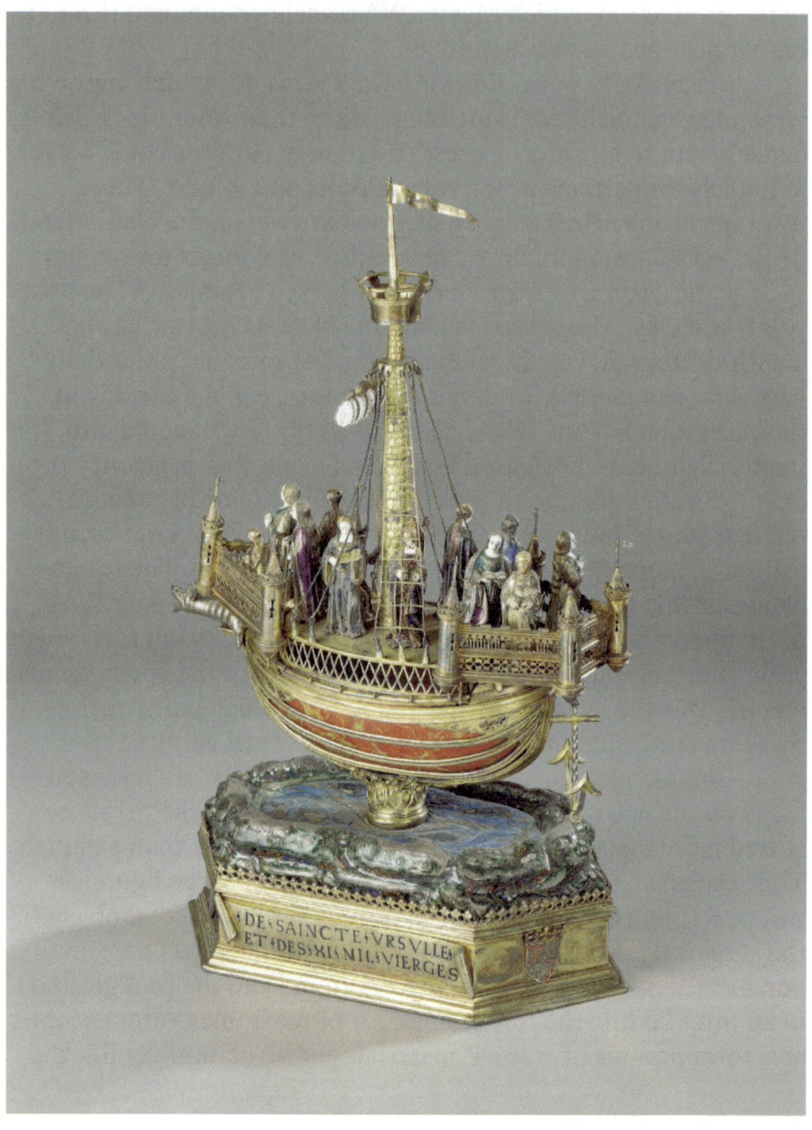

Raymond Guyonnet (attr.), Reliquary of St. Ursula, ca. 1500–1505,
gold, silver, and enamel, 46 × 28 × 16.5 cm.
Palais du Tau, inv. nr. D-TAU1972000176, Reims.

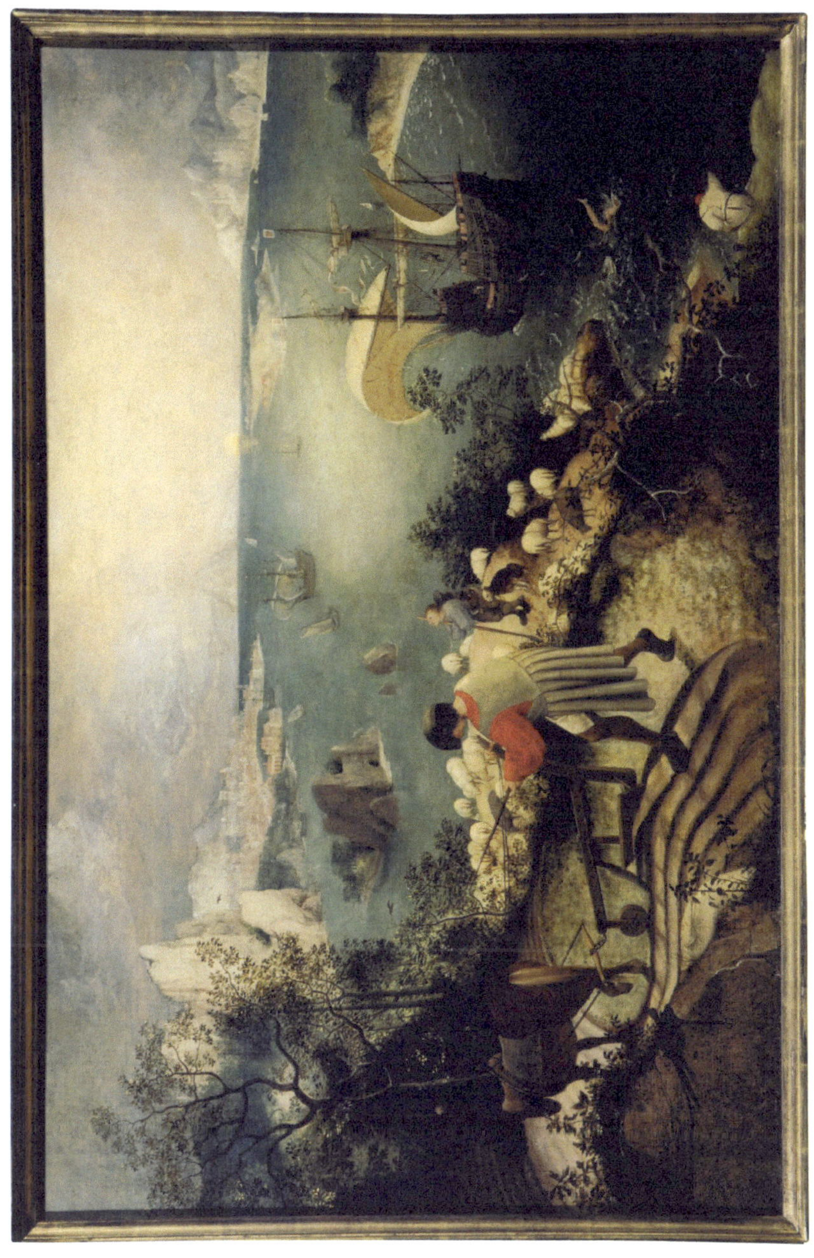

Pieter Bruegel the Elder (after?), *Fall of Icarus*, ca. 1558, oil on canvas, mounted on wood, 73.5 × 112 cm. Musées Royaux des Beaux-Arts, inv. nr. 4030, Brussels.

Fig. 75

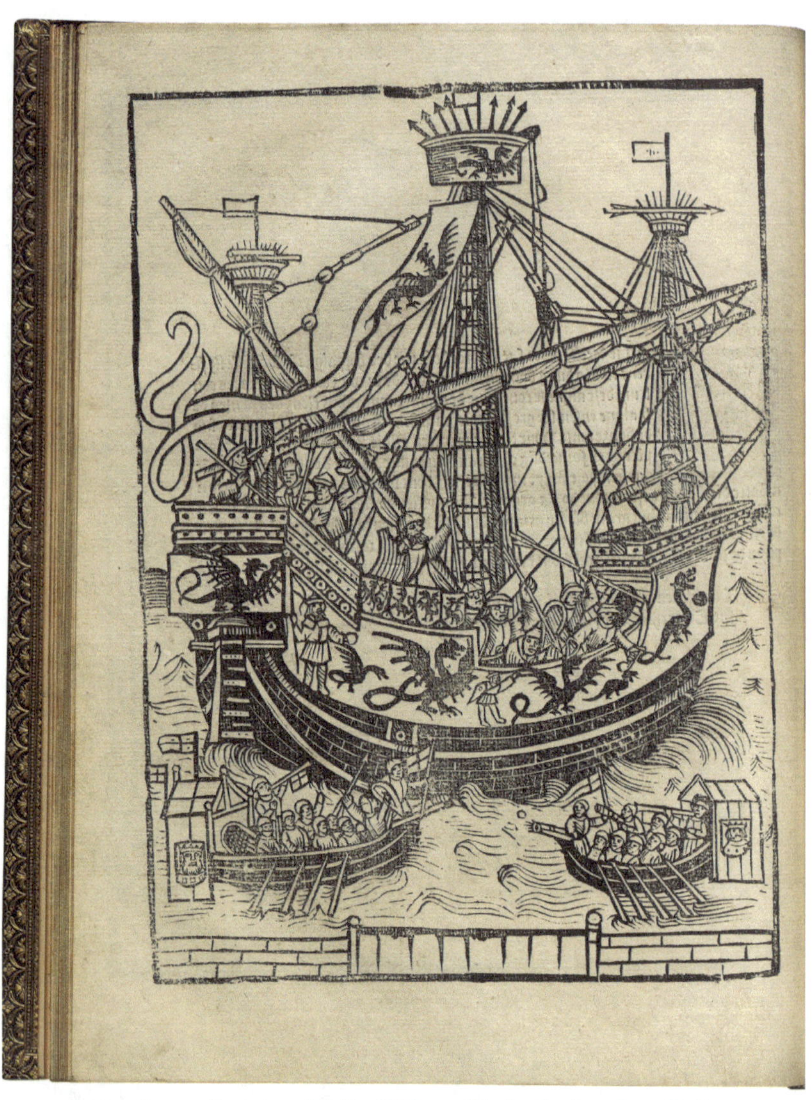

Artist unknown, Boat stage, f. D.ii. v, 1515, woodblock print from Remy Du Puys, La Tryumphante entree de Charles Prince ees Espagnes en Bruges. INHA, inv. nr. NUM 4 RES 1396, Paris.

Fig. 76

backgrounds, or inner areas, are far less structurally coherent: they are all oddly compressed and display spatial inconsistencies to the point where it is not clear how they are built. In another WA print, St. Andrew occupies the first foot or so, or indeed the structurally coherent side of an equally split space, while a great, almost accordion-like empty depth is suggested behind him [fig. 78]. One possibility is that Master WA's three figureless engravings are portraying a hybrid: a design for an actual, spatial settings for actors or sculpture in the foreground and a sort of trompe l'oeil background.

The festival book describing Charles V's 1515 entry into Bruges shows that such hybrid designs were used in theatrical productions for civic entries, and so presumably also for banquet stage sceneries.[33] The woodcut print depicting a pageant set outside the house of the Spanish *nacion* in Bruges illustrates this particularly well [fig. 79]. If the structure in this print were to be taken at face value, the stage would have three steps of depth, as in the central scene, so that the emperors on the sides might be aligned with the figures holding the wheel in the center. However, from the textual description of the pageant it emerges that it is the figure of the king in the far back of the middle section which is aligned with the emperors on the sides. The two side sovereigns are said to be set not closer to the front, but below the king ("*Ung degré plus bas*"), making the stage steep, rather than deep.[34] This suggests a total depth to the stage of about one meter rather than three. Even if the width of the street would have accommodated a three-meter stage, such depth would run the risk

33
This entry is exceptionally well documented. In addition to extensive textual documentation, including the city accounts for this enormous financial undertaking, which were printed in the nineteenth century (Louis Prosper Gachard et al., *Collection des voyages des souverains des Pays-Bas* [Brussels: F. Hayez, 1874]), two pictorial records survive: an illuminated manuscript currently at the Österreichische Nationalbibliothek (MS 2591) and a printed booklet, originally published in Paris by Gilles de Gourmont, and currently available as a digital facsimile (https://bibliotheque-numerique.inha.fr/idurl/1/58427). Both the manuscript and the booklet feature text by Remi du Puys, a court historiographer who was commissioned by the city of Bruges to record the events (see the introduction by Sydney Anglo in the 1970 facsimile: Remy du Puys, *La tryumphante entrée de Charles Prince des espagnes en Bruges 1515* [Amsterdam: Theatrum Orbis Terrarum, 1970], pp. 5–34).

34
Du Puys, *La tryumphante entrée*, pp. 33–34. The positions of the actors in the very front of the central section is also described in terms of vertical steps: "Ung degré plus bas estoient deux aultres pucelles" ("One degree lower were two other maidens"). Ibid.

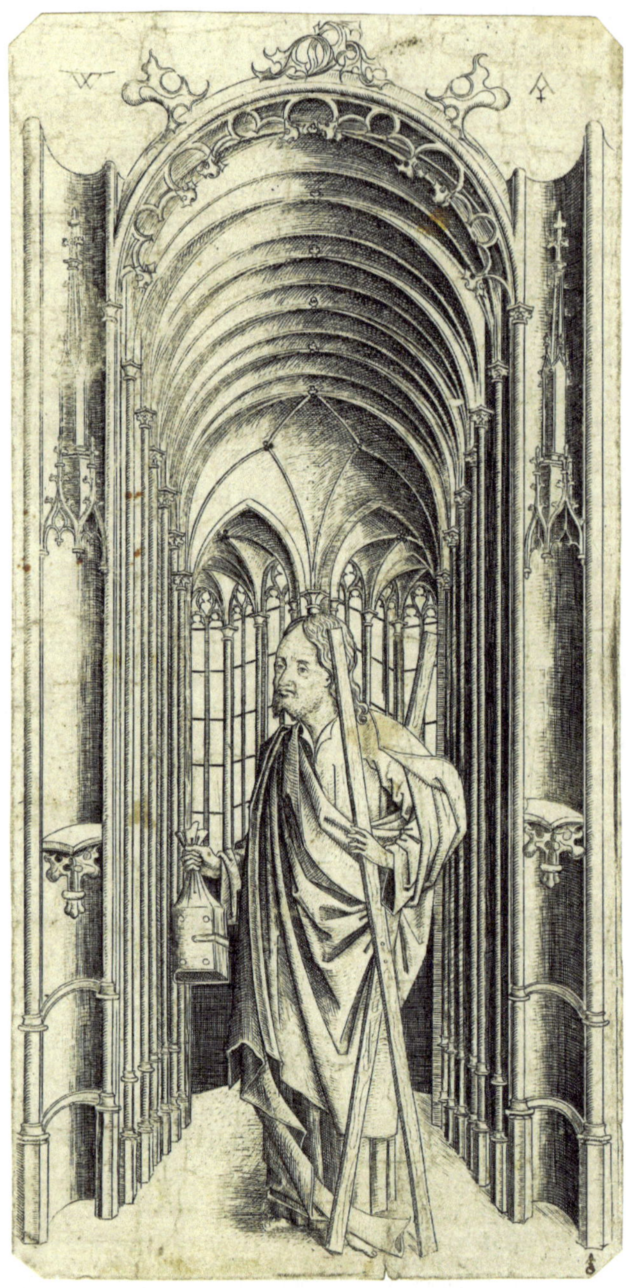

Master WA, St. Andrew, ca. 1465–1490, engraving, 22.7 × 11.3 cm.
British Museum, inv. nr. E,1.190, London.

Fig. 78

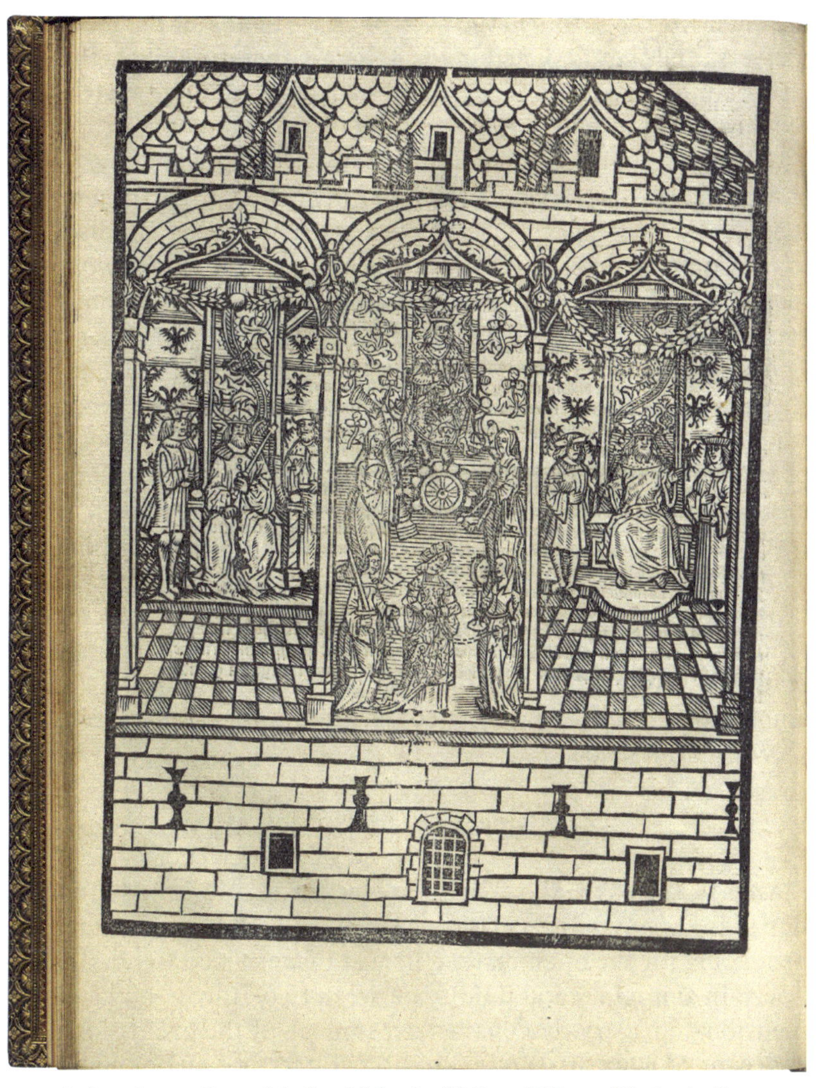

Artist unknown, Stage of the Spanish "nacion," f. D.v. v, 1515, woodblock print from Remy Du Puys, La Tryumphante entree de Charles Prince ees Espagnes en Bruges. INHA, inv. nr. NUM 4 RES 1396, Paris.

Fig. 79

of rendering the actors in the back invisible to all but the mounted viewers. The tiles depicted in the print are therefore likely illusionistic painted ones, meant to make a steep and shallow theatrical set into an illusion of a deep and level one. Master WA's prints may thus be a unique visual echo of fifteenth-century conventions in stage design, which seem to fully conform to neither the medieval *mansion* nor the later Renaissance perspective stage.[35]

Comprising patterns for media as divergent as goldwork, masonry, and stagecraft, Master WA's oeuvre visually instantiates aspects of fifteenth-century Burgundian visual culture otherwise known from texts alone. His ambiguous engravings thus reflect the cohesive nature of premodern visual culture and the crucial role painters, specifically, played within it as the primary producers of visual ideas across a variety of media. His prints also offer a glimpse into a mode of craftsmanship and viewership that has been lost with the ephemeral objects they echo. The St. Bartholomew engraving is effectively a visual demonstration of the dual denotation of the Middle French *personnage*—it is indeed either an inanimate figure or a performed character, conveying to the modern reader, in ways hardly possible through texts alone, the playful ambiguity of realistic imagery so inherent to the late-medieval viewing experience.

Dimension Ambiguity

Master WA's oeuvre sheds light on how the relationship between figure and ground differs from the modern one. As an artisan mass producing for the open market, he was incentivized to promote a certain ambiguity and fluidity between two-, three-, and four-dimensional imagery that characterizes much of the professional endeavor of many fifteenth-century painters. Media boundaries that grew quite firm in the past centuries led us to dichotomize what, in the era of paintworks, was invariably a continuum.

35
On *mansions* in medieval theater see Dunbar Ogden, *The Staging of Drama in the Medieval Church* (Newark, DE: University of Delaware Press, 2002), pp. 109–112. On the two modes of stage design see Georges Kernodle, *From Art to Theatre: Form and Convention in the Renaissance* (Chicago, University of Chicago Press, 1943). For more on this, see "Tableau-vivant curtains as mediators between figure and ground: Petrus Christus, the Salzburg Master, and Jean Fouquet" by Claudia Blümle in this volume.

Painters were sometimes tasked with accommodating actual figures in actual spaces, other times sculpted figures in miniaturized spaces, and yet in other cases were called on to produce something that we might recognize as a painting today. That, and many combinations thereof. Coupled with the historic, but not yet complete, process of painting slowly supplanting sculpture as the paradigmatic image in the West, meant that fifteenth-century painters invariably thought about painted settings neither as "space" in the modern sense of the word, nor as flat grounds or planes.

Habitually tasked with painting into being partial or complete physical environments, Early Netherlandish painters often invited viewers to actually, physically "walk around" or "walk into" one of their creations (the paintworks-packed banquet halls of the 1468 production being one example). Therefore, it is little surprising that their "flat" images likewise encode an inherently somatic viewing experience. For instance, one of the best-paid painters employed by the court in the 1468 banquet production, Lieven van Lathem, went on to produce a related set of illuminations with an innovative compositional structure that Anne van Buren described as "U-shaped"—essentially the same as the one employed by Rogier in the *Seven Sacraments.*[36]

In fact, Rogier's famed triptych is itself an echo of this transliteration of painting in the round. The iconography of the Seven Sacraments was effectively unprecedented in panel painting when Rogier was tasked with creating the altarpiece. It was, however, somewhat of a fad for about a century as a design scheme for the facets of polygonal baptismal fonts, especially (but not exclusively), in England [fig. 82].[37] Therefore, the spatial structure that compels the viewer to "walk around" closely parallels the physical experience of encircling one of those then fashionable baptismal fonts within just such a church space.

The spatial configuration is a key driver of the meaning and, more crucially, the power of Rogier's painting. The seemingly accessible circular pictorial space I discussed in the introduction,

36
See Anne Hagopian van Buren, "Van Lathem's Costumes," in *Invention: Northern Renaissance Studies in Honor of Molly Faries,* Julien Chapuis, ed. (Turnhout: Brepols, 2008), pp. 95–103; as well as Turel, *Living Pictures*, p. 111.

37
Ann Eljenholm Nichols, *Seeable Signs: The Iconography of the Seven Sacraments, 1350–1544* (Woodbridge, UK: Boydell Press, 1994).

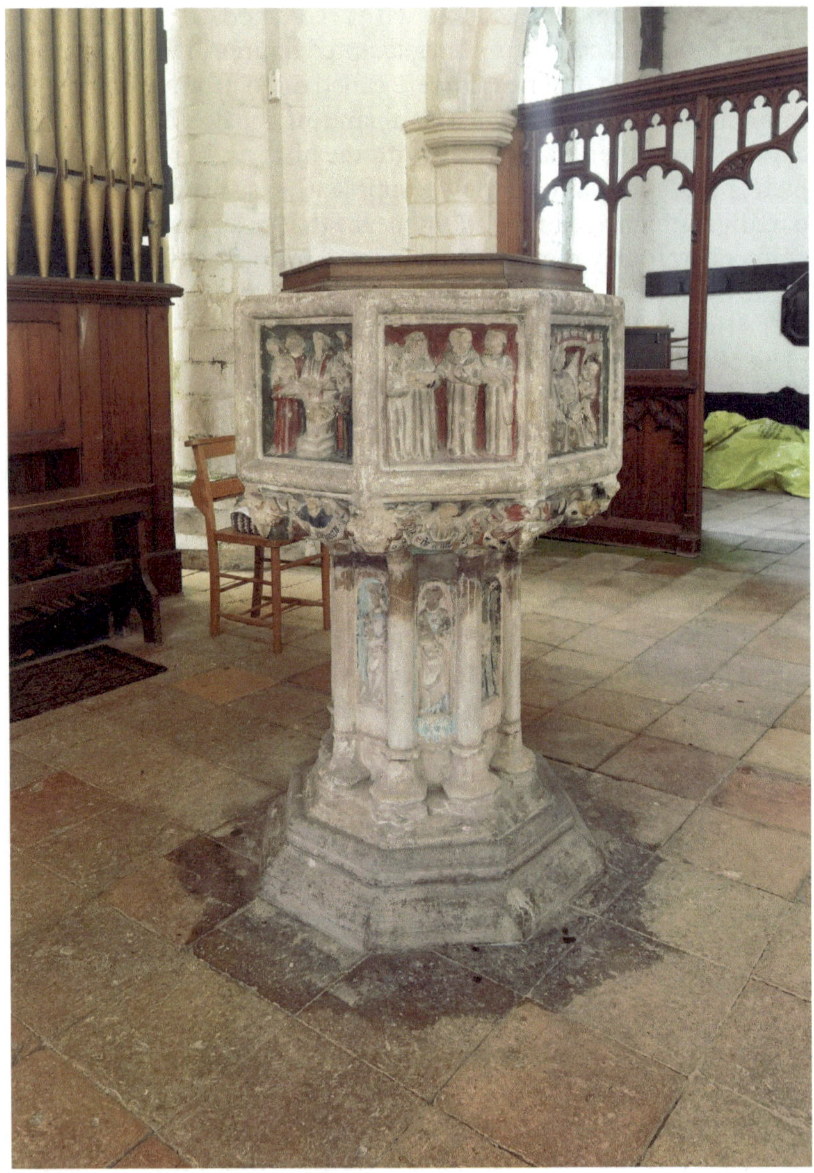

Artist unknown, Seven Sacraments Font, late fifteenth century.
St Mary's church, Great Witchingham, United Kingdom.

Fig. 82

which entwines figures and ground, is also precisely the element that does the work of persuasion here, by tethering (gratuitously, from a theological standpoint) every sacrament to the church. If the purpose of this altarpiece is to encourage church attendance and loyalty, structuring it as a simulated baptism—the one universal rite that invariably takes place in an ecclesiastical space—was a rather ingenious rhetorical maneuver. Today, it serves as a reminder of the unique and forgotten power of painting in the round.

Part 1
Staging Figures

In contrast to altar veils, which bear a connection to the altar's performativity and the presentation and concealment of paintings,[1] stage curtains restrict or allow the view of a space. However, stage curtains of the fifteenth century were not like modern theater curtains, which are opened at the beginning of a performance and closed at the end. That is because what was shown on the stage space was not a moving theater performance, but a picture. In the Roman and Byzantine ritual of *prokypsis*, for example, which was continued in the medieval period, the king did not appear in public as a full figure but was rather framed by two open curtains as a bust portrait.[2] The rite of *prokypsis* even takes its name from the wooden platform on which it took place, emphasizing the formal structure of the event. To await the appearance of the ruler, the members of the court and the public gathered in front of the closed curtain, which was not drawn aside until the emperor had entered the stage unseen through a back staircase and adopted his pose. Only now could he become an image.

As he stood motionless behind the curtains, their parting made him visible to the public as a figure on a shallow stage space before an opaque surface. In terms of construction and staging, this pictorial effect of a stage is continued in the *tableaux vivants*, which represent and reenact immobile and still images. As will be shown in the following, stage curtains depicted in paintings draw on this tension between still life and presence. Open curtains present the figures behind them in front of opaque grounds. On the other hand, they frame the figure by emphasizing the surface of a wall or textile as parallel to the picture plane, the picture frame,

I sincerely thank Saskia Quené for the productive, illuminating, and profitable exchange and central literature references she provided on the deliberations discussed here. I would also like to thank Ursula Klammer and Dorothea Douglas for their critical review of this text.

1
Joseph Braun, *Der christliche Altar in seiner geschichtlichen Entwicklung (Band 2): Die Ausstattung des Altars, Antependien, Velen, Leuchterbank, Stufen, Ciborium und Baldachin, Retabel, Reliquien- und Sakramentsaltar, Altarschranken* (Munich: Guenther Koch & Co., 1924), pp. 139–141; Alessandro Nova, "Hangings, Curtains, and Shutters of Sixteenth-century Lombard Altarpieces," in *Italian Altarpieces*, Eve Borsook and Fiorella Superbi Gioffredi, eds. (Oxford: Oxford University Press, 1994), pp. 177–189; Victor M. Schmidt, "Curtain, Revelatio, and Pictorial Reality in Late Medieval and Renaissance Italy," in *Weaving, Veiling, and Dressing: Textiles and Their Metaphors in the Late Middle Ages*, Kathryn M. Rudy and Barbara Baert, eds. (Turnhout: Brepols, 2007), pp. 191–213.

2
Ernst H. Kantorowicz, "Oriens Augusti – Lever du roi," in Dumbarton Oaks Papers, vol. 17 (1963), pp. 117–177, here pp. 156–159.

and the image itself. By positioning the figure in front of a background instead of in space, they transform the scene into a picture. Painted panels of the fifteenth century recreate this visual effect brought about by the pictorial power of the open curtain.

Opening the Curtain

In a panel of 1450 by Petrus Christus [fig. 88], open curtains allow the Man of Sorrows to step forward. Two altar boys clutch the green fabric with one hand while in the other they hold attributes identifying them as wingless angels. The white lily refers to the Annunciation by the Angel Gabriel, who turns his gaze toward the Man of Sorrows. The corresponding figure on the right can be identified as the Archangel Michael, who drove Adam and Eve out of Paradise with his flaming sword. Like the Man of Sorrows himself, he makes eye contact with us. Both angels are depicted smaller than Christ and positioned behind him. Along with the curtain, they mark the middle plane, which gives way to a dark space—a monochrome ground—behind. Brightly lit, the Man of Sorrows stands in stark relief against both the black ground and the green curtain with the angels, which adds further emphasis to his emergence. Art-historical scholarship has identified the green curtain as a "scenic curtain"[3] that allows Christ to appear close to the stage apron and thus to us. This staging of the unveiled deity combines the pictorial strategies of objective instrumentation by means of the curtain and the illuminated visualization of the figure set against a nocturnal space. The latter effect is achieved not by a supernatural aureole, but by natural, extra-pictorial light—the empirical facilitator of sight itself.[4] These pictorial elements combine to make the Man of Sorrows emerge theatrically like a figure before a black ground.

While the drapery folds of the open curtains create a sculptural play of light and shade, the pelmet is stretched smoothly and positioned parallel to the picture plane to form a monochrome

3
Ursula Panhans-Bühler, *Eklektizismus und Originalität im Werk des Petrus Christus* (Vienna: Holzhausen, 1978), p. 45. This and all subsequent quotations from German sources are my own translations.

4
Ibid., p. 52.

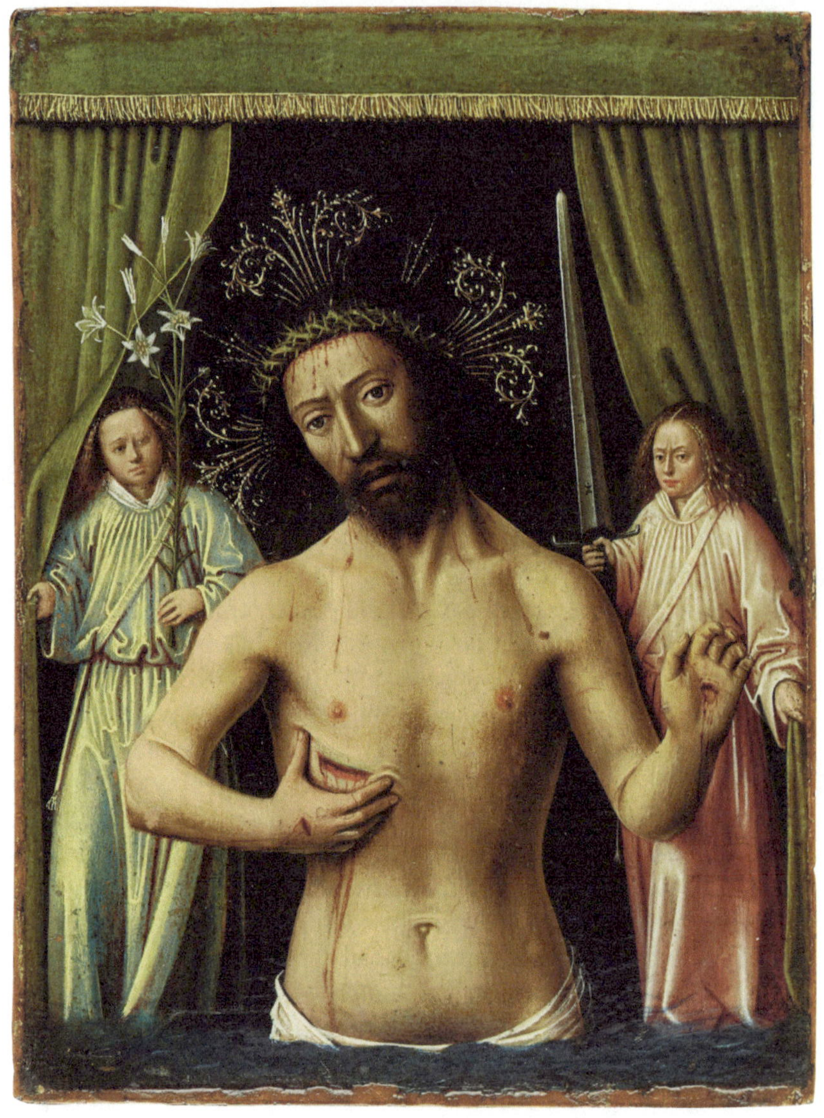

Petrus Christus, *Christ as the Man of Sorrows*, 1450, oil on panel, 11.2 × 8.5 cm.
Birmingham Museum and Art Gallery, Birmingham.

Fig. 88

color field. This element and its fringe bound the picture at the top, thus performing a framing function, while at the same time serving as a counterpart to the lower edge of the picture, to which the Man of Sorrows has moved. The green curtains, parted in the middle, thus move toward the left and right edges of the picture, taking on a framing function that resonates with the actual picture frame. At the same time, the framing function of the pelmet and open curtains make Christ appear as an image. Christ's act of stepping forward and presenting himself becomes a pictorial event. The green curtain takes on a spatial function that establishes distance as well as proximity, both within the image and between the image and the viewer.

The space in front of the curtain is further foregrounded by its illumination. The extra-pictorial light, which enters the pictorial space from the top left, lights the green curtain with its gold edging, the garments of the acolytes, and the nimbus of the Man of Sorrows. While shiny spots of light on the pelmet's gold fringe reflect the light cast from outside, this light is swallowed by the black surface behind. Here, no spatial coordinates are discernible that might provide visual orientation. As Max Raphael has noted, black as a background has no expressive value, instead forming a neutral ground. A black ground is an absolute that encompasses all content while allowing none to appear. Blackness has the vastness of indeterminacy, or omni-determinacy.[5] Raphael moreover links the black of the portrait to that of the gold of icons in terms of function.[6] It is the interplay of light, color, framing, and space that allows the Man of Sorrows to emerge pictorially. This emergence implies spatial movement, an aspect that is reinforced by the emphatic gestures with which he presents the stigmata and further emphasized by the painted curtains represented at the moment of their opening. It is in this very instant that the Man of Sorrows emerges from the black ground and comes toward us.

In the Salzburg Master's *Man of Sorrows* from the Oskar Reinhart Collection at Am Römerholz in Winterthur, dated around 1470, two green curtains and a caparison of the same color define

5
Max Raphael, *Die Farbe Schwarz: Zur materiellen Konstituierung der Form* (Frankfurt am Main: Qumran, 1984), pp. 30–31.

6
Ibid., p. 31.

the middle ground [fig. 91]. Instead of a hem with a gold fringe, gold embroidery (meanwhile faded) trims the caparison. This border, which may have originally been gilded, would have created a strong material luster effect. In contrast to the dark ground in Petrus Christus's panel, a green damask honorary cloth serves as a backdrop. The various textiles—the white linen in the foreground, the liturgical vestments, the damask in the background, and the curtains with the caparison—are all depicted with the same high degree of plasticity and tactility. They emerge in the same light, whose source is outside the pictorial space. The painted curtains do not belong to a different pictorial realm but are part of the textile plane. At the same time, they define the space within which the Man of Sorrows and the acolytes appear. However, the spatial relationship between the figures and fabrics differs strongly from that in the panel of Petrus Christus. The Man of Sorrows does not appear as clearly in the foreground, nor is he set apart from the angels behind him but on the contrary is supported by them.

The acolyte on the right is shown in profile holding Christ's vertically positioned forearm and bent elbow in his left and right hand, respectively. His opulently decked-out counterpart is facing us—as is the Man of Sorrows himself—as he grasps Christ's right elbow with both hands. Both altar boys are situated on roughly the same plane as the curtains. The brightly lit inner lining of the curtain on the right suggests that the head of the altar boy in pink is located behind the fabric, while his belt and the linen over his left arm are level with the curtain. The Man of Sorrows therefore appears slightly in front of it. All three figures are placed on the threshold and within the space between the parted curtain and the green honorary cloth. In Petrus Christus's panel, on the other hand, Christ is clearly set apart from the plane of the curtain and the black ground behind it. There, he has moved to the foreground and appears close to the viewer. Only the blue wavy area at the lower edge, which probably represents water or perhaps clouds, creates a distance.

No painting before had ever depicted the Man of Sorrows as vividly.[7] Based on sources other than the biblical narratives

7
Romuald Bauerreiß, *Pie Jesu: Das Schmerzensmann-Bild und sein Einfluss auf die mittelalterliche Frömmigkeit* (Munich: Widmann, 1931); Rudolf Berliner, "Bemerkungen zu

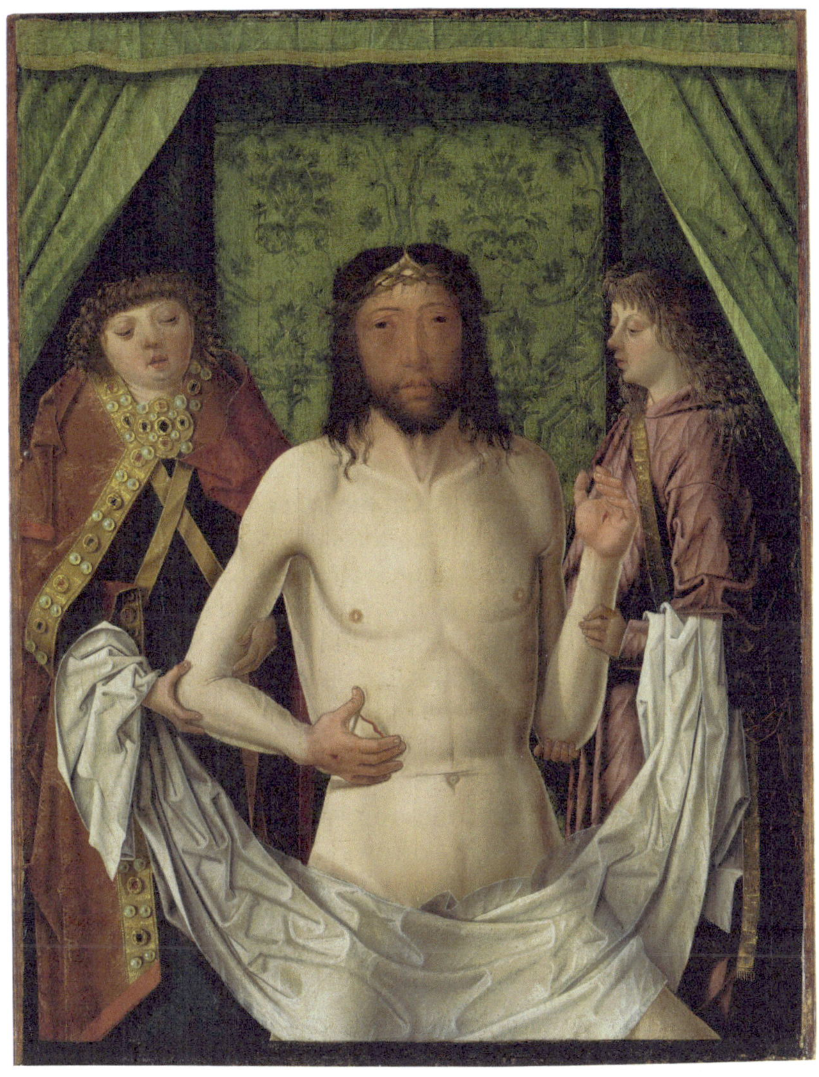

Salzburg Master, *Christ as the Man of Sorrows*, ca. 1500,
tempera on spruce wood, 41.5 × 33 cm.
Oskar Reinhart Collection Am Römerholz, Winterthur.

Fig. 91

of the Passion, the iconography of the Man of Sorrows alternates between that of the Son of God who has died and, as seen in Petrus Christus's panel, the risen and living Christ.[8] In comparison to older depictions of the Man of Sorrows, the dead Christ in Petrus Christus's panel has become animated, emancipating himself from the angels supporting him and—actively calling attention to his stigmata—ready to engage with us.[9] In the Salzburg Master's panel, both acolytes look at Christ's stigmata and turn toward the space between the open curtains and the cloth of honor stretched out behind them. In Petrus Christus's panel, the acolyte representing the Archangel Michael looks at us with a stern, even grim expression; only the Archangel Gabriel turns toward the Man of Sorrows and gazes directly at him. Here the two angels step aside, holding the brightly lit, vivid green curtain and thus adhering to the iconography of angels opening curtains. On the other hand, they lack wings and are not depicted aloft. Rather, they are acolytes identifiable as angels solely due to the attributes: the sword and lilies. Similarly, Christ's crown of thorns has been wound around his head like a black headband and looks somewhat like a theatrical prop. His elaborate halo glitters and shines like gilded metalwork and seems to be mounted on the dark band of the crown of thorns. Both the crown of thorns and the nimbus occupy their place as tangible objects and materialize as recognizable signs. Staging the figures as living performers, the costumes and props explicitly facilitate the appearance of the Man of Sorrows and the Archangels.

einigen Darstellungen des Erlösers als Schmerzensmann," in Das Münster 9 (1956), pp. 97–117; Gert von der Osten, *Der Schmerzensmann: Typengeschichte eines deutschen Andachtsbildwerkes von 1300–1600* (*Forschungen zur deutschen Kunstgeschichte* 7) (Berlin: Deutscher Verein für Kunstwissenschaft, 1935); Erwin Panofsky, "'Imago Pietatis': ein Beitrag zur Typengeschichte des 'Schmerzensmanns' und der 'Maria Mediatrix,'" in *Festschrift für Max J. Friedländer zum 60. Geburtstag* (Leipzig: E. A. Seemann, 1927), pp. 261–308; Hubert Schrade, "Beiträge zur Erklärung des Schmerzensmannbildes," in *Deutschkundliches: Friedrich Panzer zum 60. Geburtstag (Beiträge zur neueren Literaturgeschichte 16)* (Heidelberg, 1930), pp. 164–182; and Andrea Zimmermann, *Jesus Christus als "Schmerzensmann" in hoch- und spätmittelalterlichen Darstellungen der bildenden Kunst: eine Analyse ihres Sinngehalts*, PhD diss. (Martin Luther University Halle-Wittenberg, 1997).

8
Steffen Siegel, "Die Kunst der Ostentatio: Zur frühneuzeitlichen Bildgeschichte des Selbstverweises," in *Deixis: Vom Denken mit dem Zeigefinger*, Heike Gfrereis and Marcel Lepper, eds. (Göttingen: Wallstein, 2007), pp. 38–61, here p. 44.

9
This is particularly apparent in the comparison to the pictorial history of the inanimate Man of Sorrows. Panofsky, "'Imago Pietatis': ein Beitrag zur Typengeschichte des 'Schmerzensmanns' und der 'Maria Mediatrix,'" pp. 261–308.

In the Salzburg *Man of Sorrows*, the hands and face of Christ are—strikingly—painted a darker shade than the bright white upper body and arms. The transition between the hands and arms reveals the figure's natural tan, and in combination with elements such as the detailed rendering of the veins on the forearm and the wrinkles above the navel and in the left armpit depict the real-life body of Christ. The representation of tanned skin is an indication that a living, human body is presented to us as Christ. The two figures in liturgical garments, who do not hold the curtain but the Man of Sorrows himself, also take on a theatrical quality. In this reading, they become two children who, equipped with props, support the Man of Sorrows while holding his loincloth, which is draped around their arms.

Another case of a curtain depicted parallel to the picture plane is found in a panel by Jean Fouquet with a vastly different subject: a portrait of King Charles VII [fig. 94].[10] His image is framed by two white curtains, parted and fixed on either side of the pictorial space, and a red pelmet. It is considered the first portrait to depict a king on life-size scale.[11] Earlier portraits are significantly smaller in scale compared to this example by Fouquet. Dated around 1450, the painting is of pivotal importance for the portraiture genre in that it depicts the king not as an ideal type but as a living human being.[12] His individuality is indicated by bags under the eyes, wrinkles, redness of the skin, and a swelling of the right cheek, an early indication of the ulcer in the

10
Jean Fouquet, ed. Nicole Reynaud, exh. cat. Musée du Louvre (Paris: Éditions de la Réunion des Musées Nationaux, 1981). Erik Inglis has shown that the king here is not depicted praying: "he has no book of hours, his hands are not clasped in prayer, and he keeps his hat on." Erik Inglis, *Jean Fouquet and the Invention of France: Art and Nation after the Hundred Years War* (New Haven, CT: Yale University Press, 2011), p. 111.

11
Born in 1403, the king would have been about fifty years old at the time of the painting's execution. Stylistic as well as dendrochronological studies suggest the dating of the panel. Stephan Kemperdick, Stephan, "'Fouquet le peintre': Der Tafelmaler Jean Fouquet und das Diptychon von Melun," in *Jean Fouquet: Das Diptychon von Melun*, ed. Stephan Kemperdick, exh. cat. Staatliche Museen Preußischer Kulturbesitz, Gemäldegalerie, Berlin (Berlin: Imhof Verlag, 2017), pp. 11–35, here p. 22; Peter Klein, "Dendrochronologische Untersuchungen der Gemäldetafeln von *Jean Fouquet*," in Kemperdick, *Jean Fouquet*, pp. 190–191.

12
Reynaud, *Jean Fouquet*, p. 17. On the pictorial history of the portrait as an individual, see Gottfried Boehm, *Bildnis und Individuum: Über den Ursprung der Porträtmalerei in der italienischen Renaissance* (Munich: Prestel, 1985).

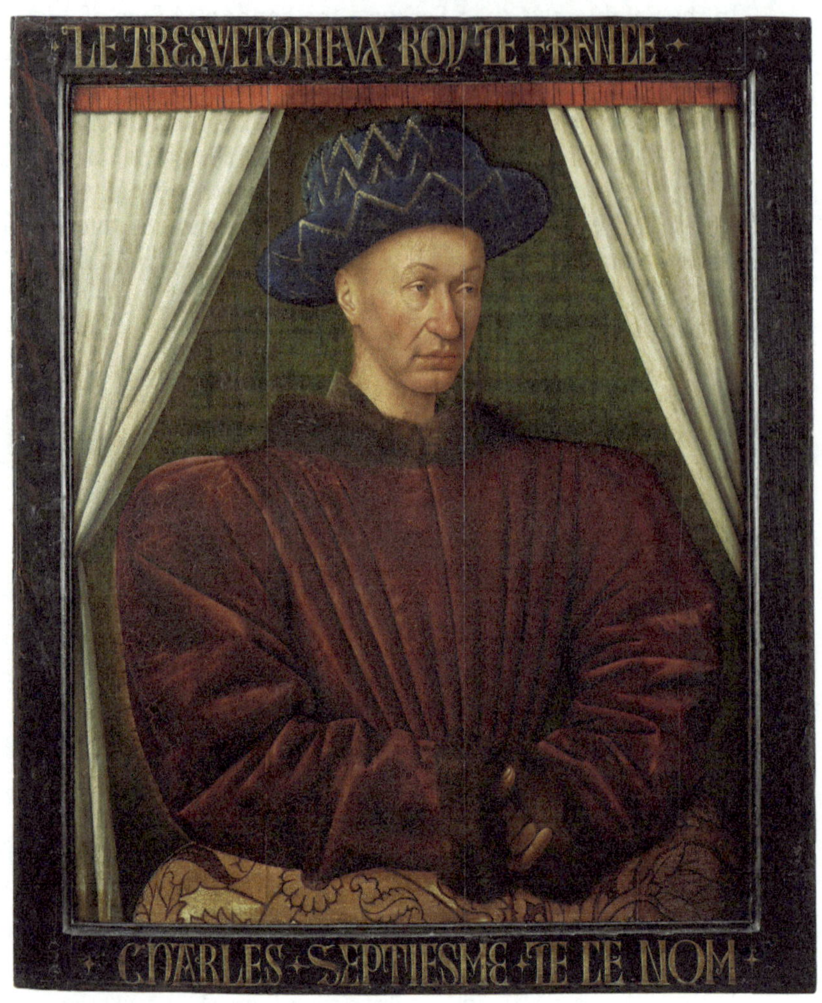

Jean Fouquet, *Portrait of Charles VII, King of France*, 1445–1450, oil on panel, 85 × 70 cm. Musée National du Louvre, Paris.

Fig. 94

regent's lower jaw that would later lead to his death.[13] The light entering the pictorial space from the viewer's left illuminates the face, especially the subject's right eyebrow, cheek, nose, and ear. This play of light and shade also distinguishes the representation of the two white curtains. Pulled to either side, they give way to a dark green background that appears as a wall behind the king and thus creates the impression of a rather shallow space. The red pelmet and black picture frame reinforce the shallow spatial layering of the planes, which evoke a relief-like space toward the front and a planar space in the background.

The configuration of an open curtain and a pelmet differ from depictions of honorary cloths or altar curtains hanging from curtain rods. In our examples, the curtains serve to call attention to the depicted figures while allowing a view into a shallow space bound at the back by a wall, or into spatially indefinite darkness [figs. 88, 91,94]. Open curtains and flat grounds serve to move the figures plastically and theatrically in front of them toward the illuminated middle- or foreground. As will be shown below, this strategy relates to the theatrical custom of unveiling *tableaux vivants* as pictures.[14]

Tableaux vivants

The French term *tableau vivant* as it is used today for the theatrical form of the living image was introduced in the German-speaking world in the nineteenth century.[15] In early theater studies, the terms "living image," "wordless performance," and "silent play"

13
The reddened eyes as well as other signs of fatigue on the face show physical suffering, which can be typologically interpreted. Just like Christ suffered for humanity, Charles VII suffered for France. Inglis, *Jean Fouquet and the Invention of France*, pp. 119–120.

14
Philine Helas, *Lebende Bilder in der italienischen Festkultur des 15. Jahrhunderts* (Berlin: De Gruyter, 1999), p. 6; Birgit Joos, *Lebende Bilder: Körperliche Nachahmung von Kunstwerken in der Goethezeit* (Berlin: Reimer, 1999); Fredrika Herman Jacobs, *The Living Image in Renaissance Art* (Cambridge, UK: Cambridge University Press, 2005); Rose Marie Ferré, "L'art des tableaux vivants au Moyen Age: Rappel de la question et enjeux," in *Le tableau vivant ou l'image performée,* ed. Julie Ramos (Paris: Mare Martin, 2014), pp. 35–52, here pp. 40–41; Hélène Visentin, "La pratique des tableaux vivants dans les entrées royales françaises," in *Le tableau vivant ou l'image performée*, ed. Ramos, pp. 53–70, here p. 57.

15
Helas, *Lebende Bilder*, p. 2.

came to be used synonymously.[16] Historically, more diverse and descriptive terms were used, such as games (*ludi*), supporting frameworks (*échafauds*), images (*edifice*), apparitions (*apparati*), and demonstrations (*vertooninge*).[17] To be sure, the notions of the "living image," "wordless performance," and "silent play" would be more accurate in that they do not suggest a false historicity through the use of a foreign term and moreover take geographical differences into account. Nevertheless, the term *tableau vivant* has become established throughout the disciplines and will be used here to denote the living image as a specific theatrical form.

Tableaux vivants appeared in public, sacred, or profane pageants and could be presented on fixed stages as well as moving processional floats.[18] There are two forms involving two different viewing modes. Whereas in Italy and France mobile *tableaux vivants* were transported on carts during processions and parades and visible from all sides without curtains, in the northern countries fixed stages with mounted curtains were preferred. When the high-ranking visitor and his retinue reached one of these structures, they were honored with a pictorial play, revealed by curtains at the sound of trumpets.[19] The scenes were concealed by curtains that only opened to the audience after the procession had begun and at the moment when the ruler was passing them.[20] The moment of opening could be announced not only musically, but also with an oral commentary about what the *tableaux vivants* would depict.[21] When revealed, the scene presented costumed figures, mute and motionless, imitating a spectacle as a living image. These figures did not interact with the audience, but represented biblical, mythological, historical, or contemporary personages and allegories with statuesque poses and fixed gestures.

16
Max Herrmann, *Forschungen zur deutschen Theatergeschichte des Mittelalters und der Renaissance* (Berlin: Weidmann, 1914), p. 370.

17
Helas, *Lebende Bilder*, p. 6; Ferré, "L'art des tableaux vivants," pp. 40–41; Visentin, "La pratique des tableaux vivants," p. 57.

18
Joos, *Lebende Bilder*, p. 28.

19
Marlis Radke-Stegh, *Der Theatervorhang: Ursprung – Geschichte – Funktion* (Meisenheim am Glan: Hain, 1978), p. 180.

20
Joel Blanchard, "Le spectacle du rite: Les entrées royales," *Revue historique* 627 (2003), pp. 475–519, here pp. 485–486.

21
Radke-Stegh, *Der Theatervorhang*, p. 180.

From the thirteenth century onward, *tableaux vivants* decorated with curtains and draperies were erected at the side of the road for a ruler's formal entry into a city.[22] It was cities who organized, designed, and paid for these ceremonial entries, which were often accompanied by processions and profane and religious games. In the first quarter of the fifteenth century, *tableaux vivants* set up along the route in front of façades, bridge pillars, and gates, on squares, and at crossroads became the central spectacles in the celebration of the sovereign's entry.[23] They evidently did not merely influence public perception, but were a reflection of the same, as it was the public who planned them.

While the routes of these processions hardly changed over the centuries, the *tableau-vivant* performances became ever more elaborate. At the end of the fourteenth and beginning of the fifteenth century, living images were moreover presented as a part of ecclesiastical mystery plays.[24] They contributed greatly to entry ceremonies and in the second half of the fifteenth century evolved into outright spectacles. As a result, they were now no longer incidental decorative elements but constitutive parts of the ceremony, which was attended by the entire urban population. *Tableau-vivant* scenes represented typological contexts and solidified allegorical programs.[25]

Most stages were placed on high trestles to make them visible from afar. However, the pictorial character of *tableaux vivants* is created primarily through the use of curtains. Curtains are constitutive for the theatrical pictorialization of *tableaux vivants* because they establish an aesthetic distance between the audience and the scene revealed by opening them. This setup created spatial distance, which meant that the *tableaux vivants* could never be touched but perceived only as pictures. Here, the relationship between touching the surface of a picture and visual perception is

22
The earliest written documents report events held by Philip the Fair in honor of Edward of England in Paris at Whitsun in 1313. Herrmann, *Forschungen zur deutschen Theatergeschichte,* pp. 367–403.

23
Cf. Blanchard, "Le spectacle du rite," pp. 475–519, here pp. 485–486.

24
Herrmann, *Forschungen zur deutschen Theatergeschichte,* pp. 367–403.

25
Visentin, "La pratique des tableaux vivants," pp. 53–70, here p. 53.

inverted. Haptic qualities are inherent to *tableaux vivants*, as they are themselves created out of flesh and blood. At the same time, they can never be experienced haptically, as that would call the "pictorial character" into question. Despite this circumstance, as Philine Helas has argued, the fascination lies precisely in the fact that the spectators and the performers share the same experiential space, the same potentiality of haptic experience. Their status as "picture" brackets a before and after in which all participants are united in the same web of social contact.[26]

The *tableau vivant*'s stage curtains take on a constitutive function for the picture because they can be closed and opened on the frontmost plane. When they are closed, the scenic picture takes shape behind them: the performers position themselves on the stage unseen for their later presentation in their immobile postures when the curtain finally opens. The curtains are the prerequisite for the scene to be revealed and perceived as a picture in its motionless state, suddenly set apart from the space surrounding it. The curtains of the *tableaux vivants* therefore not only organize the appearance of the figures on the stage as an image, but also define a space behind them as well as one in front of them—the space in which the celebration of the ruler's entry takes place. The theatrical form of the living image thus bridges the divide between eternal art and transient life.[27]

Living Images as Pictures

The earliest surviving pictorial documentation of stage curtains used for stationary *tableaux vivants* are the pen-and-ink drawings made on the occasion of Joan of Castile's entry into Brussels on December 9, 1496.[28] Fifty days after her marriage to Philip the

26
Philine Helas, "Lebendes Bild – haptisches Bild," in Markus Rath, Jörg Trempler, and Iris Wenderholm, eds., *Das haptische Bild: Körperhafte Bilderfahrung in der Neuzeit* (Berlin: De Gruyter, 2013), pp. 69–92, here p. 92.

27
Helas, *Lebende Bilder*, p. 2.

28
Herrmann, *Forschungen zur deutschen Theatergeschichte*, pp. 367–403; Paul Wescher, *Beschreibendes Verzeichnis der Miniaturen, Handschriften und Einzelblätter des Kupferstichkabinetts der Staatlichen Museen zu Berlin* (Leipzig: J. J. Weber, 1931), pp. 179–181; Wim Blockmans, "Le dialogue imaginaire entre princes et sujets: Les joyeues entree en Brabant en 1994 er 1496," in *Fêtes et cérémonies aux XIVe-XVI siècles*, ed. Jean-Maries Cauchies (Neuchâtel: Centre Européen

Fair, she celebrated and honored the city as the new queen in her husband's absence. The colored pen-and-ink drawings depicting the entry are found in a manuscript produced between 1496 and 1506 to chronicle the event. Each image fills an entire folio on the recto and is juxtaposed with Latin commentary on the verso explaining the depiction's allegorical interpretation and making reference to Philip the Fair and Joan of Castile. The manuscript thus contains not only important descriptions of the solemn procession and the *tableaux vivants* revealed by the opening of curtains, but also reproduces the images themselves in their overall conception and pictorial program in a total of sixty images. The quality of the colored pen-and-ink drawings suggests that the manuscript was not intended for the ruling couple themselves. Furthermore, it does not contain a dedication, indicating that it was probably meant to serve as a model for a more elaborate manuscript or for prints.[29] As a chronicle, these pen-and-ink drawings rank as a historical source insofar as they convey a visual impression of the theatrical form of the *tableaux vivants.*[30]

Although it is not known by name who produced the pen-and-ink drawings and the chronicle, several rhetoricians of Brussels are known to have been involved in the ceremonial processions and can be considered possible authors.[31] The first-person-plural form chosen for the texts suggests that the manuscript

d'Etudes Bourguignonnes, 1994), pp. 37–53, especially pp. 41–42; Paul Vandenbroeck, "A Bride Amidst Heroines, Fools and Savages: The Joyous Entry into Brussels by Joanna of Castile, 1496 (Berlin, Kupferstichkabinett, Ms. 78D5)," in *Jaarboek Koninklijk Museum voor Schone Kunsten* (2012/2014), pp. 153–194; Anne-Marie Legaré, "L'entrée de Jeanne de Castille à Bruxelles: Un programme iconographique au fémina," in *Women at the Burgundian Court*, Dagmar Eichberger, Anne-Marie Legaré, and Wim Hüsken, eds. (Turnhout: Brepols, 2010), pp. 43–55; Monique Chatenet, *Fastes de cour: Les enjeux d'un voyage princier à Blois en 1501* (Rennes: Presses universitaires de Renne, 2010); Laura Weigert, *French Visual Culture and the Making of Medieval Theater* (Cambridge, UK: Cambridge University Press, 2015), pp. 26–73.

29
Ibid.

30
These pen-and-ink drawings have therefore played an important role in the history of theater studies since its beginning. Already Max Herrmann, the founder of the subject of theater studies in Berlin, and subsequently Winfried Klara referred to these drawings from the Kupferstichkabinett in Berlin. Herrmann, *Forschungen zur deutschen Theatergeschichte*, pp. 367–403; Winfried Klara: Theaterbilder. Ihre grundsätzliche Bedeutung und ihre Entwicklung bis auf Jacques Callot (Berlin: Freunde der Staatsbibliothek zu Berlin, 2005.

31
They could be Colijm Cailleu, Jan Smeken, Jan Precheval, Jan Van den Dale or Hiertherot. Paul Vandenbroeck, "A Bride Amidst Heroines, Fools and Savages," p. 160.

was written in the name of the city of Brussels. A few months earlier, Jean Molinet, the official historiographer of the Burgundian dukes, had written a detailed report on the entry of Joan of Castile. He refers to the *histoires par personnaiges*, which were organized by the inhabitants of the city, merely by pointing out that listing them would take too much time.[32] The pen-and-ink drawings, on the other hand, were dedicated to precisely this feature of the event, depicting the living images mounted on the mansions and adorned with curtains visually rather than in writing.[33]

In order to grasp the general context of the *tableaux vivants* and the curtains that reveal and conceal them, it is necessary to understand the structure and narrative of the overall manuscript. The latter begins with the depiction of a wreath of clouds in which the Archangel Michael is depicted as the patron saint of Brussels raising his sword over the devil [fig. 101]. The following leaves depict the beginning of the procession, which was led by the representatives of various social groups. The commentary points out that the images correspond to the sequence of the procession and the games performed, in which context the order of the groups represented was determined by their office and rank.[34] The entry of these groups is followed by six mimic games performed by buffoons, jesters, wild men, and masked actors.[35] The procession then continues with noblemen and officials ranging from court presidents to secretaries, councilors, and mayors. They are followed by two rows of torchbearers representing the

32
"Plusieurs histories par personnaiges furent faictes par ceulx de la ville, qui long seroient à les *réciter.*" Jean Molinet, *Chroniques de Jean Molinet,* Georges Doutrepont and Omer Jodogne, eds. (Brussels: Palais des académies, 1935), p. 430.

33
Laura Weigert, *French Visual Culture,* pp. 70–71.

34
Ecclesiastical scholars precede the procession against the backdrop of the city with red flags. The following folios show Carmelite monks, followed by Minorites, senior canonized clergy, clergy of Saint Gudule, and the city regents with torches. Fol. 10r shows representatives of the guilds with torches from which the guild symbols hang.

35
The first in this group is a scene with three jesters and a monk as a musician on fol. 11r. This is followed by a depiction of the jester being mocked by boys in the marketplace on fol. 12r. Fol. 13r shows an Ethiopian princess on a white horse accompanied by green and masked wild men with clubs. This is followed by a jester with a jester's scepter and bellows on the back of a white horse against the backdrop of a castle. Fol. 15r depicts four wild men hitting each other with heavy clubs. On fol. 16r, a group of white-clad actors wearing masks with long noses and red caps ride a sleigh pulled by a mounted white horse.

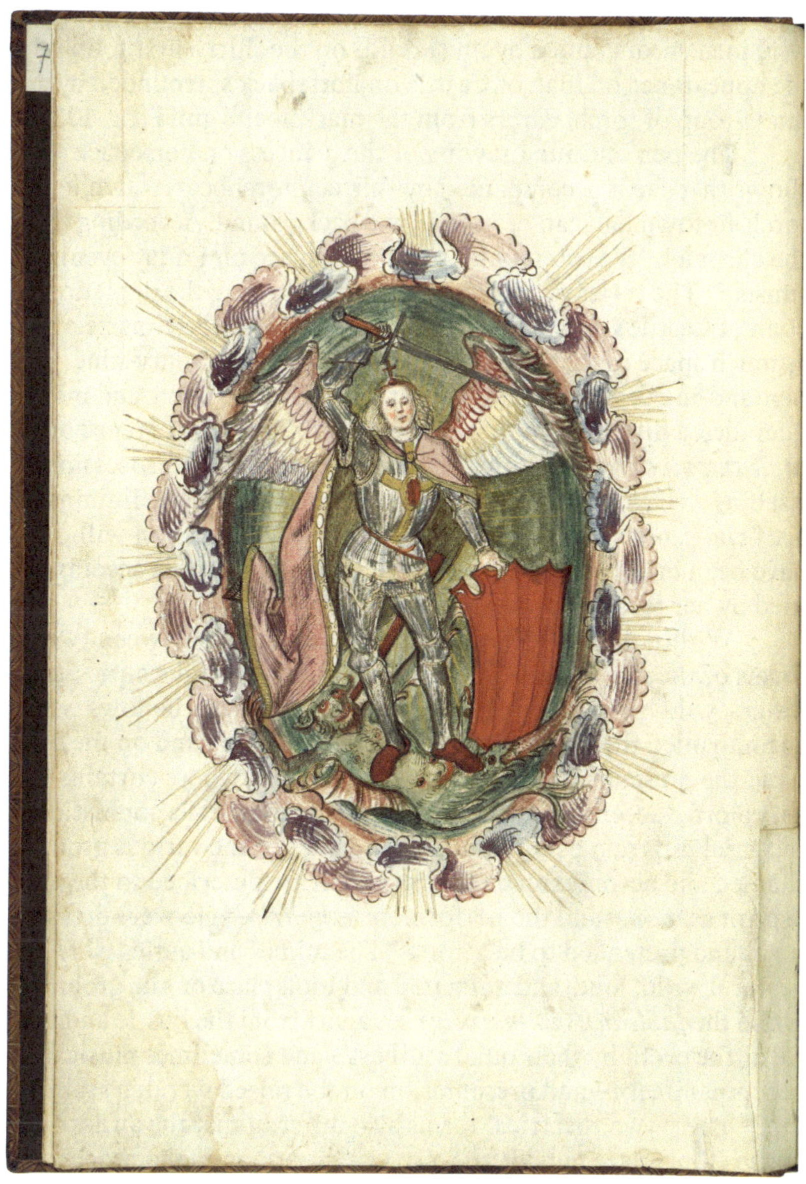

Archangel Michael rising his sword over the devil
(entry of Joan of Castile into Brussels on December 9, 1496), ca. 1496–1506, Brussels.
Berlin, Staatliche Museen, Kupferstichkabinett, 78.D.5, fol. 1v.

Fig. 101

guilds of the liberal arts. The long procession of guilds, jesters, and wild men accompanied by music ends on the thirty-first folio with the appearance of Joan of Castile on horseback surrounded by a final group of torchbearers from the marksmen's guild [fig. 103].

The pen-and-ink drawing of the princess on horseback shows that she is accompanied by thirteen torchbearers, while the torch-lit town hall can be seen in the background. According to the chronicle, the ceremonial entry took place on Friday evening at sunset.[36] The series of *tableaux vivants* following the depiction of Joan of Castile's entry into the city [figs. 106–124] claims nearly as much space in the manuscript as the previous twenty-nine pen-and-ink drawings devoted to the ceremonial entry and masquerades, a distribution that illustrates the great importance of the *tableaux vivants*. The many torches suggest that the procession itself as well as the stages revealed along the way were illuminated artificially, now more, now less brightly. The procession will have been brightest in the section with Joan of Castile accompanied by her torchbearers.

Within the procession, we must distinguish between two forms of theater—on the one hand the games with the antics of the jesters, wild men, bagpipers, and mask players with bellows which accompanied the procession and elicited laughter, and on the other hand the presentation of the *tableaux vivants*, whose curtains set colorful accents in the city and opened to reveal a sophisticated pictorial program behind them. The games of the various groups that led and accompanied the procession are described in the manuscript as *mimes* and the performers as *hystrio*, who were dressed up as and pretended to be actors.[37] The mimes and antics were gestural, wild, loud, and animated and took place on the ground, while the *tableaux vivants* were set apart from the hustle and bustle of the event by their quiet stillness—and sometimes musical accompaniment—and presentation on the raised wooden scaffolding.[38] These two theatrical forms also differ in that the antics and mimes took place outside the city walls. As soon as the procession

36
See fol. 2r.

37
Weigert, *French Visual Culture*, pp. 69–70.

38
Laura Weigert describes and contextualizes these mimes and antics in the pen-and-ink drawings of Joan of Castile in much greater detail than is possible here: Weigert: *French Visual Culture*, pp. 62–70.

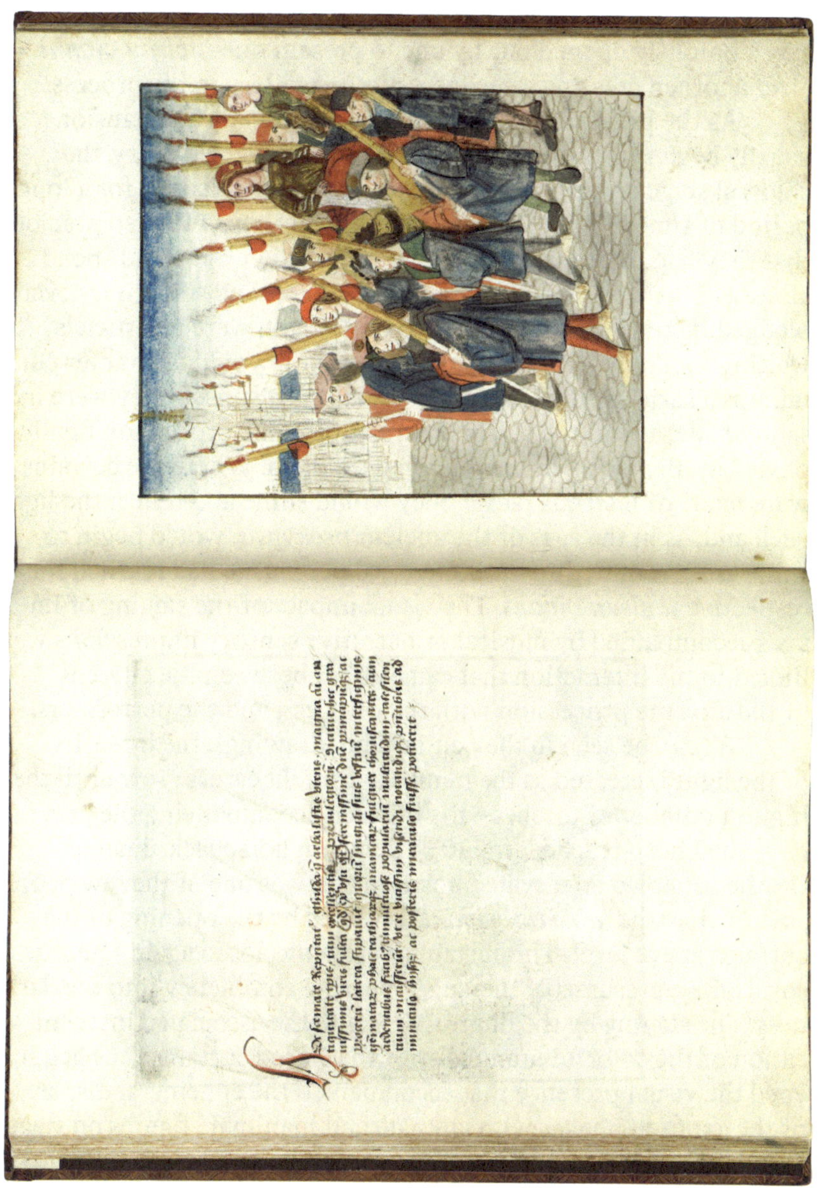

Joan of Castile on horseback surrounded by torchbearers (entry of Joan of Castile into Brussels on December 9, 1496), ca. 1496–1506, Brussels. Berlin, Staatliche Museen, Kupferstichkabinett, 78.D.5, fol. 30v and 31r.

Fig. 103

had passed through them and arrived in the city, the curtains were ceremoniously opened one by one to present one *tableau vivant* after another, creating a veritable picture gallery in the process.

As the preparations for and construction of the mansions usually began six to ten months before the expected entry, the colorful stage curtains dominated the cityscape visually for a long period of time.[39] With their valuable textiles, they were so precious that they had to be guarded day and night.[40] A city would spend all its available funds on the *tableaux vivants* and sometimes even pledged its revenue for years to come.[41] If you were in Brussels waiting for Joan of Castile's royal entry, you would encounter curtains as a series of different-colored fields. At sunset, they were in semi-shade, and as the torchbearers leading the procession finally passed by, flickering light would fall on them. Where the curtains were made of lustrous fabric, they would shine and reflect the light back and, as in the case of the ancient *prokypsis,* would begin to shine as if from within until the royal personage had reached the respective *tableau vivant*. The visual impact of the staging of images accompanied by musical or narrative sensory impressions was linked to the interaction that came about between the citizens of the city, the procession with the princess, and the performers.

As can be seen in the pen-and-ink drawings, the intensity of the light increased as the number of torchbearers grew until the highest number of torches—the thirteen accompanying the princess—had been reached [fig. 103]. Being on horseback, Joan of Castile occupied an elevated position and was one of the few people able to view the *tableaux vivants* revealed by the opening of the curtains at eye level. The curtains were only closed again after the royal entry, presumably then disappearing completely into the darkness. The staging by the illumination and the associated intensification of the colorful luminosity of the closed curtains thus heightened the visual presence that accompanied the ephemeral display of the exposed images with animate and inanimate figures on stage.

39
George Kernodle, *From Art to Theatre: Form and Convention in the Renaissance* (Chicago: University of Chicago Press, 1944), p. 60.

40
Weigert, *French Visual Culture*, p. 39 ff.

41
Kernodle, *From Art to Theatre*, p. 59.

On a total of twenty-seven leaves, the living pictures mounted on wooden structures are depicted individually. The Latin commentary informs us that the order of the drawings corresponds to the chronological sequence of the presentation of the *tableaux vivants.*[42] The first living image to be revealed depicts the *inventors of music*, as we know from the inscription on the pelmet [fig. 106]. Jubal at the anvil and Tubalcain are surrounded by a music scribe and noblemen making music. Presumably the sound of Tubal's hammer could be heard, as well as those of a lute and a flute.[43] As can be inferred from the commentary,[44] the image is an allegory of both the arts and political harmony. Just as Jubal and Tubal discovered the sweet melody of music when they heard the beating of a hammer, Joan of Castile establishes unity through her authority over thirty countries in a single peace agreement.

The image is followed by scenes from the Old Testament, among them a depiction of Esther before Ahasver. The content switches then to profane, historical themes, followed by a contemporary event: Philip the Fair kneels before Joan of Castile personifying the muse of victory, two standard-bearers, one on each side, frame the two figures at the center [fig. 107]. This image is followed by several allegorical depictions of female heroines and queens flanked by assisting companion figures and continues with a *tableau vivant* containing three living pictures revolving around the marriage of Florentius, Duke of Milan, and Meriana, Princess of Castile [fig. 108]. Here, two paintings serve as props. On the left and right, the bridegroom and bride are shown presenting their own painted portrait, complete with a gold frame, to an envoy, while the scene in which they shake hands appears in the middle.

Next in line are living pictures of war scenes, ending with a living image of the three virgins [fig. 109]. This image is the only one to show the mansion for the *tableau vivant* from the side, probably due to the fact that the central figure holds a red staff that extends into the space in front of the stage like a fishing rod.

42
Brussels School, *Entry of Joan of Castile into Brussels on December 9, 1496*, 1496 to 1506, pen-and-ink drawing, watercolor on paper, 35.6 × 25 cm, Staatliche Museen zu Berlin, Kupferstichkabinett, fol. 32 l, Berlin.

43
Björn R. Tammen, "A *Feast of the Arts*: Joanna of Castile in Brussels, 1496," in *Early Music History* 30 (2011), pp. 213–248.

44
See fol. 31v.

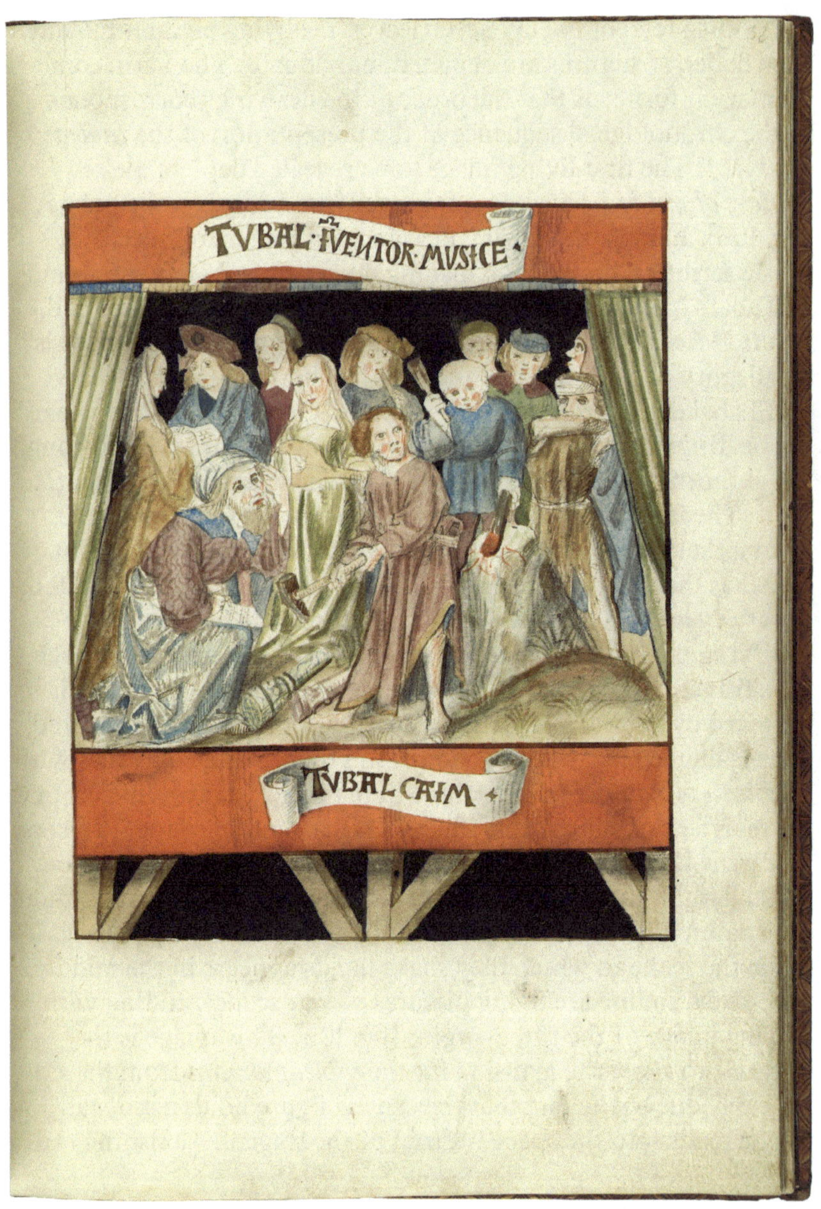

Tableau Vivant of Tubalkaim as inventor of music
(entry of Joan of Castile into Brussels on December 9, 1496), ca. 1496–1506, Brussels.
Berlin, Staatliche Museen, Kupferstichkabinett, 78.D.5, fol. 32r.

Fig. 106

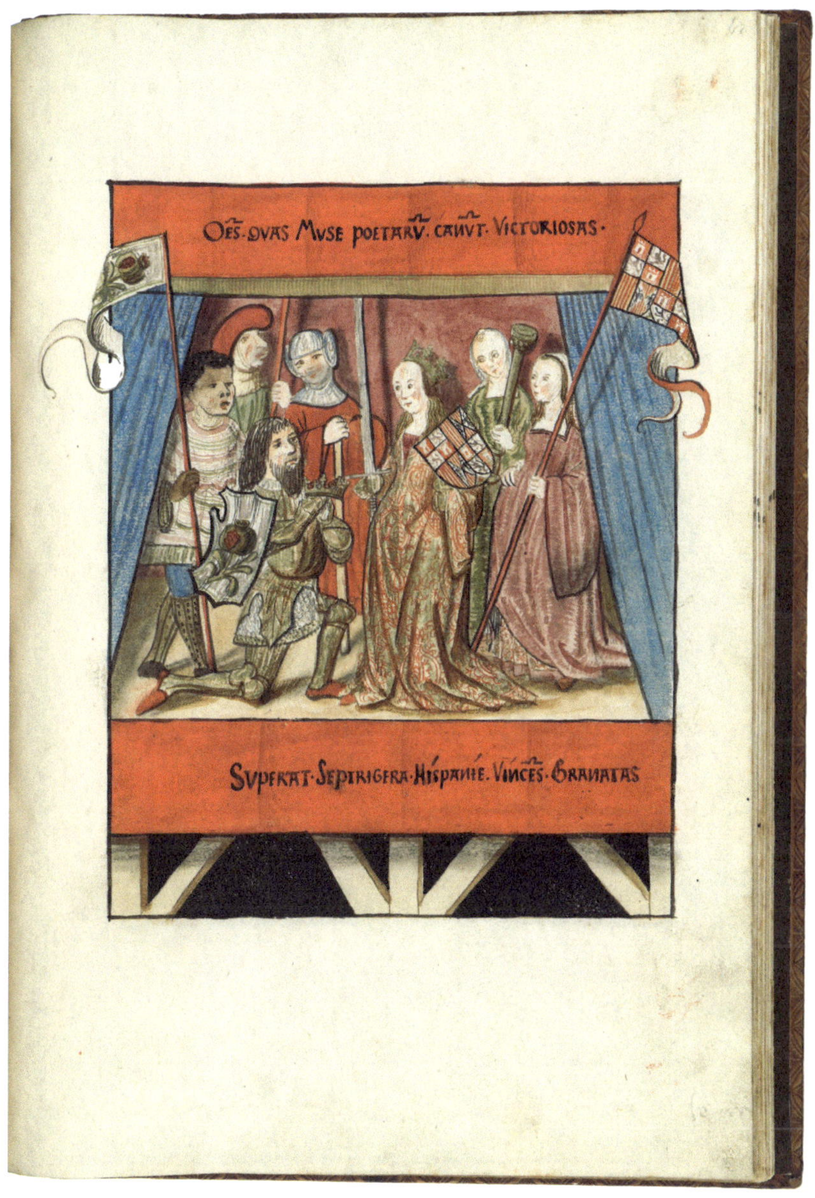

Tableau Vivant of Philip the Fair kneeling in front of Joan of Castile as the Muse of Victory (entry of Joan of Castile into Brussels on December 9, 1496), ca. 1496–1506, Brussels. Berlin, Staatliche Museen, Kupferstichkabinett, 78.D.5, fol. 42r.

Fig. 107

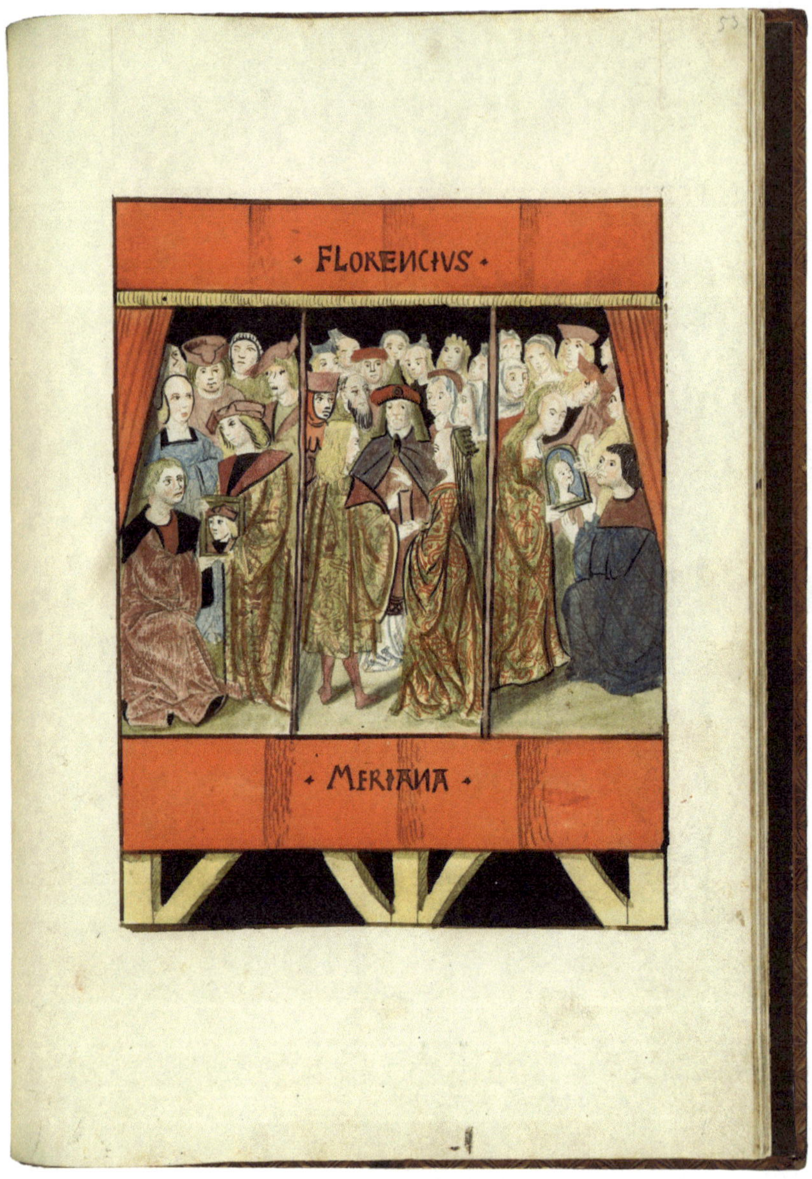

Tableau Vivant of the marriage of Florentius, Duke of Milan, and Meriana, Princess of Castile (entry of Joan of Castile into Brussels on December 9, 1496), ca. 1496–1506, Brussels. Berlin, Staatliche Museen, Kupferstichkabinett, 78.D.5, fol. 53r.

Fig. 108

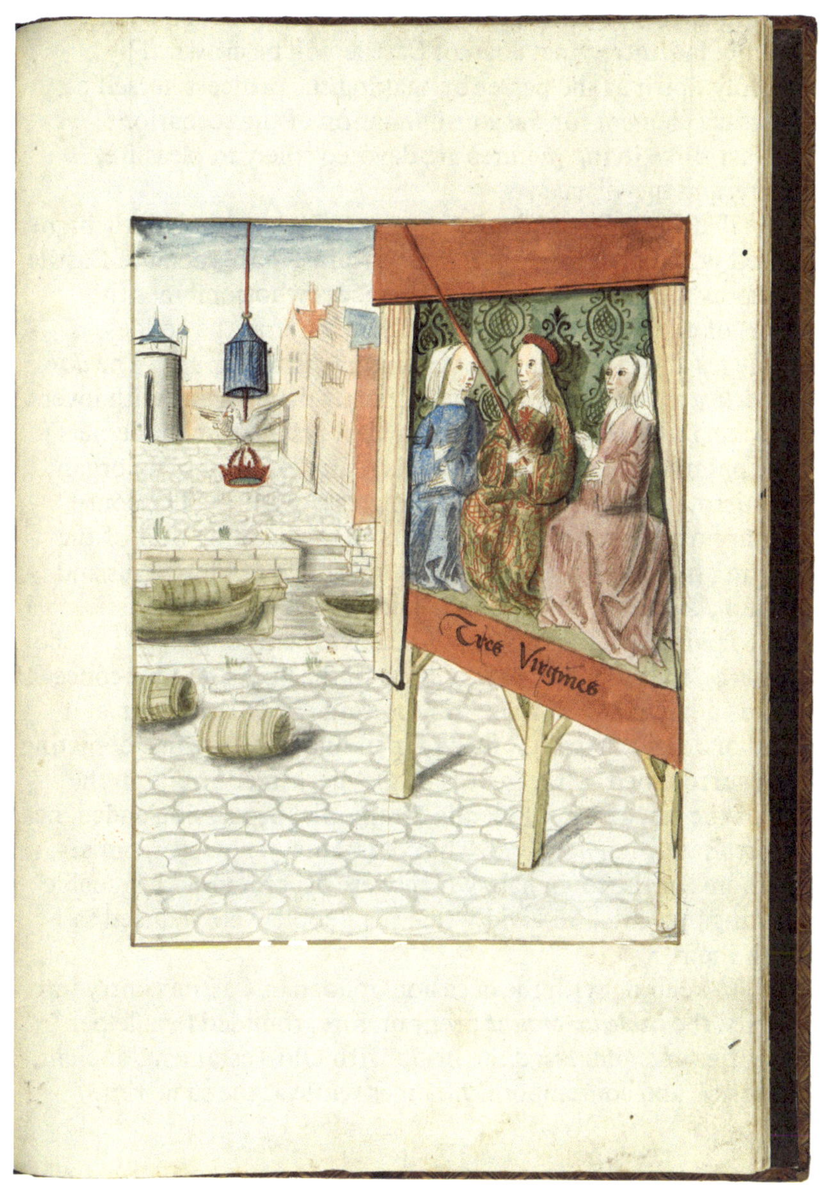

Tableau Vivant of the Three Virgins
(entry of Joan of Castile into Brussels on December 9, 1496), ca. 1496–1506, Brussels.
Berlin, Staatliche Museen, Kupferstichkabinett, 78.D.5, fol. 56r.

Fig. 109

A white dove on a crown can be seen under a small blue tent, possibly indicating that Joan of Castile will be crowned by the Holy Spirit as she passes by, making the princess herself a necessary element for the consummation of the scenario.[45] The last three living pictures are devoted solely to pleasure, beauty, and the visual arts.

The depiction of the Judgment of Paris, prominently highlighted with particularly precious curtains, makes Joan of Castile appear as the ideal and universal princess who combines the merits of all three goddesses in one person,[46] as the goddesses' privileges and gifts do not appear immaculate [fig. 111]. The *domus delice et jocunditatis* shows a courtly dance scene with lovers, musicians, and jesters [fig. 112]. The last *tableau vivant* depicts Luke painting the Madonna, who is seated in front of an organ and surrounded by musicmaking angels [fig. 113].[47] The commentary on the opposite folio refers to the handing over of the painting previously depicted in the marriage of Florencius and Meriana [fig. 108], since Luke is said to have used his artistic skill to paint a picture of Joan which was sent to Brabant. As the canvas on the easel is visible only from the back and thus conceals what is depicted on it, it might represent either the Virgin and Child or Joan's portrait. The final pen-and-ink drawing, depicting Joan surrounded by the guards of the marksmen's guild in the hall of the town hall, where the ceremonial procession ended, has unfortunately not survived. The commentary, however, praises the rooms of the town hall, which were decorated with valuable paintings executed so vividly that the people were seduced to touch them.

In keeping with the occasion of Joan of Castile's entry into the city, the *tableau-vivant* program foregrounded female personalities and addressed the bride with Old Testament, ancient, historical, and contemporary themes while at the same time

45
Weigert, *French Visual Culture*, p. 43.

46
Anne-Marie Legaré, "L'entrée de Jeanne de Castille à Bruxelles: Un programme iconographique au fémina," in *Women at the Burgundian Court*, Dagmar Eichberger, Anne-Marie Legaré, and Wim Hüsken, eds. (Turnhout: Brepols, 2010), pp. 43–55, here p. 53.

47
As in the first *tableau vivant* on fol. 32r, they play a lute and a flute in reference to the invention of music.

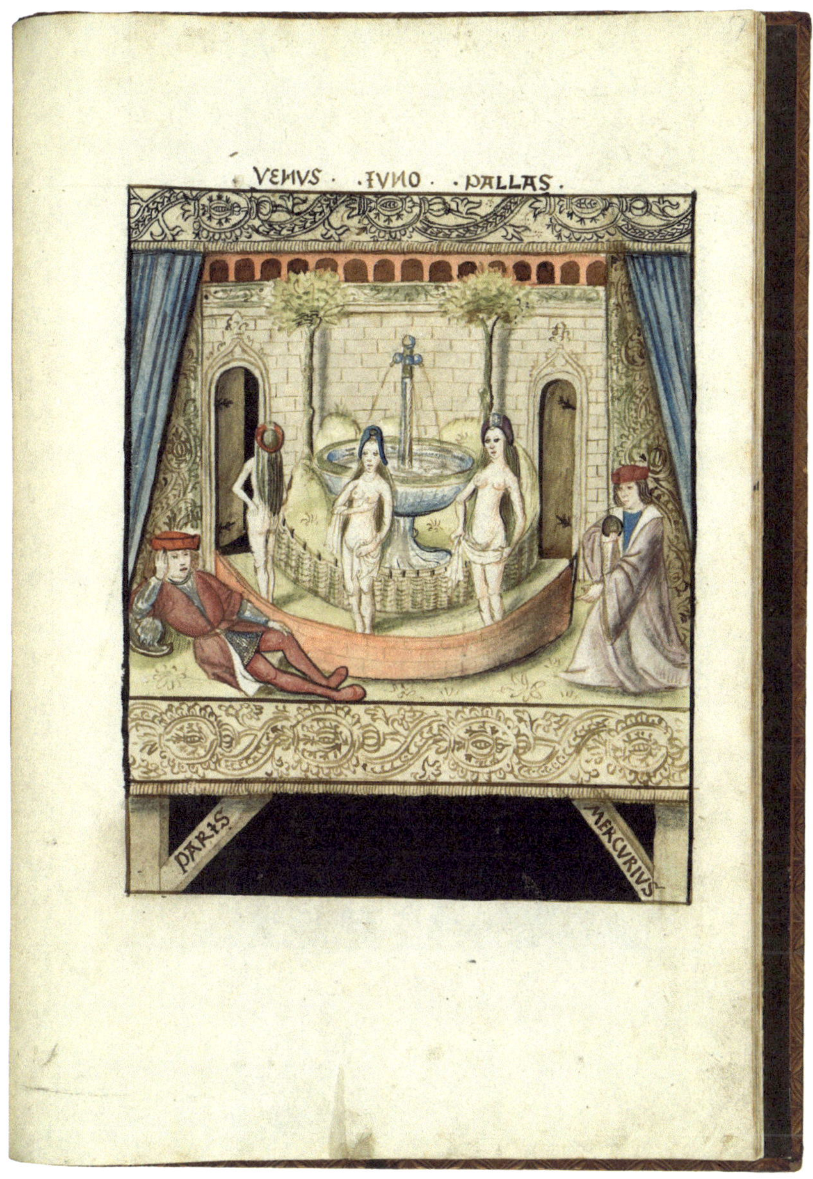

Tableau Vivant of the Judgement of Paris
(entry of Joan of Castile into Brussels on December 9, 1496), ca. 1496–1506, Brussels.
Berlin, Staatliche Museen, Kupferstichkabinett, 78.D.5, fol. 57r.

Fig. 111

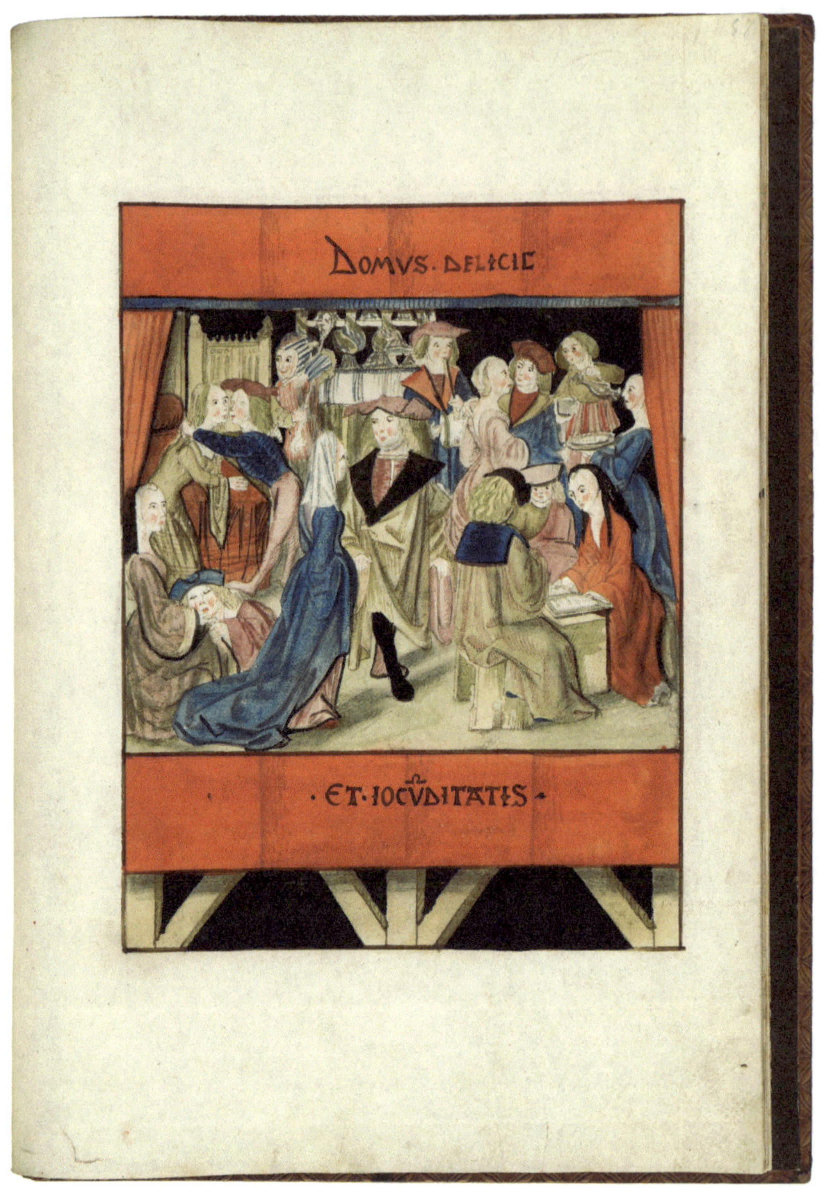

Tableau Vivant of the *domus delice et jocunditatis*
(entry of Joan of Castile into Brussels on December 9, 1496), ca. 1496–1506, Brussels.
Berlin, Staatliche Museen, Kupferstichkabinett, 78.D.5, fol. 58r.

Fig. 112

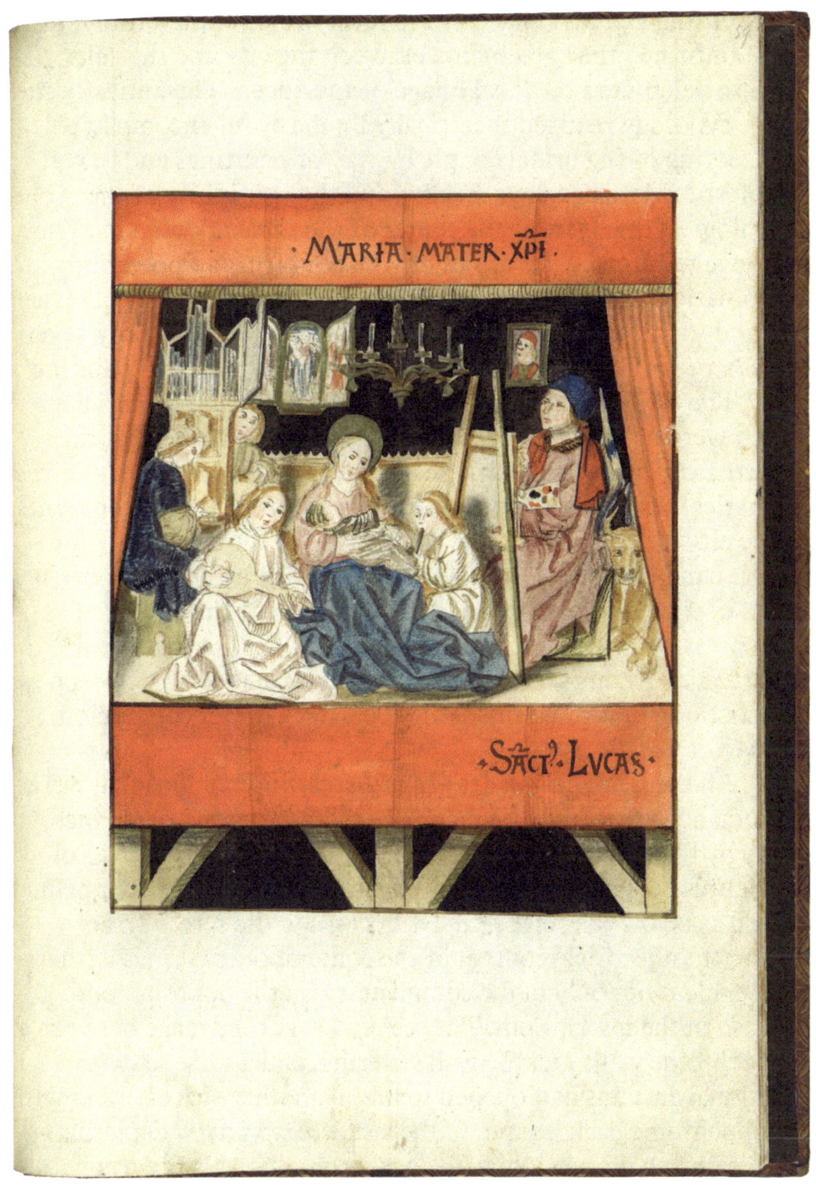

Tableau Vivant of Luke painting the Madonna
(entry of Joan of Castile into Brussels on December 9, 1496), ca. 1496–1506, Brussels.
Berlin, Staatliche Museen, Kupferstichkabinett, 78.D.5, fol. 59r.

Fig. 113

representing a public image of the future ruler. It therefore not only confirmed the agreements between the city and the ruler, but also celebrated the ideal image of the queen. Thematically, the image typology realized theatrically by the event encompassed the meeting of the bridal couple by way of paintings and in real life on site. Marriage, love, beauty, and the continuity of the genealogical line were at the center of the *tableaux vivants*. They moreover addressed the topics of war, courage, and power in combination with themes relating to the country's political security and social harmony. What is more, the series of twenty-seven *tableaux vivants* was framed by allegories of music and painting.

The skills of the visual artists, musicians, and rhetoricians, which were necessary for the conception of the content of the *tableaux vivants* and the design of the stage sets, were themselves thematically staged. In view of the depictions of the patron saints of the city of Brussels and the final image of the town hall, however, it can be said that the concern was less with the self-portrayal of the respective guilds than with that of the city itself as an expression of the *Bruxellois'* wealth and skill in these arts in general.[48] In this sense, the overall performance is to be seen as an artistic achievement of the city bearing a direct connection to Joan of Castile.[49]

All the pen-and-ink drawings display inscriptions that were presumably attached to the mansions themselves and performed orally by the commentators. In multifigural scenes, the names of the figures depicted are written in black letters on the upper pelmet as well as below the stage or in letters on a white scroll. To an extent, the allegorical content of the contemporary scenes is, therefore, evident not only in the commentary on the opposite folio, but also in the inscriptions. The scenes' backdrops range between a monochrome wall, a textile wall covering, and a stage set with additional curtains half opened to reveal another space behind with a monochrome background. In the last *tableau vivant* depicting Luke painting the Madonna, the background is a black curtain, as is indicated by the wavy hem at its lower edge [fig. 113]. In the foreground, we see how the open curtain with the pelmet plays a key role in constituting the stage that opens up behind it.

48
Weigert, *French Visual Culture*, p. 72.

49
Ibid., p. 73.

Perused from front to back, the manuscript reveals the sequence of the content, the rhythm of the curtain colors, and the changing references made by the individual *tableaux vivants.* The green, yellow-gold, red, white, and blue curtains have opened to reveal the narrow stage space of the mansions. All the valances are red except that in the *tableau vivant* of the Judgment of Paris, in which a white textile with a black floral pattern was used for both the curtain and the valance [fig. 111]. The fringed hems of the red valances vary between yellow and blue. Only the first *tableau vivant* depicting Tubal as the inventor of music has a multicolored hem that announces all the colors of the curtains to come [fig. 106]. The curtains vary in color, with individual groups also forming. At the beginning, the stage curtains are green, then red, then yellow-gold, then green again. This is followed by four blue curtains, then five yellow-gold curtains for the female allegories as the antitype to Joan of Castile before the picture gallery closes with a changing rhythm of individual red curtains, then yellow-gold, then blue again, and finally red. Green and red curtains are mainly used for the biblical themes, while the allegories, histories, and contemporary portraits of Joan of Castile and Philip I the Fair are predominantly accompanied by yellow-gold or blue curtains. Here, we can assume a semantic link between the colors of the curtains and the images behind them. While green and red refer typologically to the virtues and beauty of Joan of Castile in connection with the Old and New Testaments, the gold curtains, which shone and shimmered in the darkness due to the illumination of the procession's torches, and those in blue—a Burgundian color—stand for imperial splendor and representation. The spectacle of the coronation by the three opulently dressed virgins, for example, took place in the instant the gold curtains opened. The imperial color blue appears as a curtain color ten times and thus most frequently, so that here again the semantic focus is on Joan of Castile.

The colors of the curtains link the individual mansions on the one hand, while creating contrasts between them on the other, creating a rhythm, tension, and intensification in the process of viewing the images successively.[50] What is more, the opening and

50
Laura Weigert also makes this observation: Weigert, *French Visual Culture*, p. 50.

closing of the curtains determined the duration of the viewing of the *tableaux vivants* as paintings, which in turn was celebrated as a fleeting and special event. Within this dramaturgy, with its sheer multitude of stages and wealth of different-colored curtains and changing sets, four elements are consistent throughout. Firstly, there is always a curtain that parts in the middle to open to either side; secondly, the frame of the mansions is always covered with an upper and lower pelmet; thirdly, the stages are built on raised supporting frames; and fourthly, the stage spaces are self-contained and closed on all sides when the curtain is drawn.

The manuscript also shows how the wooden mansions were constructed as stationary street stages. As mentioned before, there is one pen-and-ink drawing that does not show the *tableau vivant* from the front—the point of view from which the theatrical pictorial effect came fully to bear—but depicts the construction of the simple wooden stage, complete with its two-part curtain, in a three-quarter view from the side [fig. 109]. Here we can see that the stage was in an elevated position on supporting scaffolding in the public space, and that its sides and backs were closed so that the picture box was visible only from the front and only when the curtains were open. The edge of the drawing cuts the depiction off exactly at the point where the curtain is pushed aside, blocking our view of the mansion from the side. The mansion stands on a paved ground on which a shadow is cast.

The figure at the center of the *tableau vivant* wears an ornate green and red dress that corresponds in hue to the red of the valance, the gold of the curtains, and the green fabric in the background. The two maidens at the left and right, for their part, wear the blue of the small tent hanging from the rod and the red of the crown that will be placed on the head of Joan of Castile in the moment she passes by. Presumably a dove, symbolizing the Holy Spirit, was trapped under the blue tent, and was suddenly revealed with the help of a mechanism on the rod that pulled up the tentlike cover. The virgin in the red dress on the right raises her eyes to look directly at the dove, while her counterpart in the blue dress on the left looks at the virgin in the center. A double spectacle thus takes place here, both based to equal degrees on the sequence of concealment and subsequent revealment.

Seeing Images

The manuscript introduces the *tableaux vivants* with the following words:

> Images (*effigies*) or schemata of the figures (*scemata figurarum*) (which we call personages [*personagias vocamus*]) followed on stages (*scenis*) or on elevated and closed platforms (*elevatis et clausis esschaufaudis*) on street corners, which were now, according to the occasion, sometimes veiled by the curtains made for this purpose, sometimes veiled, sometimes uncovered (*que pretereuntium cum oportunitate tum requesta cortinis ad hoc aptatis nunc velabantur, nunc patebant*), not to mention the appropriate fiction of the actors and the marvelous and pompous décor best suited to tropology (as will be obvious) to entertain the mind through the application of the arts (especially literature).[51]

The scribe primarily refers to images (*effigies*) and the arrangement of figures in space (*scemata figurarum*), which are then referred to as figures (*personagias*) in parentheses. The *tableau vivant* is, therefore, a theatrical form consisting in revealing and presenting still images. The *tableaux vivants* were not only pictures because they approximated actual paintings and sculptures both formally and programmatically, but also because the aim of the overall apparatus—made up of curtain, raised and framing mansion, and design of animate and inanimate figures in a closed stage space—was to achieve a pictorial effect. That is why their curtains are more akin to picture curtains than theater curtains, which only came into use later and whose origins can be traced back to this context, among others.[52]

In the case of *tableaux vivants* images, their imagery is perceived primarily pictorially, with the scenes performed on stage occasionally drawing on existing paintings. A well-known example is the entry of Philip the Good into Ghent in 1458,

51 Fol. 31v.

52 Kernodle, *From Art to Theatre*, pp. 52–110; Radke-Stegh, *Der Theatervorhang*, pp. 180–197.

for which Jan van Eyck's *Adoration of the Lamb* served as a model. The living image for Philip's entry was performed in three tiers on a fifty by twenty-eight-foot display scaffolding.[53] The stages were covered with blue cloth, creating a monochromatic blue background for the figures. The curtain, on the other hand, was white. Behind the curtain, which was pulled aside only when the ruler arrived, a three-tiered stage imitated the scenes depicted on the inside of the Ghent altarpiece. Here, the authorities of Ghent appropriated the iconographic content of a specific painting and used the famous artwork to indicate the city's position within a wider cultural landscape.[54]

Yet the painting by Petrus Christus, the panel by the Salzburg Master, and the *Portrait of Charles VII* by Jean Fouquet are not theatrical images in the narrow sense of the word [figs. 88, 91, 94]. They do not depict the unveiling and performance of a silent picture. Instead, they transfer individual theatrical elements and, in the process, the theatrical into pictorial form, transforming the imaginative element of the living image as a picture. In doing so, the main element transposed onto the picture plane is the curtain. The stage space behind the curtain, the arrangement of the bodies on the stage, and the surrounding supporting framework, are edited out. As will be discussed below, this has fundamental consequences for the conception of the pictorial ground as background and its relation to the figure.

In our manuscript, most representations appear as cutouts detached from their spatial contexts, showing only parts of the wooden scaffolding. The stage space behind the curtain is visible in its entirety and its confined dimensions are apparent. Within this space, figures occupy designated places and some cast shadows on the floor or the back wall. In doing so, they emphasize how the drawings should be understood as images preserving and documenting *tableaux vivants* and the ways in which they were perceived. When we compare the drawings to the three panels by

53
Kernodle, *From Art to Theatre*, p. 65; Radke-Stegh, *Der Theatervorhang*, pp. 180–181.

54
Jesse D. Hurlbut, "The Mystic Lamb of Ghent: Aldermen's Seal, Altarpiece, and 'Tableau Vivant,'" in *Medieval Coins and Seals: Constructing Identity, Signifying Power*, ed. Susan Solway (Turnhout: Brepols, 2015), pp. 377–396.

Petrus Christus, the Salzburg Master, and Fouquet, we notice that, in those three works, no stage floor is visible, while the figures appear almost as portraits. The proportional difference between the larger Man of Sorrows figure and the smaller acolytes representing angels in Petrus Christus's panel must be understood as theatrical. In *tableaux vivants*, children elevated on pedestals played the role of angels while adult figures could stand in as statuaries and busts.[55]

In the Salzburg Master's panel, the Man of Sorrows appears to be seated in a manner reminiscent of the three seated Virgins in our manuscript [fig. 109]. The scenic appearance of prop-like elements such as the black headband with the crown of thorns lend him a sense of theatricality. Apart from these elements, however, the representation of the space revealed by opening the curtain does not correspond to the stage boxes depicted in the manuscript. On the other hand, the curtain alludes to the curtains used to reveal *tableaux vivants*. Especially the depiction of the fringed pelmet covering the curtain rod and framing the upper edge of the picture is similar to configurations seen in the manuscript. As we have seen, a caparison with a shiny border appears particularly vivid and lively in the panel by Petrus Christus. The pelmet has the same color as the green stage curtain in the manuscript. In turn, the fringe of the caparison can be of a different color, whether gold, as in Petrus Christus, or bright red, as in the Fouquet's *Portrait of Charles VII*. Here, it is noticeable that the draperies are not made of an ostentatiously colored fabric but are plain white, like the curtains of the *tableaux vivants* used for the ceremonial entry of Philip the Good into Ghent in 1458.[56] Moreover, the white curtains in Fouquet's panel are open on both sides, while the privacy curtain of boxes in grandstands or the marquee would be drawn to only one side. In contrast, all curtains depicted in the paintings and drawings discussed here represent

55
Stijn Bussels, "Powerful Performances: Tableaux vivants in Early Modern Joyous Entries in the Netherlands," in Ramos, *Le tableau vivant ou l'image*, pp. 71–95, here pp. 72–73.

56
"Item, up den Poul stont gemaect eene groete hoghe stellagie, met drye stagien upgaende L. voeten lanc, ende XXViij voeten breedt, al verdect met blauwen lakenen, voren ghesloten met witten gordinen, de misterye diere opstont was dusdanich: Chorus beatorum in sacrificium agni pascalis." *Kronyk van Vlaenderen van 580 tot 1467*, Constant-Philippe Serrure and Philip Marie Blommaert, eds., vol. 2 (Gent: D. J. Vanderhaeghen-Hulin, 1840), p. 222.

and refer to the specific form of the bilateral stage curtain used in *tableaux vivants.*

The inscription on the original frame of Jean Fouquet's royal portrait also suggests that the curtains depicted were theatrical curtains used to reveal silent plays. At the top of the black frame, just above the pelmet, whose painted, red fringed hem is immediately adjoining, we can read: "*Le tres victorieus roy de France, Charles septieme, ce le nom*" (The very victorious king of France, Charles the Seventh, this is the name). This inscription corresponds to inscriptions on scaffold frames for the living images explored above.[57] They were helpful aids for recognizing the staged characters and understanding the scenes. However, they had to be written in large letters so that the inscription could be read from a distance. In the manuscript drawings, pelmets therefore serve as grounds for inscriptions, which corresponds to the practice of writing on the wooden scaffolds supporting the *tableaux vivants*. These written keys to the scene depicted could take the form of plaques, scrolls, or ribbons, and served to reiterate in writing what was communicated visually. What is more, the allegorical content of contemporary scenes, for example that of Archduke Philip kneeling before Joan of Castile, not only becomes evident in the supplemental commentary but is also imminently clear in the inscription, in which Joan is honored as the Muse of Victory [fig. 107].

Inscriptions and names were indispensable because they were part of the scenic arrangement, whether they specified the identity of the figures or explained the scenes represented with the help of a short motto or the transcription of verses. The *tableaux vivants,* as silent pictures, interacted with written as well as spoken commentaries. In addition to the inscriptions, narrators explained and described the narratives and contexts of the revealed scenes. Emerging in a scholarly and humanistic cultural climate, the allegorical character of the *tableaux vivants* could usually only be fully understood with the guidance of inscriptions and oral explanations.[58] The inscription on Fouquet's picture frame alone likewise does not convey the allegorical complexity

57
Radke-Stegh, *Der Theatervorhang,* p. 141.

58
Visentin, "La pratique des tableaux vivants," pp, 53–70, here pp. 66–67.

in the sense of a commentary, which would be capable of forging links to other narratives.

Fourteenth-century passion plays and Corpus Christi processions served to demonstrate sensorily and ostentatiously the literal emanation of the mystical body of Christ and the Church.[59] They shared this feature and their focus on individual events to capture the attention of their audiences with *tableaux vivants*.[60] Acting as mirrors producing ideal images while centering on the arts, virtues, and good government,[61] the four most important and elaborate ceremonies serving to reinforce the legitimacy of the constitution and affirmation of the state were the entry into the city, the anointment, the parliamentary assembly, and the burial. The entry differed from the other ceremonies and displays of power in its juxtaposition of the sovereign and the people. The interaction between the queen or king and the city took place in the synchronization of their arrival with the opening of curtains to reveal pictures.[62] Through the act of opening the curtains, *tableaux vivants* were not only presented to the sovereign's gaze, but the presentation endowed the royal viewer with the character of a theatrical performer in a public living image him- or herself.

59
Mario Longin, "Conventions de lecture: L'exemple de la pausa dans le Mystère de sainte Barbe en cinq journées," in *Langues, codes et conventions de l'ancien théâtre: Actes de la troisième rencontre sur l'Ancien théâtre européen*, Jean-Pierre Bordier, ed. (Paris: Honoré Champion, 2002), pp. 83–92. One could also place Steffen Siegel's art-historical observations on the Ostentatio of the Man of Sorrows by Petrus Christus in this theatrical context: "Above all, the tense posture of the erect body as well as the gaze resting on the viewer mark the act of ostentatio vulnerum that becomes visible here as an active action of the Savior showing himself. Here, both the penetrating gaze of the Man of Sorrows and the double pointing gesture of the stopped side wound on the right half of the body as well as the raised and pierced hand divide the viewer as the addressee of this small devotional picture. The acts of pointing and seeing directed at him are parallelized and in this way mutually reinforce each other in their appellatory character." Siegel, "Die Kunst der Ostentatio," pp. 38–61, here p. 45. Translation C. B.

60
Longin, "Coventions de lecture," pp. 83–92.

61
Joel Blanchard and Jean-Claude Mühlethaler, *Ecriture et pouvoir à l'aube des temps modernes* (Paris: Presses Universitaires de France, 2002), pp. 7–32; Lyse Roy, "'Justice tient de noble cueur entier': Les entrées comme miroirs des princes sour le regne de François Ier," in *Des entrées solennelles de l'Ancien Régime et des rituels imaginaires*, Marie-France Wagner, ed. (Montreal: Groupe de recherche sur les entrées solennelles, Montréal, 2008), pp. 27–42.

62
Visentin, "La pratique des tableaux vivants," pp. 53–70, here p. 55; Blanchard and Mühlethaler, *Ecriture*, pp. 7–32; Roy, "Justice tient de noble coeur entier," pp. 27–42.

Stage scaffolds were erected for ceremonial processions outdoors, while rulers could take their place in festival halls and churches during major indoor festivities.[63] In this context it is of interest to consider that Fouquet was active as a stage designer for *tableaux vivants* performances for the entry of Louis XI. According to the commission, he was requested to design the "*chafaux et des misteres ou faintes*," which, however, were not realized owing to the king's rejection.[64]

The entry ceremony or *entrée solennel* for Charles VII, which marked the liberation of France after years of occupation, took place on November 12, 1437, in Paris and included living images depicting the Passion of Christ. Unfortunately, no designs or representations of these *tableaux vivants* have survived. Chroniclers describing the ephemeral spectacle mention Charles appearing on a white horse. After a child dressed as an angel had greeted the ruler and presented him with three golden lilies, chants of "*Vive le roi!*" resounded throughout the crowd.[65] In Fouquet's portrait, the figure of the king is brought to life through the transformation of the theatrical curtains, but also through the allegorical depiction of the acclamation "*Vive le roi!*" Here, the inanimate medium of painting connects with the theatrical installment of the king through the becoming of an image and its permanent solidification as a material picture. For the duration of the procession and ceremonial entry into the city, the *tableaux vivants* are removed from the motions of the living, from time itself, and endowed with permanence in the sense of becoming a picture.[66]

This link between (theatrical) still life and (painterly) presence set in perpetuity is connected to the Man of Sorrows as a resurrected body. Petrus Christus chose the iconography of the Man of Sorrows to bring home the complexity of this relationship. Equally, Fouquet negotiated this very tension in his portrait

63
The chronicler Oliver de la Marche, for example, reports on a magnificent feast that Adolf of Cleve hosted for Philip the Good in 1453 with tableaux vivants in a large hall. Herrmann, *Forschungen zur deutschen Theatergeschichte*, p. 369.

64
Ferré, "L'art des tableaux vivants," pp. 35–52, here p. 43.

65
Bernard Guenée and Françoise Lehoux, *Les entrées royales françaises de 1328 à 1515* (Paris: Éditions du Centre national de la recherche scientifique, 1968), pp. 72–75.

66
Helas, "Lebendes Bild – haptisches Bild," pp. 69–92, here p. 92.

of King Charles. As will be shown, there are parallels to be drawn semantically between the figure of the Man of Sorrows and the king's portrait revealed by the opening of the curtains. First, the narrativizing power of a *parcours* with a multiplicity of pictures is missing in both panels. Not as part of a gallery of pictures but as a single picture, these figures are revealed only through the depiction of painted curtains on picture planes. Through the omission of the room's floor or the stage, a monochrome ground without measurable depth opens up behind the curtain. This realm is either treated as a color surface and can be understood as a reference to the shallow space of the stage and its backdrop, or, as in Petrus Christus's panel, the backdrop appears black, just as it does in the drawing of the *tableau vivant* depicting Queen Penthesilea in front of a black wall [fig. 124].

In Jean Fouquet's painting, the backdrop is a dark green slightly shaded toward the left. The opaque green color takes on the function of a wall that can be located somewhere close behind the figure. The view of the depicted space framed by the curtains is interrupted by the three-quarter portrait of King Charles VII. With precise detailing and "sharply modeled forms," the king's portrait appears almost like a high relief or "a three-dimensional sculpture"[67] set off against a bare wall or monochrome surface of the kind common for backdrops accompanying living pictures. In the panel by the Salzburg Master, the textiles constituting the opaque background of the shallow space are shown quite explicitly. The cloth of honor behind the Man of Sorrows appears like a textile stretched on a board suspended from above. Shadows at the edges indicate only minimal distance, while the textiles in the background and the curtain in the foreground have been given the same green color. Green silk fabric with a similar pomegranate pattern also lines the shallow stage of a *tableaux vivant* in the Berlin manuscript [fig. 109].

While the elevation and the associated distance are necessary to allow the *tableaux vivants* to become images on the stage, in painting, conversely, the main focus is on the effect of haptic

67
Claude Schaefer, *Fouquet: An der Schwelle zur Renaissance* (Dresden: Verlag der Kunst, 1994), p. 153.

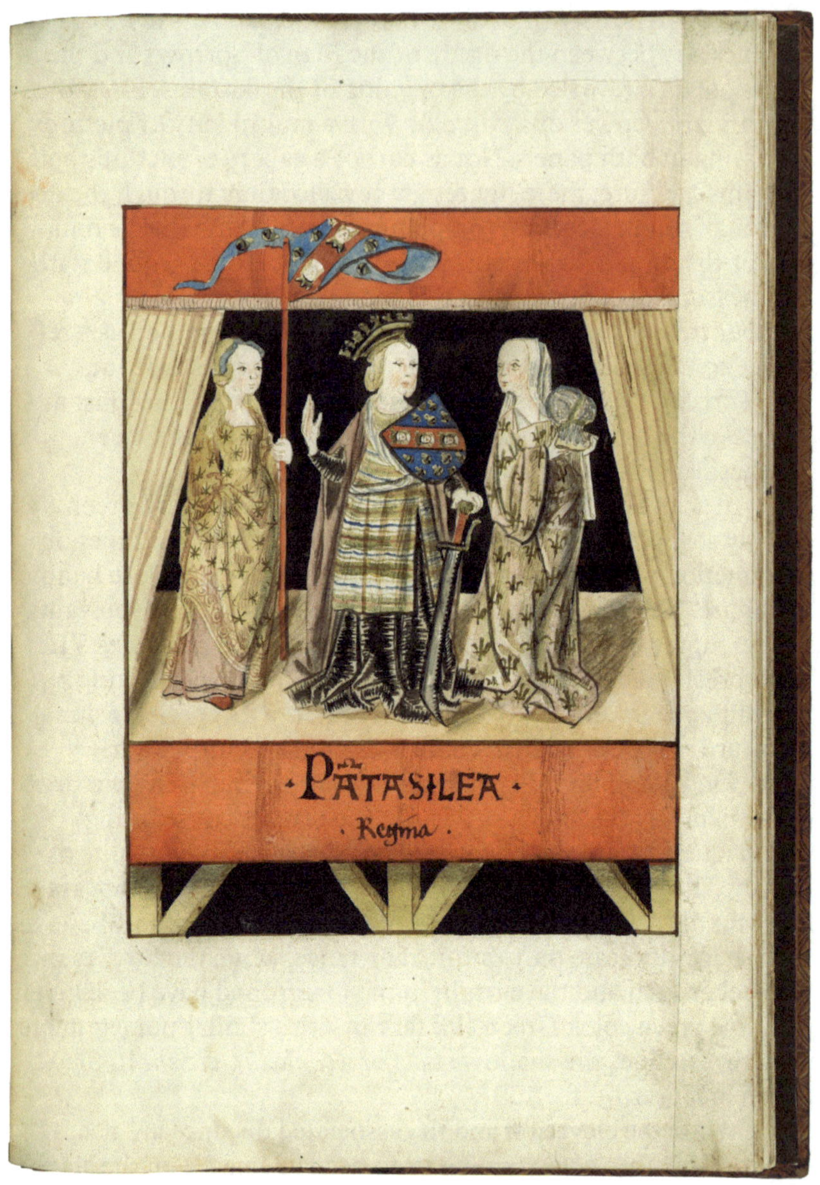

Tableau Vivant of Queen Penthesilea
(entry of Joan of Castile into Brussels on December 9, 1496), ca. 1496–1506, Brussels.
Berlin, Staatliche Museen, Kupferstichkabinett, 78.D.5, fol. 51r.

Fig. 124

proximity with simultaneous visual and spatial distance through the painted stage curtains. This difference between paintings and the depiction of theater images suggests that, in the painted panels by Petrus Christus, the Salzburg Master, and Jean Fouquet, only the depiction of the curtain was included in the painting as a theatrical means of creating a presence and presenting images. In painted form, the stage curtain represents the unveiling of a picture within a picture. The creation of images in the theater and the theatricalization of images is a connection that would also be realized in different pictorial concepts in the following centuries. Painted curtains continued to serve to theatricalize the image, which refers to a way of dealing with the image and aims at seeing *in* and *of* images.

Mediating Twofoldness

The painted stage curtain takes on a spatial, and indeed a separating function serving primarily to distinguish the space in front of the picture from the ground behind the curtain. In the paintings under discussion here, it sets the king and the Man of Sorrows, respectively, at a distance. At the same time, especially in comparison to the manuscript drawings, these curtains are set apart from the vicinal ground of the colored drapery or wall, which brings them closer to the viewer. While the portrayed King Charles VII seems to be on the same plane as the open curtains, it is unclear whether he would disappear behind the curtains if they were closed or remain visible in front of them. Petrus Christus's Man of Sorrows, on the other hand, is clearly situated in front of the black ground. The altar boys/archangels pushing the curtain aside and placing themselves spatially behind Christ are decisive here. If we consider the angels to be represented by children, the distance between them and the Man of Sorrows becomes smaller yet.

The small dimensions of both panels depicting living images of the Man of Sorrows indicate that they were most likely commissioned as private devotional paintings. They refer to the theatrical veiling practice of *tableaux vivants* in close proximity to the viewer as they are not proportioned to life size. In its dimensions, Petrus Christus's panel (11.2 by 8.5 centimeters) comes close to the format of a modern day postcard, suggesting "that the earliest viewers were to hold this picture in their own hands and could therefore bring it extremely close to their bodies and especially their eyes."[68] The panel painting by the Salzburg Master, measuring 41.5 by 33 centimeters, is a bit larger and was most likely intended for close viewing during devotional practice. The format and ratio of the figures do not correspond in scale to real *tableaux vivants*, but instead to the perception of living images from a distance. Indeed, the small-scale projections of the figures appear even more immediate while the curtains emphasize and frame their immediate presence. The possibility of making direct eye contact with the depicted figure is decisive and Petrus Christus offers it not only through the gaze of the Man of Sorrows but also through those of the altar boys with their inviting quality.

In contrast to these small panel paintings, which require a close-up view, we can assume that the life size portrait of king Charles VII would have been seen from a distance and hung in an elevated position, "close and yet unreachably distant, separated in its majesty from all the living."[69] In the eighteenth century, Fouquet's portrait most likely hung above the tomb of his great-uncle, the Duke of Berry, in the Sainte-Chapelle at Bourges.[70] Its original location has yet to be determined. Accordingly, it is no longer possible to reconstruct whether a real curtain covered the painting.[71] Moreover, we do not know who commissioned the portrait.[72] As already discussed in connection with the stage curtains of the *tableaux vivants*, the maintenance of spatial

68
Siegel, "Die Kunst der Ostenatio," pp. 38–61, here p. 43.

69
Wescher, *Beschreibendes Verzeichnis der Miniaturen*, pp. 55–56.

70
The tomb was commissioned by Charles VII. Cf. Reynaud, "Nicole: La radiographie du Portrait de Charles VII par *Fouquet*," in *Revue du Louvre* 33 (1983), pp. 97–99; Schaefer, Fouquet, pp. 153–159. Cornelia Logemann, "Des Königs neue Räume: Genealogie und Zeremoniell in den 'Grandes Chroniques de France' des 14. Jahrhunderts," in *Ausmessen – Darstellen – Inszenieren: Raumkonzepte und die Wiedergabe von Räumen in Mittelalter und früher Neuzeit*, Ursula Kundert, Barbara Schmid, and Regula Schmidt, eds. (Zurich: Chronos, 2007), pp. 41–72; in particular Inglis, *Fouquet and the Invention of France*, pp. 105–140.

71
Wolfgang Kemp, *Rembrandt: Die Heilige Familie mit dem Vorhang* (Frankfurt am Main: Fischer, 1992), p. 56.

72
With the *Portrait of Charles VII,* Fouquet would have risen to the position of court painter, provided that it was a commissioned work by his own hand and not executed in his circle. The fact that such a portrait would most likely have had to be executed by the court painter Jacob de Litemont would seem to be an argument against the speculation of a

and aesthetic distance was vital to the pictorial character of the image. In painted form, such images possess an appearance that evokes even more presence through their proximity. Taking into account that what is revealed behind the curtains was understood as a picture, the relationship between distance and proximity negotiates the question of how paintings encounter and engage with space. It is the painting that stands out as a flat object in front of a wall to allow figures to emerge. This comprehension of a painting itself as a ground and figures therefore also provides an answer to the question "What is an image?"[73]

In the painted panels of Petrus Christus, the Salzburg Master, and Jean Fouquet, the external theatrical curtain of the *tableau vivant* becomes part of the picture plane, incorporating simultaneous distance and proximity into the picture and making auratic that which is revealed. With the introduction of the theatrical curtain, the depiction of the Man of Sorrows is no longer a sacred picture. In stark contrast to altar veils, what we have encountered here is a profane pictorial element deriving from pageants and plays and finding its continuation in ceremonial and courtly theater. The *tableaux vivants* establish a way of perceiving pictures in public spaces that allows important life events to emerge as and transform into images through the opening of a curtain. Since the entire city became theatrical space during the procession, the curtain demarcated and revealed a way of being that was different from that of street. The curtain thus served a deictic function, its opening pointing to a second-order world of play visible within the play.[74]

personal commission by the king. Over the course of his career, Fouquet's work evolved substantially, especially as regards the design of the miniatures. This transformation took place under the influence of the court and aristocratic circles, for whom Fouquet worked ever more exclusively. On the other hand, Litemont himself commissioned Fouquet to color the death mask he had made, the *effigie* of Charles VII after the king's death in 1461. Schaefer, *Fouquet*, p. 346.

73
Gottfried Boehm, "Zur Hermeneutik des Bildes," in *Seminar, Die Hermeneutik und die Wissenschaften*, Boehm and Hans-Georg Gadamer, eds. (Frankfurt am Main: Suhrkamp, 1978), pp. 444–471; ed. Volker Bohn, *Bildlichkeit* (Frankfurt am Main: Suhrkamp, 1990); ed. Gottfried Boehm, *Was ist ein Bild?* (Munich: Fink, 1994); Sebastian Egenhofer, Inge Hinterwaldner, and Christian Spies, eds., *Was ist ein Bild? Antworten in Bildern: Gottfried Boehm zum 70. Geburtstag* (Munich: Fink, 2012).

74
Radke-Stegh, *Der Theatervorhang*, 1978, 184–185.

The stage curtains of the *tableaux vivants* are conceived of as temporal events linked to the performative act of revelation. In the manuscript on the celebratory entry of Joan of Castile, these moments of opening and closing according to circumstances and prescribed requirements is explicitly described: "*elevatis et clausis… quea pretereuntium cum oportunitate tum requesta cortinis*" (fol. 32v). In the midst of the festive celebration, the opening of the curtains disrupts the procession to carve out a new temporal and visual realm. The three panels by Petrus Christus, the Salzburg Master, and Jean Fouquet do precisely the same in a different medium. When this theatrical picture play, developed in public urban spaces, is translated into painting through the transfer of the *tableau-vivant* stage curtain into another artistic medium, it is the calm moment of "becoming-picture" that sets the image apart from the hustle and bustle of everyday life. The curtains, which frame the picture and place the figures in concrete relation to the ground behind them, make them appear relief-like and projects them into the foreground, creating a specific effect of presence. In doing so, they still bear a relation to the display of *tableaux vivants* in public spaces, despite their different size. Set against a backdrop-like ground, the motionless but animate figures convey the very impression of presence the *tableaux vivants* are meant to produce. Like the living bodies in *tableaux vivants*, as images the panel paintings create not only a tension between play and representation but also between figure and ground.

In keeping with this concept, the *Journal d'un bourgeois de Paris* from 1405 to 1449 describes how the living images stand out as if positioned against a wall: "*comme si ce fussent images élevées contre un mur*."[75] This perception of the statuesque performers in front of a wall as pictures bears upon the entire image, which is mounted on the wall as a flat object revealed through the removal of a curtain. Behind the curtain, the pictorial surface becomes a ground while the figure emerges into real space. In this configuration, the painted stage curtain becomes the intermediary responsible for producing the theatrical relationship between

75
Julien P. de Gaulle and Charles Nodier, *Nouvelle histoire de Paris et des environs* 3 (Paris: Hachette Livre, 2017; orig. pub. 1839), p. 78.

figure and ground described here. The curtain defines the ground, presenting itself as a two-dimensional picture plane parallel to the panel it is painted on. In the equation of picture frame to stage frame, it is the curtain that coincides with picture plane, mediating between figure and ground as an interplay between the image and its theatrical form of presentation.

Part 1
Staging Figures

Miracles of Mediation:
Staging the Sacred in the Annunciation by Pedro da Córdoba

Beate Fricke

131

An unusually staged annunciation scene is infused by artistic reflections about the relation between liturgical vessels and narrated scene, between sculpture and painting, between imagination and experience. The painting, made for the *mezquita* in Córdoba, Spain, a former mosque, is featuring the artist Pedro da Córdoba himself in the midst of saints accompanying the scene and might have been used for Corpus Christi processions. This unique mise-en-scène is discussed with regard to late medieval discourses on divine acts of creation and their relationship to the work of human *artifex*. Medieval thinkers' thoughts go so far as to compare visual and mental reflection to the power of insemination and creation.

As beholders, our gaze is ensnared by a sacred spectacle unfolding on a tidy, tilted stage and directed by a complex web of gazes among the eleven protagonists internal to the panel painting itself [fig. 133]. Three figures occupy the tiled stage in the middle ground, and eight linger in the "orchestra pit," or the foreground. On this stage set of a bedchamber, we encounter a mixture of profane and sacred objects. Mary is the only figure whose gaze is directed outward, beyond the surface of her own panel painting. She rests in a chamber and is sitting in front of her bed next to a bench with a built-in bookcase. A rich still life of dishes filled with fruit, wine, and water is spread out in front of her feet. Two wooden doors open behind her to another room, revealing a monstrance on a table piled high with manuscripts. To her right kneels the Archangel Gabriel, holding a lavishly ornate staff in his left hand. He points with his right index finger toward Mary. She has paused to turn her upper body toward the angel, away from the open book on her reading bench. What we can see, but she cannot, is a bundle of golden rays barely penetrating her nimbus.

The rays are sent by God, who hovers outside a window, nestled in heavenly clouds and holding an orb [fig. 134]. The window is located behind Mary's back, along the left side of the chamber. The dove, i.e., the Holy Ghost, glides along the rays. Below the dove's belly glares a golden cross attached to Gabriel's diadem. Pointing with its top toward Godfather, a "golden triangle" of Godfather, the hallowed Holy Ghost, and the Crucified yet invisible son renders further emphasis to the Trinity as origin of the salvation for mankind. Gabriel has yet to reach the knotted

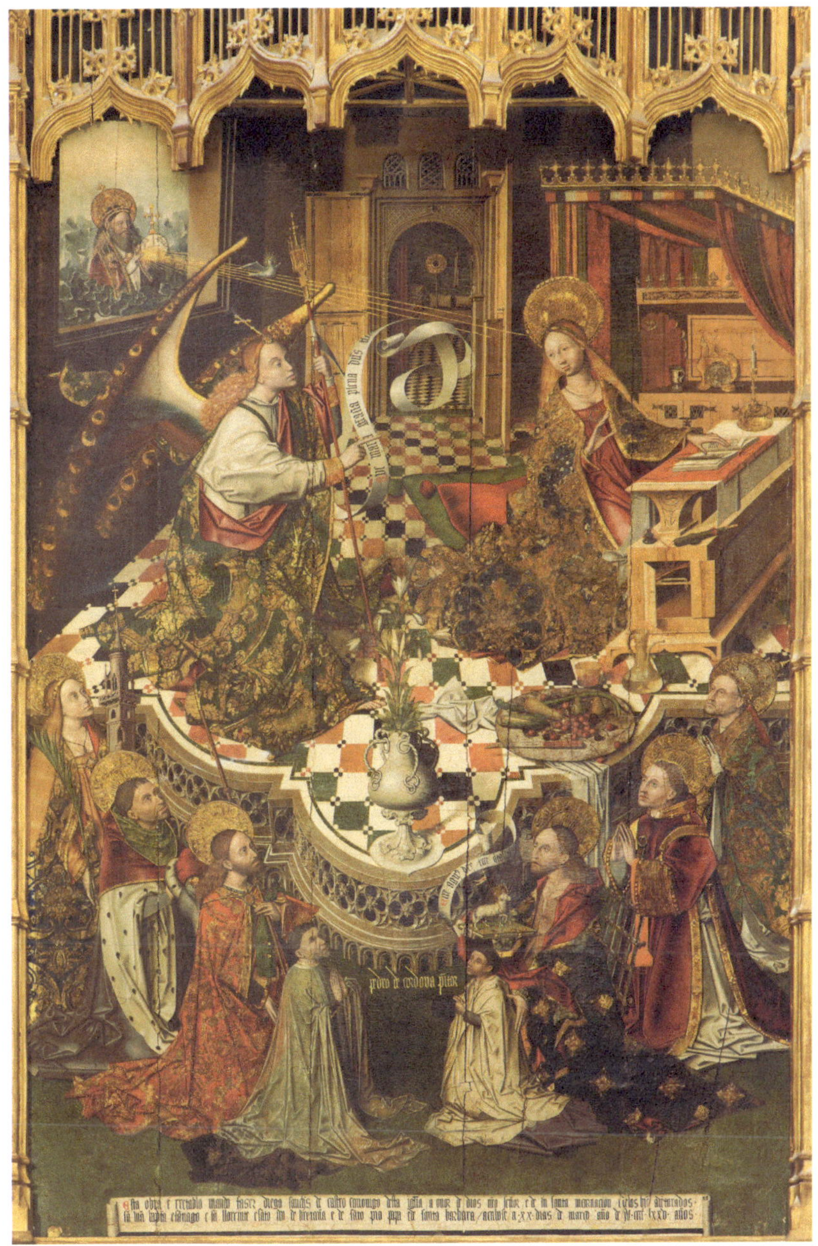

Pedro de Córdoba, *The Annunciation/Incarnation*, 1475, oil on panel, 271 × 156 cm. Mezquita, Córdoba.

Fig. 133

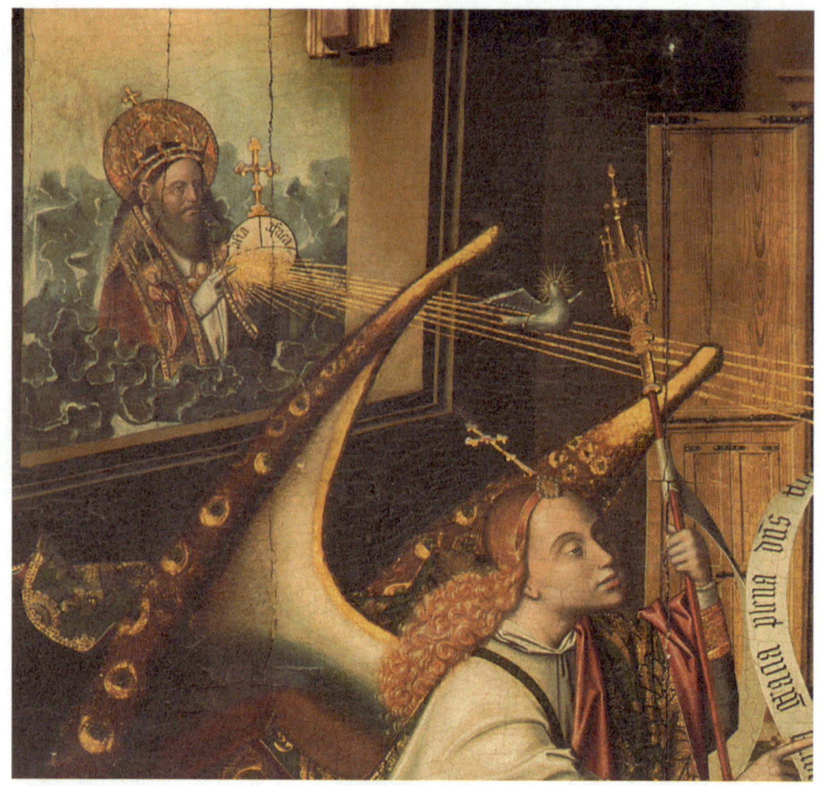

Detail of Fig. 133.

Fig. 134

white scroll in the middle of the room verbally announcing the Incarnation [fig. 136]. Tilting our head to the left, we can easily read *Ave Maria gratia plenus*. While we are able to decipher the abbreviation for *Dominus*, we have to supply the *tecum*. As in many contemporary panels of the annunciation, the beholder is prompted to complete the verse from memory "*Benedicta tu in mulieribus, et benedictus fructus ventris tui, Iesus*." After all, many will know the following words of the prayer by heart.

Beyond both the knotted, though blank section of the scroll and the golden rays, the open doors guide our gaze into another room. The golden glow of a monstrance shimmers in the darkness of this "tabernacle." In these ostensories, sacred hosts were kept, i.e., the bread that turned into the body of Christ during the act of the priest blessing. Solar-shaped monstrances are known from depictions in illuminated manuscripts and from inventories since the beginning of the fifteenth century.[1] However, the oldest surviving exemplars and the earliest records of their commission date to the time of this panel, to 1475 [fig. 137]. This visual focal point draws our attention, evidencing an important aspect of the artwork's theological program.

Pedro de Córdoba's panel is not only a depiction of an annunciation scene. The composition places particular emphasis upon two aspects of Christian narrative. Pictured here is the annunciation highlighting the act of the Incarnation. Most frequently, the annunciation is depicted with the dove representing the Holy Spirit overcoming Mary, as for example in the left wing of Rogier van der Weyden's Columba Altar [fig. 138]. In Córdoba, it is not the baby on the beam, which occasionally accompanies

1
Frédéric Tixier, *La monstrance eucharistique: Genèse, typologie et fonctions d'un objet d'orfèvrerie XIIIe–XVIe siècle* (Rennes: Presses Universitaires de Rennes 2014), pp. 135–140. An early example is shown in the Exaltation of the Croix in the Très riches Heures du duc de Berry, ms. 65, fol. 193, Condé, Chantilly, and in the Ms III B 10, Narodni Museum, Prague, ca. 1420, showing people venerating a solar monstrance. An early mention in an inventory of a treasure can be found in the inventory dating to May 10, 1405, for the Sainte-Chapelle de Bourges: "grand vaissel ront de cristal, de deux pieces pareilles faites en manière d'un soleil, garnie d'or." Tixier, *La monstrance eucharistique*, p. 137, note 314. An early commission is preserved for the fraternity of pilgrims to Santiago in Paris, ordering a "ung joyau d'argent dore a porter corpus domini le jour de la feste du saint sacrament" from the goldsmiths Jehan Brisset et Jehan Enguerran. This ostensory should include "deux angels tenant ung soleil couvert de crestaulz, ou ce assiet le corpus domini," see Tixier, *La monstrance eucharistique*, p. 137, note 317.

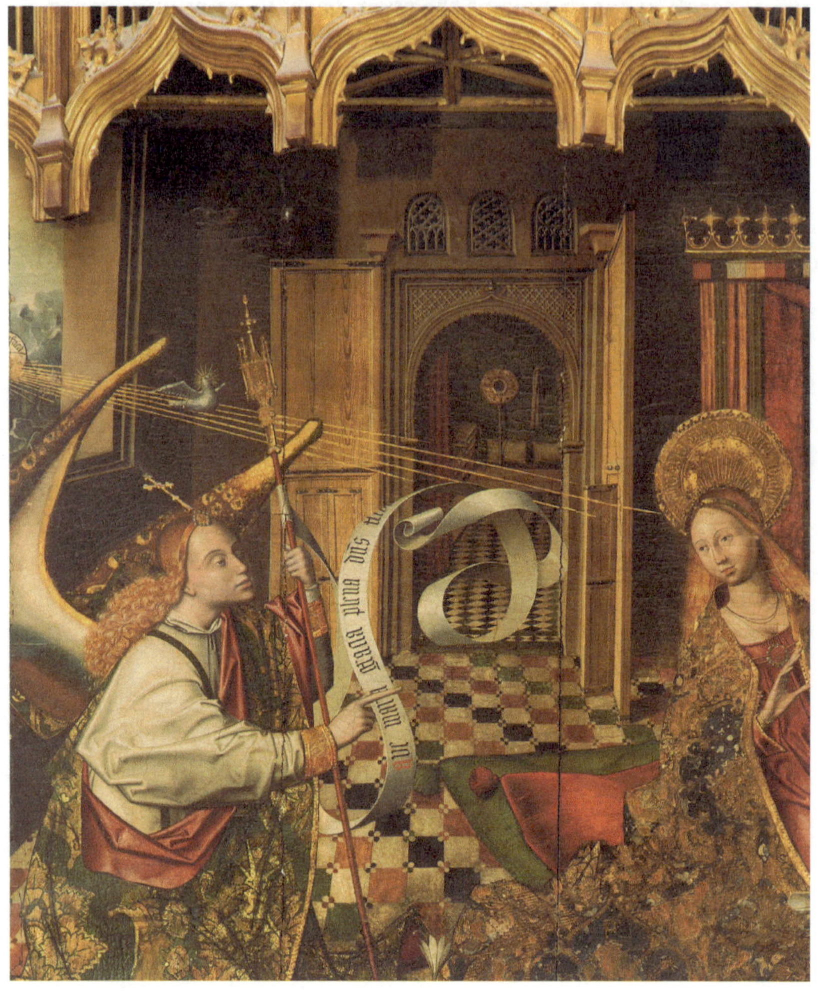

Detail of Fig. 133.

Fig. 136

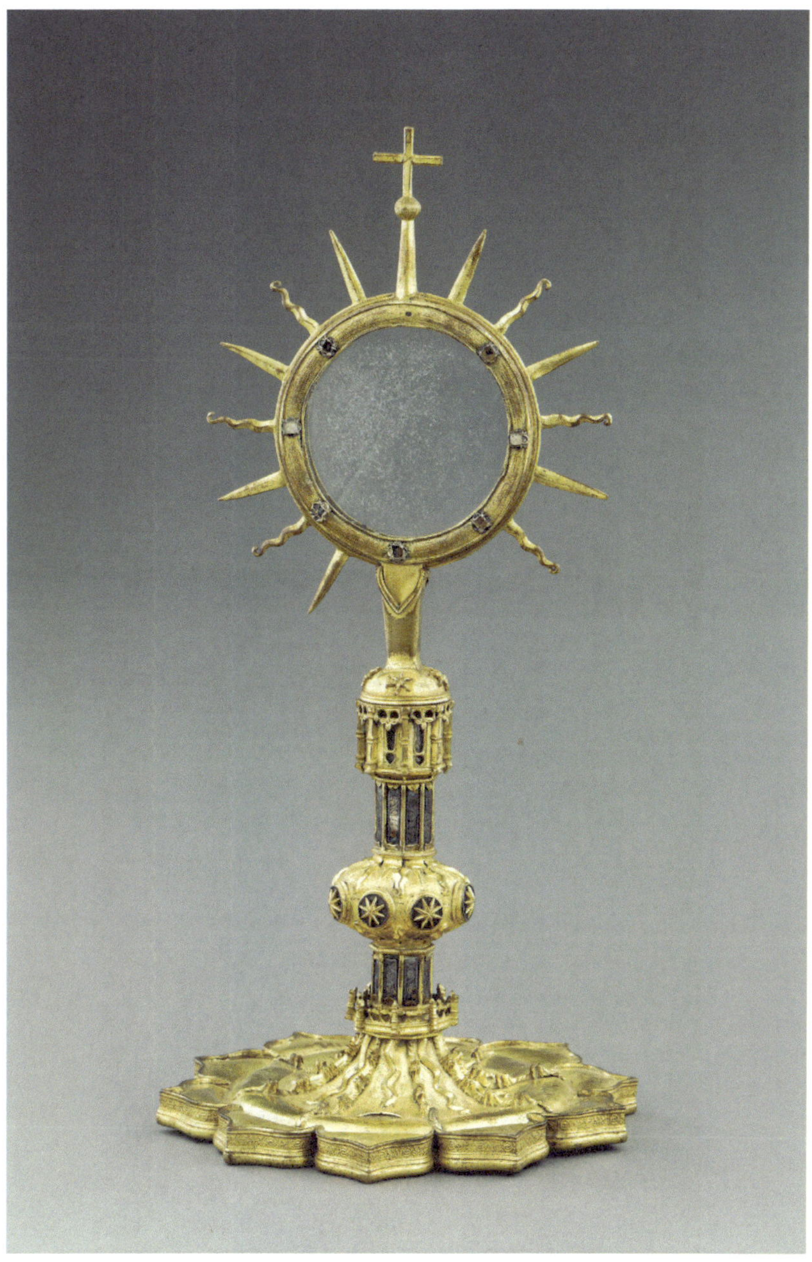

Solar monstrance, second half of fifteenth century, gilded copper, height: 45 cm.
Musée de Cluny, inv. nr. MC 922, Paris.

Fig. 137

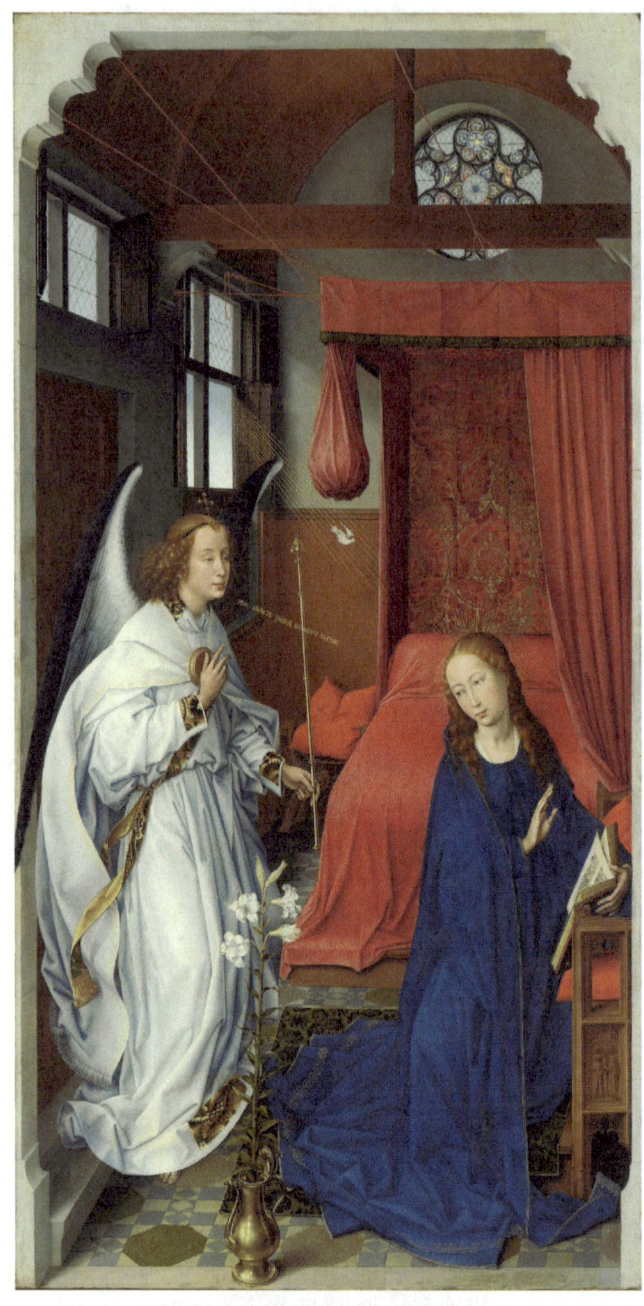

Rogier van der Weyden, *Columba Altarpiece*, left wing, 1399/1400, oil on oak, 139.4 × 72.9 cm. Bayerische Staatsgemäldesammlungen, Alte Pinakothek, inv. nr. WAF 1190, Munich.

Fig. 138

or is sometimes depicted instead of the dove, as for example in the case of contemporary painting by the Master of the Marienleben [fig. 140]. Rather, in the painting at Córdoba, there are other explicit references to the Incarnation and the salvation, with the host in the solar monstrance in the back, and wine and water in the front [fig. 133]. The pictorial references to the entry of Christ's blood and soul into the vessel of Mary's virginal body is a unique addition to the more standard iconography for the annunciation scene. The regular pattern of the green, white, ocher, black, and cinnabar tiles on the floor of Mary's study continues into this back room, unifying the space traversed by the devotee from annunciation to monstrance. In the lower half of the painting, these same floor tiles conform to shape a scalloped, trefoil platform with a white vase at its pinnacle.

Clearly separated from the annunciation, eight figures are gathered in a half circle at the edge of the stage [fig. 141]. The four on the left (back to front) are the three saints Barbara, St. Yves, and Jacob, while a smaller kneeling person at the front of the stage is the altar's donor, canon Diego Sánchez de Castro. His name, also in the inscription below, is first mentioned in a bull by Pope Pius II in 1463.[2] The sequence of the saints continues on the right behind a small man in a white cloak with John the Baptist, followed by S. Laurence and Pope Pius I.

The identity of the man in white has been subject to speculation. He is depicted even smaller than Diego Sánchez de Castro. Maria Angeles Raya Raya suggests that he represents the former donor of the chapel, the canon Juan Muñoz, who commissioned the altar.[3] Muñoz established the first altar on September 9, 1390, to which a fresco belongs [fig. 142]. It shows the Baptism and was

2
The bull by Pope Pius II mentions an altar in the church cathedral of Córdoba dedicated to the virgin, the apostle Jacob, the martyr Laurence, St. Pius, and the confessor St. Yves. In 1475, when the panel for the altar was completed, further donations occurred, see Maria Angeles Raya Raya, *Catálogo de las pinturas de la Catedral de Córdoba* (Córdoba: Publicaciones del Monte de Piedad y Caja de Ahorros de Córdoba, 1988), p. 24. He is also mentioned in the *Actas Capitulares* (1455–1476), tomo 2, fol. 190v and 191r.

3
Raya Raya, *Catálogo de las pinturas de la Catedral de Córdoba*, p. 24: "Juan Muñoz, canónigo de la Catedral de Toledo y oriundo de Córdoba, ya que en su testamento, dado el 9 de septiembre de 1390, creaba una capellanía en este lugar, dado por el cabildo para su enterramiento."

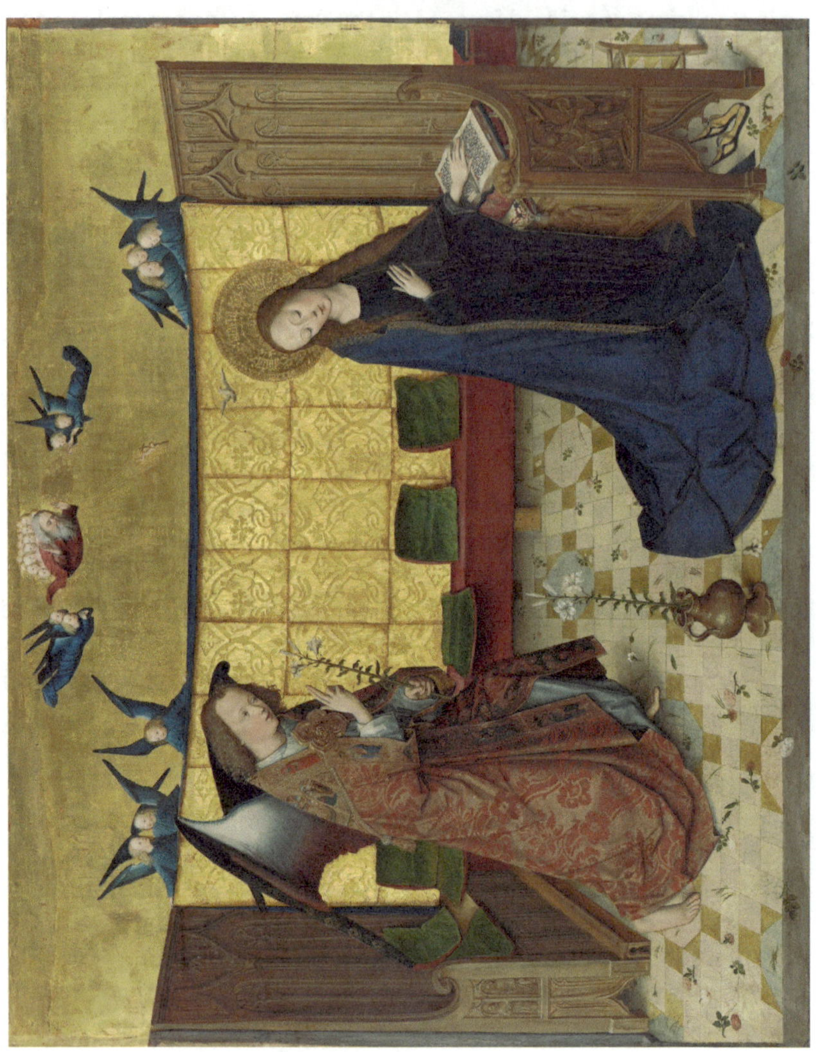

Master of the Life of the Virgin, *The Annunciation*, ca. 1470,
mixed materials on oak, 85 × 105.1 cm.
Bayerische Staatsgemäldesammlungen, Alte Pinakothek, inv. nr. WAF 622, Munich.

Fig. 140

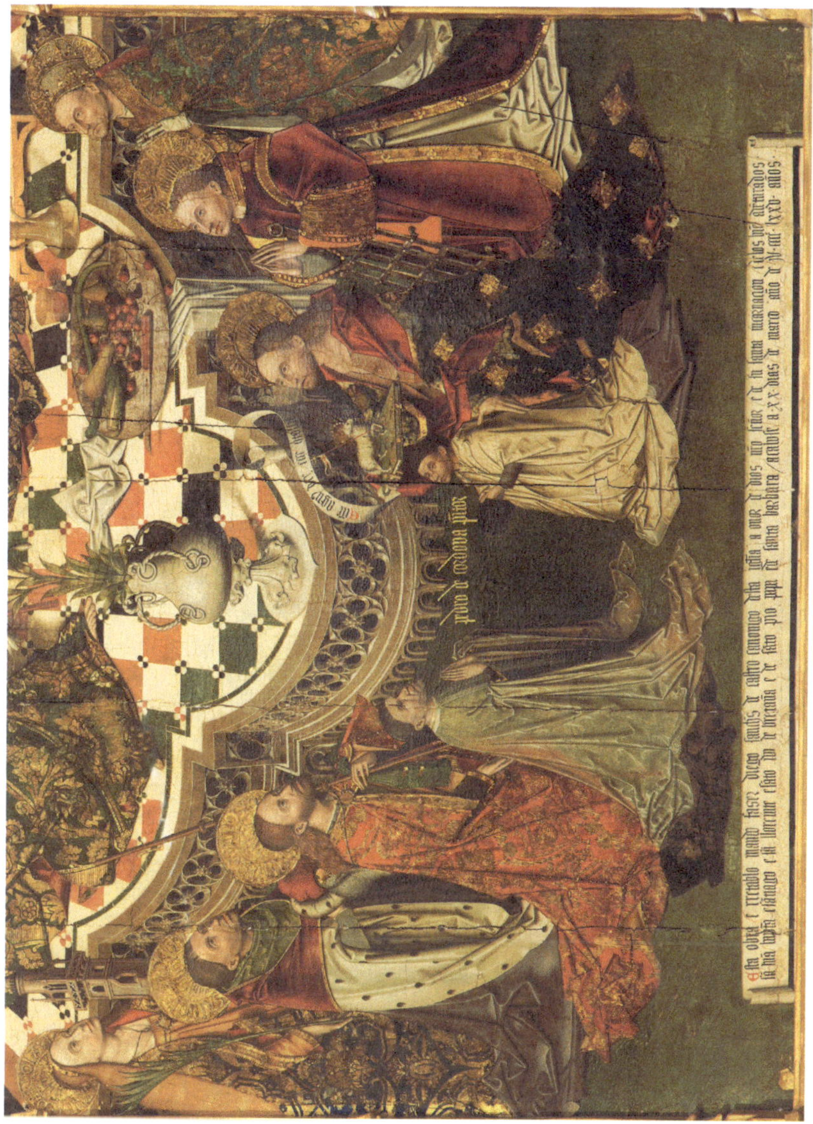

Detail of Fig. 121.

Fig. 141

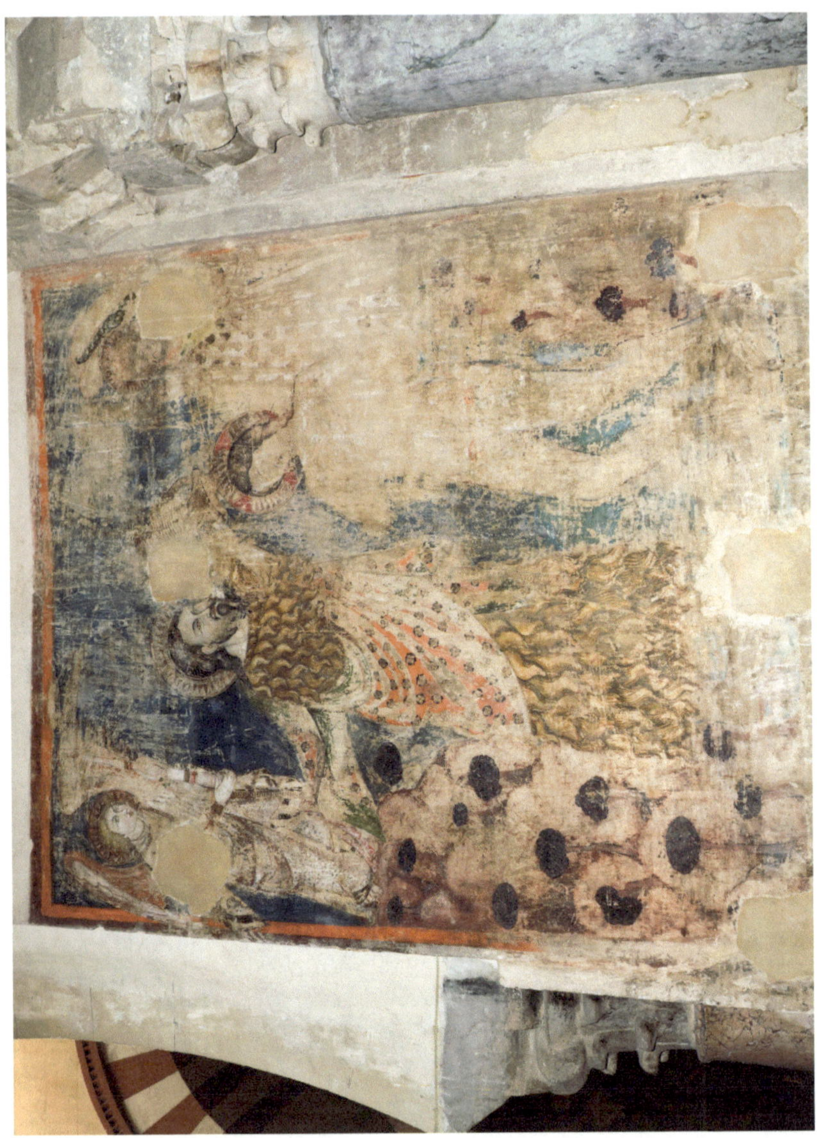

Artist unknown, *The Baptisim of Christ*, ca. 1390, fresco of the former altar, later covered by the painting by Pedro of Córdoba, 2.20 × 1.88 cm. Mezquita, Córdoba. [fig. 133].

Fig. 142

discovered in 1989 during the restoration works, when the painted panel was moved to its current location. However, the location of an inscription reading "*Pedro de Córdoba pintor*" right next to the kneeling figure in white combined with his reduced scale, suggests that this could be a unique representation of the panel's artist himself.

The Medieval Artist and Medieval Ideas about Creation

It is interesting that the inscription referring to the painter is prominently placed, lending it significance in pictorial space: "Pedro of Córdoba painter" is to be read as if these golden letters spell out words from the white clothed figure's mouth. These are the only words "spoken" in the foreground—together with St. John's scroll coiling upward to the edge of the stage. Of all the attentive saints, only John the Baptist speaks, contributing to the "oral" layer of dialogues embedded in the scene. However, the oral elements in this panel are clearly distinct from each other, i.e., the scroll is a visual speech indicator and notes known prayer and eternal or timeless biblical speech, whereas the donor speaking the painter's name in golden letters marks a human, temporally bound speech.

St. John's words serve to connect the realms of the martyrs, saints, and biblical figures in the foreground with the beholder in front of it. John is, of course, the link between Old and New Testament and thus his painted scroll reads "*ecce agnus dei, ecce qui tollis,*" with the ending "*peccata mundi*" again left to the beholder's memory. Whereas John's prayer aspires to ascend to the holy stage, the text referring to the painter is positioned in the empty realm at the lower center of the panel most available to the beholder's eyes. This unusual prominence for an inscription naming a painter is striking.[4]

Inscriptions in paintings containing the name of the artist participate in a lengthy tradition spanning the entire Middle Ages, as Peter Cornelius Claussen and Albrecht Dietl, among others, have analyzed. However, inscriptions usually appear on the frame,

4
"Esta obra e retablo mando faser diego sanch[e]s de castro canonigo desta igl[es]ia ... acabose a XX dias de março año de MCCCCLXXV años."

as in the famous works by Jan van Eyck, in the Tiefenbronner Altar, and elsewhere.[5] Placing the inscription in golden letters in the middle of the green ground between the only two figures who are not saints is, in contrast, highly unusual and points to the pride and prominence of the artist and his ideas about artistic inspiration and creativity manifest in the panel itself.

The most widely known authority on the relationship between divine acts of creation and the work of a human *artifex* was Thomas Aquinas, whose *Summa* is still preserved in a manuscript at the archive of the church, still located inside the building.[6] "God is cause of things through His intellect and will, just as a maker of artificial things [acts through his intellect and will]. The *artifex*, however, crafts (*operatur*) through the word conceived with his intellect, and through the love and will to refer to something."[7]

My translation of *operatur* is as wrong as it is simplifying. It is one of the verbs that has experienced a significant change of meaning from the classical period to post-classical Latin texts. Its original meaning (as an active verb) was "being busy," "working," "being occupied" with something, for example with performing a religious ritual or a sacrifice, to honor or serve the gods. The effect of that action is embedded in the very same word now used as an intransitive verb in post-classical periods. In the works of scholastic theologians, the word means now "to operate," "to have an effect," "to produce" by working, or by a cause. In other words, the act of the *artifex*, either human or divine, became one with the idea for what one wants to create. With love he carries it into effect, and labors to craft and to render it a visible shape. The nature or medium of the *opus*, the work, remains undetermined.

5
Beate Fricke, "Artifex and Opifex—The Medieval Artist," in *A Companion to Medieval Art: Romanesque and Gothic in Northern Europe*, Conrad Rudolph, ed. (Hoboken, NJ: Wiley-Blackwell, 2006), pp. 45–70; *Signaturen – Auktoriale Präsenz zwischen Bild und Schrift, 1400–1700*, Alessandro Della Latta and Karin Gludovatz, eds. (Berlin: De Gruyter, 2023), and Karin Gludovatz, *Fährten legen – Spuren lesen: Die Künstlersignatur als poetische Referenz* (Paderborn/Munich: Fink 2011).

6
Timothy Lee Smith, *Thomas Aquinas' Trinitarian Theology: A Study in Theological Method* (Washington, DC: Catholic University of America Press), p. 31.

7
Thomas Aquinas, *Summa Theologica I*, q 45, a. 6: "Deus est causa rerum per suum intellectum et voluntatem, sicut artifex rerum artificiatarum. Artifex autem per verbum in intellectu conceptum, et per amorem suae voluntatis ad aliquid relatum, operatur."

A brief look into thoughts by Thomas Aquinas can clarify these connections. *Operor* can be used for both, for creating texts *and* creating images. Reading Thomas Aquinas's thoughts alongside Pedro of Córdoba's annunciation suggests that we view the words of Gabriel on the knotted scroll in the panel's center as having something to do with the mediating of divine origins, and the conception of an idea or an act of creation. Both scrolls in the painting are in fact mediating elements—one between the announcement and the inception of our knowledge of what God is doing, and the other, St. John's scroll, between the human registers of the "orchestra pit" and the holy stage, or between the artistic act of creativity and the creation of a human being. Both scrolls are dependent on the active viewer completing the words; they are the two lynch pins holding the composition in relationship with itself as a painting created by a painter and with God. This solidifies the entanglement of visual composition and verbal completion, of divine origins and human fruits. Thomas Aquinas further explains that the origin of creativity is perfection and that mankind—because of its divine-like nature—can also create like God.[8] Medieval thinkers such as Giles of Rome inspired by the renaissance of Aristotelian thought drew intrinsic ties between perception and conception, and between both artistic and divine inspiration and creation. They go so far as to compare visual and mental reflection to the power of insemination and creation. Giles specifically compares sperm carving an embryo out of maternal blood with the work of a sculptor.[9]

8
He then goes on to discuss the role of the Holy Spirit and of wisdom. Aquinas, *Summa Theologica, I*, q 45, a. 5: "what is perfect can make its own likeness. But immaterial creatures are more perfect than material creatures, which nevertheless can make their own likeness, for fire generates fire, and man begets man. Therefore an immaterial substance can make a substance like to itself. But immaterial substance can be made only by creation, since it has no matter from which to be made. Therefore a creature can create."

9
Aegidius Romanus, *De formatione humani corporis in utero*, R. Martorelli Vico, ed. (Florence: Sismel-Edizioni del Galluzzo, 2008), pp. 135–137: "Sanguis enim convertitur in membra virtute membrorum cum animal nutritur et sanuis convertitur in membra virtute spermatis cum animal generatur.... Actio enim huiusmodi virtutis, sive huius spiritus, assimilatur artificiato et quasi potest dici actio artis et actio intellectus.... Actio tamen artis et actio intellectus ex una et eadem materia facit quecumque diversa, ut idem artifex ex eodem ligno faciet ydolum equi et ydolum hominis et multa alia varia et diversa." See also Beate Fricke, "A Liquid History: Blood and Animation in Late Medieval Art," *RES* 63/64 (2013): 53–69, here 53 note 2.

As I will elaborate later, in this panel the divine procreative forces originating in sacred blood of Christ and the creation of golden sacred vessels used in the Christian liturgy are also connected.

The Metaphor of the *Vis Solaris*

The beholder's negotiation between the visual assertion of divine origins and human craftmanship used in its celebration can help us unfold the different layers of the represented space in this fifteenth-century painting. In the painting by Pedro da Córdoba, it seems no coincidence, that several golden rays are sent into the depicted room accompanying the dove of the Holy Spirit, but only *three* of those rays are reaching toward Mary, underscoring the Trinitarian idea. Each of these three rays seems connected to a particular aspect—the lower to the word—as seemingly to transgress behind the empty part of the scroll. The upper ray shields off the chamber with the host, the solar monstrance, and piled manuscripts and objects used for the liturgy. Only the middle one is reaching Mary and the virginal vessel for the miracle of the Incarnation.

In this painting, the pictorial space is constituted through the shifting relationships between caused miracle (Incarnation), interlocutors (saints), and mediated miracle (communion), as well as between painted objects (liturgical objects) and invisible things (annunciation, conception, transubstantiation). The key mediator among these elements, weaving them into a discursive whole, is the Holy Spirit—if we focus on the causes—or the *artifex*—if we focus on the effect's mise-en-scène. The Holy Spirit's *and* the *artifex'* efforts and efficacy are perceived through the active imagination of the beholder. Furthermore, the visual references to liturgical vessels, moved and processed during the mass, enhance this effect of blurring between cause and effect, i.e., between object vision and enactment.

For our context, the Spanish author Ramon Sibiuda, or Raimundus Sabundus, is particularly relevant when aiming to reconstruct the intellectual context of the panel. He was widely read in the region and was the authority for identifying potential theological thoughts under consideration at the time of the creation of the panel at Córdoba. His *Liber Creaturarum*, a tract considering the book of nature and the bible as divine revelations, the first general and immediate, the second specific and mediate. The *Liber Creaturarum* was written in 1434 until shortly before his death in 1436 and was printed in its most popular version from 1485 and later translated into French by Michel Montaigne.

A key passage in this work deals with the fact that God's ability to create out of nothing continues after the creation of the cosmos, just like the sun continues to create rays of sun in the air ("*et ideo ipsum continue creat, sicut sol suos radios continue creat in aere*"). Sibiuda notes that even when there are no rays of sun in the night air, God does not desist creating them; Sibiuda argues that the world would have ceased, if God would not have continued to create and to preserve ("*ita mundus esse desineret, si non a Deo continue crearetur et conservatur*"). Cusanus, who owned a manuscript with Sibiuda's *Liber Creaturarum*, goes a step further in his use of the metaphor. For him, the divine Spirit shines like the sun's rays (*vis solaris*) onto and in the human spirit; it actually "is sent into the human spirit by God" ("*quod immittis in spiritum hominis*").[10] One of the fruits of these divine rays is human creativity.[11]

According to Cusanus, the absolute sight and power of God remains inextricably entangled with the act of generation: "To see is to create."[12] But it takes not only the ability to see—love and sex are, after all, essential for acts of creation, human or

10
Nicolaus Cusanus, *De visione dei*, ch. 25 (1453): "Sed quid est hoc, domine, quod immittis in spiritum hominis quem perficis? Nonne spiritum tuum bonum, qui penitus est in actu virtus omnium virtutum et perfectio perfectorum, quoniam ille est qui omnia operatur? Sicut enim vis solaris, descendens in spiritum vegetabilem, movet ipsum ut perficiatur et fit, gratissima et naturalissima decoctione caelestialis caloris, fructus bonus medio boni arboris, ita spiritus tuus, deus, venit in spiritum intellectualem boni hominis, et calore divinae charitatis decoquit virtualem potentiam, ut perficiatur et fiat sibi gratissimus fructus."

11
Cusanus is the theologian in the fifteenth century who draws intrinsic ties in his work between perception and conception, as well as between both artistic and divine inspiration and creation. He was papal legate on the council of Basel, very well attended by Spanish theologians and in close touch with pope Pius the II. Cusanus was deeply indebted to and familiar with the writings of medieval scholars reflecting on the origins of procreative powers, and the brink between perception and conception, such as those cited already: Thomas Aquinas and Ramón Sibiuda. In his famous work *De visione dei*, he compares visual reflection, mental reflection, and the reflection of mirrors to the power of insemination and creation. Cusanus was in Padua from 1420 to 1425. He first traveled to Rome in 1427 and was a cardinal and a papal legate starting in 1448. *De visione dei* was written in 1453. For Cusanus's concept of vision as active and passive process as well as an act of self-reflection see Werner Beierwaltes, *Visio absoluta: Reflexion als Grundzug des göttlichen Prinzips bei Nicolaus Cusanus: Vorgetragen am 5. Nov. 1977* (Heidelberg: Winter 1978).

divine, according to Cusanus. He elaborates further on the relation of concepts (ideas) and conception explicitly comparing them to the sexual act of procreation.[13] Cusanus concludes with a comparison between divine creation and an artist's creation, drawing an analogy between the painter mixing different colors for his self-portrait and the Holy Spirit mediated through Gabriel's spoken words. The former is making figures that inspire the creation of further pictures: in other words, the first generation that initiates manifold acts of procreation.[14]

Returning to the panel at Córdoba, the painter witnessing the divine Incarnation through directing his gaze upward, toward the divine creator, illuminates two abilities that link divine and human creativity in a particularly evident way; the ability to make and the ability to connect. God's power of making is visualized through the painted sun rays which cross perpendicular to the imaginary rays of our gaze in order to connect annunciation, Incarnation, and the miracle of the Eucharist with the solar monstrance at our focal point.

This painting of an annunciation scene is, therefore, informed by artistic reflections about the relationship between figures and their grounds, between three-dimensional liturgical vessels and the two-dimensional narrated scene, between

12
Ibid., ch. 12, p. 175: "Your seeing is Your creating; and You do not see anything other than Yourself but Your own object, for You are the perceiver, that which is perceived, and the act of perceiving. If so, then how is it that You create things that are other than yourself?"

13
Cusanus, *De visione dei*, ch. 19: "Nam conceptus tuus est filius, et omnia in ipso. Et unio tui et tui conceptus est actus et operatio exsurgens, in qua est omnium actus et explicatio. Sicut igitur ex te deo amante generatur deus amabilis–quae generatio est conceptio–ita procedit ex te deo amante et conceptu tuo amabili a te genito actus tuus et tui conceptus. Qui est nexus nectens et deus uniens te et conceptum tuum, quemadmodum amare unit amantem et amabile in amore. Et hic nexus spiritus nominatur. Spiritus enim est ut motus procedens a movente et mobili. Unde motus est explicatio conceptus moventis."

14
Cusanus, *De visione dei*, ch. 25, p. 265 (trans.): "You, O Lord, who work all things for Your own sake, created this whole world on account of the intellectual nature. |You created| as if You were a painter who mixes different colors in order, at length, to be able to paint Himself—to the end that He may have an image of Himself wherein He Himself may take delight and His artistry may find rest. Although the Divine Painter is one and is not multipliable, He can nevertheless be multiplied in the way in which this is possible: viz., in a very close likeness. However, He makes many figures, because the likeness of His infinite power can be unfolded in the most perfect way only in many figures. And all intellectual spirits are useful to each |intellectual| spirit" (emphasis in the original).

sculpture and painting, between imagination and experience, and last, but not least, between inspiration and conception. Each of these constellations connects divine origins with incarnations in human flesh or objects as speaking metaphors. The painting sets up the coordinates of crossing lines, producing direct intersections between causes and effects.

Annunciation and Incarnation— Interlacing Liturgical and Pictorial Space

While the theme of the annunciation is comprehensible at first glance, references to the Incarnation are supplied to the viewer through the surrounding, painted objects [fig. 141]. Attending more closely to the objects painted on the chamber's floor cues us into the double theme of annunciation and Incarnation. Vessels are included here that are not usually depicted as part of an annunciation scene.

Similar vessels made of glass and filled with water or vases can be found in other annunciations, such as in a panel by Petrus Christus [fig. 150]. However, the choice of fruit with potentially sexual allusions (cherries, three pears, a cucumber, white-flower gourds next to a long knife resting on a large silver platter next to two glass vessels filled with water and red wine) is a highly unusual addition. Less than a decade later, another member of the gourds, the *Curcubita*, which will be placed as significant detail in front of Gabriel's feet by Carlo Crivelli [fig. 151]. Daniel Arasse has read the paradoxical placement of these fruits as "figuration of the irrepresentability of the Incarnation."[15] The fruit of the gourd has been interpreted as metaphor for sin based on Isaiah 1.8.[16] The gourd also plays a role in vanitas depictions (most famously in Albrecht Dürer), possibly referring to the fast growth and decay of the plant, as described in the tale of the prophet Jonah

15 Daniel Arasse, "Gott im Detail: Über einige italienische Verkündigungsszenen," in *Der liebe Gott steckt im Detail: Mikrostrukturen des Wissens*, Wolfgang Schäffner, Sigrid Weigel, and Thomas Macho, eds. (Munich: Fink, 2003), pp. 73–90, here p. 82.

16 Anna Degler has studied the role of fruits of *Curcubita* plants in the meaningful parerga of contemporary paintings in Italy (Cosmè Tura, Bellini, Crivelli), see Anna Degler, *Parergon: Attribut, Material und Fragment der Bildästhetik des Quattrocento* (Munich: Fink, 2015), pp. 81–83.

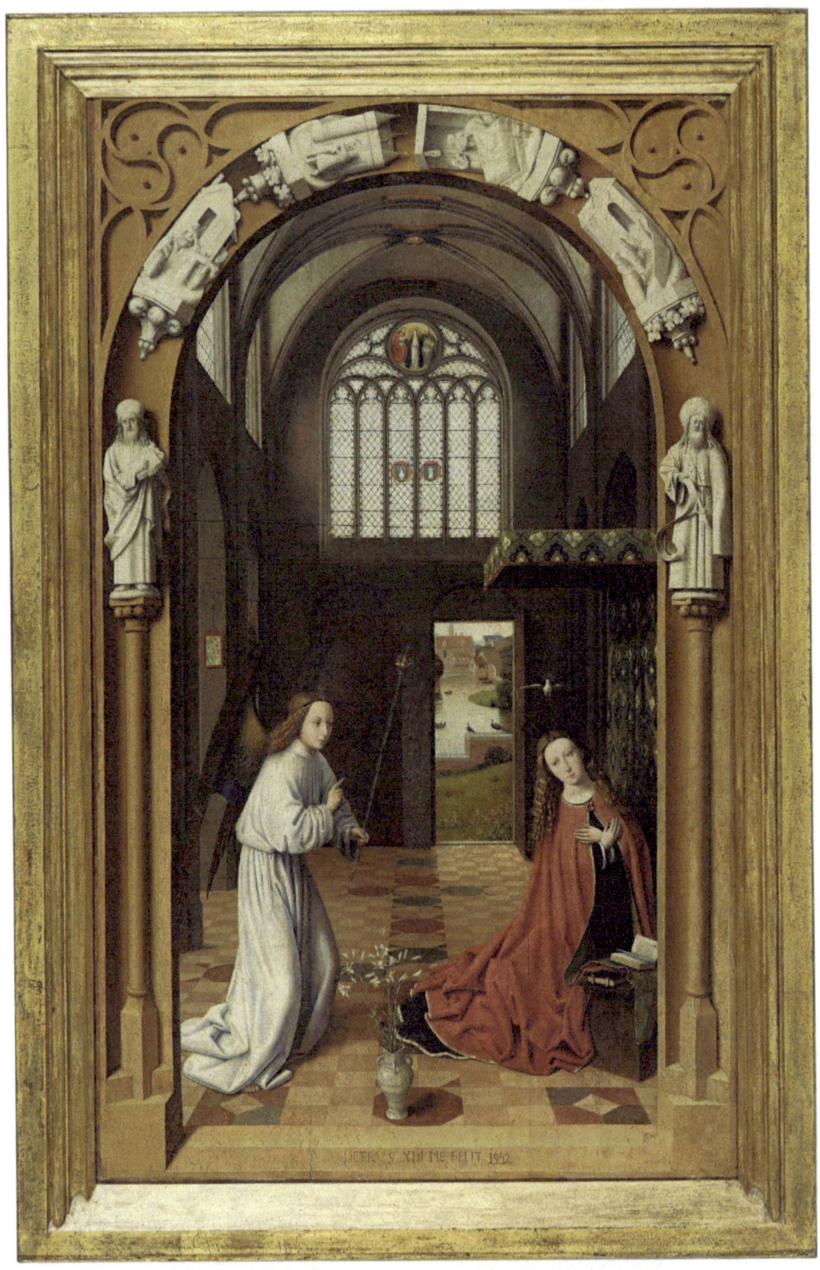

Petrus Christus, *The Annunciation*, 1452, oil on panel, 85.5 × 54.8 cm.
Groeningemuseum, inv. nr. 1983.GRO0019.I, Bruges.

Fig. 150

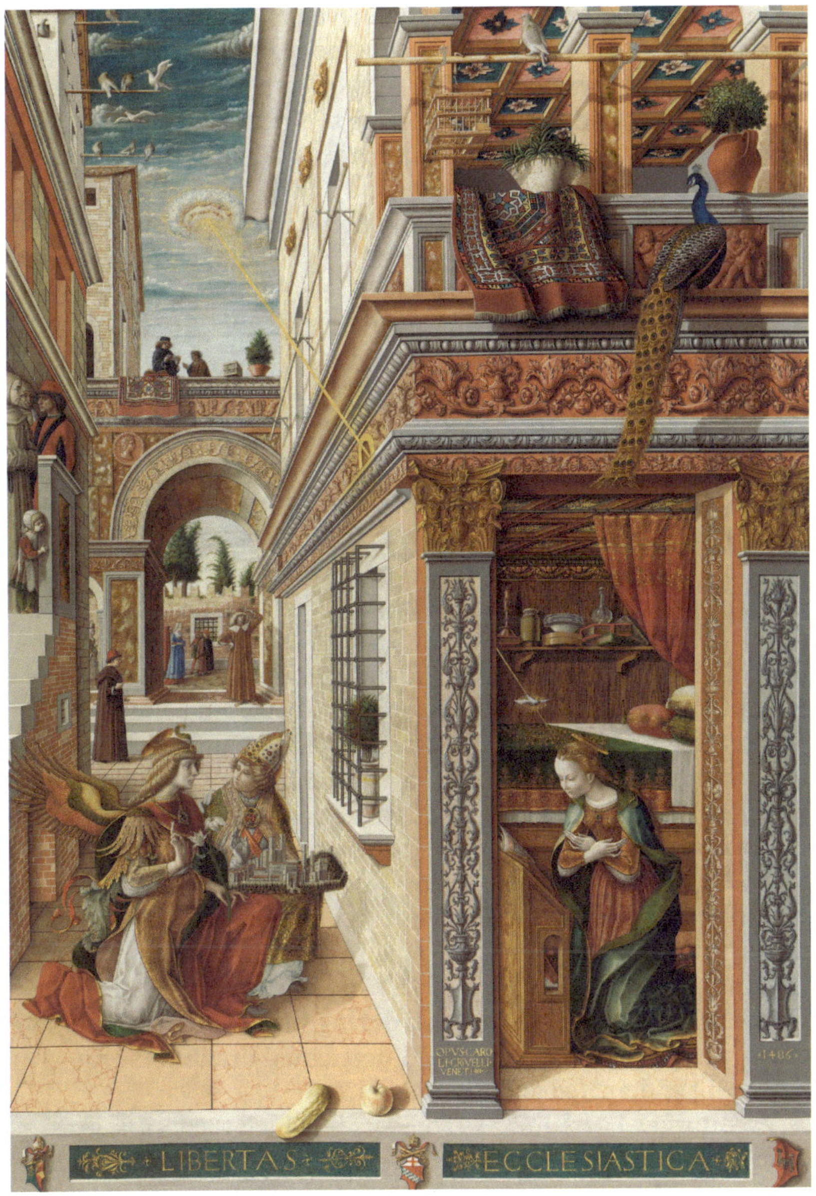

Carlo Crivelli, *The Annunciation, with Saint Emidius*, 1486, egg tempera and oil on canvas, 207 × 146.7 cm. The National Gallery, inv. nr. NG739, London.

Fig. 151

seeking shade before the walls of Nineveh.[17] Particularly striking is the long strip of white linen below the platter. In concert with other profane elements, it points to the death of the incarnated son of God—the white linen referring to the shroud and/or immaculate conception, the vessels with red and clear liquid to the blood, and water from the side wound and so forth. A crumpled cloth shifts seamlessly in our vision between the potential to cover a table and cover a man. On the other hand, we do not expect a monstrance to be part of Mary's household goods. Yet, we find one through the open back doors.

So, while other annunciation scenes do provide us with references to Christ's passion too, as in the example by Rogier van der Weyden in the Louvre shows [fig. 153], the question arises how this panel combines these elements in an entirely new way. Many panels depict Mary in her bedchamber receiving the visit of Gabriel, often complete with rich testimonies of domesticity, precious objects kept by a proud houseowner in the late Middle Ages. However, the manner in which the barbed quatrefoil stage simultaneously divides and connects Christian narrative from the beginning of the gospels with the row of saints and martyrs in the foreground to the announcement of Christ's impending birth and death is a unique pictorial strategy. Significantly, the specific repertoire of forms—for example, the standing quatrefoils and the row of double-layered arches supporting and enclosing the painting's stage—can be found in gothic liturgical vessels ornamenting the lower registers and the stands. However, neither the combination of standing quatrefoils with arches, nor arches stemming directly out of the ground are found to have “real” counterparts in extant liturgical objects [figs. 154 and 155]. Yet, the resemblance is striking, suggesting that during the ceremonies, beholders of both the painting and the liturgy could draw connections between the depicted and the real objects.

Liturgical acts are key moments in which the visible presence of vessels containing a sacred object, such as a monstrance for a sacred host, is connected to invisible causes, i.e., the Holy

17
The name of the plant *Qiqayon* in the Book of Jonah has also been translated as ivy. I owe this observation, comparison and reference to Saskia Quené.

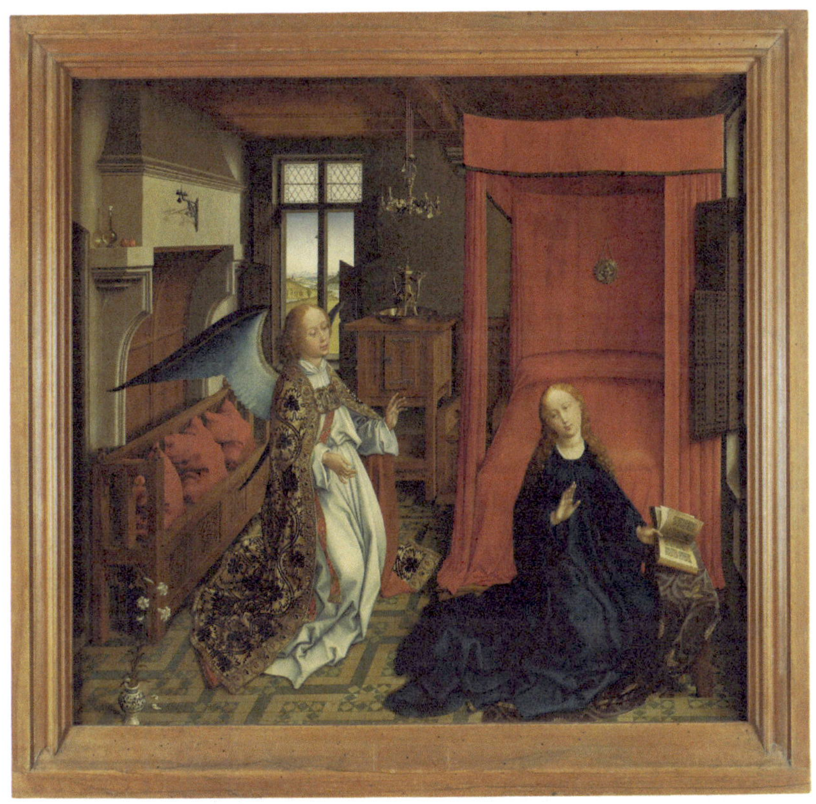

Rogier van der Weyden, *The Annunciation*, oil on panel, 86 × 93 cm.
Musée du Louvre, inv. nr. INV1982, Paris.

Fig. 153

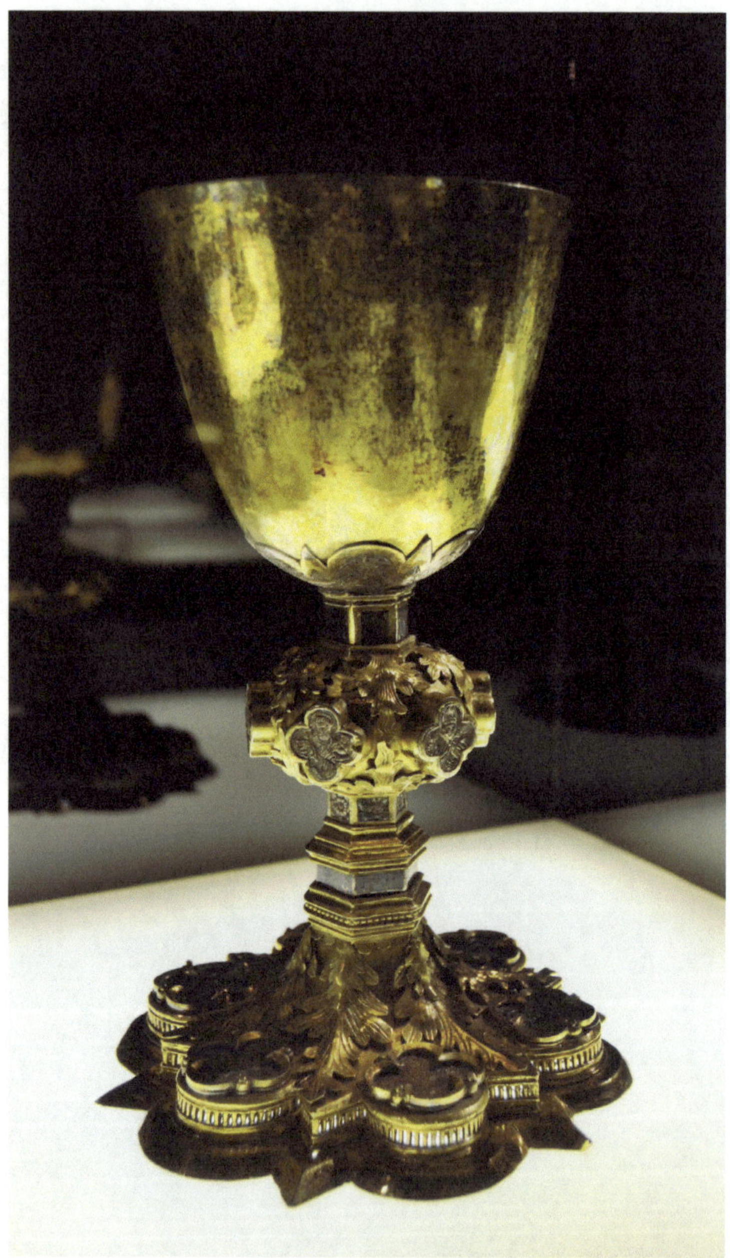

Valencian workshops, *Chalice of Pope Callixtus III*, ca. 1455–1458,
gilded, embossed and chiseled silver, with missing enamels, height: 24 cm, diameter: 18 cm.
Museo de la Colegiata, Xàtiva.

Fig. 154

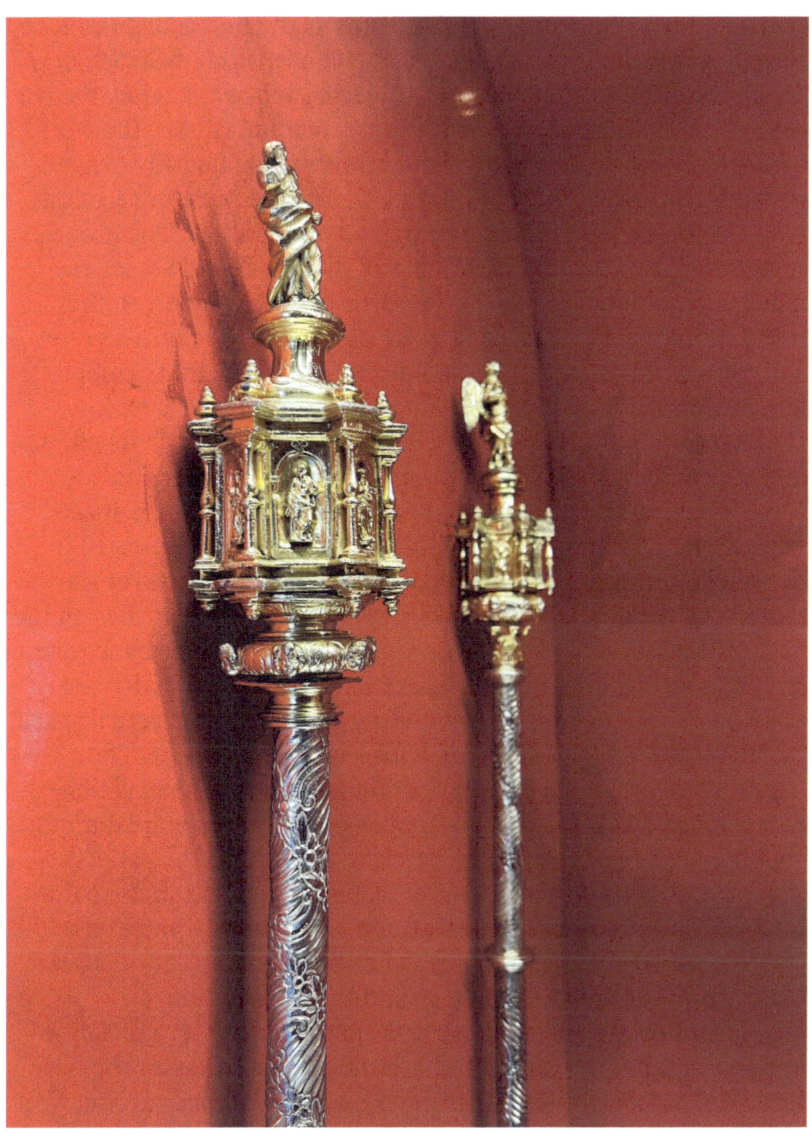

Artist unknown, *Liturgical Staff*, 18th century, gilded silver.
Tesoro de la Mezquita-catedral, Córdoba.

Fig. 155

Spirit and God, and abstract ideas, such as the immaculate conception of Mary, the Incarnation, i.e., the conception of Christ, or transubstantiation. The depicted objects such as the wine, the water, and the monstrance refer to transcendental causes, the works of the Holy Spirit. Our mental eye traverses the lavishly ornate pedestal, following and completing the knotted prayer scrolls as it works to grasp the miracle contained on the stage. The miracles of annunciation and Incarnation mix in the painted vessel, the panel as a goblet, filled with divine inspiration, yet left to the beholder to create and incarnate those inspirations into a vessel. This effect of the painting as a liturgical vessel with its ambivalent motif oscillating between annunciation and Incarnation is even further enhanced, if we imagine the panel with its unique architectonic frame in live motion, as part of processions.

The tiles in the painting have a counterpart in the space where the beholder moves [fig. 133]. The colors are repeated in the tiled altar upon which the panel was installed. The regular pattern of the green, white, ocher, black, and cinnabar tiles on the floor of Mary's study are not only continuing into the back room but are also reaching into the space of the beholder—with the addition of a light blue—and building a bridge to the actual space of the former mosque, the *mezquita* [figs. 157 and 158]. The decisive feature of the baseless columns in the mosque, which forms long rows of reiterating arches, seems to resonate with the striking feature of the row of baseless columns in the panel [fig. 159]. The viewer is thus at once away from and in the painting, positioned to view the painting's scene, taking place on a stage, as an object of sorts, a goblet or liturgical object filled with the miracles of the annunciation and the Incarnation.

But how do we explain the double theme of annunciation and Incarnation in relation to both the panel's use as a processed liturgical object, as well as the panel's own references to liturgical objects within it? I recall the before-mentioned similarity of liturgical objects used in Córdoba and items depicted on the panel, e.g., the solar monstrance, Gabriel's staff, the forms used for the stage design as floor for the main scene, and, last but not least, the explicit connection between the stage and the liturgical site of the church itself, the tiled bridge. A fifteenth-century beholder would have most likely recognized the solar monstrance depicted

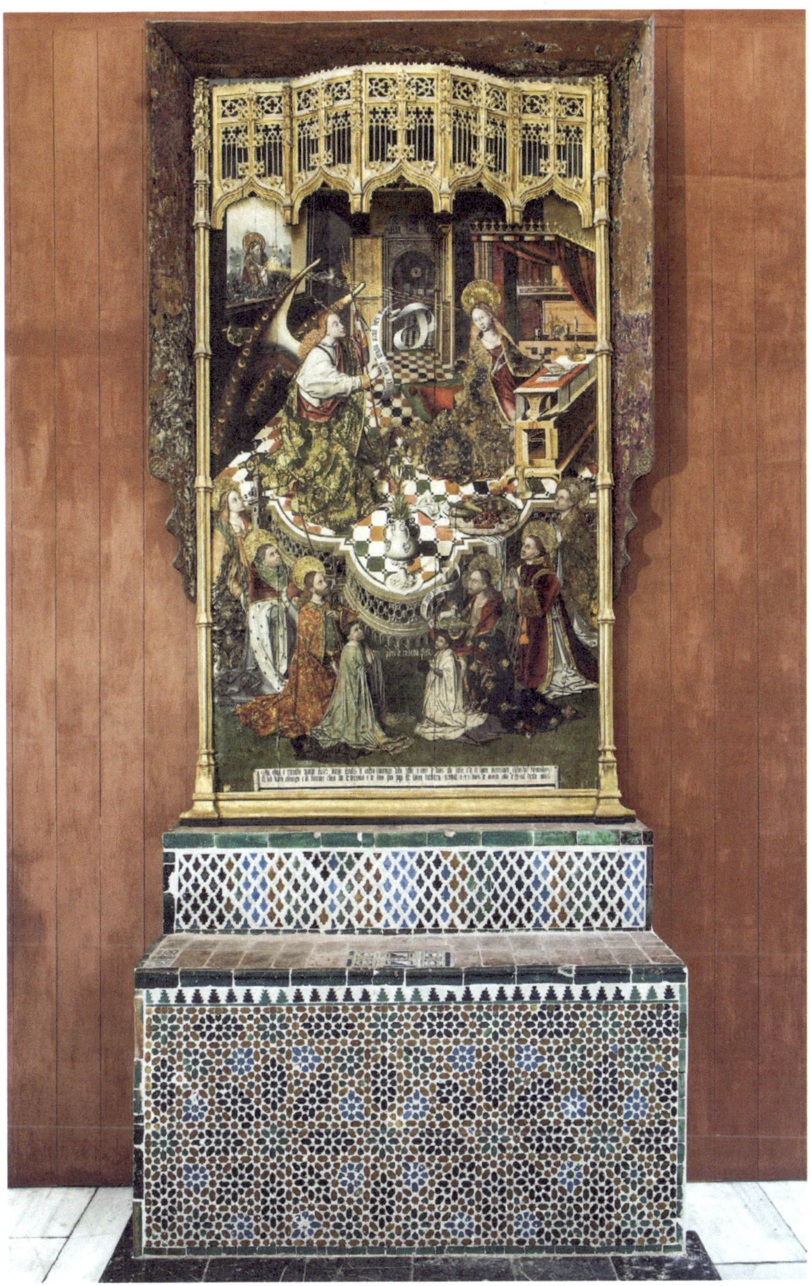

View of Fig. 133 in its current location. Mezquita, Córdoba.

Fig. 157

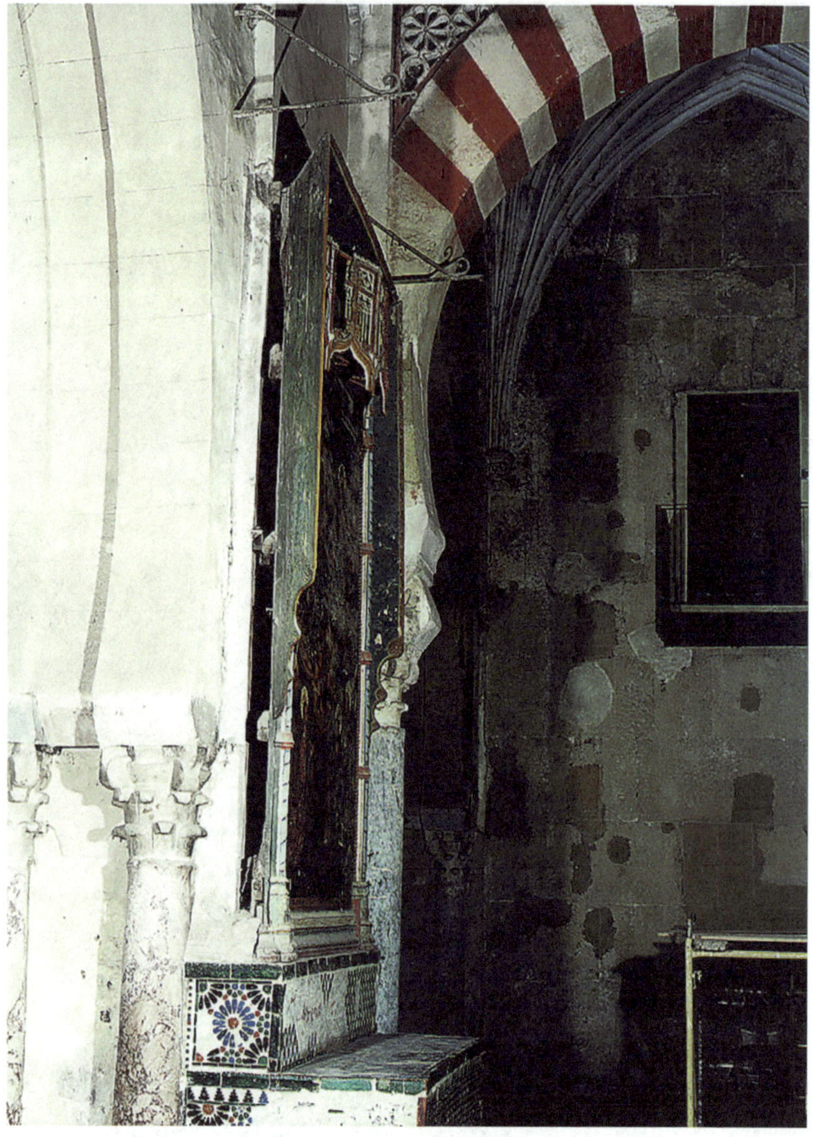

View of Fig. 133 in its current location. Mezquita, Córdoba.

Fig. 158

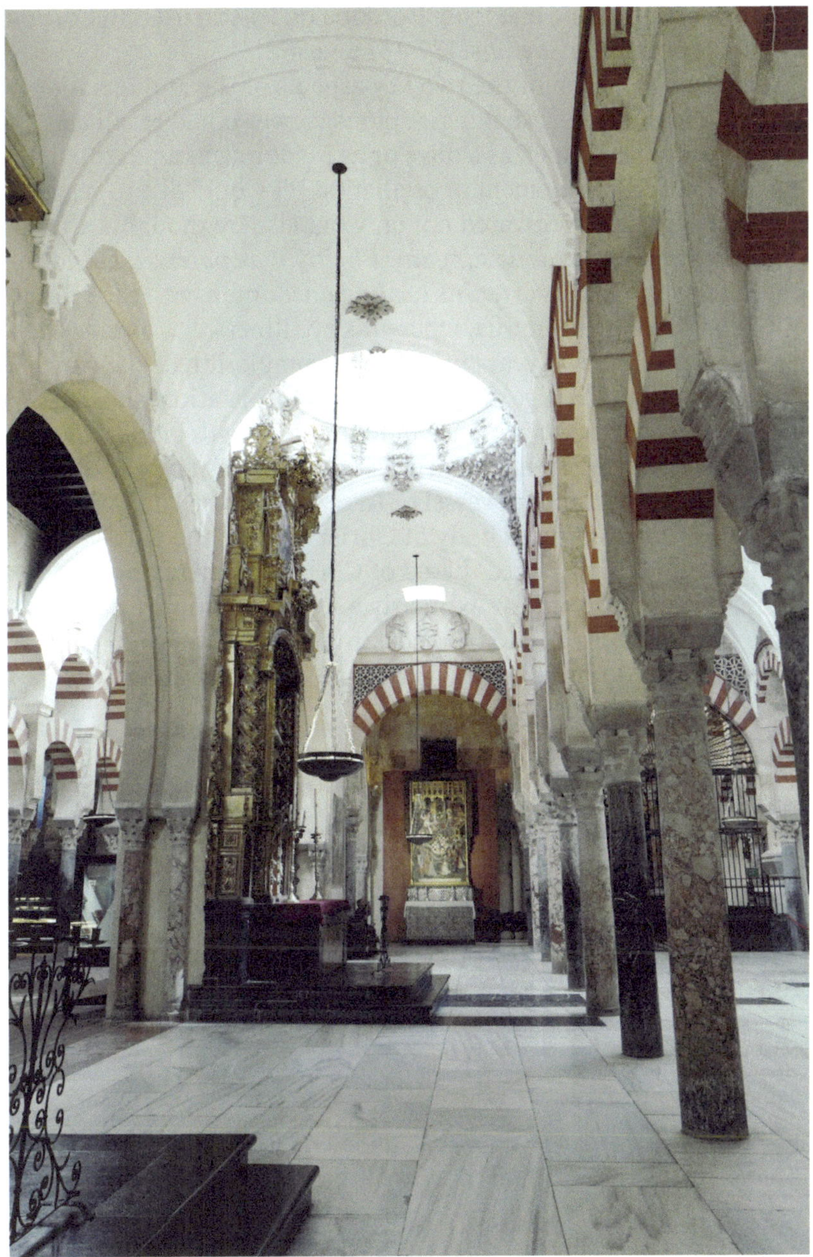

View of Fig. 133 in its current location at the northern wall. Mezquita, Córdoba.

Fig. 159

in the painting as the one from Córdoba or Toledo used in Corpus Christi processions [see figs. 137, 161 and 162].[18]

The oscillation of the two key aspects of the annunciation and the Incarnation is striking. A pious viewer could recall containers for hosts shaped as a dove or as Madonna as a potential inspiration for this moment of oscillation.[19] I would like to suggest that this shift was motivated not only but also by thoughts articulated in the *Tractatus de sanguine Christi et de potentia dei* composed for Pope Sixtus after his healing encounter with the relic of Christ's blood at Mantua, where his eye illness was cured. The tract was printed two years prior to the completion of the panel at Córdoba, in 1473 [fig. 163]. It discusses Incarnation, substantiation, and the divine presence in relics of Christ's blood. It also explicitly addresses the formation of Christ's body and his Incarnation into the pure vessel of Mary's embryo.[20] It clarifies that when the prefigured body of Christ entered the pure vessel of Mary's body, the (sacred) blood of Christ was there, too. In this paragraph the author explicitly quotes the words of John: "*Ecce ancilla domini*."[21] After discussing the generation of semen from blood, the tract turns to the Eucharist and to the

18
There is no solar monstrance preserved in the treasure of Córdoba dating prior to the painting by Pedro de Córdoba, but there are monstrances mentioned in the inventory of the Capilla Real written in 1512, unfortunately without describing their shape, see the *Inventario de la yglesia mayor a Córdoba*. For the history of Corpus Christi processions see Miriam Rubin, *Corpus Christi: The Eucharist in Late Medieval Culture* (Cambridge, UK: Cambridge University Press, 1991) and Miriam Rubin, "Symbolwert und Bedeutung von Fronleichnamsprozessionen," in *Laienfrömmigkeit im Späten Mittelalter*, Klaus Schreiner, ed. (Berlin: De Gruyter, 1992), pp. 309–318.

19
Otto Nussbaum, *Die Aufbewahrung der Eucharistie* (Bonn: Hanstein, 1979), pp. 323–326.

20
Sixtus IV, *Tractatus de sanguine Christi et potentia dei* (Nuremberg, 1473), 31.2nd problem: "videt enim que sanctissimus C(h)risti corpus prius tempore (tempe) organizatum fuerit quem assumptum ex hoc. Quoniam in ipsius organizacione (hic!) opus erat ut sanguines purissimi virginis intemerate ad locum generacionis reducerentur cum ex ipsis formatum fuerit xpi corpus in tali loco. Talis autem reductio facta fuit per motum localem. Necesse insuper fuit que xpi corpus ex eisdem sanguinibus generatum eis deum. Sius efficeretur alteriusque forme & figure. Cum in eo partes eterogenee formande essent quem (queim) sanguine non prefuerant. Hec autem cum sine motu locali non possint fieri."

21
Sixtus IV, *Tractatus*, pp. 32–33: "Virtute sanctus spiritus sancti infinita purissimi illi sanguines Virginis intemerate ad locum generacionis delati fuerunt condesatis & figurati atque forma toci in sacratissimu Christi corpus sic dispositum inducta & demque in eodem met tempis momento totum cum qualibet sui parte simul & sanguine fuit a verbo assumptu facto sive expresso gloriosissime virginis matris consensu Cum dixit. Ecce ancilla domini tecum."

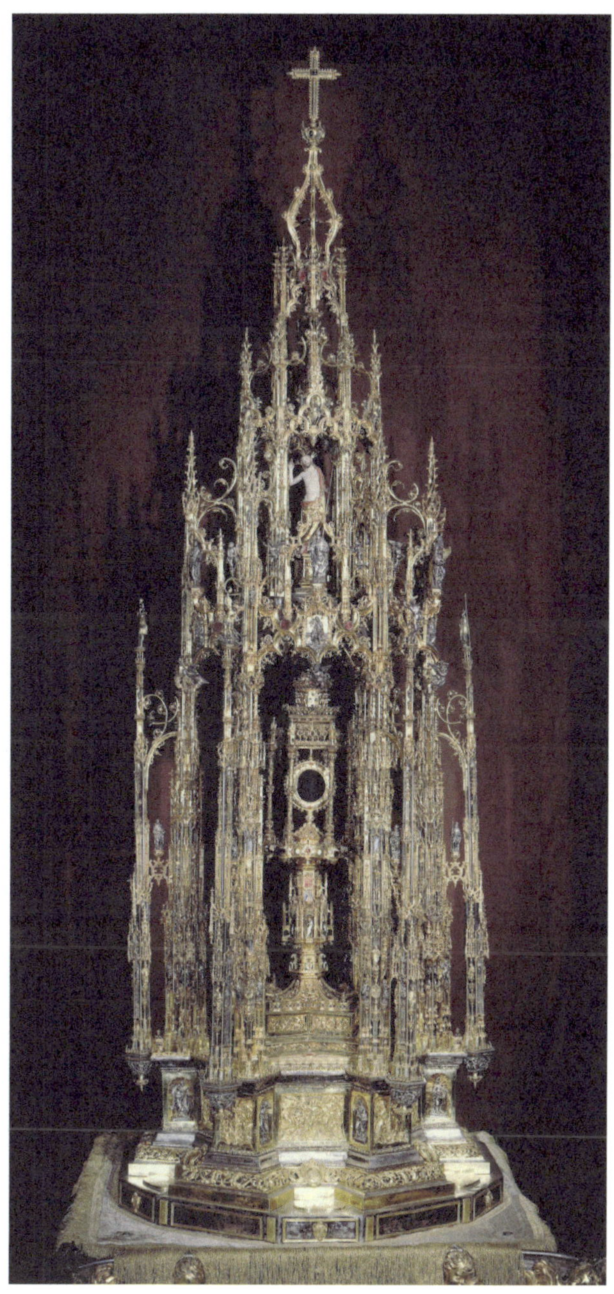

Enrique de Arfe (Heinrich von Harff), *Custodia*, ca. 1515–1523, gilded silver, height: 309 cm. Toledo Cathedral, Toledo.

Fig. 161

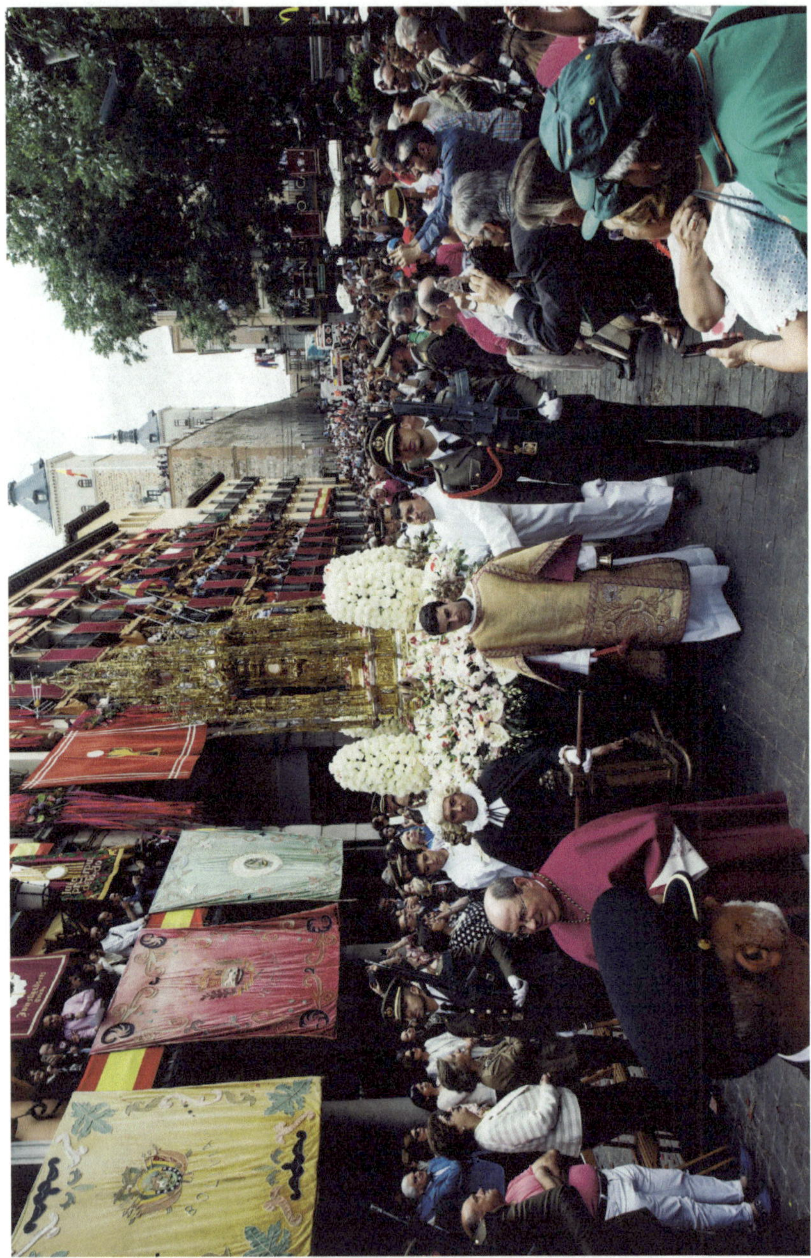

The *Custodia* [fig. 161] in procession.

Fig. 162

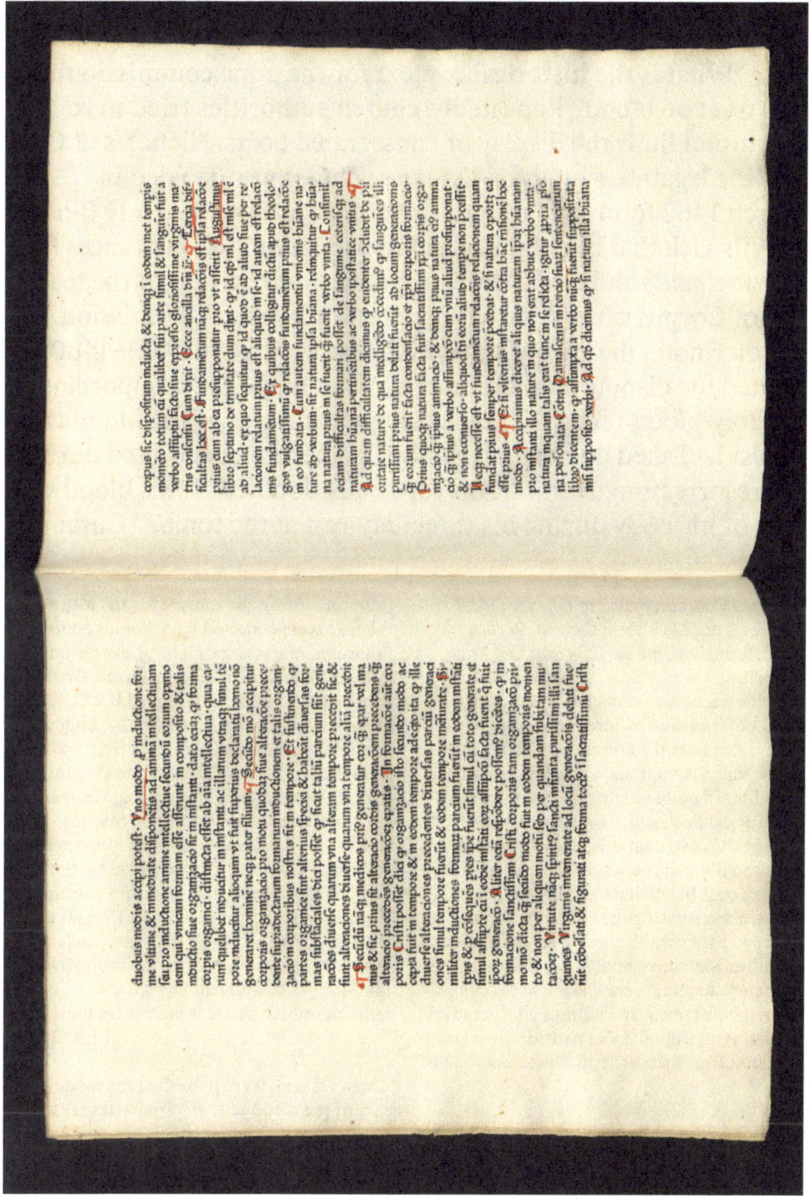

Pope Sixtus IV, *De sanguine Christi et De potentia Dei*, pp. 32–33, printed by Friedrich Creussner in Nürnberg, 1473.
Biblioteka Uniwersytecka w Warszawie, XV.F.1056,1, Warsaw.

Fig. 163

question of what happens to Christ's shed blood in the moment of his resurrection.

What is the historical context for the pope commissioning this tract on blood? Repeatedly, church authorities tried to regulate and limit the display of consecrated hosts. Nicholas of Cusa was the legatine synod for Cologne when it was decided in March 1452 following the controversy regarding the Holy Blood at Wilsnack that blood relics had to be placed in monstrances (*in monstranciis*) and could be displayed just once a year at the feast day of Corpus Christi, or with the bishop's special permission.[22] Furthermore, the stay of pope Pius II at Mantua in 1459–1460 ignited the dispute about the authenticity of the most important of all Holy-blood relics.[23] The crucial question was, if the blood that Christ had shed during his passion had been incorporated during the resurrection. Dominicans especially doubted if this blood was part of his body during his three-day-rest at the tomb.[24] Cusanus,

22
Nicolaus Cusanus, *Synod of Cologne (1452 March 8)*, no. 2343 (*Acta Cusana: Quellen zur Lebensgeschichte des Nikolaus von Kuess* [Hamburg: Felix Meiner, 2016]), p. 1504, https://actacusana.de/quellenverzeichnis/2343.pdf: "Item ad maiorem honorem sanctissimi sacramenti statuimus, quod deinceps ipsum sanctissimum sacramentum nullatenus visibiliter in quibuscunque monstranciis ponatur aut deferatur, nisi in sanctissimo festo Corporis Christi cum suis octavis et extra huiusmodi festum cum suis octavis semel in anno in qualibet civitate aut oppido seu 150 parrochia vel ex singulari indulto ordinarii aut alias pro pace vel alia necessitate imminente ex indisposicione rempublicam pregravante, et tunc cum summa reverencia atque devocione, in premissis tamen laudabilibus consuetudinibus huius metropolitice et cathedralium ecclesiarum suffraganeorum eiusdem semper salvis."

23
The Dominican Giovanni Turrecremata doubted the authenticity of the relic while the Franciscan Francesco da Savona argued in favor of it. For a summary of all related arguments in this debate see Sixtus IV, *De sanguine Christi et De potentiae Dei* (Rome, 1471) as well as from a Mantuan perspective: Francesco Maria Caraccioli, *Discorso nell'espositione del pretioso sangue che si conserva nella citta di Mantova* (Mantua, 1666); the sources for the history of the relic were collected by Antonius Nerli, cf. Francesco Maria Caraccioli, "Breve chronicon monasterii mantuani sancti andreae, Ord. Benedict. ab anno MXVII usque MCCCCXVIII," in *Rerum Italicarum Scriptores* 24, Lodovico Antonio Muratori, ed. (Milan, 1738), pp. 1071–1084, here p. 1073: "Carlo Magno Pippini Regis filio imperante, translato ad Germanos in personam ejus Imperio, apud Mantuam hoc eodem loco, quo praesens hodie Monasterium cernitur, parvo tunc Oratorio cum Hospitali domo in jam dictae urbis suburbio constituto, Sacratissmum Sanguinem Dei & Domini nostri Jesu Christi, ex ipsius in Cruce pendentis effusum latere, a beato Longino milite & glorioso Martyre delatum atque reconditum, primi inibi innotuisse patribus nostris tradunt."

24
Three volumes were published for the anniversary of the blood relic at Weingarten; *Festschrift zum Heilig-Blut-Jubiläum am 12. März 1994*, 3 vols., Norbert Kruse, ed., with collaboration by R. Schaubode (Sigmaringen: Thorbecke, 1994). Herein see especially the contributions in the first volume by Norbert Kruse, "Der Weg des Heiligen Bluts von Mantua nach Altdorf-Weingarten," pp. 57–76 and by Lukas Weichenrieder, "Das Heilige Blut von Mantua," pp. 331–336.

who as papal legate was directly involved in the dispute, answers the question of Christ's corporeal integrity at the resurrection, and whether blood is present in the transfigured body of Christ positively, with the following argument:

> The blood and the body of Christ are an indissoluble unity which is taken in heaven. For those, who believe that the blood in the consecrated chalice is his, this is certainly so. Since the body cannot be nourished without it, ... the body of every human has to resurrect together with the blood.[25]

The decisive question, if *all* of Christ's blood has returned to his body has not been addressed by Cusanus. He chooses not to do so, because as one of the most prominent critics of the veneration of miraculously bleeding hosts (e.g., at Wilsnack), he was in the delicate position to act for a pope who was a declared friend of relics of the True Blood.[26]

The occasions for the painting set into motion in 1475 were either on March 18 for the procession and fiesta of San Gabriel,[27] on March 25 for the celebration of the annunciation, for the installation of the panel on March 20 in 1475, or during the Corpus Christi procession on Maundy Thursday on April 1 in 1475, the feast for which Thomas Aquinas composed not only the Vespers but the entire Office for the Mass. These papal debates around the presence of blood in general and the related ceremonies of the Corpus Christi processions are centered on the question of verifying miraculousness and questioning where it comes from, which is something that the

25
Rudolf Haubst, *Die Christologie des Nikolaus von Kues* (Freiburg: Herder, 1956), p. 296. For the fourteen Christological questions (Cod. Cus. 40, 144r–146v) see the appendix, pp. 315–328, here p. 322. In these Nicolas of Cusa discusses why what rises was never separated from the person of the risen ("resurget in ipsa quidquam, quod desiit esse suum per separationem a persona"), in which his implicit critique of Holy-blood relics become evident.

26
Cusanus has articulated his opinion toward this issue in the last of fourteen questions regarding the three deaths of Christ and the afterlife of his blood. See Caroline Walker Bynum, *Wonderful Blood: Theology and Practice in Late Medieval Northern Germany and Beyond* (Philadelphia: University of Pennsylvania Press, 2007), pp. 125–127 and pp. 142–151.

27
Alonso Rodriguez Gamarra, *Flos Sanctorum: Fiestas, i santos naturales de la Ciudad de Cordova* (Seville, 1615), pp. 57–67.

painting by Pedro de Córdoba is also doing through its complex networks of gazes, mirrors, and plays with what the viewer can and cannot see, as well as what the members of the painting itself can see and not.

Imagination and Experience

The plurality of gazes of those in the painting (Mary, Gabriel, God, and the lineup of saints, donor, and artist) is essential for guiding the viewer within the depicted space, in which visible and invisible acts of divinity occupy different dimensions, layers, and levels of the stage. Between imagination and experience, we complete our access to the play of staged figures and figurations through the mental and verbal completion of prayers.

In the painting by Pedro da Córdoba, the pictorial space is constituted through the shifing relationships between caused miracle (Incarnation), saintly interlocutors, and mediated miracle (communion), as well as between the painted objects (specifically liturgical objects) and invisible things (annunciation, conception, transubstantiation). The key mediator knitting these (invisible) connections is the Holy Spirit. His efforts and efficacy are perceived through the imagination of the beholder. His or her imagination is enhanced through the movement of actual liturgical vessels during the mass and the visual references to these objects on the panel. The Holy Spirit also plays a decisive role in the medieval discourse on the origins of human creativity. Scholastic reflections about the causes and the nature of human creativity align divine acts of creation and the works of human artifices. Again, it is the Holy Spirit who relates perception of concepts (ideas) and conception with explicit references to the Incarnation as well as to procreation.

This contribution, therefore, showed how art historians dealing with art in second half of the fifteenth century can address and reveal pictorial challenges and artistic solutions without using established terms and paradigms such as perspective, figure, and ground. The close reading of this hitherto little discussed painting, embedding it in the potential visual and ceremonial use at the turn of the century and unfolding possible relations to contemporary intellectual and theological debates enables to distance us from the historical baggage these terms carry. Our analysis has shown how theological ideas about creation, revelation inspired artistic creations, and reflections on the potentials of painting as a mediator between form, idea, and spirit.

Part 2
Describing and Translating

"I will teach you differences."
—Wittgenstein, after Shakespeare[1]

Since 1978, I and others have been developing the category of iconic difference to analyze the explicatory power particular to images.[2] The first task of this category is not just to speak of images in vague generalities but to reflect on the huge historical and factual diversity of images. Articulating the resonant concepts that result from thinking about difference goes hand in hand with being close enough to an image to look at it. Linking images together, weighing them against each other, and examining their materiality is the task of an academic discipline whose appropriate name is image criticism.

An insistence on exact appearance follows from a phenomenological impulse that reveals the forms of experience unique to images, forms that Plato first describes in the words of Theaetetus in the *Sophist* as the συμπλοκή (*symploké*, interweaving) of being and nonbeing. Plato has the visitor in the dialogue formulate a question that still confronts today's thinking about images: "So it's not really what is, but it really is what we call an image?"[3] The enigma of the image has a thousand faces and yet always has to do with how something factual manifests an effect, how materiality discloses lucid meaning. The criterion of difference is first applied, however, in an external and descriptive manner, which leads to an incomplete interpretation. It provides, for example, an overview of family resemblances between images or of genre associations and functional contexts, specifying how and by what means images differ. As much it must rely on previous work, the approach of image criticism is not trivial because it sharpens the eye for peculiarities and for the enormous spectrum of

1
Quoted in Maurice O'Connor Drury, "Conversations with Wittgenstein," in *Recollections of Wittgenstein*, Rush Rhees, ed. (Oxford: Oxford University Press, 1984), pp. 97–171, here p. 157.

2
See Gottfried Boehm, "Zu einer Hermeneutik des Bildes," in *Seminar: Die Hermeneutik und die Wissenschaften*, Hans-Georg Gadamer and Gottfried Boehm, eds. (Frankfurt am Main: Suhrkamp, 1978), pp. 444–471; and Gottfried Boehm, "Bildsinn und Sinnesorgane," *Neue Hefte für Philosophie* 18/19 (1980): pp. 118–132.

3
Plato, *Sophist*, trans. Nicholas P. White, in *Complete Works*, John M. Cooper, ed. (Indianapolis, IN: Hackett, 1997), pp. 235–293, here 240b; translation modified.

pictorial phenomena, including iconic latencies. As an inventory, it explores the open boundaries of the pictorial in its historical contexts, which different materials and media also contribute to. Thinking about iconic difference thereby leads to ascertaining the historical and anthropological preconditions of its objects, as well as the objects' places in the discursive field. The "pictorial turn"[4] was not coincidental but based on the profound transformations images underwent in the twentieth-century avant-gardes, transformations that exponentially multiplied their modes of appearance and representation. Digital technologies have further ensured that images have become what they never were before: fluid and interactive means of communication.

Since then, the generalizing singular entity of "the image" has found an adequate content. But thought about iconic difference is just as much based on more recent developments in philosophy and other disciplines. Above all, the discovery of nonverbal forms of symbolization, of showing as opposed to saying (Ludwig Wittgenstein, Martin Heidegger, Ernst Cassirer, Karl Bühler) is of great interest. At the same time, linguistics, neuroscience, paleontology, research on primates, and child psychology have been able to clarify which gestural, iconic capacities precede or accompany language.[5] As a theoretical figure, iconic difference attempts to do justice to the iconic in logos or as logos.

The constitutive characteristics of the pictorial are only imperfectly revealed by vivid description. A more profound, critical study of images is required to uncover how their recognizable meanings and the effects we experience are generated.

With iconic difference, we propose a hypothesis that should be valid for each particular pictorial work. It states that every iconic artifact is organized in the form of a visual, intelligent, and deictic (that is, nonlinguistic) difference. Their constitutive aspects differ in each case depending on whether they are, for example,

4
See Gottfried Boehm, "Die Wiederkehr der Bilder," in *Was ist ein Bild?*, Gottfried Boehm, ed. (Munich: Wilhelm Fink, 1994), pp. 11–38.

5
See Ludwig Jäger, "Bild/Sprachlichkeit: Zur Audiovisualität des menschlichen Sprachvermögens," *Sprache und Literatur* 98, no. 2 (2006): pp. 2–24; Michael A. Arbib, "Grounding the Mirror System Hypothesis for the Evolution of the Language-Ready Brain," in *Simulating the Evolution of Language*, Angelo Cangolesi and Domenico Parisi, eds. (London: Springer, 2002), pp. 229–254; and Michael Tomasello, *Origins of Human Communication* (Cambridge, MA: MIT Press, 2010).

cave paintings, icons, masks, panel paintings, three-dimensional pictorial works, drawings, photographs, imaging processes, diagrams, or moving images. But they all have one thing in common: in their heterogeneous manifestations, they activate a structural moment that links them together and turns them into images. Structurally speaking, all images work with the interplay of a contrast between continuous moments and discrete elements; they are a continuous discontinuity. This general hypothesis, clothed in the form of a vivid description—one might also call it a summary definition—seems to resemble the figure–ground relation of gestalt theory, but it points in a completely different direction. For iconic difference proves not to be a two-part, visually oriented figure of opposition; it rather represents a three-part transition that conceptualizes the image as an event. Defining this transition is a matter for a second step, which we will now turn to.

Anyone who works with the category of difference participates in a central field of philosophy. Gilles Deleuze recently conceived of a way of thinking about difference; with *différance*, Jacques Derrida brought into play a groundless ground for every distinction; one notes a linguistic proximity of our iconic difference to Martin Heidegger's ontological difference; and a dialectical turn of the argument about difference refers to Georg Wilhelm Friedrich Hegel.[6] One could add to these four references. In fact, however, iconic difference does not attempt to shift questions about images to the terrain of one of these thinkers and to work them out there. This is not to deny that they provide a lot of insights for us to consider, offer intellectual resistance, and present arguments that are helpful for developing iconic difference. The reasons for our abstinence in this regard lie in a diagnosis of Western thought, which has never really managed to grant logos a preverbal, iconic meaning.

6
See Gilles Deleuze, *Difference and Repetition*, trans. Paul Patton (New York: Columbia University Press, 1994), e.g., pp. 28–29, pp. 262–263; Jacques Derrida, *Of Grammatology*, trans. Gayatri Chakravorty Spivak, corr. ed. (Baltimore, MD: Johns Hopkins University Press, 1997), p. 24; Martin Heidegger, "On the Essence of Ground," trans. William McNeill, in *Pathmarks*, William McNeill, ed. (Cambridge, UK: Cambridge University Press, 1998), pp. 97–135; Martin Heidegger, *Identity and Difference*, trans. Joan Stambaugh (Chicago: University of Chicago Press, 2002); and Georg Wilhelm Friedrich Hegel, *Phenomenology of Spirit*, trans. A. V. Miller, rev. ed. (Oxford: Clarendon, 1977), pp. 46–57.

In other words, the role of the image in the hominization of humans has not been sufficiently considered; it has been completely obscured by the definition of the human as the ζῷον λόγον ἔχων (*zoon logon echon*).[7] What is more, the meaning and legitimacy of such a question—which does not challenge the linguistic proposition but does transcend it—is highly controversial; paths into this terra incognita have rarely been taken. Iconic difference attempts to breach this iron wall, to initiate a different way of thinking about meaning, not only out of a justified, specialized interest in images, but even more so to find a more suitable and complex definition of human beings as a creature capable of images, a being who is always in the process of linking *imaginatio* with *imago*.

As a visual *dispositif*, iconic difference thus becomes a theoretical explanatory process. It offers moments of differentiation and unity, which have been traditionally interpreted as, for example, energeia, *physis*, τὸ ἕν (*to hen*), or intentionality. Above all, the interplay in difference needs to be considered. We will expressly avoid speaking of a dialectic or synthesis and refrain from using the model of a linguistic proposition (*S–p*) or of semiotic relations as a basis. Instead, the category of embodiment, of chiasmus (Maurice Merleau-Ponty), should take us further.[8] It is very important only to include concepts and explanatory figures that fit the iconic and that do not immediately incorporate it into language or a general process of symbolization.[9]

Talk of interplay, transition, and process or of iconic difference as an open space does not yet determine the nature or functioning of iconic logic. But it does bring to bear that it is a standing process of differentiation, that temporality dominates at the core of images.

7
See Hans Jonas, "Homo Pictor: Von der Freiheit des Bildens," in Boehm, *Was ist ein Bild?*, pp. 105–124; Gottfried Boehm, ed., *Homo Pictor* (Munich: K. G. Saur, 2001); and Hans Belting, *An Anthropology of Images: Picture, Medium, Body*, trans. Thomas Dunlap (Princeton, NJ: Princeton University Press, 2011).

8
See Maurice Merleau-Ponty, "Eye and Mind," trans. Carleton Dallery, in *The Primacy of Perception, And Other Essays on Phenomenological Psychology, the Philosophy of Art, History and Politics*, James M. Edie, ed. (Evanston, IL: Northwestern University Press, 1964), pp. 159–190; and Maurice Merleau-Ponty, *The Visible and the Invisible*, trans. Alphonso Lingis, Claude Lefort, ed. (Evanston, IL: Northwestern University Press, 1968).

9
See, for example, Nelson Goodman, *Languages of Art: An Approach to a Theory of Symbols*, 2nd ed. (Indianapolis, IN: Hackett, 1976).

In other words, images represent a form of event, albeit a highly specific one.[10] They encompass not only entangled visual contrasts between figure and ground but also implicate the space of history. For all the determinations that flow into images—not just iconography and iconology or form and style—derive from work performed in history and in a culture. And, as is well known, it is not only the content of representation that has changed along the way but also the pictorial concepts, that is, the very modes of representation. In other words, image criticism, which analyzes the modes of iconic representation, must refer to the productivity of history and of those who make images.

According to Bernhard Waldenfels, image theory tends to start too high or too low.[11] It also tends to forgo the labor of developing its own concepts, to take up the repertoire of existing philosophies, to use the language of, for example, Ferdinand de Saussure, Charles Sanders Peirce, Wittgenstein, Ernst Cassirer, Heidegger, Nelson Goodman, John Searle, Derrida, Deleuze, and others. In doing so, it should of course bear in mind that these theorists pursued completely different epistemological interests and that it is therefore necessary to examine in each case which claims are useful and which are not. For concepts are, as we know, not just words but decisive for what one claims.

Elaborating iconic difference as an explanatory figure can therefore greatly benefit from the elementary descriptive work already mentioned. If images follow a logic, then the operators involved should be demonstrable in the visual field and in the example in question. It is therefore insufficient, for instance, to place images under the category of potentiality and then to use Aristotelian arguments. It is insufficient as long as it is not made clear what specific kind of dynamis or energeia images possess and what operations materially organize them. The power of iconic difference consists in how it works with structures of

10
Horst Bredekamp recently conceptualized them as an image act in Horst Bredekamp, *Image Acts: A Systematic Approach to Visual Agency*, trans. and ed. Elizabeth Clegg (Berlin: Walter de Gruyter, 2018).

11
"Most conceptions of the image suffer from starting too high, namely, on the level of pictorial works and media. They thereby lose sight of the fissures and abysses of experiencing images." Bernhard Waldenfels, "Spiegel, Spur und Blick: Zur Genese des Bildes," in Boehm, *Homo Pictor*, pp. 14–31, here p. 14; trans. by Anthony Mahler.

visibility and is therefore very specific. Not only does it not imitate a verbal predicate ("is"), it also opens up an asymmetry whose significance can hardly be overestimated.

The continuous ground is sustained and uninterrupted, whereas the elements that appear before and in the contrast to it are always singular and distinguishable. To see the one under the condition of the other—to speak with Edmund Husserl, to relate the subject and the horizon reciprocally to one another—presupposes that they each belong to fundamentally different realities.[12] The continuum of the ground shows itself to be impenetrable and for this very reason can give the distinct elements a place in which they make a view visible and configure meaning. This is precisely what asymmetry means: the visually organized relationship of what could never be substituted. The continuous and simultaneous continuum can never be completely reduced to the distinct, successive elements. The visual asymmetry establishes a gradient that mobilizes the power of the ground and brings it to bear in the presence of the respective figuration as clear evidence, emotional emphasis, or in other forms of visualization.

Asymmetry is also associated with the phenomenon of inversion. Pictures turn what they present toward us. They do not simply extend the lines of the reality in which we act but present them in such a way that they can engage and enter into a dialogue with the beholder, such that they can look at us. This also means that the gap or rift that iconic difference tears through and turns into an event interacts in a constitutive way with the beholder's eyes, their sensory organs. The beholder is, according to a common expression, "in the image," not because they have to put themself in it but because iconic difference has already created their place there in advance.

12
We do not yet have an image theory that adapts Husserl's category of the horizon, which he developed in his phenomenology of perception as a place of nuance, implications, nonthematic ramifications, expectations, and fulfillment. Husserl characterizes the logic of the world as a background or field. In the logic of the image, this background returns transformed. See Edmund Husserl, *The Crisis of European Sciences and Transcendental Phenomenology: An Introduction to Phenomenological Philosophy*, trans. David Carr (Evanston, IL: Northwestern University Press, 1970), p. 149; and Edmund Husserl, *Experience and Judgment: Investigations in a Genealogy of Logic*, trans. James S. Churchill and Karl Ameriks, rev. and ed. Ludwig Landgrebe (Evanston, IL: Northwestern University Press, 1973).

The argumentative figure of iconic difference is successful when it is able to explain how images generate meaning and from what they draw their power, without making use of linguistic models or analogies. As mentioned, its inherent oscillation between identity and difference does not follow the pattern of predication, nor does it pursue a dialectical synthesis that strives for a higher conceptual form in order to sublate the moments involved. Iconic difference thus brings into play a gradient that is always turned toward the viewer. The build-up or surplus sedimented in it explains why a representation is endowed with liveliness and self-evidence, why it presents itself. Iconic difference generates meaning without saying "is"; it provides access to a reality that "manifests itself," that "shows itself." Images are deictic events; their meaning is the effect of a material structure and disposition.

It is precisely this temporality that allows something visible to emerge in the image, presents meaning to our eyes, places it in the light of evidence. Materiality is indispensable to this. It not only provides the continuum of representation but also gives that basic distinction a body. Only where an opaque impenetrability comes into play can the meaning of an image be revealed, can the spark of difference light up.

We understand iconic difference as an event in the sense of an oscillation or a logic of contrast. Pictures create their space of meaning by enabling the eye to move back and forth in a complex way, by allowing it to oscillate between simultaneous comprehension and successive movement. It therefore also does not seem helpful to distinguish the (material) image carrier from the always immaterial image object, as Lambert Wiesing has in mind.[13] We do not adopt a rigid ontological demarcation that separates the dull material from the "pure visibility" that becomes manifest in it, because what is truly pictorial consists in the event of that manifestation. What beholder would be satisfied with distinguishing the imaginary of a picture from its carrier? Even the most suggestive magic that a picture is capable of triggering, even its most seductive simulation, is nourished by the fact

13
See Lambert Wiesing, *Artificial Presence: Philosophical Studies in Image Theory*, trans. Nils F. Schott (Stanford, CA: Stanford University Press, 2009), pp. 24–59.

that we can always see the paint and the facture, the chemistry of painting. The degree of differentiation, however, implies vibration and subtlety.

In chapter 7 of his *Thousand Plateaus*, which is dedicated to the face, Deleuze interprets what we call iconic difference as an "abstract machine." It is already manifested in the difference between a "white wall" and a "black hole" and is capable of generating something like an answering gaze or an expression of affect.[14] One could say that the power of this simple image machine begins with the inevitability of the confrontation it forces on the beholder. The beholder encounters, in our language, the asymmetry between the ground and the pattern of holes. Here we will not further pursue Deleuze's thinking about how difference is endowed with the early childhood dyad of mother and child so as to explain the power of the face or the image,[15] despite the fact that one should note the intimate connection between iconic difference and physical birth.[16]

For the moment, we will instead only draw on Deleuze's "abstract machine," which introduces a (transcendental) schematism, a term that he admittedly does not employ. In fact, a genealogy of images could be deduced from an iconic difference interpreted in this way, an approach that would be based not only on the difference between a white wall and a black hole but also on other mechanisms operative in the history of images and image theory.

These mechanisms include dots and scatterings of dots, stains and stain patterns (in the sense of Leonardo da Vinci's *macchia* or Rorschach tests), the energy of a line or of a color that spreads out. They organize the genesis of pictorial meaning from its beginnings and have largely determined the appearances of images throughout their history. By their very nature, these mechanisms involve setting various differences, each of which schematizes

14
See Gilles Deleuze and Félix Guattari, *A Thousand Plateaus*, trans. Brian Massumi (Minneapolis, MN: University of Minnesota Press, 1987), pp. 167–191.

15
See Deleuze and Guattari, *A Thousand Plateaus*, pp. 167–191.

16
On the relation of iconic difference to the process of gesticulation, see Gottfried Boehm, "Die Hintergründigkeit des Zeigens: Deiktische Wurzeln des Bildes," in *Wie Bilder Sinn erzeugen: Die Macht des Zeigens* (Berlin: Berlin University Press, 2007), pp. 19–33.

the world in a different way and thereby creates a different access to it. It is in the construction of iconic difference that different configurations of meaning—what we might call the logos of images—become manifest. We are dealing with the fact that the grounding element and what is grounded develop out of each other as an event. The ground plan that iconic difference reveals outlines the task of image criticism.

Translated from German
by Anthony Mahler

Part 2
Describing and Translating

When we try to describe and interpret artifacts of the past, we easily believe that descriptive categories are neutral and that their use does not influence what we see. Every painting, every "image" seems to imply a relation between something like a "ground" and a "figure." The relation between "figure and ground" almost seems to be a general anthropological fact.[1] Yet, this volume asks whether the terms "figure" and "ground" are adequate to describe works of art from the medieval period, since there are good reasons to believe that this terminology leads to an anachronistic perception of historical paintings provoking errors on different levels, from the general appreciation of lexicography to the specific interpretation of individual artworks and their contexts. In this article, I will introduce the notion of *campus* in four steps: I will first describe a number of methodological problems; second, I will give an account of "*campus*" as opposed to "ground" in its relation to the conception of space and "*locus*" in natural philosophy that underlie pictorial practices; third, I will illustrate the medieval use of *campus* by a detailed analysis of a stained-glass window in Chartres; and fourth, I will provide a close reading of passages from Theophilus's treatise *Schedula diversarum artium* paralleling these observations.

Methodology

Many recent authors express a need to rethink the history of pictorial space, especially in its late medieval and early modern period, feeling that our current categories may not be sufficient to do justice to pre-Albertian perspective devices.[2] With the present article, I contribute to this discussion by introducing the concept of *campus* that permits a shift in the appreciation of devices

1
Gottfried Boehm, "Der Grund: Über das ikonische Kontinuum," in *Der Grund: Das Feld des Sichtbaren*, Gottfried Boehm and Matteo Burioni, eds. (Munich: Fink, 2012), pp. 28–92, with an analysis of "ground" very much indebted to twentieth-century approaches (especially Heidegger, Pollock, and others), applied to prehistoric and antique objects. In his contribution to the same volume, Matteo Burioni discusses the terminology of "ground" and "campo" in fifteenth-century treatises: "Grund und campo: Die Metaphorik des Bildgrundes in der frühen Neuzeit oder: Paolo Uccellos *Schlacht von San Romano*," ibid., pp. 94–149, especially pp. 96–99. See also Gottfried Boehm, *Wie Bilder Sinn erzeugen: Die Macht des Zeigens* (Berlin: Berlin University Press, 2007), pp. 21–28, and Gottfried Boehm, "Das Zeigen der Bilder," in *Zeigen. Die Rhetorik des Sichtbaren*, Gottfried Boehm, Sebastian Egenhofer, and Christian Spies, eds. (Munich: Fink, 2010), pp. 19–53.

creating volume and pictorial space. Some remarks on methodology will help to orient the reader in an argument admittedly complicated because it combines theoretical elements from the history of philosophy, art-historical observations, and technical information derived from written sources.

Descriptive categories are never neutral, they are part of a *Sprachspiel* (Wittgenstein) that predetermines what can be seen and said.[3] A first step in shifting a given *Sprachspiel* consists in criticizing, negating, and recombining old categories. But the negation of a given term remains dependent on its semantic horizon, and the general epistemic frame stays unchanged as long as we avoid a more fundamental analysis. My approach of *campus* is based on an adapted version of Charles Sanders Peirce's *semiotic triangle*.[4] The semiotic triangle helps handling text-image relationships because as long as this relation is considered binary, and their confrontation based on comparison, the interpretation of both, word and image, cannot outrun the limits of our own (anachronistic) preconceptions. This diagnosis rests on the semiotic triangle and the fundamental *law of the interpretant*, as we may call it. The content and meaning of a given theory has no existence in itself; its existence takes place only in the interpretant, i.e., in a reformulation or "translation" in our own words. These words should

2
See for example Hans Belting, *Florenz und Bagdad: Eine westöstliche Geschichte des Blicks* (Munich: Beck, 2008); David Summers, *Vision, Reflection, and Desire in Western Painting* (Chapel Hill, NC: University of North Carolina Press, 2007); Thomas Puttfarken, *The Discovery of Pictorial Composition* (New Haven, CT: Yale University Press, 2000), with an account of the history of art-historical discourse on pictorial spatiality, or, more recently Bertrand Prevost, *Peindre sous la lumière: Leon Battista Alberti et le moment humaniste de l'évidence* (Rennes: Presses Universitaires de Rennes, 2013), Saskia Quené, *Goldgrund und Perspektive: Fra Angelico im Glanz des Quattrocento* (Berlin/Boston: Deutscher Kunstverlag, 2022), and Thomas Le Gouge, *Schémas de cosmologie et géométrie de l'image du monde: XIIIe – XVIe siècles* (Rennes: Presses Universitaires de Rennes, forthcoming), with new material on the use of geometry in perspective before Alberti.

3
Ludwig Wittgenstein, "Über Gewißheit," in *Werkausgabe* 8 (Frankfurt am Main: Suhrkamp, 1984), especially the aphorisms on color, pp. 7–112. There has been much discussion on the relation between words and perceptional differences in linguistics. For a summary of relevant positions see Caleb Everett, *Linguistic Relativity: Evidence across Languages and Cognitive Domains* (Berlin: De Gruyter, 2013).

4
I am referring here to Peirce's discovery of the structural "threeness" of the sign relation. See Charles Sanders Peirce, *Collected Papers* II (1932), ed. Charles Hartshorne and Paul Weiss (Cambridge, MA: Harvard University Press), especially the texts under the title "Speculative Grammar," pp. 129–269.

not modernize or adapt a given theory but should take the distance between its author's and our own frame of mind into account, thus providing us with an idea of their fundamental differences.[5]

Paintings can help producing corresponding evidence, *iconic evidence*. Iconic evidence is not self-evidence; it is the result of a long discipline of looking. It necessarily implies engagement with original artifacts. Many main features of medieval imagery cannot be represented with the aim of photographs because these modern devices simply do not function in the same way as the medieval images we engage with.[6] On the other hand, iconic evidence depends on the descriptive categories we use when we *see* what we *say* and *think*. Seeing can be learned through the functional analysis of pictorial syntax,[7] based on historically informed terminologies. Rigorously defined categories of iconic syntax would constitute a relevant contribution to the dimension of the interpretant in historical hermeneutics.[8] As will be demonstrated here, medieval paintings provide us with iconic evidence about "space," "place," "figure" etc. and are able to illustrate medieval philosophical positions that are

5
In fact, the *Sprachspiel* is not a question of conviction; it is rather a frame to possible convictions, a horizon the participants normally cannot and do not overpass, a sort of *episteme* (Foucault). This does not mean that there be no communication at all between *Sprachspiele*. Art-historical research is very much about this problem. The productive nature of translation is underlined by Jacques Derrida, *Qu'est-ce au'une traduction "relevante"?* (Paris: L'Herne, 2005), without explicit reference to Walter Benjamin's fundamental essay "Die Aufgabe des Übersetzers," in *Gesammelte Schriften* IV (Frankfurt am Main: Suhrkamp, 1972), pp. 9–21.

6
This is the necessity of what has been called "historische Ausstellungspraxis." Readers are meant to examine the present contribution by confronting its results with original artifacts in autopsy.

7
We are far from disposing of a developed scientific semiology of iconicity comparable to linguistics. See the seminal book by Francis Edeline, Jean-Marie Klinkenberg, Philippe Minguet, *Traté du signe visuel* (Paris: Seuil, 1992), that does not address the problems of iconic historicity, limiting itself to the analysis of extremely reduced and simple forms of iconicity. For the notion of iconic evidence, see Gottfried Boehm, "Augenmaß. Zur Genese der ikonischen Evidenz," in *Movens Bild. Zwischen Evidenz und Affekt*, Gottfried Boehm, Birgit Mersmann, and Christian Spies, eds. (Munich: Fink, 2008), pp. 15–43. On functional deixis see Bruno Haas, "Über deiktisch-funktionale Werkanalyse: Hegel – Duchamp – Van Gogh," in *Wendepunkte: Interdisziplinäre Arbeiten zur Kulturgeschichte*, Pommersfeldener Beiträge 11, Claus Bussmann and Friedrich A. Uehlein, eds. (Würzburg: Königshausen und Neumann, 2004), pp. 139–172, and Bruno Haas, "Von der Phänomenologie zur funktionalen Deixis," in *Deixis – Zeigen – Pointing: Interdisziplinäre Perspektiven, Schriften zur Phänomenologie und Anthropologie* 4, Erik Norman Dzwiza-Ohlsen, ed. (Darmstadt: WBG, forthcoming).

8
On the theory of historical hermeneutics and anachronism, see Carlos Spoerhase, *Autorschaft und Interpretation: Methodische Grundlagen einer philologischen Hermeneutik* (Berlin: De Gruyter, 2007), with a critical review of relevant literature, especially pp. 145–157.

otherwise very difficult to access intuitively. This evidence thus contributes not only to art history, but also to the history of ideas.

As far as texts are concerned, we cannot limit ourselves to the study of written sources directly available to artisans or patrons. We must also turn to fundamental philosophical theories.[9] Philosophical texts (such as those by Albert the Great or Roger Bacon) provide us with decisive clues when it comes to the question of how language was used and understood in a given time and place. Ever since, a large part of philosophy has been concerned with the explicit analysis of the implicit structure and logic of the spoken language.[10] If we take philosophy and iconic evidence into account mutually, we are provided with a richness of information on iconic functionalities. Moreover, if we want to understand what pictorial or real "space" might be, if we want to know what is to be understood by "place" (*locus*), and if we want to interpret the horizon line in a painting in respect to "infinity," we have to cope with philosophers' use and analysis of these terms.

In this paper, my first aim is to outline a conceptual frame in which "ground" and "*campus*" can be understood in order to uncover the iconic evidence that can be obtained from a paradigmatic study of two main examples, a stained-glass window from Chartres and Theophilus's treatise *Schedula diversarum artium*. Therefore, I will try now to give an introduction to the conceptual background of pictorial *campus* in thirteenth-century painting on the basis of a very condensed summary of philosophical approaches to space and *locus* from the same period.

9
In his doctoral thesis, Thomas Le Gouge has studied the cosmological tradition and diagrams in the context of philosophical theories of space. This work permits the author to give a very new account of how cosmological diagrams actually function, when they are adapted to paintings (thirteenth to fifteenth century). Le Gouge shows that the diagrams in Sacrobosco have had a very precise use in the constitution of something like a pictorial space from the thirteenth century onward providing us with very interesting insights into the early history of "perspective."

10
This is what Robert Brandom suggests in the title of one of his major works: *Making It Explicit* (Cambridge, MA: Harvard University Press, 1994).

Defining *Campus*

As the notion of *campus* is to be profiled here against the concurrent notion of "ground," I will begin this section with a short sketch of the meaning and intrinsic logics of ground and its implicit spatiality in painting.

The descriptive category of "ground" does not emerge before the sixteenth century. The ground is then linked to the technique of *imprimatura*, a mostly brownish preparation used in order to unify the chromatic atmosphere and to produce the projective spaces typical of tonal painting.[11] When this ground becomes Wassily Kandinsky,[12] its originally spatial character has vanished. But Kandinsky's *Grundfläche* does not turn back to a state of affairs prior to the elaboration of ground in the late sixteenth century. In his time, the notion of ground had acquired an unrivalled multiplicity of meanings not least because of its massive introduction in vernacular German philosophy.[13] Gottfried Boehm's interest in "*Grund*," I believe, can be understood on behalf of this modern development, and his concern with "gesture" reflects his uninterrupted interest in the art of Paul Klee.

11
The structure of this kind of "grounding" is linked to what I have called the "ground chord," *Grundakkord*, G, the unity of three related color shades; see *Die ikonischen Situationen* (Paderborn: Fink, 2015), ch. 3, especially p. 164. By the term "tonal painting," I designate a particular functional organization of color, typical of European painting in the seventeenth century and based on the use of essentially three "pure" or "primary" colors, their mixtures, and of brown instead of gray as the chromatic center. What follows is a short summary and reformulation of an argument developed in chapter 3 on projective imagery and its structure in seventeenth-century painting. See also the chapter "Lineage of a Paradigm: 'Figure and Ground' in Encyclopedic Sources" by Veronica Peselmann in this volume.

12
Kandinsky occupies a very important place in modern art theory; he combined an outstanding pictorial practice with an intense pedagogic and literary activity. I here refer especially to his *Punkt und Linie zu Fläche* (*Point and Line to Plane*), first published in the *Bauhausbücher* IX (1926). On the historical context of Kandinsky's theory, see especially the very well informed Nadja Podzemskaia, *Colore, simbolo, immagine: Origine della teoria di Kandinsky* (Florence: Alinea, 2000).

13
Essentially since Kant's decision to publish in German (1781). Important formulations introduced by Schelling since his *Untersuchungen über das Wesen der menschlichen Freiheit* as early as 1809, *Werke* 4, ed. Schröter (Munich: Beck, 1925), pp. 223–308. For further information on the history of *Grund* since Leibniz, look especially the influential essay by Martin Heidegger *Der Satz vom Grund* (Pfullingen: Neske, 1957).

To seize the specific difference between these two concepts, it will be enough to go back to the origin of ground in European painting as observable in seventeenth-century painting and documented in Carel van Mander's *Schilderboek*.[14] Van Mander uses the word "ground" first and foremost to speak about foreground, middle-ground, and background in landscape painting. Ground emerges whenever a figure is detached from a surface. Between this figure and the ground, there is a distance and a space that has no existence outside the image and constitutes, thus, what we call a "pictorial space." Pictorial and real space are, therefore, *incommensurate*, i.e., they have no common measure, so that pictorial space has no limit in real space. In this sense, it is structurally unlimited, i.e., *infinite*. To illustrate this point, let us remember one of Claude Lorrain's classical landscape paintings. Even though we do not see what is behind the far mountains, we intuitively feel that there is still space; and although the frame cuts our vision on all sides, we feel that the imaginary landscape continues. The mountains are material obstacles in space, limiting our vision, but space itself is no material object. Wherever between figure and ground there appears some pictorial space incommensurate with real space, it will be intrinsically infinite and experienced as a reality distinct from corporeal limits and objects placed within, even though the place actually represented may be extremely narrow. The gap between pictorial and real space is marked by the *frame*.

Depth in a pictorial space based on a ground has specific characteristics. The ground of a figure is always *relative* to an observer's standpoint, it is *remote*. Remoteness is necessarily defined in relation to a beholder and to *hicceitas* as his special mode of being-in-space.[15] The "here" correlative to pictorial remoteness

14
Carel van Mander, *Het Schilderboek* (Haarlem: Passchier van Wesbusch, 1604), especially ch. 8. A thorough investigation on his use of the term would show important differences from the use in later painting and writing, his "ground" being linked to the peculiar technique of *imprimatura* and the ground chord, but this cannot be developed here.

15
Hicceitas is derived from latin: *hic*, "here." The logics of remoteness (*Ent-fernung*) and *hicceitas* as fundamental structures of "space" have been analyzed by Heidegger in *Sein und Zeit* (Halle/Saale: Niemeyer, 1927), and later by Maurice Merleau-Ponty in his *Le visible et l'invisible* (Paris: Gallimard, 1964). Remoteness is defined only in relation to a "here" impossible to situate in a coordinate system. Whenever we try to situate a point in space, we treat it as a "there" (remote). "Here" is not a point in space, but the structural correlate of remoteness. Remoteness in this sense is a structure of pictorial spaces as can be realized in a ground.

never does coincide with the beholder's real standpoint, it is the imaginary place the beholder is invited to project himself or herself in, when confronted with the remoteness of pictorial (tonal) grounds.[16] In the Lorrain painting, we are projected into an arcadian landscape or antique city. The very standpoint of the beholder is never directly represented; it is always located a little bit in front of the painting's soil. Whatever can be represented is "there," remote; the beholder's "here" is the logically necessary correlate of remoteness, a structure of seventeenth-century imagery and ground.

So, the main characteristics of ground in pictorial space can be summed up as follows: 1) There is a distance between figure and ground *incommensurate to real space*, so that we speak of *pictorial space* as an (imaginary) entity on its own. 2) As incommensurate, pictorial space is not limited in real space; it is unlimited, *infinite*.[17] 3) As pictorial space continues even outside the limits of the picture plane, the gap between the two is marked by a *frame*. No object inside pictorial space can reach out of this frame.[18] 4) There is a *radical difference* between space itself and the corporeal things that exist in space. 5) In pictorial spaces, things always appear *remote* in respect to imaginary "*hic*." In the imagination, the beholder is *projected* to this place.

Infinity appears as a structure of pictorial spaces inasmuch as they are incommensurate with real space and thus cannot be limited in real space. In this sense, spatial infinity is specifically an imaginary structure. However, we intuitively attribute the

16
In certain cases of decorative painting, however, the projective standpoint can coincide with the real one (seventeenth century, Andrea Pozzo), but this case can be understood as a special application of the same paradigm of great interest, but too complicated to be explained here.

17
Argument used by Kant in the *Critique of Pure Reason*. I do not consider here the relative finitude of non-Euclidian spaces not known before the eighteenth century. Space as a metrical system has a structural relation to infinity. When we learn that medieval thought does not accept infinity in nature, this has very much to be nuanced as there are several exceptions (Johannes Jandunus, Nicolas of Cues, the "calculators" etc.). The opposition between acceptance or not of infinity is not sufficient to characterize medieval natural philosophy and theory of space/*locus*. My point is that before coping with the difficult questions of infinity, we have to elaborate on the vocabulary of space, site, place etc. and their philosophical background.

18
In decorative painting, figures sometimes reach out of a frame, but this is possible only because in these cases, pictorial space continues in the decorative parts surrounding the frames. About illusionism see also note 16.

aforementioned characteristics of pictorial space to real space: infinity, difference between space itself, and the corporeal beings inside space, remoteness, and *hicceitas* as structures of being-in-space. As we will see, these seemingly necessary or universal characteristics of space shape our appreciation of medieval painting, but do not respond properly to medieval art and thought.

At first sight, *campus* does not seem to say anything substantially different from ground or surface. A *campus* is a plane on which to place a figure (*figura, imago*) thus creating some kind of pictorial space. If we turn to medieval natural philosophy, however, we notice that there is no word for what we call "space" today. The Latin word *spatium* designates a distance, but not space itself.[19] As we have seen, space is something separate from the spatial: it is structurally infinite, so that a pictorial space is necessarily incommensurable with real space, necessitating a form of framing to cover the inevitable hiatus.

None of these necessary implications of space prove to be valid for premodern and early modern imagery. Medieval natural philosophy considers space to be finite and never void (*horror vacui*). Writers never refer to *space* (i.e., a system of coordinates), but exclusively to "place," i.e., τόπος or *locus*. When we speak of "space" and its metrical characteristics, medieval philosophers speak of *loci* and their relations. "Space" is an abstract term in itself, indifferent to the fact of being void or plain. *Locus*, in contrast, is defined as the place of something and therefore cannot even be conceived as being devoid of anything. The Aristotelian *horror vacui* thus is not just a hypothesis to be proved or rejected by empirical experimentation. On the basis of some Aristotelian primary assumptions, its contrary would just be self-contradictory. There cannot be a distance or a place (τόπος, *locus*) in itself without being the place of something.

19
This has been correctly noted by Rudolf Kuhn in his important book *Komposition und Rhythmus* (Berlin: De Gruyter, 1980); also: Rudolf Kuhn, *On Composition as Method and Topic* (Frankfurt am Main: Lang, 2000). Since then, Thomas Puttfarken has pointed out the anachronistic character of most modern approaches to Giotto, but without mentioning Kuhn's historically well-informed study (Puttfarken, *The Discovery of Pictorial Composition*, p. 842), with instructive remarks on "space" and "projection" as such (pp. 26–29). Even though Puttfarken tries to enrich our conception of "pictorial space" with a renewed attention to the spectator's place, he misses the more fundamental difference between "space" and *spatium* as underlined by Kuhn.

The Aristotelian and scholastic conception of *locus* instead of space confronts us with severe difficulties. Whoever wants to grasp the profound gap between modern and medieval conceptions should turn to the two first books of Bernardino Telesio's *De rerum natura*, a highly important sixteenth-century treatise on space and *locus*.[20] Telesio tries to establish a modern conception of space as independent of what it contains. As he writes in a context of late Aristotelianism, he unfolds a complicated argument to explain a point that may seem trivial to modern readers; the difficulty being to understand why the argument could have appeared so awfully contra-intuitive at the time.[21]

Before Telesio, space was considered in terms of "place," *locus*, or τόπος. There is no pictorial space, there are only pictorial *loci*. The profoundness of a painting must not be conceived in terms of a three-dimensional pictorial space structurally incommensurable with "real space," but as a place (*locus*) within a real constellation of real places, apt to contain a "figure" of limited magnitude. Thus, there is no need and no possibility of a subjective projection of the beholder into pictorial space. The image refers directly to the beholder in his or her corporeal presence in the same real space, i.e., constellation of places. In this sense and compared to seventeenth-century illusionism, the medieval image possesses a superior force and capacity of suggesting presence.

The figure is usually the image of a human being: in the language of natural philosophy, their detachable *species*. The *species* is to be considered, first, as an authentic part of being itself, the visible form of a saintly person for example. Second, the same *species* can be detached from the real body, transformed into a more "spiritual" entity able to pass through the "transparent medium" (air or water), and finally entering vision. Natural philosophers then speak of "visible species," as there are other kinds of *species* as well. This ontological transformation of *species visibiles* from a property of a body to an entity freely passing through the medium

20 Bernardino Telesio, *De natura iuxta propria principia libri II* (Naples: Salviano, 1565). One may still consult the masterly study by Alexandre Koyré, *From the Closed World to the Infinite Universe* (Baltimore: Johns Hopkins University Press, 1954).

21 Our own preconception of space is much more contradictory than usually recognized. As Kant points out in the *Critique of Pure Reason*, space as such cannot be considered as something different from an image without reality in itself (see *Kritik der reinen Vernunft*, 2nd ed. [Riga: Hartknoch, 1787], p. 182).

is realized by light (*lumen*), "*actus* of the transparent medium" as the Aristotelian commentators put it, so that air is full of different *species* that nevertheless do not hamper each other while progressing. This spiritual nature of *species* makes their appearance at another place possible, where they can be fixated by the craftsman to remain visible on the *campus*.[22] The *campus* itself is a *locus* quite much like other *loci*, a place between real places, peculiar only in respect to the fact that it is apt to receive a visible *species*.[23] What is called "pictorial space" in these historical contexts is not incommensurable with real space, but rather part of it.

The premodern *campus* is not considered a plane or surface waiting for a mark, but rather a limited place and *locus* ready to accommodate an image or figure. This figure has a certain volume, and so does the *locus* where it will literally take its place, somewhat like in a niche. The architectural niche receiving the body of a sculpture can, therefore, be seen as a model for painting throughout the period under examination.[24] As the *locus* and *campus* of the image is well integrated in the intricate system of *loci* constituting reality, its size is rather limited. To give an example: if the image is placed in the *campus* of a stained-glass window, its size is given by the size of the opening of that window. As we will see, this is the reason why painters of the thirteenth and fourteenth centuries avoid representing distant objects. There is literally not enough space (*spatium*) in the *campus*.

22
On the notion of *species*, see Katherine H. Tachau, "Seeing as Action and Passion in the Thirteenth and Fourteenth Centuries," in *The Mind's Eye: Art and Theological Argument in the Middle Ages*, Anne-Marie Bouché and Jeffrey F. Hamburger, eds. (Princeton, NJ: Princeton University Press, 2006), pp. 336–359, and her still fundamental study, *Vision and Certitude in the Age of Ockham: Optics, Epistemology and the Foundations of Semantics 1250–1345* (Leiden: Brill, 1988). See also Leen Spruit, *Species intelligibilis* 1, *Classical Roots and Medieval Discussions: From Perception to Knowledge* (Leiden: Brill, 1994).

23
For an interesting theoretical account of *locus* as such in medieval art, see Jérôme Baschet, "L'image et son lieu: quelques remarques générales," in *L'image et son lieu: Fonctions dans l'espace sacré et structuration de l'espace cultuel*, Eric Palazzo, ed. (Turnhout: Brepols, 2011), pp. 179–204.

24
Christopher Lakey, *Sculptural Seeing: Relief, Optics, and the Rise of Perspective in Medievl Italy* (New Haven, CT: Yale University Press, 2018), pp. 102–103, ch. 3, "The Geometry of Vision," pp. 78–119, gives an interesting account of the spatiality of iconic situations in Italian Romanesque sculpture with much new insight into the organization of the beholder space in respect to the visual effect *in situ* of sculpture.

As has been shown, modern space is conceived in terms of metrical continuity. But *loci* are conceived in terms of mutual countenance. One *locus* is contained in the other. While the *campus* is contained in the niche, the niche is in the portal, the portal in the larger architecture, and so on. Every *locus* is a body containing another body. The figure as a *species* can be detached from its actual material body and traverse the transparent medium. It can enter a new place, a *campus* and be fixed there by the artist. The specificity of *campus* is that it receives no ordinary corporeal objects, but *species*. The relation between figure and *campus* is essentially the relation between two bodies, of which one can contain the other. This is why the *campus* should not be identified too quickly with a surface or a plane, although technically, a surface may sometimes be used and function as a *campus*. As they remain relatively independent from one another, the image can easily exceed the boundaries of its *campus*.

Let me now briefly illustrate the described figure-*campus* relation. Valuable examples can be found in stained-glass windows representing an individual saint [fig. 191]. The color surrounding the figure suggests a certain intrinsic depth as it is made of glass and is thus transparent. The *campus* here functions as a light color volume able to receive the *species* in its three-dimensional corporeality. Here, the figure of Saint Catherine is placed in a blue *campus*.[25] On the photograph, we do not have the impression of intrinsic depth, but the original glasses do produce this effect, although the figure is not entirely contained in the blue as it exceeds the framing. As we have discussed, this is not unusual. The idea of *campus* as *locus* and thus a certain intrinsic depth and corporeality is always presupposed. The *campus* almost becomes an artificial gemstone, intrinsically translucid and crystalline.[26]

25
The Cologne window is usually dated end of first quarter of the thirteenth century. Similar examples in Strasbourg Cathedral, bay S I, 1240–1245, the prophets from the clerestory in Lyon Cathedral or the older clerestory windows of Troyes Cathedral (for example bay 207 dating from the first decoration campaign of the cathedral around 1228).

26
See Albertus Magnus, *De mineralibus*, especially book I, ch. 2. See also the Salomo window in Strasbourg Cathedral, north transept (Trans n III), end of the twelfth century, or the roses from the south transept (S E and O). In the well-preserved panel of the seven branched candelabrum, the main object is placed on a red *campus* surrounded by a blue border with a very characteristic effect of relative independency and corporeality.

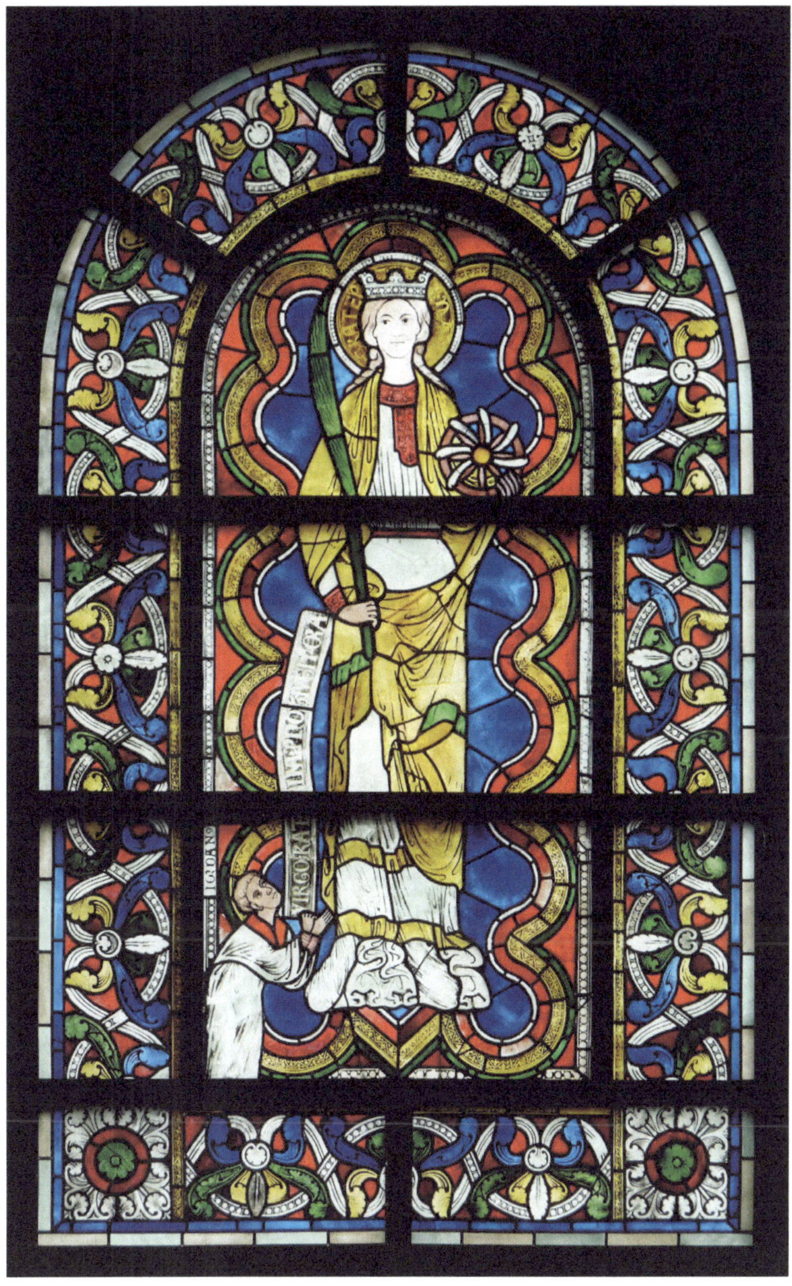

St. Catherine with Donor Figure, ca. 1220, stained glass and lead.
St. Kunibert, northern transept, Cologne.

Fig. 191

In older examples, figures often seem to float as they do not rest on a firm soil; an impression that is the consequence of anachronistic viewing rather than of intentional craftsmanship. The figure does not "float," it is just posited in a *campus*. Another solution is found in the Bourges Cathedral, e.g., bay 202 [fig. 193]. Here, the *campus* is framed by a rudimentary architectural structure. This framing of *campi* develops during the following decades, but remains a secondary feature even where it is prominently elaborated. It always serves the main structure of a figure in a *campus*, as can be observed in the prophet series of Saint Urbain in Troyes [fig. 194].[27] In the clerestory windows in Cologne Cathedral [fig. 195], the architectural setting is even more developed, but remains accidental; it is still a decorated *campus*.

The *campus* as *locus* is not a phenomenon found in stained-glass windows alone. In fact, we are describing a fundamental feature of premodern imagery, which can be seen in enamels from the twelfth and thirteenth centuries such as the Eilbertus portative altar in Berlin showing a conception very similar to contemporary stained-glass windows with a *campus* as *locus* receiving figures that at the same time exceed the *campus* [fig. 196]. Under good light conditions, enamels present effects of transparency quite similar to stained glass.

Although realized with different materials, manuscript miniatures imply quite the same relation between figure and *campus* [fig. 197].[28] Here, the apostles are quite typically placed in front of a green *campus* overlapping its blue border. These examples correspond, once again, strikingly to glass painting from the same period [fig. 198].[29] In all cases, the *campus* is

27
The comparison between the original glasses of 1270 and Didron's Abraham from 1879 shows that Didron naturally has no intuition any more of the specific spatiality of *campus* as *locus*; his blue field is just a schematic background. This difference is, however, almost not apparent in the photographical reproduction.

28
See Paris, BnF lat. 17325, fol. 28r, dating from 1120–1130 and compared by Andrea Worm in her monographic study to the Gerlach window in Münster (*Das Pariser Perikopenbuch und die Anfänge der romanischen Buchmalerei an Rhein und Weser* [Berlin: Deutscher Verlag für Kunstwissenschaft, 2008, p. 227]) and other manuscripts from the middle Rhine such as the lost gospel of Lippoldsberg, the prayer book of Hildegard, Munich, Clm 935, the gospel from St. Pantaleon in Cologne (Historisches Archiv, W 312a, fol. 110v, our fig. 197) etc., with blue, green, and gold leaf *campi*.

29
However, there is no good reason to believe that the idea of a *campus* as (corporeal) *locus* was first developed in this medium, as our examples seem to suggest.

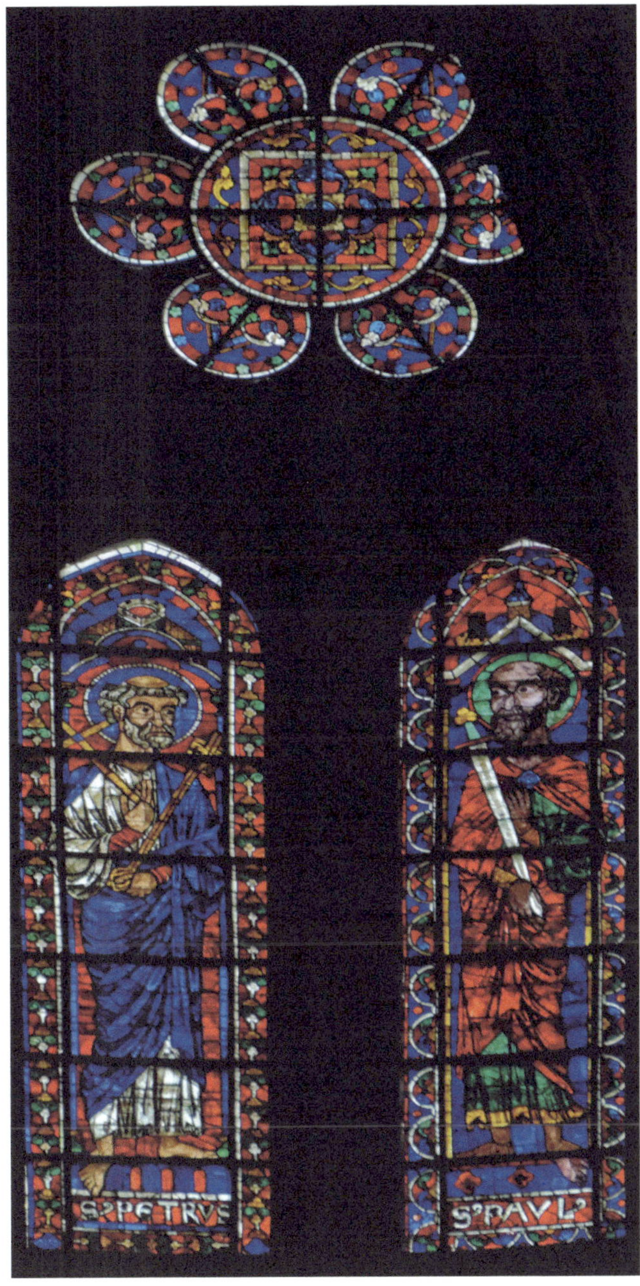

St. Peter and St. Paul, ca. 1220–1225, stained glass and lead. Bourges Cathedral, choir clerestory bay 202, Bourges.

Fig. 193

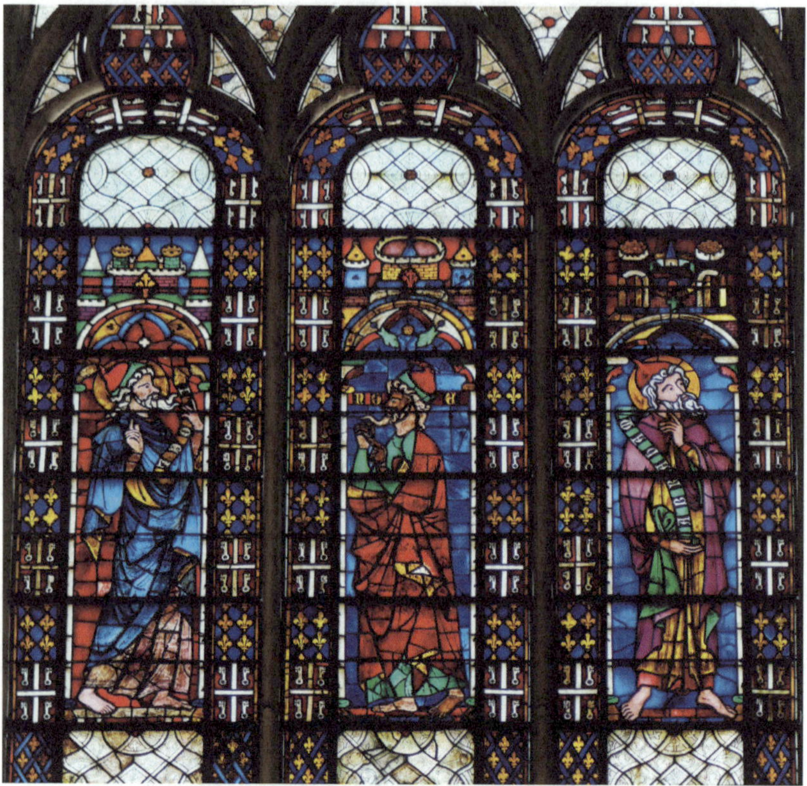

Joel, Noah and Abraham, ca. 1270, stained glass and lead.
Saint Urbain, choir clerestory, bay 101, Troyes.

Fig. 194

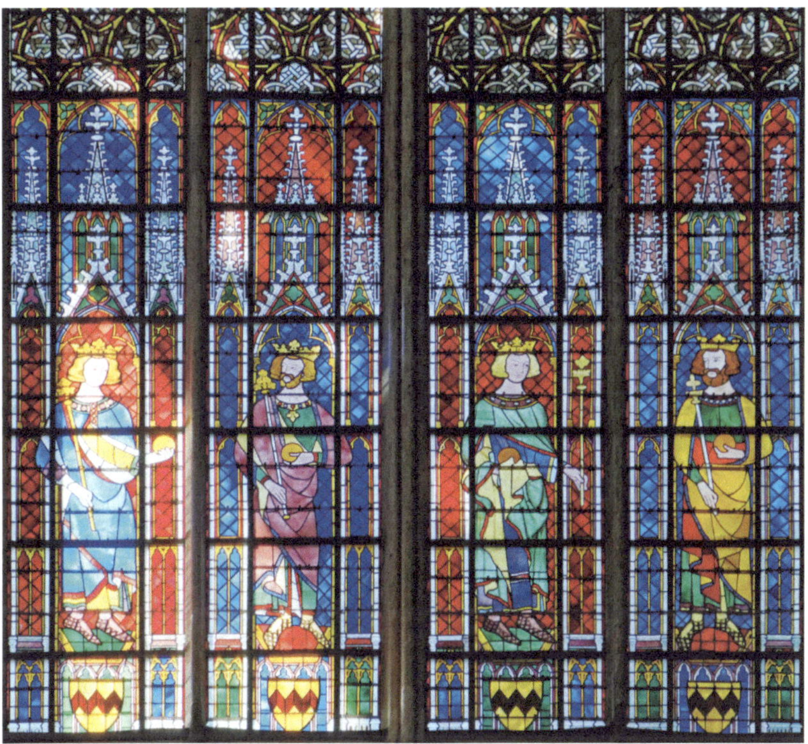

Cycle of Kings, ca. 1310, stained glass and lead.
Cologne Cathedral, choir clerestory, Cologne.

Fig. 195

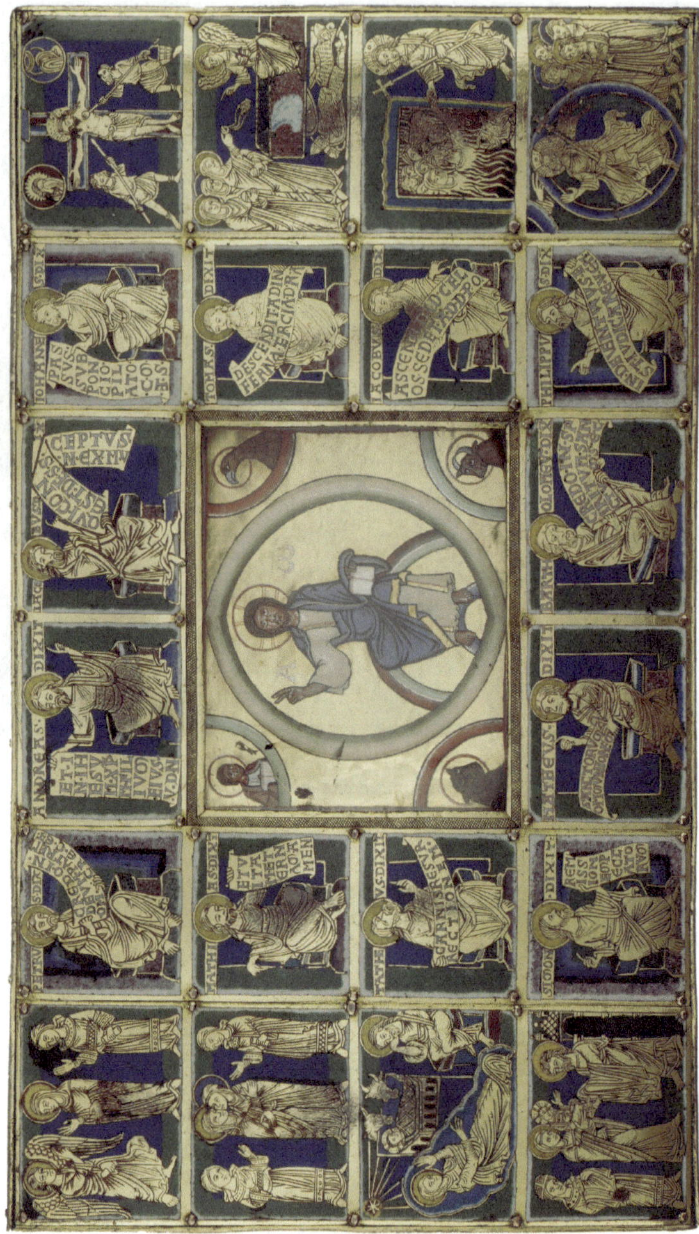

Mensa of the Eilbertus Portable Altar, ca. 1150,
enamel champlevé, rock crystal, and painting on parchment, 13.3 × 35.7 × 20.9 cm.
Kunstgewerbemuseum, inv. nr. W 11, Berlin.

Fig. 196

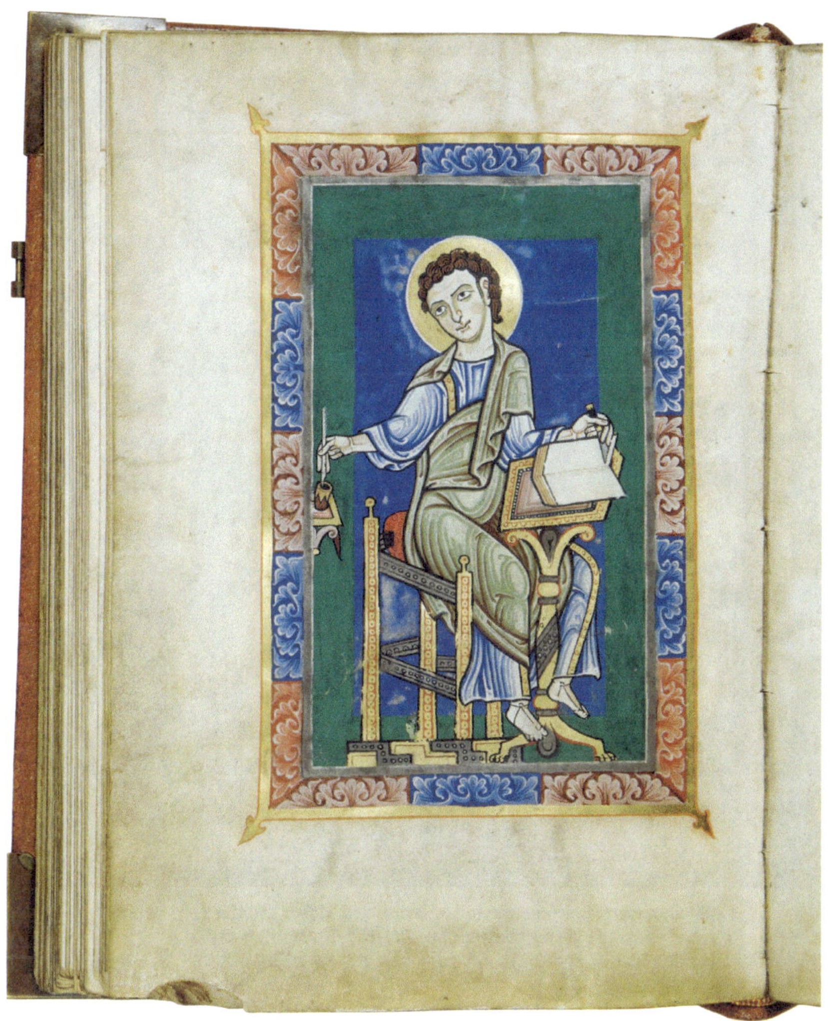

St. Luke, Gospels from St. Pantaleon, ca. 1140, parchment, 30.7 × 21.3 cm.
Cologne, Historisches Archiv, inv. nr. W 312 a, fol. 110v.

Fig. 197

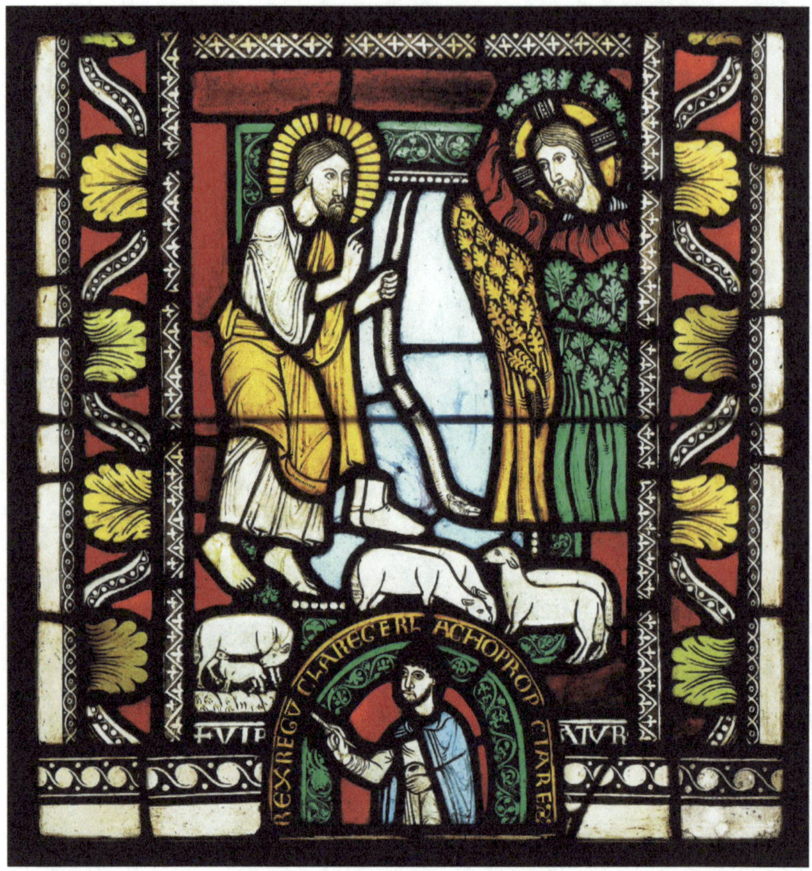

Master Gerlachus, Self-portrait of Gerlachus and Moses and the Burning Bush, ca. 1150–60, stained glass and lead, 51.8 × 49.8 cm. LWL-Landesmuseum für Kunst und Kulturgeschichte, inv. nr. L-1002 LM, Münster.

Fig. 198

never to be seen or understood as a background, but as a *locus* large enough to receive the three-dimensional *species* of a figure.

As the modern conception of space linked to the phenomenon of "ground" and "pictorial space" in the sense specified above emerges in philosophy only from Bernardino Telesio onward, it seems to be worth considering that late medieval and early modern painting may have remained in touch with the logics of *campus* as *locus* well beyond the reutilization of linear perspective.[30] In stained-glass windows from the fourteenth and fifteenth century, we can easily trace the same sensibility. Heavy curtains are used to build something we would be tempted to consider a background, but contemporary viewers must still have appreciated them as *campi*. In the Annunciation of the Behaim window in Nuremberg [fig. 200], the main figures' profile in the red *campus* of a curtain is backed with an architecture that has, in fact, only a decorative function. The same curtain motif with a very similar pictorial function is found in the famous Annunciation window in Bourges Cathedral, painted for Jacques Coeur [fig. 201]. We may even add Grünewald's version of the same topic in the Colmar altarpiece and many other paintings, such as Rogier van der Weyden's Crucifixion from the Philadelphia Museum of Art [fig. 202]. In this late painting, Rogier goes back to the fundamentals of his art. The red curtains are still conceived as *campi* and *loci*, the representation of "naturalistic" details constitutes only a secondary finishing.

The Syntax of *Campus* in a Narrative Stained-glass Window

The interpretation of *campus* as *locus* does not only modify the way we see and enjoy medieval artifacts in general, but deepens the appreciation and interpretation of singular works of art and their allegorical sense. The efficacious employment of the *campus* in relation to figure in a narrative context at the beginning of the thirteenth century is, therefore, the topic of the following paragraphs. The *campus*-figure entanglement proves to be an important feature of narration that enabled artists to depict human relations and actions.

30
Cf. lastly Quené, *Goldgrund und Perspektive*, and further bibliography in note 2.

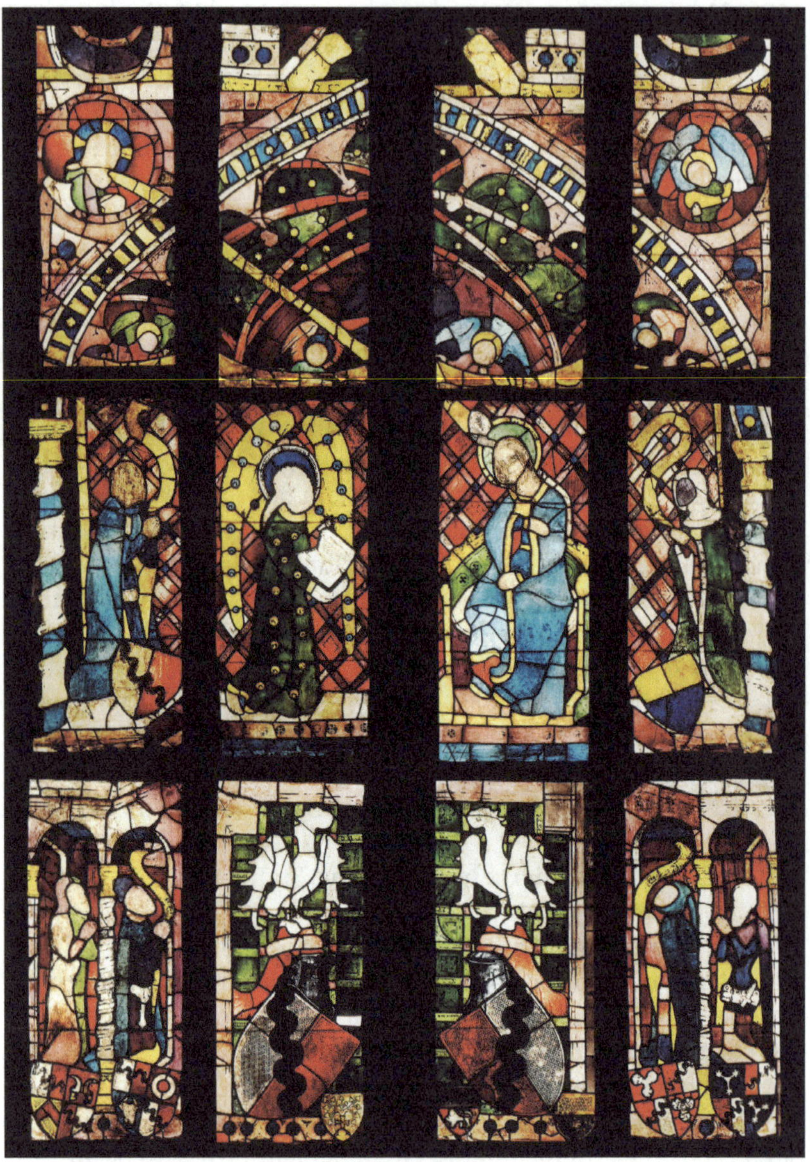

Annunciation with Donors, so-called Behaim Window, ca. 1380–1390, stained glass and lead.
St. Sebaldus, Nuremberg.

Fig. 200

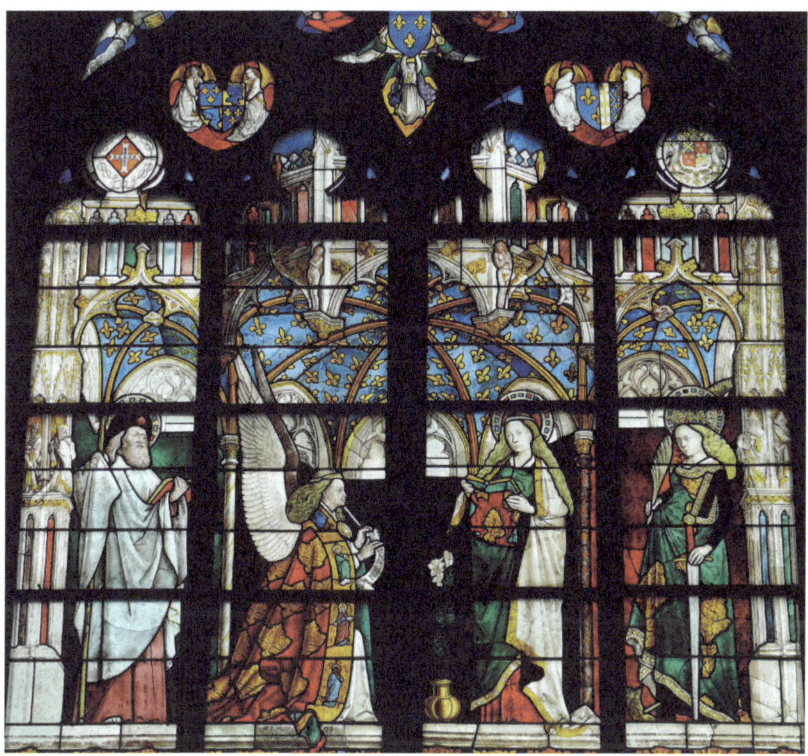

Annunciation with St. James the Great and St. Catherine, ca. 1450, stained glass and lead. Bourges Cathedral, chapel of Jacques Coeur, Bourges.

Fig. 201

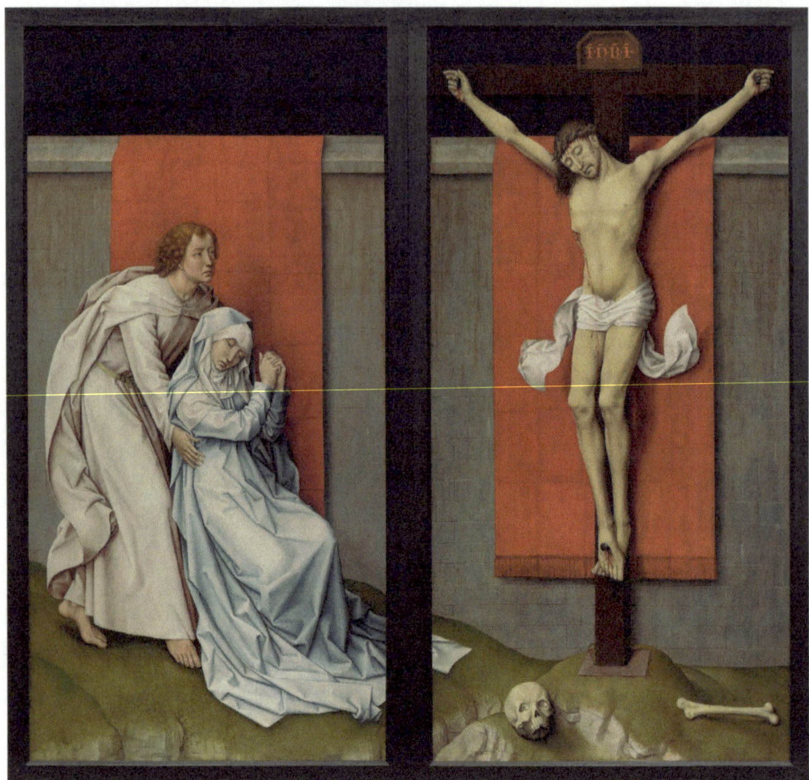

Rogier van der Weyden, *The Crucifixion, with the Virgin and Saint John the Evangelist Mourning*, ca. 1460, oil on panel, 180.3 × 92.2 cm (left panel) and 180.3 × 92.5 cm (right panel). Philadelphia Museum of Art, inv. nr. John G. Johnson Collection, 1917, Cat. 335.334, Philadelphia.

Fig. 202

In the Joseph window of Chartres Cathedral in bay 41 [fig. 204],[31] the *campi* of all narrative scenes are blue and the figures are mostly situated inside the *campi*, now and then exceeding them. The blue *campi* all suggest a crystalline volume apt to receive the *species* of figures in their corporeal three-dimensionality. Inside these blue *campi*, there are several smaller red *campi* serving as a *locus* of reference for a given figure inside the larger blue *campus*. These red *campi* represent doors or doorways. In the following, we will consider the use of these red *campi* in respect to the image or figure they refer to. This will permit us to discover a much more specific and less universal or fundamental use of *campus* and show that a conceptually rigorous use of *campus* (instead of ground) does not restrict the possibilities of empirical observation but enlarges them with new perspectives on the way medieval images can produce sense. Let us, therefore, turn to the biblical narrative of Joseph leaving his father's home, his arrest, and selling as an enslaved person to the Egyptians, his misfortunes, imprisonment, and liberation until the arrival of his brothers, and finally the reunion with his father.[32]

In scene 3,[33] Joseph's dream is foretelling his future advantage over his brothers [fig. 205]. There is a red *campus* on the right, another one behind his head on the left. Both areas are well distinguished, two *loci* or places Joseph may belong to. The aspect of repeated relocating is underlined by the *campus* behind his feet.[34] Joseph will have to use his feet to travel far away and will

31
Colette Manhès-Deremble, *Les vitreaux narratifs de la cathédrale de Chartres: Etude iconographique*, Corpus vitrearum, France, études 2 (Paris: Le léopard d'or, 1992). For a more comprehensive study on the iconography of the Joseph narration in thirteenth-century French narrative cycles, see Marie-Dominique Gauthier-Walter, *L'Histoire de Joseph* (Bern: Lang, 2003), especially pp. 165–183 on Chartres, and pp. 154–165 on the Bourges Cathedral series.

32
For more on the iconography see Gauthier-Walter, *L'Histoire de Joseph*.

33
Numbering as in the *corpus vitrearum*.

34
The use of prepositions like "behind" may surprise here. Didn't we suggest that a *campus* is a *locus* the figure can be placed in? In what precise sense can we speak of a *campus* behind the figure? If we understand the logics of *campus* as a pictorial function as related to scholastic topology (the science of *topos* and spatial relations), prepositions can change their meaning. Joseph's *campus* is behind the figure not because it functions as a ground, but quite simply because the figure is not inside this *campus* but slightly beside and in front of it. There is, therefore, a relative freedom in determining the relation between a *campus* and an image in the thirteenth century. As I have shown elsewhere, this rather loose connection between image and *campus* survives in graphic syntax at least until the sixteenth century.

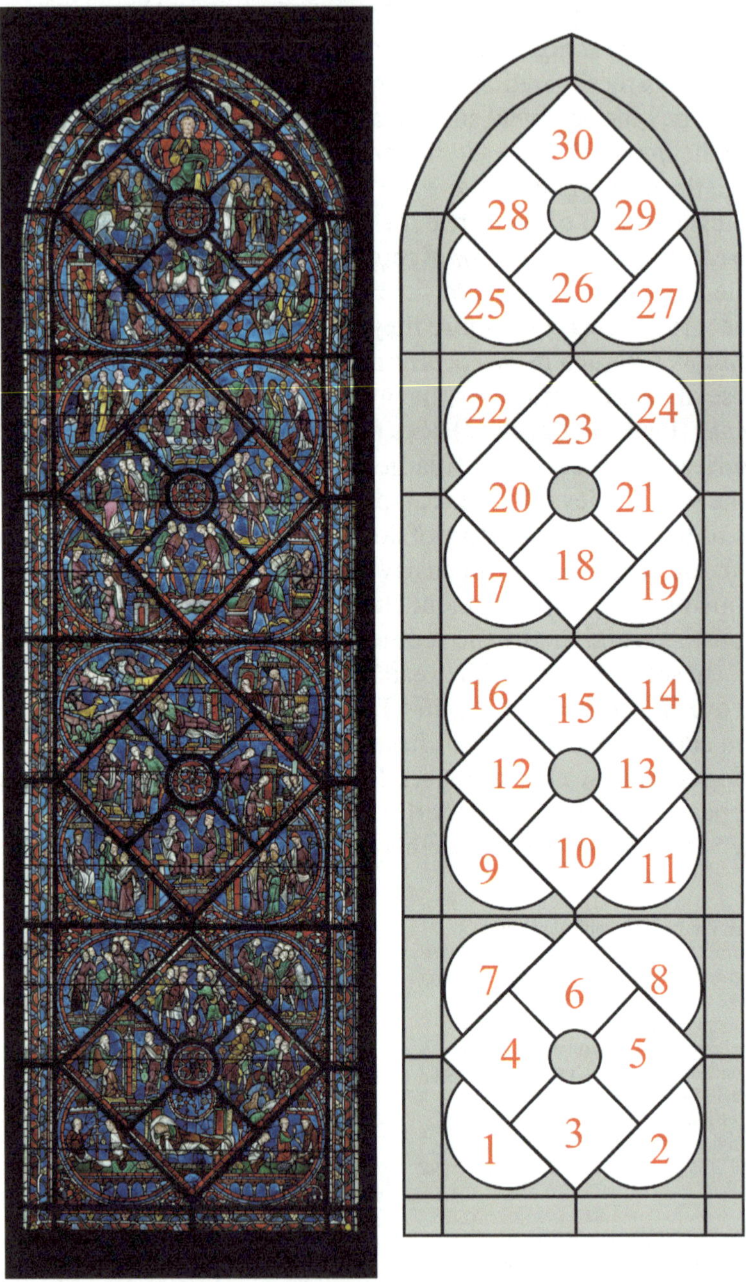

Lancet Window with the Life of Joseph, early 13th century, stained glass and lead. Chartres Cathedral, northern aisle of the nave, bay 41, Chartres.

Fig. 204

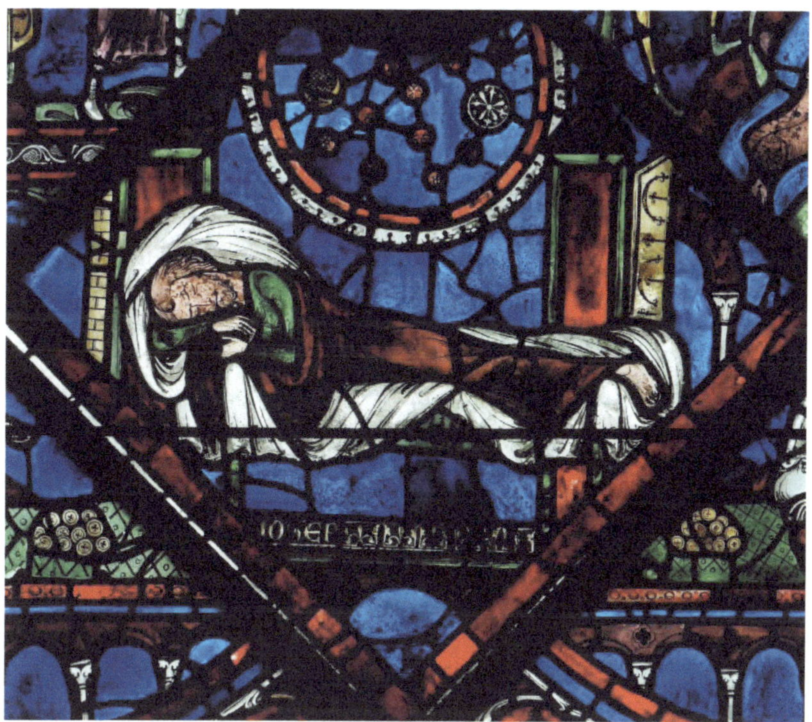

Scene 3 from the Life of Joseph, early 13th century, stained glass and lead.
Chartres Cathedral, northern aisle of the nave, bay 41, Chartres.

Fig. 205

make others travel as well. His story is about separation and loss, reunion and glory. Joseph's head, on the other hand, is isolated in a glorious stature, relating to his inner value and vision, symbolized by the dream depicted amid this scene. The two *campi* distinguish these two aspects of Joseph's story.

In scene 4 depicting Jacob sending Joseph to his brothers, the seated figure of Jacob is placed in a blue arched *campus* and appears as the main person, the one who commands [fig. 207]. Joseph is leaving and is, on the other hand, placed in a blue rectangular *campus*. The arch gives stability and frontality to Jacob who is, in fact, represented *en profil*. Joseph's move to the right interprets his blue *campus* as a *locus* designed to contain a moving image, moving from the left to the right. However, his brothers are waiting for him in a separate *campus*. Nothing here, therefore, suggests a specific distance between Jacob's house and the pastureland, but we understand that the scene on the right (scene 5) indicates Joseph's destination. A tiny red *campus* is placed between father and son. It appertains to Joseph, not to Jacob since Joseph is leaving while Jacob is staying.

The tiny red *campus*, therefore, marks a *locus* in which the figure of Joseph had been located. While he has left the place, the place itself still persists where it was before. The distance between the red *campus* and the corresponding figure of Joseph, therefore, helps expressing the departure of Joseph. The *campus* functions as the place where a given figure (a *species*) really *is* (and does not only seem to be). While the figure of Joseph now *is* in the blue *campus* in scene 5, he *was* in the red *campus*. The distance between scenes 4 and 5 do not (naively) represent a larger distance; there is no need to represent this distance. In fact, the image and *species* of Joseph has been fixed in one *campus*, and the images and *species* of his brothers have been determined in another.

However, the *campi* are brought together because Joseph is still attached to his brethren while leaving his father, they might even be waiting for him. When we think of something absent, we can present it to our attention by making an image, by enclosing the *species* of a person in a *campus*. This proximity is suggested by the *campus* in front of him. What is depicted here is, therefore, not the distance between Joseph and his brothers, but the

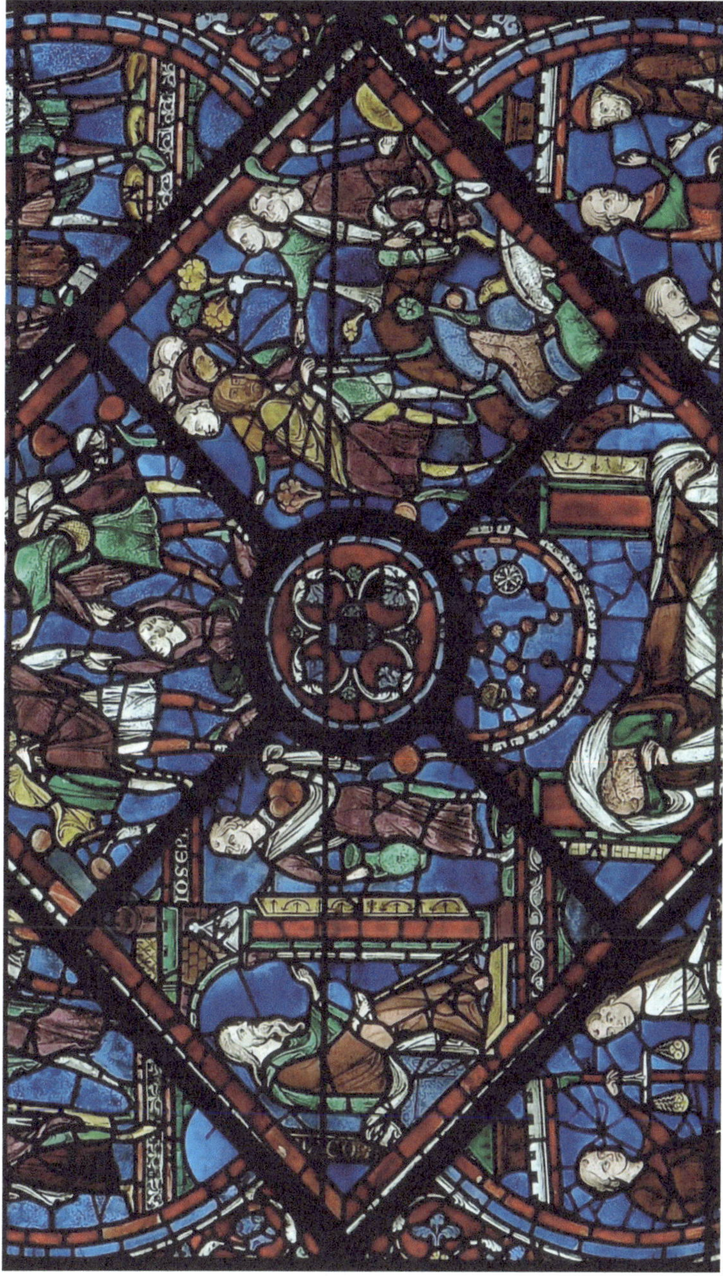

Scenes 4 and 5 from the Life of Joseph, early 13th century, stained glass and lead. Chartres Cathedral, northern aisle of the nave, bay 41, Chartres.

Fig. 207

proximity in thought. Nonetheless, the proximity is so telling because we know there is a distance and there will be still other, even greater distances later. However, we can be "near" to something or someone far away in space due to the fact that our mind can be absorbed with them. This kind of proximity has been discussed by various philosophers around 1900, like Henri Bergson, in contrast to surrounding positivist convictions. Yet, in medieval imagery the logical articulation between proximity and distance is implied by the way images work. In a *campus* as *locus*, long distances can only be symbolized because there is not enough place inside any *campus* to represent them.

In scene 9, Joseph is sold to "Butifar" (according to the inscription) and accused of adultery [fig. 209]. Here, the small red *campus* on the right indicates the door Joseph crossed when arriving at Butifar's throne, while the *campus* on the left in scene 11 represents the door through which he would like to leave in order to not be unjustly accused in front of his master. The red *campi* serve as references specifically to the figure of Joseph even though he is not materially present in them.

In scene 10, Butifar's wife is depicted trying to seduce Joseph. Here, the red *campus* door is found on the right. This indicates that it is not Joseph, but Butifar's wife who took the initiative. There is a difference of authority between her and Joseph. She is the mistress in her home, and he is the servant. We do not see her coming in from the right and addressing Joseph; the reading direction from left to right suggests otherwise.[35] In controlling the door, her *campus*, she does not give way to him whose gestures show his confusion.

In scene 12, Butifar sends Joseph to prison. There is no red doorway here as there was in scene 4 depicting Joseph being sent to his brothers by his father [fig. 207]. The two departure scenes are admirably differentiated. In scene 4, the very core of separation is represented and expressed by the red *campus* and door between

35
The reading direction does not automatically dominate the narrative structure, as we can observe in scene 9, where Joseph is presented in front of Butifar. Joseph is entering the scene from the red *campus* on the right. A more complete analysis of narrative devices would have to cope with other elements than the *campus*-image relationship. Still, we note that this relationship is always quite suggestive, even though the precise reasons for this might not always be obvious. Their elucidation would presuppose a functional analysis of graphic and pictorial syntax.

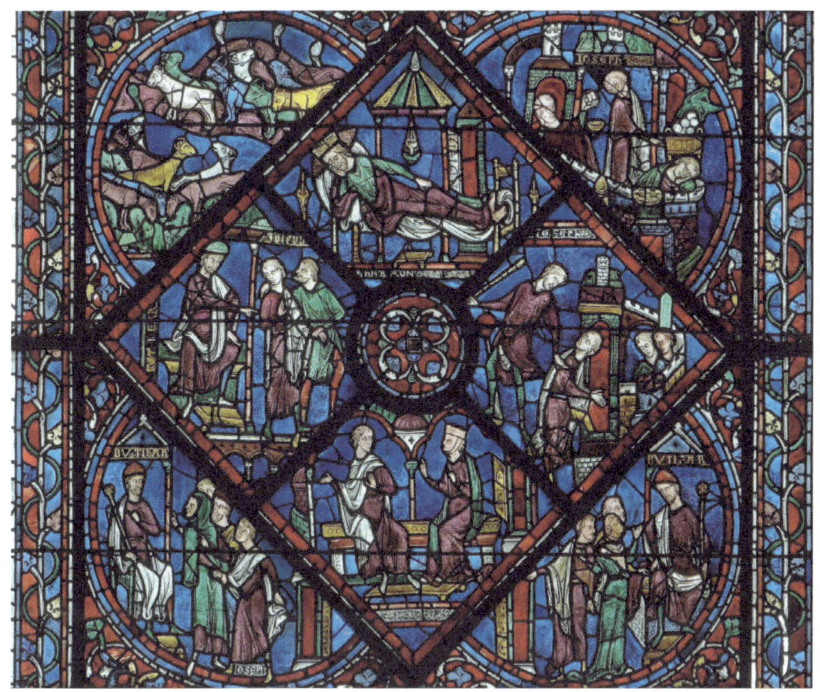

Scenes 9 to 16 from the Life of Joseph, early 13th century, stained glass and lead.
Chartres Cathedral, northern aisle of the nave, bay 41, Chartres.

Fig. 209

father and son. Joseph and Jacob will be separated for many years to come. The red door is a separation motif, not because it is placed between Joseph and Jacob, but because it is understood as the *campus* Joseph originally belongs to, but that has been left by its inhabitant. Now, in the judgment scene (scene 12), there is no such sign of separation, no red *campus* between the two protagonists. However, the red doorway motif appears again in scene 13. Here, Joseph enters prison. It is not his departure, but his arriving in jail that dominates the narrative. The red *campus*, again, marks the *locus* Joseph belongs to, the place at which he will first encounter his final destiny.[36]

Scene 13 marks the turning point of the story and constitutes its climax. For the first time, a figure enters her red *campus*. The great economy of pictorial effects makes this detail so intense; imprisonment is humiliating and may be lethal. For Joseph, however, it is the decisive path to his destination, a mystical event. The chromatic detail of his left yellow leg producing a peculiar color concordance gives this scene a marvelous, promising, and even tender atmosphere, reminiscent of a paradise garden.[37] We should note here that Joseph entirely ignores his destination and that this serene sacrifice makes his confidence all the more gracious.[38]

36
The soil motif is investigated by Steffen Bogen in his article "Imaginäres Eindringen: Schwellen- und Schleierfunktionen von Bildern (um 1100–1400)," in *Mobile Eyes: Peripatetisches Sehen in den Bildkulturen der Vormoderne*, David Ganz and Stefan Neuner, eds. (Munich: Fink, 2013), pp. 90–130, see especially the suggestive examples from the St. John's door of the Florentine Baptistery, pp. 100–102.

37
Some readers will be surprised about such detailed a description of color effects on a stained-glass window that is to be seen from rather far away. Still, all these effects are perfectly visible to the naked eye from below and there is no reason to believe that they were not made to be appreciated in detail. In other words, I do not find very much empirical confirmation of the myth of medieval art being addressed to God alone. The somewhat "subjective" character of this description may nevertheless necessitate some supplementary explanation. In this particular case, I would like to stress that the peculiar mood of this and other scenes is accessible to our appreciation because of our effort to correctly understand the syntactical functioning of *campus*.

38
Ignorance of the future is an essential element of faith as allegorically represented in the narrative. We notice here that this allegorical dimension emerges in the context of an emotionally highly charged event. From an anthropological point of view, we cannot avoid recognizing that Joseph has just escaped from a structurally incestuous situation veiled by a series of substitutions and inversions easy to decipher (Butifar himself being a substitute of the father, and his wife's love an inverted representation of Joseph's own desire). Successful resistance, and thus obedience to the law, is unjustly sanctioned by prison. On the difference between "literal" allegory (allegory intended by the author) and allegory in the proper sense (i.e., not intended, ignored, but real) in Saint Thomas, see Jean Pépin, *La*

The following three panels, in which Joseph interprets the dreams of his coprisoners (scene 14) while the pharaoh is depicted asleep (scene 15) and experiencing himself in a dream (scene 16), are to be seen together. Scenes 14 and 15 are linked by a very subtle interplay of red *campi*. First, Joseph is depicted between his two co-prisoners. The cupbearer is depicted *amidst* his red *campus*. As we know, he will be reprieved whereas the baker, *below* his red *campus*, is weighed down by the burden of his breadbasket and the bird. Their positions in relation to their *campi* indicate their fate.

Joseph is placed in between, in the center of the encompassing blue *campus*. He is connected to the red *campus* accompanying the pharaoh depicted in scene 15 and placed similarly to scene 3 in which Joseph was the one sleeping and dreaming [figs. 205 and 212]. Yet, whereas the right *campus* in scene 3 is situated at the level of Joseph's feet, the corresponding door in scene 15 is positioned a little more to the left. This slight variation produces a relevant shift in meaning. In scene 3, Joseph is invited to leave, to begin his long journey. It marks a decisive departure, even though he ignores what is to come. The pharaoh, on the other hand, is waiting for help and advice. His door is open to welcome Joseph who did not yet arrive.

As we have seen, the *campus* is a place and a *locus* apt to receive an *imago* or figure, just as in scene 4, where Joseph is leaving his father while leaving a red *campus*, and as in scene 12, where Joseph is attracted by the red *campus* of scene 13. The red *campus* of scene 15 offers a place for Joseph, who will leave prison and return to a state of grace. Moreover, the narrative unfolds from right to left, so that the scenes 13 and 15 appear linked together by the curved frame of scene 14, highlighting the dramatic chain of events through prison and the benign face of the pharaoh. The inversion of the narrative's direction literally stresses the character of this episode as a turning point.[39]

tradition de l'allégorie de Philon d'Alexandrie à Dante (Paris: Etudes Augustiniennes, 1986), pp. 282–285. On typology and allegory, see the remarkable doctoral thesis by Christoph Bellot, *Zu Theorie und Tradition der Allegorese im Mittelalter*, PhD diss. (University of Cologne, 1996).

39
A similar inversion will follow in scenes 25 to 27.

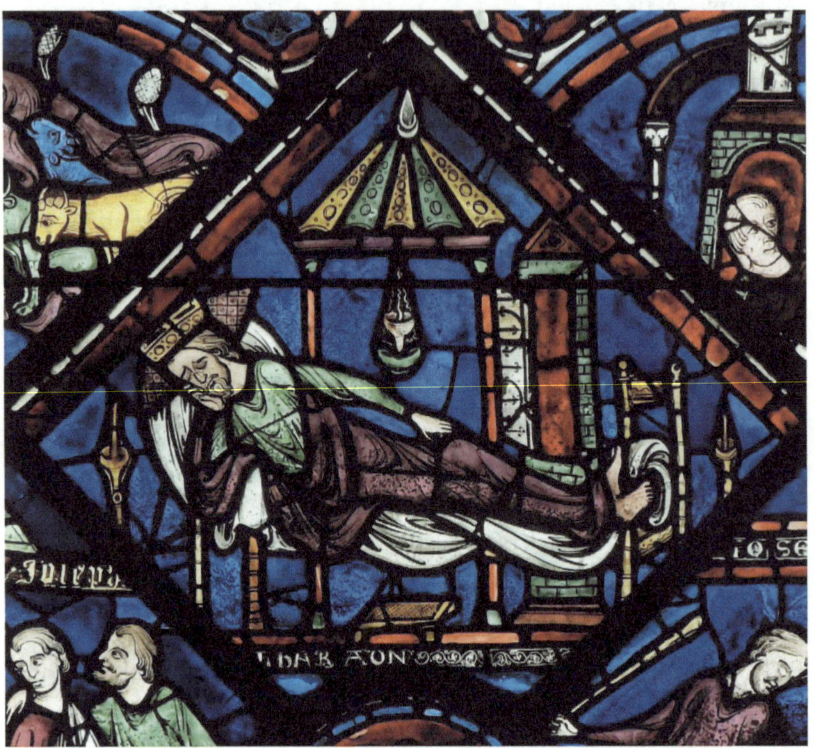

Scene 15 from the Life of Joseph, early 13th century, stained glass and lead.
Chartres Cathedral, northern aisle of the nave, bay 41, Chartres.

Fig. 212

The red *campus* in scene 15 [fig. 212] functions as *locus* for the image of Joseph. Yet, both the pharaoh and Joseph ignore what will follow. Guided by biblical knowledge, the viewer expects the red *campus* to receive the image of Joseph as suggested by the subtle variation of its position in comparison to scene 3 [fig. 205]. Although the distance between two *campi* does not *represent* the spatial distance between their figures (just as the distance between Joseph and his brothers is not represented between scenes 4 and 5), it does suggest proximity of thought and, in this case, of time. The very rhythm of the narrative is quickening at this turning point of the narrative.

There is no red *campus* in the next group of eight scenes [fig. 214]. Only the tiny doorway towards the pharaoh in scene 17 indicates Joseph's arrival in front of him before he is summoned to organize food storage. The last group of scenes, however, already begins with the event contrasting the dramatic moment of Joseph's imprisonment, anti-climax and response: the brothers travel back to their father's after having met incognito with Joseph [fig. 216]. The narrative moves from right to left before going back to Egypt in the opposite direction, from left to right in scene 28. Their old father seems eager to take the long and tiring journey upon him and just as his sons arrive, he has already left his red *campus* [fig. 217]. A second middle aged, bearded man remains in the door. We can easily grasp that the red *campus* belongs to Jacob and that the other person is present to replace him in his absence. Vested in blue and yellow, the same colors Joseph is wearing in the recognition scene (scene 29), these are also the traditional colors of Saint Peter.

While the narrative began with a son leaving his father on the latter's command, it ends with a father leaving his home in order to find his son again. While it is challenging to grasp the desire and grief, hope and joy that comes with departure, long separation, and reunion, the narrative recounts this in a straightforward way.[40] Nevertheless, the recognition scene does not take up much space compared to the other scenes, nor is it

40
A similar highly emotional expressivity is found in a novel by Hartmann von Aue, *Der arme Heinrich*, and the intense final joy and love at the moment in which the parents find their child again after her long and adventurous journey with Heinrich to the doctors of Salerno.

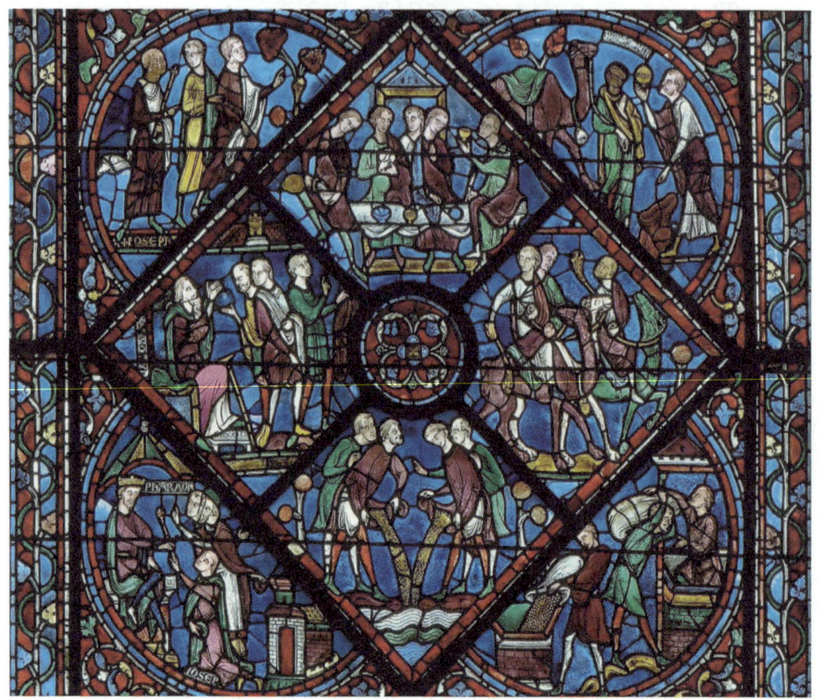

Scenes 17 to 24 from the Life of Joseph, early 13th century, stained glass and lead.
Chartres Cathedral, northern aisle of the nave, bay 41, Chartres.

Fig. 214

stressed by other pictorial strategies. The emotional charge of this decisive final scene, instead, is expressed by allegory. Above the last scenes, the triumphant image of God appears in a large red *campus*, the only one of its kind in the window [fig. 218]. It hints at the typological dimension of the story of Joseph insofar as it foretells aspects of the relationship between God the Father and his son.[41]

Stylistically different from the rest of the window, Christ in majesty could have been employed here in substitution of a lost panel.[42] The heterogeneous *trèfle* motif framing the figure of God may originally have been part of another window. Nevertheless, the panel successfully suggests the sudden appearance of Christ *on another level of being*. Unseen by the protagonists, the visibility of Christ for the beholder instantiates the glory and joy felt by father and son while recognizing each other.

As we can see in Chartres, one of the most fundamental medieval narrative devices consists in *splitting* one emotional event between different participants, the beholder himself participating actively. In this case, the joy felt by Joseph and Jacob is elaborated in a triangulation engaging the participation of Christ, invisible to them, and of the beholder, actually seeing what they do not and thus giving reality to their emotions. The sober treatment of the recognition scene is part of this splitting [fig. 216]. What today appears as a matter of inner (subjective) feeling and consciousness once occurred as an affair of social interaction and interrelations. In a modern (e.g., "romantic") version of the same theme, the joy of filial love would have to be expressed by the protagonists themselves. Here, it is expressed through a constellation. This point of our interpretation is particularly difficult to transform

41
See the classical study by Manhès-Deremble, *Les vitreaux narratifs de la cathédrale de Chartres*, pp. 163–164, who, on the contrary, thinks that the typological aspects of the Joseph story do not appear so much in this window, more concerned, she believes, with the literal sense and the story in itself.

42
Stylistic discrepancies do not necessarily imply a loss or a modification of an "original" plan; there are examples in Chartres of glasses produced by another workshop inserted in an otherwise stylistically coherent whole, for example the original sin in the window of the Samaritan (bay 42) that is to be ascribed to the master of Saint Lubin. While waiting for Claudine Lautier's recension of the Chartres windows, we do not know exactly what kind of intervention has to be supposed in the Joseph window.

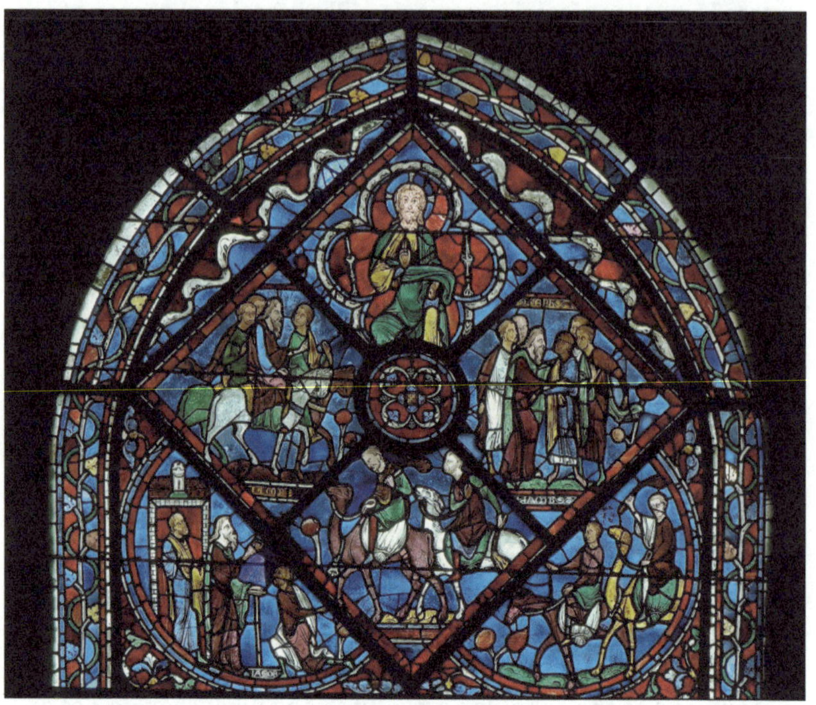

Scenes 25 to 30 from the Life of Joseph, early 13th century, stained glass and lead.
Chartres Cathedral, northern aisle of the nave, bay 41, Chartres.

Fig. 216

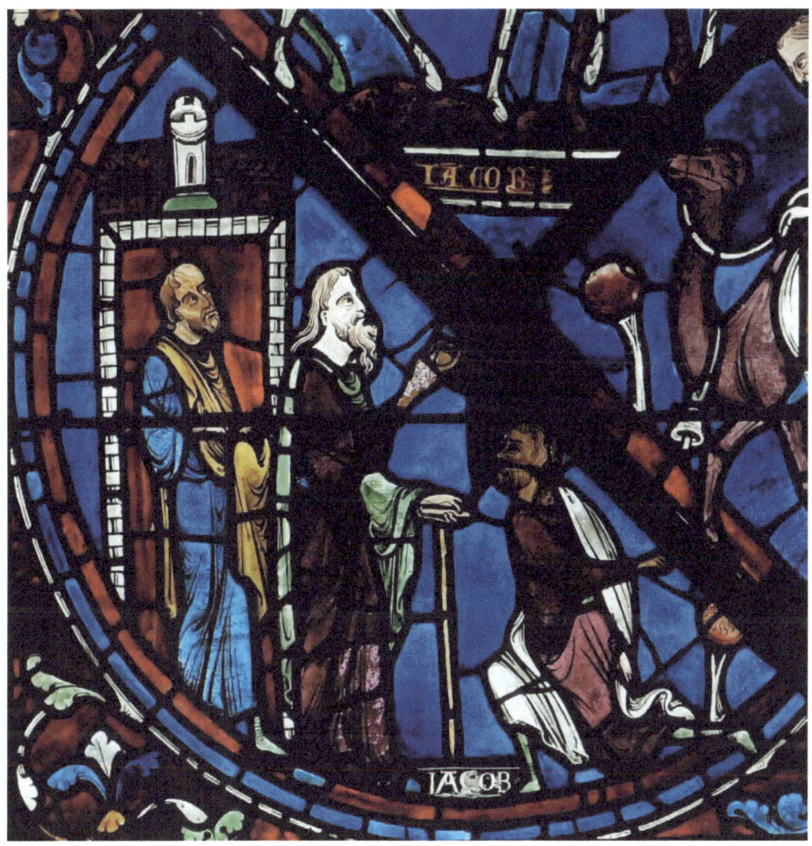

Scene 25 from the Life of Joseph, early 13th century, stained glass and lead.
Chartres Cathedral, northern aisle of the nave, bay 41, Chartres.

Fig. 217

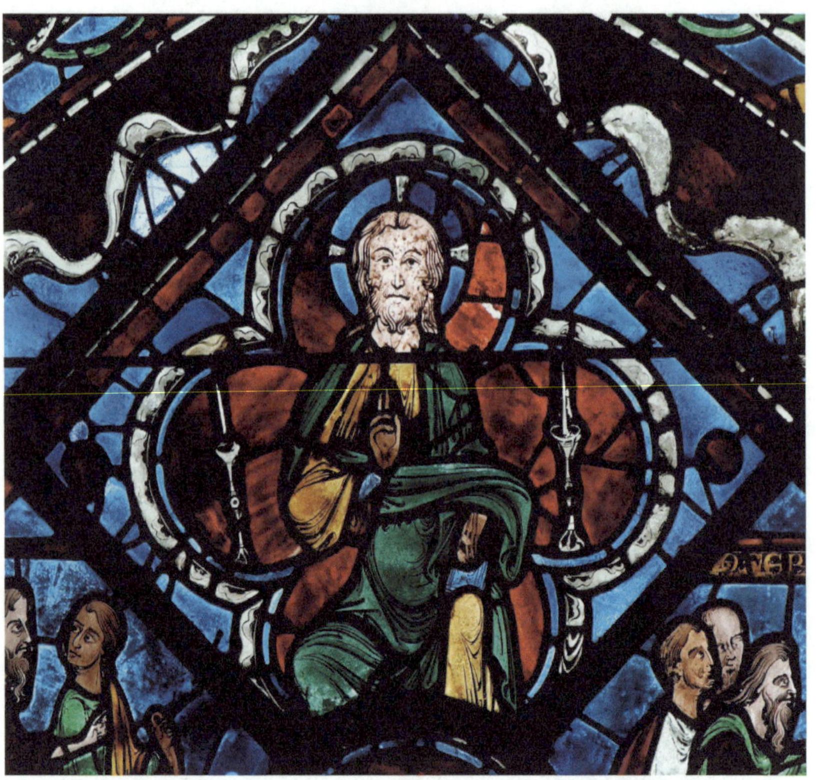

Scene 30 (Christ in Majesty), early 13th century, stained glass and lead.
Chartres Cathedral, northern aisle of the nave, bay 41, Chartres.

Fig. 218

into discourse, yet it is fundamental for a historically informed understanding of medieval allegory. If we want to see the human emotions between Joseph and Jacob, we must try to access to its iconic evidence through a thorough study of its syntax and functional structure. This presupposes a proper understanding of *campus* as *locus*.

In his red *campus*, Christ in majesty is present to the recognition scene, because of a series of other red *campi* that had to be passed through at different decisive moments of the narrative. The intensity of all these *campi* (the door between father and son in the departure scene 4, the entrance of prison in scene 13, the door in pharaoh's dream in scene 15, the place Jacob is leaving in scene 25), procures the necessary emotional charge to the red *campus* of God in scene 30 [fig. 218]. We intuitively grasp the highly affective moment of recognition when we look at the image of God after having noticed the red *campi* series in the narrative. Whoever tries to do so in front of the original window will be able to catch this allegorical sense that does not have much to do with academically learned reading, but nourishes the strong emotions enacted in the narrative.[43]

If we want to understand how the very idea of transcendency takes its place within the Christian myth and its pictorial realization in the thirteenth century, we have to acknowledge thirteenth-century imagery as a constitutive moment of this religion. We can try to deduce some metaphysical fundamentals from iconic syntax, in the present case the structure of transcendency in its (typological) relation to earthly events. The red doorways marking the main turning points of Joseph's story (Joseph's departure, seduction, imprisonment, Jacob's departure) all mark a difficult path realized with obedience, faith, and confidence, although without any knowledge of the future. Young Joseph *enters* the red *campus* of his prison with confidence, faith, and serenity, whereas Jacob *leaves* home at his old age without any certainty about his journey's outcome, but also without hesitation. In fact, God is watching over their individual destiny in particular, and

43
In his overview of early typological imagery, Christoph Bellot has marked a sort of climax or turning point around 1200. He puts the focus on cycles with clearly opposed images rather than on the interrelations between typologically linked topics in one narrative as observed in our case (Bellot, *Zu Theorie und Tradition der Allegorese im Mittelalter*, p. 803).

man's destiny in general. God's reality is evident to the beholder, insofar as he is looking at the stained-glass windows. The value and holy character of Joseph's and Jacob's actions, however, depend on their ignorance. Or, rather, it depends on their intimate confidence and faith in something real they nevertheless ignore.

Transcendency implies certainty of what we ignore. The beholder, in contrast, does not ignore. He is the third term in this triangular relation between Joseph (and Jacob) on the one hand and God (Christ in majesty) on the other. What is ignored, however, is just the same as what is known, even though not by the same person: in all the red *campi* with their high emotional charge, the figure of God in his equally red *campus* is copresent. The very divinity of God as it appears in the iconic evidence of this stained-glass window—a reality accessible to human emotional experience—is the result of the method of "splitting" the narrative and of combining its different aspects in an extremely sophisticated pattern of *campi* as *loci*. The two levels (the earthly father and son narrative and the heavenly one) correlate. Transcendency would be void if it could not reappear in earthly reality. Christ's transcendent appearance in majesty is the *return* of the most intimate human desire as expressed in the narrative, the love between a father and his son, told through the son's leaving on the father's command, his symbolic ordeal, his inverted incestuous relation to his master's wife, imprisonment, grace, and reunion with his father.

At this point, however, we encounter a difficulty. If panel 30 [fig. 218] has been integrated in substitution of an older one, our whole interpretation seems to become hazardous. It seems to be hazardous to suppose a meaning that has not been the intention of the original artists, but only the effect of some later intervention. What I would like to stress here, nevertheless, is the fact that certain pictorial effects and their iconographic consequences can be produced by the syntactical properties of the elements used. They are not necessarily the effect of deliberate intention. To put it differently; the intention and content of a work of art is as much produced by a deliberate choice as by the syntactical properties of a functional system. The intrinsic logics of iconic syntaxes, thus, can *produce* dimensions of content and doctrine that otherwise would not exist. This implies that the study of iconic functionality is of major interest to anthropology in general and historical anthropology in particular.[44] This strong consequence has to be considered when we address problems of the image-text relation.

Let us, therefore, consider briefly the syntactical rule at work in the specific case of the Joseph window. In thirteenth-century stained-glass painting, blue and red are the only colors eligible for a *campus*. They are used alternately in order to produce difference where necessary.[45] As the main *campi* in stained-glass narratives are always blue,[46] a subordinate *campus* (the many doorways we observed) will necessarily be red. So does an individual main *campus* whenever meant to be differentiated from the surrounding blue ones. The small subordinate *campi*, therefore, cannot be of any other color than the larger coordinate *campus* of Christ, so that two different levels of *campus* are necessarily found to be of the same color. The alternate use of blue and red produces a sort of identification between two otherwise distinct narrative levels permitting to *see* the one (Christ in glory) allegorically in the other (the many doorways).

In Chartres bay 41, the door motif always functions as a *campus* for an image. However, there are different ways in which the *campus* relates to its figure. While it happens that another figure occupies the *campus* belonging to a main protagonist who has just left (scene 25), the *campus* of a figure can also be placed within another scene (scenes 14 and 15). Only a slight alteration of its

44
The essential message of G.W. F. Hegel's *Aesthetics* is that *content is a function of its mediation by a signitive act*, such as symbolization, iconic representation or one of the more abstract sorts of functional production of sense (as in iconic or musical syntax). Signitive activities, or semiosis in an encompassing sense, *produces* reality, human reality. This is the profound meaning of Horst Bredekamp's "image act:" *Image Acts: A Systematic Approach to Visual Agency* (Berlin: De Gruyter, 2018).

45
The principle of alternation has been observed by Eva Frodl-Kraft in her classical studies, "Die Farbensprache der gotischen Malerei," in *Wiener Jahrbuch für Kunstgeschichte* XXX/XXXI (1977–78), pp. 89–178, and Frodl-Kraft, "Farbendualitäten, Gegenfarben, Grundfarben in der gotischen Malerei," in *Von Farbe und Farben, Albert Knoepfli zum 70. Geburtstag* (Zurich: Manesse, 1980), pp. 293–302, and interpreted as part of a binary color system.

46
In twelfth-century stained-glass windows blue is still treated as an eventually neutral color. The "rise of blue" during the thirteenth century, as observed by Michel Pastoureau ("Et puis vint le bleu," in Pastoureau, *Figures et couleurs – étude sur la symbolique et la sensibilité médiévale* (Paris: Léopard d'or, 1987), pp. 15–22, see also Pastoureau, *Bleu: Histoire d'une couleur* (Paris: Seuil, 2002), can be linked to observable changes in the use of blue in stained-glass windows around 1200. Blue is getting more intense and is more and more seen as a color in its own right.

position in respect to the related figure can change its meaning, as in scenes 3 and 15. These elegant pictorial solutions to narrative problems cannot be appreciated in their iconic evidence as long as the function of *campus* and its peculiar topological rather than spatial character remains unnoticed.

There are many interrelated sources coming from different areas of experience and thinking that corroborate our observations, proving that we are coping with a fundamental anthropological phenomenon. Apart from theories of *locus* and *situs* in natural philosophy and descriptions of *campus* by artisans, innumerable uses of the same or similar pictorial strategies in relation to specific uses and appearances in architecture and sculpture can be found elsewhere.[47] We can trace these appearances in color theories, in explications on the theory and use of gemstones,[48] geography,[49] in sources discussing life and its movement,[50] and so forth. The pictorial function of the *campus* was intuitively accessible to virtually all members of thirteenth-century society.

Reading Theophilus

In this final section, I will shortly turn to some formulations in Theophilus's treatise *Schedula diversarum artium*, a recipe collection with prologues, known through a large number of manuscripts diverging from one redaction to the other.[51] We will show that the understanding of *campus* as *locus* corresponds

47
As shown by, for example, Christopher Lakey in his book on *Sculptural Seeing*.

48
Especially the *De mineralibus* by Albert the Great (see my *Histoire des systèmes chromatiques*, forthcoming).

49
Barbara Obrist, *La cosmologie médiévale, I: Les fondements antiques* (Florence: Sismel, 2004); Kathrin Müller, *Visuelle Weltaneignung: Antronomische und kosmologische Diagramme in Handschriften des Mittelalters* (Göttingen: Vandenhoek und Ruprecht, 2008); Alessandro Scafi, *Mapping Paradise: A History of Heaven on Earth* (Chicago: University of Chicago Press, 2006). David Summers has tried to establish a link between the geographic tradition and painting in the fifteenth century: *Vision, Reflection, and Desire* (University of North Carolina Press, 2007), especially ch. 3, pp. 78–111.

50
Extensively treated by Thomas Le Gouge, *Schémas de cosmologie et géométrie*.

51
The Theophilus treatise can be consulted online on the "schedula-Portal" of the Thomas-Institute, University of Cologne. I will cite from the Dodwell edition (Theophilus, *De Diversis Artibus: The Various Arts*, ed. C. R. Dodwell [London: Thomas Nelson and Sons, 1961]),

closely to workshop habitudes as far as they can be grasped from Theophilus's discourse. Chapter one and two describe the production of *membrana* (literally skin color) and *prasinus*, the only color not included in the catalogue of *membrana*'s ingredients, but to be added in the case that a *pallid* face (for example of a dead person) is to be represented.[52] Theophilus writes: "*Cum vero mambranam miscueris et inde facies et nuda corpora impleveris, admisce ei prasinum etc.*"[53] The verb *implere* occurs invariably at the beginning stage of execution, when the limited and well circumscribed surface that has to be painted to become an "image" (a figure) is "filled in" with color serving as a foundation to the other layers, as described in the following chapters. After having "filled" the figure to be painted with this first layer (*implere*), Theophilus tells the artisan to prepare a second color he calls "*posc*" or "*posch*," made of *membrana*, green, and red. The outcome is a dark gray, brown, or black tone used to draw the facial features such as eyes, the nose, the mouth etc. With this color, Theophilus says, "*designabis supercilia et oculos*."[54] *Designare* can be translated as "drawing" (Ital. *disegnare*), but literally means something like "indicating" or "defining." Two of the oldest manuscripts read "*signabis*" instead of "*designabis*" suggesting an intimate relation between drawing and *signum* (sign).[55] In chapter 4, Theophilus

also accessible online. The new edition by Erhard Brepohl (*Theophilus Presbyter und das mittelalterliche Kunsthandwerk: Gesamtausgabe der Schrift De Diversis Artibus in einem Band* [Cologne: Böhlau, 2013]) does not improve the text given by Dodwell but proposes a thorough new German translation and many valuable technical explanations. An overview of the use of *campus* in other sources (Heraclius, Mappae clavicula, Göttinger Musterbuch, Cennino Cennini etc.) can be found in Thomas Le Gouge, "Art et illusion au XIIIe siècle," in *Art et philosophie: De la mimesis à l'imago*, Emanule Iezzoni and Elisabeth Ruchaud, eds. (Paris: Cerf, forthcoming).

52
Monika E. Müller in her critical account of the relation between the written advice and real application in illuminated manuscripts ("Das erste Buch der 'schedula diversarum artium': Distanz zwischen Text und buchmalerischer Wirklichkeit," in *Zwischen Kunsthandwerk und Kunst: Die "Scheldula diversarum artium,"* Andreas Speer, Maxime Mauriège, and Hiltrud Westermann-Angerhausen, eds. (Berlin: De Gruyter, 2014), pp. 225–243, with further reading) shows a rather convincing relation between the two even though she does stress the fact that Theophilus, namely in his description of carnation (*membrana*), introduces a more complicated differentiation between layers than can be observed in the illuminations. Theophilus's text refers to more monumental painting; the miniatures clearly are based on a simplified pattern.

53
"When you will have mixed flesh color and with it filled in the faces and nude figures, mix with it green earth etc." Theophilus, *De Diversis Artibus*, ch. 3, p. 5.

54
Theophilus, *De Diversis Artibus*, ch. 3, p. 6.

uses the term "*rubricabis*" to describe the act of putting on "*rosa prima,*" i.e., the first layer of red color to give life to the figures. "*Rubricare*" designates "coloring" as linked to life. In chapter 5, then, Theophilus describes how to put on light and calls it "*illuminare.*" With the expression "*facere subtiles tractus*" in chapter 8,[56] Theophilus refers to very fine lines and hatchings underlining contours and volumes not visible from afar, and not applied in works of smaller dimensions. The four main terms indicate, therefore, four painterly functions: *implere*, *designare*, *rubricare*, and *illuminare*.

I will discuss now how the function of *impletio* is intimately linked to the function of *campus*. In chapter 14, Theophilus enumerates different ways of "*mixtura vestimentorum,*" of preparing colors for vestments. The terms he uses to describe these processes are standardized. We read "*Misce menesch cum folio*"[57] or "*purum viride cum ogra*"[58] followed by "*et imple vestimentum.*" When there is no color to be mixed and the *impletio* is done with a pure pigment, the text begins directly with "*imple vestimentum cum rubeo/cum cenobrio.*" The *impletio* is invariably followed by the expression "*fac tractus,*" and by a (double) *illuminatio* ("*illumina primum – illumina superius*").[59] The last working stage is described by the expression "*facere umbram.*"[60] *Tractus* is a "trait," as derived from the Latin *trahere*: to draw, to pull, sometimes: to cut, a graphic device that permits to limit an area or to sign a mark. *Tractus* and *signum* are marks limiting a field you can fill in (*implere*), the *signum* serving to define the *campus* before it is filled, the *tractus* serving to underline the limits once the *campus* has been filled or marking a point or a crest.

55
British Museum Ms Egerton 840A and Paris BnF Ms lat 6741, the reading is "*signabis*" instead of "*designabis*" as Dodwell notes in his edition.

56
Theophilus, *De Diversis Artibus*, p. 7, a bit later, writes "*linies subtiles tractus,*" ch. 9, p. 8

57
Ibid., p. 10.

58
Ibid.

59
Ibid., ch. 14, pp. 10–13, on coloring of vestments repeating several times the same formulations.

60
We are not concerned here with *umbra*, the underlining of dark "shadows." In fact, *umbra* does not refer exactly to what we would call a shadow, even though it always is of a dark (mostly black or gray) color. *Umbra* is the color of a graphic underlining of folds in clothing or dark parts in the face as mouth, nostrils, eyelids etc.

In chapter 15, when writing about blue vestments,[61] Theophilus tells us:

> Cum imagines vel aliarum rerum effigies pertrahuntur in muro sicco, statim aspergatur aqua tamdiu, donec omnino maditus sit. Et in eodem humore liniantur omnes colores qui supponendi[62] sunt, qui omnes calce misceantur et cum ipso muro siccentur, ut haereant. In campo sub lazure et viridi ponatur color qui dicitur veneda, mixtus ex nigro et calce, super quem, cum siccus fuerit, ponatur in suo loco lazur tenuis cum ovi mediolo abundanter aqua mixto temperatus, et super hunc iterum spissior propter decorem.[63]

Theophilus specifies that there is underpainting in blue vestments, "*in campo sub lazure.*" *Campus* here signifies the area to be underpainted, i.e., the surface or field the figure is occupying. In most cases, however, *campus* refers to the surrounding area of a figure and not just to the area the figure is exactly occupying. And while this double sense may be counter-intuitive to modern readers, for readers of the twelfth to fifteenth century, it must have been self-evident, especially considering their premodern understanding of "space" as "place."

Theophilus's formulation indicates unambiguously that *impletio* concerns *campus*. Every figure constitutes itself within the *campus* it actually fills (*implere*). At the same time, a *campus* can be inscribed in and contained by another, larger *campus*, just like one *topos* can be situated in the other.[64] A *topos* (or *locus*, place) is a container containing a smaller *topos*. The exact *locus* (and *campus*) of a figure is, therefore, defined by the exact volume

61
No blue color is mentioned in chapter 14 (*de mixtione vestimentorum in laqueari*).

62
Dodwell prefers "*superponendi.*"

63
"As a field, under azure blue and viridian, a color called veneda is laid, mixed of black and chalk-white. On this color, when it is dry, a thin glaze of azure blue, mixed with the yolk of an egg which has been diluted with a lot of water, is laid, and on top of this again a thicker glaze for beauty." Theophilus, *De Diversis Artibus*, ch. 15, p. 13.

64
This double sense of *campus* can be verified until at least the fifteenth century, when Cennino Cennini still uses the Italian words *campo*, *campire*, and *campeggiare* in the same double sense. See Thomas Le Gouge, "Art et illusion au XIIIe siècle."

containing it. In a larger sense, however, a niche, a larger *campus*, can also be considered as its *locus*. In this case, there is some space (distance) between the figure and the inner surface of its containing *locus*. This field can be "filled in," decorated, or even cut out, as Theophilus describes respectively in chapter 42 and 93.[65]

Between Theophilus's *Schedula diversarum atrium* and the Albertian writings on *locus* lies at least a century and the arrival of the *Corpus Aristotelicum* in the West. It is quite possible that Alberti's reading of Aristotle rests on an intuitive response to phenomena of spatialization familiar to him from sculpture and painting. At any rate, Alberti's writings give access to some anthropological fundamentals relevant for the understanding of iconic syntax that have been in place before him and that we have traced here in a stained-glass window from the beginning of the thirteenth century in Chartres.

65
Theophilus, *De Diversis Artibus*, pp. 93 and 167. The term "*campus*" does not signify the surfaces not filled by the images or figures the artisan has to decorate, but the whole *campus* as occupied by the figure. One cannot decorate the part of a *campus* occupied by the figure but only the parts left aside.

Part 2
Describing and Translating

Lineage of a Paradigm: "Figure and Ground" in Encyclopedic Sources

Veronica Peselmann

227

Language affects the way we approach and examine art. Assessing visuality to describe, analyze, or exchange ideas about art deeply entrenches terms and concepts. The field of art history draws on a set of technical terms that has been established over time facilitating disciplinary discourses. However, this terminology not only serves as a tool to explain artworks but also pre-shapes a viewer's attention and observations. In art-historical scholarship, the terms "figure" and "ground" became particularly fundamental and advanced to basic terms over time. Conceptually, the terms "figure" and "ground" refer to two distinct areas of a picture, distinguishable by shape, material, color, or position.[1] Seemingly detached from historic and artistic transformations, figure and ground are part of almost every formal and visual analysis, especially when referring to artifacts such as paintings and drawings. The use of figure and ground as a descriptive model thereby focuses on certain aspects while neglecting others.

In 1894, the German-Swiss artist Ottilie Roederstein painted a self-portrait in which figure and ground form the crucial compositional arrangement [fig. 229]. The close-up bust portrait solely comprises the painter's face in front of a monochromatic field, clearly distinguishing the area of the figure and the area of the ground. The matte shade of brownish tint behind her face recedes to emphasize the glowing flesh tone and the painter's red cap. Leaving a formal point of view, the strict, almost motionless facial expressions of the self-portrait are reminiscent of old master's male portraits from the early sixteenth century.[2] Furthermore, Roederstein chose an anachronistic material and painting technique that was fairly unusual for the late nineteenth century: tempera on wood panel. Instead of prefabricated tubed oil colors that dominated the art supplies market since the mid-nineteenth century, Roederstein used tempera, the predecessor to oil-based paints.[3] Likewise, wooden panels were used only occasionally by the end of the nineteenth century. However, the material qualities of wood are, as it goes for any other material, unique. Sanded down,

1
Stefan Neuner, "Figur und Grund," in *Lexikon Kunstwissenschaft: Hundert Grundbegriffe*, Stefan Jordan and Jürgen Müller, eds. (Stuttgart: Reclam, 2012), pp. 112–116.

2
Marianne Koos, *Bildnisse des Begehrens: Das lyrische Männerportrait in der venezianischen Malerei des frühen 16. Jahrhunderts – Giorgione, Tizian und ihr Umkreis* (Emsdetten: Edition Imorde, 2006).

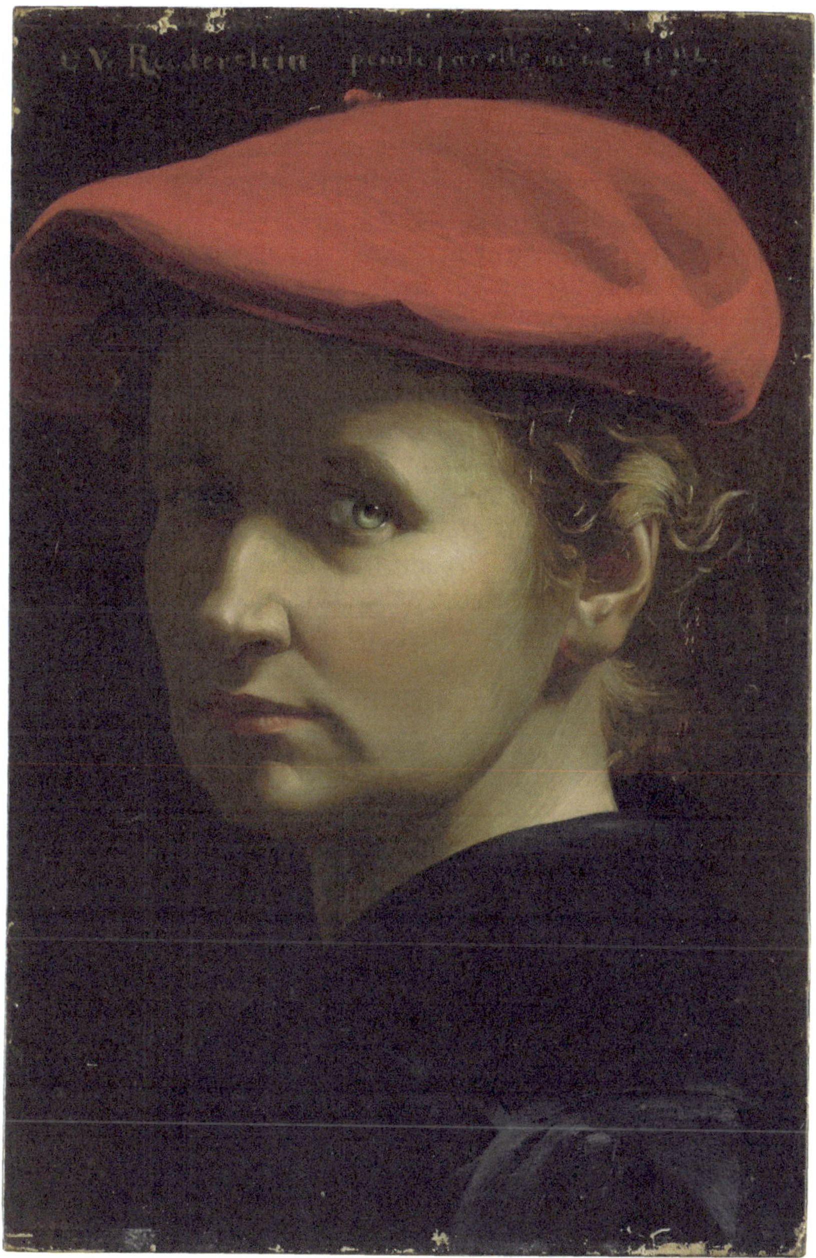

Ottilie W. Roederstein, *Selbstbildnis mit roter Mütze*, 1894, tempera on wood, 36 × 44 cm. Kunstmuseum, Basel.

Fig. 229

wood panels provide remarkably even and glossy surfaces that canvas, yet carefully smoothed and primed, would not be able to achieve. The velvety depiction of the figure's flesh tones is thus dependent on the material precondition of the ground and the respective preparation of the wooden carrier. The fact that the figure's appearance inseparably connects to a material interplay of myriad levels—support, grounding, and layers of paint—is not subject of a modernist analysis addressing figure-and-ground (a combined noun) as a formal paradigm. In turn, deentangling and disconnecting the ground's material and depictional means forms a crucial shift in nineteenth and twentieth-century terminology.[4] Roederstein's famous auto portrait exemplifies what we can observe when referring to figure and ground as formal categories and what we respectively exclude from our analytical approach following a modernist understanding of figure-and-ground.

The terms figure and ground have been verifiable as pictorial elements for centuries, as the contributions of this volume discuss in manifold ways. However, since the late nineteenth and early twentieth centuries, figure and ground were established as a dichotomy that did more than describing relationalities. Instead, the terms started to presuppose analyses that aimed to separately identify forms and areas. In examining "figure" and "ground" as terms used in the nineteenth century, this contribution detects lineages of this paradigm. To which historical pictorial understandings of figure and ground refers the dichotomy in the first place, and which concept are reflected and eventually preserved?

Perusing French and German dictionary lemmata and entries in encyclopedias from between 1780 and 1890, I will follow the conceptual lineage and formation from "figure" and "ground" to "figure-and-ground." This shift can be observed in different

3
Alain Bonnet, *L'enseignement des arts au XIXe siècle: La réforme de l'École des Beaux-Arts de 1863 et la fin du modèle académique* (Rennes: Presses Universitaires de Rennes, 2006), p. 16. Anthea Callen, *The Art of Impressionism: Painting Technique and the Making of Modernity* (New Haven, CT: Yale University Press, 2000), pp. 25–29. Anthea Callen, *Techniques of the Impressionists* (Edison, NJ: Chartwell Books, 1993).

4
Veronica Peselmann, *Der Grund der Malerei: Materialität im Prozess bei Corot und Courbet* (Berlin: Reimer, 2020).

languages both in dictionaries as well as encyclopedias.[5] These textual sources reflect a standardized understanding of terms that circulate as normative knowledge. Therefore, lexicons and encyclopedias allow us to pinpoint terminological shifts that go beyond individual or subject-specific debates. Instead, they manifest meanings that are set and perceived as "common knowledge."

In the following, I will focus on French and German entries from the late eighteenth to the late nineteenth centuries that can represent current understandings of how figure and ground were perceived in those languages. The selected entries discuss the two terms at length and demonstrate how the shift toward a binary terminology occurred. The key sources encompass Watelet's *Dictionnaire des Arts de Peinture, Sculpture et Gravure* (1792), Bouillet'ss *Dictionnaire universel des sciences, des lettres et des arts* (1854), *La Grande Encyclopédie* (1887–1902); Sulzers's *Allgemeine Theorie der Schönen Künste. Lexikon der Künste und Ästhetik* (1771), Brockhaus editions, such as the *Handbuch für die gebildeten Stände* from 1814, 1875, and 1884, as well as *Meyers Konversations-Lexikon* from 1876.

Tracing Lineage

In the late eighteenth and early nineteenth centuries, entries on ground entailed lengthy explanations of material means. The lemmata sketch the relationship between figure and ground by mapping a distinct conceptual difference of a multifaceted ground contrasting a two-dimensional "figure" defined as a self-contained entity. However, starting mid-nineteenth century, the lemmata increasingly address a compositional and complementary placing of figure and ground. In these rather formal implications of the terms, the vocabulary designates contrasting color zones as complementary shapes, thereby distinguishing a spatial difference between the front (the figure) and the back (the ground). The back, hence, the ground, enhances the figure's visibility by consequently shifting most of the viewer's attention

5
I examined French, German, and English entries between 1790–1900 to detect a terminological shift of the term "ground." See Peselmann, *Der Grund der Malerei*. Comparing languages enabled me to indicate a more conceptual shift that is not only relevant to one specific language.

toward the figure. Regarding the medium of painting, I will argue that material preconditions have contributed to that semantic change, leading to the modernist paradigm of "figure-and-ground" used in art criticism and art-historical research of the twentieth century.

Modernist pictorial theory conceives figure and ground as formally contrasting areas.[6] However, in terms of painting practice, figure and ground are inextricably linked. Accordingly, recent art-historical scholarship has drawn increased attention to the "ground" and has mapped its etymological history to encompass the complexity of this crucial (technical) term.[7] Related to emerging approaches focusing on material iconography, the material aspects of ground have been put forth in particular.[8] In research on medieval and Renaissance art specifically, comprehensive examinations of the gold ground emphasize material implications of ground. Notably, Ellen J. Beer advertizes a reading of gold as a metal and, therefore, as a distinct material.[9] By connecting "gold ground" and "perspective," Saskia Quené shows how the gold ground as an active ground may inhere and not

6
Clement Greenberg's notion of ground was particularly influential in highlighting the flatness of the depiction. Ground and background conceptually describe areas beyond the material. Clement Greenberg, "Modernist Painting," *Art and Literature* 4 (1965): 193–201; Clement Greenberg, "Collage" (1948), in *Die Essenz der Moderne: Ausgewählte Essays und Kritiken*, Karlheinz Lüdeking, ed. (Hamburg: Philo Fine Arts, 2000), pp. 157–162.

7
Jeroen Stumpel, "On Grounds and Backgrounds: Some Remarks about Composition in Renaissance Painting," *Simiolus* 18 (1988): 219–243; Thomas Puttfarken, *The Discovery of Pictorial Composition: Theories of Visual Order in Painting, 1400–1800* (New Haven, CT: Yale University Press, 2000); Bastian Eclercy, *Nimbendekor in der toskanischen Dugentomalerei*, PhD diss. (University of Münster, 2007). Gottfried Boehm and Matteo Burioni, eds., *Der Grund: Das Feld des Sichtbaren* (Munich: Fink Verlag, 2012); Peselmann, *Der Grund der Malerei*; David Young Kim, *Groundwork: A History of the Renaissance Picture* (Princeton, NJ: Princeton University Press, 2022). Saskia Quené, *Goldgrund und Perspektive: Fra Angelico im Glanz des Quattrocento* (Berlin/Boston: Deutscher Kunstverlag, 2022).

8
Günter Bandmann, "Bemerkungen zu einer Ikonologie des Materials," in *Städel-Jahrbuch* 2 (1969), pp. 75–101. Günter Bandmann, "Der Wandel der Materialbewertung in der Kunsttheorie des 19. Jahrhunderts, in *Beiträge zur Theorie der Künste im 19. Jahrhundert* 1, Helmut Koopmann and J. Adolf Schmoll genannt Eisenwerth, eds. (Frankfurt am Main: Klostermann, 1971), pp. 129–157. Thomas Raff, *Die Sprache der Materialien: Anleitung zu einer Ikonologie der Werkstoffe* (Münster: Waxmann [Münchner Beiträge zur Volkskunde, 37], 2008). Monika Wagner, *Das Material der Kunst. Eine andere Geschichte der Moderne* (Munich: C. H. Beck, 2001).

9
Ellen Beer, "Marginalien zum Thema Goldgrund," *Zeitschrift für Kunstgeschichte* 46, no. 3 (1983): 271–286; Quené, *Goldgrund und Perspektive*, pp. 40–43.

necessarily exclude perspectival forms of representation.[10] Attempting to link multiple connotations of ground, David Young Kim uses the term "groundwork" to highlight a process consisting of various material layers revealing or withdrawing figuration. As groundwork is "what artists do,"[11] Kim suggests that art historians should consider a significantly more complex approach to ground. The renewed scholarly interest in the interconnectedness of material and compositional means of the term links, therefore, to its early terminological conception.

Dictionaries and encyclopedias of the late eighteenth and nineteenth centuries attest to a multifaceted perspective on ground and the interdependence between figure and ground. They reveal a conceptual transition that inheres material and technical means toward an orientation that favors the degree of formal difference.[12] Early entries do not solely address formal criteria or the pictorial surface. Instead, the materiality of the support was inevitably part of its concept.

Encyclopedic Entries and Their Epistemic Potential

The number of printed dictionaries and encyclopedias drastically increased during the eighteenth century, distributing and familiarizing knowledge to a broader audience.[13] New entries started to exceed simple terminological definitions by offering comprehensive treatises written by experts and published carrying the authors' names. Replacing these individualized approaches with anonymous entries in the nineteenth century marks a significant shift that advanced the dictionaries' status toward general knowledge.[14] However, examinations and terminological descriptions outlined contemporary discourses. Hence, earlier entries display

10
Quené, *Goldgrund und Perspektive*, pp. 27–47.

11
Kim, *Groundwork*, p. 6.

12
See Gottfried Boehm's "Iconic Difference" in this volume.

13
Nico Dorn, "Zedlers Universal-Lexicon und das Problem seiner inhaltlichen Erschließung," in *Kulturen des Wissens im 18. Jahrhundert*, Ulrich Johannes Schneider, ed. (Berlin: De Gruyter, 2008), pp. 183–190, 183. See also Peselmann, *Der Grund der Malerei*, pp. 43–45.

14
Ulrich Johannes Schneider, *Die Erfindung des allgemeinen Wissens* (Berlin: De Gruyter, 2013), pp. 8–9.

which definitions got canonized and thus conveyed as "common" knowledge.[15] Lexical entries engage in prevailing opinions and debates; however, manifested terminologies transgress the limits of simply summarizing preceding discussions. They act as formative tools, affecting the knowledge of future generations.

The historian Reinhart Koselleck has decisively coined the history of concepts or conceptual history (*Begriffsgeschichte*) that examines terminological alterations over time. Koselleck claims that terms both trace social knowledge and shape what they describe. He defines these terms as "basic concepts in history" (*geschichtliche Grundbegriffe*) and has collected them in a dictionary comprising eight volumes.[16] Koselleck highlights the relevance of conceptual history, as language provides an in-depth comprehension: "Conceptual historical research does not understand language as an epiphenomenon of so-called reality ..., rather as a methodologically irreducible final instance. Without [language], one cannot obtain any understanding nor science of the world or society."[17] As part of his research, he extensively studied the significance of historical dictionaries and encyclopedias and describes them as a crucial source for gaining insight into temporal discourses: "The knowledge and self-understanding of generations is reflected on this level. First the scholarly, then the educated world, finally the journalistic public."[18] Hence, the importance of historic lexical terms is grounded in the increasing expansion of terminological knowledge that equally transmits

15
Ulrich Johannes Schneider, "Der Aufbau der Wissenswelt: Eine phänotypische Beschreibung enzyklopädischer Literatur," in *Kulturen des Wissens im 18. Jahrhundert*, Schneider, ed., pp. 81–100, here p. 82.

16
Geschichtliche Grundbegriffe: Historisches Lexikon zur Politisch-sozialen Sprache in Deutschland, Otto Brunner, Werner Conze, and Reinhart Koselleck, eds. (Stuttgart: Klett-Cotta, 1972–ongoing), 8 vols. Hartmut Lehmann and Melvin Richter, eds., "The Meaning of Historical Terms and Concepts: New Studies on Begriffsgeschichte," *Occasional Paper*, no. 15 (Washington, DC: German Historical Institute Washington, DC, 1996).

17
"Konzeptgeschichtswissenschaftliche Forschung, die Sprache nicht als Epiphänomen der sogenannten Wirklichkeit ..., sondern als methodisch irreduzible Letztinstanz versteht, ohne die keine Erfahrung und keine Wissenschaft von der Welt oder von der Gesellschaft zu haben sind." Reinhart Koselleck, *Begriffsgeschichten. Studien zur Semantik und Pragmatik der politischen und sozialen Sprache* (Frankfurt am Main: Suhrkamp, 2010), p. 99.

18
Reinhart Koselleck, "Einleitung," in *Geschichtliche Grundbegriffe*, XIII–XXVII. Peselmann, *Der Grund der Malerei*, pp. 43–45.

a specific vocabulary. It channels attention to matters related to the term and feeds into altered terminological understanding.

To ultimately grasp all layers of why meanings change certainly surpasses a lexical analysis and would include newspaper articles, contemporary reviews, treatises, and scientific papers.[19] Often, dictionaries reflect on terminological alteration with a certain time lag, as even a high frequency of printed new editions not necessarily included a rewrite of all lemmata. Focusing on historic lexical entries rather enables identifying and tracking terminological shifts and allows pondering which terminological use eventually became canonic. Hence, the epistemic potential of terms in historic dictionaries does not necessarily lie in the fact that the entries *explain* terminological shifts. However, they *determine* these shifts and detect concepts that form and structure imminent perspectives.

A Proper Ground

The extent to which a terminological analysis not only depicts a surface but goes beyond an "epiphenomenon," to quote Koselleck, highlights a French dictionary published in 1789. The entry on ground, French: *fond*, written by Claude-Henri Watelet (1718–1786), a member of the Royal Academy of Painting and Sculpture in Paris, is one of the most comprehensive and detailed accounts of the eighteenth century [fig. 236].[20] A few years prior, large parts of the entry had already been published in Diderot's famous *Encyclodpédie*, for which Watelet wrote several entries.[21] Translations diffused his statements internationally from there, a German dictionary from 1814, for example, repeats Watelet's distinctions in almost identical wording.[22]

19
That entailed a comprehensive history of discourses and concepts encompassing articles outside of artistic or art-historical debates.

20
Dictionnaire des Arts de Peinture, Sculpture et Gravure (Paris: L. F. Prault, 1792), vol. 2, entry: "*Fond*", pp. 333–343.

21
Denis Diderot and Jean le Rond D'Alembert, eds., *Encyclopédie, ou Dictionnaire Raisonné des Sciences, des Arts et des Métiers* 7 (1757–1772), https://gallica.bnf.fr/ark:/12148/bpt6k5785794x.r=Encyclop%C3%A9die%2C%20ou%20Dictionnaire%20Raisonn%C3%A9%20des%20Sciences%2C%20%20des%20Arts%20et%20des%20M%C3%A9tiers?rk=21459;2.

DICTIONNAIRE

DES ARTS DE PEINTURE, SCULPTURE ET GRAVURE.

Par M. WATELET, de l'Académie Françoiſe, Honoraire de l'Académie royale de Peinture & Sculpture ; & M. LÉVESQUE, de l'Académie des Inſcriptions & Belles-Lettres, Aggrégé à l'Académie des Beaux-Arts de Saint-Peterſbourg.

TOME SECOND.

A PARIS,

Chez L. F. PRAULT, Imprimeur, Quai des Auguſtins.

1792.

Dictionnaire des Arts de Peinture, Sculpture et Gravure, Paris: L. F. Prault, 1792, vol. 2.

Fig. 236

Watelet's entry on ground, which includes collaborative passages with an unknown Monsieur Robin, signifies a broad scope of meaning, highlighting the multivocality of ground:

> This term has several meanings in painting. The material on which the painting is made is called ground: a ground of wall, plaster, copper, wood, marble, etc. The primer or coating printed on these materials is also called [ground]. In this sense, we say an oil ground, a glue ground, a white, gray, red ground, etc.... The ground is not only what is seen behind the figures, nor the last plane of the composition; often he interrupts the scene & anticipates it, he animates the subject, gives him rest, & indicates the shots.[23]

The terminological range encompasses the supports' raw material (*matière*), second, the priming of the material (*préparation*), and third, the background or generally the area behind the figures (*dernier plan*). According to Watelet, the composition of figure and ground is one of multiple configurations of the ground. Despite being of particular relevance, "figure and ground" only results from previous preparatory layers.

Watelet's examinations of the terminological multitude, addressing the ground as material as well as visual component, dates back to early modern sources.[24] In his important work on fifteenth-century sources on ground and *campo*, Matteo Burioni puts forth how crucial and remarkable this differentiation was:

22
Brockhaus: Conversations-Lexicon oder Handbuch für die gebildeten Stände (Leipzig: Im Verlag des Kunst und Industrie-Comptoirs Amsterdam, 1814), entry: "*Grund*," pp. 101–102.

23
"Fond. Ce terme a plusieurs acceptions en peinture. On appelle fond la matière sur laquelle on fait le tableau: un fond de mur, de plâtre, de cuivre, de bois, de marbre, & c. On nomme de même l'apprêt ou l'enduit imprimé sur ces matières. En ce sens, on dit un fond de l'huile, un fond à la colle, un fond blanc, gris, rouge, & c.... Le fond n'est pas seulement ce qui se voit derrière les figures, ni le dernier plan de la composition; souvent il entrecoupe la scène & la devance, il anime le sujet, lui donne du repos, & en indique les plans." *Dictionnaire des Arts de Peinture, Sculpture et Gravure* (1792), pp. 337–339.

24
Jilleen Nadolny, "European Documentary Sources before c. 1500 Relating to Painting Grounds Applied to Wooden Supports. Translation and Terminology," in *Preparation for Painting: The Artists Choices and Consequences*, Joyce Townsend et al., eds. (London: Archetype Books, 2008), pp. 1–13.

a visually detectible ground, hence the discernible surface, is also part of a technical term, describing the support's preparation, and vice versa.[25] Such terminological distinction highlights both a differentiation between and an inseparability of various ground layers. While the ground signifies a solid and essential layer of the entire painting process, this preparation is inevitably inscribed in the visible result. This early modern understanding has been preserved and is included in Watelet's entry. Watelet's article is enriched with evaluative remarks that draw upon early modern descriptions of a multifaceted ground encompassing different layers. Watelet had previously published in the *Dictionnaire des Arts de Peinture* making the entry an important contemporary resource for how and what aspects were taught in artists' education.[26] In the form of lexical entries, academic knowledge, and instructions, this knowledge spread to a broader lay audience even outside of France.

Hence, the entry also underlines prevailing connotations implying a normative understanding of what counts as a painting and, more importantly, as a successful painting. Watelet advertized a harmonious interplay of all layers that ultimately constitute the ground and its shape. For him, synchronizing picture layers is essential to achieve artistic and not just mediocre results. The entry insists on considering *all* layers with the same care as compositional outlines since the ground prepares the light and dark areas of the painting. Therefore, the ground is unavoidably part of the final result, causing particularly brilliant colorfulness and nuanced depictions.

Watelet mainly criticizes the carelessness of artists' process of examining the priming and first layer of paint: "It seems to me that artists often leave it to habit or to a random chance how they

25
Matteo Burioni, "Grund und *campo*. Die Metaphorik des Bildgrundes in der frühen Neuzeit oder: Paolo Uccellos *Schlacht von San Romano*," in *Der Grund. Das Feld des Sichtbaren*, Gottfried Boehm and Matteo Burioni, eds. (Munich: Fink, 2012), pp. 94–149, here p. 96.

26
See France Nerlich and Alain Bonnet, eds., *Apprendre à peindre: Les ateliers privés à Paris 1780–1863* (Tours: Presses Universitaires François-Rabelais, 2013). Alain Bonnet, *L'enseignement des arts au XIXe siècle: La réform de l'École des Beaux-Arts de 1863 et la fin du modèle académique* (Rennes: Presses Universitaires de Rennes, 2006). Albert Boime, *The Academy and French Painting in the Nineteenth Century* (London: Phaidon, 1971).

decide on the color on which they begin to sketch out the works."[27] He underlines that the first application—the grounding—needs to be thoroughly considered and produced with attention equal to the composition, as the priming layers affect the following layers and, crucially, the ultimately visible surface: "I truly think that this part of their art, as well as several others that lead to mediocre results, ought to be the object of their research, their investigations and their thoughts."[28] All paint layers interact and are inseparable from each other: the first primer prepares the light and dark areas of the surface and is therefore involved in the result. This preparatory layer should be treated with immense attention and care to achieve highly valuable artworks. A thoughtful and consciously chosen priming, to summarize Watelet's advice, increases the quality of the painting. This demand for a more profound awareness highlights the importance of such preparatory layers, which form a technical necessity and directly impact the quality of the artwork.

Another example in a well-known German dictionary stresses the relevance of the prepared ground to achieve a visually appealing result. Published at the end of the eighteenth-century Sulzer's *General Theory of the Fine Arts* imbues its entry on "*Grund*" with a similar meaning highlighting the proper usage in a recipe-like terminology:

> The safest way to create a good painting, seems this way: Firstly, use a wide brush to place the lights and afterwards the shadows equally side by side.... This first step must give ground to a good stand and fluent blend of lights and shadows. And this will never be obtained, if the first grounding steps have already failed.[29]

27
"(Fond): Il me semble, que les artistes laissent souvent à l'habitude, à l'exemple ou au hasard, à décider de la couleur sur laquelle ils commencent à ébaucher les ouvrages." *Dictionnaire des Arts de Peinture, Sculpture et Gravure*, p. 333.

28
"(Fond): Je crois cependant que cette partie de leur art, ainsi que plusieurs autres qui paroissent de médiocre conséquence, devroit être quelquefois l'objet de leurs recherches, de leurs épreuves et de leurs réflexions." *Dictionnaire des Arts de Peinture, Sculpture et Gravure*, p. 333.

29
"Der sicherste Weg, ein Gemählde gut anzulegen, scheint dieser zu seyn, daß man mit einem breiten Pinsel zuerst die Lichter, denn die Schatten gleich stark neben einander seze, und hernach an den Gränzen zwischen beyden gelinde hin und her fahre, um sie etwas mit einander zu vereinigen. Diese erste Anlage

Without careful handling and preparation of the material, the result can hardly be considered "good" art. Qualitative and highly valued results can only be achieved by using the right recipe. Therefore, entries repeatedly aim to achieve a good result by following the instructions correctly. However, a well-executed ground does not stand alone but always relates to its composition. Thus, a "good" result depends on proper preparation, while the final composition to which the ground contributes is subject to evaluation. Nevertheless, the ground forms the basis for all subsequent paint layers and is both part of the surface and, within the surface, a compositional ground to the figures.

Two-dimensional Figures on Multidimensional Grounds

In the eighteenth and early nineteenth centuries, entries address a ground that runs through all layers of a painting, ultimately intending to provide a proper foundation for the figures that are arranged on them. Entries outline the principle of "figure and ground" and set out possible functions and requirements in relation to the figure. It is striking that lemmata on figure, in turn, do not reference the ground. Accordingly, painting explanations conceptualize an asymmetrical relation between figure and ground. Conceptually, it is the ground that ought to take the lead to form a complementary figure-and-ground composition.

For example, the entry "*figure*" in Diderot's *Encyclopédie* encompasses almost forty large-scale pages with a two-column printed text. The descriptions address various disciplinary fields that use the word "figure" as a key term.[30] In addition to the rhetorical, geometric, theological, or mathematical figure, the figure in painting is one of many subentries. Under "*Figure – terme de peinture*," the entry briefly defines the figure's relevance for

muß den Grund einer guten Haltung und Verfließung der Lichter und Schatten geben. Und diese wird man schwerlich erhalten, wenn man es in der ersten Anlage verfehlt hat." Johann Georg Sulzer, *Allgemeine Theorie der Schönen Künste. Lexikon der Künste und Ästhetik* (Leipzig: Weidmanns Erben und Reich, 1771), entry: "*Anlegen*," vol. 1, pp. 56–57, col. 253–254. This description follows in accuracy and style medieval and early modern recipe books like Cennino Cennini's *Il libro dell'arte*, in which several chapters are dedicated to how to prepare the ground for painting on different materials like wooden panes and walls.

30 Diderot, *Encyclpédie*, vol. 16, entry: "figure," pp. 748–783.

painting in generalizing words: "To paint the figure or to make the image of man is first of all to imitate all the possible forms of his body."[31] According to the artistic understanding, figure is geared toward representing a human body. The article continues by elaborating on the proper depiction of a man by first painting the body with varied light and shadow accents and second by aiming to express the human's emotional state.[32] As the inner emotion of the soul largely follows the posture of the body, the entries on figure in Diderot's *Encyclopédie* and subsequently in Watelet's *Dictionnaire* mainly focus on detailed descriptions on how to represent bodily proportions and muscles in order to achieve an aptly anatomic representation.[33]

References to the position of the figure and its relation to the surrounding space are absent in Diderot's and Watelet's examinations as well as in later entries such as the German *Handbuch für die gebildeten Stände* from 1814. Aspects on the figure's spatial context are only included in the entry on ground. While the concept of figure predominantly refers to the shape of the human body, the entry on ground indicates a complex multilayered model. The entry in Watelet's *Dictionnaire* even drafts a "theory of ground": "The theory on the ground keeps to some general principles: for example, the composition of the ground must contrast with the figures & highlight them."[34] The tone of the entry reflects the (self-)assigned authority of the French *académie* taking the position to enact rules. Addressing "general principles," the theory of ground mostly comprises a set of standardized tenets. Using the term "theory" claims an approach of overall validity that is not only true for one specific artwork but may even apply to the entirety of paintings.

31
"Peindre la figure ou faire l'image de l'homme, c'est premièrement imiter toutes les formes possibles de son corps," Diderot, *Encyclopédie*, vol. 16, p. 775.

32
"C'est secondement le rendre avec toutes les nuances dont il est susceptible, & dans toutes les combi-naisons que l'effet de la lumière peut opérer fur ces nuances. C'est enfin faire naître, à l'occasion de cette re-préfentation corporelle, l'idée des mouvemens de l'ame." Diderot, *Encyclopédie*, vol. 16, p. 775.

33
Diderot, *Encyclopédie*, vol. 16, p. 775; Watelet, *Dictionnaire des Arts de Peinture*, entry: "figure," p. 282.

34
"La théorie sur les fonds se borne à quelque principes généraux: par exemple, la composition du fond doit contraster avec les figures & les mettres en valeur." *Dictionnaire des Arts de Peinture, Sculpture et Gravure*, entry: "*Fond*," p. 339.

The ultimate rule was to contrast the ground with figures to make them visible. While "figure" and "ground" are not yet conceptualized as stable binary terms, the entry notes a hierarchy between figure and ground: the ground, in its multiple means, mainly serves the figure, providing a platform to come forth. This requirement is met by maintaining a formal discrepancy between the ground and the figure. The entry continues by explaining the basic rules of creating an appropriate contrast. The livelier the arrangements of the figures, the calmer and more static the ground. If, on the other hand, the figures are more restrained, the ground becomes more dynamic:

> If the general plane of the arrangement of the figures is parallel to the edge of the picture, the background must be circular or triangular; & on the contrary, if the plan of the figures is tormented, the ground of the painting must be characterized by grandeur & simplicity.[35]

The French original notably uses four different phrases to describe the ground and the complementary relation: "*plan général*," "*plan de fond*," "*plan de figure*," and "*fond du tableau*." "*Plan*" refers to aspects of the overall arrangement as, for instance, the area of the background, the area of the figures, or the general display of the painting. Such elaborations particularly touch upon compositional means to combine figure and ground. However, this paragraph is still part of the entry "*fond*" with its extensive discussion of preparation techniques. Hence, before figure and ground may even serve as a compositional pair, the ground inheres multiple layers and preparing tints.

A German entry in the *Brockhaus: Conversations-Lexicon oder Handbuch für die gebildeten Stände* from 1814 approves Watelet's set of rules. The descriptions demand creating a ground following the laws of harmony:

35 "[Q]ue si le plan général de la disposition des figures est parallèle au bord du tableau, il faut que le plan du fond soit circulaire ou triangulaire; & au contraire, si le plan des figures est tourmenté, il faut que le fond du tableau se caractérise par la grandeur & la simplicité de son plan." *Dictionnaire des Arts de Peinture, Sculpture et Gravure*, entry: "*Fond*," p. 339.

> The painter [must] take to heart that certain colors destroy one another while others enhance one another. Flesh color becomes pale on a red background, pale red appears vivid and fiery on a yellow background. One, therefore, must select a ground favorable for the objects represented, according to the laws of harmony and contrast. Often the ground determines the general effect of the scene, supports the masses, asserts the characters in the details, enlivens or destroys the claim.[36]

For the ground to fulfill this task and correctly stage the overall effect of the painting, the ground ought to follow the outlined rules by creating different background variants and respective color applications. All aspects jointly form the lemma "ground" and emphasize its versatile functions for paintings. These comprehensive instructions to achieve a proper ground stand in stark contrast to entries on the figure.

The entries on ground comprise notions of material preparation, composition, color theory, and perception. Each of these conceptions is distinct. However, they connect and merge in the term. This unity of aspects builds a multidimensional ground for paint applications. A spatial ground forms the basis for the figure to appear and come to the fore. Compared to the complexity of the ground, the notions of figure are direct and clearly outlined. One could argue that the required compositional contrast is also reflected in a conceptual contrast of a mutidimensional ground complementing a two-dimensional figure.

Another entry in the German dictionary *Brockhaus* from 1813 underlines the figures as a two-dimensional layer in contrast to a spatial surrounding. Without referring to figure and ground

36
"Der Maler [hat] wohl zu beherzigen, dass gewisse Farben einander zerstören, andere einander heben. Fleischfarbe wird blaß auf einem rothen Grunde, blaßroth erscheint lebhaft und feurig auf einem gelben Grunde. Man muß also den für die dargestellten Gegenstände vorteilhaften Grund nach den Gesetzen der Harmonie und des Contrastes auswählen. Oft bestimmt der Grund, die allgemeine Wirkung der Scene, unterstützt die Massen, macht die Figuren in den Details geltend, belebt oder zerstört den Anspruch." *Brockhaus: Conversations-Lexicon*, entry: "*Grund*," pp. 101–102. Such "laws of harmony and contrast" can be found, for example, in chapter 48 of Leon Battista Alberti's treatise *Della Pittura*.

as a compositional pair, the figure is defined as an external shape whose existence depends on the surrounding space:

> The term figure is used in several arts, some with a proper meaning, others with an improper or figurative meaning. The actual meaning is external shape, which arises from every limited and circumscribed space, be it with surfaces (surface figures) or with bodies (physical figures).[37]

The entry depicts the "figure" as a single entity that solely results from the immediate context, which would be the ground in painting. A further terminological specificity lies in the distinction between figure and form: "In the fine arts, the term figure is usually restricted to the human figure, and the expression form is used for the other figures."[38] The term "figure" only applies to the human appearance; without the gestalt of a human, the shape is defined as "form."

The entry does not refer to the terminology of ground, even when addressing the spatial relation of the figure in the arts. Sculpture, for instance, requires a surrounding space. In painting, the outline of a figure is placed on a flat surrounding surface that is, according to these lexical entries, supposed to create a spatial context for the figure. The entry, therefore, demonstrates how the figure's visibility relies on space; however, it is anticipated that the "ground" or rather "area" already exists and is prepared for the positioning of the the figures.

Regarding painting, this "area" is de facto equivalent to the ground that carries the figures. The ground, therefore, is closely associated with material means serving as a base for placement.[39] Matteo Burioni examined the terminological proximity between

37
"Des Ausdrucks Figur bedient man sich in mehreren Künsten, bei einigen in eigentlicher, bei anderen in uneigentlicher oder figürlicher Bedeutung. Die eigentliche Bedeutung ist äußere Gestalt, welche entsteht durch jeden beschränkten und umschriebenen Raum, sey dies nun bei Flächen (Flächenfiguren) oder bei Körpern (Körperliche Figuren)." *Brockhaus: Conversations-Lexikon*, entry: "*Figur*," pp. 603–604.

38
"Bei der bildenden Kunst schränkt man den Begriff Figur meist auf die Menschenfigur ein, und bedient sich für die übrigen Gestalten des Ausdrucks Form." *Brockhaus: Conversations-Lexikon*, entry: "*Figur*," pp. 603–604.

39
See "*Campus* as *Locus* and Narrative Stained Glass" by Bruno Haas in this volume.

"ground" and "*campo*" in the fifteenth century that enables acknowledging the ground in painting "as a regular, architectural process" starting with the foundation.[40] Wolfram Pichler, in turn, introduces the term "image field," (*Bildfeld*) to differentiate between a ground that enables visibility and a ground that provides an area, a field or *campo* for figures to stand on and to be positioned.[41] Early dictionaries gather these different conceptual facets of enabling visibility under the lemma ground.

However, it is noticeable that a different understanding of figure and ground was feasible too. The visual and material connection between figure and ground is particularly pronounced in cloth painting, a technique from the fifteenth and sixteenth centuries that dispenses with a primer and a final varnish [fig. 246]. The material is evidently inscribed in the figure since the number of layers of paint is reduced due to the fragile materiality of the fabric [fig. 247]. Figure and ground, therefore, primarily consist of the textile support and the figure comprising one or few layers of paint. This example shows, therefore, how different materials and media adapted the concepts of figure and ground and additional examples would enable other aspects to come into focus. However, all painting practices on the ground are directed toward the figure, and in turn, the figure is conceptually almost unmarked. As the focal point, the figure is mainly subject to iconographic and hermeneutical interpretations.

The difference between figure and form, as highlighted in the entry of 1814, implies an animistic understanding of figure. In contrast to the form, the figure appears as a living being in front of a serving carrier, the ground. The ground forms layers of material and color contrasts, while the figure marks the vital, the *anima*, the creature, and the living. The ground is technically constructed and multilayered while the figure appears in her *individuality*, hence in her unity as a being. The figure in her entirety is placed on the ground. Yet, achieving a well-balanced constellation weighs on the side of the multilayered ground.

40
Burioni, *Grund und campo*, p. 96.

41
Wolfram Pichler, "Zur Kunstgeschichte des Bildfeldes," in *Der Grund*, Boehm and Burioni, eds., pp. 441–472, here p. 442.

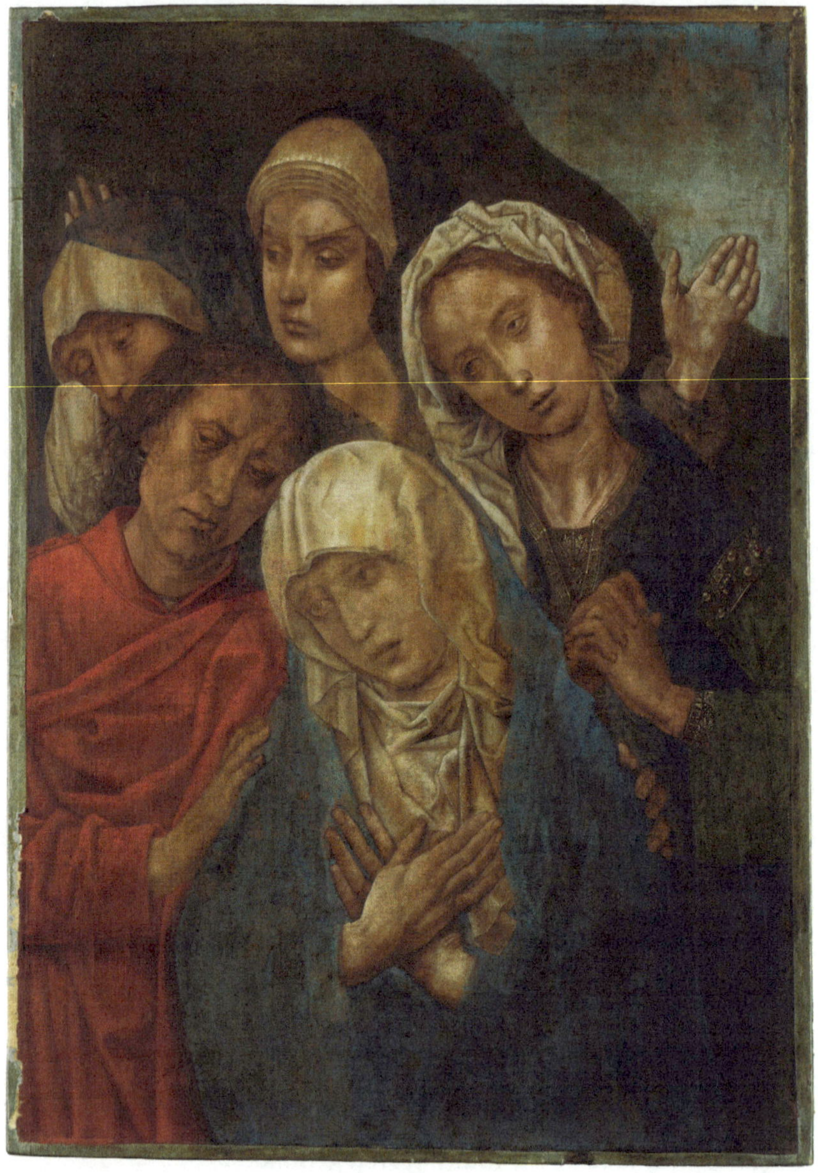

Hugo van der Goes, *Beweinung Christi*, 1480, tempera and cloth, 53.6 × 38.7 cm.
Gemäldegalerie, Berlin.

Fig. 246

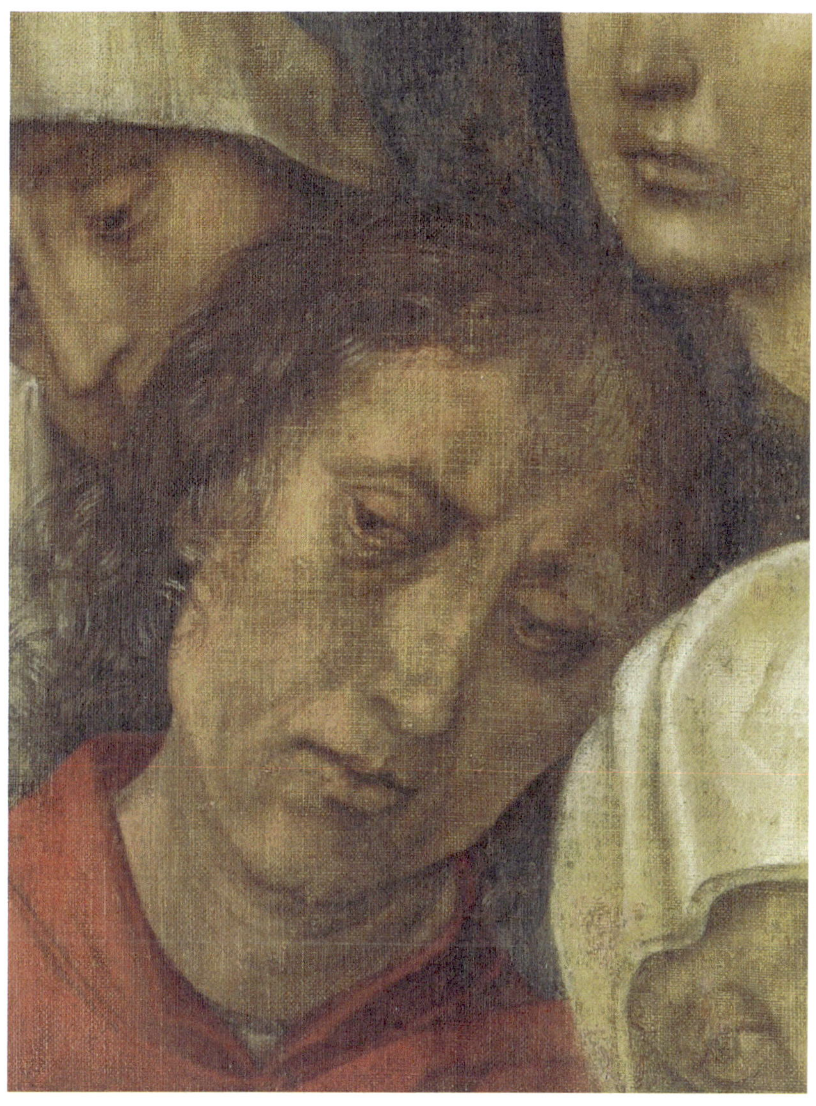

Detail of Fig. 246.

Fig. 247

The terminological difference between a multifaceted ground and the figure associated with the human shape raises questions about two different spatial notions. The figure appears as a two-dimensional and spatially well-defined unit. The ground, in contrast, meets the figure's plane with an expansive spatiality. Semantically as well as in technical means, the ground is multivocal and consists of multiple paint layers. Accordingly, the ground not only represents a pictorial space or a level to stand on but forms a multilayered spatiality. Designated as "the ground" in its singular form, historical sources conceptualize the ground as a multidimensional model, an idea that has given way to a ground as a two-dimensional equivalent to the figure in the twentieth century.

The rawness of the ground's material and its preparation techniques are repeatedly mentioned in historical entries on ground. This implies that, historically, the conception of the ground went far beyond the modernist focus on compositional and formal aspects, including all painting processes, even those that are often separated as technical preparation, such as smoothing and priming. The binary terminology of "figure" and "ground" is less dichotomous in its historical understanding. Instead, the dichotomy consists of the figure on the one hand and of a multilayered, complex ground on the other. Material connotations and technical elaborations, which for a long time filled large parts of the lexical entries on ground, steadily declined over the course of the nineteenth century. The question of which modifications have contributed to this altered understanding is particularly central to the formation of the concept of figure-and-ground.

Pre-primed Canvases in the Studio

At the beginning of the nineteenth century, a drastic change concerning painting supports altered centuries-old painting practices. Industrially pre-primed and mounted canvases, available in different formats, rapidly entered and changed the art supplies market.[42] This industrial mass production originated in Paris.

42
Pascal Labreuche, *Paris, capitale de la toile à peindre, XVIIe – XIXe siècle* (Paris: CTHS – INHA, 2011), p. 20. Beatrix Haaf, "Industriell vorgrundierte Malleinen: Beiträge zur Entwicklungs-, Handels- und Materialgeschichte," *Zeitschrift für Kunsttechnologie und Konservierung* 1, no. 2 (1987): pp. 7–72, here p. 11.

Factories carried out all preparatory steps, such as washing, smoothing, and priming, creating ready-to-use canvases. In harmony, the workers manually applied the primer on lengths of textile and cut the material in various formats. As specialized workers handled meter-long canvases, the priming proved to be more evenly and precise than applications by painters. Finally, the workers mounted the canvas pieces on a stretcher, which notably increased the sale of prefabricated canvases.[43]

Large parts of long-existing painting procedures transformed thoroughly, making traditional painting processes gradually obsolete. Whether artists were trained academically or rejected academic guidelines and guidance, artists across all principles used the ready-to-paint canvases. From a conservational perspective, Paul Labreuche, Anthea Callen, and others were able to show how quickly artists switched to these products, which enabled them to immediately start with compositional layers without washing, pressing, and priming the canvas first.[44]

A steady decline of traditional painting techniques can be observed in a shift in meaning for the term "ground." Instead of material discussions of priming methods and recipes, descriptions of the compositional tasks of the ground dominated the entries. For instance, the entry "*fond*" in Bouillet's *Dictionnaire universel des sciences, des lettres et des arts* from 1854 only briefly includes material and priming aspects. Practical instructions and the importance of material preparation for the effect and outcome of the painting are missing.[45] The entry in *La Grande Encyclopédie* from 1886–1902 emphasizes on the *fond* as a compositional layer, highlighting the *fond*'s contrastive means to shift attention toward the figure:

43
Pascal Labreuche, "The Industrialisation of Artists' Prepared Canvas in Nineteenth Century Paris. Canvas and Stretchers: Technical Developments up to the Period of Impressionism," in *Zeitschrift für Kunsttechnologie und Konservierung* 22, no. 2 (2008,): pp. 316–332, here p. 316.

44
Callen, *The Art of Impressionism*, p. 21. Callen, *Techniques of the Impressionists*; Haaf, "Industriell vorgrundierte Malleinen"; Labreuche, *Paris, capitale de la toile à peindre*; Labreuche, "The Industrialisation of Artists' Prepared Canvas."

45
Marie-Nicolas Bouillet, *Dictionnaire universel des sciences, des lettres et des arts* (Paris: Libraire de L. Hachette et Cie, 1854), entry: "*Fond*," p. 688.

> The ground must remain absolutely neutral to allow all the interest to focus on the main subject of the painting or to highlight this subject in a more active way, by a skillful contrast of lines or tones.[46]

In this determination, the fond is part of the surface and the depiction but only as a neutral or merely supportive ground in favor of the main representation. In earlier dictionaries, as we have seen, material-practical aspects were still emphasized and minimized or absent in the entries from the late nineteenth century. From now on, the ground hardly appears in favor of the figure.

In German dictionaries, the notion of ground as background took over progressively, with "background" becoming a synonym for "ground." Ultimately, the term "background" gained so much significance that it led to a linguistic separation between ground and background. The *Brockhaus* from 1875 and *Meyers Konversationslexikon* from 1876 eventually introduced "background" as a separate lemma no longer associated with the previous superordinate term "ground." The entries on "*Hintergrund*" focus on perspective and spatial dimensions as well as on the relation between foreground, middle, and background. *Meyers Konversationslexikon* from 1876, for instance, addresses how these three should be connected: "Background (distance), in paintings, that, which is shown behind and apart from the main subjects; both foreground and background are harmoniously brought together by the middle ground."[47] Equivalent to earlier descriptions of ground, the contrast between figure and ground is particularly crucial: "In particular, where individual figures or objects form the main focus of the representation, background is the designation for the rest of the surface from which they stand out."[48]

46 "Le fond doit rester absolument neutre pour laisser tout l'intérêt se porter sur le sujet principal du tableau ou faire valoir ce sujet d'une manière plus active, par un habile contraste de lignes ou de tons." *La Grande Encyclopédie* (Paris: H. Lamirault et Cie, 1886–1902), entry: "*Fond,*" pp. 710–711, here p. 710.

47 "Hintergrund (Ferne), bei Gemälden das, was hinter den Hauptgegenständen und von diesen abgesondert dargestellt ist; beide, Vordergrund und Hintergrund, werden durch den Mittelgrund in harmonische Verbindung gebracht." *Meyers Konversationslexikon*, entry: "*Hintergrund,*" p. 936.

48 "Insbesondere ist Hintergrund da, wo Einzelfiguren oder Einzelgegenstände die Hauptsache der Darstellung ausmachen, die

As a distant area, the background forms contrast and therefore enables visibility. However, the background has no distinct formal or spatial qualities anymore. It is regarded as the "rest," the undesignated area whose contour and shape lacks precise determination. No longer referring to material and preparatory aspects, the term "background" replaces "ground." In the description of the *Brockhaus* from 1884, the background even resembles definitions of figure, taking the shape of a two-dimensional area that contrasts another two-dimensional area.

Entries from the late nineteenth century demonstrate how the meaning of ground has changed over time. While the term originally included multiple aspects, such as material and painting techniques, perspective, and spatial connotations, time favored an understanding of the ground that analytically excluded these facets and increasingly focused on questions of representation. By the end of the nineteenth century, the terms figure and ground conceptually converged, moving toward a binary structure of figure-and-ground in the twentieth century.

Outlook

The terms "figure" and "ground" were listed separately until the beginning of the nineteenth century. While "figure" was largely described as a precise formal and spatial unit, the term "ground" included aspects of material, technique, composition, and pictorial space. Drawing upon fifteenth-century understandings of the ground as a foundation that is inscribed in the visible result, entries from the eighteenth and nineteenth centuries are in line with the French Academy and its concepts of what a successful classicist painting should be. Throughout the nineteenth century, the ground becomes less concerned with material matters. Instead, compositional aspects of ground come to the fore, paving thc way for the introduction of the lemma "background." Descriptions under the term "ground" no longer necessarily link to painting or cross-reference a different lemma. In Meyer's lexicon from 1876, the entry "*Grund*" refers to the lemma "*Hintergrund*"

Bezeichnung für das übrige der Fläche, von der sich jene abheben." *Brockhaus Conversations-Lexikon*, entry: "*Hintergrund*," p. 252.

to obtain more information about painting: "In painting, finally, [that what] is behind the individual painted objects (fore- middle- background), see "*background.*"[49]

Modified art supplies of the nineteenth century with pre-primed canvasses enabled one to paint without the former preparatory steps that required time and specific knowledge. Because of these innovations, priming recipes, extensive explanations of how to prepare a canvas that matches the anticipated depiction of the figure became obsolete and outdated. An increasingly rather compositional and formal understanding of both figure and ground opened room for new conceptualizations of these terms.

Gestalt and perception psychology at the beginning of the twentieth century, for instance, prominently refer to figure and ground. Based on color and form constellations, gestalt psychology explored the laws of perception and imagery.[50] Confining the figure as clearly outlined, the figure's perceptibility stems from the contrasting difference to the ground, which in turn equally consisted of precise shapes and colors. Edgar Rubin's face-vase, for example, advertized interchangeability between figure and ground that did not imply a hierarchy between the two components. In transgressing artistic discourses, gestalt psychology acquainted a broader audience with the concept of figure-and-ground while manifesting its terminological dichotomy that became a prominent formal-analytical criterion.

The historical entries of figure and ground provide insight into the wide variety of conceptual dimensions that became less and less relevant in the nineteenth century. Altered meanings showed that figure-and-ground is and was a traditional and much-described paradigm, which, however, did not keep its validity over time. Instead, the paradigm of figure-and-ground is, in itself, subject to historical change. No study can or should replace object-based analyses, especially since terms may act statically and literally in prescriptive manners. Figure and ground should not be perceived nor used as a template that makes us see and analyze.

49
"In der Malerei endlich, [das] was sich hinter den einzelnen gemalten Gegenständen befindet (Vorder-Mittel-Hintergrund, s. Hintergrund)." *Meyers Konversationslexikon*, entry: "*Grund*," p. 289.

50
Rudolf Arnheim, *Art and Visual Perception: A Psychology of the Creative Eye: The New Version* (Berlin: De Gruyter, 1979. See also the contribution by Tom Steinert in this volume.

Their variability should rather inform their usage. The terms' variance and historical changeability contrasts the twentieth century utilization of the terminology. Taking this into account might help expand the vocabularies and perspectives for analyzing premodern (and modern) artifacts.

Part 3
Beyond the Surface

Stained glass is usually composed of several variously colored or colorless glass pieces, painted with vitreous paints and then fired. The pieces of glass are assembled into the desired motif or ornament with lead came. A key feature of stained-glass painting is that glass is not merely the material support to which paint is applied;[1] it is also visible in its emergence as figure and an integral part of the image field.[2] The glass is never completely covered with paint, enabling light to filter through and penetrate into the space of the viewer.[3] The material ground remains visible and becomes part of the figure. Wojciech Bałus goes even further and reinforces this aspect of materiality and light by defining the glass ground as

> a support that, in the technical sense, is "self-supporting," being the construction of the window with its frame, *ferramenta* and a network of lead bars, and a support, that, by virtue of being translucent, is capable of opening up the "abyss" (*Abgrund*) behind it, from where the *lumen* comes.[4]

1
On the different appearances of ground see Gottfried Boehm and Matteo Burioni, "Einleitung: Nichts ist ohne Grund," in *Der Grund: Das Feld des Sichtbaren,* Gottfried Boehm and Matteo Burioni, eds. (Munich: Brill, 2012), pp. 11–24, here pp. 16–17; Étienne Jollet, "Introduction," in *Le fond de l'œuvre,* Émilie Chedeville, Étienne Jollet, and Claire Sourdin, eds. (Paris: Edition Sorbonne, 2020), pp. 13–26, here p. 13.

2
Wojciech Bałus, "Diaphanum: Bildwissenschaftliche Überlegungen zur Glasmalerei," in *Licht(t)räume: Festschrift für Brigitte Kurmann-Schwarz zum 65. Geburtstag,* Barbara von Orelli-Messerli, Eva-Maria Scheiwiller-Lorber, Angela Schiffhauer, and Katharina Georgi, eds. (Petersberg: Michael Imhof, 2016), pp. 11–17, here p. 13; Wojciech Bałus, "A Matter of Matter: Transparent – Translucent – Diaphanum in the Medium of Stained Glass," in *Investigations in Medieval Stained Glass: Materials, Methods, and Expressions,* Brigitte Kurmann-Schwarz and Elizabeth Carson Pastan, eds. (Leiden: Brill, 2019), pp. 109–188, here p. 113. For further remarks on glass painting and *Bildwissenschaft,* cf. Brigitte Kurmann-Schwarz, "'Fenestre vitree ... significant Sacram Scripturam'": Zur Medialität mittelalterlicher Glasmalerei des 12. und 13. Jahrhunderts," in *Glasmalerei im Kontext: Bildprogramme und Raumfunktionen,* Rüdiger Becksmann, ed. (Nuremberg: Germanisches Nationalmuseum, 2005), pp. 61–73.

3
The aspect of light and its effect on the viewer has been explored in research mainly on medieval stained glass; cf. Bałus, "Diaphanum," p. 12; Bałus, "A Matter of Matter," p. 112; Eva Frodl-Kraft, *Die Glasmalerei: Entwicklung, Technik, Eigenart* (Vienna: Schroll, 1970), pp. 10–12; Christine Hediger and Brigitte Kurmann-Schwarz, "[...] et *faciunt inde tabulas saphiri pretiosas ac satis utiles in fenestris*: Die Farbe Blau in der 'Schedula' und in der Glasmalerei von 1100–1250," in *Zwischen Kunsthandwerk und Kunst: Die "Schedula diversarum artium,"* Andreas Speer, ed. (Berlin: De Gruyter, 2014), pp. 256–273.

4
Bałus, "A Matter of Matter," p. 116; Bałus, "Diaphanum," p. 16.

In the following exploration of stained glass, it is crucial to remember that glass painting does not rely on an opaque support that needs to be covered up or concealed, but that instead the material is intended to be visible in the completed work of art. The pieces of painted glass in works of stained glass oscillate between figure and pictorial ground, but they also remain material support. Focusing on examples of later medieval and early modern stained glass from Switzerland, the aim of this contribution is to describe various relations of figure and ground in stained glass, while taking into account the technical processing of the material ground.

Colored and Colorless Glass, Lead Came, and Grisaille Painting

To produce a work of stained glass, colored or decolorized pieces of glass are first cut into the required shape. Contours and outlines are then usually painted on the front of the glass using grisaille. Grisaille or *Schwarzlot* is a black or brown glass paint that can also be applied over a wide area on both the front or back to model halftones, or to etch shapes and motifs into the area coated with it (more on this below). From the fourteenth century onward, silver stain is more commonly used and from the sixteenth century onward, various vitreous enamels are added (see below for examples). These enamel paints are used to paint in color onto the front of the glass pieces and fired in the kiln to fuse them to the glass. After firing, the pieces are assembled using lead came, which unites the glass pieces into a larger whole.[5]

5
This abbreviated presentation of the production process does not take into account that even in the middle ages, pot-colored stained glass was supplemented with paints applied cold that were not fired into the glass. For more on this see Germanisches Nationalmuseum / Corpus Vitrearum Deutschland, eds., *Originale Kaltmalerei auf historischen Glasmalereien* (Freiburg: Nationalkomitee des Corpus Vitrearum Medii Aevi Deutschland und Germanisches Nationalmuseum Nürnberg, 2018). On the technique of glass painting see, among others, Uta Bergmann, *Die Zuger Glasmalerei des 16. bis 18. Jahrhunderts* (Bern: Benteli, 2004), pp. 141–144; Barbara Butts and Lee Hendrix, "Drawn on Paper, Painted on Glass: Introduction," in *Painting on Light: Drawings and Stained Glass in the Age of Dürer and Holbein*, Lee Hendrix and Barbara Butts, eds. (Los Angeles: J. Paul Gettty Museum, 2000), pp. 1–16, here p. 4; Musée Suisse du Vitrail, ed., *Glasmalerei: Eine Einführung mit Beispielen des Vitromusée Romont und Glasfenstern in der Region von Romont* (Romont: Vitromusée Romont, 2006).

It should be added that the design of the motif or figure takes place in a different medium, namely on paper, cardboard or on a whitewashed wood panel, for which there is evidence in the Middle Ages. In accordance with this preliminary drawing, the glass was cut to the requisite size and shape and painted with grisaille. In his reflections on the concept of the image in relation to stained glass, Bałus maintained that the process of transferring the design to glass detaches the image from its support.[6] All the characteristics of the image field are retained in the process, he argues, but behind it there is now an empty space instead of the ground. This interpretation, however, should be differentiated to account for the fact that traces of preliminary drawings that were directly applied to the glass have been preserved in the medieval stained glass in the choir of the Bern Münster.[7]

On a heraldic stained glass in the Bern Münster an angel stands on a green field of grass carrying a shield with an unknown coat of arms [fig. 259].[8] His upper body with wings extended is turned slightly to the right from a frontal viewpoint. The angel is framed by a round arch supported by narrow columns, decorated with branch tracery with acanthus leaves. The background is filled with a blue-black damask pattern. Viewing the panel in reflective light foregrounds the material elements [fig. 260].[9] The lead came with soldered joints is clearly visible, covering the stained glass with a protruding net.[10] The colors of the individual glass fragments, such as the yellow of the angel's robe or the green

6
Bałus describes the process as iconic difference and refers to Boehm. Bałus, "Diaphanum," pp. 13–14; Bałus, "A Matter of Matter," p. 113; Cf. Gottfried Boehm, "Ikonische Differenz," in *Rheinsprung 11: Zeitschrift für Bildkritik* 1 (2011), pp. 170–177, https://rheinsprung11.unibas.ch/archiv/ausgabe-01/glossar/ikonische-differenz/.

7
Sophie Wolf and Stefan Trümpler, "Rückseitige Vorzeichnungen und Kaltbemalungen: Untersuchungen an den Chorfenstern des 15. Jh. im Berner Münster," in *Das Berner Münster: Das erste Jahrhundert: von der Grundsteinlegung bis zur Chorvollendung und Reformation (1421–1517/1528)*, Bernd Nicolai and Jürg Schweizer, eds. (Regensburg: Schnell & Steiner, 219), pp. 405–431.

8
Brigitte Kurmann-Schwarz, *Die Glasmalereien des 15. bis 18. Jahrhunderts im Berner Münster* (Bern: Benteli, 1998), pp. 432–433.

9
According to Bałus the "anatomical parts" of stained glass are revealed in reflected light: Bałus, "Diaphanum," p. 16.

10
The lead came of this panel was replaced in the nineteenth century: Kurmann-Schwarz, *Die Glasmalereien des 15. bis 18. Jahrhunderts im Berner Münster*, p. 429 and p. 433.

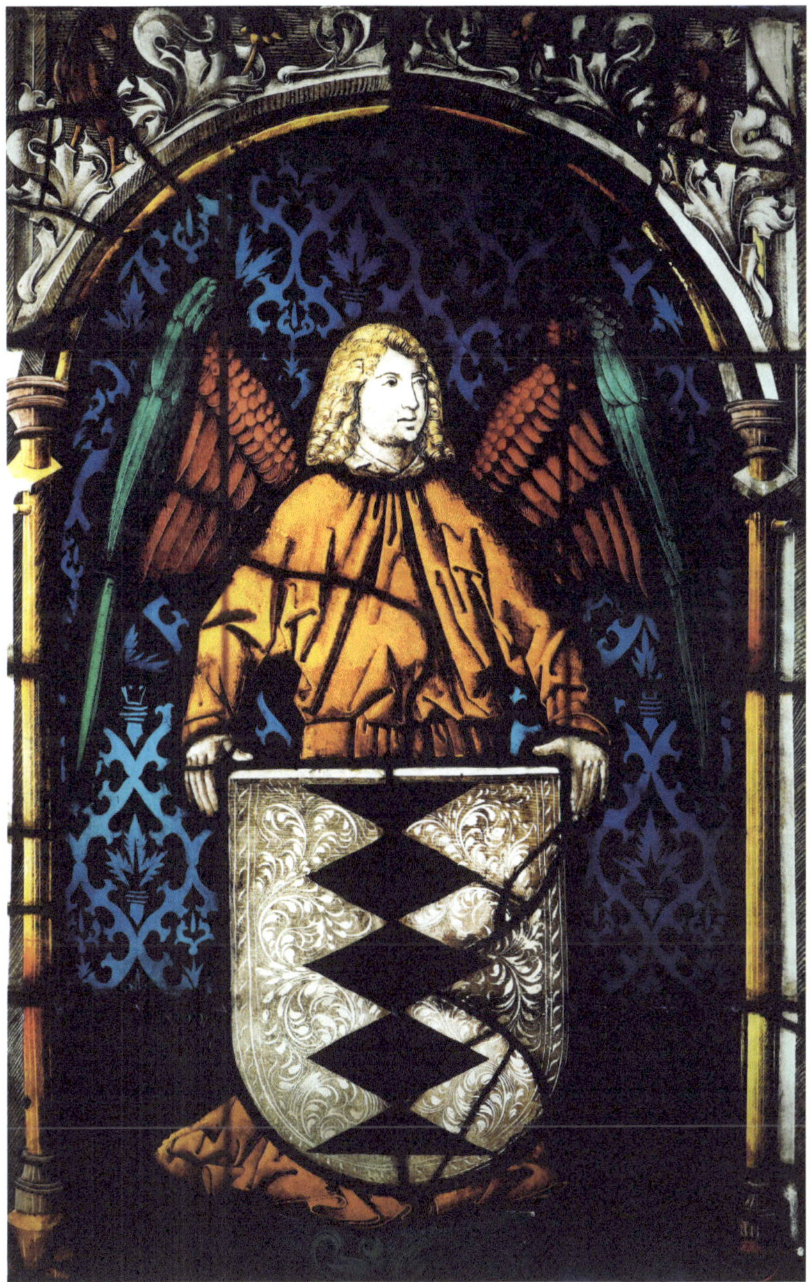

Heraldic stained glass with angel and unknown coat of arms, in transmitted light, ca. 1500–1520, 98 × 66.5 cm. Münster N VII, 1b, Bern.

Fig. 259

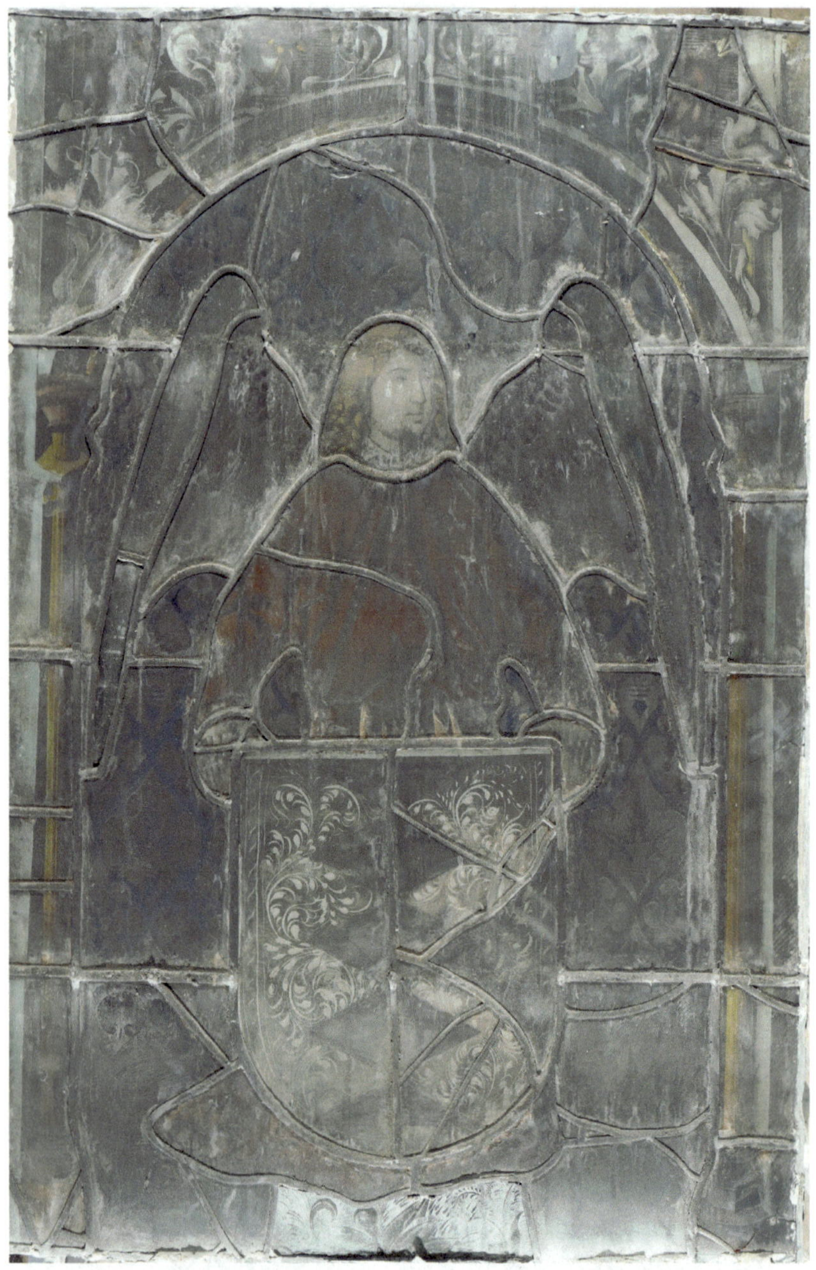

Heraldic stained glass with angel and unknown coat of arms, in reflected light, ca. 1500–1520, glass painting, 98 × 66.5 cm. Münster, N VII, 1b, Bern.

Fig. 260

of the grass, can be surmised more than perceived. The grisaille is visible where it is applied to the brighter glass pieces but disappears with the darker colors. On the angel's upper body, for example, the black outlines of the folds are distinguished from the yellow robe. In reflective light, the silver stain applied to the reverse also appears on the front as a lighter and more yellow area, as seen with the hair of the angel.

However, this processing of the glass pieces by the glass painter as well as the color of the glass only unfold their impact as imaging elements in transmitted light.[11] The individual glass pieces, produced in various colors and cut into the desired shape, combine in the light to create a colorful mosaic.[12] The grisaille lining and shading applied to the front and back of the glass transform the colored glass fragments into parts of clothing, a head, architectural elements or an ornamental background. Bałus rightly counts not just the physically permanent materials such as glass, vitreous enamels, iron rods, or lead came among the media of stained glass, but also the light.[13] In this case, it is not reflected light, but transmitted light—that is, light that must penetrate through the glass. Only in this modality does stained glass in all its details and facets become truly visible.

The technical necessity of lead came also fades into the background when the heraldic glass panel is viewed in transmitted light. The came lead loses its materiality and is perceived as black lines that outline the represented figures. The net of black lines cast by the leading across the entire surface of the stained glass impacts the way it is seen, from the foreground to the background

11
See also Bałus, "Diaphanum," p. 15; Frodl-Kraft, *Die Glasmalerei*, p. 6; Brigitte Kurmann-Schwarz and Angela Schiffhauer, "Bildmodelle in der Glasmalerei des 12. und 13. Jahrhunderts: Vom vollfarbig zum teilfarbig verglasten Fenster," *Das Mittelalter* 15, no. 2 (2010): 114–133, here 114.

12
This type of stained glass is also called "musivic" or "glass mosaic": Rebekka Gysel, *Glasmalerei im Dienste der Nation: Standesscheibenzyklen als Zeugnisse des schweizerischen Bundesstaats* (Bern: Peter Lang, 2020), pp. 38–39; Jenny Schneider, *Die Standesscheiben von Lukas Zeiner im Tagsatzungssaal zu Baden (Schweiz): Ein Beitrag zur Geschichte der schweizerischen Standesscheiben* (Basel: Birkhäuser, 1954), p. 123; Christine Hediger and Angela Schiffhauer, "Werkstoff Glas: Überlegungen zur Materialität von Glasmalerei in Moderne und Mittelalter," *Kunst und Architektur in der Schweiz* 58, no. 4 (2007): 15–23, 16.

13
Bałus, "Diaphanum," p. 12. Frodl-Kraft had already described the translucent ground of stained glass and postulated light as a prerequisite medium for viewing stained glass: Frodl-Kraft, *Die Glasmalerei*, p. 8.

and beyond the figure. The leading unites the angel with the ornamental ground and the architectural frame on a single surface plane. In this sense it directs the focus of the viewer either to the material properties or to the motif or figure. This phenomenon of lead came oscillating between figure and ground is demonstrated particularly clearly in the example of ornamental glazing.

Lead Came Between Figure and Ground

The clerestory windows of the basilica on the castle mount of Valère in Sion are among the largest and oldest ensembles of medieval ornamental windows in Switzerland. The glazing was restored in the early twentieth century and partially amended, but retains much of the original inventory, which was created between 1225 and 1260.[14] In total, four windows in the clerestory of the nave contain medieval remnants. Two of these feature a pattern of scales, for which parts of the original leading has been preserved in the workshop of the restorer Richard Nüscheler.[15] The ornament in the two other windows is composed of tracery with intersecting rings and diagonal bands [fig. 263].[16] The diagonal bands run alternately above and below the circles and intertwine with them, forming a weaving pattern at their intersection. The geometrical ornament is created by the specific cut of the glass pieces and lead came which darkly frame the former. This lead glazing is divided at regular intervals horizontally and vertically by iron rods in the window axis, which also anchor the glass in the window opening.

The ornamental windows draw the attention of the viewer as a bright, light-flooded area in contrast to the rest of dark, built architecture. The structure of the lead came is a focal point

14
Chantal Ammann-Doubliez, Ludovic Bender, Karina Queijo, and Romaine Syburra, *Le bourg capitulaire et l'église de Valère à Sion* (Bern: Société d'histoire de l'art en Suisse, 2022), pp. 177–179.

15
Ammann-Doubliez, et al., *Le bourg capitulaire et l'église de Valère à Sion*, p. 180. Today, they are kept in the collection of the Valais History Museum.

16
Ellen J. Beer, and Hans R. Hahnloser, *Die Glasmalereien der Schweiz vom 12. bis zum Beginn des 14. Jahrhunderts* (Basel: Birkhäuser, 1956), p. 123. The browning of individual glass pieces is due to the oxidation of manganese in the glass. Ammann-Doubliez, et al., *Le bourg capitulaire et l'église de Valère à Sion*, p. 179.

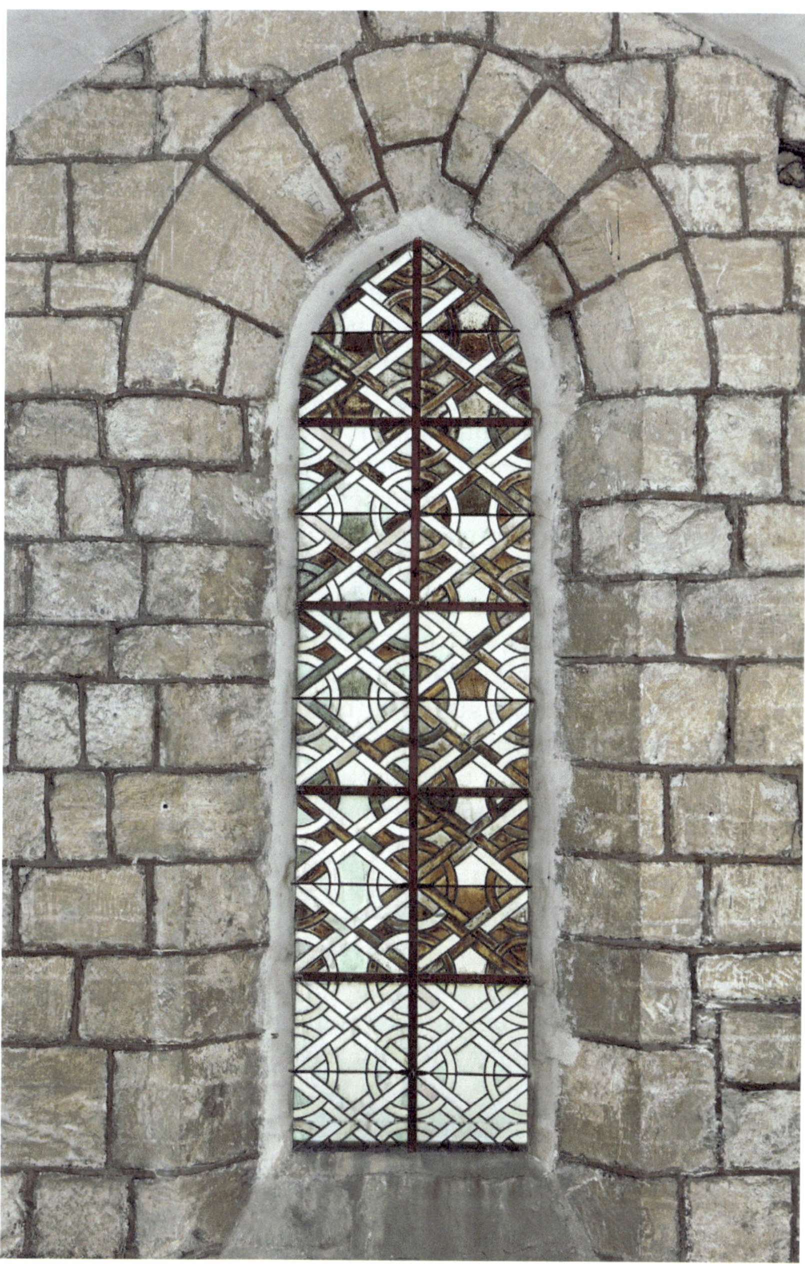

Ornamental window, ca. 1225–1260, 290 × 90 cm.
Valère Basilica on the castle mount, clerestory on the north, Sion.

Fig. 263

perceived as a pictorial ornament. Only the thicker iron rods connect the individual windows with the dark frame of the window embrasure. The exterior space that exists beyond the glass panel—the clouds, the landscape, the mountains—lies beyond the viewer's field of vision, despite the glass being colorless. Such purely ornamental windows are most commonly linked with the aesthetic principles of the Cistercian order, which required a restrained and modest artistic concept.[17] The example above among others proves that ornamental glazing of this kind was also integrated in other ecclesiastical buildings, be it for aesthetic or economic reasons.

If the glass serves as a support for painting, the attention of the viewer remains focused on the stained glass image consisting of its ornaments. The surrounding architecture, in which the glass painting is embedded, becomes a vague backdrop in contrast to the luminous image. As mentioned before, grisaille or *Schwarzlot* is the black, gray, or sometimes brown paint used to apply lines, patterns, and shading. It consists of very finely powdered glass mixed with iron and copper oxide to give a dark color. The powder is liquified using vinegar, water, and a binder such as gum arabic. For example, the ocular window on the north side of the basilica in Sion above the portal is glazed with colorless glass combined with a few colored elements and painted with a grisaille ornament [fig. 265]. The window is a patchwork of pieces of the original glazing from the late thirteenth century amended with remnants of older glass from the same church. According to the most recent study, the window was probably originally decorated entirely with a uniform grisaille ornament.[18]

The central square with a herringbone pattern and a blue quatrefoil from the fifteenth to sixteenth century was not part of the original window. It is joined on all four sides with an ornament of large quatrefoil flowers with leaves interwoven with

17
Ammann-Doubliez, et al., *Le bourg capitulaire et l'église de Valère à Sion*, p. 179; Kurmann-Schwarz and Schiffhauer, "Bildmodelle in der Glasmalerei des 12. und 13. Jahrhunderts," pp. 115–116. Angela Schiffhauer, "Strategien der Beleuchtung im gotischen Sakralraum: Überlegungen zur Farbigkeit der Glasfenster und zur Funktion von Grisaillen," in *Manipolare la luce in epoca premoderna: Aspetti architettonici, artistici e filosofici*, Daniela Mondini and Vladimir Ivanovici, eds. (Mendrisio: Mendrisio Academy Press, 2014), pp. 252–271, here p. 256.

18
Ammann-Doubliez, et al., *Le bourg capitulaire et l'église de Valère à Sion*, p. 182.

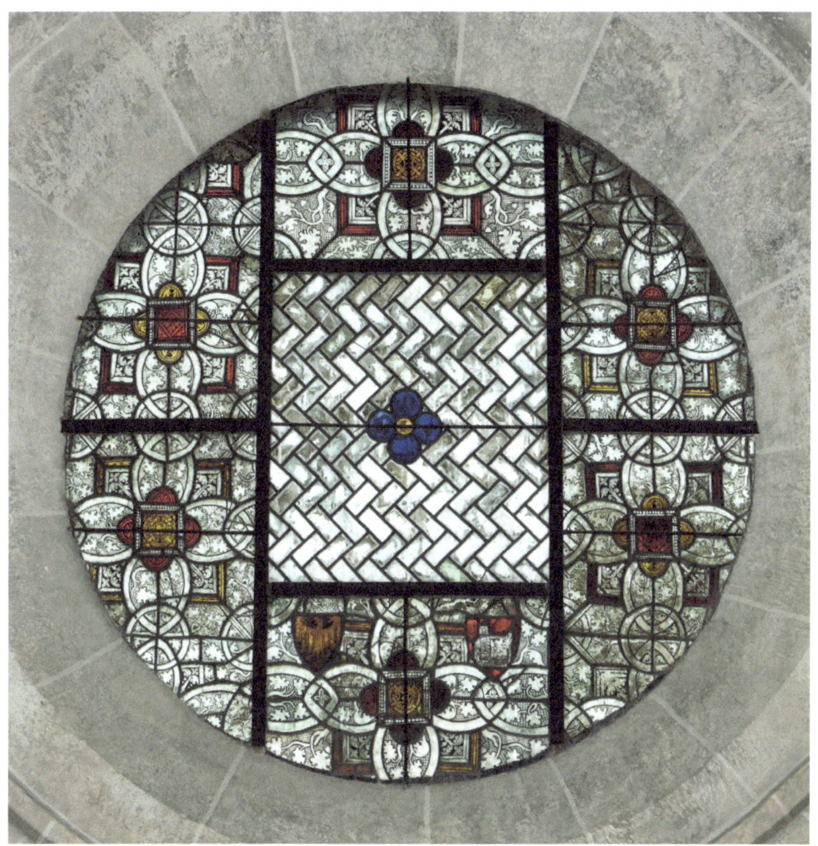

Ocular grisaille-window, end of the thirteenth century, 170 cm diameter.
Valère Basilica on the castle mount, clerestory on the north, Sion.

rings, to form a circle. Below the flower leaves there is a square red border. A red or yellow square, outlined in white and underlaid with a colored quatrefoil, decorates the center of the flowers. The white flower petals and shapes are filled in with oak leaves and crosshatching. The defining aspects of the ornamental window are the course of the lead cames, which define the large shapes such as the quatrefoil and squares, as well as the more delicate leaf ornaments and crosshatching in grisaille. Through skillful layering of surfaces and borders as well as sporadic colorful accents there emerges an interplay between foreground and background. The lead came as part of the material ground loses its inherent materiality and merges with the ornament. In other words: the grisaille painting applied to the surface of the glass is seen simultaneously with the lead came that holds the pieces together; forming a single ornament composed of thicker and thinner black lines. The individual colored glass pieces accent parts of the pattern, although they too are a part of both the material ground and the image field. When the ocular window is seen in transmitted light, the various materials and the ground merge with the ornament that takes shape.[19]

Lead Came, Pot-Colored Glass, and Grisaille

On windows with pot-colored glass the relationship between figure and ground is configured differently again. In stained glass, the color (with the exception of vitreous enamel, which I discuss below) is not externally applied to the material support, but the pieces of glass themselves are tinted. The material ground therefore already contains color, the intensity of which depends on the thickness of the glass and on the brightness of the light. In contrast to the regular, colorless ornamental windows, the glass pieces are cut individually to the desired shape, which is determined by the motif of the image.

The three-lancet tracery window from the second quarter of the fourteenth century in the chancel of St. Laurentius church

19
On this see also the observations by Kurmann-Schwarz and Schiffhauer, "Bildmodelle in der Glasmalerei des 12. und 13. Jahrhunderts."

in Frauenfeld, Switzerland, serves as an instructive example of the interplay of pot-colored and ornamental background, as well as of stained glass and architectural context [fig. 268].[20] It features a very high percentage of original substance and is extremely well preserved. This is partly due to the circumstance that the stained glass was walled in from the outside and covered with a baroque high altar on the inside during the early modern period.[21] The leading also largely dates to the period of the window's creation.

The upper third of the middle lancet depicts the crucified Christ. He is flanked in the outer lancets by Mary and John the Evangelist. Below, the left and central fields are dedicated to the annunciation, while the church patron St. Lawrence is depicted on the right. In the bottom third, ornamented quatrefoils and six-pointed stars form a circular arrangement.

The color of the figures' robes, the yellow of the architectural framing, and the accents of color are made of pot-colored glass. For each new color, a new piece of glass was cut to the requisite size and matched with others, like a mosaic, to assemble the figure of a saint, the frame, or an ornament. The size and shape of stained glass artwork is defined by the opening in the wall. The volume of the figures of the saints is modeled through grisaille shading and garment folds, which are painted onto the pot-colored glass. The layout of the lead came is also determined by the picture motif. The leading follows the fold of a robe or an outline, in the latter case separating various colored-glass pieces from each other. Progressive color gradients are therefore not possible. Each colored surface has a clear contour. The effect is a strong schematization of the figures.[22] The material ground—the glass—the lead and the grisaille are perceived as the colors and

20
Rolf Hasler and Sarah Keller, "St. Laurentius-fenster," *Vitrosearch* 2020, https://vitrosearch.ch/de/objects/2660478; Sarah Keller and Kathrin Kaufmann, *Die Glasmalereien vom Mittelalter bis 1930 im Kanton Thurgau* (Berlin: De Gruyter, 2022), p. 29.

21
Sophie Wolf, "Das Chorfenster von St. Laurentius in Frauenfeld-Oberkirch: Eine aussergewöhnlich gut erhaltene Glasmalerei," in *Licht- und Farbenzauber: Glasmalerei im Thurgau*, Amt für Denkmalpflege des Kantons Thurgau, ed. (Basel: Denkmalpflege im Thurgau, 2022), pp. 108–115, here p. 113. In the mid-nineteenth century this wall was removed and just a few glass pieces were replaced.

22
See also the work on this by Hediger and Schiffhauer on the example of the Flums Madonna: Hediger and Schiffhauer, "Werkstoff Glas," p. 20.

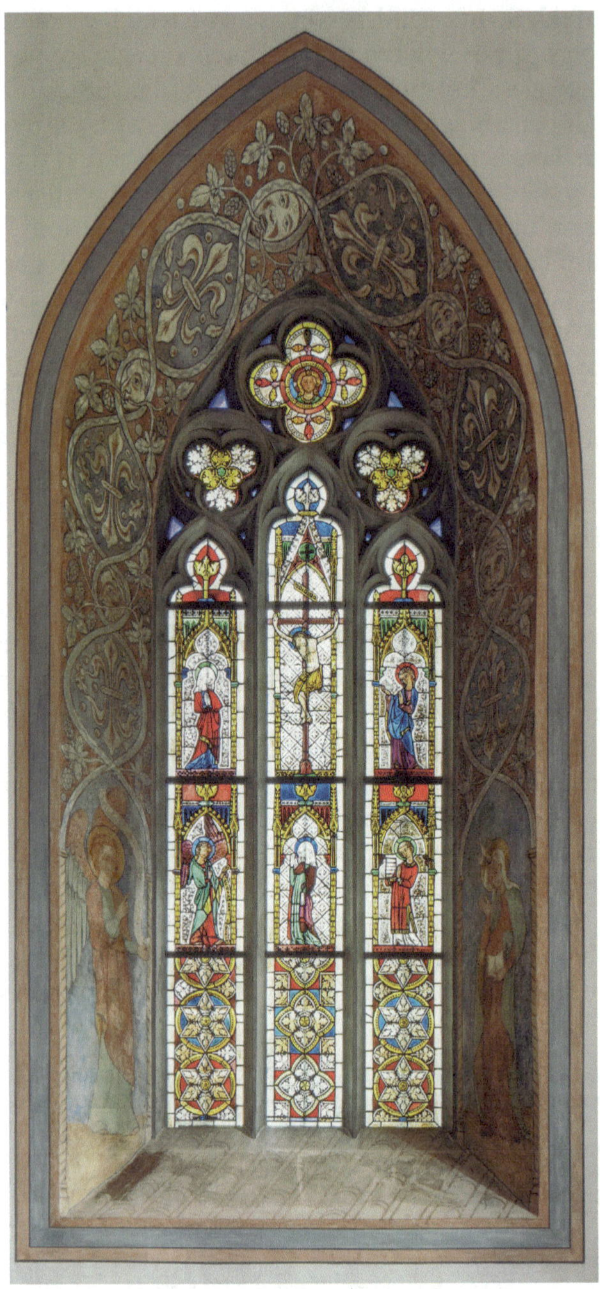

St. Laurentius window, 1320–1344, 400 × 140 cm.
St. Laurentius church, chancel, Amt für Denkmalpflege des Kantons Thurgau, Frauenfeld.

Fig. 268

contours of a figure. It is the simultaneous visual perception of these aspects that creates the appearance of the saints in the window.

The biblical figures in the Laurentius window are divided among its three lancets and take up almost the entire width of the glass surface. The stone tracery and the painted tabernacle frame separate them from each other. This built and painted framing focuses the gaze on each field of glass, although the crucifixion and the annunciation are distributed across several lancets. Depending on the intensity of the daylight or the interior lighting, the stone tracery that limits the pictorial surface fades into the background to a greater or lesser degree, becoming part of the image field or part of the architecture.[23]

In the middle lancet, geometric ornaments with diamond shapes containing quatrefoils fill the surface bounded by the glass painted tabernacles. Lozenge patterns are a wide-spread ornament for stained glass in the first third of the fourteenth century, found, for example, in several windows of the abbey at Königsfelden, where they are painted on colored glass.[24] In the example of the St. Laurentius church, they structure the field behind the figures, forming a closed-off space with the crowning baldachin. The backgrounds of the two lateral lancets are decorated with stylised leaves and foliage, which were not yet widespread at the time.[25] To create this effect, colored glass was densely covered in grisaille before etching out the foliage. White dots also break up the black surface, filtering the light more strongly on the two lateral lancets than in the bright central lancet with the lozenge ornament. The two different ornamental grounds, the lozenge and the foliage, were not used to formally connect the iconographically linked pictorial fields that transcend the lancets. Rather, the brighter lozenge pattern emphasizes the vertical with Christ on the cross and Mary in the scene of the annunciation.

23
Cf. in particular, Kurmann-Schwarz and Schiffhauer, "Bildmodelle in der Glasmalerei des 12. und 13. Jahrhunderts," pp. 120–122.

24
Brigitte Kurmann-Schwarz, *Die mittelalterlichen Glasmalereien der ehemaligen Klosterkirche Königsfelden* (Bern: Stämpfli, 2008), p. 132 and pp. 148–150.

25
Hasler and Keller, "St. Laurentiusfenster"; Kurmann-Schwarz, *Die mittelalterlichen Glasmalereien der ehemaligen Klosterkirche Königsfelden*, p. 132.

Filling "empty" image field areas with ornaments was already described by the monk Theophilus Presbyter in the twelfth century. In the second book of his *Schedula diversarum artium* he writes about stained glass and advises that ornaments be painted on garments and seating as well as on background fields.[26] He explains that vacant glass ground should be coated with grisaille and scraped with a brush handle to bring forth rings, branches with blossoms and leaves, or even small animals. The same procedure was used for the stained glass in Frauenfeld.[27]

Another remarkable feature is the clear gap between grounds that include architectural frames, landscapes as well as ornamental diapering. On the example of the stained glass in the choir of the Bern Münster, Brigitte Kurmann-Schwarz has described in-depth the varied pictorial backgrounds and integrated them with the interpretation of the pictorial narrative.[28] She emphasizes that the ornamental grounds were intended to evoke the materiality of textiles and ascribes to the painted damask backdrops a function comparable to that of textiles in sacred spaces.[29] The following section therefore discusses the use of textile backgrounds in single stained-glass panels.

26
Erhard Brepohl, *Theophilus Presbyter und das mittelalterliche Kunsthandwerk: Gesamtausgabe der Schrift* De diversis artibus *in zwei Bänden* (Cologne: Böhlau Verlag, 1999), p. 158; Brigitte Kurmann-Schwarz, "The Role of Ornament in the Conception and Significance of Medieval Figurative Stained Glass," in *The Concept and Fabrication of Stained Glass from the Middle Ages to Art Nouveau*, International Colloquium Corpus Vitrearum, ed. (Barcelona: Corpus Vitrearum Catalunya, 2022), pp. 13–21, here p. 19; Hediger and Kurmann-Schwarz, "[…] et faciunt inde tabulas saphiri pretiosas ac satis utiles in fenestris."

27
Cf. also the remarks by Brigitte Kurmann-Schwarz on the colored ornamental backgrounds in the stained glass at Königsfelden Abbey: Kurmann-Schwarz, *Die mittelalterlichen Glasmalereien der ehemaligen Klosterkirche Königsfelden*, pp. 147–150.

28
Brigitte Kurmann-Schwarz, "Rahmen, Bilder, Ornamente: Die Glasmalereien des Berner Münsterchors (1441 – ca. 1455), in: Nicolai and Schweizer, *Das Berner Münster*, pp. 373–403; Kurmann-Schwarz, "The Role of Ornament in the Conception and Significance of Medieval Figurative Stained Glass," p. 14.

29
Kurmann-Schwarz, "Rahmen, Bilder, Ornamente," p. 400; Kurmann-Schwarz, "The Role of Ornament in the Conception and Significance of Medieval Figurative Stained Glass," p. 13.

Damask-Patterns in Small-Scale Stained Glass

The dispositions of the relationship between figure and ground change around 1500 with the emergence of so called *Einzelscheiben*, painted glass panels intended to be viewed relatively close-up and showing a self-contained motif.[30] In the late fifteenth and sixteenth centuries, the backgrounds of pictorial spaces in glass painting were increasingly covered with textile patterns. The heraldic panel from the Bern Münster mentioned at the outset includes such a damask ornament as a backdrop for the shield-wielding angel [fig. 259]. It is also found in two other panels that are part of the same donation.[31] Small differences in the execution of the pattern suggest that they were not applied with the assistance of a stencil.[32]

The link between damask patterns in glass painting to objects of textile art is illustrated clearly by the examples where a wall hanging is visible behind the figures. In a pictorial heraldic stained glass from the reformed church in Neuenegg, Saint Vincent stands on a narrow stage in front of a painted red tapestry suspended from a bar behind him, with a round arch supported by columns above [fig. 272].[33] The dark red wall hanging with a colorful fringe and a poorly discernible damascene pattern is stretched behind the saint as a cloth of honor. To the side of the painted tapestry, the damask ornament ground is visible; it is also red but in a glowing shade. The layering with the figure in

30
For an overview of the development of heraldic glass panels see, among others, Gysel, *Glasmalerei im Dienste der Nation*, pp. 38–239; Butts and Hendrix, "Drawn on Paper, Painted on Glass"; Stefan Trümpler and Valérie Sauterel, eds., *Les panneaux de vitrail isolés – Die Einzelscheibe – The Single Stained-glass Panel* (Bern: Peter Lang, 2010).

31
Kurmann-Schwarz, *Die Glasmalereien des 15. bis 18. Jahrhunderts im Berner* Münster, pp. 428–429.

32
As one example among many for a damask pattern painted on with the help of a stencil, we might mention the panel "Erhard Kastler with St. Bernhard" in the reformed church in Utzenstorf: Rolf Hasler, Sarah Keller, and Patricia Sulser, "Figurenscheibe Erhard Kastler, Abt von St. Urban, mit hl. Bernhard," *Vitrosearch*, 2016, https://vitrosearch.ch/de/objects/2467378. Earlier examples for the use of stencils are found in the Cathedral of Évreux among others: Kurmann-Schwarz, "The Role of Ornament in the Conception and Significance of Medieval Figurative Stained Glass," p. 17.

33
On the conservation status of the panel see Rolf Hasler and Sarah Keller, "Figurenscheibe Stand Bern mit hl. Vinzenz." For the development of the damask background in the coats of arms, see Schneider, *Die Standesscheiben von Lukas Zeiner im Tagsatzungssaal zu Baden (Schweiz)*, pp. 55–56.

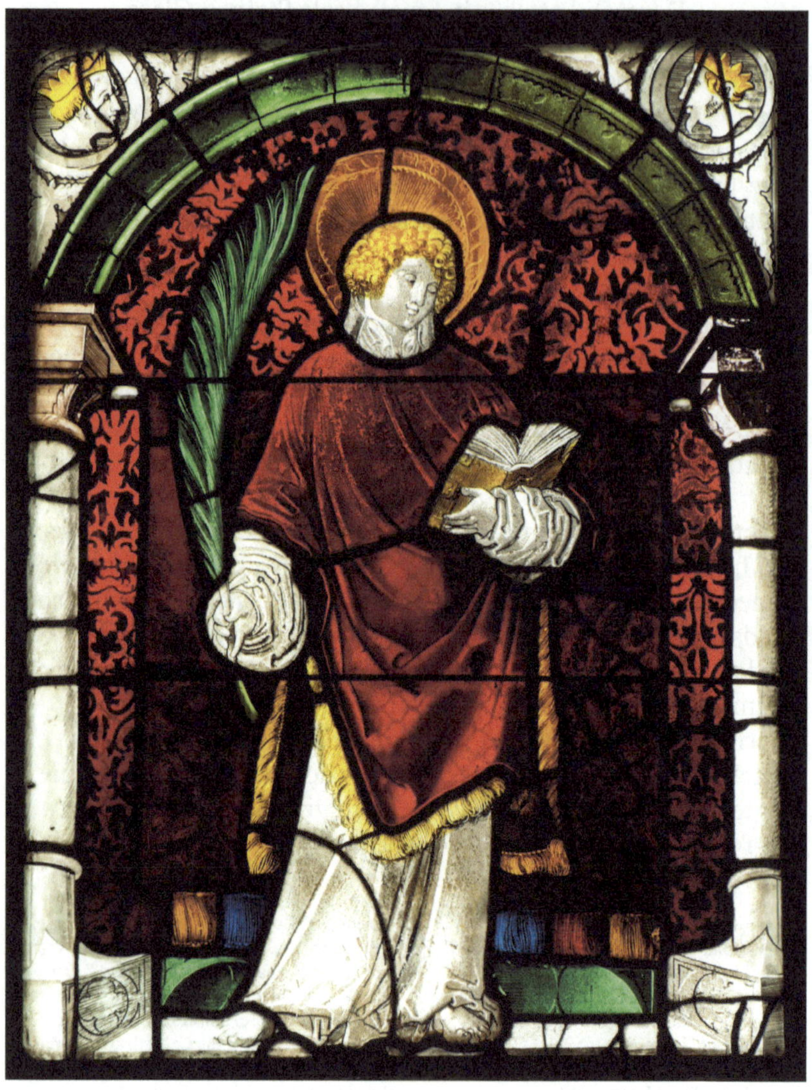

Heraldic stained glass with St. Vincent, around 1516, 82.5 × 60.5 cm.
Reformed church, s II, 3a, Neuenegg.

Fig. 272

front of the tapestry and the ornamental background creates spatial differentiation.[34]

This stained-glass panel has a counterpart that depicts Bern's heraldic pyramid. Saint Vincent is therefore shown as the city's patron saint and together with the heraldic panel represents a donation by the Canton of Bern. Heraldic glass painting was very popular in Switzerland from the end of the fifteenth century and this was the most widespread form of glass painting until 1800. Its popularity is also due to the custom of gifting such panels, which was intensively cultivated in the old Swiss Confederacy.[35] The donor of the heraldic glass panel paid not only for the glass painting, but also for the rondel or rhombus glazing of the entire window, thereby financing a newbuild or a renovation. In return the donors—who might be cantons or municipalities, but also dignitaries or private individuals—represented themselves prominently by displaying their arms.

Among the earliest and most influential examples are the cantonal heraldic panels created by Lukas Zeiner in 1501 for the chamber of the Tagsatzung (federal diet) in Baden.[36] The glass panels have a straightforward composition, showing the canton's coat of arms in the foreground, each presented by two shield bearers, as seen for example in the heraldic panel for Zug [fig. 274]. The coat of arms and the shield bearers stand under a round arch on a tiled floor in front of a red ornamental ground. Both shield bearers hold the banner of the Canton of Zug in their hands. The one on the left faces the viewer, while the one on the right looks back toward the banner. The fringe at the rear boundary of the floor reveals that the red damask pattern is part of tapestry.

34
Schirra and Kondor, "Das bildphilosophische Stichwort 24: Figur/Grund-Differenzierung," p. 185.

35
Uta Bergmann, "Glasmalerei in der Schweiz, 1500–1800," SIKART – Lexikon zur Kunst in der Schweiz 2019, https://recherche.sik-isea.ch/sik:text_file-15392299:exp/in/sikart/; Ariane Mensger, "Wie 'Tannenzapfen im Schwarzwald': Schweizer Glasgemälde und ihre Vorzeichnungen im 16. Jahrhundert," in *Lichtgestalten: Zeichnungen und Glasgemälde von Holbein bis Ringler*, Ariane Mensger and Kunstmuseum Basel, eds. (Munich: Hirmer, 2020), pp. 15–29, here pp. 18–19.

36
In 1501 Zeiner made ten heraldic panels that represented the ten Cantons of the Old Confederacy and one for the City of Baden. The entire cycle with the exception of the Baden panel was sold in 1812 and is now part of various different collections. Schneider, *Die Standesscheiben von Lukas Zeiner im Tagsatzungssaal zu Baden (Schweiz)*.

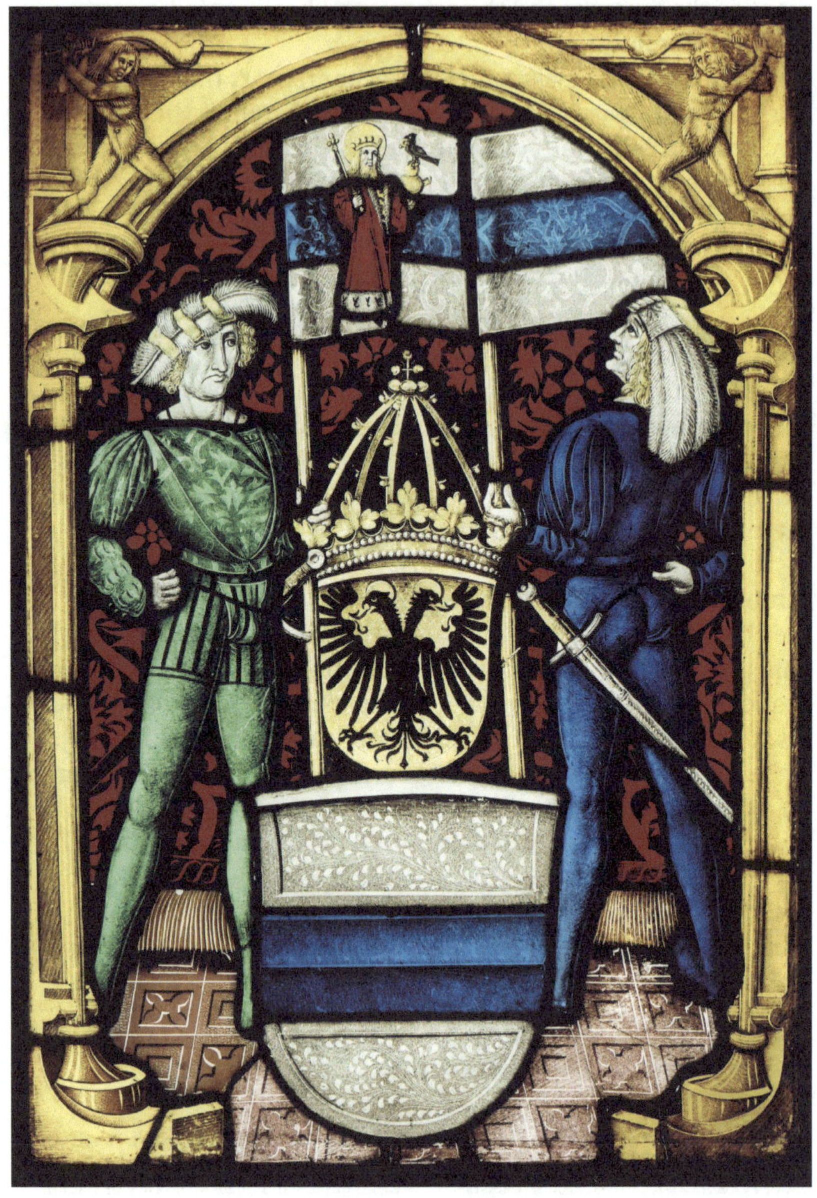

Lukas Zeiner, heraldic stained glass canton Zug (Standesscheibe Zug), 1501, 50 × 35 cm.
Historisches Museum, inv. 1870.1272, Basel.

Fig. 274

This stretches across the entire surface of the space demarcated by the round arch, so that the damask ornament is perceived less as a painted textile work and more as a flat delimitation of the ground. Zeiner has decorated the shield with a beautiful, delicate feathered damask. To visually imitate fabric, the banners and the upper body garments of the shield bearer on the left were decorated with various textile patterns. The additional modeling of volume through the use of shading differentiates the clothing and the banners from the flat red damask in the background. Moreover, the white sections on the banners and the shield are adorned with distinctive ornaments to denote the difference between their materials, wood and fabric. Painting the glass pieces with textile patterns therefore serves not merely to fill out the background of the pictorial field, but also to accentuate the surfaces of objects.

Throughout the sixteenth century, textile patterns remained popular as ornamental backgrounds for heraldic stained glass. An intricate feathered damask on blue glass features on a 1586 heraldic panel donated by David Michel of Schwertschwendi, today at Schlossmuseum Burgdorf [fig. 276].[37] The coat of arms is displayed in the foreground in front of a round arch with an enlarged, decorated keystone. The blue feather damask serves as a ornamental element between the coat of arms and the arch, and counterpoints the spatial illusion of the architectural frame. In this example, the blue ornamental ground serves less to demarcate a spatially conceived pictorial background, as was the case in the Canton of Zug panel [fig. 274], but rather it seems to be a loose reference to the tradition of stained glass. The diapering ensures that the surface is not left empty and groundless, but defined as part of the glass painting.

A large number of contemporary preliminary drawings (*Scheibenrisse* in the Swiss and German context) have been preserved for the single stained-glass panels of the early modern period. These designs, templates, and prototypes can only rarely be linked to a still extant heraldic panel. For the discussion of the figure-ground relationship in stained glass, their significance lies

37
Rolf Hasler and Sarah Keller, "Wappenscheibe David Michel von Schwertschwendi," *Vitrosearch*, 2016, https://vitrosearch.ch/de/objects/2252046.

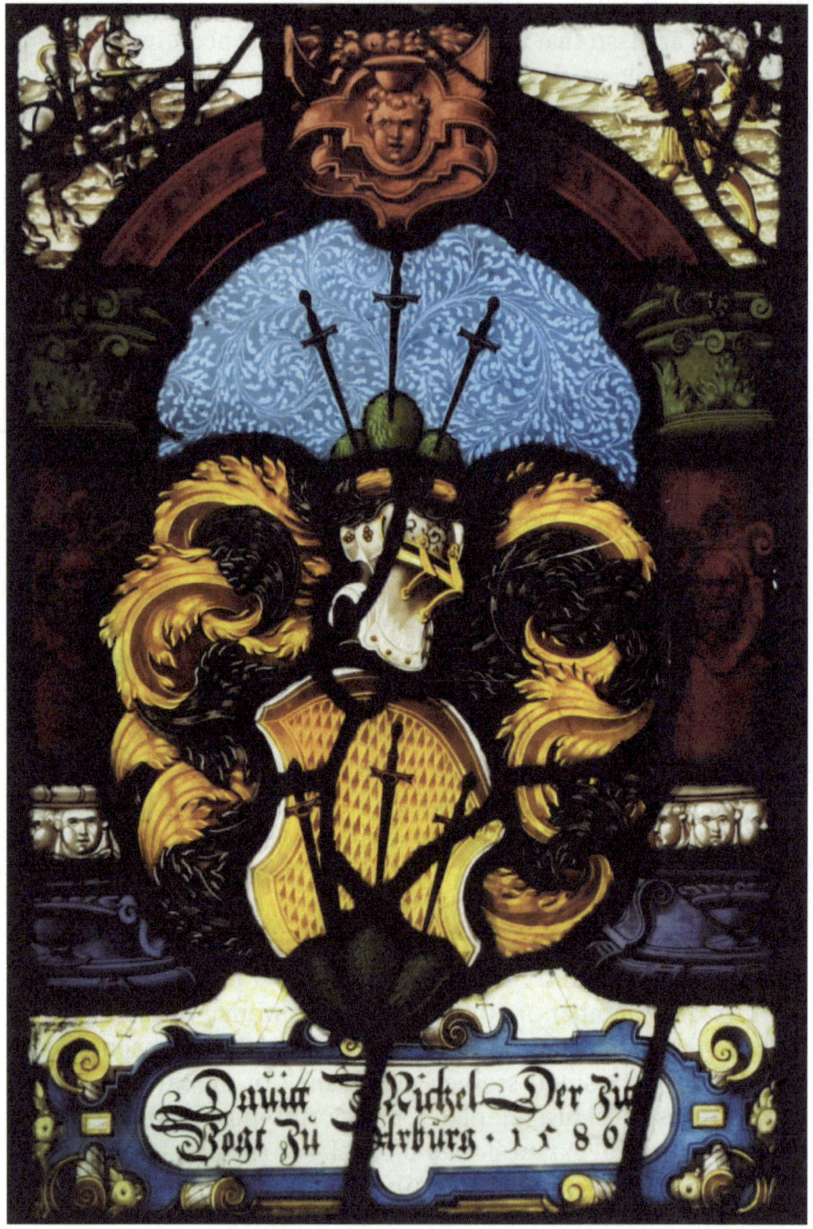

Peter I Balduin (ascribed), heraldic stained glass David Michel von Schwertschwendi, 1586, 33 × 21.4 cm. Schlossmuseum, inv. 4.1367, Burgdorf.

Fig. 276

in the fact that in historical preparatory drawings, the ornamental grounds are not part of the design. The drawings leave the background either empty or sketch a landscape, as we will examine below. By way of illustration we might mention the work of glass painter Abraham Bickhart (1535–1577), by whom several preliminary drawings have been preserved, as well as several glass paintings with damask diapering, including a signed 1577 heraldic panel for the Canton of Bern in the reformed church of Aarwangen [fig. 278].[38] In the center of the glass panel, the heraldic pyramid of Bern-Reich (the arms of the free city of Bern as part of the Holy Roman Empire) is topped by the imperial crown. The pyramid is flanked by two lions holding the imperial sword and the imperial orb respectively. Behind them two pillars support an architrave. The space between the heraldic pyramid, the lions and the architectural frame is lined in blue damask. A signed preliminary drawing by Bickhart for a 1555 heraldic panel for the Canton of Zurich is kept at the Kunstbibliothek Berlin [fig. 279]. Its composition and motif are comparable to the stained glass panel in Aarwangen. The pictorial ground between the architectural frame and the lion is left empty in Bickhart's drawing. Considering the panel mentioned above, it is possible that the final glass painting based on the drawing would have filled the empty space with a textile pattern. These observations suggest that textile grounds were familiar templates in stained glass art and were not designed for specific commissions.[39]

Heraldic Panels and Landscape

In addition to heraldic panels with damask backgrounds we also find panels where the coat of arms and the shield bearers are

38
Rolf Hasler, Sarah Keller, and Uta Bergmann, "Standesscheibe Bern," *Vitrosearch*, 2016, https://vitrosearch.ch/de/objects/2246213. Rolf Hasler, "Abraham Bickhart," SIKART – Lexikon zur Kunst in der Schweiz, 2017, https://www.sikart.ch/kuenstlerInnen.aspx?id=4027054. Several preliminary drawings by Bickhart are kept in the collection Wyss in the Bern Historical Museum: Rolf Hasler, *Die Scheibenriss-Sammlung Wyss* 1, Depositum der Schweizerischen Eidgenossenschaft im Bernischen Historischen Museum Katalog, 1996–1997 (Bern: Stämpfli, 1996), pp. 182–190.

39
Kurmann-Schwarz has made the same argument for medieval stained glass. Kurmann-Schwarz, "The Role of Ornament in the Conception and Significance of Medieval Figurative Stained Glass," p. 17.

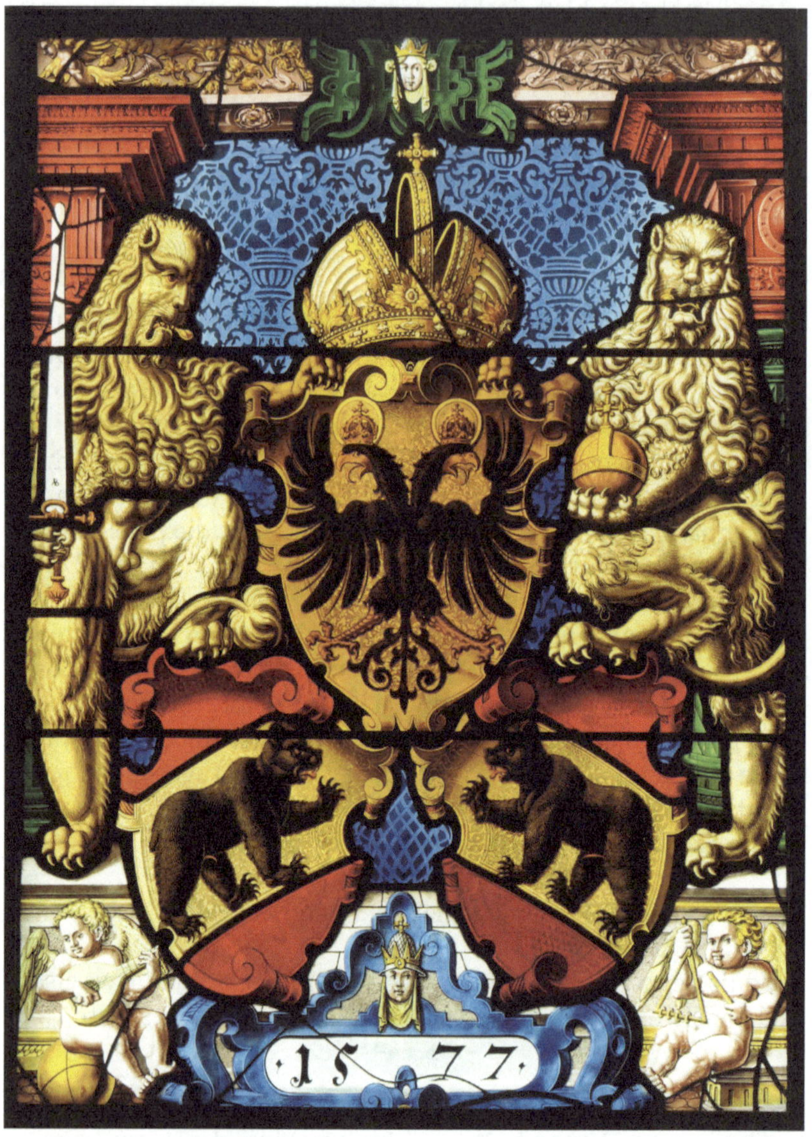

Abraham Bickhart, heraldic stained glass canton Bern (Standesscheibe Bern), 1577, 71 × 53 cm.
Reformed church, I, 2a, Aarwangen.

Fig. 278

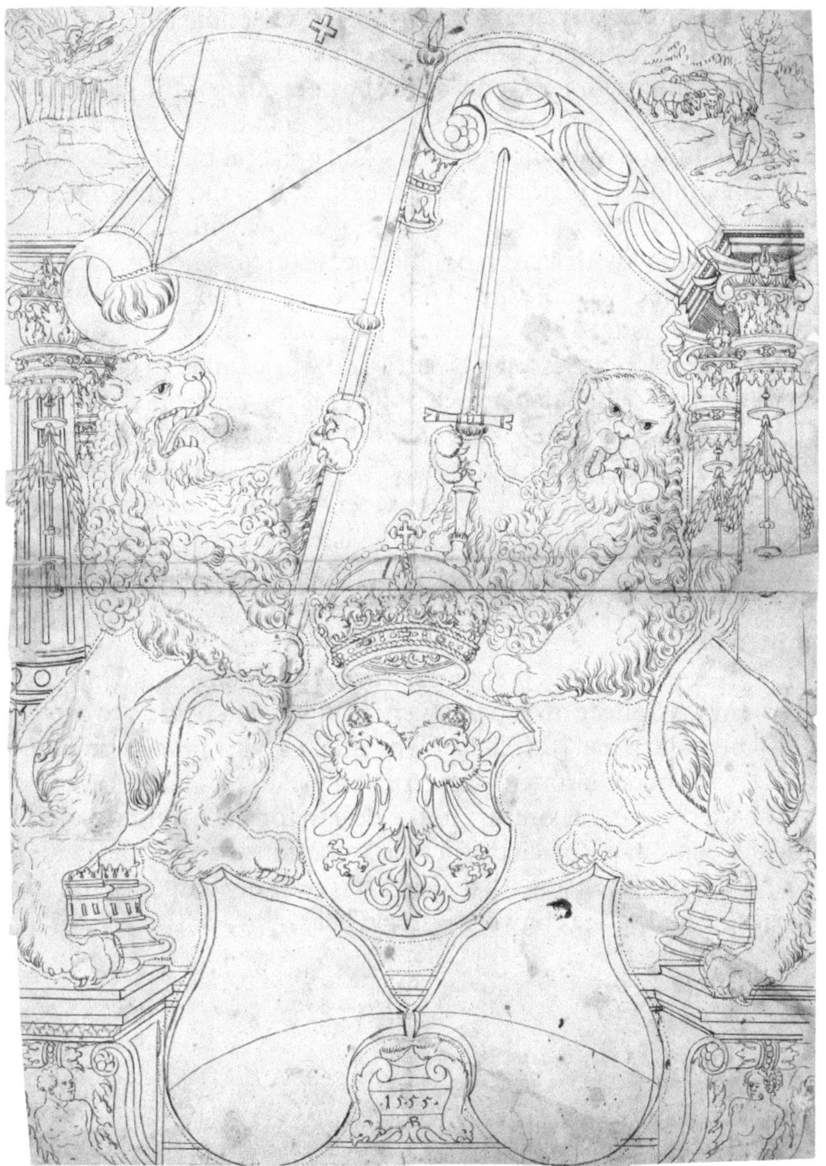

Abraham Bickhart, preliminary drawing for a Heraldic stained glass canton Zurich, 1555, 41.9 × 30.6 cm. Kunstbibliothek, Hdz 1767, Berlin.

Fig. 279

presented in or in front of a landscape. In a heraldic panel of the Canton of Bern from 1508–1509 the shield bearer with a feathered hat stands with legs apart at the bottom edge of the stained glass [fig. 281].[40] He is framed by a round arch that is decorated with an illusion of branches, leaves, and graceful pillars. Beneath the arch unfolds a pictorial space that underlies the figure like a foil. In the foreground is an abundant meadow with a path leading to a wood with a river. Behind the wood to the right, we can make out a rocky landscape in the distance, and on the left the towers of a castle. The meadow was painted with grisaille on green pot-colored glass, while the wood was painted in grisaille on blue glass, on the same piece of glass as the rocky landscape. To achieve a green tint for the trees, this area was coated with silver stain on the back of the glass. Silver stain is a silver oxide that stains the surface of the glass yellow when fired—see, for example, the head of the angel on the heraldic panel in the Bern Münster discussed above [fig. 259].[41] When the paint is applied to blue glass, however, the painted areas appear green in transmitted light.

A contemporary preparatory drawing by an unknown artist in the Wyss Collection shows a very similar composition to the Bern heraldic panel [fig. 282].[42] The shield bearer in the drawing also stands under a round arch on a stony path that leads to a wood on the left. In contrast to the design for the heraldic panel for the Canton of Zurich by Bickhart mentioned above, the landscape here is sketched with delicate and restrained lines of ink as a background to the combative shield bearer.

40
The panel is today in the collection of the Bern Historical Museum, inv. nr. BHM 366. It is originally from the church in Lenk and was probably donated by the City of Bern for the rebuild of the church in completed in 1505. Cf. Hasler and Keller, "Standesscheibe Bern mit Bannerträger," *Vitrosearch*, 2016, https://vitrosearch.ch/de/objects/2465612.

41
On the painting of heraldic panels with silver stain see: Schneider, *Die Standesscheiben von Lukas Zeiner im Tagsatzungssaal zu Baden (Schweiz)*, p. 123; Bergmann, *Die Zuger Glasmalerei des 16. bis 18. Jahrhunderts*, p. 143.

42
Hasler, *Die Scheibenriss-Sammlung Wyss* 1, pp. 137–138.

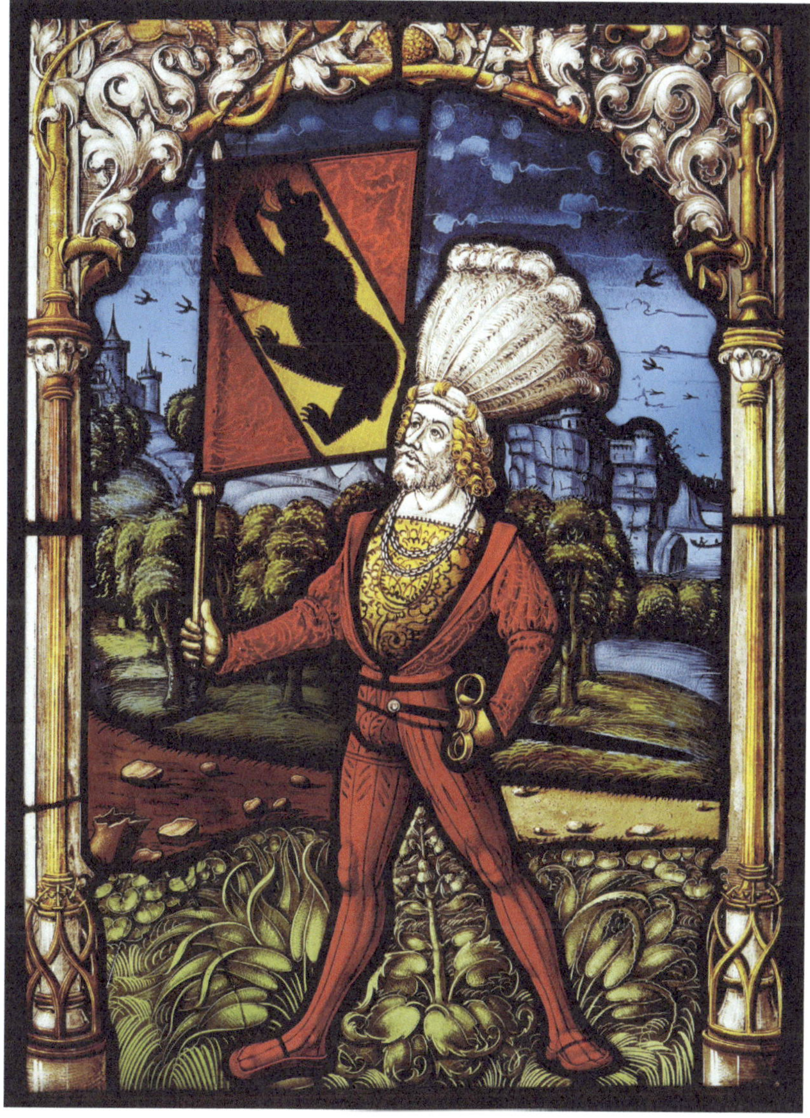

Heraldic stained glass canton Bern with standard-bearer, around 1508–1509, 59 × 43.1 cm.
Bernisches Historisches Museum, BHM 366, Bern.

Fig. 281

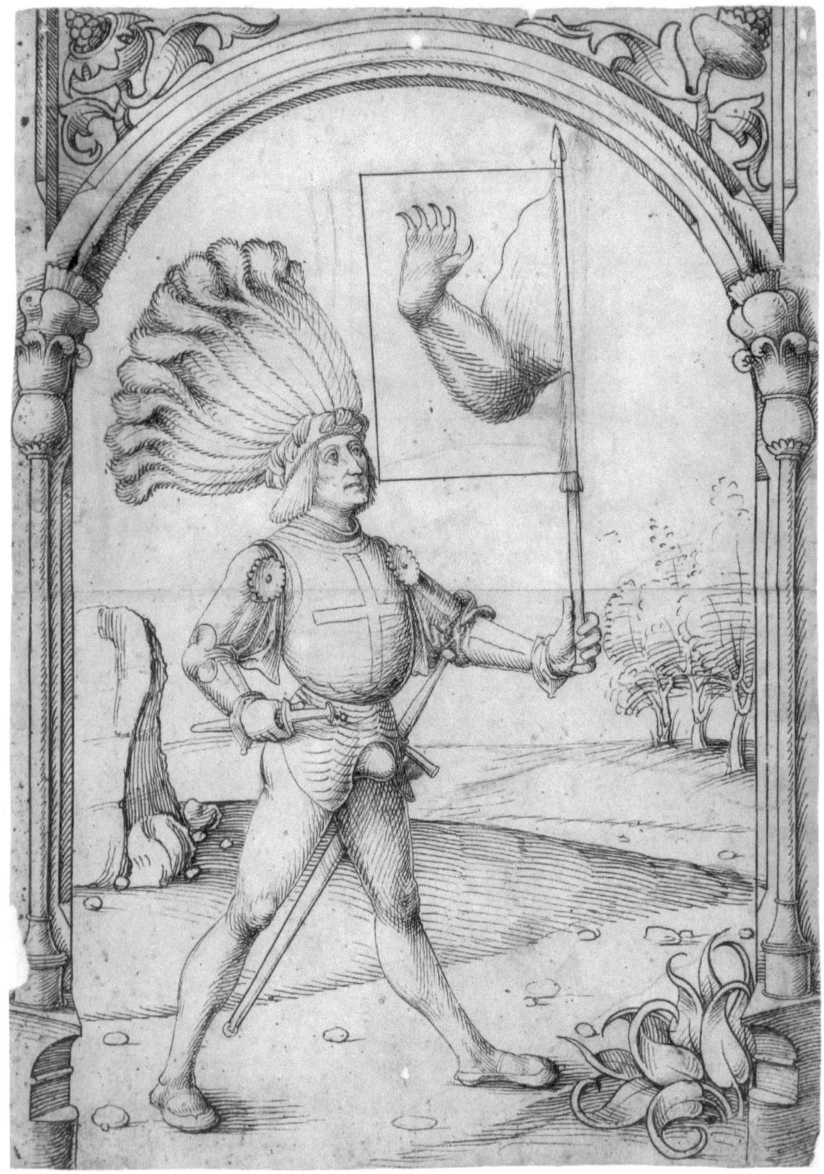

Preliminary drawing for heraldic stained glass with standard-bearer, 1509–1510, 43 × 31.8 cm. Bernisches Historisches Museum, BHM 20036.1, Bern.

Fig. 282

Narrative Panels and Landscape

However, the space under the arch was not utilized just to present the coat of arms, but also as a pictorial field for biblical or instructive narratives. In a single stained-glass panel from 1563 in the Bern Historical Museum, the coat of arms of the donor, Sulpitius Haller, is placed at the center bottom edge beside the inscription [fig. 284].[43] This leaves the space under the arch free for a representation of the biblical tale of Christ meeting the Samaritan woman at a well. Richly decorated colorful columns frame the story on each side. They support a scrolled gable with horn-blowing angels that form the upper border. At the bottom, the two pedestals of the columns flank the coat of arms with a ribbon scroll. These elements frame the biblical scene and open up a pictorial space. The scene shows the Samaritan woman fetching water with a pail from a hexagonal well. To her right, Christ sits on the edge of the well facing her. A landscape with a river, towns, green fields, and woods unfolds in the background. In the distance, a bright mountain landscape lines the horizon.

The landscape with its white, green, and blue tones is painted on a single piece of glass. In addition to the grisaille shading and line painting on colorless glass, a blue vitreous enamel was used to color the river and the sky blue.[44] For the green grass and wood, the reverse of the glass was also coated in silver stain. It should be noted that with the expanding use of enamel paints, the color in stained glass was no longer produced only by assembling pot-colored pieces of glass, but increasingly by painting in color on glass. Comparing this process to medieval, mosaic stained glass art, we might argue that the glass is progressively treated as a material support for painting, to be covered and thereby concealing the unique properties of the material. It is also noticeable that, through these possibilities of coloring, the lead came loses its significance as a conceptual element of the pictorial design. In the stained glass with Christ and the

43
Rolf Hasler, Sarah Keller, and Uta Bergmann, "Bildscheibe Sulpitius Haller mit Christus und der Samariterin am Brunnen," *Vitrosearch*, 2016, https://vitrosearch.ch/de/objects/2467901.

44
Various Enamel paints are documented from the mid-sixteenth century onward on Swiss stained glass: Bergmann, *Die Zuger Glasmalerei des 16. bis 18. Jahrhunderts*, p. 143.

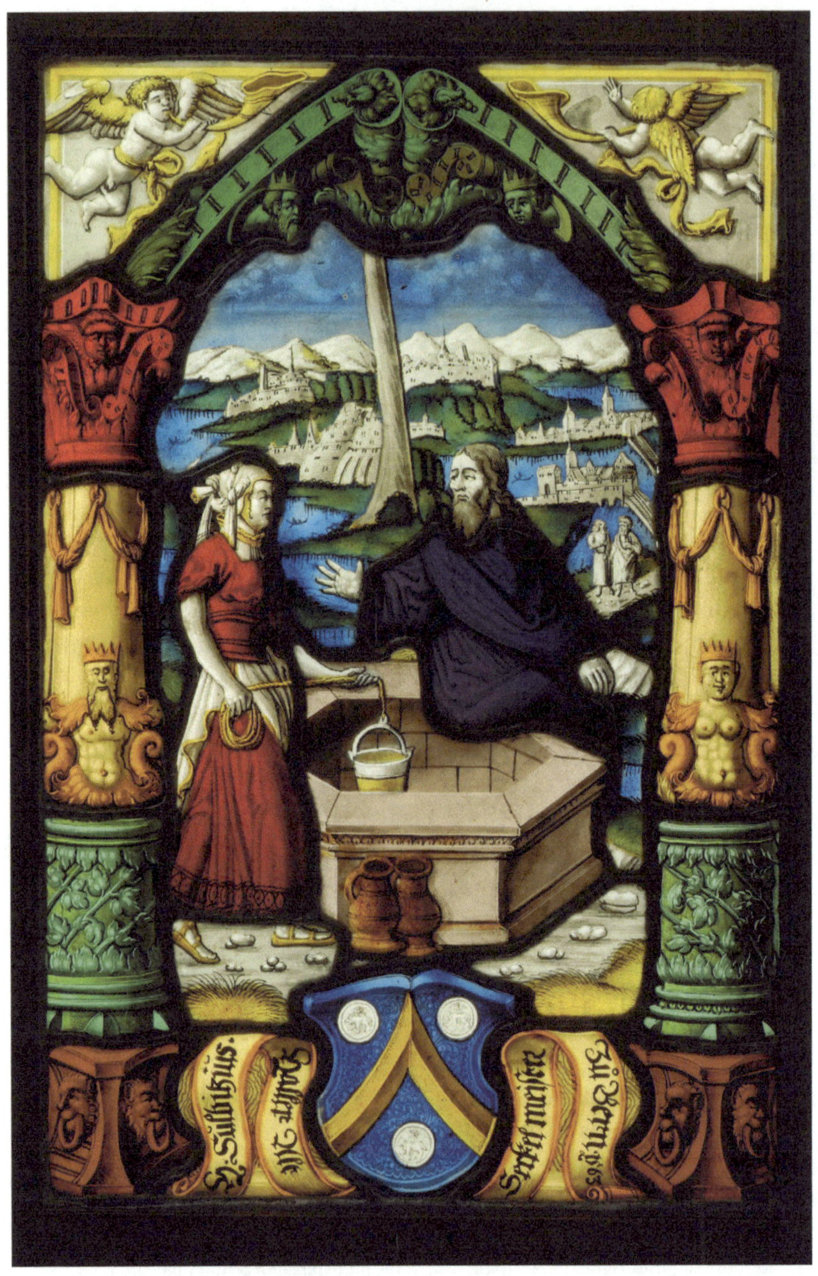

Pictorial glass panel for Sulpitius Haller with Christ and the Samaritan at the Well, 1563, 32 × 21.4 cm. Bernisches Historisches Museum, BHM 2288, Bern.

Fig. 284

Samaritan, the black leading is clearly distinct from the fine lines of the grisaille painting. The lead was placed deliberately to follow the outlines of figures or objects, as we saw with medieval stained glass [fig. 259]. The Samaritan consists of a single piece of red flashed glass that has been abraded for the head, the arm, and the apron. Christ's robe also consists of a single piece, and as a result his head is painted separately on the piece of glass showing the landscape. The separating effect of the lead came is softened in transmitted light by the dark color of Christ's clothing.

The introduction of vitreous enamels provided the glass painter with new possibilities, leading to innovative, more complex arrangements of space in the early seventeenth century, as seen for example in the donation by Daniel Lerber with Justitia in the central field [fig. 286].[45] The personification of Justice stands in a rich and detailed landscape with a variety of colors, which extends far into the depth of the image. A large piece of glass contains the upper body of Justitia and the landscape running into the background on her left.[46] To achieve this, colorless glass was painted with silver stain, iron oxide red as well as blue, violet, and green enamel. The shading, lines, and outlines were done with grisaille. Justitia is framed by a column arcade that allows a narrow view of the landscape on each side. The spatially staggered framing architecture, with projecting fluted columns and a projecting entablature, prepares the spatial depth of the landscape.

Dissolution of the Background

Besides ornaments and landscapes as pictorial ground, we should end our exploration by including some examples that leave the colorless glass entirely unpainted. The 1608 heraldic stained glass of Fribourg by Josias Murer shows the two shield bearers in armour standing on a tiled floor, with the coat of arms between them [fig. 287].[47] Behind them columns support an arched beam

45
The figure panel is in the reformed church of Münchenbuchsee and is attributed to glass painter Abraham Sybold. Rolf Hasler and Sarah Keller, "Figurenscheibe Daniel Lerber mit der Justitia," *Vitrosearch*, 2016, https://vitrosearch.ch/de/objects/2253040.

46
Today, the glass piece contains several pieces of replacement lead that date to a later restoration. Cf. Halser and Keller, "Figurenscheibe Daniel Lerber mit der Justitia."

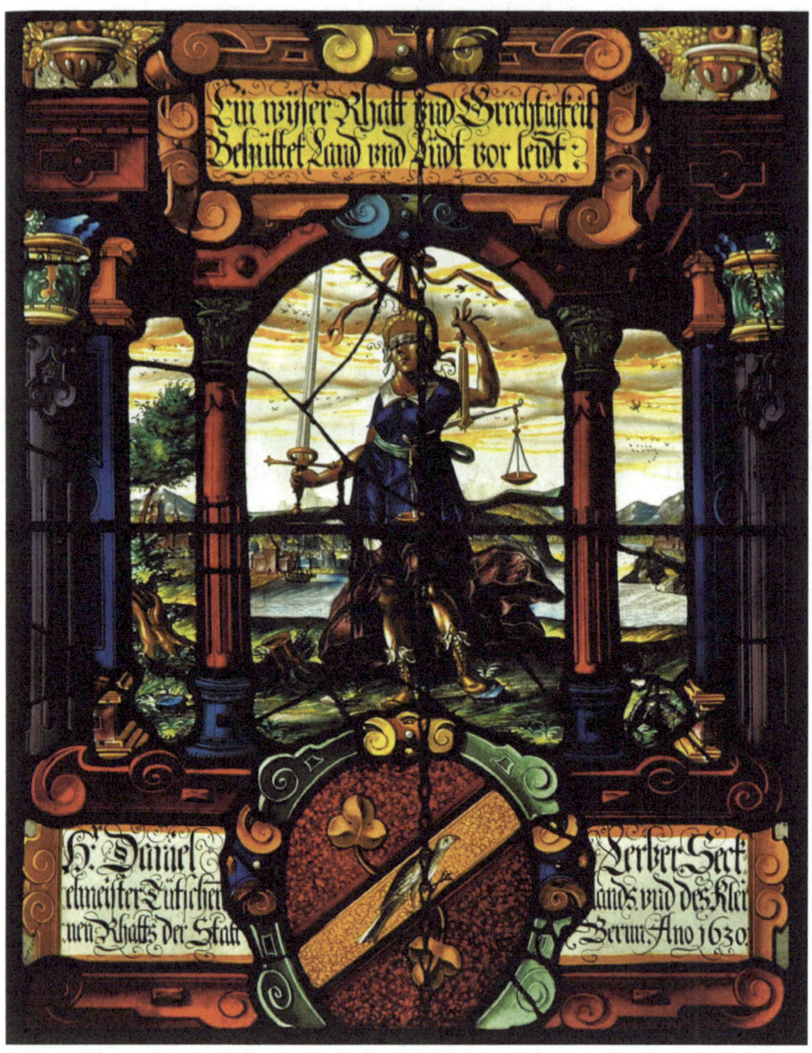

Abraham Sybold (ascribed), pictorial glass panel for Daniel Lerber with with Justitia, 1630, 66.8 × 50.7 cm. Reformed church, s VI, 2, Münchenbuchsee.

Fig. 286

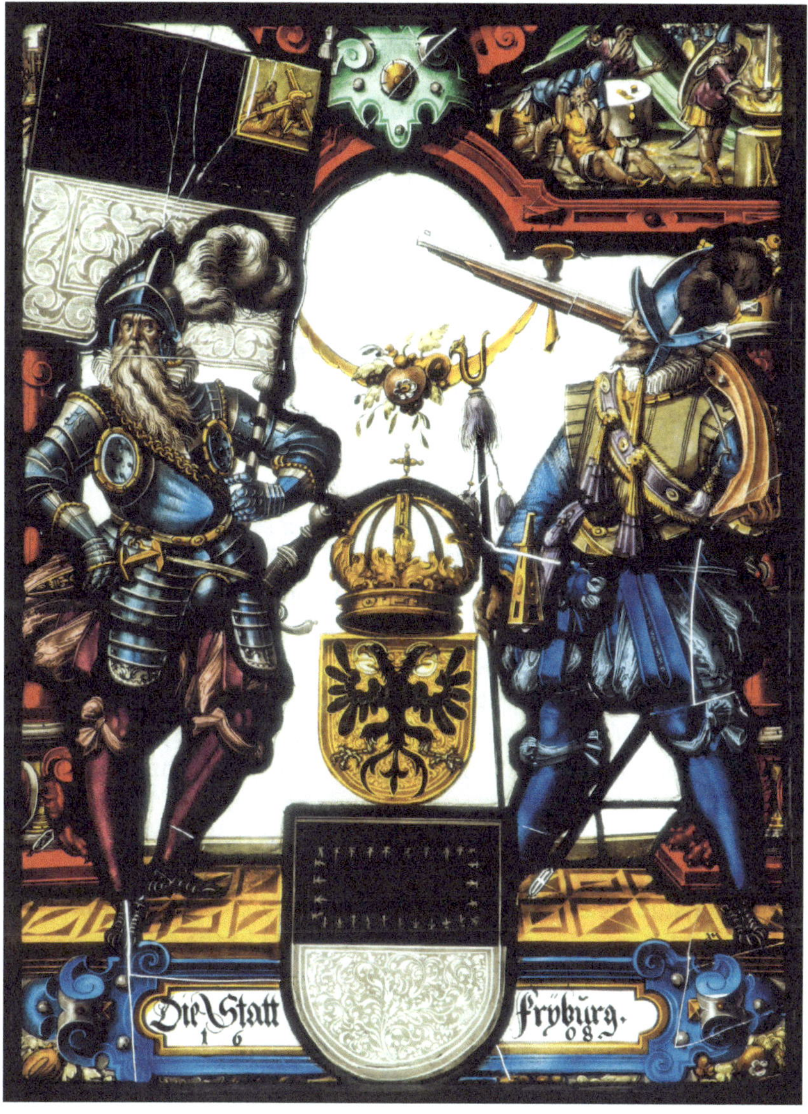

Josias Murer, heraldic stained glass canton Freiburg, 1608, 40.7 × 30.7 cm.
Maison de Fégely, Freiburg.

Fig. 287

from which a garland with a bouquet of flowers is suspended. Between the shield bearers and the coat of arms, a large surface of glass remains unpainted. The basic composition, the arms in the centre flanked by two shield bearers set within an architectural frame, is the same as the compositional scheme of the panels by Lukas Zeiner for the Tagsatzungs chamber in Baden [fig. 274]. It is notable for the more dynamic representation of the figures but also for its lack of a damask ground.

The background, or the imaginary back wall of the space that is evoked by the presence of the tiled floor, is dissolved. The materiality of glass as both pictorial ground and material support for stained glass seems to dissipate into transparency.[48] This effect is enhanced by the shadows of the shield bearers. The men's legs cast a shadow on the tiled floor toward the back, assuming a frontal source of light outside the image. There are no shadows to be detected on the back wall. The shield bearers therefore seem to stand in a space that is open at the back. For the lighting scheme of his image, the artist Josias Murer did not take into consideration the daylight that falls through the window from the outside in. This may suggest that transmitted light, which was significant and meaningful for medieval stained glass, played a secondary role for early modern heraldic panels. Although the colorless, fully transparent glass brightens the interior with plenty of light, the figure in the pictorial ground is conceived independently of its effect.

To conclude, it should not be forgotten that the larger, unpainted glass surfaces in the stained glass panels allow a view of the outside space. This effect is demonstrated by a snapshot of a panel from 1620 at Schloss Altenklingen in the Canton of Thurgau, which depicts the donors Bernhard Brägger and his wife

47
Uta Bergmann, "Standesscheibe Freiburg 1608," *Vitrosearch*, 2016, https://vitrosearch.ch/de/objects/2565289; Uta Bergmann, *Die Freiburger Glasmalerei des 16. bis 18. Jahrhunderts: Le vitrail fribourgeois du XVIe au XVIIIe siècle* (Bern: Peter Lang 2014), pp. 728–729.

48
Here the term "transparency" is used in its proper meaning of translucency without implying any further hidden meaning. On the terms "transparency" and "diaphane" in glass painting see Bałus, "Diaphanum," p. 13; Bałus, "A Matter of Matter," p. 115. About the relationship between the transparent background and the framing architecture in the heraldic glass paintings of Ludwing Ringler, cf. Michael Schaffner, "Through the Stained-Glass: The Basel 'Schützenhaus' as a Site of Encounter," in *Sites of Mediation: Connected Histories of Places, Processes, and Objects in Europe and Beyond, 1450–1650*, Susanna Burghartz, Lucas Burkart, and Christine Göttler, eds. (Leiden: Brill, 2016), pp. 125–156, p. 139.

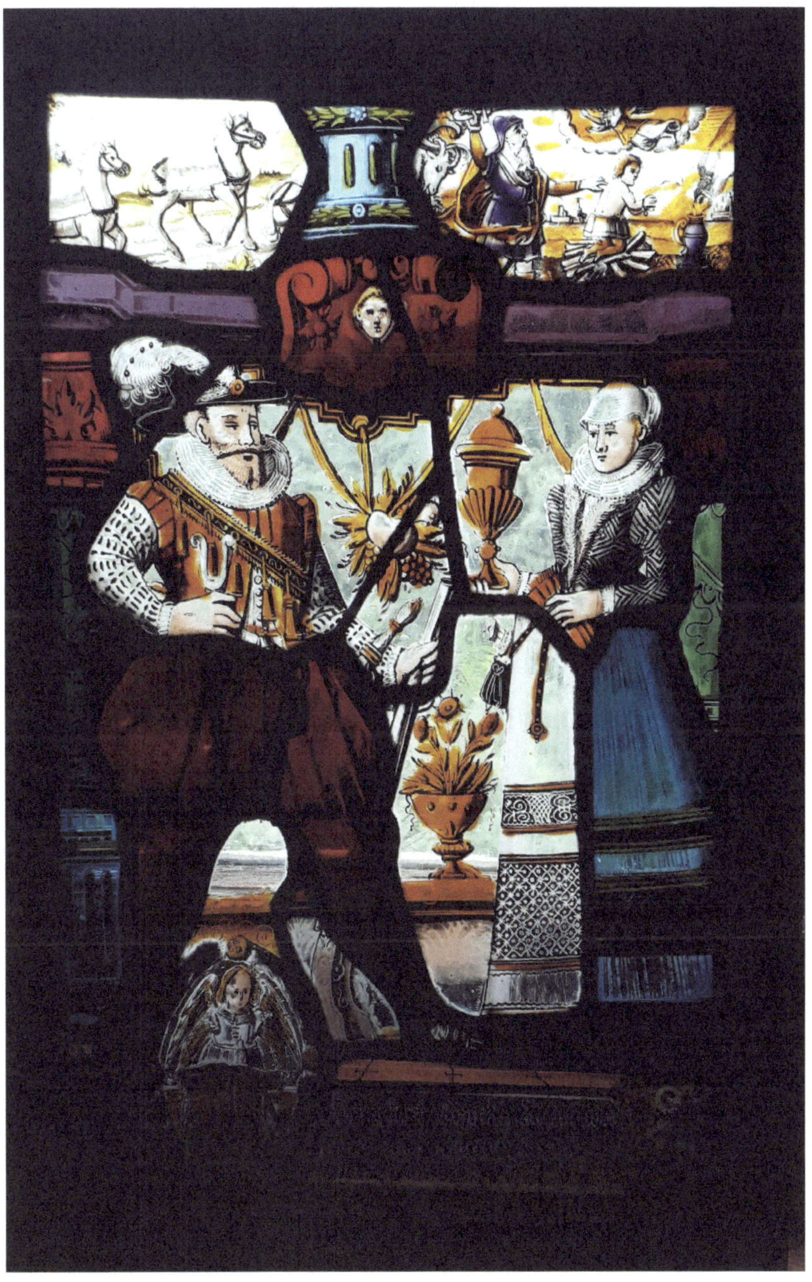

Hans Jegli (ascribed), welcome panel Bernhard Brägger and Elisabeth Geering (Willkommscheibe), 1620, 30.5 × 19.5. Wigoltinen Schloss Altenklingen, Mühlestube.

Fig. 289

Elisabeth Geering [fig. 289].[49] Although the current location of the panel in the Mühlestube at Schloss Altenklingen does not correspond to the originally intended site, the panel was probably created for display in private space.[50] This genre of panels, so-called *Willkommscheiben*, document alliances between families. The wife welcomes her husband by presenting him with a golden goblet. The couple stands facing each other on a tiled floor in front of a low balustrade with a vase. The ground behind them is empty. The photograph records the view of the observer in situ through the unpainted colorless glass into exterior space. Trees and a green landscape are visible beyond the glass. The real space outside and beyond the image thus becomes the ground of the image field.

49
Rolf Hasler and Sarah Keller, "Willkommscheibe Bernhard Brägger (Bräcker) und Elisabeth Geering (Gerig)," *Vitrosearch*, 2020, https://vitrosearch.ch/de/objects/2659041.

50
Keller and Kaufmann, *Die Glasmalereien vom Mittelalter bis 1930 im Kanton Thurgau*, p. 35.

Part 3
Beyond the Surface

Gold leaf, inasmuch as it so often dominates what one sees of a premodern panel painting, opens a passage from reading, or interpreting, into the physical act of seeing. Seeing in premodernity is a bodily experience, an encounter shaped by materials and light. Gold's reflexivity, transparency, and malleability encouraged painters and artisans to explore strategies addressing the beholder we would anachronistically describe today as phenomenological. Gold has the potential to emphasize the three-dimensional nature of panel painting by protruding pictorial spaces into real spaces.

One particularly striking example that can clarify this point has been discussed by art historians for almost a century, as we will discuss throughout the following pages. In Ambrogio Lorenzetti's *Annunciazione,* on view today at the Pinacoteca Nazionale in Siena, gold leaf dominates the picture plane [fig. 293]. Numerous squared leaves delineate the smooth surface of the gesso- and bole-covered wooden panel, allowing the red undertones to shine through the translucent precious metal while the squared gilded frame divides the panel through a double arcade in two equal parts. The archangel Gabriel encounters the virgin Mary in a squared space, which is emphasized by a checkboard pavement. While the angel, approaching Mary from the left, kneels down on his right knee, Mary has folded her hands before her chest, raising her gaze up towards God himself, appearing in the arcade's pendentive and, therefore, within the frame and outside the space in which Mary and Gabriel are exchanging words as described by Luke (Lk 1:26–38). In Lorenzetti's visualization of the miraculous scene, God has sent a white dove figuring the Holy Spirit to allow the virgin's pregnancy and the Incarnation of God in Christ, son of Mary: "NON ERIT I[M]POSSIBLE APUD DEU[M] O[MN]E V[ER]BUM" ("No Word Shall Be Impossible With God"), the angel Gabriel speaks to Mary, to which she replies, "ECCE A[N]CILLA D[OM]INI" ("Here Is God's Maid").

But God's gesture, which is returned by Mary's gaze and connected by the dove and Mary's words, does not mark the only place where pictorial architecture and architectural framework intertwine. On the central axis of the panel, the double arcade of the frame ends in a protruding console heightened in pastiglia. Immediately below, however, a likewise golden, slender capital appears, resting on a spirally twisted column shaft incised into

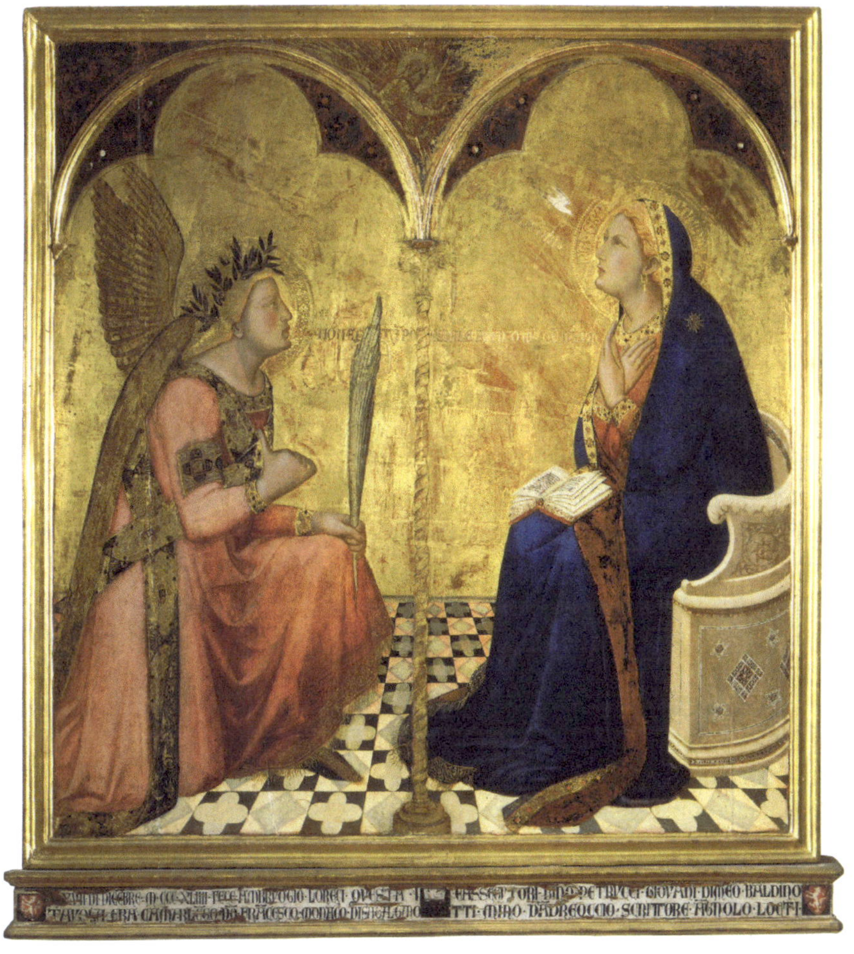

Ambrogio Lorenzetti, Annunciation to Mary, 1344, tempera and gold leaf on wood, 130 × 152 cm. Pinacoteca Nazionale, inv. 88, Siena.

Fig. 293

the gold ground [fig. 295]. While the column together with the pedestal and the capital can be assigned to the pictorial space and is located between the angel and Mary, the architecturally unfeasible connection between the capital and the console dissolves foreground and background, figure, ground, and gold ground.

The present article offers a new reading of Lorenzetti's *Annunciazione* beyond binary structures like "figure and ground" or "foreground and background," and challenges descriptive categories like "picture plane," "pictorial space," and "real space" to capture what Lorenzetti presented visually almost seven hundred years ago. In doing so, our aim is to guide our reader's eyes toward remarkable details in the artifact itself while critically discussing how Lorenzetti's panel has been perceived and theorized in art-historical scholarship. By looking into the panel's reception history, it becomes clear how important traits of the gilded panel could have been overlooked, while other pictorial elements were emphasized, and, therefore, decontextualized. Erwin Panofsky, who discusses the panel in his extensive article "Perspektive als 'Symbolische Form'" mentions its "old," or "traditional," and therefore "medieval" gold ground without describing it,[1] but discusses the panel's checkboard pavement at length, attributing the "discovery of the vanishing point" to Lorenzetti. While the "discovery" of any form of "central perspective" as well as the historicity of the "vanishing point" as such has been successfully contested,[2] his article is still a good example for how "gold ground" and "perspective" have been played out against each other as being incommensurable, illustrating the distinctiveness between "medieval" and "Renaissance" art. Pushing against these divides, this chapter argues how Lorenzetti's panel displays a complex tiled pavement in foreshortening, albeit without running toward one vanishing point or zone, while predominantly using gold leaf as an artistic material

1
Erwin Panofsky, *Perspective as Symbolic Form*, trans. Christopher S. Wood (New York: Zone Books, 1991), p. 57. Erwin Panofksky, "Die Perspektive als 'symbolische Form'" (1924/1925), in *Erwin Panofsky: Deutschsprachige Aufsätze* 2, Karen Michels and Martin Warnke, eds. (Berlin: Akademie Verlag, 1998), pp. 664–757, here p. 718.

2
See most recently Dominique Raynaud, *Studies on Binocular Vision: Optics, Vision and Perspective from the Thirteenth to the Seventeenth Centuries* (Cham: Springer, 2016); Sven Dupré, ed., *Perspective as Practice: Renaissance Cultures of Optics* (Turnhout: Brepols, 2019); Saskia Quené, *Goldgrund und Perspektive: Fra Angelico im Glanz des Quattrocento* (Berlin/Boston: Deutscher Kunstverlag, 2022).

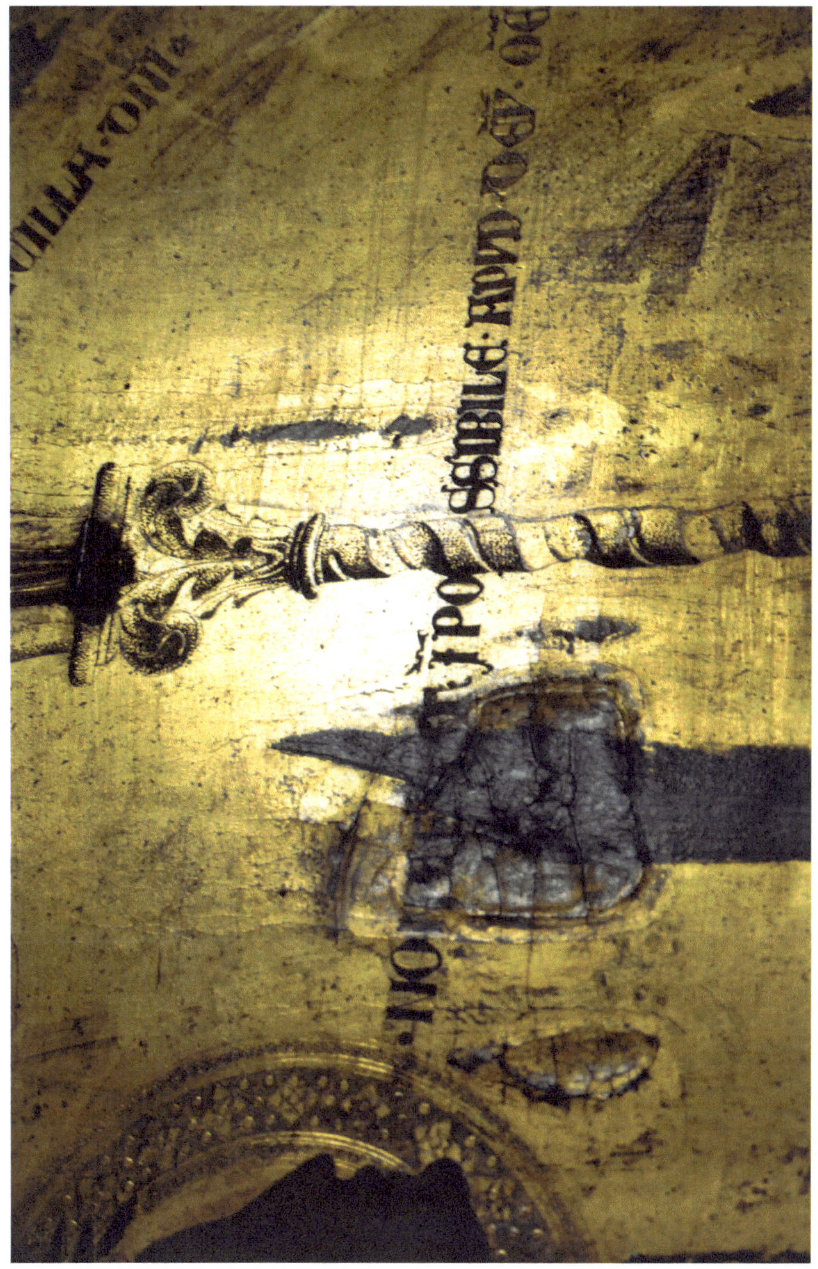

Detail of Fig. 293.

Fig. 295

to present "space." In doing so, we conclude that Lorenzetti's premodern space is shaped by spatial, visual, and allegorical proximity and distance, both within and beyond the picture plane.

Luminous Phenomena

In Lorenzetti's panel painting, the Incarnation takes place in an imaginative and, therefore, multidimensional space, in which the heavenly and earthly realms convene. Based on biblical precedent, gold can represent heaven and divinity. As such, it was an appropriate material with which to depict saints and martyrs: it could anagogically move from base materialism to divine revelation.[3] In this capacity, we might think of analogies between reliquaries' metal work and painting. However, as a natural agent of light itself, gold has to be understood as the artistic, material manifestation of what makes things visible.

Theories and metaphors of light and optics pervaded all aspects of intellectual and spiritual life. Light, of course, had important biblical associations with Christ that were equally bound up in image theories. To take but one example, Wisdom 7:26 reads "For she [i.e., Christ] is the brightness of eternal light, and the unspotted mirror of God's majesty, and the image of his goodness." And one only has to think of the importance of light and vision in the works of Dante and Guido Cavalcanti to understand its importance to poetics. Moreover, for writers on optical theory, light consisted of three main categories. *Lux* was its formal cause; it is the source of natural light, its pure form that humans could not see. *Lumen* replicates lux in all directions; it is the physical actualization of *lux*, or its *species*. Roger Bacon made this clear in his *De multiplicatione specierum* (ca. 1260) stating: "And to explain the meaning of 'species' with an example, we say that the *lumen* of the sun in the air is the species of the solar lux in the body of the sun, and *lumen* falling perchance through a window or an aperture is sufficiently visible to us, and it is the species of the lux of a star."[4] The *lumen* then radiates through a transparent medium,

3
See, most recently, on the iconography and iconology of gold and gold leaf: ibid., pp. 27–75, "Prolegomena zu einer anderen Geschichte des Goldgrundes."

4
De multiplicatione specierum, 1.1, ln. 29–32: "Et, ut in exemplo pateat hec species, dicimus lumen solis in aere esse speciem lucis solaris que est in corpore suo; et lumen forte cadens

such as air, and illuminates an opaque body. Illumination is the third category, sometimes referred to as splendor. Gold, as a specular material, was an agent through which divine light could manifest itself on earth, a belief upheld well into the Baroque period.[5]

Theologians often describe the process outlined above regarding how one could see the divine. For instance, according to Saint Bonaventure (d. 1274) the ability to understand how God participates in the material world requires divine illumination. He explores this powerful metaphor in his sermon *De altitudine perfectionis christianae* where he explains the three principal operations of corporeal light (*lux visibilis*): to exorcise darkness, to make forms manifest (i.e., to reveal them), and to delight in the power of sight. Spiritual light (*lux spiritualis*) has three parallel operations: to purge, to illuminate, and to perfect. This concept spread throughout high scholastic circles. For instance, Bartholomew of Bologna (d. 1294), one of Bonaventure's followers, wrote the treatise *De luce* (probably composed in the 1280s), which was a "compendium for students and preachers [and] draws a tight web of parallels between certain properties of natural luminous phenomena in the sensible world and corresponding qualities in spiritual light."[6] In this text, he explains the concept of exemplarism by way of the notion that God impressed human souls with divine illumination. This divine illumination could only be revealed in the world if one concerned oneself with acts of faith and prayer. Bartholomew's theory of material light developed out of his engagement with both natural philosophers and moral theologians. He understands material light to flow down from

per fenestram vel formam nobis satis est visibile, et est species lucis stelle." See *Roger Bacon's Philosophy of Nature*, ed. and trans. David C. Lindberg (Oxford: Clarendon Press, 1983), pp. 2–5.

5

See Christopher R. Lakey, "The Materiality of Light in Medieval Italian Painting" "in *Medieval Materiality*, Anne E. Lester and Katherine C. Little, eds. (Boulder, CO: University of Colorado, 2015), pp. 119–136; Roland Betancourt, "The Icon's Gold: A Medium of Light, Air, and Space," *West 86th: A Journal of Decorative Arts, Design History, and Material Culture* 23, no. 2 (2017): 252–280, Marjolijn Bol, "The Emerald and the Eye: On Sight and Light in the Artisan's Workshop and the Scholar's Study," in *Perspective as Practice: Renaissance Cultures of Optics*, Sven Dupré, ed. (Turnhout: Brepols, 2019), pp. 71–102, Fabio Barry, "Lux and Lumen: The Symbolism of Real and Represented Light in the Baroque Dome," *Kritische Berichte* 4 (2002): pp. 22–37.

6

Francesca Galli, "The *Perspectiva ad usum praedicatorum* in Late 13th-Century Florence," *Micrologus* 29 (2021): 189. On this text, see Francesca Galli, *Il "De luce" di Bartolomeo da Bologna: Studio e edizione* (Florence: SISMEL–Edizioni del Galluzzo, 2021).

heavenly bodies to earthly bodies. It was the cause for humankind's seeing all things in the world, including the workings of the divine.

Artists understood the power of gold and harnessed its reflective qualities. The decision to manipulate surfaces demonstrates a knowledge of optical theory. One reason artists tooled, incised, or otherwise worked to break up the reflective and refractive surface of burnished halos and other gilded areas was to limit its strong glare. The glare from pure gold in natural light could even be blinding, and artists knew this.[7] Thus, roughing up the surface of gold leaf scatters the light, a natural phenomenon that Alhazen in his optical treatise referred to as *scintillatio* or "dazzle."[8] Thomas Aquinas referred to this type of light as *refulgere* or shine.[9] Unlike pigments, gold, silver, and tin are naturally specular, transmitting light from the surface back to the beholder with "little or no diminution of intensity,"[10] according to Norman Muller, making the appearance of natural light in space via candles and the sunlight streaming through windows a crucial aspect of their display.

Seeing and Being-Seen

Lorenzetti's *Annunciazione* was originally commissioned by the *carmarlingo*, or treasurer, of the Ufficio della Gabella (the Office of the Tax), a Cistercian monk named Don Francesco di San Galgano, as specified by a two-line signature on the predella [fig. 293]. The *carmarlinghi* during this period were often drawn from the ranks of the religious orders in the city to provide, theoretically at least, a more pious account of finances than the tax officers themselves who came from the ranks of the city's merchants. Its original location was in the Sala del

7
See Norman Muller, "In a New Light: the Origins of Reflective Halo Tooling in Siena," *Zeitschrift* für *Kunstgeschichte* 75 (2012): p. 157; see on gold and burning mirrors also Quené, *Goldgrund und Perspektive*, pp. 276–289.

8
Alhacen's Theory of Visual Perception: A Critical Edition, with English Translation and Commentary, of the First Three Books of Alhacen's De aspectibus, trans. A. Mark Smith (Philadelphia: Transactions of the American Philosophical Society, 2001), vol. 91 (5), book. 1: 6.108.

9
Thomas Aquinas, S.T. III, q. 45. a.1.

10
Muller, "In a New Light," p. 156.

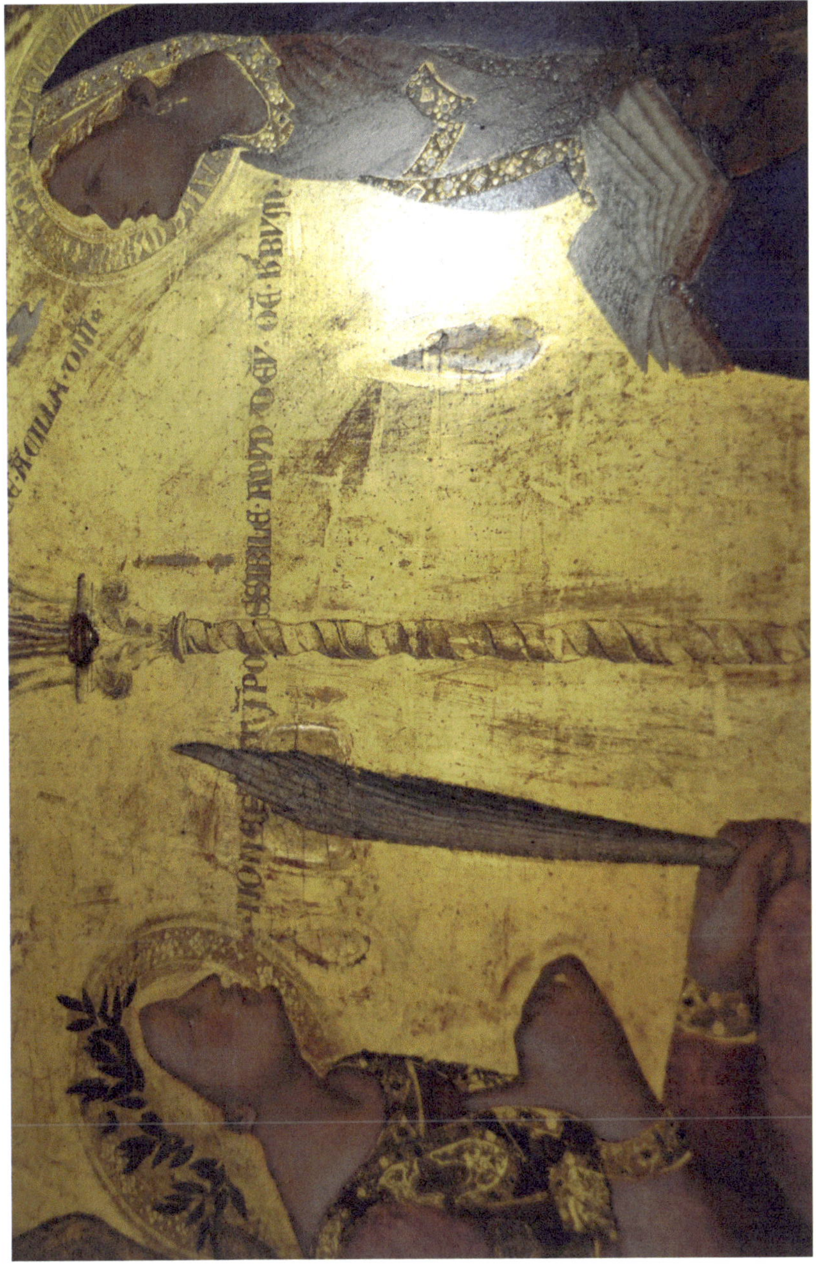

Detail of Fig. 293.

Fig. 299

Concistoro of the Palazzo Pubblico, which, since the construction of the Palazzo, was used as a venue for the meetings of the government of the republic, a function maintained until the establishment of the modern Municipality in 1786.[11]

While we do not know how precisely Lorenzetti's panel functioned in the Sala del Concistoro (e.g., whether it was an altarpiece or not), we do know from conservators that there are at least two candle burns in Lorenzetti's Annunciation: one just below and to the right of the angel's chin and halo, and the other above Mary's book [figs. 295 and 299]. A further example that demonstrates how the relationship between gold leaf and natural light effected viewership has been revealed by a team of scientists and art historians from the University of Bristol on their study of Duccio's *Annunciation* (1311). By comparing Duccio's panel under two different lighting conditions, the typical diffuse light found in museum settings and a recreation of its original lighting conditions using candles, showed "how the density of observers' eye fixations changed under [these] different lighting conditions, and how the glow of the gold induced shifts in fixations when lit by candle."[12] They found that under candlelight their subject's eyes moved away from the brightest parts of the panel—that is, where the reflection of the gold was most intense—to less dense areas of the panel. This type of behavior is consistent with what we know about how premodern artists' used a variety of techniques to mitigate the blinding potential of gold on their beholders.

11
It has been suggested that the panel was commissioned for the office of the Gabella itself, located in the Malborghetto, which was part of the Mercato di Campo. See Allesandra Caffio, "*L'Annuciazione* Per L'Ufficio di Gabela," in *Ambrogio Lorenzetti*, Alessandro Bagnoli, Roberto Bartalini, Max Seidel, eds. (Milan: Silvana Editoriale, 2017), cat. no. 29, pp. 346–348. The inscription reads: "AD XVII. DI. DICE[M]BRE. M. CCC. XLIIII. FECE. AMBRUGOGIO. LORE[N]ÇI. QUESTA. // TAVOLA. ERA. CAMARLE[N] GO. DO[N]. FRA[N]CESCO. MONACO. Di SA[N] GALGANO //. E ASSEGUTORI. BI(N)DO. PETRUCCI. GIOVANNI. DI MEO. BALDINO // TTI. MINO. D'A[N] DREOCCIO. SCRITTORE. A[N]GNOLO. LOCTI. On the history of *carmarlengi* see, Alessandra Ghidoli, "Ragionando di carmarlinghi e altri boni homines," in *Le Biccherne di Siena. Arte e Finanza all'alba dell'economia moderna*, Allessandro Tomei, ed. (Rome: Retablo, 2002), pp. 54–59.

12
Uta Leonards, Roland Baddeley, Beth Williamson, et al. "Medieval Artists: Masters in Directing the Observer's Gaze," *Current Biology* 17, no. 1 (2007): R8–R9.

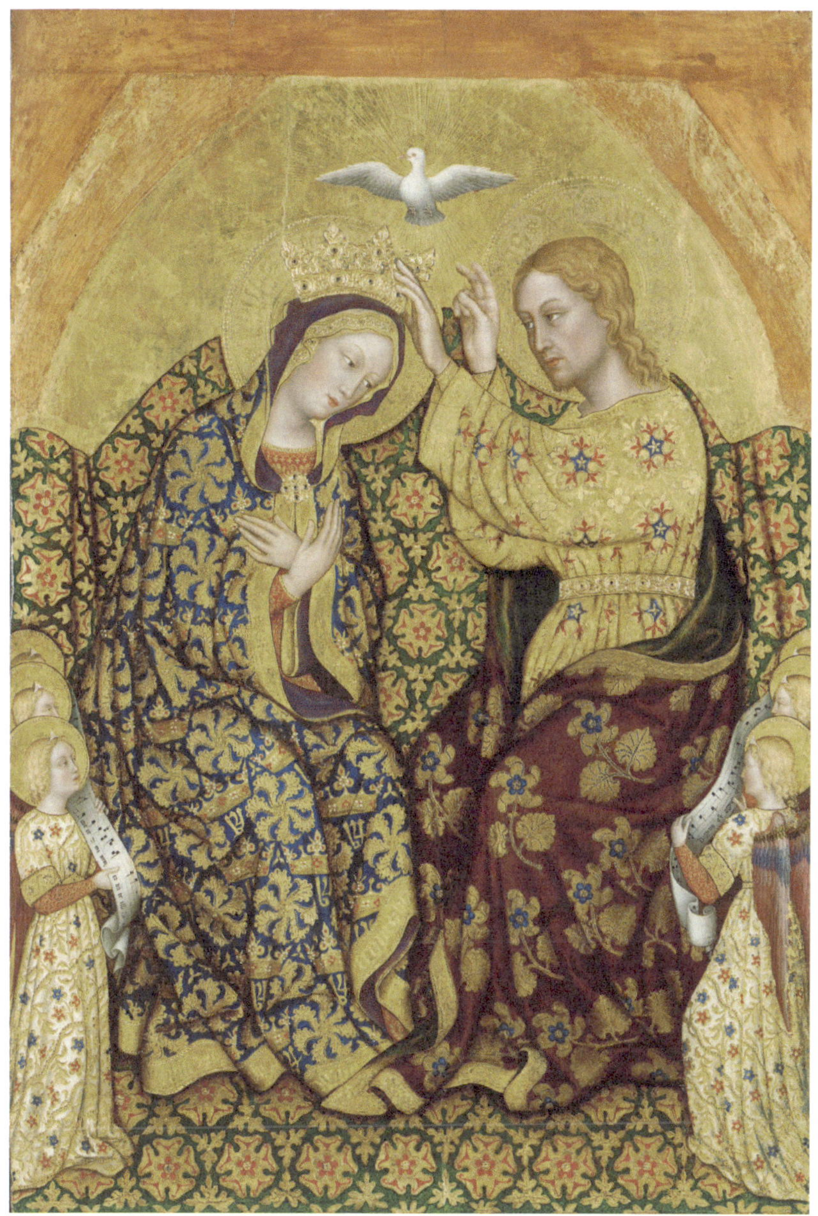

Gentile da Fabriano, Coronation of the Virgin, ca. 1420, tempera and gold leaf on wood, 93 × 64.1 cm. The Getty Museum, inv. 77.PB.92, Los Angeles.

Fig. 301

Lumen, therefore, was an active participant in the beholder-object relationship. And gold was a mediating factor, interlocking the figure, or the beholder, with their ground, the pictorial surface they were encountering while looking at a gilded panel. As a counter to interpretations that ignore gold leaf altogether, or deem its use value only iconologically, much can be gained from interpreting Lorenzetti's panel, or medieval and early modern paintings in general, along these phenomenological lines. One other example, which sums up the use of gold for allegorical purposes as much as it takes into account the subject-object relation is a double-sided processional standard by Gentile da Fabriano, painted for a confraternity linked to the church of San Francesco in his hometown of Fabriano [fig. 301]. One side depicts the Coronation of the Virgin. Gold leaf is distributed throughout the panel to depict the heavenly sphere in which the coronation takes place and to amplify the regality of both Christ and the Virgin through their sumptuous garb. As the concentric incisions insinuate, God himself as the source of all light remains hidden behind the haloed Holy Ghost, presented as a white dove right above Mary's crown and Christ's blessing hands [fig. 303].[13]

The other side of Gentile's panel is dedicated to the Stigmatization of St. Francis [fig. 304], a depiction for which the painter was placed firmly in "Vasari's Second Age," because of its high degree of naturalism, especially in the depiction of the landscape. In his analysis, Keith Christiansen does not address the gold ground upon which the flaming seraph appears,[14] which produces a double effect of light. On the one hand, a light source from the right, located in front of the picture plane illuminates the vegetation behind the Saint and Francis himself, who casts shadows on the grass on which he is kneeling. Christiansen, therefore, praised the artists for "embracing the idea of painting as mimesis."[15] On the other hand, there is the seraph's glow, casting a second,

13
See for other examples Quené, *Goldgrund und Perspektive*, ch. 6, pp. 251–289.

14
Keith Christiansen, *Gentile da Fabriano* (London: Chatto & Windus, 1982), pp. 93–96; Emanuela Daffa, "Gentile da Fabriano, *Stigmatization of St. Francis*," in *Gentile da Fabriano and the Other Renaissance*, Laura Laureati and Lorenza Mochi Onori, eds., exh. cat. (Milan: Electa, 2006), pp. 182–184.

15
Christiansen, "The Art of Gentile da Fabriano," in *Gentile da Fabriano and the Other Renaissance*, pp. 30–31.

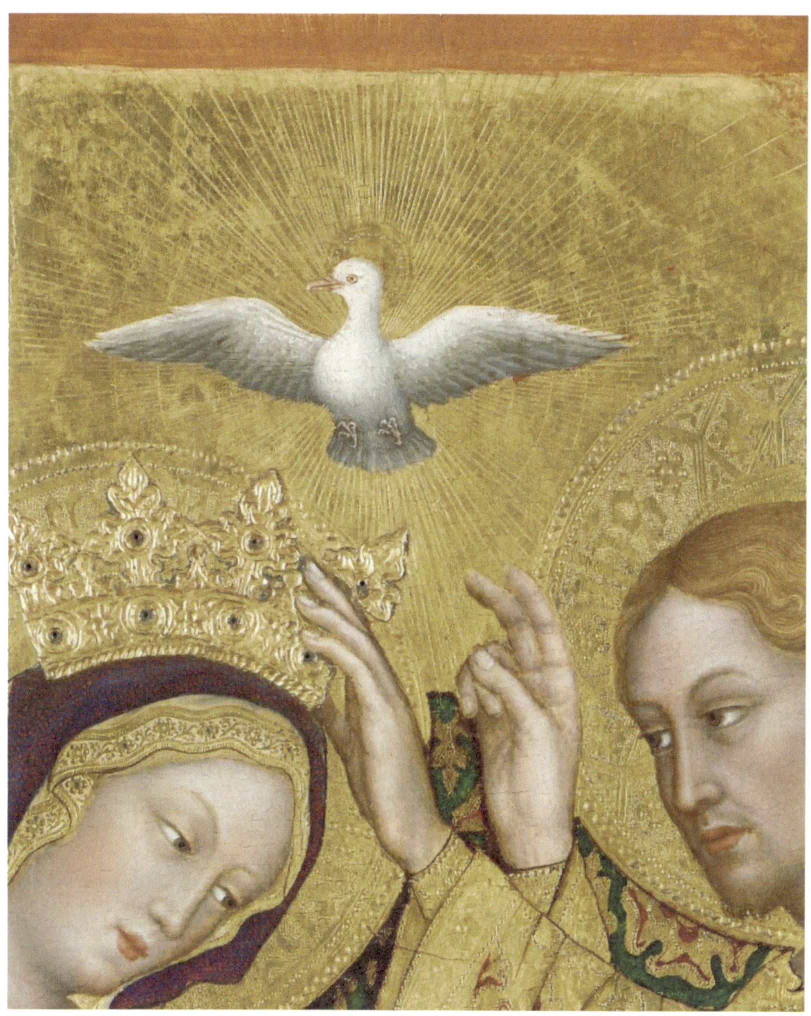

Detail of Fig. 301.

Fig. 303

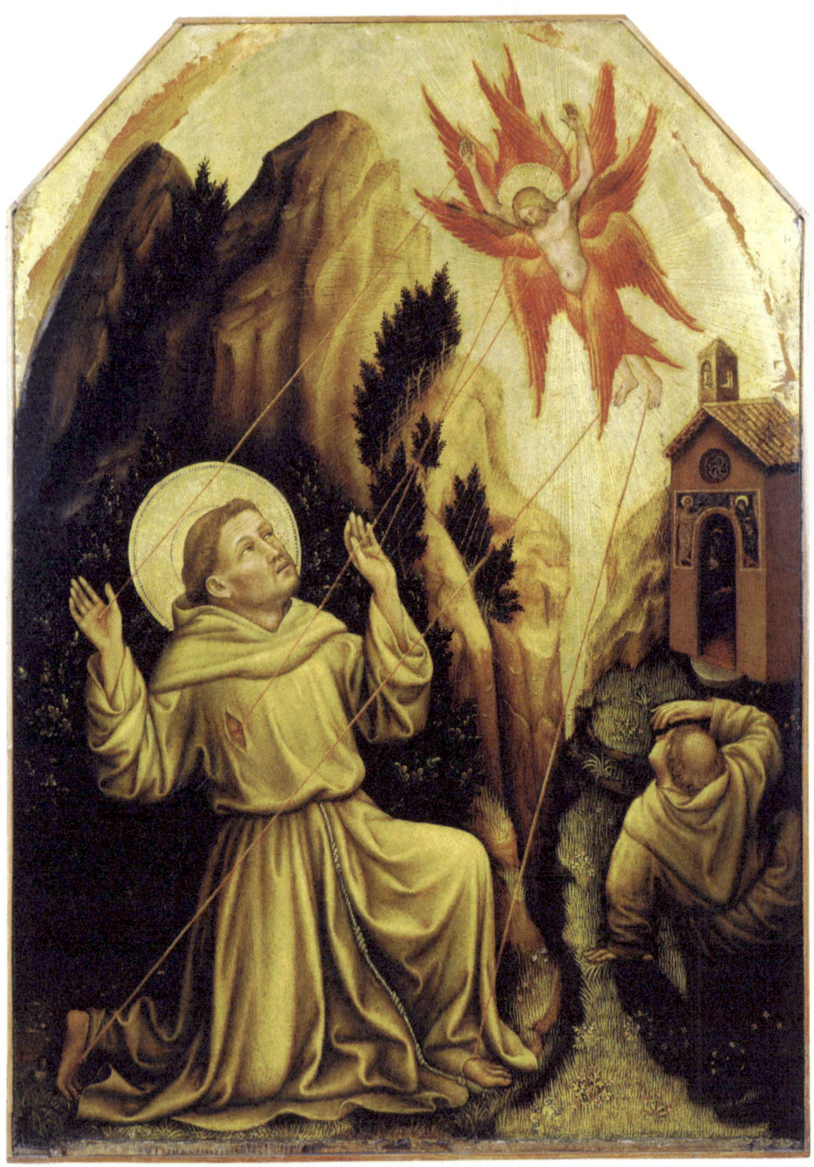

Gentile da Fabriano, Stigmatization of St Francis, ca. 1420, tempera and gold leaf on wood, 89 × 65 cm. Magnani Rocca Fondazione, Mamiano di Traversetolo, Parma.

Fig. 304

distinct shadow towards the viewer. Sitting on the ground on the other side of a slender but dark abyss, Brother Leo is shielding his eyes with his right hand from the golden light piercing through the gilded surface.

In both paintings by Gentile da Fabriano, natural light touching the surface would have been scattered in all directions. As a processional standard, both paintings would have been processed around the town (and perhaps elsewhere) in honor of the virgin (probably on certain feasts days)—this was its primary function. We can imagine that under the Italian sun beholders might have temporarily been blinded if the light hit at the right angle, quite literally reproducing the blinding effects of the divine light that Brother Leo shields his eyes from. Anachronistically, Jacque Lacan's description of a glittering sardine can floating at sea, seeing him more as he sees the can in his fisher boat, might illuminate this point: "It was looking at me at the level of the point of light, the point at which everything that looks at me is situated—and I am not speaking metaphorically."[16] Lacan continues:

> That which is light looks at me, and by means of that light in the depths of my eye, something is painted—something that is not simply a constructed relation, the object on which the philosopher lingers—but something that is an impression, the shimmering of a surface that is not, in advance, situated for me in its distance. This is something that introduces what was elided in the geometrical relation—the depth of field, with all its ambiguity and variability, which is in no way mastered by me. It is rather it that grasps me, solicits me at every moment, and makes of the landscape something other than a landscape, something other than what I have called this picture.[17]

16
Jacques-Alain Miller, ed., "The Seminar of Jacques Lacan, Book XI: The Four Fundamental Concepts of Psychoanalysis," trans. Alan Sheridan (Harmondsworth: Penguin, 1977), p. 95.

17
Ibid., p. 96.

Lacan's ambiguous and variable depth of field becomes, nevertheless, a prerequisite for the being-seen as well as for the seeing. The ephemeral moment in time in which a spark appears can only derive from a ground or field receptive to light.

On Time and Place

Lorenzetti inherited a tradition of painting in Siena and elsewhere on the peninsula that since the mid-thirteenth century replicated the techniques and iconographies of Byzantine icons that had been brought to western Europe after Crusaders pillaged the city during the sack of Constantinople in 1204. Typically, these early examples depicted the Virgin and Child on panel surrounded by gold leaf, as exemplified by Berlinghiero of Lucca's *Hodegetria*, now at the Metropolitan Museum in New York [fig. 307]. What began as literal replications of icons in terms of their format, grew into larger and multipaneled altarpieces, especially in the fourteenth century. This story might sound familiar, but it is important to remember that the relationship between Byzantine icons and Italian painting fostered an art-historical teleology for writers like Hans Belting that understood artists in the fifteenth century to have shaken-off the "cult status" of works in favor of "art"—in other words, the "medieval," in which gold leaf as a predominant artistic material for icons played a key role. Art-historiographical narratives like these were eager to brush over the fact that Gentile's two paintings were created by one and the same artist.

In other ways, Lorenzetti's painting was a response to the incredibly popular depiction of the Annunciation by Simone Martini and Lippo Memmi in 1333, which was originally located on the altar in the chapel of Sant'Ansano, just to the north of the high altar in the Siena Duomo [fig. 308].[18] Although the painting's inscription names both artists as painters, and payment records indicate the two artists and brothers-in-law collaborated,

18
Irene Hueck, "*L'Annunciazione e Santi* di Simone Martini e Lippo Memmi," in *Simone Martini e L'Annunciazione Degli Uffizi*, Alessandro Cechhi, ed. (Milan: Silvana Editoriale, 2001), p. 11. For the history of this debate, see Hueck, pp. 19–22. For the records of payment, see Monika Butzek and Allessandro Cecchi, "Appendice documentaria," in *Simone Martini e L'Annunciazione Degli Uffizi*, p. 129; Kavin M. Frederick, "The Dating of Simone Martini's S. Asano Altar-Piece: A Re-Examination of Two Documents," *The Burlington Magazine* 131 (1989), pp. 468–469.

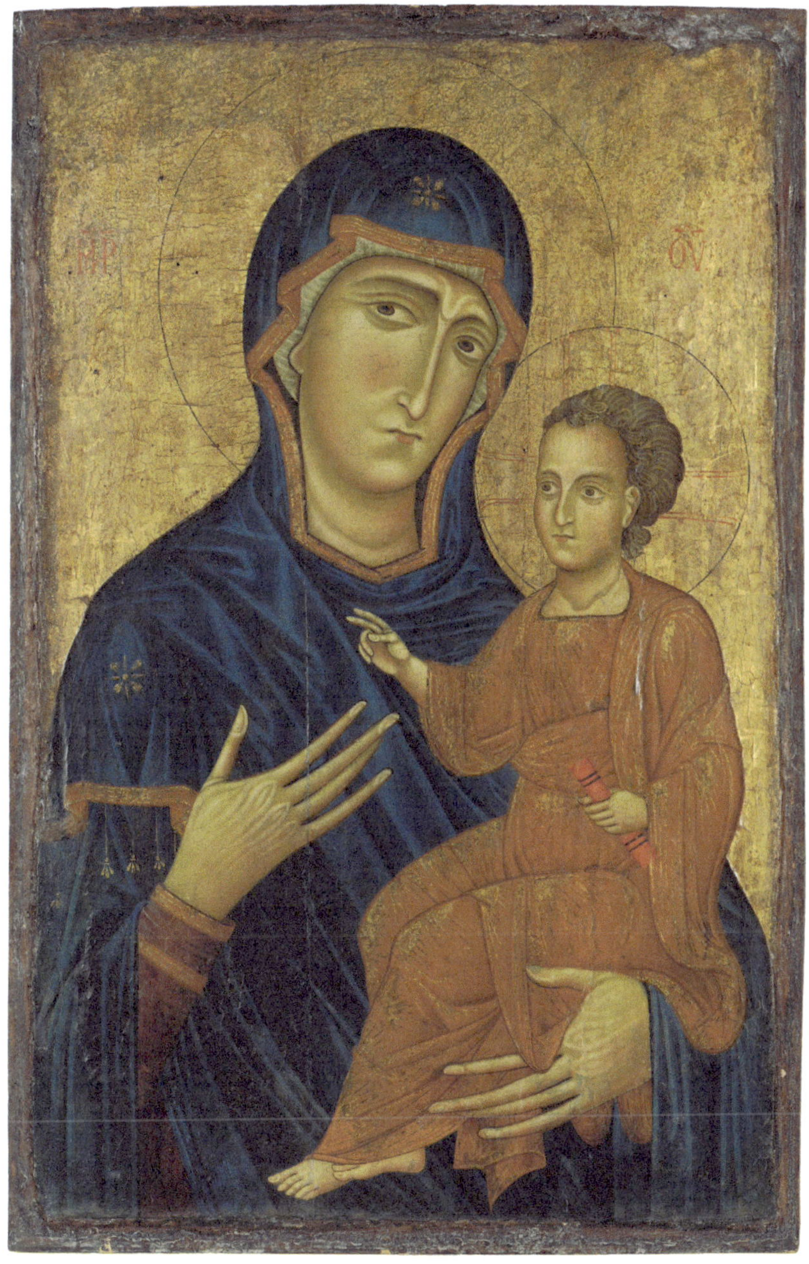

Berlinghiero, Madonna and Child (*Hodegetria*), ca. 1230, tempera and gold leaf on wood, 76.2 × 49.5 cm. The Metropolitan Museum, 60.173, New York.

Fig. 307

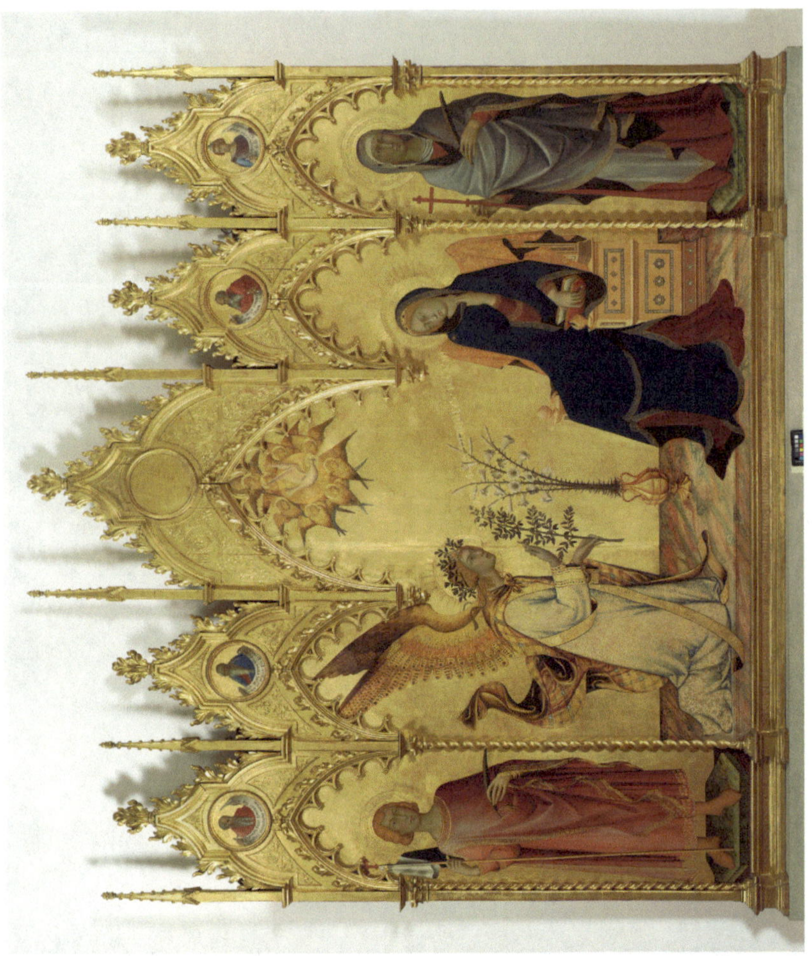

Simone Martini and Lippo Memmi, Annunciation to Mary, 1333, tempera and gold leaf on wood, ca. 184 × 168 cm. Gellerie degli Uffizi, inv. 1890 no. 451, 452, 453, Florence.

Fig. 308

it is debatable to what extent Lippi was involved in its conception and design. Nevertheless, for all intents and purposes, the central panel of the polyptych appears to be by Simone's hand. Here, the archangel appears to the Virgin Mary and greets her with "AVE GRATIA PLENA DOMINUS TECUM" ("Hail, Full of Grace, the Lord is With Thee"), raised in pastiglia within, or rather underneath, the gold leaf surface. Above, in the center of the scene, the Holy Spirit is depicted as a dove surrounded by seraphim, while golden rays flow out of the bird's beak toward Mary. Between her and the angel, the virgin's vase filled with an abundance of white lilies scarcely leaves room for the angel's green twig, the *virga* from the Tree of Jesse.

In Siena in 1333, "the impact of Simone's Annunciation [was] overwhelming,"[19] as Henk van Os has demonstrated. Nevertheless, or maybe just because of it, Lorenzetti's 1344 painting deviates from Simone's configuration in important ways. To borrow van Os's words, Lorenzetti was an "ostentatious individualist among the Sienese artists," and we can see this playing out in at least two of his Annunciations. The first, a fresco on the wall behind the high altar at the Chapel of San Galgano, Montesiepi, originally depicted the Virgin dramatically clinging to a column, reminiscing the averting turn of Mary's body toward Gabriel as depicted by Simone. Mary is depicted in fear, who is separated from her by a window [fig. 310]. At some point, however, the Virgin's figure was modified, perhaps for decorum's sake, to show a calmer Mary, bowing toward Gabriel with her arms crossed [fig. 311].

For the panel painting, Lorenzetti or his patrons chose a different moment from Luke's account (Lk 1:37–38). It is not the initial greeting of the archangel that is depicted (though the phrase "AVE MARIA GRATIA PLENA DOMINU[S] TE[CUM]" is tooled within the Virgin's halo), but the moment after Gabriel explained to Mary how the conception would happen and when it would occur. A confident, not frightened, Mary leans forward in her throne and looks up at the holy ghost who God sends forth

19
Henk van Os, *Sienese Altarpieces 1215–1460: Form, Conent, Function, Volume Two: 1344–1460* (Groningen: Egbert Forsten Publishing, 1990), p. 99.

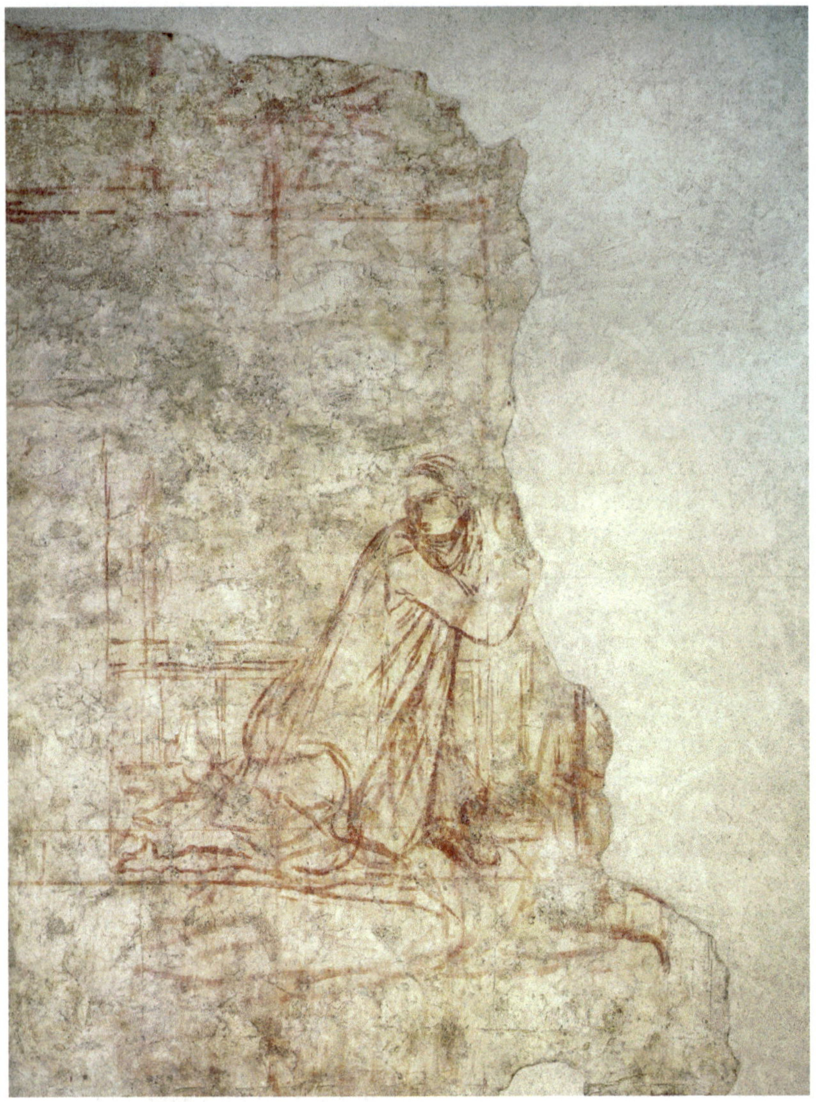

Ambrogio Lorenzetti, detail of a study in sinopia for the Annunciation, ca. 1334–1336.
Chapel of Saint Galgano in Montesiepi, Chiusdino, Siena.

Fig. 310

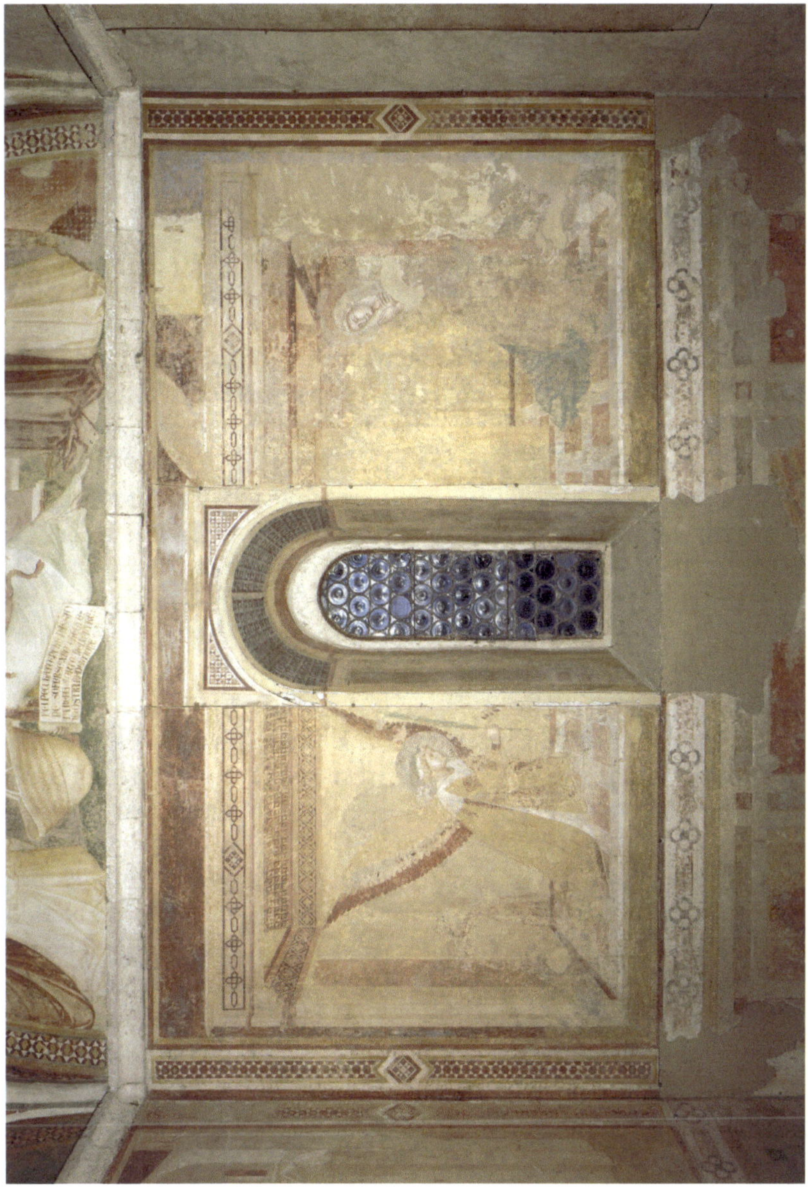

Ambrogio Lorenzetti, Annunciation, ca. 1334–1336, fresco, ca. 220 × 170 cm.
Chapel of Saint Galgano in Montesiepi, Chiusdino, Siena.

Fig. 311

from the pendentive above the central axis of the panel and accepts her fate. Here, not only does Lorenzetti deviate from the normal iconography of the scene—he also defied theologians.

That Mary is not afraid of the bodily appearance of Gabriel was a concern for Thomas Aquinas, the great Dominican master. In the *Summa* he addressed this pointing to a hymn sung during the Feast of the Annunciation, "and the Virgin seeing the light was filled with fear."[20] Moreover, what is on the axis beneath God the Father is not a vase of lilies, but the central column that divides the scene vertically and acts as a spring for the two triumphal Roman arches that frame the protagonists. Originally, the words "NON ERIT" (the "est" was the mistake of a restorer) would have passed in front of the angel's palm branch, as Norman Muller has demonstrated, and the following "I[M]POSSIBLE" behind the column [figs. 299], thus creating depth on the front plane through what he calls "spatial indicators."[21] That is to say, Lorenzetti located the inscription in front of the palm branch held by Gabriel's left hand and the column between the two figures resting on a base on the lower edge of the panel, where the gilded frame coincides with the horizontal border of the floor's black, white, and gray tiles [fig. 313].

Simone painted a marble floor veined with touches of black that slopes slightly upward on the front plane and dramatically cuts off to the left and right of the main scene where two golden columns delimit the framing saints, St. Ansano to Gabriel's right and St. Margaret (or Maxima) to the left. Lorenzetti's ground plane, on the other hand, is divided into geometrically ornamented orthogonal tiles that, according to Erwin Panofsky "are here for the first time all oriented toward a single point undoubtedly with full mathematical consciousness;" and "in a sense, the concrete symbol for the discovery of the infinite itself." Moreover, Lorenzetti invented a "completely new meaning ... upon the ground plane as such."[22] Compared to his predecessors like Giotto and Duccio,

20
Thomas Aquinas, S.T. III, q. 30. a.3.

21
Norman Muller, "Ambrogio Lorenzetti's Annunciation. A Re-Examination," *Mitteilungen des Kunsthistorischen Institutes in Florenz* 21, no. 1 (1977): pp. 1–12.

22
Panofsky, *Perspective as Symbolic Form*, p. 57.

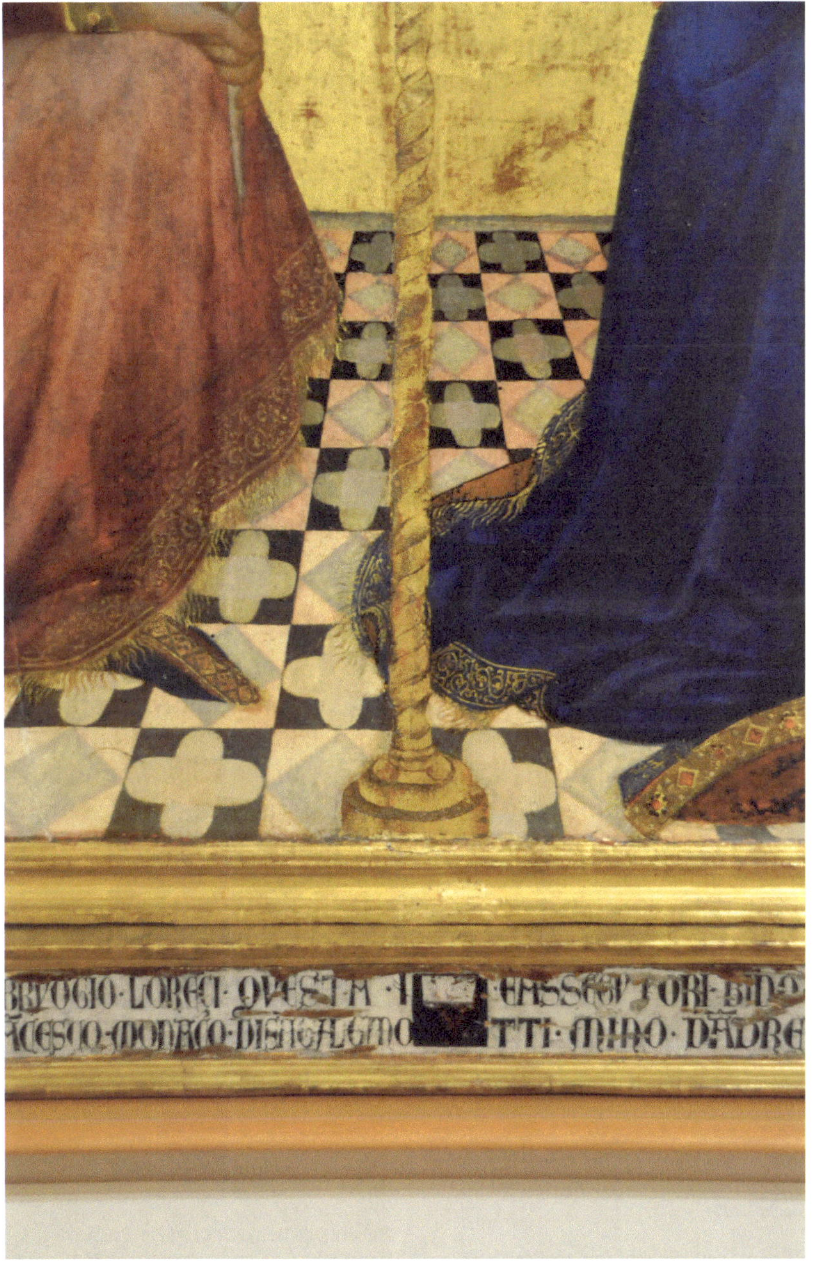

Detail of Fig. 293.

Fig. 313

who employed the technique of a "Raumkasten"[23] or "space-box," which terminates the image's edges at the left and right, Lorenzetti notionally extended the image by cutting off the Virgin's throne and by showing just enough of the ground plane behind the Angel to suggest a lateral expansion.

However, the orthogonals do not in fact meet at one point, and we have no evidence Lorenzetti utilized any form of geometry to design the work. Nevertheless, Panofsky's account of this painting remains pivotal and has shaped art-historical periodization. Along these lines, Miriam Schild Bunim and John White largely agreed with Panofsky that Lorenzetti contributed to the development of perspective.[24] Though Hubert Damisch and others have questioned Panofsky's thesis concerning Lorenzetti's geometrical interests, there is, however, a scant analysis of the large surface of gold leaf. Panofsky only explains that the picture "is still bounded (*begrenzt*) at the rear by the traditional gold ground," as if it needed to be freed from its gilded, medieval prison.

Dissimulation

Damisch does discuss the gold briefly, but importantly. His focus is mainly on the column as a disruptive element in the picture as it stands precisely in the center of the composition where the supposed vanishing point would appear: "But the point toward which its orthogonals converge doesn't appear as such; it is dissimulated, or, to be more precise, obliterated, obstructed by a column in low relief that corresponds with the panel's axis of symmetry."[25] He then goes on to make an important point: "In its spatial ambiguity, functioning as is does as a kind of mask or screen, this architectonic element is the lynchpin of an eminently contradictory structure in which the paving's recessions is in open conflict with the flattening effect created by the gold ground."[26]

23
Ibid., Wolfgang Kemp, *Die Räume der Maler: Zur Bilderzählung seit Giotto* (Munich: C. H. Beck, 1996).

24
Miriam Schild Bunim, *Space in Medieval Painting and the Forerunners of Perspective* (New York: Columbia University Press, 1940), pp. 145–146; John White, *The Birth and Rebirth of Pictorial Space* (London: Farber and Farber, 1957), p. 100.

25
Hubert Damisch, *The Origin of Perspective*, trans. John Goodman (Cambridge, MA: MIT Press), p. 80.

26
Ibid., p. 81.

Dissimilitude, a slight of hand, or a deception, functions here as a crucial aspect of early perspectival constructions. Lorenzetti understood how to orient a painting geometrically to create an illusory space. However, by creating such an illusion, a deception in itself, his "obliteration" of this space by the column acts as a commentary on the sacred subject. How can the divine truly reveal itself in the world of the beholder? Another commentator worth noting in this regard is Daniel Arasse.

Arasse, in his tour-de-force account of the history of perspective in paintings of the Annunciation also understood the gold as a disruptive element. According to him, the gold would negate any true sense of perspectival depth and does not attend to its real, material spectral qualities but would rather seek to explicit the Incarnation of the divine in the human world.[27] He analogizes Lorenzetti's Annunciation to others in which natural light separates Gabriel and Mary through fenestration. One example is Lorenzetti's Annunciation fresco, yet there are many others from the eighth century onwards that could be cited. For Arasse, this symbolic function of gold as light, is held in contrast to perspectival paintings that, according to him, better allow for the depiction of the mystery of the Annunciation exemplified by Fra Angelico, Fra Filippo Lippi, and others. It, therefore, seems somewhat contradictory that for Arasse, both gold and linear perspective impart to the manifestation of the Incarnation.[28]

What stands out in these analyses of Lorenzetti's painting, despite each author's different theoretical and historical horizons, is something that earlier writers like Panofsky missed. Namely, the manifold possibilities to create and present spatiality and distance through the use of different materials and techniques to emphasize the convocation of the heavenly and the earthly, the spiritual and the bodily realms through the Incarnation. Lorenzetti had many options at his disposal, for just a few years earlier he depicted Mary's Presentation in the Temple where he demonstrates an understanding of the ground plane as a plane of projection, however geometrically accurate [fig. 316]. Painted for the chapel

27
Daniel Arasse, *L'Annonciation Italienne: Une Histoire de Perspective* (Parais: Hazan, 1999), pp. 59–99.

28
See Quené, *Goldgrund und Perspektive*, pp. 221–224, "Sakraler Goldgrund – Profane Perspektive?"

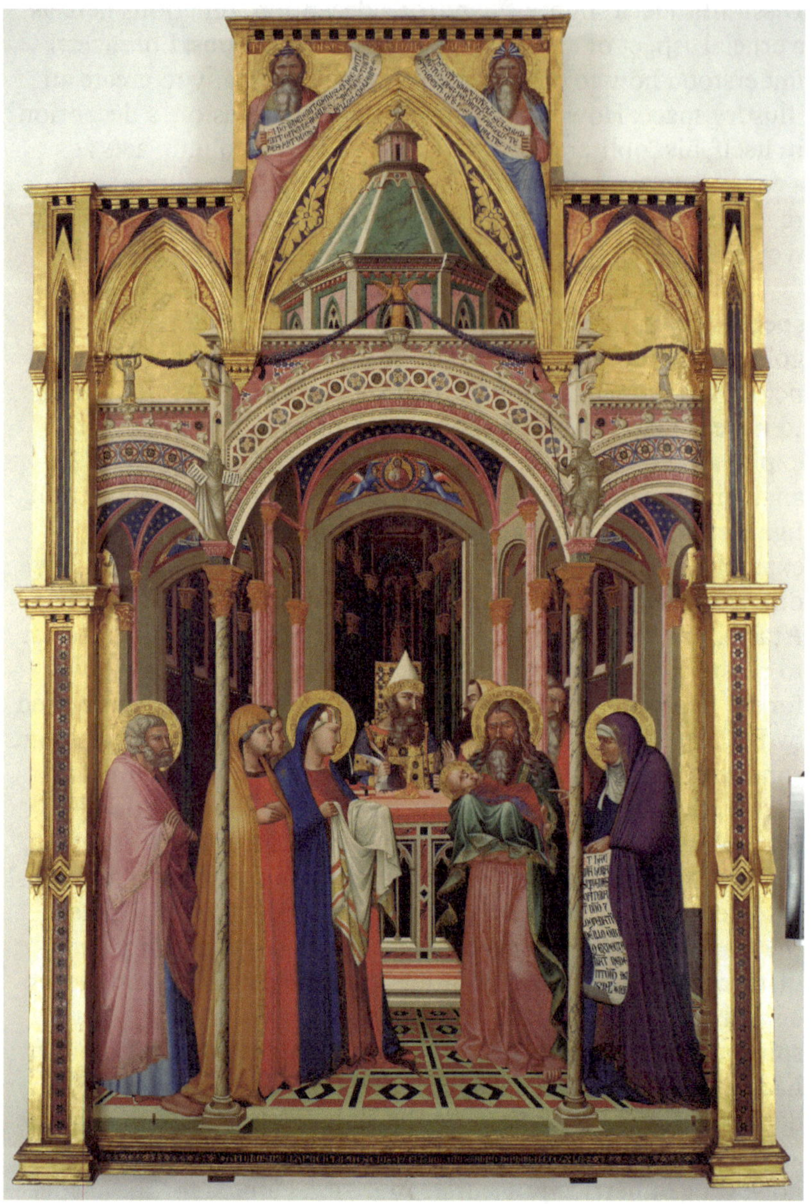

Ambrogio Lorenzetti, Presentation at the Temple, 1342, tempera and gold leaf on wood, 257 × 168 cm. Gellerie degli Uffizi, inv. 1890 no. 8346, Florence.

Fig. 316

of San Crescenzio in the transept of the Cathedral of Siena, his Presentation was part of a small group of altar pieces painted by Siena's most important artists of the first half of the fourteenth century. Dedicated to the Virgin Mary and her life, these five transept altars in the cathedral included Simone Martini's Annunciation. Clearly, then, two years later he faced another choice: paint an Annunciation in the same manner as his Presentation, opting for a more geometrical, quasi-naturalistic setting, or produce something so ostentatious that it would gesture to *and* deviate from older models (i.e., Simone's) by including a paradox in its spatial coherence to challenge the boundaries of the iconography of the Annunciation. As we have argued, he clearly chose the latter.

Visual Dialethism

Whether in debt to Lorenzetti or not, Lorenzo Monaco decided on a similar and most remarkable path for his Annunciation for the Bartolini Salimbeni chapel in Santa Trinità, Florence [fig. 318]. Lorenzo responds to architectural elements for Mary's domicile, opting for a Giotto-esque "space-box," albeit more complex, and a tiled floor that we could anachronistically describe as rendered "reversed." Here, as much as in Byzantine icons, the analytical gaze is compelled to construct a vanishing point in front of the picture plane instead of within the pictorial space, since the squared tiles taper towards the lower edge of the panel. Moreover, Lorenzo not only applies gold to depict numerous halos, the rays of light on which the Holy Ghost flies toward Mary, and details in the depicted architecture, but also to cover entire surfaces. The space "behind" Mary consists of solid gold. While Gabriel and Mary are communicating through a squared portal framed by two slender columns, another portal at the back wall of Mary's domicile allows us to sneak a peek into Mary's *hortus conclusus*, her enclosed paradisial garden [fig. 319]. Three trunks of trees rise vertically across the surface, remaining materially as well as spatially in front of the gilded background. Standing before the panel, however, the in-between gold pushes to the front, now appearing as four bright brush strokes, whose contours fade toward the lower end, where the grass rises from the ground. Emphasizing spatial instability—or rather miraculousness—through

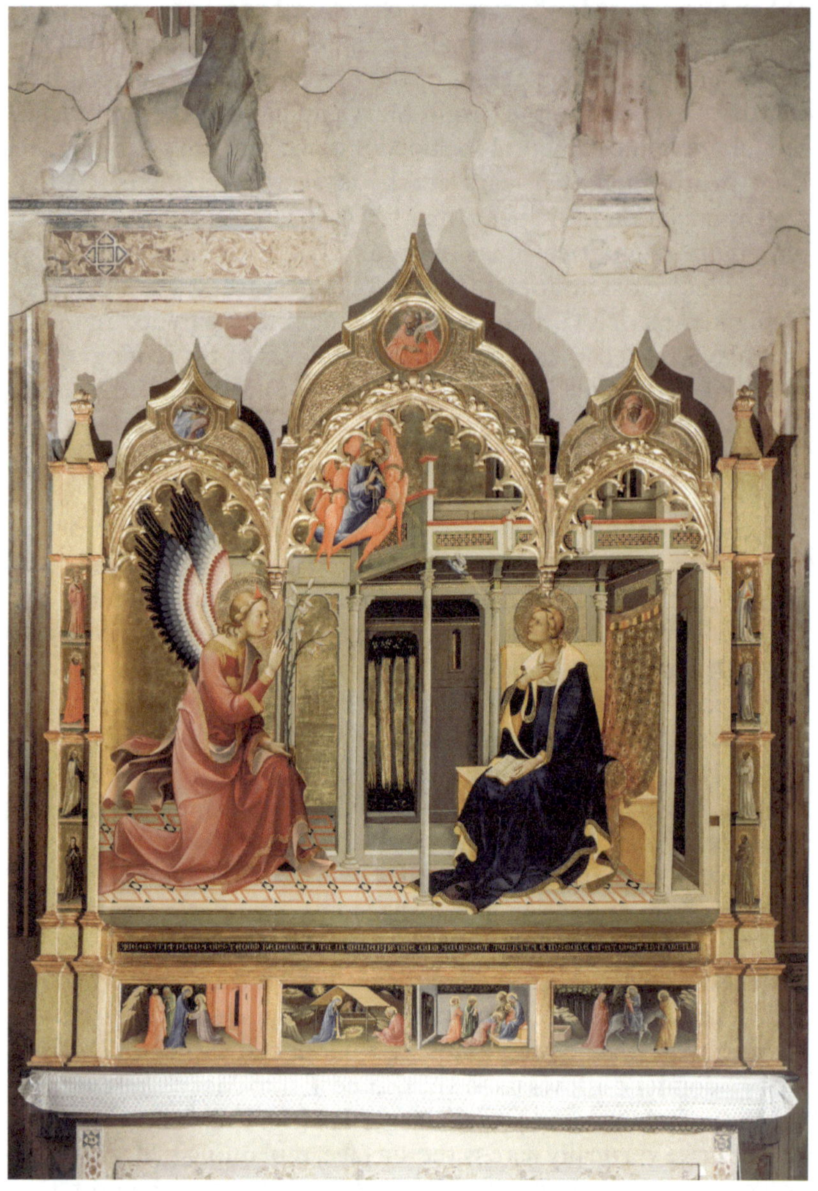

Lorenzo Monaco, *Bartolini Salimbeni Annunciation*, ca. 1420–1424, tempera and gold on wood, ca. 300 × 274 cm. Santa Trinità, Florence.

Fig. 318

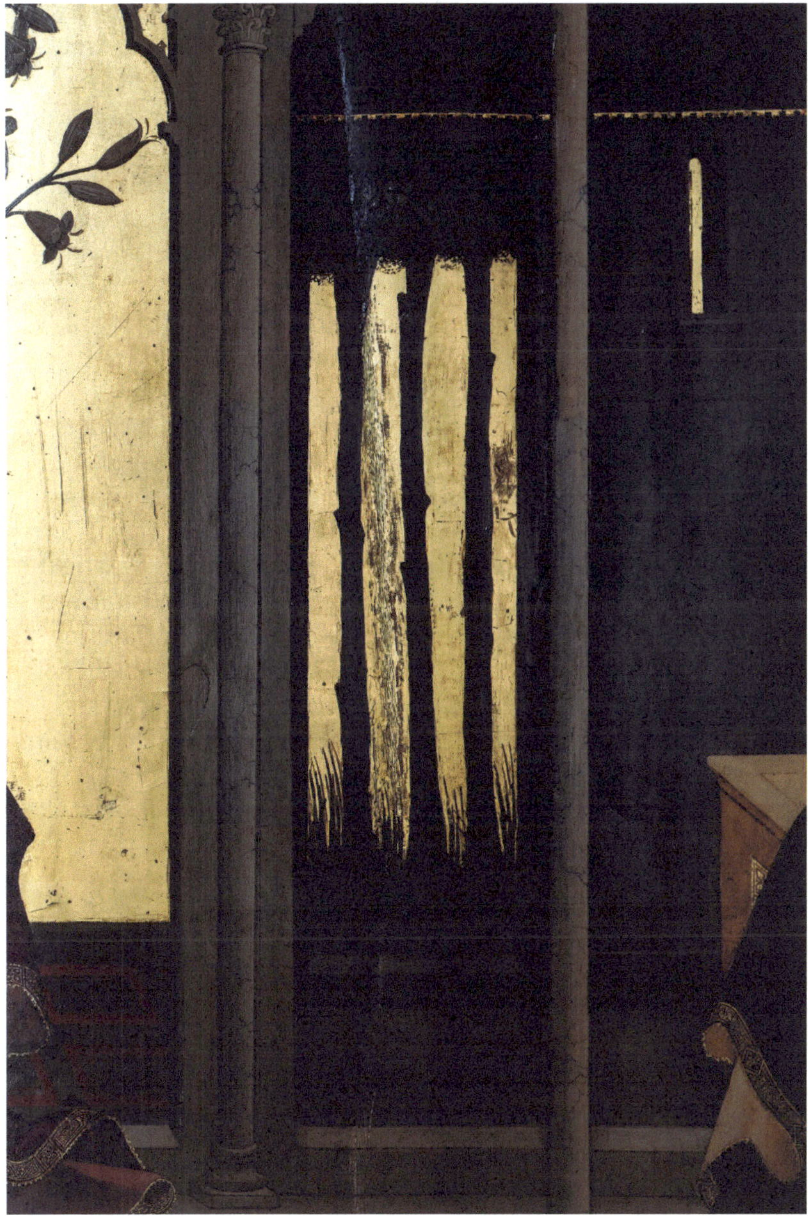

Detail of Fig. 318.

Fig. 319

inviting us to partake in a complex play unfolding between figure and ground, both Lorenzetti and Lorenzo are invested to argue visually that spaces and places can be both earthly and heavenly, maidenly and motherly, human and divine. As true contradictions, or double truths (διάλήθεια), the panel paintings discussed in this chapter are not just traces of artistic struggles in a "late medieval" or "early modern" period in which gold leaf applications and newer forms of perspectival modes of depiction clash. They are visual statements in favor of the power of art.

In Andrea del Castagno's Assumption of the Virgin [fig. 321] for the non-extant church of San Miniato Fra le Torri in Florence (1449–1450) we are, however, provoked to see a "combination of old-fashioned and forward looking:"[29] that is to say, the gold ground and the tomb decisively foreshortened. While gold leaf could have been desired by the patron (though this is not mentioned in the contract) or the space (e.g. the darkness of the church required an altarpiece in which luminosity would better enable its viewing), the foreshortened tomb leads the eye across the ground and into the suggested depth of the painting, from which a gilded aureole arises, in which Mary has taken her seat amid red-and-orange clouds. Flanked by Saint Minias and Saint Julian standing beside the tomb, the aureole is held by four flying angels. The Assumption is a visionary experience, and Castagno, like Lorenzetti and Lorenzo Monaco, provides us with a foray into the paradoxical nature of different spatial systems in one painting.[30]

The question of how many different systems we can decipher, or how we can distinguish and understand these competing

29
John R. Spencer, *Andrea del Castagno and his patrons* (Durham, NC: Duke University Press, 1991), p. 71.

30
On this point, see Anne Dunlop who argues that the aureole (or mandorla) "embodies a paradox: it is as much a disruption in the pictorial field as a delimited form ... on the one hand, this is clearly a physical object, at least for supernatural beings: four angels lift it upward ... yet it is figured as intense striations of pattern and color against which Mary rises, orange light streaked with clouds, and it reads as a flat area against the gold ground even as short bands of clouds trail, crimson red, at the bottom right, denying the closed edges that the angle grasps ... all this happens against the mitigating space of a gold ground, but where gold meets the green grass behind the lower angels, the green space bends upward, incoherently, around their forms, in a confusion that suggests the painter's own indecision about how these spaces might conceptually coexist." Dunlop, *Andrea del Castagno and the limits of painting* (London: Harvey Miller Publishers, 2015), p. 105.

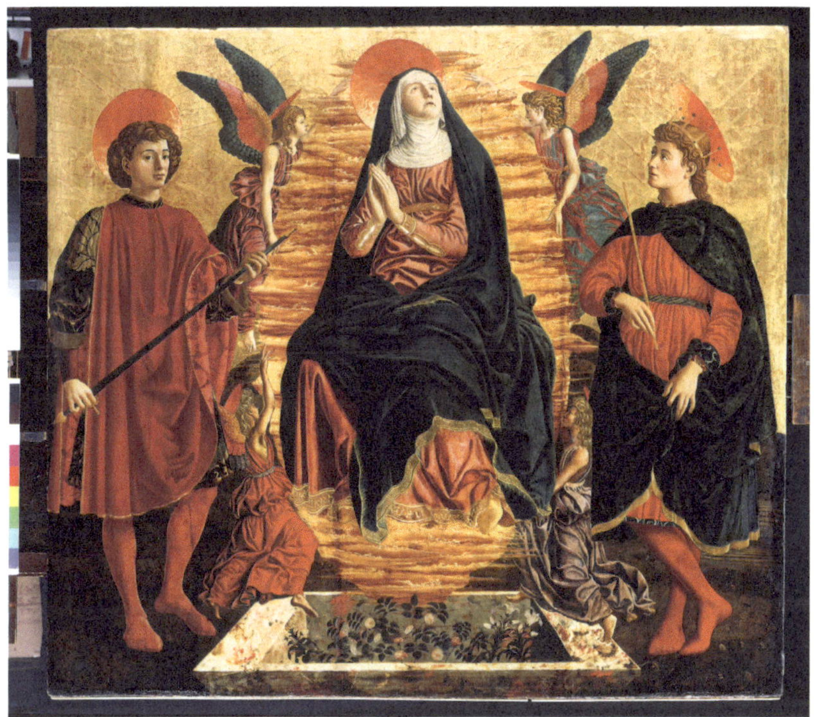

Andrea del Castagno, The Assumption of the Virgin with Saints Julian and Minas of Florence, 1449–1450, tempera and gold leaf on poplar wood, 131.3 × 150.3 cm. Staatliche Museen, Gemäldegalerie, inv. 47A, Berlin.

Fig. 321

systems to coexist, is, however, a question formed and informed by modernity. Instead, as a viewer, we should be eager to experience how manifold forms of spatial configuration can shape and manifest equally real spaces next, inside, and in between each other. Spaces between figures and grounds are shaped by proximity and distance, be it spatial, visual, or allegorical both within and beyond the picture plane, pictorial places, and real spaces. Whoever becomes part of these spaces, is invited to enjoy premodernity's visual dialethism.

Part 3
Beyond the Surface

Wie nimmt im Entwurfsprozess etwas Gestalt an und auf welcher Grundlage? Der materielle Träger der Skizze hat Anteil an der Visualisierung der Bildidee. Das Format des Papiers legt das Spielfeld für die Aufzeichnung eines Gedankengangs fest, während seine Farbigkeit untergründig an der plastischen Gestaltung der Figuration mitwirkt. Beide Aspekte sind effektiv, jedoch nicht konstitutiv für den Entwurfsprozess. Sie mögen in den Arbeitsprozess hineinspielen oder auch nicht, denn sie sind als akzidentiell einzustufen und nicht grundlegend für das Bild, an dem die Skizze arbeitet.

Die Generierung des Möglichkeitsspektrums einer Bildvorstellung, die sich in der groben Figuration des Entwurfs ankündigt, geschieht vornehmlich in der Vorstellungskraft des Künstlers oder der Künstlerin. Die Skizze externalisiert und dokumentiert eine Etappe innerhalb eines Gedankengangs, zu welchem wir über die Skizze jedoch nur mittelbar Zugang haben, denn der Papierbogen neutralisiert die Matrix der Figur, welche sich in der Skizze abzeichnet. Die Vorstellung, dass wir in der Skizze die freie Formulierung eines Bildgedankens finden, ist somit richtig, aber nicht hinreichend, denn sie unterschlägt seinen Ermöglichungsgrund.

Die Matrix der Figur als der formgebende Untergrund des Entwurfs ist, wie wir im Folgenden sehen werden, verborgen und liegt versteckt ‚hinter' dem Bogen Papier, welcher allein hilft, die Figur von diesem ‚Nährboden' abzuheben und freizustellen. Das Liniengefüge der Skizze bleibt, trotz der im meisterlichen Strich demonstrierten Unabhängigkeit, diesem Grund verhaftet. Die künstlerische Handschrift, die sich vor allem in der schnell hingeworfenen Skizze artikuliert, ist als Loslösungsbewegung diesem substanziell verbunden. Die Vorstellung, der Zeichner entwickele eine Bildidee auf dem Blatt *ex nihilo*, ignoriert das vielschichtige Netz an Bezügen, das sich zwischen den Linienverläufen und diesem latenten Grund entspinnt.

Scharfsinn, Methode, Fleiß

Martin Kemp hat in seinem wegweisenden Aufsatz „From Mimesis to Fantasia" zur Vorsicht geraten, solche Vorstellungen künstlerischer Kreativität, welche die Kunsttheorie des 19. und 20. Jahrhunderts bestimmt haben, auf die Kunst des

15. Jahrhunderts zu übertragen, denn diese orientierte sich theoretisch an antiken und mittelalterlichen Konzepten der Imagination, welche Fantasia und Mimesis nicht kategorisch gegeneinander abgrenzten; vielmehr sind sie hier eng verbunden. Die Skizze als das primäre Medium der künstlerischen Erfindung schöpfte in der Frühen Neuzeit auf der Grundlage dreier Fähigkeiten, welche die frühneuzeitliche Kunsttheorie maßgeblich der antike Rhetoriklehre entnommen hat: Scharfsinn (*acumen*), Methode (*ratio*) und Fleiß (*diligentia*) bilden für Cicero die „ganze Kunst", „aus eigener Kraft Formulierungen hervorzubringen, die immer [...] wirkungsvoll genug sind, wenn sie so sind, dass sie die Sache selbst hervorgebracht zu haben scheint."[1]

Diese drei Fähigkeiten, die sich schwer mit der Genieästhetik der Moderne verbinden lassen, helfen den kausalen Nexus zwischen Naturstudium und künstlerischer Erfindung, den der Linienzug der Skizze zwangsläufig herstellt, zu erklären, denn die Zeichnung ist nicht nur das primäre Medium der Erfindung, sondern auch dasjenige des Studiums. *Acumen*, *ratio* und *diligentia* führen zur Präzision der Linie, welche den schmalen Grat bildet, der *fantasia* und *mimesis* eint. Für Cicero hat, wie Kemp betont, *diligentia* eine herausragende Bedeutung, denn „für [den Fleiß] ist nichts unerreichbar. Um einen Fall [oder Gegenstand] [...] durch und durch zu kennen, braucht es Fleiß. [...] Zwischen Begabung (*ingenium*) und Fleiss (*diligentia*) bleibt nur sehr wenig Spielraum für die Wissenschaft."[2]

Oscar Büdel, der in seinem Aufsatz „Leonardo da Vinci: Medieval Inheritance and Creative Imagination" erklärt, dass Leonardo eher als ein „debtor of the old" denn ein „creditor of the new" zu betrachten sei, weist auf Leonardos enge Definition der Malerei als Nachahmung der Natur hin und zitiert eine Passage aus dem Codex A von 1487: „die Malerei ist die einzige Nachahmerin aller sichtbaren Werke der Natur (*sola imitatrice di tutte*

1 Cicero: *De Oratore: Über den Redner*, hg. u. übers. v. Harald Merklin, Stuttgart 1997, 299 [Buch 2; 146–147]. Vgl. Kemp, Martin: From ‚Mimesis' to ‚Fantasia': The Quattrocento Vocabulary of Creation, Inspiration and Genius in the Visual Arts, in: *Viator* 8, 1977, 347–398: 351.

2 Cicero, *De Oratore*, 299, 301 [Buch 2, 148, 150].

l'opere evidenti di natura)". Doch ist die Nachahmung nicht geistlos, denn ihre *diligentia* artikuliert zugleich die mit ihr verbundenen kognitiven Fähigkeiten – ganz im Sinne Ciceros. Leonardo fährt fort mit der Erläuterung der Malerei als einer *sottile inventione* (scharfsinnige Erfindung); ihre Nachahmung beinhalte eine „philosophische und feinsinnige Spekulation, welche sämtliche Qualitäten der Formen [der Natur] bedenkt".[3] Die *inventione* (Erfindung) der Malerei artikuliert also ein *Formbewusstsein*, das die Gestaltungsgrundlage der künstlerischen Darstellung der Natur ist.

Zur Gestalt des Randgangs

Auf einem um 1478 datierten Skizzenblatt Leonardo da Vincis aus der Sammlung Windsor Castle, welches zentral an der Vorstellung einer knienden *Madonna lactans* mit Johannesknaben arbeitet, materialisiert sich eine derartige *„speculatione"* als Randgang in der Gestalt von zwölf menschlichen Profilköpfen von unterschiedlicher Größe, von deren drei sich zur linken Seite Mariens befinden, während neun weitere die untere Blatthälfte füllen [Fig. 327]. Der Exkurs wird am unteren Bildrand durch zwei Löwenköpfe mit aufgesperrtem Maul erweitert, die demjenigen eines Drachen begegnen, der sich der allgemeinen Ausrichtung nach rechts widersetzt und als Geschöpf der Fantasie den Rahmen des Randgangs sprengt. Dieser die zentrale Skizze umgebende Gedankengang bezieht im Sinne eines Exkurses klar eine Außenposition, die jedoch, wie gezeigt werden soll, als Peripherie den Kernbereich der Skizze einkreist.

Auf dem Verso nehmen die Profilköpfe, welche hier deutlich an Größe gewonnen haben, das ganze Blatt ein [Fig. 328]. Hier brechen der Kopf eines Schreienden, ein aus dem Profil in Ober- und Dreiviertelansicht gedrehter Kopf in der linken oberen Ecke und der nach vorn geneigte Profilkopf am rechten Rand in der unteren Hälfte aus der strengen Ausrichtung der neun übrigen

3

Vgl. „[…] la quale con filosofica e sottile speculatione considera tutte le qualità delle forme." Oscar Büdel zitiert aus dem 1487 datierten R 13; Codex A, 100r. „Se tu sprezzarai [isplezzerai] la pittura, la quale è sola imitatrice di tutte l'opere evidenti di natura, per certo tu sprezzarai una sottile inventione, la quale con filosofica e sottile speculatione considera tutte le qualità delle forme." Büdel, Oscar: Medieval Inheritance and Creative Imagination, in: *Romanische Forschungen* 73, 1961, 285–299: 290.

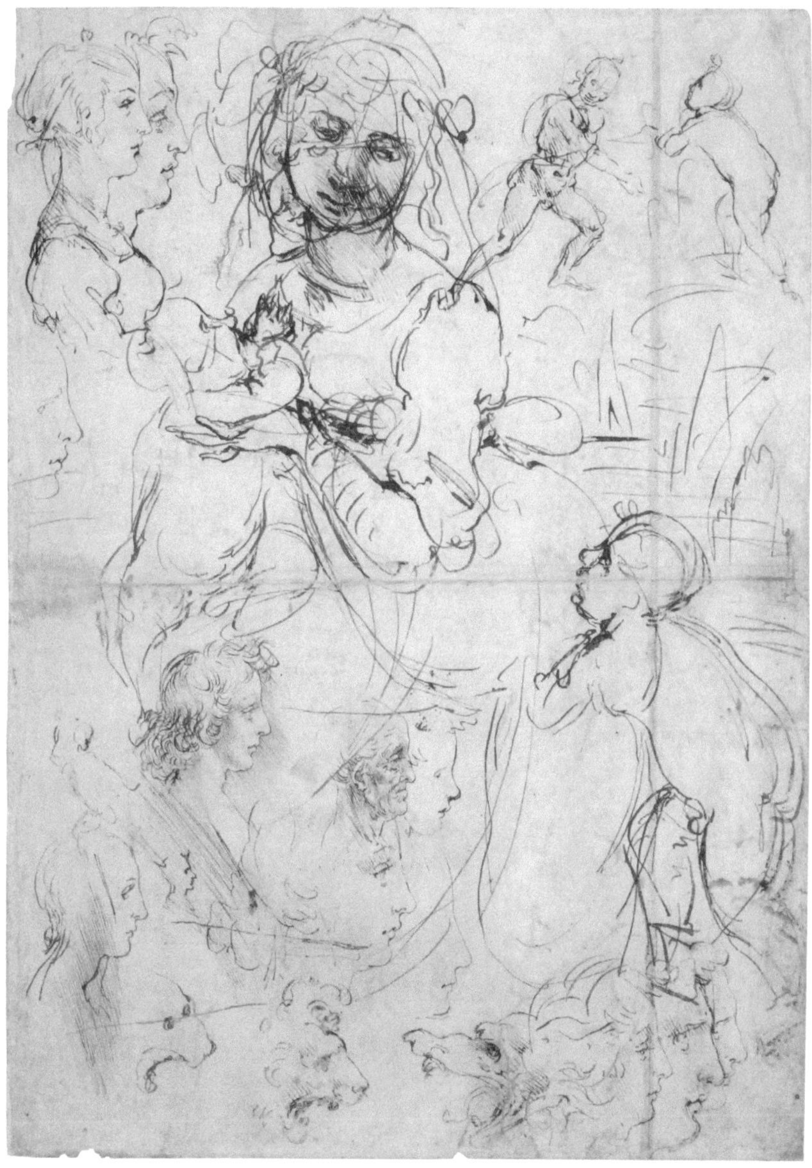

Leonardo da Vinci, *Maria Lactans* mit dem Johannesknaben [recto], ca. 1478, Federzeichnung, 40.5 × 29.0 cm. Windsor Castle, The Royal Collection, inv. Nr. RCIN 912276, Windsor.

Fig. 327

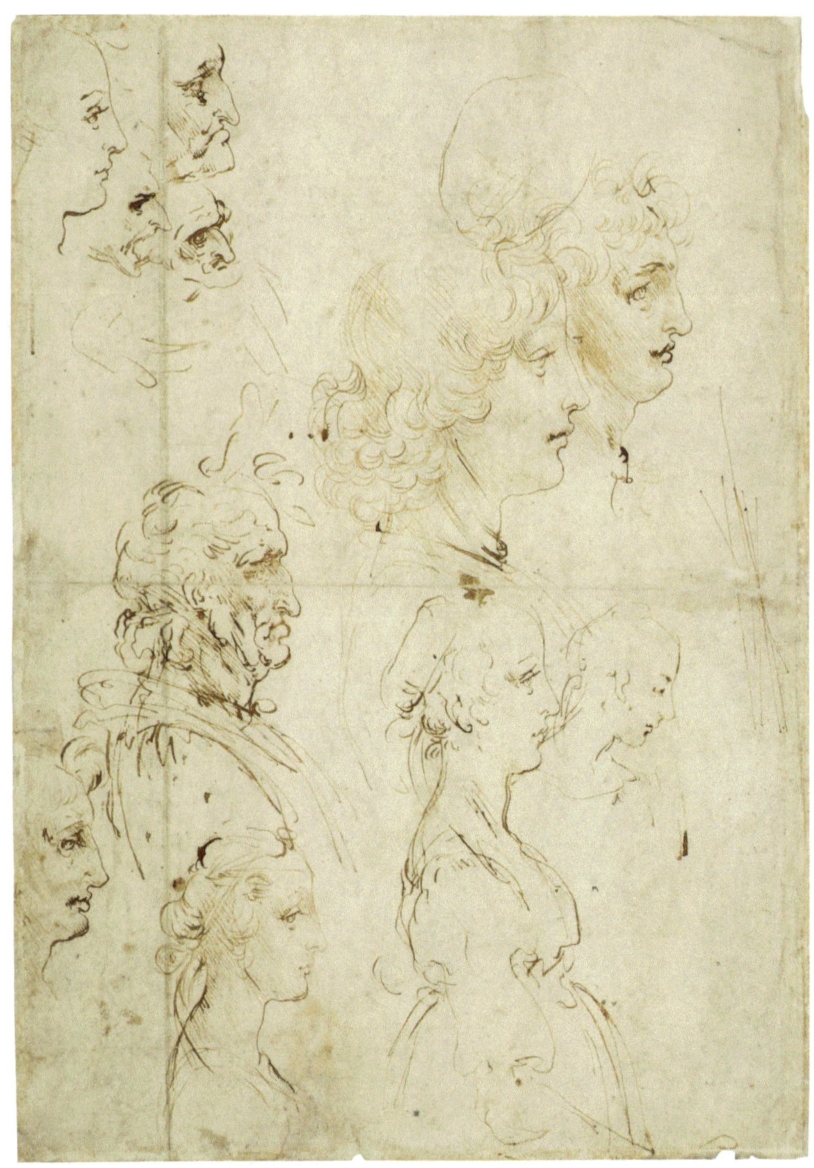

Leonardo da Vinci, *Maria Lactans* mit dem Johannesknaben [verso], ca. 1478, Federzeichnung, 40.5 × 29.0 cm.
Windsor Castle, The Royal Collection, inv. Nr. RCIN 912276, Windsor.

Fig. 328

Köpfe aus, die untereinander allein in ihrer physiognomischen Charakterisierung und Größe divergieren. In der Literatur sind die insgesamt vierundzwanzig Profilköpfe wiederholt als *doodle* bezeichnet worden, als hätte Leonardo sich hier von der den Geist beanspruchenden Tätigkeit des Entwurfs einer Madonna mit Kind und Johannesknaben erholt und der Hand freien Lauf gelassen, um sein Repertoire unterschiedlicher Profile selbstvergessen abzuspulen.[4] Demnach wäre die Armada an Köpfen als eine unabhängige Fingerübung zu betrachten, ohne direkten thematischen Bezug zur zentralen Skizze. In seiner umfassenden Analyse des Blattes bestimmt David Rosand Leonardos Spiel mit den Profilköpfen, das sich nicht nur über beide Seiten des Blattes, sondern über sein gesamtes zeichnerisches Œuvre erstreckt, genauer als „marginalia", denn dieses Spiel sei „niemals bloß eine ziellose Übung", sondern ein „wohlüberlegter graphischer Vorgang."[5] Für Rosand haben Leonardos Zeichnungen von Profilen „im Laufe ihrer Entwicklung eine systematische Logik angenommen", deren Zweck die Gewinnung von „archetypischen Bildern in Leonardos graphischem Gedächtnis" sei.[6]

Wiederholung und Reminiszenz

Tatsächlich werden über Jahrzehnte das ideale Profil des Jünglingskopfes wie dasjenige des durch Alter und mürrischen Ausdruck gekennzeichneten sogenannten ‚Galba'-Typs

4
Vgl. Carmen Bambach in: *Verrocchio: Leonardo's Master* (Ausstellungskatalog Palazzo Strozzi, Florenz), hg. v. Andrea de Marchi und Francesco Caglioti, Venedig 2019, 106. Rosand verwendet den Terminus, um ihn allerdings umgehend zu relativieren: „That the artist's pen reached deep into his self to give graphic form to psychic preoccupations and fantasies is further confirmed by the sketches surrounding the main figural group on the folio and those on the verso. Leonardo's favorite and most typical doodle—although that must now seem hardly an adequate word for such an accomplished performance—took the form of an odd and old, beautiful and ugly, male and female." Rosand, David: *Drawing Acts: Studies in Graphic Expression and Representation*, Cambridge 2002, 79–80.

5
Vgl. Rosand, *Drawing Acts*, 86.

6
„The alignment of parallel profiles, variations on an initial theme, becomes in Leonardo's marginalia more than a doodle precisely because it is never quite an aimless exercise. [...] Leonardo's drawing of profiles assumes a systematic logic and purpose in the course of its development." Ibid.

(die Bezeichnung ist hergeleitet von dem Profilkopf des Kaisers auf römischen Münzen) immer wieder am Rande von Studien auftauchen. Doch kein weiteres Blatt weist eine derartige Häufung der Profilköpfe auf wie dieses wohl früheste Beispiel seiner Art. Die ‚systematische Logik' des gestalterischen Gedankengangs der Profilköpfe, welcher auch auf anderen Blättern als Reminiszenz aufscheint, ist, wie wir sehen werden, hier bereits vollumfänglich entfaltet.

Auch wenn die „programmatische Untersuchung der Profilköpfe" (Rosand) als Randgang einer Eigenlogik folgt, so schlagen einige der Profile nichtsdestotrotz eine Brücke zur zentralen Skizzierung der Madonna mit Kind. Denn auch wenn der Kopf Mariens nicht ins Profil gewendet ist, baut die ins Profil gedrehte Halbfigur zu ihrer Rechten durch die Ähnlichkeit ihres Typs und ihrer Bekleidung einen Bezug zur Hauptfigur auf. Und auch wenn auf dem Verso der Randgang der Profilköpfe schließlich das ganze Blatt einnimmt und damit vom Thema der *Maria lactans* wegführt, ist der Bezug hier nicht abgebrochen, sondern setzt sich über die zweifache Wiederholung dieses weiblichen Profils in der unteren Blatthälfte fort.

Eine weitere Korrespondenz zwischen Exkurs und zentraler Skizze schafft das kindliche Profil, das, unmittelbar unterhalb des rechten Oberschenkels Mariens positioniert, dem Umriss der Köpfe des Jesuskinds und Johannesknaben gleicht [Fig. 327]. Dieses Köpfchen ist jedoch mit seiner Einreihung in die über das Blatt gestreuten Profilköpfe in einen Gedankengang eingepasst, der von der Skizze der *Maria lactans* zugleich wegführt. Es ist gepaart mit dem gleich großen Gesicht eines Greises, der mit dem herrisch dreinblickenden Galba-Typus und einer Trias mürrischer Greise auf dem Verso als physiognomische Ausnahmefiguren die Regel bestätigt, welche sich in der starken Familienähnlichkeit der übrigen Köpfe abzeichnet. Der Polarisierung von jung und alt muss die Darstellung des Idealbilds eines schönen Jünglings links von ihnen vorangegangen sein, dessen Profilkopf offensichtlich zeitlich *vor* dem ungleichen Paar gezeichnet wurde, denn die Konturierung des Oberschenkels Marias endet hier abrupt, während die beiden anderen Profilköpfe dessen Konturlinie überschneiden. Ein aus feinen Parallelstrichen aufgebautes nuancenreiches Helldunkel verleiht den Gesichtszügen des Schönlings Plastizität und hebt zugleich sein Profil effektvoll von dem ihn umgebenden dunklen Hintergrund ab. Das Gesicht des alten Mannes ist ebenfalls schattiert, jedoch geht das Helldunkel hier in die plastische Ausgestaltung der alten Haut ganz auf und grenzt sie von dem im wahrsten Sinne ganz ‚unfertigen' weichen Gesicht des Kleinkindes ab.[7]

Wie stark der Profilkopf des Jünglings den Arbeitsprozess des Blattes gleichsam grundiert haben muss, zeigt sich nicht nur in seiner wohl frühen Präsenz auf dem Blatt und in der Modellhaftigkeit der Linie seines Profils, welche über das Blatt in verschiedenen Größen und Stufen der Konkretion und Modifikation mannigfach gestreut ist, sondern bestätigt sich vor allem auf der Rückseite [Fig. 328]. Singulär in seiner Größe dominiert das Motiv des Jünglingskopfs das Verso. Womöglich ging diese Studie der kleineren Version auf dem Recto sogar voraus, denn die Proportion und Positionierung des Auges sind hier stimmiger. Die Linie, welche Stirn und Nase motivisch eint, ist differenzierter. Die Visualisierung der Sinnlichkeit der vollen Lippen ist in den verschatteten Lippenschluss mit den deutlich markierten Mundwinkeln verlegt, welcher in der kleineren Version noch in eine einzige Zickzacklinie zusammengefasst ist.

Die Ausdruckskraft der Mundwinkel hat Leonardo wiederholt beschäftigt. Sie definieren die zwei Profilköpfe auf dem Verso, deren abstehender gelockter Pony sie mit den beiden Versionen des Jünglings motivisch verbindet, jedoch nur, um die Differenz, die ihre Profile zu dem Idealbild aufbauen, thematisch werden zu lassen. Beide Köpfe ähneln eher demjenigen männlichen Profil mit Pony, welches dem weiblichen Kopf links von Maria hinterlegt ist, der seinerseits jenem des prominenten Knabenporträts zwillingshaft gleicht.

Neben dem Lippenschluss ist es die Positionierung und Konturierung des Auges, welche dem Gesicht Ausdruck verschaffen. Die Linie, welche die Achse des Oberlids und Wimpern zu einem charakteristischen Zug verbindet, zeigt die Blickrichtung

7
Ein späterer Stich von Wenceslaus Hollar nach Leonardo, der das Paar des greisenhaften und des kindlichen Gesichts mit dem des Jünglings von den anderen Profilköpfen losgelöst als unabhängige *„inv:[entione]“* (siehe Inschrift) präsentiert, unterstreicht den thematischen Zusammenhang der drei Köpfe als einen Exkurs über die drei Lebensalter des Mannes. Vgl. Wenceslaus Hollar, 1644–1652, Radierung, 6 × 11.1 cm. The Metropolitan Museum, acc. Nr. 17.50.18-249, New York.

an, welche nach unten weisend eine gewisse Niedergeschlagenheit in das Gesicht einschreibt. Des Weiteren wird die Differenzierung des Gesichtsausdrucks durch die kurvigen Linien bewirkt, welche den Bogen der Augenbraue wie denjenigen der Deckfalte des Auges und den der unteren Lidfalte kennzeichnen. Doch die deutlichste Differenzierungsmaßnahme ist die leichte Biegung der Stirn- und Nasenlinie. Die physiognomische Abweichung vom Idealbild scheint diese Gesichter zu affizieren; ihr Ausdruck wirkt gequält.

Der mittlere Kopf in der Dreiersequenz unten links liegt auf einer ersten mit feinem Strich gezogenen idealen Profillinie auf, welche wohl der bewusst vollzogenen Abweichung als Richtlinie diente. Die Stirn war erst, wie bei einigen der anderen Köpfe, steiler angelegt, wurde dann deutlich reduziert, so dass die Partie der Augenbraue hervortritt; der Augenaufschlag, welcher das Oberlid vollständig verdeckt, weicht deutlich von dem in sich gekehrten Blick des ersten Profils ab; die Nasenspitze wurde nach unten verlängert, das Kinn offensichtlich verstärkt, wie der doppelte Kontur verdeutlicht. Diese Veränderungen sind unmittelbar in den Zug des dritten Profils in der Reihe eingegangen, wobei, wie die Größe vermuten lässt, womöglich auf die zugrundeliegende Kopiervorlage des ersten Kopfes zurückgegriffen wurde.

Die neutrale Folie des Möglichkeitsspektrums zur Darstellung der Gesichter bietet eine Hohlform oberhalb eines Drachenmauls am unteren Rand des Versos, welche aus zwei Linienzügen gebildet ist, deren eine von der Stirn über die Nase zu dem Mundwinkel geführt ist, während die zweite Kinnpartie und Unterlippe umreißt. Eine dritte Linie, die unterhalb des Kinns verläuft, zeigt, wie Leonardo die knöcherne Struktur des Kinns von der weichen Textur der submentalen Region und damit das Gesicht vom Hals unterscheidet.

Die Konturen des Nasenflügels, der Augenbraue und des schematisierten Profilauges als die darauffolgenden Markierungen sind die Variablen, die in die Gleichung eingetragen sind und in der Streuung der Profillinie über das Blatt durchgespielt werden. Die durch diesen engen Spielraum erwirkte Familienähnlichkeit macht die Köpfe vergleichbar und deren Unterschiede deutlich wahrnehmbar. Die Aufnahme von Ausnahmen, die in Form von als hässlich definierten Köpfen die Regel bestätigen, mag hingegen als Schlussfolgerung verstanden werden: Dass Schönheit ein schmaler Grat ist, ist an den weniger gelungenen Profilköpfen deutlich zu sehen, die doch kaum von dem Modell abweichen. Wir können also schließen, dass die Wiederholung der Profillinie gleichsam forschend der Fragilität der schönen Proportion des Gesichts nachgegangen ist.

David Rosand hat in seiner umfassenden Analyse des Blattes bereits auf die generelle Doppelfunktion der Konturzeichnung („to create and record") und auf Leonardos graphisches Gedächtnis im Speziellen hingewiesen, das er in den bemerkenswerten Kontinuitäten und Wiederholungen von Formen verortet, wie beispielhaft derjenigen des laut Rosand „archetypischen Bildes" des Jünglingsprofils, dessen Linien er sich fest eingeprägt haben muss.[8] Rosand verweist auf Leonardos schriftliche Aufzeichnungen und seine Empfehlung der Gedächtnisübung, vor dem Schlafen im Dunkeln die Konturen derjenigen Formen in Gedanken („*con imaginativa*") nachzuzeichnen, die tags gezeichnet und studiert wurden, und insbesondere die Konturen derjenigen Formen, die ihm am schwersten zu verstehen und festzuhalten erschienen: „Und diese Tätigkeit ist lobenswert und dient dazu, sich dieser Dinge im Gedächtnis zu versichern (*confermarsi*)."[9]

Gedächtniskunst

Das wiederholte Abspulen der gleichen Linienbahn als Kurzschrift des Profils auf Leonardos Skizzenblatt erscheint wie die Materialisierung einer solchen Erinnerungsspur [Fig. 327 und 328]. Die sich zugleich in der Wiederholung abzeichnenden minimalen Variationen des erinnerten Bildes könnten demnach als eine kreative Antwort auf die neurologische Tatsache verstanden werden, dass jede einzelne Aktivierung der Erinnerung das Engramm als die neuronale Erinnerungsspur überschreibt und dessen Bahn damit zwangsläufig verändert. Erinnerungen sind, wie die

8
Rosand, *Drawing Acts*, 93.

9
Vgl. Leonardo da Vinci: *Trattato della Pittura condotto sul Cod. Vaticano Urbinate 1270*, hg. v. Marco Tabbarini, Rom 1890, [parte 2, 64. 40 „Dello studiare insino quando ti desti, o innanzi tu ti dormenti nel letto al scuro. Ancora ho provato essere di non poca utilità, quando ti trovi allo scuro nel letto, andare colla immaginativa ripetendo i lineamenti superficiali delle forme per l'addietro studiate, o altre cosenotabili da sottile speculazione comprese, ed è questo proprio un atto laudabile et utile a confermarsi le cose nella memoria." [Lu 67]. Vgl. Rosand, *Drawing Acts*, 93.

Gehirnforscherin Hannah Monyer feststellt, keine „festen Bestandteile des Gedächtnisses, sondern dessen flexibel angelegtes, beinahe flüssiges Medium."[10] Als Medium aufgefasst, bestehen die Erinnerungen also allein aus den Beschaffenheiten der Spuren und nicht aus der Materialität dessen, was die Spuren hinterlassen hat. Aristoteles hat bekanntlich hierfür eine kulturgeschichtlich prägende metaphorische Beschreibung geliefert: Der Abdruck des Siegelrings im Wachs – als der Eindruck des Wahrgenommenen – empfängt nur die Form und nicht das Material des Eisens oder Golds, aus dem der Ring besteht. Als flexibel und flüssig aufgefasst, sind die Erinnerungen wie Wachs dehnbar und der Auflösung preisgegeben.[11]

Der Richtungswechsel in der gegenwärtigen Gedächtnisforschung vom *priming* hin zur Erforschung des Vergessens als aktives kognitives Vermögen, welches das Potential hat, engrammatische Spuren zu verflüssigen und damit zu lösen, hilft, die Doppelrolle der Zeichnung als Mnemotechnik *und* Entwurfspraxis zu klären: Der phänomenale Aspekt der Kritzelei in der Konturierung artikuliert die Eröffnung ihres Spielraums.

Leonardos Zeichnungspraxis *materialisiert* jedoch nicht nur den Prozess der Konsolidierung einer Gedächtnisspur, sondern *bestimmt* und *leitet* ihn auch. Die Profillinien gleichen sich nicht nur, sondern sind sogar deckungsgleich. Würde man zwei Fotokopien gleichen Formats aus transparenter Folie übereinanderlegen und die Profillinien gleich großer Köpfe vergleichen, so wird die Passförmigkeit selbst bei Köpfen erstaunen, die sich deutlich in Ausdruck, Alter und Geschlecht unterscheiden. Die Kongruenz der Profile hat eine äußere, technische Ursache, an der sich das Spektrum der Charakterisierung durch Abweichung bemessen lässt. Denn sie sind nicht, wie allgemein angenommen, aus dem Handgelenk heraus frei skizziert, sondern durchgepaust, wobei es zwei unterschiedlich große graphische Vorlagen gegeben haben muss, die unterlegt wurden: eine mittelgroße, die selbst den mürrisch dreinblickenden sogenannten Galba-Typ einschließt, und

10
Monyer, Hannah/Gessmann, Martin: *Das geniale Gedächtnis: Wie das Gehirn aus der Vergangenheit unsere Zukunft macht*, München 2015, 46.

11
Aristoteles verband mit der Metapher des fließenden Wassers bekanntlich den Mangel an Gedächtnisvermögen.

eine kleinere, auf dessen Grundlage auch der Greis und das Kindergesicht als deren Abweichungen entworfen sind.

Die Ausnahme, die die Regel bestätigt, ist der an Größe singuläre Knabenkopf auf dem Verso, dessen kleine Version auf dem Recto ihm wie aus dem Gesicht geschnitten zu sein scheint [Fig. 336]. Im Gegensatz zum mechanischen Verfahren des Abpausens demonstriert die starke Ähnlichkeit zwischen dem kleinen und dem großen Jünglingskopf jedoch künstlerisches Können, wie eine Anekdote aus der Vita des Malers Carlo Maratta (1625–1713) illustriert. Sein Freund, der Kunsttheoretiker Gian Pietro Bellori, berichtet, wie Marattas älterer Bruder Bernabeo dem zehnjährigen Carlo einige mit der eigenen Feder gezogene „Prinzipien der Zeichnung" in Form von Augen, Nasen, Mündern und Ohren postalisch geschickt habe, damit dieser sich in der Nachzeichnung üben könne.[12] Doch Carlo kopierte sie nicht freihändig, sondern legt ein halbtransparentes Blatt darüber, um die Umrisse durchzupausen. Der ältere Bruder erkannte jedoch sogleich den Trick, als er die ihm zugesandten Zeichnungen seines Bruders sah, und forderte ihn im nächsten Brief auf, sie erneut zu zeichnen, aber diesmal solle er die Größe variieren, sie sowohl kleiner als auch größer nachzeichnen, was Carlo bestens gelang, worauf er zu seinem Bruder nach Rom kommen durfte.

Die beiden Größen des Jünglingskopfes bei Leonardo lassen auf ein allen Profilen gleichermaßen zugrundeliegendes Muster schließen, das in diesen zwei Versionen als Kopierunterlage diente. Und selbst die sehr verschiedenen Löwenköpfe teilen sich ihren Umriss und haben folglich an der Übung Anteil.

Das wiederholte mechanische Durchpausen artikuliert das Ziel der Übung: Die Einschreibung eines Engramms, das ja als ‚Einzeichnung' im Gedächtnis des Künstlers selbst keine faktische Größe hat und also in jeder Größe entäußert werden kann. Die frappierende Gleichförmigkeit des Linienzugs der verschiedenen Profilköpfe ist demzufolge nicht Resultat einer Einprägung, sondern geht ihr voraus, denn der Vorgang des wiederholten Abpausens arbeitet

12 Vgl. Bellori, Giovan Pietro: *Le Vite de' Pittori, Scultori ed Architetti Moderni*, Rom 1672, 574–575. Übersetzung N.S. Vgl. hierzu Steinhardt-Hirsch, Claudia: Version – Kopie – zeichnerische Nachschöpfung? Zu zwei Zeichnungen von Cristofano Allori, in: Brahms, Iris (Ed.): *Marginale Zeichentechniken: Pause, Abklatsch, Cut & Paste als ästhetische Strategien in der Vormoderne*, Berlin/Boston 2022, 29–43: 40–41.

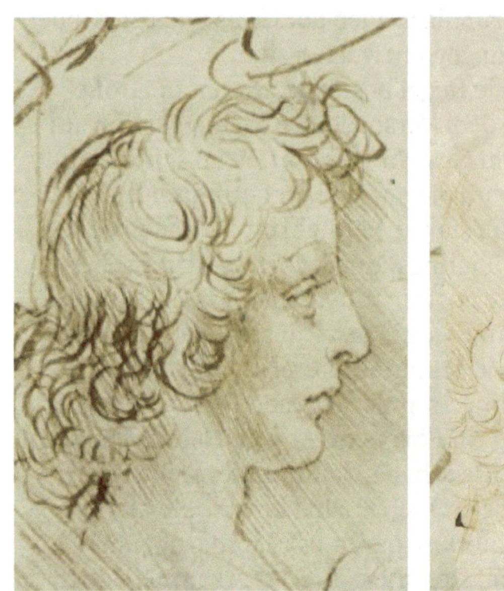

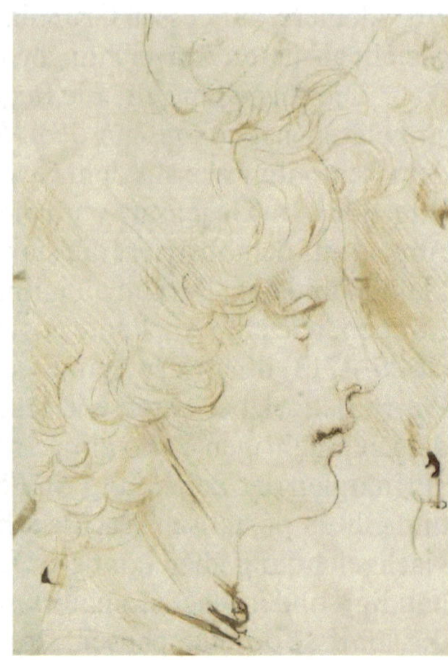

Details Fig. 327 und 328.

an der *Gewinnung* eben eines solchen Engramms. Anstatt also die Profillinien als eine in die Handbewegung eingelagerte Erinnerungsspur zu lesen, die hier gleichsam selbstvergessen abgespult wird, gilt es nach der analytischen Funktion der Praxis des Abpausens zu fragen. Sie ist eng verknüpft mit der Vorstellung der Einprägung, wie sie die Metapher der *memoria* als Wachstafel bereithält.

Konkretion und Modifikation

Schon vor Aristoteles nutzte sein Lehrer Platon in seinem Dialog *Theaitetos* das Bild des Siegelrings, der einen Abdruck auf der Wachstafel hinterlässt, um die Einprägung von Gehörtem, Gesehenem und Gedachtem vor Augen zu stellen.[13] Die Wahrnehmung produziert Eindrücke, diese wiederum Erinnerungen, welche die Grundlage unserer Vorstellungen sind. Erkenntnis jedoch erwächst erst aus den Schlüssen, die aus den Eindrücken gezogen werden, indem sie die Wahrnehmung mit einem Gedankengang verbinden, der zur identifizierenden Unterscheidung führt. Platon erklärt diesen Erkenntnisprozess anhand der gedanklichen Vorstellung des Gesichts seines Gesprächspartners:

> Vorausgesetzt, ich habe eine richtige Vorstellung von dir, so erkennen ich dich doch nur, wenn ich noch deine Erklärung dazu auffasse... Deine Erklärung aber war die Bezeichnung deiner Verschiedenheit... Allein wenn ich mir auch nicht bloß einen Nase und Augen Habenden denke, sondern auch wohl einen Krummnasigen und mit heraustretenden Augen, werde ich dann mehr dich vorstellen als mich selbst und wer sonst noch so beschaffen ist? [...] Sondern nicht eher, glaube ich, wird Theaitetos in mir vorgestellt werden, bis diese Krummnasigkeit selbst ein sie von anderen Krummnasigkeiten, die ich auch schon gesehen, unterscheidendes Merkmal in mir abdrückt und zurückläßt, und so alles übrige, woraus du bestehst...

13 Platon, *Theaitetos* 191d; in: Platon, *Sämtliche Werke*, vol. 3, übers. v. Friedrich Schleiermacher, Reinbek bei Hamburg 2021, 222.

> Also die richtige Vorstellung von einem jeden geht schon auf die Verschiedenheit.[14]

Die Kenntnis dieser Textstelle oder zumindest ihres Arguments legt Leonardos methodischer Zugriff in der Kodifizierung von „Krummnasigkeit“ nahe. In einer Passage aus dem Codex Urbinas teilt Leonardo das Profil in die signifikanten Abschnitte „Nase, Mund, Kinn und Stirn“ (Leonardos Reihenfolge) und erklärt die Vielfalt der Nasenform wie folgt:

> Zuerst zur Nase, von der es drei verschiedene Arten gibt, gerade, konkav und konvex. Von der geraden gibt es nur vier Variationen, kurz oder lang, hoch am Ende oder niedrig. Von den Konkaven gibt es drei Arten; manche Nasen haben die Konkavität oben, manche in der Mitte und manche am Ende. Die konvexen Nasen variieren auch auf drei Arten; einige ragen im oberen Teil hervor, einige in der Mitte und andere unten. Die Natur, die sich an der unendlichen Vielfalt zu erfreuen scheint, gibt den Nasen, die in der Mitte einen Höcker haben, wieder drei Veränderungen; denn manche haben ihn auf einer geraden, manche auf einer konkaven und manche auf einer konvexen Nase.[15]

Leonardo entwickelt also seine systematische Unterscheidung der verschiedenen Nasenprofile anhand dreier Formkategorien, welche nicht der Anschauung der Natur, sondern der Terminologie der Geometrie entnommen sind.[16]

In seinem *Trattato della pittura* findet sich zudem die Beschreibung einer kreativen Aneignung des plastischen Vorgangs des mechanischen Abdrucks als Methode, sich etwas im Geiste einzuprägen. Und auch sie ist engstens verknüpft mit den gedanklichen Akten des Vergleichs und der Unterscheidung:

14
Platon, *Theaitetos* 209a–d; ibid, 248–249.

15
Vgl. Leonardo, *Trattato della Pittura*, [parte 3, 285], 104–105 [Codex Urbinas Latinus, 1270, 108v mit Abbildung]

16
Siehe auch Fig. 84 in Rosand, *Drawing Acts*, 89. Vgl. Pardo, Mary: Memory, Imagination, Figuration: Leonardo da Vinci and the Painter's Mind, in: Kuchler, Susanne/Melion, Walter (Ed.): *Images of Memory: On Remembering and Representation*, Washington/London 1991, 47–73: 57–58.

> Wenn Du eine Sache, die Du gut studiert hast, im Kopf behalten möchtest, folge der folgenden Methode: Wenn Du ein und dieselbe Sache viele Male abgezeichnet hast, und es dir scheint, dass du sie im Kopf [*mente*] hast, versuche sie ohne das Modell vor Augen zu zeichnen. Und nachdem Du eine Pause auf einer feinen Glasscheibe abgenommen hast, ziehe dann die Pause über deine Zeichnung. Markiere, wo die Pause nicht mit deiner Zeichnung übereinstimmt. Merke Dir, wo Du fehlgingst, und wende dich wieder deinem Modell zu. Zeichne mehrere Male den Teil, der Dir nicht gelungen ist, so dass Du ihn gut in dem Vorstellungsvermögen [*immaginativa*] behältst.[17]

Und sollte der Maler kein Glas haben, so könne er stattdessen ein in Öl getränktes und damit semi-transparentes Pergamentpapier benutzen.[18]

Das Abgleichen von Linien, die aus dem Gedächtnis gezeichnet sind, mit denen der Vorlage arbeitet an der Passgenauigkeit der gezeichneten Linien mit dem inneren, eingeprägten Bild. In seinen theoretischen Aufzeichnungen zur Wahrnehmung als Gehirnfunktion führt Leonardo den Begriff der „*imprensiva*" ein, um den Umschlagplatz des äußeren in ein inneres Bild hirnphysiologisch zu umreißen.[19] Der Begriff legt eine semantische Assoziation mit dem Vorgang des ‚Eindrückens' (von lat. *imprimere*; Partizip: *impresso*) nahe. Lorenzo Pericolo hat jüngst diese Lesart kompliziert, indem er eine mögliche Herleitung des Begriffs von

17 Leonardo da Vinci, *Trattato della pittura* [parte 2, 69], 42; Übersetzung N.S. „Modo di bene imparare a mente. Quando tu vorrai sapere una cosa studiata bene a mente, tieni questo modo: cioè quando tu hai disegnato una cosa medesima tante volte che ti paia averla a mente, prova a farla senza lo esempio; ed abbi lucidato sopra un vetro sottile e piano lo esempio suo, e lo porrai sopra la cosa che hai fatto senza lo esempio; e nota bene dove il lucido non si scontra col disegno tuo; e dove trovi avere errato, lì tieni a mente di non errare più, anzi ritorna all'esempio a ritrarre tante volte quella parte errata, che tu l'abbia bene nella immaginativa."

18 Ibid.: „E se per lucidare una cosa tu non potessi avere un vetro piano, togli una carta di capretto sottillissima e bene unta e poi seccata; e quando l'avrai adoperata per un disegno, potrai colla spugna cancellarla e fare il secondo."

19 Vgl. die grundlegende Untersuchung von Klemm, Tanja: *Bildphysiologie: Wahrnehmung und Körper in Mittelalter und Renaissance*, Berlin 2019, und Fehrenbach, Frank: *Leonardo da Vinci: Der Impetus der Bilder*, Berlin 2019, insbes.: 39–44.

imprendere (= *apprendere*; dt. ‚lernen') ins Spiel brachte. Seine sich daraus ergebende Definition der *„imprensiva"* als Vermögen nicht nur der passiven Aufnahme der Seheindrücke, sondern auch ihrer aktiven Beurteilung erhellt die hier beschriebene Praxis Leonardos.[20] Der Vorgang des mechanischen Abpausens baut ein Bewusstsein für das mimetische Potential der Linie auf, denn er entnimmt die Konturen aus der hinter dem Blatt befindlichen Vorlage, und dieser konzentrierte Akt extrahiert die einzelnen Linien.

Die technische Möglichkeit der Loslösung der Konturlinie vom Bild, um – wie auf Leonardos Skizzenblatt ersichtlich – das Erinnerte im kreativen Sinne zum Spielball der Imagination werden zu lassen, hat bereits Aristoteles in Aussicht gestellt, wenn er in *De memoria et reminiscentia* schreibt:

> Ein auf einer Tafel dargestelltes Lebewesen z. B. ist sowohl ein Lebewesen wie ein Abbild, und beides ist ein und derselbe Gegenstand. Wesensmäßig sind die beiden Gegebenheiten freilich verschieden und man kann den Gegenstand sowohl als Lebewesen als auch als Abbild betrachten: Ebenso muss man das Vorstellungsbild in uns sowohl als selbständiges Wesen für sich auffassen wie auch als von einem anderen abhängig. Als selbständiges Wesen ist es ein Gegenstand der Betrachtung oder ein Vorstellungsbild, als abhängig von einem anderen ist es gleichsam ein Abbild und ein Gegenstand des Gedächtnisses. Ist nun das Vorstellungsbild in seiner Wirkung lebendig, so nimmt es die Seele in einem Fall als selbständiges Wesen für sich wahr; da meinen wir, wir haben ein Objekt des Denkens oder ein Vorstellungsbild vor uns. Im anderen Fall nimmt man es als abhängig wahr, als Abbild.[21]

20
Pericolo, Lorenzo: Knowing through the Eye. Leonardo da Vinci's Imprensiva and Alhazen's Intuitio, in: *Römisches Jahrbuch der Bibliotheca Hertziana* 44, 2019/2020, 205–261: 225 f.

21
Aristoteles: De memoria et reminiscentia, in: Id.: *Kleine naturwissenschaftliche Schriften*, Stuttgart 1997, 91.

Die Übersetzung des Erinnerungsbildes in ein Objekt des Denkens geschieht bei Leonardo über den Prozess des Abpausens. Dieser rein technische Prozess lenkt die Aufmerksamkeit weg vom Abgebildeten hin auf den Verlauf der Linie und eröffnet damit ein Bewusstsein für die Flexibilität des Konturs. Die Wiederholung der Profillinie auf Leonardos Skizzenblatt entspinnt einen bildlichen Diskurs der Reihung und Differenzierung und weicht damit die als Matrize fungierende fixe Vorlage auf. Diese wird zur Folie eines kreativen Prozesses, welcher sich in der Linienführung artikuliert. Die im Akt des Abpausens bewusst vollzogene Extrahierung und Freilegung der Linie arbeitet mit der Trefflichkeit des flüssigen Linienzugs am Aufbau der visuellen Vorstellung aus dem Verlauf des Konturs heraus.

Der enggesteckte Rahmen seiner Entfaltung zeigt uns, wie aus dem Einen eine Vielzahl an Möglichkeiten entstehen kann, denn dieser schafft erst die Wahrnehmbarkeit der sich zwangsläufig in der Wiederholung herausbildenden Differenz.

Michael W. Kwakkelstein hat auf die Eigentümlichkeit hingewiesen, dass Leonardo, als er bereits als unabhängiger Maler tätig war, mit dem Nachzeichnen auf eine Praxis rekurrierte, die dem absoluten Anfänger in der Ausbildung vorbehalten war, und dabei zudem auf Idealköpfe zurückgriff, die sein Lehrer Verrocchio, neben anderen, entwickelt hatte. Er bezeichnet Leonardo zurecht als transitorische Figur und erklärt dies damit, dass er sich nicht von der Musterbuchtradition löste, um seiner Imagination freien Lauf zu lassen.[22]

Die ein bestimmtes Formenvokabular zum Einstudieren schematisch festlegende mittelalterliche Tradition der Musterbücher wirkte hier *praktisch* unterschwellig fort, auch wenn die sich im Laufe des 15. Jahrhunderts herausbildende *Auffassung* der Zeichnung als eines vornehmlich geistigen Prozesses in eine andere Richtung wies.

Die für den heutigen Blick ‚unkünstlerische' Technik des Abpausens war fester Bestand der Werkstattausbildung, wobei die zugrunde gelegte Vorlage der Hand des Meisters entstammte, die

22 Kwakkelstein, Michael W.: Leonardo da Vinci's recurrent use of patterns of individual limbs, stock poses and facial stereotypes, in: Id./ Melli, Lorenza (Ed.): *From Pattern to Nature in Italian Renaissance Drawing: Pisanello to Leonardo*, Florenz 2012, 175–191.

durch das Abpausen zur Aneignung quasi weitergereicht wurde.[23] Das Kopierverfahren sicherte jedoch nicht nur die stilistische Kohärenz der Werkstatt, sondern vermittelte zugleich dem Lehrling Kunst. In seinem *Libro dell'Arte*, dem ersten frühneuzeitlichen Malereitraktat, erklärt Cennino Cennini, dass es darum gehe, „die Substanz einer guten Figur oder Zeichnung" herauszuziehen.[24] Um diese rein visuelle „Substanz" zu gewinnen, bedürfe es jedoch einer materiellen Grundlage und ihrer spezifischen Eigenschaft, dem *„lustro"* (Glanz, Licht) der *„carta lucida"* (Transparentpapier), durch welches die darunterliegende Figur oder Zeichnung deutlich zu sehen sei. Cennini führt die auch in späteren Traktaten stets genannten drei Verfahren zur Gewinnung einer *„carta lucida"* auf: die Herstellung eines Pergaments, eines eher dunklen, aber transparenten Blattes aus Fischleim und eines weißen, extrem dünnen und durch Tränkung mit Öl transparent werdenden Papiers (*„carta bambagina"*).

Der Vorgang des Durchzeichnens wird wie folgt beschrieben: Der Lehrling solle daran gehen, mit feiner Feder oder feinem Pinsel die Konturen und Umrisse (*„lle stremità"*) der darunterliegenden Zeichnung „heraus[zu]finden"[25] – Cennini benutzt den Begriff *„richercare* [sic]" und insinuiert damit ein klares Bewusstsein im Vollzug des mechanischen Verfahrens. Nachdem der Lehrling die Schatten, die er durch das Pauspapier sehen könne, eingetragen habe, solle er das Paper abnehmen und Licht- und Schattensetzungen nach eigenem Gutdünken eintragen. Unmittelbar anschließend behandelt Cennini die Frage, ob man zur Gewinnung der eigenen *„maniera"* nach einem oder mehreren Meistern nachzeichnen solle und empfiehlt, statt der vielen sich an einen Meister zu binden.

Das ‚unkünstlerische' Verfahren ist also engstens verknüpft mit der Herausbildung eines eigenen künstlerischen Stils. Dies ist nur vordergründig eine Paradoxie: Das, was sich herausbildet, ist der Forschergeist, ganz im Sinne von Cenninis Wortwahl *„richercare"*, den Raffaelo Borghini knapp zwei Jahrhunderte

23
Melli, Lorenza: L'uso della carta lucida nel Quattrocento, in: *Paragone–Arte* 36, 2001 (März), 3–9.

24
Vgl. Cennini, Cennino: *Il libro dell'arte*, hg. v. Fabia Frezzato, Vicenza 2003, 77–78.

25
Ibid.

später in seinem *Il Riposo* (1585) ganz phänomenologisch auffasst, auch wenn er mit der Beschreibung des Vorgangs als „*ricavare*" (‚herausarbeiten', wörtlich: ‚heraushauen') diesen selbst als einen bildhauerischen beschreibt.[26] Es ist wohl kein bloßer Zufall, sondern eine praxeologische Folgerichtigkeit, dass diejenigen Werkstätten, in denen im Quattrocento das Abpausen breit praktiziert wurde, vom Goldschmiedehandwerk herkamen. Zu nennen wären Verrocchio, Dominico Ghirlandaio, Maso Finiguerra und die Pollaiuolo-Brüder. Viele dieser Künstler, die mit langen und mit Nachdruck durchgezogenen und damit leicht abpausbaren Konturlinien operierten, waren mit der Niello-Technik vertraut, eine Form der Zeichnung auf Metallplatten, deren Lineament eingeritzt und mit schwarzer Farbe ausgefüllt wurde. Von ihr leitete Giorgio Vasari den Kupferstich her, von dem in der Folge breit abgepaust wurde.

Borghini beschreibt als initialen Moment des Vorgangs des Abpausens die Wahrnehmung des Inerscheinungtretens der Umrisse und Linien auf dem Blatt („*vedete apparir di sopra tutti i dintorni, e tutte le linee che vi saranno*"). Der Maler müsse dann mit dem Stift oder der Feder sorgfältig die Profile und Linienzüge, die sich dort abzeichneten (wörtlich: ‚zeigen'), nachzeichnen. Der Wechsel der Begriffe – von „*dintorni*" zu „*profili*" und von „*linee*" zu „*lineamenti*" – zeigt den Übertragungsvorgang an, der die Pause von ihrem Untergrund abhebt und auf der *carta lucida* eine eigene Zeichnung schafft. Die mechanische Praxis des Abpausens hat die pädagogische Aufgabe, ein Bewusstsein für die ästhetischen und mimetischen Potenzen der Linie aufzubauen. Da Hand und Auge bereits in den nachzuahmenden Kontur eingegangen sind, wird mit der Linie nicht nur der Kontur des abgebildeten Körpers, sondern auch das, was den persönlichen Stil des Vorbildes ausmacht, nachvollzogen. Kunst- und Naturnachahmung greifen ineinander.

Die durch den Kopiervorgang freigelegten Linien können eine künstlerische Emanzipation einleiten, wenn die Urteilskraft es schafft, die Linienzüge von der Hand des Meisters zu entbinden, um sie sich zu eigen zu machen – ganz im wörtlichen Sinne

26
Borghini, Raffaelo: *Il Riposo (1584)*, Hildesheim 1969, 145.

von *„emancipatio“* (aus *manus*: Hand, *capere*: nehmen). Die Vorlage bildet also das Sprungbrett für eine eigene künstlerische Artikulation, die sich erst einmal in der Trefflichkeit des meisterhaften Vorbildes bemisst.

Die damit zwangsläufig einhergehende Inkorporation einer fremden Anschauung wurde in der Frühen Neuzeit stets als eine notwendige Etappe in der Herausbildung eines eigenen Stils begriffen. Nicht idiosynkratische Abweichungen, sondern ein eigenes künstlerisches Bewusstsein, das sich in dem motivierten Nachvollzug der Linien auf der Pause gleichermaßen vom Vorbild ablöst, formt die Urteilskraft, von der bekanntermaßen Giorgio Vasari die Geistigkeit des *disegno*, dessen höchste Form die eigene bildnerischen Erfindung ist, ableiten wird.[27]

Es ist bemerkenswert und spricht für eine Neuausrichtung der Technik, dass der scheinbar so mechanische Prozess des Durchzeichnens bei Leonardo und anderen Künstlern seiner Zeit und darüber hinaus auch in den Bildfindungsprozess einging. Der durchgezeichnete ‚extrahierte‘ Umriss konnte in einem zweiten Schritt wiederum zu einer selbst gewonnenen Kopiervorlage werden, welche den Abstand zum Vorbild durch die wiederholte Aneignung erheblich vergrößert, um Freiraum für das eigene Bild zu schaffen.

Die mit feinem sicherem Strich und äußerst feiner Parallelschraffur ausgeführte Kopfstudie Leonardos aus dem Louvre, [Fig. 345] welche bekanntlich seine *Madonna Litta* vorbereitete, ist auf der Grundlage der Umrisszeichnung in Feder auf dem Verso entstanden, welche zur Durchzeichnung von unten beleuchtet worden sein musste [Fig. 346].

Auch wenn der fein modellierte Kopf auf der Basis der groben Umrisszeichnung aufgebaut ist, zeigt die Korrektur der Stirnlinie, die anfänglich erst in den Scheitel mündete, an, dass Leonardo in der Metallstiftzeichnung durchaus kreativ mit der Vorlage umging, indem er die Stirn im nächsten Schritt steiler anlegte. Die Mundwinkel wurden etwas mehr nach unten gezogen,

27
Vasari, Giorgio: *Le vite de' più eccellenti pittori, scultori e architettori*, Florenz 1550, vol. 1, 111: [Cap. XV *Che cosa sia disegno, e come si fanno e si conoscono le buone pitture et a che; e dell'invenzione delle storie*]: „Perché il disegno, padre delle tre arti nostre architettura, scultura e pittura, procedendo dall'intelletto cava di molte cose un giudizio universale simile a una forma overo idea di tutte le cose della natura.“

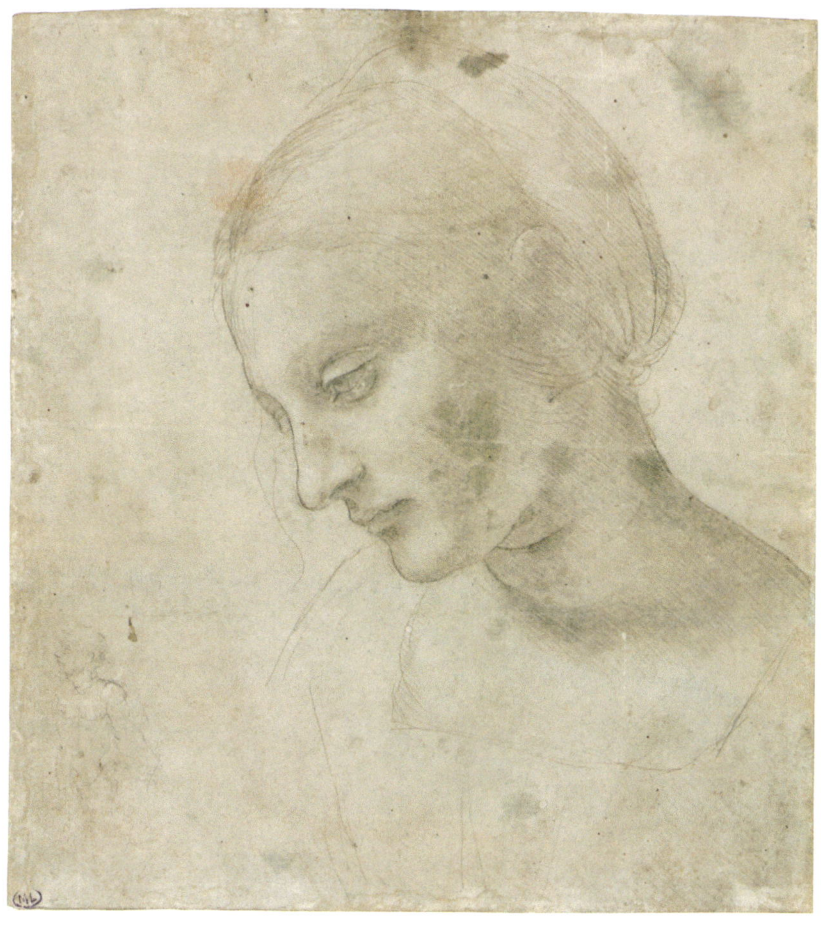

Leonardo da Vinci, Studie eines weiblichen Kopfes [recto], ca. 1490,
Silberstift auf grünlichem Papier, 18 × 16.8 cm. Musée du Louvre, inv. Nr. 2376, Paris.

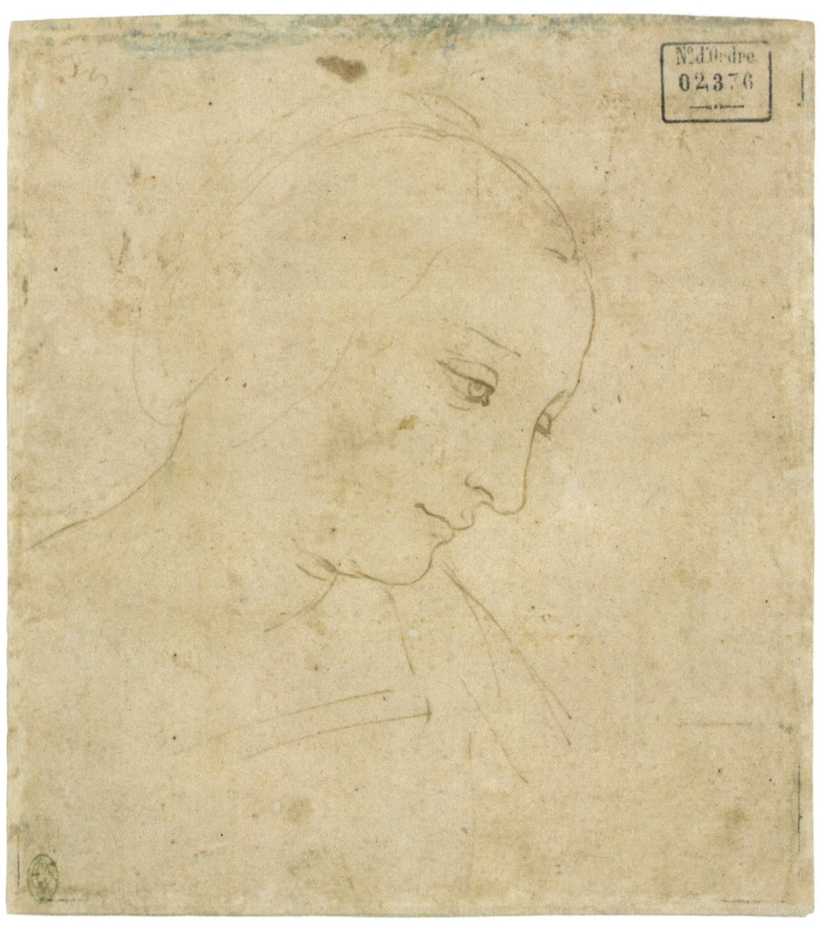

Leonardo da Vinci, Kopfstudie [verso], Federzeichnung, 18 × 16.8 cm.
Musée du Louvre, inv. Nr. 2376, Paris.

Fig. 346

was den Ausdruck des Gesichtes veränderte. Der Kontur, welcher auf dem Verso vom Ansatz der Augenbraue zum Mundwinkel durchgezogen ist, ist an der Unterseite der Nasenspitze unterbrochen und damit vom Philtrum plastisch abgehoben. Zudem hat Leonardo die Helix der Ohrleiste eingezeichnet und damit veranschaulicht, wie sich das Ohr, das auf der Umrisszeichnung fehlt, durch das eng am Kopf anliegende Haar hindurchdrückt. Was beide Seiten jedoch grundsätzlich unterscheidet, ist die Differenz des Zeichenmaterials und seines technischen Einsatzes. Während die flüssige Federzeichnung in groben Zügen die Konturen des Kopfes festlegt, arbeitet die feine Silberstiftzeichnung an seiner plastischen Ausgestaltung, wobei die Konturen in das Helldunkel eingehen, das, in feinen parallelen Linien angelegt, sich wie ein Schleier über die Konturen legt und sie einspinnt. Die in gerader Richtung schräg von links oben nach rechts unten geführte Parallelschraffur beugt sich nicht der plastischen Modellierung, welche eben nicht durch die Linienbahnen, sondern allein durch die mimetische Kraft des Helldunkels erzeugt ist. Leonardo hat sich an der Umrisslinie der Augenbraue orientiert, ohne ihren Kontur jedoch durchzuzeichnen.

Die grobe Federzeichnung muss wiederum auf der Grundlage einer Studie entstanden sein, deren graphische ‚Substanz' herausgezogen wurde [Fig. 348]. Die kunstvoll ausgeführte Bleistiftzeichnung, so natürlich sie auch erscheint, ersetzt die Naturstudie Verrocchios, welche möglicherweise der groben Federzeichnung auf dem Verso als Kopiervorlage zugrunde lag. Die Umrisszeichnung ist das mimetische Rückgrat, das Leonardo „nach eigenem Gutdünken" mit Helldunkelsetzungen (Cennini) körperlich ausfüllt, um das Vorbild vergessen zu machen – mit Erfolg, denn die Silberstiftzeichnung wird gemeinhin als Studie nach der Natur betrachtet, eine Sicht, welche die graphische Leistung der Arbeit der Verso-Seite notwendig ignorieren muss.

Die Lichtbahn, welche die Kinnpartie markiert, ist steiler zum Ohr hochgezogen; das Gesicht erscheint dadurch schmaler und weicher. Man kann auch die Wahl der ‚sauberen' Metallstiftzeichnung anstelle der ‚schmierigen' Kreidezeichnung Verrocchios als Versuch der künstlerischen Überwindung seines Lehrers lesen, die statt durch Verwischung mit äußerst feinen Parallelschraffuren Schattenpartien schafft. Der Abstand, der hier in

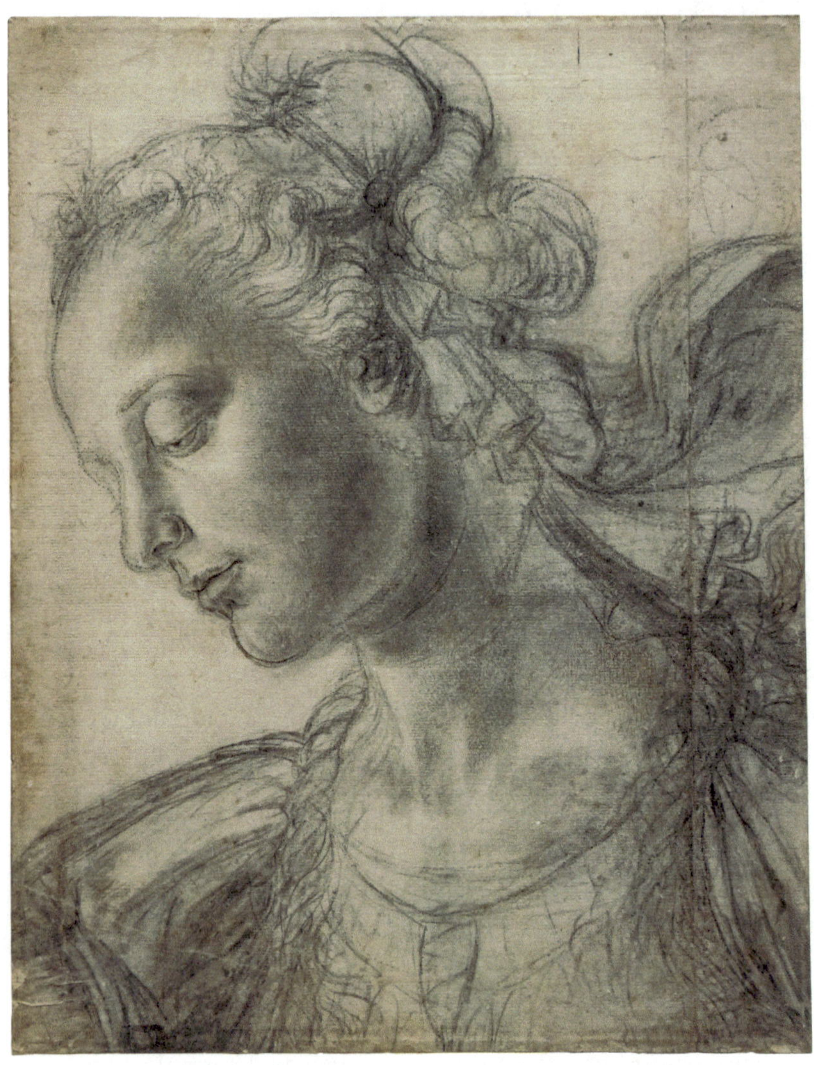

Verrocchio, Studie eines weiblichen Kopfes, schwarze Kreide mit Weißhöhungen, Umrisse durchgestochen, 40.8 × 32.7 cm. Christ Church, Oxford.

Fig. 348

der Trefflichkeit der graphischen Umsetzung aufgemacht wird, ist zugleich eine Distanzierung von der Natur als Lehrerin des Künstlers. Die natürliche Erscheinung des Kopfes ist ein Produkt höchster Kunst, wobei das Studium der Natur sowohl in das künstlerische Vorbild als auch in die Beherrschung der Technik im Vorfeld eingegangen ist.

Leonardos Pause

Der scheinbar so unkünstlerische Vorgang der Kopie sensibilisiert den Künstler für die Differenz, die sich zwangsläufig unter der Hand abzeichnet, und zwar nicht nur in der Abweichung, sondern in der Sache selbst. Denn die minimalen Abweichungen schaffen ein Bewusstsein für die logische Differenz, welche die Beziehung der Ähnlichkeit zwischen dem Einen und dem Anderen zugleich herstellt. Leonardo mag dieser Sachverhalt, den seine Zeichnung exemplifiziert, im Vorfeld klar gewesen sein. Möglicherweise hatte er während seiner Schulzeit den römischen Rhetor Quintilian gelesen, der in seiner Schrift zur Ausbildung des Redners zu bedenken gibt:

> Hinzu kommt, dass es meistens leichter ist, mehr zu leisten, als das Gleiche; denn Ähnlichkeit ist so schwer zu erreichen, dass dieser Schwierigkeit nicht einmal die Natur selbst so völlig gewachsen ist, dass sich nicht Dinge, die am ähnlichsten und gleichwertigsten aussehen, doch immer an einer Abweichung unterscheiden ließen.[28]

Indem nun im Vorfeld des Vorgangs des Abpausens das Vorbild notwendig unter dem Blatt verschwindet und damit auch die volle Ansicht des dargestellten Gegenstands, kann sich der Künstler ganz auf den Nachvollzug der Linienbahnen konzentrieren. Die Form, die er dabei schafft, ist insofern jedes Mal eine neue

28
Quintilian: *Die Ausbildung des Redners. Zwölf Bücher*, hg. u. übers. v. Helmut Rahn, Darmstadt 1988, vol. 2 [X, 2. 10]. Siehe ferner: „Hinzu kommt, dass alles, was einem anderen ähnlich ist, zwangsläufig geringer ist als das Nachgeahmte; so etwa der Schatten geringer gegenüber dem Körper, das Abbild gegenüber dem Gesicht.“ Ibid., Bd. 2 [X, 2. 11].

Schöpfung, als sie sich aus eigenen Liniensetzungen aufbaut, die eine präsentische und keine erinnernde Dimension haben. Leonardos Hand zeichnet sich also in dem Moment ab, in welchem sich Gedächtnisspuren in der bewussten Modifikation des Erinnerten aktualisieren und damit zum Potential des Künstlers werden.

Das Durchpausen ist eingestandenermaßen *prima vista* eine unkünstlerische Praxis, doch sie entspricht der frühneuzeitlichen Praxis der Herausbildung der eigenen Handschrift, die sich auf antike Quellen berufen kann. In seiner Schrift zur Ausbildung des Redners erwähnt Quintilian, wie man Kinder im Schreiben unterrichten solle:

> Wenn aber das Kind schon so weit ist, den Schriftzügen zu folgen, wird es nicht unnütz sein, diese so gut wie möglich auf einem Täfelchen eingraben zu lassen, damit der Griffel durch sie wie durch Furchen gezogen werden kann. Denn dann kann er nicht abrutschen wie bei den Wachstafeln – er wird nämlich auf beiden Seiten durch die Ränder festgehalten und kann nicht aus der Schriftbahn herauskommen –, kräftigt dadurch, dass er schnell und oft festen Spuren folgt, das Handgelenk und braucht keinen Helfer, der mit seiner Hand die des Schreibenden führt.[29]

Es mag erstaunen, dass Quintilian ein Hilfsmittel anpreist, das an eine Buchstabenschablone erinnert, deren Rigidität den Spielraum der Handbewegung extrem einengt. Doch diese Einschränkung ist die Bedingung der Herausbildung der Lesbarkeit des Schriftbildes. Wird jedoch die Hand stattdessen von einer anderen geführt, kann sie dabei keinen eigenständigen Bewegungsablauf ausbilden. Aus dem mechanischen Prozess der Verinnerlichung der im Wachs eingeprägten Linien durch aufmerksamen Nachvollzug entwickelt sich die persönliche Handschrift.

Selbst in den Passagen, in denen Quintilian die Erfindung thematisiert, kommt er auf die elementare Praxis des Kopierens zurück:

29 Ibid., vol. 1 [I, 1.27].

> So richten sich die Knaben nach den Führungslinien der Buchstaben, um Schreiberfahrung zu gewinnen, so richten sich die Musiker auf die Stimme der Lehrer, der Maler auf die Werke der Vorgänger. [...] [K]urz, wir sehen, dass die Anfangsgründe in jedem Lehrfach ihre feste Form in einer Vorschrift finden, die ihnen schon vorliegt. [...] Aber gerade die Tatsache, dass die Nachahmung die Ausführung aller Aufgaben so viel leichter macht, als sie für die war, die nichts hatten, wonach sie sich richten konnten, kann Schaden stiften, wenn man hierbei nicht behutsam und mit eigenem Urteil vorgeht.[30]

Die pädagogische Beschränkung der Bewegungsfreiheit führt also zur Verfestigung des Schriftzugs, die dessen persönlichen Ausdruck schließlich prägen wird. Die, wie gezeigt wurde, unzutreffende Bezeichnung der Profilköpfe als *doodles* benennt eben diese Gewinnung des eigenständigen Zugs, welche sich jedoch erst aus dem auf die Linie fokussierten Prozess des Abpausens nachträglich ergibt. Denn die Praxis des Pausens verfolgt eigentlich ein anderes Ziel, nämlich das der mimetisch korrekten Abzeichnung und, damit einhergehend, der gedanklichen Abspeicherung des Gesehenen. Da es jedoch keine Wiederholung ohne Differenz geben kann, eröffnen die sich zwangsläufig ergebenden Abweichungen der Fantasie Spielraum. Dieser Gestaltungsspielraum ist jedoch ebenfalls abgezirkelt, denn der den Profilköpfen zugrundeliegende Gedankengang ist in Profilreihen und Cluster kanalisiert, welche Leonardos analytische Urteilskraft veranschaulichen; sie leitet die Bildung der Linienzüge und gibt jeder Wendung und Differenzierung der Gesichter Bedeutung und Struktur.

In der tentativen Korrelation des heterogenen Spektrums der Kopfbildung zeichnet sich also Leonardos graphisches Formbewusstsein konkret ab. Dabei dissoziiert sich die in den Durchzeichnungen abzeichnende generelle Form des idealen Profils von der materiellen Matrix der Vorlage, um sich assoziativ mit der Skizzierung der *Maria lactans* zu verbinden. Die Feminisierung des Profils markiert diese konzeptuelle Wende. Doch warum kaprizierte sich Leonardo in diesem Randgang, welcher die

30 Ibid., vol. 2 [X, 2.2].

Skizzierung der *Maria lactans* mit Johannesknaben einbettet, auf das *Profil*? Die Bildvorstellung, an der die zentrale Skizze arbeitet, hat diese Ansicht offensichtlich an keiner Stelle vorgesehen. Doch bevor diese Frage beantwortet werden kann, muss die bildliche Vorstellung, an der die Skizze arbeitet, eruiert werden.

Bewegungsspielräume

Das imaginierte Bild ist das folgende: Maria hat ihr Kind auf ihren erhobenen rechten Oberschenkel gesetzt und stillt es, während der Johannesknabe an Maria herantritt, um – wie es die äußerst grobe Skizzierung dieser Stelle nahezulegen scheint – an ihrem Oberschenkel lehnend und mit in Anbetung gekreuzten Armen zu Jesus emporzuschauen [Fig. 327]. Die kniende Beinstellung Mariens ist mit kursorischen Linien angelegt; bauschige Züge, welche Gewandfalten vorstellen sollen, durchkreuzen und verschleiern die Skizzierung ihrer nackten Oberschenkel; langgezogene Linien, die eine Art Schürze umreißen, leiten unseren Blick nach links unten. Die Wendung des Oberkörpers des Kindes hin zu ihrer Brust unterstützt die Mutter mit beiden Händen, wobei sie mit der einen Hand dem Kind unter den Arm greift und mit der anderen den Oberschenkel seines hinter ihrem Knie verschwindenden rechten Beins an ihr Knie presst.

Wie stark selbst kursorische Linien Erinnerungsspuren nachspüren, legt ein vergleichender Blick auf die rechte Hand Mariens auf der wenige Jahre später entstandenen *Felsgrottenmadonna* nahe [Fig. 353]. Auch wenn sie hier nun den knienden Johannesknaben in seiner Anbetung Jesu stützt, erstaunt doch die Ähnlichkeit ihres Konturs, die sich noch erhöht, kippt man die Skizze ein wenig nach rechts. Weitere motivische Reminiszenzen sind Marias Kopfwendung, ihre gesenkten Augenlider wie auch die Kniehaltung des assistierenden Engels, die, wenn auch verhüllt, die Beinstellung Mariens wiederholt.

Während die Finger ihrer feingliedrigen Hände in der Skizze aus der Sammlung Windsor klar umrissen sind, zeichnen sich zwei verworfene Optionen unter dem mit entschiedenem Strich entworfenen Händchen ihres Säuglings ab: Zwei feine parallele Linien eröffnen die vage Vorstellung eines Greifens nach der Taille der Mutter [Fig. 354]. Diese Vorstellung wurde jedoch,

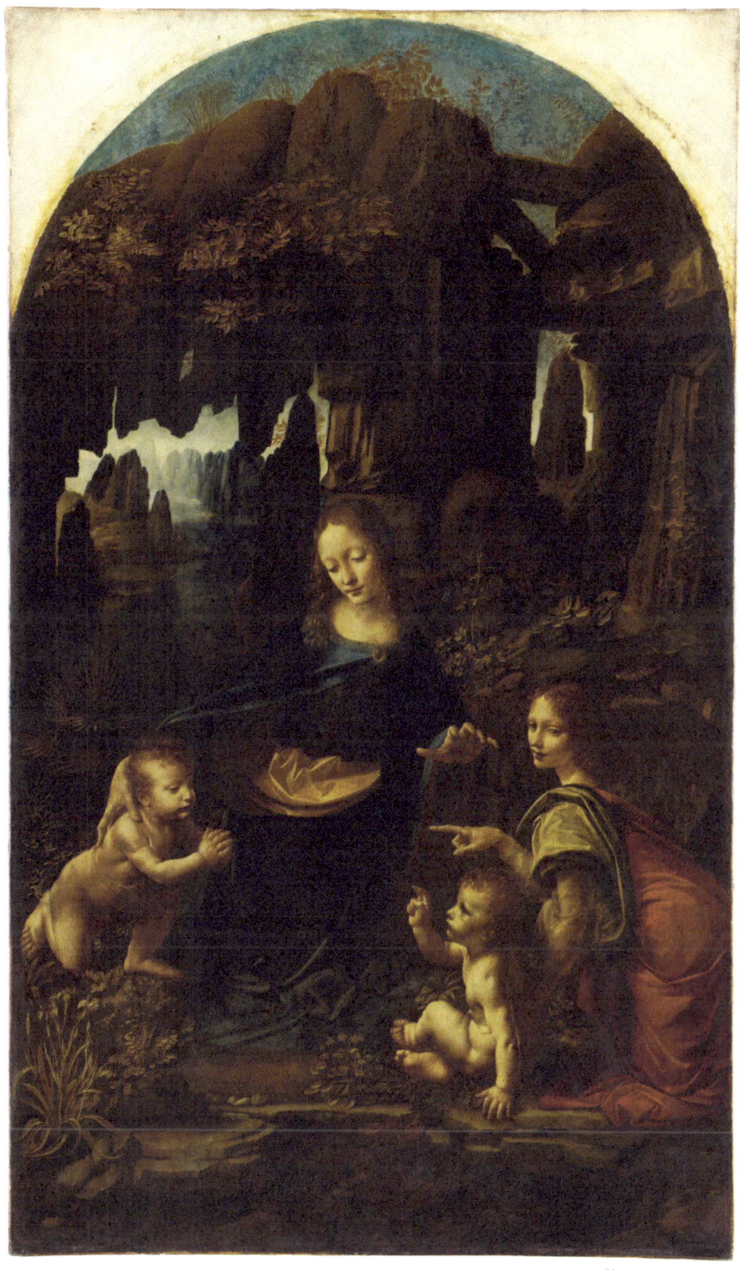

Leonardo da Vinci, *Felsgrottenmadonna*, erste Version, 1483–1486, Öl auf Holz, 199 × 122 cm. Musée du Louvre, inv. Nr. 777, Paris.

Fig. 353

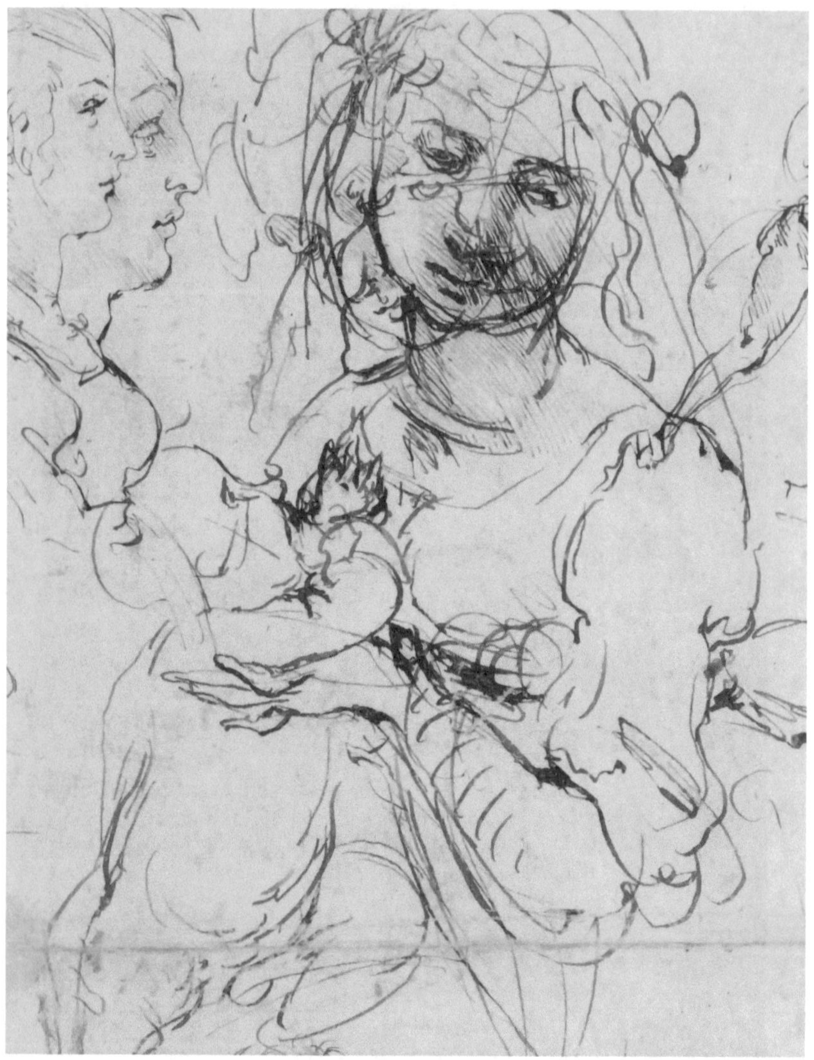

Detail Fig. 327.

Fig. 354

wie es scheint, schnell verworfen, um das Motiv der *Maria lactans* mit dem zur Brust erhobenen Ärmchen aufzurufen. Ein bogenförmiger, mit Nachdruck gezogener Strich oberhalb des Ellenbogens, der wohl das Unterärmchen markiert, hat die Position des Händchens in einer nächsten Konkretisierung nach oben verschoben.

Der Prozess des Umdenkens innerhalb des Entwurfsprozesses ist in der Gestalt Mariens noch augenfälliger, doch ist er ausschließlich auf ihren Kopf beschränkt. Während die Haltung ihres Körpers in wenigen flüchtigen Strichen klar umrissen ist, eröffnet die Skizzierung des Kopfes einen erheblichen Radius an Bewegungsspielraum. Maria senkt ihr Haupt einerseits und womöglich anfänglich auf das Jesuskind, anderseits zu dem wahrscheinlich erst nachträglich eingefügten Johannesknaben, der dem Jesuskind wie aus dem Gesicht geschnitten gleicht – eine motivische Auffälligkeit, die auch Leonardos *Felsgrottenmadonna* bestimmt. Sie ist von theologischer Signifikanz: Die in der Überblendung greifbare Wendung der Aufmerksamkeit Mariens öffnet die innige Blickbeziehung zwischen Mutter und Kind, die nun über Johannes als den ersten Zeugen der göttlichen Natur Christi in einer Dreieckskonstellation neu geschlossen wird; Johannes schaut zu Jesus auf, der zu Maria hochblickt, welche auf Johannes herunterschaut. Indem sie durch die Wendung ihres Blicks die Präsenz des Johannes als Verkünder der göttlichen Natur in die Szene aufnimmt, verschiebt sich ihre Liebe. Die irritierende Gleichheit der Gesichter von Johannes und Jesus (welche auch in der *Felsgrottenmadonna* aufgenommen ist) mag veranschaulichen, dass ihre Liebe nicht allein ihrem leiblichen Kind gilt, sondern kraft dieses Umwegs über den Dritten im Bunde auf den göttlichen Sohn gerichtet ist.

Die gleichzeitige Präsenz der Hinwendung Mariens zu Jesus *und* Johannes in der Skizze, wobei der letzteren offensichtlich Nachdruck gegeben wurde, schafft irritierende Überlappungen. So zeichnet sich der seitliche Haarknoten der ersten Variante als ovale Form auf der Stirn der zweiten ab. Ein mit mehreren dünnen und unterbrochenen Strichen gezogenes Oval markiert die Vorstellung einer frontalen Sicht eines nach vorne geneigten Kopfes, die sich jedoch kaum als dritte Variante artikuliert. Eine die Positionierung der Augen fixierende horizontale Linie dient hier als

Ausgang, diesen dritten, äußerst rudimentären Kopf durch die Einzeichnung einer zweiten geraden, jedoch leicht ansteigenden Linie, welche die Positionierung der ersten Horizontalen korrigiert, erst einmal nach links im Bild leicht zu neigen. Eine dritte Gerade, welche das Gefälle der Linie umkehrt, bewirkt die entschiedene Neigung des Kopfes nach rechts. Die Einzeichnung einer diese Diagonale mittig im rechten Winkel durchschneidenden vierten Geraden legt das Kreuz fest, an dem sich die Wendung des Gesichts aus der Frontalansicht orientiert hat.[31]

Das anfängliche Schwanken innerhalb der Positionierung ihres Kopfes tangiert jedoch kaum die Konturierung der beiden plastisch ausgestalteten Optionen, deren Sicherheit in der Skizzierung ein doppeltes Netz verrät. Die Parallelschraffuren verleihen dem Kopf eine Plastizität, welche die grobe Skizzierung des Körpers vermissen lässt. Die Sicherheit des Umrisses *beider* Kopfhaltungen spricht für die Klarheit zweier Vorstellungsbilder, die hier in der Skizzierung nicht erst geschaffen werden, sondern nur in Erscheinung treten. Was hat jedoch diese Klarheit ermöglicht?

Giorgio Vasari erwähnt in der Vita Verrocchios, dass er selbst einige Zeichnungen Verrocchios besitze, welche Frauenköpfe mit schönen Mienen („*bell'arie*") und schönen Frisuren darstellen; diese habe Leonardo wegen ihrer Schönheit stets kopiert.[32] Die beiden Kopfhaltungen Mariens, deren rechte der 1475 datierten Studie eines weiblichen Kopfes Verrocchios aus dem British Museum erstaunlich gleichkommt [Fig. 357], während die linke Ansicht seiner *Maria mit Kind* von 1470 aus der Gemäldegalerie Berlin stark ähnelt [Fig. 358], reflektieren dieses Studium. Die Herstellung des Gemäldes fällt in den Zeitraum, in welchem

31
Der Schematismus, der an der Verräumlichung der Vorstellung auf dem flachen Papier arbeitet, leitet bereits den Einprägungsprozess des Studiums. So rät Leonardo, stets eine Hauptlinie in der Vorstellung zu formen. Um die Teile des Körpers zueinander räumlich bemessen zu können, solle der Künstler darauf achten, ob deren Konturen von dieser Hauptlinie überschnitten werden oder sich parallel oder in Schieflage zu ihr befinden. Auch wenn Leonardo in dieser Passage möglicherweise eher eine lotrechte Linie vor Augen stand, hat das Fadenkreuz, mit welchem bekanntlich die räumliche Verkürzung der einzelnen Gesichtspartien beherrschbar wird, eben diese beschriebene Funktion. Leonardo, *Trattato* [171], 71.

32
„Sono alcuni disegni di sua mano nel nostro libro fatti con molta pacienza e grandissimo giudizio, in fra i quali sono alcune teste di femina con bell'arie et acconciature di capegli, quali per la sua bellezza Lionardo da Vinci sempre imitò." Vasari, Giorgio: *Le vite de' più eccellenti pittori, scultori e architettori*, hg. v. Paola Barocchi, Florenz: 1971, vol. 3, 538.

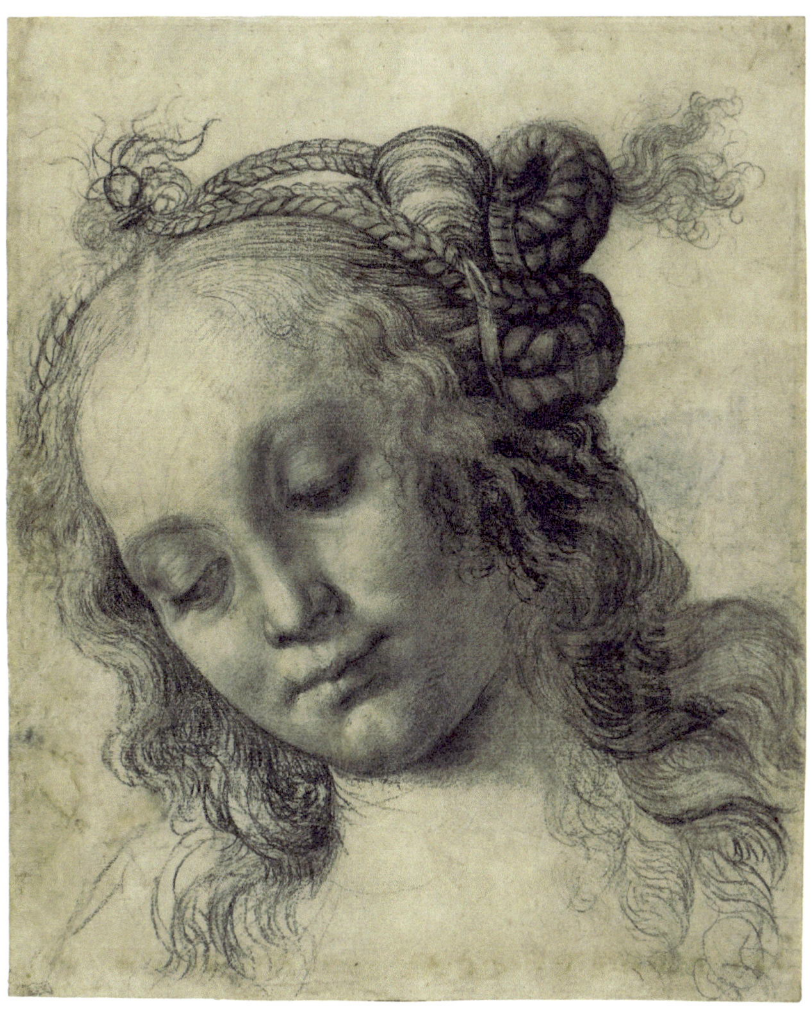

Verrocchio, Weiblicher Kopf, 1475, Kohlezeichnung, 32.5 × 27.2 cm.
The British Museum, London.

Fig. 357

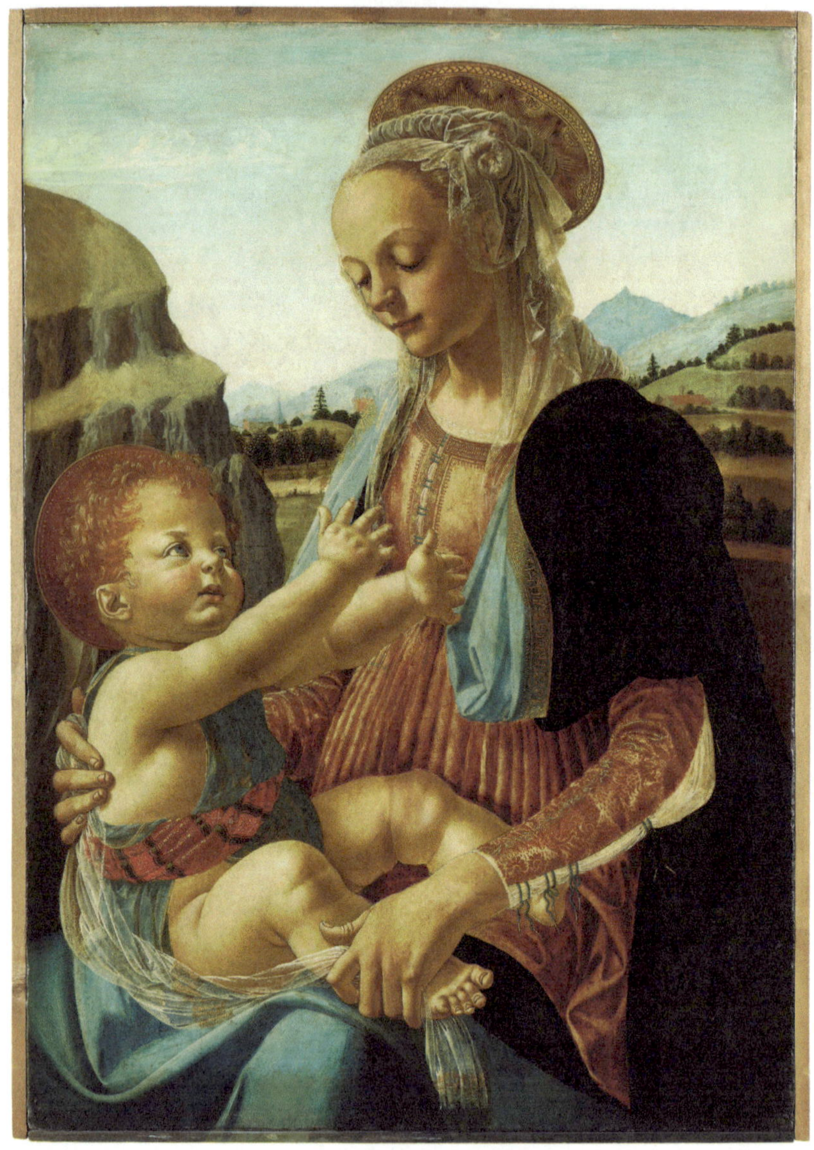

Verrocchio, Maria mit Kind, ca. 1470, Öl und Tempera auf Pappelholz, 75.8 × 54.6 cm.
Gemäldegalerie, Berlin.

Fig. 358

Leonardo in der Werkstatt Verrocchios arbeitete. So kann vermutet werden, dass Leonardo im Entwurfsprozess Bildvorstellungen aufgriff, die maßgeblich sein Lehrer entworfen hatte. Leonardo griff demzufolge für die Skizze auf verschiedene Vorbilder Verrocchios zurück, die er im Entwurfsprozess gleichsam übereinanderlegte. Die konstruktiven Linien, die in seiner Skizze an der konkreten Verräumlichung des Erinnerungsbildes arbeiten, verschränken beide Optionen miteinander und eröffnen damit ein Bewegungsspektrum der Kopfneigung Mariens.

Doch Verrocchio war nicht die alleinige Inspirationsquelle. Mit dem männlichen nackten Figürchen auf Marias rechter Schulter fügte Leonardo einen Fremdkörper ein, um ein Modell für die Beinstellung zu gewinnen, die, in seinem kindlichen Gegenüber gespiegelt, schließlich in die Skizzierung des an Marias linken Oberschenkel lehnenden Johannesknaben eingehen wird. Diese markante Beinstellung ist auf einem weiteren Skizzenblatt Leonardos, das neben zwei Sitzenden eine männliche Figur zeigt, die eine Trompete ins Ohr eines nackten Mannes bläst, bereits erprobt [Fig. 360]. Sie ist sehr wahrscheinlich Antonio Pollaiuolos kurz zuvor entstandenem Gemälde *Hercules mit der Hydra* abgeschaut.[33] Die eigenartige eingeschnittene Taille von Leonardos Figürchen gilt sogar als Indiz, dass Leonardo hier ein Holzmannequin gebrauchte,[34] jedoch, wie der Vergleich mit Pollaiuolo zeigt, nicht zum Entwurf, sondern allein als technisches Hilfsmittel, das den Aufruf des Erinnerungsbildes stabilisierte – ähnlich den Konstruktionslinien auf dem Blatt selbst.

Formbewusstsein

Wie interveniert nun die Armada an Profilköpfen, welche sich über die äußerst flüchtige Gestaltung des Unterkörpers Mariens schiebt, ihn visuell in den Hintergrund drückt, in den Sachverhalt der Skizze? Oder ist sic als cin übcr sie hinausgehender und damit wegführender und also selbstständiger gestalterischer Gedankengang aufzufassen?

33
Antonio del Pollaiuolo, *Herkules mit der Hydra*, ca. 1475, Tempera und Öl auf Holz, 15 × 12 cm. Uffizi, inv. Nr. 1890 no. 8268, Florenz.

34
Rath, Markus: *Die Gliederpuppe. Kult – Kunst – Konzept*, Berlin/Boston 2016, 306–307.

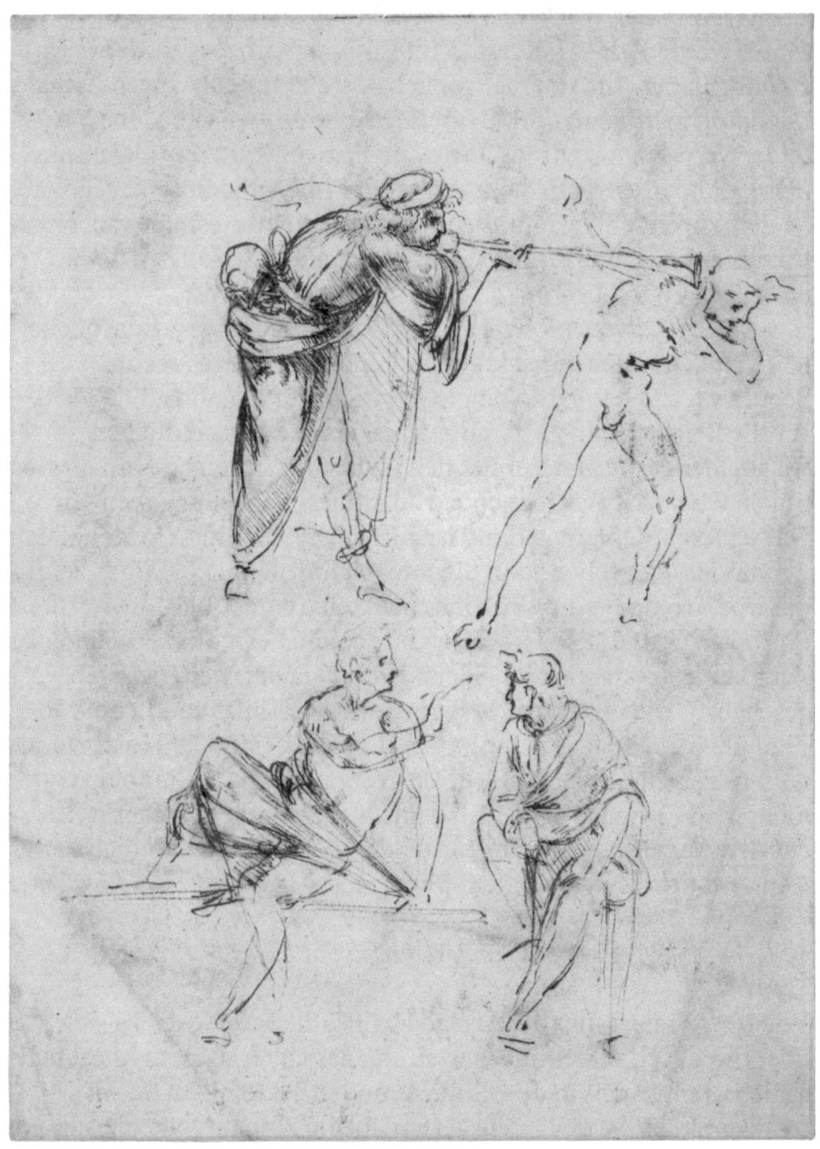

Leonardo da Vinci, Mann, der einem nackten Mann eine Trompete ins Ohr bläst und zwei sitzende Männer, Feder und braune Tinte über Bleistiftskizze, 25.8 × 19.3 cm. The British Museum, London.

Fig. 360

Wiederholt wurde auf den prominenten Jünglingskopf hingewiesen, der porträthaft das Schönheitsideal seiner Zeit und sicherlich auch Leonardos repräsentiert.[35] Als Bildnis aufgefasst, wurde er mit seinem Schüler Salaì identifiziert, dessen „liebliche Anmut" und „schöne Ringellocken" Leonardo erfreut haben sollen.[36] Aber da dieser Kopf immer wieder und über weite zeitliche Strecken in seinen Skizzen auftaucht und also nicht altert oder sich aus dem strengen Profil wendet, können wir davon ausgehen, dass Leonardo nicht in der Person selbst, sondern in eben diesem, seinem Profilkopf das Bild von Schönheit verwirklicht sah, das er auf die fixe graphische Formel der idealen Profillinie brachte.

Seine ‚Formel', die auf verschiedenen Skizzen der Maria mit dem Jesuskind auftaucht, erscheint beispielsweise am Rande eines Blattes, das fünf Bewegungsstudien eines Kleinkindes umfasst, welches eine Katze umarmt, wobei ihm zweimal die Mutter zugesellt wurde [Fig. 362]. Einmal erscheint es, als würde Maria die Katze füttern, das andere Mal ihr Kind, und zwar mit erstaunlich wurstigen Fingern. Während in der oberen Skizze Maria im Dreiviertelprofil dargestellt wurde, dessen Ausdruck von Schönheit von der Augenbraue und Nase zusammenbindenden Konturlinie erwirkt ist, ist Leonardo das strenge Profil der zweiten Version trotz Nachdruck des Stifts offensichtlich misslungen. Der auf den ersten Blick arbiträr erscheinende Jünglingskopf scheint hier nun zu intervenieren und als Erinnerung an die ideale Proportionierung zu fungieren. Der Missstand der ‚fliehenden' Stirn Mariens, die vom Idealbild ganz offensichtlich abweicht, ist in der schwachen Kreidezeichnung unterhalb des Jünglingskopfes vergrößert und durch Überspitzung karikiert. Wir können also folgern, dass der Profilkopf hier als ein die graphische Vorstellung korrigierender Maßstab eingefügt ist. Was die Kombination des Jünglingskopfes mit einer Skizze der Maria mit Kind, in welcher das Bewegungsspektrum der Umarmung der Katze in den

35
Michael W. Kwakkelstein vergleicht beispielsweise den Jüngling mit den später entstandenen knabenhaften Engeln auf Botticellis *Madonna mit Kind, sechs Engeln und dem Johannesknaben*, ca. 1490 in der Galleria Borghese. Kwakkelstein, Michael W.: *Leonardo da Vinci as a physiognomist. Theory and drawing practice*, Leiden 2014, 144.

36
Vasari, Giorgio: *Das Leben des Leonardo da Vinci*, hg. u. übers. v. Victoria Lorini, Berlin 2006, 36.

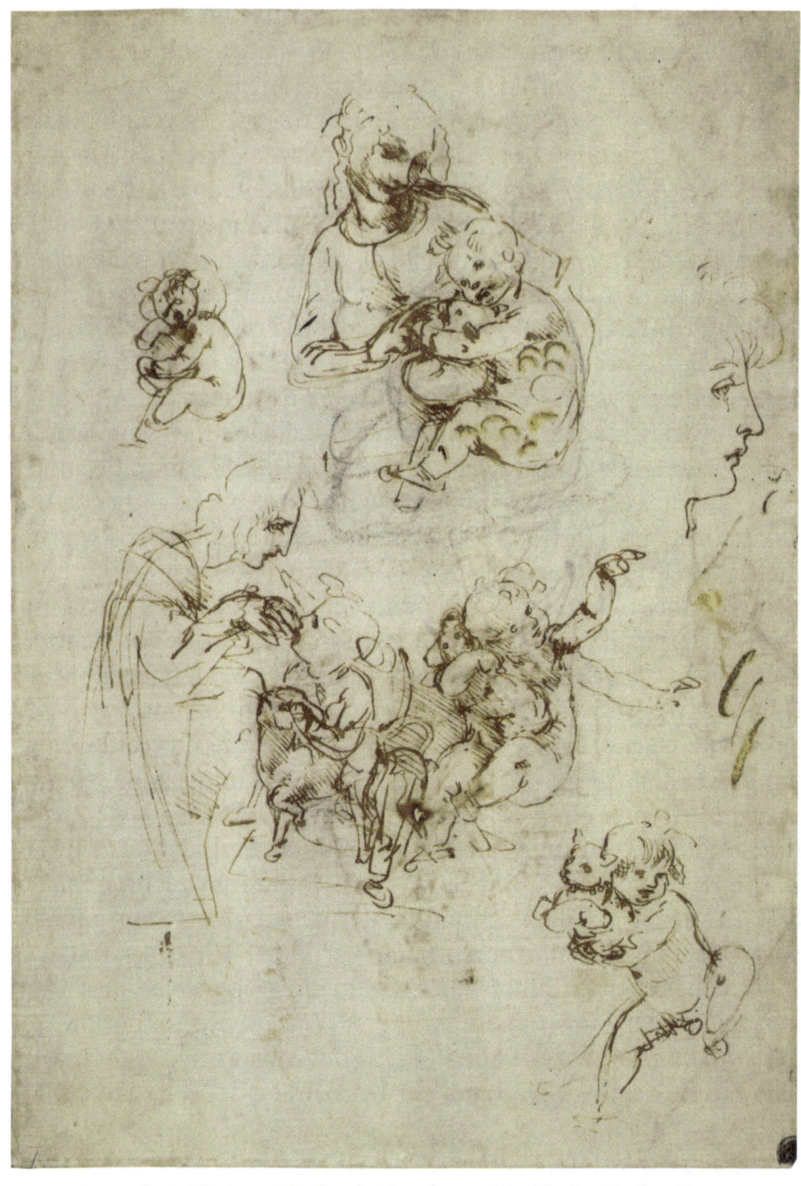

Leonardo da Vinci, zwei Studien der Jungfrau und des Kindes mit einer Katze und drei Studien des Kindes mit einer Katze, Feder und braune Tinte, über schwarzer Kreide und Bleigriffel, ca. 1475–1481, 28 × 19.7 cm. The British Museum, London.

Fig. 362

Einzelskizzen variationsreich durchgespielt wird, jedoch so bemerkenswert macht, ist der Sprung der Ebenen, der sich in der stilistischen Differenz zwischen freier Skizze und fixem Profil zeigt: Entwurfs- und Erinnerungsarbeit greifen scheinbar nicht ineinander, sondern stehen sich gegenüber.

Die Einzelskizzen erarbeiten verschiedene Ansichten, die sich auf der Grundlage des kurzfristigen Arbeitsgedächtnisses einstellen. Nicht die reproduktive Evokation eines konkreten Bildes, sondern die kreative Aktivierung eines motivischen Spielraums kraft variierender Wiederholungen bestimmter Linienzüge auf dem Blatt ist hier im Einsatz. Die kleinere Variation links oben wiederholt in verkürzter Form die Kopf- und Beinstellung des Kleinkindes, den Umriss der Rückenbahn wie auch die hakenförmige Markierung der beiden Pobacken, welche die Konturierung der Rundung unterbricht, die Po und Oberschenkelchen verbindet. Der linke Arm ist hingegen stärker angewinkelt und auch das Motiv des Umschlingens der Katze wurde verändert. Die beiden Ärmchen schließen sich nicht zu einer Umarmung, denn der rechte Arm setzt höher an und umschlingt nun den Nacken des Tieres, dessen Kopf wir – mit Blick auf die mittlere Skizze – zur linken Seite seines Köpfchens in der ovalen Markierung vermuten dürfen, während die wenigen Linien auf der rechten Seite Hinterkopf und Pony markieren und so eine alternative, jedoch nur kursorisch vollzogene Wendung des Köpfchens umreißen. Der Umriss des rechten Ärmchens wiederholt in verknappter Form die Armhaltung in der mittleren rechten Unterskizze. Schwer lesbare Formen, wie etwa diejenige, die sich in der mittleren Zone zwischen die Hinterbeine der Katze der linken Skizze und die Babybeinchen der rechten Skizze schiebt, lassen sich nur auf der Grundlage ihrer Wiederholungen entziffern: Hier ist es das aufgestellte Beinchen in der unteren Skizze, welches die Erkennbarkeit des Motivs in der oberen Skizze herstellt. Die Kombination eines auf dem Boden aufliegenden mit einem aufgestellten Beinchen wiederholt wiederum das durch die Federzeichnungen gleichsam in den Untergrund gedrückte und mit schwarzer Kreide grob entworfene Sitzmotiv der Maria mit Kind in der oberen Hälfte des Blattes. Allein die Konturierung ihrer linken Hüfte, die derjenigen auf der Skizze der Maria mit Kind und Johannesknaben überraschend gleichkommt [Fig. 354], ist mit der Feder nachgezogen und umreißt nun den Rücken ihres Kindes, weshalb der Umriss ihres Unterkörpers gleichsam aus dem Blick gerät. Der Spielraum der Imagination, wie er sich auf diesem Blatt entfaltet, ist also klar durch die Struktur der Wiederholung geprägt. Der aus der Erinnerung extrahierte Profilkopf des Jünglings stellt dem flüchtigen und flüssigen Entwurfsprozess ein fixes Bild gegenüber, das wie ein Anker funktioniert, der das Entwurfsgeschehen an die Verpflichtung zur Schönheit zu binden scheint.

Die Kombination einer Maria-mit-Kind-Skizze mit einem Profilbild findet sich auch auf einem anderen Blatt aus dem British Museum, das darüber hinaus verschiedene Diagramme aufweist [Fig. 365]. Ähnlich wie auf dem Blatt aus der Sammlung Windsor arbeitet die Überblendung gegenläufiger Kopfhaltungen Mariens an der Gewinnung eines Bewegungsspektrums, wobei jedoch die drei Phasen hier materiell voneinander abgehoben sind: Das frontal ausgerichtete und mit Bleigriffel gezogene Fadenkreuz des Gesichts war auch hier die technische Grundlage, welche die räumliche Bewegung auf der Fläche des Papieres verankerte. Das Kreuz wurde leicht nach rechts und dann deutlich nach links geschwenkt, wobei in beide Kopfwendungen die Markierungen von Augen, Nase und Mund eingetragen wurden. Die Wendung zur gegenüberliegenden Seite ist vor allem durch den mimetisch konkreten und mit Tinte Nachdruck verliehenen Umriss des Kiefers und Halses vorgestellt, welcher die Gesichtsfläche der alternativen Wendung durchkreuzt. Die Skizzierung ihrer Augen, Brauen und Nase konfligiert wiederum mit dem seitlichen Haarknoten des sich am stärksten abzeichnenden Kopfes.

Die im Vergleich zum Blatt aus der Sammlung Windsor deutlich kleinere Skizze auf lachsfarbenem präpariertem Papier zeichnet sich somit nicht nur durch den Wechsel des Mediums vom Metallstift zum Bleigriffel und zur Tintenfeder aus, welcher die drei Phasen des Entwurfs kenntlich voneinander abhebt, sondern auch durch die Drehung des Blattes innerhalb des Zeichnungsprozesses, die den Randgang klar von der Hauptskizze abhebt.

Der idealschöne Profilkopf, dem die Haarlocke an der Stirn fehlt und der damit als geschlechtsneutral definiert ist, rahmt hier nicht die Skizzierung des Gesichts Mariens, sondern bildet den Ausgangspunkt eines bildnerischen Gedankengangs, der sich entlang einer mit Lineal gezogenen Horizontalen entwickelt.

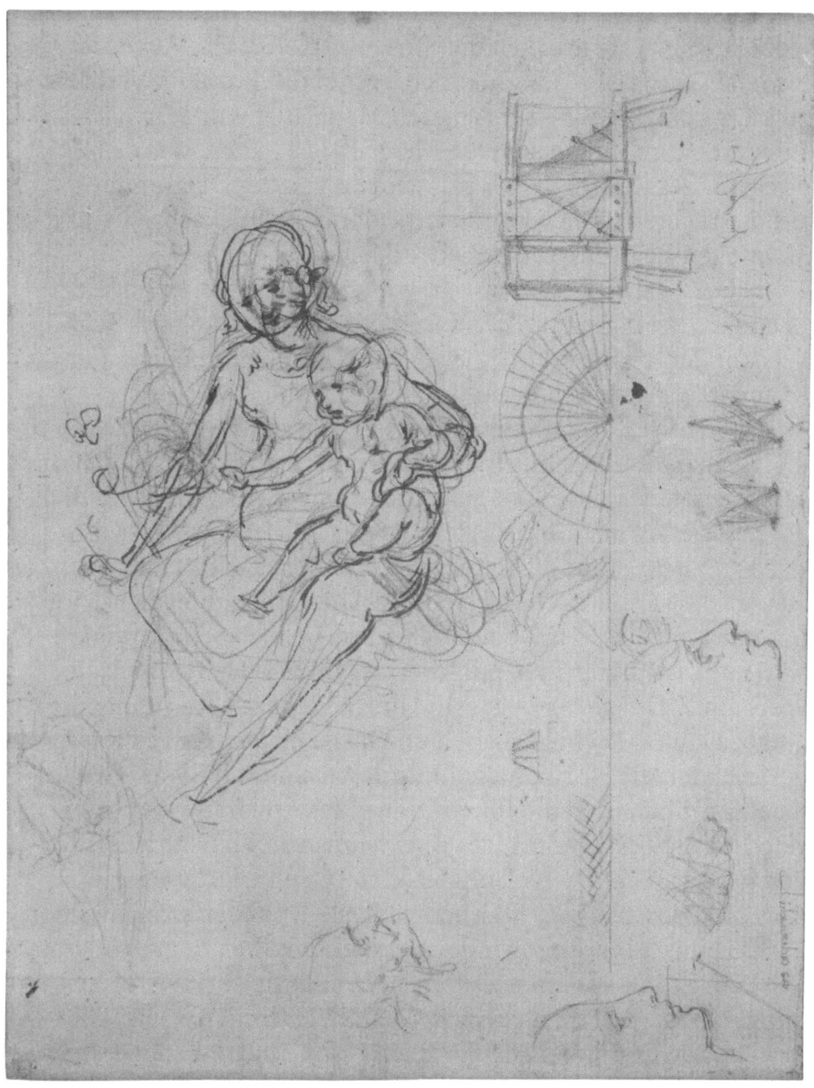

Leonardo da Vinci, Jungfrau mit Kind, drei Köpfe im Profil und andere Skizzen, Metallstift und Bleigriffel, mit Feder und brauner Tinte, auf blasslachsrosa präpariertem Papier, ca. 1478–1480, 20.3 × 156 cm. The British Museum, London.

Fig. 365

Der Kopf wiederholt sich ein weiteres Mal unterhalb der Geraden, wobei diesmal Haarlocken die Stirn umspielen. Das Auge ist maßstabgerecht wiederholt, doch ist hier das Profil im Verhältnis zu klein geraten. Statt zum spitzen Metallstift wurde in der Wiederholung zum weicheren Bleigriffel gegriffen, was den Zeichnungsprozess dieses Profils mit demjenigen der Diagramme auf der rechten Seite verbindet, die doppelte Blickachsen und ihre Sichtfelder bei Blickwechsel vorstellen.

Der Kontur der Stirn war, wie so oft, erst steiler angelegt; Leonardo hat dann im nächsten Schritt die Rundung des Schädels mit der die Stirn korrigierenden Linie eingezeichnet. Für die Kinnpartie setzte Leonardo dreimal neu an.

Auf der Horizontalen liegt ein Diagramm auf, das zweiundzwanzig Radien um einen Mittelpunkt auffächert, wobei drei verschiedene Reichweiten eingekreist sind. Sehr wahrscheinlich handelt es sich um die Unterteilung der „Dicke der Luft" („*grossezza del'aria*"), auf die Leonardo in seinem Traktat mehrfach zu sprechen kommt. Die sich aus der Überschneidung der beiden inneren Kreislinien mit den Radien ergebenden Schnittpunkte sind mit der Zirkelspitze punktiert. Während der äußere Halbkreis mit Zirkel gezogen ist, sind die beiden inneren freihändig eingezeichnet. Rechts daneben und quasi in den fiktiven Raum gestellt, den die Horizontale hiermit zur unteren Blattkante aufmacht, befindet sich die Illustration eines Apparates, der offensichtlich die Festlegung eines Spektrums von Radien mit Hilfe von Fäden an ein Dreieck bindet, das – wenn wir die Diagramme der Blickachsen erklärend hinzuziehen – wohl den sich auf einen Distanzpunkt hin verengenden perspektivischen Raum vorstellt. Die dem Profilkopf am nächsten stehende zopfförmige Verschränkung schräg zusammengeführter paralleler Linien erklärt die irritierende Dissoziierung der Radien von einem sie bündelnden Mittelpunkt in dem darunterliegenden Diagramm. Es mag sein, dass in diesem abgegrenzten Bildfeld Leonardo sich selbst oder einem Schüler die aus der Verdoppelung des Sehstrahls resultierende Komplizierung der Perspektive vor Augen führen wollte. Doch wie haben der Profilkopf und seine Wiederholung an diesem theoretischen Exkurs Anteil? Oder ist ihre Eingliederung in den visuellen Gedankengang rein zufällig?[37] Ein Indiz für Letzteres mag ein dritter Profilkopf sein, der Leonardos Galba-Typus aufruft und oberhalb und also außerhalb des eigentlichen Randgangs skizziert ist.

Auch wenn die Einzelskizzen in ihrer Streuung auf dem Blatt es also auf den ersten Blick nicht nahelegen, so eröffnet sich doch zwischen den beiden Profilköpfen und den Diagrammen ein assoziativer Denkraum. Wie bereits dargestellt, arbeiten Leonardos Diagramme an dem Verständnis der Koordination der Blickbahnen beider Augen und illustrieren dabei den Wechsel der Fokusse bei Augenbewegung – ein Sachverhalt, den Leonardo in seinen Notizen anhand des Vorgangs des Lesens erklärt, bei dem das Auge von Wort zu Wort springt.[38] Die irritierende Schrägstellung des rechten Auges auf dem linken Diagramm folgt dabei dem albertischen Konzept des zentralen Sehstrahls. Dieser muss von der Pupille aus senkrecht auf die Oberfläche des Anschauungsgegenstandes treffen, damit der Gegenstand in aller Schärfe betrachtet werden kann. Die eigenartige Perforierung der Kreuzungspunkte der Radien mit den Umrissen der inneren Halbkreise in dem Diagramm darüber scheint dem Faktum Rechnung zu tragen, dass die zugespitzte Schärfe nur punktuell möglich ist, während die schwach gezeichneten multiplen Blickachsen in den beiden Diagrammen darunter Abweichungen von dem zentralen Sehstrahl und damit die Entschärfung des Blicks insinuieren. Das geradezu physische Eindrücken der Nadel des Zirkels ins Papier lässt vermuten, dass Leonardo hier von der Vorstellung geleitet war, dass diese Punkte eine einprägende Wirkung haben.

Das auf den ersten Blick willkürlich anmutende Zusammentreffen diagrammatischer Illustrationen mit Profilköpfen ist auf einer späteren Zeichnung aus einem zerlegten Notizbuch aus der Sammlung Windsor Castle zu einer Illustration verschmolzen, welche den Lichteinfall auf einem Gesicht behandelt [Fig. 368]. In dem begleitenden Text schreibt Leonardo dem senkrecht auf

37
Carmen Bambach spricht von „unrelated technological studies“. *Leonardo da Vinci: Master Draftman* (Ausstellungskatalog The Metropolitan Museum of Art, New York), hg. v. Carmen Bambach, New Haven 2003, 298.

38
„Noi conosciamo chiaramente che la vista è delle più veloci operazioni che sieno, ed in un punto vede infinite forme; nientedimeno non comprende se non una cosa per volta. Poniamo caso, tu, lettore, guardi in una occhiata tutta questa carta scritta, e subito giudicherai questa esser piena di varie lettere … onde ti bisogna fare a parola a parola“ Leonardo, *Trattato* [parte 2, 47], 34.

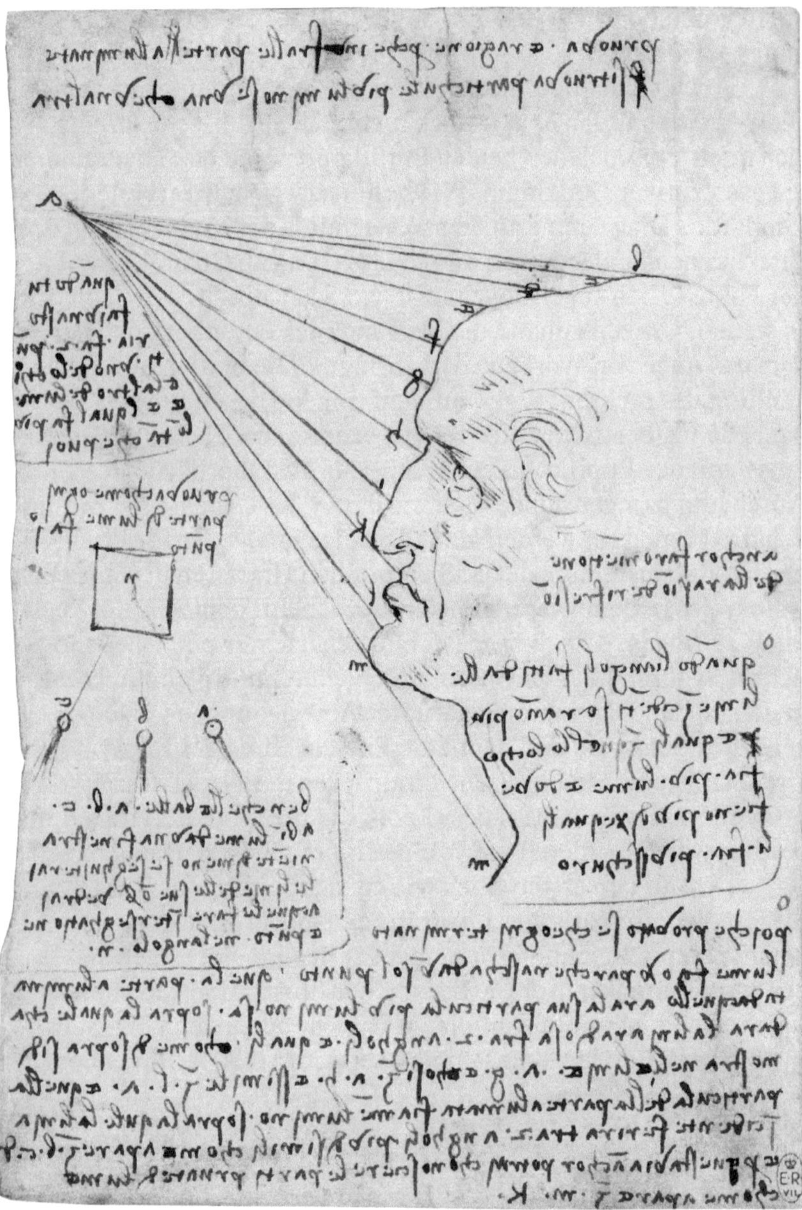

Leonardo da Vinci, Lichteinfall auf ein Gesicht, ca. 1488, Federzeichnung, 20.3 × 14.3 cm.
Windsor Castle, The Royal Collection, Windsor.

Fig. 368

die Oberfläche treffenden Lichtstrahl die stärkste Wirkung zu, welche mit zunehmender Brechung abnimmt. Mit dieser Aussage inkorporiert Leonardo gleichsam den zentralen Sehstrahl in die Brechung des Lichts und verschränkt in logischer Weise damit die zwei Bereiche der Optik, welche in Leon Battista Albertis *De Pictura* (1435) noch separat behandelt wurden. Wie schon in Leonardos Blickdiagrammen [Fig. 365] fehlt auch hier die Einzeichnung einer Trennfläche (wie beispielsweise eine von Leonardo empfohlene Glasscheibe), auf der sich die Linien bildhaft abzeichnen. Die Linien konstruieren keine *perspectiva artificialis*, sondern visualisieren vielmehr die natürliche Wahrnehmung. Wenn nun Leonardo mit dem Galba-Profil ein engrammatisches Bild aufruft, um den Vorgang des Sehens zu illustrieren, dann scheint er den Prozess paradoxerweise vom Ende her zu denken: vom Erinnerungsbild als Abdruck eines Seheindrucks in der *memoria* des Künstlers.

Amors Pfeil

Wie stark Leonardos eigene Überlegungen zum Wahrnehmungsvorgang durch die Sehstrahltheorie des arabischen Naturwissenschaftlers Ibn al-Haytham angeregt worden waren, zeigen, wie in der Forschung breit diskutiert, seine theoretischen Aufzeichnungen im Codex Atlanticus, in welchem er auf die herausgehobene Stellung des zentralen Sehstrahls im verstandesgeleiteten Einprägungsprozess zu sprechen kommt.[39] Leonardos Praxis der Wiederholung von Linienzügen deckt sich mit Ibn al-Haythams Auffassung, dass die wiederholte Wahrnehmung eines Objektes zur Verfestigung seiner Einprägung führe.[40]

Martin Kemp hat in seinem Aufsatz „Leonardo and the Visual Pyramid" als eine weitere mögliche Informationsquelle auf Dantes *Convivio* hingewiesen, in welchem der Dichter die einzigartige

39 Leonardo da Vinci: *Codice Atlantico*, vol. 2, hg. v. Augusto Marinoni, Mailand 2000, 661 (380v): „Chiaro si complende l'occhio non intendere li obietti se le spezie non vengon a quello per linia retta, e quella cosa fia manco intesa che più si partirà da detta linia." Siehe hierzu weiterführend Pericolo, Knowing through the Eye, 236–244.

40 Alhazen, *De li aspecti*, 54r: „E le forme de' modi di visibili le quale el viso comprende rimanghono ne l'anima e se figono ne l'imaginatione, e quanto più se iterarà la comprensione de esse dal viso tanto più serano fisse ne l'anima e in l'imaginatione." Zit. n. Pericolo, Knowing through the Eye, 244.

Stellung des zentralen Sehstrahls damit erklärt, dass allein das, was kraft des Sehstrahls in gerader Linie auf die Pupille trifft, wahrhaft wahrgenommen werde und sich wie ein Siegel in die Imagination einpräge.[41] Der Grund dafür sei die direkte Verbindung des zentralen Sehstrahls mit dem Sehnerv. Interessanterweise steht Dantes Exkurs zur Sehstrahltheorie im Kontext seines Liebesdiskurses. So leitet er aus dem zentralen Sehstrahl, den er kurz darauf metaphorisch mit Amors Pfeil verbindet, die Erklärung ab, weshalb der intensive Augenkontakt Liebe entfachen kann. Dante kommt wiederholt auf seine große Liebe zu Beatrice zu sprechen, die, prospektiv gesehen, als Inbild und Maßstab allen folgenden Wahrnehmungen zu Grunde liegt und zugleich retrospektiv auf die Jungfrau Maria als das christliche *exemplum* idealer Schönheit rekurriert. Indem Leonardo nun den Jünglingskopf als sein eigenes Inbild quasi an den Anfang seiner visuellen ‚Abhandlung' über den Sehstrahl setzt [Fig. 365], assoziiert auch er frei den physikalischen Vorgang der Wahrnehmung mit demjenigen der geistigen Einprägung.

Der thematische Riss, der beide Diskurse so unvermittelt aufeinandertreffen lässt, geht bei Dante im Fluss der Abhandlung unter, während er sich bei Leonardo gleichsam als Bilderrätsel formiert. Die Verbindung der einzelnen disparaten Diagramme leistet die Horizontale, die sowohl die Unterseite des Halbradius ausmacht als auch als konstruktive Linie den Boden der Perspektivapparatur bildet. Indem die Schrägen des ersten Diagramms genau hier abbrechen, tragen sie der Verbindungslinie Rechnung, deren Abstraktheit den Riss materialisiert, über welchen die freie Assoziation springt.

Die lose Zusammenstellung der drei Motivgruppen – Maria mit Kind im Längsformat, Diagramme und Profilköpfe im Querformat – wird durch die grobe Skizzierung zweier Körperhaltungen erweitert, die sich jeweils einer der beiden Blattausrichtungen

41
Kemp, Martin: Leonardo and the Visual Perspective, in: *Journal of the Warburg and Courtauld Institutes* 40, 1977, 128–149: 131. Dante, *Convivo*, 2, ix: „E qui si vuol sapere, che avegna che più cose nell'occhio a un'ora possano venire, veramente quelaa che viene per retta linea nella punta della pupilla, quella veramente si vede e nella imaginativa si sugegella solamente. E questo è però che'l nervo per la quale corrre lo spirito visivo, è diritto a quell aparte, e veduto da lui. [...] e molte vole, nel dirizzare di questa linea, discocca l'arco di colui al quale ogni arme è leggiere." Dante, *Convivio. A Dual-Language Critical Edition*, hg. v. Andrew Frisardi, Cambridge 2018, 91.

fügen und, da sie wohl an einem Gedankengang zusammenarbeiten, diese zugleich verklammern. Eine solche motivische Verlinkung widerspricht der generellen Forschungsmeinung, der zufolge thematisch divergierende Ebenen in einer Skizze als unzusammenhängend zu betrachten seien. Die Unverbundenheit kann aber auch als Artikulation von Gedankensprüngen und Digressionen aufgefasst werden, welche eine unterschwellige, zwischen den disparaten Ebenen zirkulierende Bewegung des Geistes anzeigen. Auf dieser hypothetischen Grundlage erscheint die befremdliche wie rätselhafte Kombination der Elemente als Ausweitung eines Denkhorizonts, der das Ikonische des Erinnerungsbildes an das Prozessuale des Wahrnehmungsvorgangs gleichsam fragend heranführt, indem sie den Entwurf eines Bewegungsspielraums nebst der Visualisierung des Radius der Wahrnehmung erarbeitet. Der Randgang ist folglich als ein kritischer Rahmen zu verstehen, der den Bedingungen der Möglichkeit der Konkretion einer inneren Bildvorstellung in einem sie entäußernden Entwurf nachgeht.

Am Anfang dieses Gedankengangs steht enigmatisch der idealschöne Profilkopf, der sich, mit Metallstift gezeichnet, in einer Technik materialisiert, die, da keine Korrektur zulassend, höchste Reinheit der Form beansprucht. Leonardo griff erneut zu diesem Zeicheninstrument, um unterhalb des idealschönen Bildnisses die in Spiegelschrift verschlüsselte Inschrift *„inprincipio era“* hinzuzusetzen. Eine zweite Inschrift auf der linken Seite ist hingegen durch den kalligraphischen Schwung beinahe unleserlich. Seine ausufernde Linienbahn hat nicht nur beide Initialen ergriffen, sondern das zweite Wort in Gänze mit sich fortgerissen, das nur aus dem ersten „Jesus“ als *„Vergine“* zu entziffern ist. Das Wort „Jungfrau“ scheint – wie *„inprincipio era“* – in seiner Lesbarkeit verhüllt. Indem Leonardo nach *„era“* abbricht, lässt er das *verbum* (Wort) als das, was im Sinne der ersten Zeile des Johannesevangeliums („im Anfang war“) in der Schwebe.

Der daran anschließende visuelle Gedankengang liest sich wie das Grübeln des Doktor Faust in seinem Studierzimmer über die Frage, wie *logos* als das Wort des Anfangs genauer zu übersetzen sei.[42] Ihm vorausgeschickt erscheint Leonardos Idealbildnis wie ein figürliches Schema unter lauter abstrakten Diagrammen, welche mit ihrer Thematisierung des Wahrnehmungsprozesses die schwer lösbare Aufgabe der notwendigen räumlichen Relativierung seiner Form, wie sie in der Skizze zu Tage tritt, anstoßen. Als *principium* seiner Kunst ist der Profilkopf Ausdruck bzw. Abdruck der *figura* des Idealbilds, das Leonardos eigenem Verständnis zufolge in seiner *memoria* fest eingeprägt ist.[43] Dieses Bild scheint dem Bildfindungsprozess für die Jungfrau Maria als die schönste aller Frauen beizustehen, ohne mit ihm vereinbar zu sein.

Diese strukturelle Unvereinbarkeit des Umrisses der Köpfe mit dem Skizzierungsprozess der Madonna mit Kind hat, wie eingangs dargestellt, zur Auffassung einer gleichermaßen abgespalteten zeichnerischen Handlung geführt, die mit der Bezeichnung *doodle* sogleich ins Aus der Betrachtung verwiesen wurde, auch wenn die Massierung ihres Auftretens doch immerhin als aufsehenerregend wahrgenommen wurde. Die spektakuläre Streuung auf dem Blatt mit Maria, Jesus und Johannesknaben [Fig. 327] verriet ihre unterschwellige Verankerung in einer darunter befindlichen Vorlage, an deren Fixierung im Prozess des Durchpausens gerüttelt wurde, um die Linie von diesem verpflichtenden Untergrund zu lösen. Leonardo hat mit dem ‚unkünstlerischen' Prozess der Pause eine Sperre eingeführt, welche das Vorbild von dem Nebeneinander der Köpfe separiert, um mit dieser Vorlage eine zugrundeliegende Idee von Schönheit zu schaffen, welche den Denkprozess der Skizzierung der Madonna mit Kind untergründig trägt.

42
„Geschrieben steht: ‚Im Anfang war das Wort!' | Hier stock' ich schon! Wer hilft mir weiter fort? | Ich kann das Wort so hoch unmöglich schätzen, | Ich muss es anders übersetzen, | Wenn ich vom Geiste recht erleuchtet bin | Geschrieben steht: Im Anfang war der Sinn. | Bedenke wohl die erste Zeile, | Dass deine Feder sich nicht übereile! | Ist es der Sinn, der alles wirkt und schafft? | Es sollte stehn: Im Anfang war die Kraft! | Doch, auch indem ich dieses niederschreibe, | Schon warnt mich was, dass ich dabei nicht bleibe. | Mir hilft der Geist! Auf einmal seh' ich Rat | Und schreibe getrost: Im Anfang war die Tat!" Goethe, Johann Wolfgang von, *Faust. Eine Tragödie*, Tübingen 1808: 80–81.

43
Nach Leonardo prägen sich in der *memoria* nur ausgezeichnete Dinge ein [„li si ferma et li muore se la cosa imaginata non e de molta eccellentia". Siehe Fehrenbach, Frank: Leonardo's Dark Eye, in Galley, Nicolas u. a. (Ed.): *Senses of Sight. Towards a Multisensorial Approach of the Image. Essays in Honor of Victor I. Stoichita*, Rom 2015, 67–82: 67.

Part 4
Navigating Dichotomies

Für die komplementäre Paarung von ‚Figur' und ‚Grund' kann eine ausgesprochen verzweigte und weit zurückreichende Ideen- und Begriffsgeschichte geltend gemacht werden. Die äußeren Enden dieser Geschichte werden einerseits durch die antike Erzählung zur *Erfindung der Kunst* markiert; am anderen Ende steht die fortschreitende Überwindung disziplinärer Grenzen, welche dem Begriffspaar ‚Figur und Grund' im Verlauf des 20. Jahrhunderts schließlich zu erstaunlichem Erfolg verhalf. Als Kristallisationspunkte auf unterschiedlichen Etappen dieser Geschichte erscheinen Berlin und Weimar, London und Paris.

Im ersten Teil des folgenden Essays wird das komplexe Beziehungsgeflecht, welches mit dem Begriffspaar ‚Figur und Grund' assoziiert ist, anhand der gemeinsamen Betrachtung von Eduard Daeges Gemälde *Die Erfindung der Malerei* (1832) und des nach Edgar Rubin benannten ‚Rubinkelches' (1912–1915) greifbar. Das Gemälde verkörpert die erwähnte antike Erzählung und steht damit für die Sphäre der Kunst. Beim ‚Rubinkelch' handelt es sich hingegen um eine Darstellung aus der Inkunabel der wahrnehmungspsychologischen Fachliteratur zur Figur-Grund-Beziehung. Während der Kelch einen bleibenden Platz in unserem kollektiven Bildgedächtnis einnimmt, ist seine Herkunft bislang nie genauer untersucht worden. Dabei hat auch der ‚Rubinkelch' seine eigene, bis in die Zeit der Französischen Revolution zurückreichende Ideengeschichte, wenngleich die Erfindung des so überaus markanten Bildmotivs ganz offenkundig auf einen Briten zurückgeht – der wiederum von der Darstellungskonvention inspiriert worden sein dürfte, welche zu jener Zeit von Johann Caspar Lavater in seinen europaweit verbreiteten *Physiognomischen Fragmenten* geübt wurde.

Im zweiten Teil meines Beitrags wird das Figur-Grund-Phänomen, das der Wirkung derartiger Darstellungen zugrunde liegt, in das System der Gestaltpsychologie eingeordnet. Die Gestaltpsychologie hat im 20. Jahrhundert eine Reihe von Gestaltgesetzen erkannt und beschrieben, welche dafür verantwortlich sind, dass wir sehen, wie wir sehen, und die Wolfgang Metzger 1936 so treffend als *Gesetze des Sehens* betitelte. Diese Gestaltgesetze sind wiederum Grundlage verschiedener Gestaltphänomene, zu welchen auch die Figur-Grund-Unterscheidung zu zählen ist.

Im dritten Teil wird angedeutet, wie insbesondere Rudolf Arnheim das Wissen um die Gestaltgesetze für die Kunstwissenschaft fruchtbar machte. Anknüpfend an den Tagungsaufruf zur Konferenz *Between Figure and Ground: Seeing in Premodernity* (2019) gehe ich nur ganz exemplarisch der Frage nach, worin das Selbstverständnis einer Kunstgeschichte liegt, die auf modernen Erkenntnissen und Methoden aufzubauen gedenkt. Mit Arnheim kommt auch der Ideentransfer zur Sprache, welcher eine notwendige Folge des erzwungenen Exodus der bedeutendsten Vertreter der Gestaltpsychologie nach 1933 war und der die weitere Entwicklung und Rezeption der Forschungen zu ‚Figur und Grund' letztlich bis heute mitbestimmt. Doch auch schon vor 1933 erscheint die Gestaltpsychologie als ausgesprochen transatlantisches Projekt. Ausgehend vom Psychologischen Institut der Berliner Universität entfaltete sie mit Schriften wie Wolfgang Köhlers *Gestalt Psychology* (1929), Kurt Koffkas *Principles of Gestalt Psychology* (1935), George W. Hartmanns *Gestalt Psychology. A Survey of Facts and Principles* (1935) und Willis D. Ellis' *Source Book of Gestalt Psychology* (1938) auf dem amerikanischen Kontinent eine wohl nachhaltigere Wirkung als an ihrem Entstehungsort. Insbesondere mit seinem Standardwerk *Art and Visual Perception. A Psychology of the Creative Eye* (1954) sorgte Arnheim dann für eine ungeheure Popularisierung gestaltpsychologischer Ideen in der Kunstwissenschaft – und damit auch von ‚Figur und Grund'.

Im vierten Teil werden drei sehr unterschiedliche Schlüsselwerke im Zusammenhang diskutiert, aus denen die dauerhafte Präsenz wahrnehmungs- und gestaltpsychologischer Erkenntnisse in der kunstwissenschaftlichen Literatur weiter erhellt. Bereits zehn Jahre vor Arnheims *Art and Visual Perception* erschien György Kepes' *language of vision* (1944), sechs Jahre danach Ernst Gombrichs *Art and Illusion. A Study in the Psychology of Pictorial Representation* (1960). Während Arnheim ein bestimmtes Vokabular in Umlauf brachte, das er mit einer Unmenge wahrnehmungspsychologischer Fachliteratur untermauerte, und Kepes die pragmatische Anwendbarkeit wahrnehmungspsychologischer Erkenntnisse auf die visuelle Gestaltung verfolgte, demonstrierte Gombrich auf intellektueller Ebene, dass das Begriffspaar von ‚Figur' und ‚Grund' einen ganz beiläufigen, selbstverständlichen und somit kaum mehr wahrnehmbaren Eingang in die kunstwissenschaftliche

Fachliteratur gefunden hatte. Die begriffsgeschichtliche Absorption von Rubins wahrnehmungspsychologischem Forschungsgegenstand durch die Kunstwissenschaft war damit vollzogen.

Anstelle eines Fazits führt der abschließende fünfte Teil noch einmal ins Offene, indem er vor Augen führt, dass die Ideengeschichte von ‚Figur' und ‚Grund' keineswegs zu Ende erforscht und berichtet ist. So wenig diese Ideengeschichte als Schwarzweißkontrast greifbar wird, sind in ihr immer weitere Schattierungen wahrnehmbar, vergleichbar dem irisierenden Grund mancher antiken Kameen.[1]

Die Erfindung der Kunst – Figur, Grund, Kontur

Unter dem Stichwort „Erfindung der Zeichenkunst" referiert Hans Wille (1926–1999) 1967 im *Reallexikon zur Deutschen Kunstgeschichte* die antike Butades-Erzählung folgendermaßen: Die „Tochter eines kunstreichen Töpfers [...] sah, als sie von ihrem in ferne Länder scheidenden Geliebten Abschied nahm, den Schlagschatten seines Gesichtsprofiles an der Wand, umriß die dunkle Fläche mit einem Stift und füllte sie schwarz aus. Damit habe die Zeichenkunst und mit ihr die bildende Kunst überhaupt ihren Anfang genommen."[2]

1
Ich denke hier an den Blacas Cameo im British Museum.

2
Wille, Hans: Stichwort „Erfindung der Zeichenkunst", in: Heydenreich, Ludwig Heinrich/Wirth, Karl-August (Ed.): *Reallexikon zur Deutschen Kunstgeschichte,* vol. 5, Stuttgart 1967, Sp. 1235–1241: 1236. Plinius der Ältere, auf welchen die verschiedenen Varianten der Butades-Erzählung zurückgehen (cf. ibid., 1235), teilt nur knapp mit: „De picturae initiis incerta nec instituti operis quaestio est. [...] Graeci [...] alii Sicyone, alii apud Corinthios repertam, omnes umbra hominis lineis circumducta; itaque primam talem, secundam singulis coloribus et monochromaton dictam, postquam operosior inventa erat" bzw. in der Übersetzung Roderich Königs: „Die Frage über den Ursprung der Malerei ist ungeklärt und gehört nicht in den Plan meines Werkes. [...] die Griechen [...] lassen sie teils zu Sikyon, teils bei den Korinthern ihren Anfang nehmen, alle jedoch sagen, man habe den Schatten eines Menschen mit Linien nachgezogen; deshalb sei die erste Malerei so beschaffen gewesen, die nächste habe nur je eine Farbe verwendet und sei [...] die einfarbige [...] genannt worden, nachdem eine kunstvollere Malerei erfunden war". – König, Roderich (Ed.): C. Plinii Secundi *Naturalis Historiae Libri XXXVII,* Liber XXXV/C. Plinius Secundus d. Ä.: *Naturkunde. Lateinisch–deutsch,* Buch XXXV: *Farben, Malerei, Plastik,* München 1978, 20–23 (Kapitel V bzw. § 15). Die Stelle zu Butades lautet bei Plinius: „De pictura satis superque. contexuisse his et plasticen conveniat. eiusdem opere terrae fingere ex argilla similitudines Butades Sicyonius figulus primus invenit Corinthi filiae opera, quae capta amore iuvenis, abeunte illo peregre, umbram ex facie eius ad lucernam in pariete lineis circumscripsit; quibus pater eius inpressa argilla typum fecit et cum ceteris fictilibus induratum igni proposuit" bzw. in der Übersetzung: „Über die

Wille erwähnt hier, viel konkreter, als sein Gewährsmann Plinius (23/24–79) dies tut, jene drei Elemente, welche selbst in den reduziertesten Figur-Grund-Darstellungen, wie sie unten noch zu sehen sein werden, immer präsent sind: die Wand als den *Grund*, die schwarz ausgefüllte Fläche als die *Figur* sowie die Umrisslinie, die als *Kontur* Figur und Grund voneinander scheidet.[3]

Malerei ist nun genug und übergenug gesagt worden. Es mag zweckmäßig sein, dem Bisherigen auch [...] die Plastik beizufügen. Mit einem Erzeugnis des gleichen Erdmaterials erfand in Korinth der Töpfer Butades aus Sikyon als erster ähnliche [das heißt porträtähnliche] Bilder aus Ton zu formen, und zwar mit Hilfe seiner Tochter, die aus Liebe zu einem jungen Mann, der in die Fremde ging, bei Lampenlicht an der Wand den Schatten seines Gesichtes mit Linien umzog; den Umriß füllte der Vater mit daraufgedrücktem Ton und machte ein Abbild, das er mit dem übrigen Tonzeug im Feuer brannte und ausstellte". – Ibid., 108 f. (Kapitel XLIII bzw. § 151).

3

Cf. im vorliegenden Zusammenhang erhellend auch die Plinius' Überlieferung weiter ausschmückende Darstellung bei Joachim von Sandrart d. Ä., welcher besonders die Bedeutung der Umrisslinie bzw. des Konturs hervorhebt: „Dann [denn] die erste Mahlerey ware eine geraume Zeit nur ein bloser Umriß / und hieße bey den Latinern Linearis Pictura, in gezogenen Linien bestehend. Wie man darfür gehalten / so hat solche erfunden einer / mit Namen Philocles aus Egypten / oder Cleanthes ein Corinther / oder ein anderer Corinther / Namens Ardices, oder Telephanes von Sicyon: Diese alle sollen nichts / als nur den bloßen Umriß / ohn einigen Gebrauch der Farben oder Schattirung / bloß mit Kohlen gemachet haben. Darnach soll eine unbekandte Hand erfunden haben / den bloßen Umriß mit einerley Farbe zu füllen: welche Art vom Mahlen bey den Griechen genennet war Monochroma, das ist / Mahlerey mit einer Farbe. Es vermeinet aber Plinius, dieses heise mahlen mit zweyerley Farben / als grau in blau / oder Liecht in Dunckel / und schreibet / solches habe lang / ja biß auf seine Zeit gewehret. Er kan aber wol hierinn fehlen / in ansehung / daß die alte Meistere / so in der Wissenschaft noch nicht so hoch gestiegen waren / ihre Werke / mit verhöhen und schattiren auszufärtigen / den Umriß nur mit einerley Saft oder Farbe mögen ausgefüllet haben. Und obwol die Griechen / als Ehrsüchtig / sich unterstanden / die Ehre der ersten Erfindung ihnen selber zuzueignen / so haben sie doch damit nichts anders gethan / als daß sie andern ihre Ehren-Kron rauben wollen. Ich beharre demnach auf der Meinung / daß der Lydische Gyges, in Egypten wohnend / der erste gewesen seye / der die Zeichen-Kunst herfürgebracht / und gleichsam gebohren habe / da er im profil seinen selbst-eigenen Schatten / an der weisen Wand / mit einer Kohle / die er vom Feuer genommen / abgerissen / und daß dieser Polygnotus der erste diese Kunst vermehret / und den Umriß mit Farben gefüllet habe." – [Sandrart auf Stockau, Joachim von]: *Der Teutschen Academie Zweyter Theil. Von der alt- und neu-berühmten Egyptischen / Griechischen / Römischen / Italiänischen / Hoch- und Nieder-Teutschen Bau- Bild- und Mahlerey-Künstlere Lob und Leben. Der Teutschen Academie Zweyten Theils Erstes Buch: Von der ur-alt-berühmten Egyptischen / Griechischen und Römischen Ersten Kunst-Mahlere Leben und Lob*, (gedruckt bey Johann-Philipp Miltenberger) Nürnberg 1675, 13. Zu Gyges heißt es in der *Vorrede:* „Nach der Aussage Plinii, lib. 35. ist Gyges Lydius in Egypten der erste gewesen / der ein Bild gezeichnet. Er soll hierzu veranlasset worden seyn / als er / beym Feuer stehend / seinen Schatten ersehen: da er dann / mit einer Kohle / an der Wand sich selber abgerissen. Also haben auch andere von dem Schatten derer / so in der Sonne stunden / die äuserste Linien abgezeichnet / wie Quintilianus schreibet / und das / mit Lit. B. bezeichnete und hie beygefügte / Kupferblat weiset. [...] Andere halten darfür / daß dieser Edlen Kunst Anfang herrühre aus den unvollkommenen Bildern / welche die gütige Natur in Marmor- und andere Steine gebildet. So sind auch viele / welche glauben / daß die erste Künstlere ihr Absehen genommen haben / aus denen in den Wolken jezuweilen erschienenen mannigfältigen Figuren. Etliche machen die Liebe zur ersten Erfinderin dieser schönen

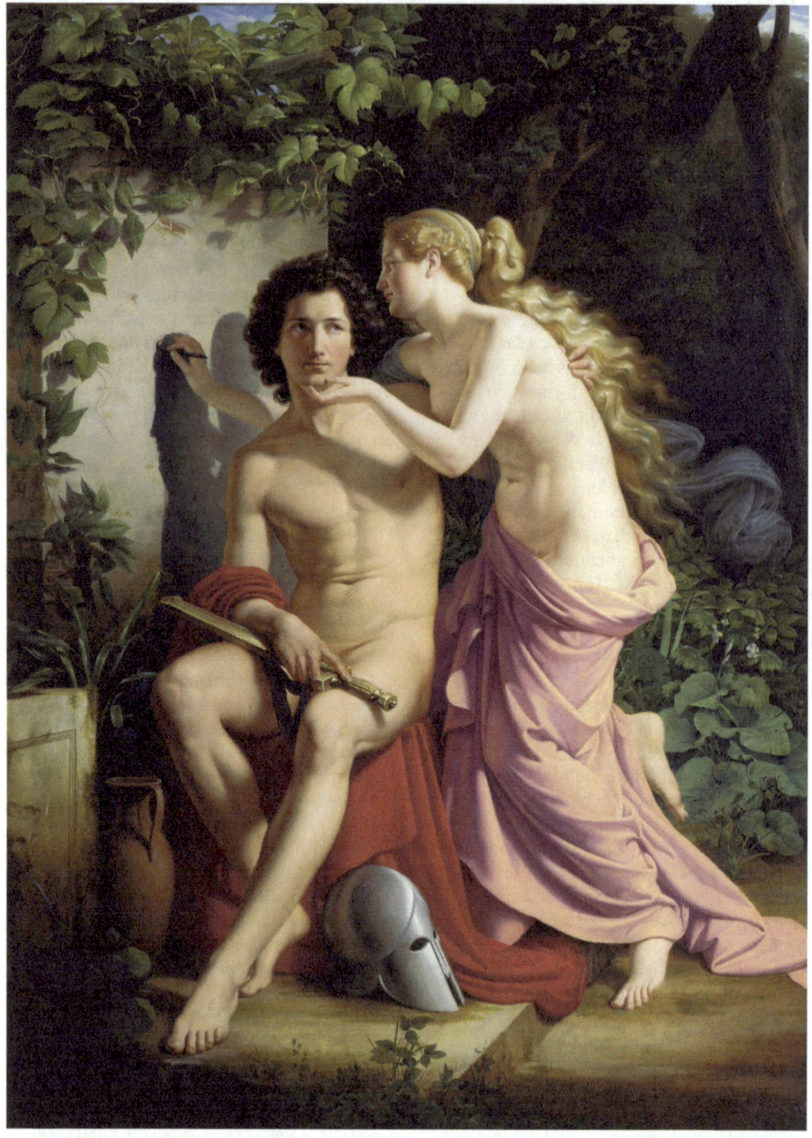

Wilhelm Eduard Daege, *Die Erfindung der Malerei*, 1832, Öl auf Leinwand, 176.5 × 135.5 cm. Staatliche Museen zu Berlin, Nationalgalerie, inv. A I 216, Berlin.

Fig. 378

Wille erwähnt weiterhin, dass die bildlichen Darstellungen der *Erfindung der Kunst* „in den Jahren zwischen 1770 und 1830 ihre größte Dichte erreichte[n]", „ausgelöst" durch Joachim von Sandrart d. Ä. (1606–1688).[4] Eduard Daeges (1805–1883) zu diesem Genre gehörende Gemälde *Die Erfindung der Malerei* (1832) entstand wenige Jahre danach [Fig. 378]. Wir erhaschen ebenjenen Augenblick, in welchem der Kontur, der die Figur aus dem Hintergrund ausgrenzt, ‚nach der Natur' gezogen wird. Die Darstellung legt nahe, dass die ersten Werke der bildenden Kunst als dezidiertes Figur-Grund-Thema in die Welt gekommen seien, noch dazu in der reduktionistischen Darstellungsweise der wahrnehmungspsychologischen Experimente um 1900 – nämlich als Schwarzweißkontrast von Figur und Grund.

Der bekannte ‚Rubinkelch' [Fig. 380] entstand zwischen 1912 und 1915 für wahrnehmungspsychologische Experimente, welche der aus Dänemark stammende Edgar Rubin (1886–1951) als Doktorand beim Psychologen Georg Elias Müller (1850–1934) in Göttingen begann.[5] Müller, 1881–1921 Professor an der Göttinger Universität, hatte dort ein experimentalpsychologisches Laboratorium eingerichtet. Rubins 1915 auf Dänisch, 1921 auf Deutsch erschienene Dissertation[6] gilt bis heute als Inkunabel

Wissenschafft / wann sie wollen / daß ein verliebtes Mägdlein / nämlich die Tochter des Dibutade Stovigliaio, eines ungemeinen irdenen Geschirr-Arbeiters / den Schatten ihres von ihr in ferne Länder scheidenden Liebsten an der Maur / vermitelst eines Latern-Liechts / erblicket / desselben Angesicht zu Behuff ihrer Gedächtnis / mit Kohlen umrissen / nachgezeichnet / und also diese Zeichnungs-Kunst erfunden haben solle / wie von diesen mancherley Meinungen handeln Leo Baptista Alberti lib. I. della Pittura, Cœlius Rhodiginus und andere. Von Polygnoto Thasio schreibet Plinius, er habe die Zeichnung verbässert / und die Farben hinzu gethan". – Ibid., 2 f.

4
Wille, Erfindung der Zeichenkunst, 1239.

5
Rubin begab sich im Oktober 1911 nach Göttingen, arbeitete wohl spätestens ab Mai 1912 am Problem der visuellen Wahrnehmung von Figuren und kehrte Ende 1913 nach Kopenhagen zurück, wo er seine Untersuchungen fortsetzte. Im August 1914 wurde er zum Militärdienst eingezogen und erhielt im März–April 1915 zwei Monate Dienstfreiheit, die er für die Fertigstellung seiner Dissertation verwendete, welche er Anfang Mai 1915 an der Universität Kopenhagen einreichte. – Cf. Pind, Jörgen L.: *Edgar Rubin and Psychology in Denmark. Figure and Ground*, Cham/Heidelberg/New York/Dordrecht/London 2014, 83 und 88–90, sowie Rubin, Edgar: *Visuell wahrgenommene Figuren. Studien in psychologischer Analyse*, 1. Teil (kein 2. Teil erschienen), København/Christiania/Berlin/London 1921, VII und XI f. Zur Frage der Datierung des ‚Rubinkelches' cf. auch Anm. 27.

6
Rubin, Edgar: *Synsoplevede Figurer. Studier i psykologisk Analyse. Første Del* (kein 2. Teil erschienen; = Diss. phil., Universität København), København/Kristiania 1915. Deutsche Ausgabe: Rubin, *Visuell wahrgenommene Figuren.*

Afbildn. 3.

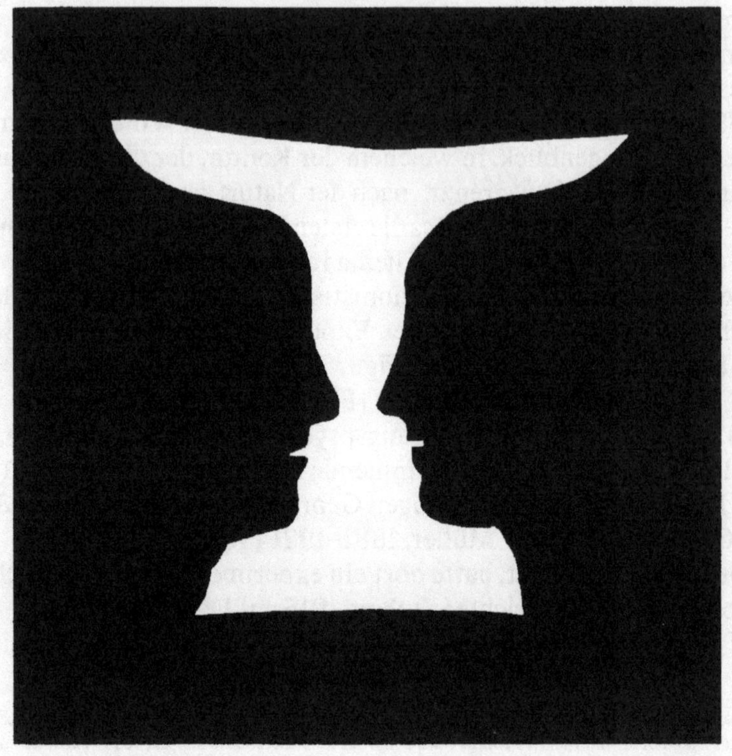

Edgar Rubin, [‚Rubinkelch'] zwischen 1912 und 1915, in: Edgar Rubin: *Synsoplevede Figurer. Studier i psykologisk Analyse,* Første Del, København/Kristiania 1915, Afbildn. 3.

Fig. 380

des Figur-Grund-Themas in der Wahrnehmungspsychologie.[7] Beim darin enthaltenen ‚Rubinkelch' sind Schwarz und Weiß auf den ersten Blick vertauscht: Schwarz ist nicht die Figur – also der Kelch –, sondern der Grund. Das Größenverhältnis zwischen Kelch und Grund ist so gewählt, dass das notwendige visuelle Gleichgewicht entsteht, welches die intendierte Figur-Grund-Umkehrung erst ermöglicht. Die mangelnde Symmetrie der Darstellung war kein Unvermögen, sondern offenkundig beabsichtigt. Da Rubin die Darstellung aus Karton ausschnitt, wäre es ihm ein Leichtes gewesen, mit Hilfe eines senkrechten Falzes eine exakt symmetrische Darstellung zu erhalten – die allerdings konstruiert und weniger lebendig gewirkt hätte. Er schuf eine Versuchsdarstellung, welche unserer alltäglichen Wahrnehmung, die üblicherweise oblique, nicht frontparallel orientiert ist, näher kommt als eine präzise konstruierte Figur. Paradoxerweise würde eine perfekte Symmetrie in vielen Fällen die Wahrnehmung der Gesichtsprofile in den Vordergrund drängen, während der dann weniger charaktervolle Kelch eher zum Grund tendierte. Rubin, der in seiner Dissertation damit kokettiert, dass er künstlerisch völlig unbegabt sei,[8] gelang es, eine geradezu ikonische Darstellung zu erschaffen, welche die verschiedenen Faktoren, die unsere Wahrnehmung mitbestimmen, gekonnt ausbalanciert. Die vielen Nachzeichnungen dieser scheinbar so einfachen Versuchsdarstellung lassen diese

7

„There are not many doctoral theses that have attained the status of classics in psychology. One such is Edgar Rubin's thesis *Synsoplevede Figurer, Visually Experienced Figures,* defended at the University of Copenhagen in 1915. In this book the figure-ground distinction, which still plays a highly important role in perceptual psychology, was first elucidated." Pind, *Edgar Rubin and Psychology in Denmark,* VII. Das Figur-Grund-Verhältnis war allerdings auch schon vor Rubins Untersuchungen im wahrnehmungspsychologischen Diskurs (und nicht nur dort) präsent. – Cf. Steinert, Tom: *Komplexe Wahrnehmung und moderner Städtebau. Paul Hofer, Bernhard Hoesli und ihre Konzeption der ‚dialogischen Stadt',* Zürich 2014, Anm. 4.70 f. auf 365–367. Rubin erwähnt zu Beginn seiner Dissertation (*Visuell wahrgenommene Figuren,* XII), dass ein Teil seiner Ergebnisse bereits 1914 veröffentlicht wurde: Rubin, E.[dgar]: Die visuelle Wahrnehmung von Figuren, in: Schumann, F.[riedrich] (Ed.): *Bericht über den VI. Kongreß für experimentelle Psychologie in Göttingen vom 15. bis 18. April 1914,* Leipzig 1914, 60–62. Es handelt sich um eine knappe Zusammenfassung der wichtigsten Ergebnisse von Rubins Forschungen zum Figur-Grund-Phänomen. Einen grundlegenden Überblick zum heutigen Forschungsstand geben Wagemans, Johan/Elder, James H./Kubovy, Michael/Palmer, Stephen E./Peterson, Mary A./Singh, Manish/Heydt, Rüdiger von der: A Century of Gestalt Psychology in Visual Perception, Teil 1: Perceptual Grouping and Figure–Ground Organization, in: *Psychological Bulletin* 138, 2012 (6), 1172–1217.

8

Cf. Rubin, *Visuell wahrgenommene Figuren,* Anm. 1 auf 7 f. sowie 189.

Punkte häufig außer acht, so dass ich noch keine Darstellung zu Gesicht bekommen habe, die der Beiläufigkeit und ästhetischen Überzeugungskraft des ursprünglichen ‚Rubinkelches' gleichkäme. Zu diesen wahrnehmungspsychologischen Faktoren tritt schließlich noch die Erfahrung, also unsere Kenntnis dieses populär gewordenen Vexierbilds, hinzu, welche unsere Wahrnehmung mitprägt. Nur selten dürfte noch die Verblüffung eintreten, die Rubin anhand seiner leicht jugendstilhaften Darstellung beschreibt:

> Wenn man die […] Figur, die einem etwas schiefen Pokal am nächsten kommt, einer Versuchsperson vorlegt, wird diese in der Regel sagen: „Es gibt nichts Merkwürdiges an der Figur." Auf die Aufforderung hin, das schwarze umschließende Feld als Figur aufzufassen, wird gewöhnlich, wenn dies gelingt, mit einem kleinen erstaunten Lächeln reagiert: „Es sind ja zwei Gesichter, die einander anblicken."[9]

Was Rubin hier beschreibt, ist eine Figur-Grund-Umkehrung, also die Vertauschung dessen, was als Figur und was als Grund gesehen wird.[10] Es wird deutlich, dass der ‚Rubinkelch' gewissermaßen als Verdoppelung des Gesichtsprofils, das für die *Erfindung der Kunst* so bedeutungsvoll war, entstand. Die gemeinsame Betrachtung von Daege 1832 und Rubin 1915 ist geeignet zu demonstrieren, dass Kunst und Wahrnehmungspsychologie sich bezüglich des Themas ‚Figur und Grund' auf vielfältige Weise gegenseitig beeinflusst haben – mit jeweils weit zurückreichenden Traditionslinien: von der Kunstwissenschaft,[11] der Kunst, Literatur und

9
Ibid., 32.

10
Die Schwierigkeit bei Rubins wahrnehmungspsychologisch verwendeter Darstellung – wie bei allen ähnlichen Vexierbildern – ist, beide Lesemöglichkeiten hinreichend gleichwertig zu gestalten, um den spontanen Wechsel der Wahrnehmung, also die Vertauschung von Figur und Grund, überhaupt zu ermöglichen. Der Kontur sollte bei beiden Lesemöglichkeiten annähernd gleiche Prägnanz haben. Der Objektcharakter weder des Kelches noch der Gesichtsprofile darf sich besonders in den Vordergrund drängen. Mit der genau ausbalancierten Gleichwertigkeit seines ‚Rubinkelches' berücksichtigte Rubin die wenige Jahre später formulierten Gestaltgesetze in ihrem Zusammenspiel wenn nicht bewusst, so doch mindestens intuitiv.

11
Versuche zur Übernahme wahrnehmungs- und gestaltpsychologischer Erkenntnisse in die Kunstwissenschaft erfolgten, mit unterschiedlicher Zielrichtung, unter anderem durch Hans Sedlmayr (1896–1984), Rudolf Arnheim (1904–2007) und Ernst H. Gombrich (1909–2001).

Philosophie[12] sowie der Gestaltpsychologie des 20. Jahrhunderts über die Wahrnehmungsexperimente vor und nach 1900[13] bis hin zum Klassizismus und der Goethezeit mit ihrer Vorliebe für Silhouetten und Scherenschnitte.[14] Daeges Gemälde lässt sich letztendlich auf zwei – wenn auch vage – Stellen in Plinius' *Naturalis historia* zurückführen,[15] während der populäre Grundsatz der Gestaltpsychologie ‚Das Ganze ist *mehr* (oder: etwas *anderes*) als die Summe seiner Teile' sich wiederum bei Aristoteles (384–322) vorweggenommen findet.[16] Die Verbindung zwischen der

12
Hier sind neben anderen Paul Klee (1879–1940), Josef Albers (1888–1976), Bridget Riley (geb. 1931) und der ganze Bereich der Op Art zu nennen. Doch wurde das Figur-Grund-Thema nicht nur in der bildenden Kunst aufgegriffen. Für ein Beispiel aus der Literatur cf. Steinert, Tom: Regaining Complex Perception. Gestalt Thinking in 20th Century Architectural Theory, in: *gestalt theory. An International Multidisciplinary Journal*, 2014 (4), 325–337: 325–327. Auf dem Gebiet der Philosophie ist Maurice Merleau-Ponty (1908–1961) zu erwähnen, dessen *Phénoménologie de la perception* mit Überlegungen zur Figur-Grund-Unterscheidung einsetzt. – Cf. Merleau-Ponty, M.[aurice]: *Phénoménologie de la perception*, [Paris] 1945, 9 f. Zuletzt erschien das Transkript eines 1981 von Gilles Deleuze (1925–1995) abgehaltenen Hochschulkurses, in welchem er wiederholt von ‚figure' bzw. ‚forme', ‚fond' und ‚contour' handelte: Lapoujade, David (Ed.), Deleuze, Gilles: *Sur la peinture. Cours mars–juin 1981*, Paris 2023. Cf. auch id.: *Francis Bacon. Logique de la sensation*, vol. 1, Paris 1981. Nicola Suthor danke ich für ihre Frage nach Merleau-Ponty.

13
Hier sind unter anderem die Arbeiten Friedrich Schumanns (1863–1940) zu nennen. Zu den vorbereitenden Schriften zählen beispielsweise Mach, E.[rnst]: *Beiträge zur Analyse der Empfindungen*, Jena 1886, und Ehrenfels, Chr.[istian] v.[on]: Ueber ‚Gestaltqualitäten', in: *Vierteljahrsschrift für wissenschaftliche Philosophie* 14, 1890 (3), 249–292. Cf. ferner Steinert, *Komplexe Wahrnehmung*, 192–199 sowie Anm. 4.54–4.97 auf 365–368 und Anm. 4.235 auf 380 f. Die Gestaltpsychologen legten gleichwohl Wert darauf, dass ein Unterschied zwischen ihrer neuen Theorie und Vorläufern wie Ehrenfels bestehe, denn „they all [die Vorläufer] left the traditional concepts intact". – Koffka, Kurt: Perception. An Introduction to the Gestalt-Theorie, in: *The Psychological Bulletin* 19, 1922 (10), 531–585: 536. Koffka schreibt weiter: „I must [...] warn the reader not to confound the old term of *Gestalt-Qualität* with the term *Gestalt* as it is employed in the new theory." – Ibid.

14
Diese Vorliebe geht nicht zuletzt auf Johann Caspar Lavaters (1741–1801) Physiognomik zurück. Die erste, reich mit Abbildungen versehene Ausgabe seiner *Physiognomischen Fragmente, zur Beförderung der Menschenkenntniß und Menschenliebe* erschien 1775–1778 in vier Bänden in Leipzig und Winterthur. Es folgten eine vierbändige niederländische (Amsterdam 1780–1783) und eine vierbändige französische Ausgabe (La Haye 1781–1786, vol. 4: 1803). Zwischen 1789 und 1798 konnte ich nicht weniger als drei jeweils mehrbändige, in London erschienene englische Übersetzungen ausmachen (1789, 1789–1798 und 1797). In diese Zeit fällt auch eine gekürzte amerikanische Ausgabe (Boston 1794). Zu Lavaters Wechselwirkung mit dem Weimar der Goethezeit cf. den Exkurs am Ende meines Beitrags (429–433).

15
Cf. Anm. 2.

16
Cf. Steinert, *Komplexe Wahrnehmung*, Anm. 4.52 auf 364 f. Zu den bis in die Antike zurückreichenden Bezügen des Gestaltbegriffs cf. ferner Gelb, Adhémar: Theoretisches über ‚Gestaltqualitäten' [= Diss. phil., Universität Berlin], in: *Zeitschrift für Psychologie* 58, 1910–1911 (1–2) (November 1910), 1–58: 4–7. Zu den unterschiedlichen Auffassungen ‚Das

Erfindung der Kunst und der Wahrnehmungspsychologie erscheint noch enger, wenn man bedenkt, dass griechisch ψῦχή auch als ‚Schattenbild' übersetzt werden kann, im Sinne der „Seele [...] in der Unterwelt, welche als Schattenbild die Gestalt des Körpers [...] behielt".[17] Dass die gegenseitige Beeinflussung von Kunst und Wahrnehmungspsychologie durchaus unbewusst geschehen kann, macht Rubin mit einer lapidaren Anmerkung deutlich, in der er zu seiner später berühmt gewordenen Darstellung bemerkt: „Ich habe einmal in einem Raritätenkabinett eine Vase gesehen,

Ganze ist *mehr* als die Summe seiner Teile' und ‚Das Ganze ist etwas *anderes* als die Summe seiner Teile' cf. zusammenfassend Wagemans et al., *A Century of Gestalt Psychology*, 1175, wobei man allerdings konzedieren darf, dass auch schon Christian von Ehrenfels (1859–1932) in seinem grundlegenden Aufsatz die zweite Lesart – etwas *anderes* – nicht etwa ausschließt, wenn er „jene ‚Gestalten' nicht als blosse Zusammenfassung von Elementen, sondern als etwas (den Elementen gegenüber, auf denen sie beruhen,) Neues und bis zu gewissem Grade Selbständiges" beschreibt. – Ehrenfels, Ueber ‚Gestaltqualitäten', 250. Wenn es über den Gestaltpsychologen Wolfgang Köhler (1887–1967) heißt, er habe „noch 1920 gesagt, daß die untersuchten physischen Systeme ‚mehr' sein müßten als die Summe ihrer Teile; er modifiziert diese These später mit dem Hinweis auf die ‚Andersartigkeit' der Wahrnehmungsgestalten, die unabhängig vom Material transponierbar sind und Eigenschaften haben, die den einzelnen Teilen nicht zukommen" (Bergius, Rudolf: Stichwort „Köhler, Wolfgang", in: Historische Kommission bei der Bayerischen Akademie der Wissenschaften (Ed.): *Neue Deutsche Biographie*, vol. 12, Berlin 1980, 302–304: 303), dann klingt hier Ehrenfels' ‚Selbständigkeit' der Gestalt gegenüber ihren ‚Elementen' durch. Köhlers spätere Positionsnahme erscheint folglich weniger als Konfrontation denn als Weiterentwicklung und Präzisierung Ehrenfels' im Rahmen des wissenschaftlichen Diskurses. Im Übrigen spricht bereits Aristoteles davon, dass das Ganze „etwas anderes" (ἕτερόν) sei. – Cf. Steinert, *Komplexe Wahrnehmung*, Anm. 4.52 auf 364 f., dazu ferner den griechischen Text: Schwegler, Albert [Ed.]: *Die Metaphysik des Aristoteles. Grundtext, Übersetzung und Commentar nebst erläuternden Abhandlungen*, vol. 1: *Grundtext und kritischer Apparat*, Tübingen 1847, 170 f. (liber VII, caput 17, § 19/1041 b).

17 Clausing, A.[dolf]/Eckstein, F.[ranz]/Haas, H.[ans]/Schroff, H.[elmut]/Wohleb, L.[eo] (Neubearb.), Kaegi, Adolf (Bearb.): *Benselers Griechisch-Deutsches Schulwörterbuch*, Leipzig/Berlin [15]1931, 862. Die Erläuterungen zu diesem Thema werden umso ausführlicher, je weiter man in den lexikographischen Werken zurückgeht. 1886 vermerkt der *Benseler* unter dem Lemma ψῦχή unter anderem: „die durch den Tod vom Leibe getrennte Seele, Seele der Abgeschiedenen in der Unterwelt, der Geist, welcher zwar körperlos war, aber doch als Schattenbild oder Schemen die Gestalt des Körpers an sich behielt". – Autenrieth, Georg (Bearb.), Benseler, Gustav Eduard: *Griechisch-Deutsches Schul-Wörterbuch [...]*, Leipzig [8]1886, 902. Als philologisch erschöpfend erscheint der Vorläufer des *Benseler*, welcher mit zahlreichen Quellenhinweisen und avant la lettre ideengeschichtlich den Bedeutungswandel miterzählt. Dort heißt es: „Wenn aber der Lebenshauch den Menschen verlassen hat, so zerfällt der Leib, die Person hört auf zu existiren, das geistige Wesen [...] hört auf zu seyn [...], nur jener Lebenshauch dauert als Schattenbild ohne Fleisch und Bein, selbst ohne Bewusstseyn [...] im Hades fort, doch ähnlich an Gestalt dem Lebenden". – Lemma ψυχή, in: Rost, Val.[entin] Chr.[istian] Fr.[iedrich]/Palm, F.[riedrich]/Kreussler, O.[tto]/Keil, K.[arl]/Peter, Ferd.[inand]/Benseler, G.[ustav] E.[duard] (Bearbb.), Passow, Franz: *Handwörterbuch der griechischen Sprache*, vol. 2 · 2, Leipzig [5]1857, 2587–2590: 2588. Hier begegnen sich altgriechische ψῦχή und die Schattenrisse und Vexierbilder der Neuzeit fast unmittelbar.

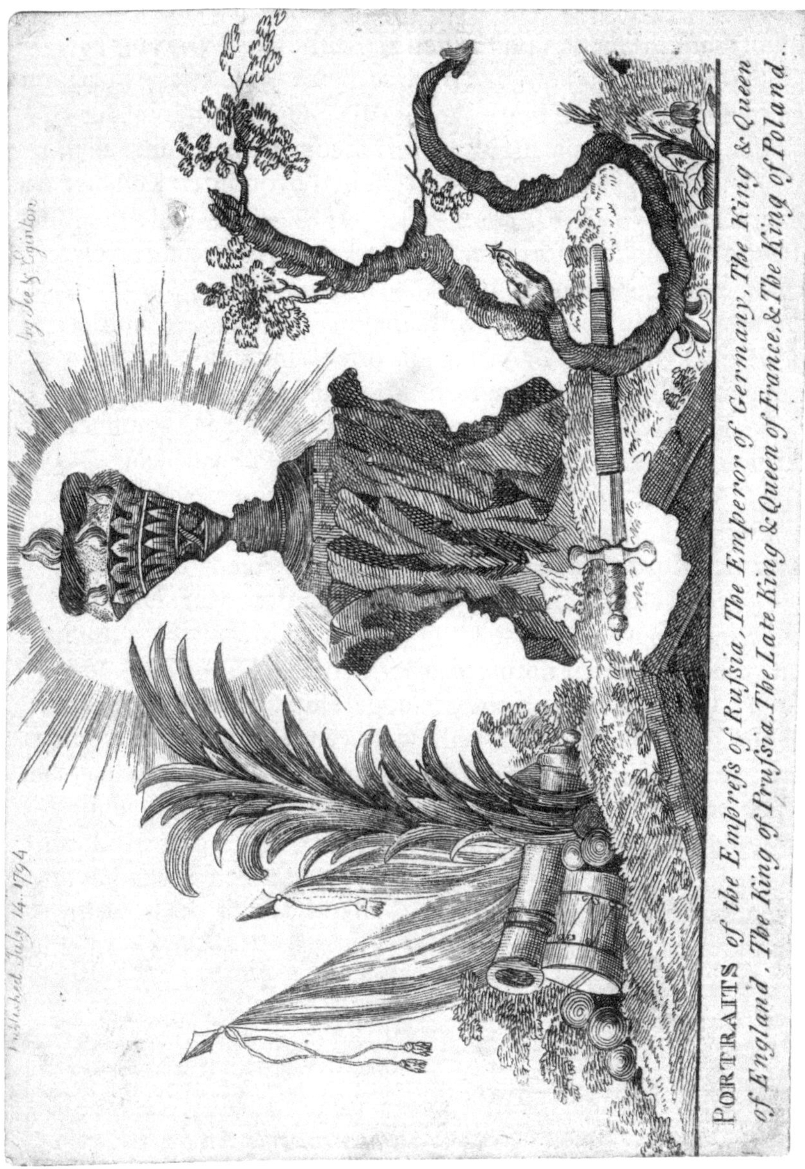

Anonym (verlegt bei [Edward] Jee und [John] Eginton, [Birmingham]),
Portraits of the Empress of Russia, The Emperor of Germany, The King & Queen of England, The King of Prussia, The Late King & Queen of France, & The King of Poland. Published July 14.th. 1794 by Jee & Eginton, 1794, Radierung, 10.9 × 15.1 cm.
British Museum, inv. 1856,0712.1126, London.

Fig. 385

wo eben von diesem Witz Anwendung gemacht worden war."[18] En passant räumt er damit gleich zu Beginn der Wirkungsgeschichte des ‚Rubinkelches' ein, dass dieser – wie stets – Vorläufer hatte, und macht uns bewusst, dass die enge Verbindung der beiden Sphären zunächst als Übertragung von der Kunst auf die Wahrnehmungspsychologie stattfand,[19] bevor durch Künstler wie Paul Klee (1879–1940), Josef Albers (1888–1976) und schließlich die Op Art ein Ideentransfer in umgekehrter Richtung erfolgte. Um diese Feststellung zu untermauern, möchte ich zu Rubins Darstellung einige wenige Vorläufer aus einer ganzen Abfolge erwähnen, die ihren Ursprung alle offenkundig in den Nachwirkungen der Französischen Revolution hatten.

Einer der frühesten Drucke, die ich in diesem Zusammenhang ausfindig machen konnte, trägt die Adresse „Published July 14.th. 1794 by Jee & Eginton",[20] ist also ein politisch-emblematisches Vexierbild anlässlich des fünften Jahrestages des Sturms auf die Bastille [Fig. 385]. Auf dem Blatt sind acht sogenannte *puzzle portraits* versteckt, allesamt gekrönte Häupter. Man darf daher annehmen, dass die Darstellung von einem Royalisten stammt und die Silhouetten Katharinas der Großen (1729–1796) und Franz' II (1768–1835) nicht von ungefähr von einer Korona umgeben sind. An dieser Darstellung ist vergleichsweise deutlich zu erleben, wie der Fels und der darauf stehende Pokal auf den ersten Blick ‚vorne' zu sein scheinen, *vor* dem weißen Hintergrund. Wenn die Wahrnehmung kippt und man die Gesichtsprofile als Figur wahrnimmt, treten Fels und Pokal deutlich in den Hintergrund, während man nun die Gesichtsprofile als ‚vorne' wahrnimmt. Das geht so weit, dass Fels und Pokal als Ausschnitt eines

18
Rubin, *Visuell wahrgenommene Figuren*, Anm. 1 auf 32.

19
Rubin rekurriert in seiner Dissertation immer wieder einmal auf künstlerische Aspekte des Figur-Grund-Themas, einzelne Vorbilder in der Kunstgeschichte und die entsprechende Fachliteratur. So verweist er passim beispielsweise auf Alois Riegl (1858–1905, cf. ibid., 34) und Adolf von Hildebrand (1847–1921, cf. 186) und stellt Überlegungen zum künstlerischen Schaffensprozess und zum Zeichenunterricht an (cf. 176–189 *(Zweiter Abschnitt, § 12 Zeichenversuche)*, insb. 186–189), nicht ohne wiederholt seine eigene vollkommene künstlerische Unbeholfenheit zu konstatieren (wie Anm. 8). Riegl hatte 1892 Bordüren beschrieben, die sich durch eine Figur-Grund-Umkehrbarkeit bei völliger Kongruenz der beiden Teilfelder („reciproke Muster") auszeichnen. – Cf. Riegl, Alois: Spanische Aufnäharbeiten, in: *Zeitschrift des bayerischen Kunst-Gewerbe-Vereins in München*, 1892 (11–12), 65–73 sowie Taf. 34.

20
Cf. Fig. 385. Edward Jee (fl. 1792–1799), John Eginton (fl. 1775–1804), beide Birmingham.

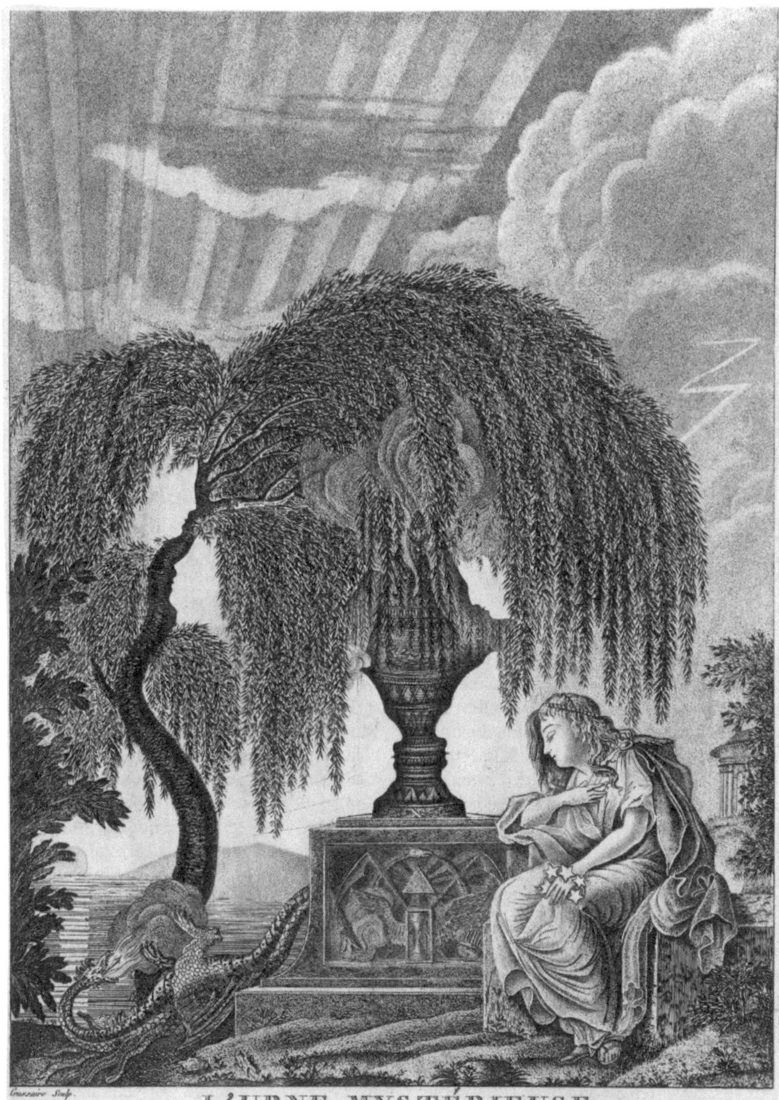

François-Joseph Crussaire, *L'urne mystérieuse,* zweiter Zustand, wohl nicht vor 1814,
Punktierstich, 23.6 × 15.4 cm.
Metropolitan Museum of Art, inv. 56.558.56, New York.

Fig. 387

sich seitlich weiter fortsetzenden, von den Gesichtsprofilen lediglich verdeckten Hintergrundes erscheinen. Diese Wahrnehmung wird dadurch befördert, dass die Formen von Fels und Pokal weniger prägnant sind als die der Gesichtsprofile, wenn man Letztere erst einmal gesehen hat.

Diese Art der Darstellung verfestigte sich innerhalb kurzer Zeit zum weitverbreiteten Topos, wofür ich exemplarisch das klassisch zu nennende Blatt François-Joseph Crussaires (1759–1831) anführen möchte [Fig. 387].[21] Erneut begegnet uns die strahlende Sonne als Sinnbild der Monarchie bzw. ihrer erhofften Wiederkehr, aus dem Pokal ist eine Urne geworden, und eine Trauerweide ist hinzugekommen. Zum besseren Auffinden sind die fünf Silhouetten, welche das französische Königshaus repräsentieren, in der Bildlegende angegeben. Die Profile Ludwigs XVI (1754–1793) und Marie Antoinettes (1755–1793) formen den Kontur im unteren Teil der Urne. Beide waren 1793 guillotiniert worden. Ein Londoner Druck von 1793 zum selben Thema zeigt

21
Die Darstellung trägt den bekanntgewordenen Titel *L'urne mystérieuse* sowie die Namensangabe „Crussaire Sculp.[sit]". Es ist davon auszugehen, dass es sich hierbei um die ursprüngliche Fassung der vielfach kopierten Motivkombination von Urne, Trauerweide und allegorischer Figur handelt, die ab 1794 oder 1795 in einem ersten Zustand avant la lettre verbreitet wurde. Über Crussaire wird berichtet, dass ihm der royalistische Gehalt des anonymen Blattes im August 1795 eine entsprechende Denunziation und polizeiliche Verfolgung eingebracht habe. – Cf. Guelliot, O.[ctave]: Joseph Crussaire. Dessinateur et Graveur, in: *Nouvelle revue de Champagne et de Brie*, 1924 [2–3] (März–Juni), 71–81: 74 f. Der dort (76) berichtete Zustand avant la lettre hat mir bislang nicht vorgelegen. Guelliots Fazit zu Crussaires Blatt lautet: „[Au Cabinet des Estampes] on y peut voir, dans les cinq volumes des portraits de Louis XVI, des quantités de variations ou d'imitations […] La plupart sont anonymes, et pour cause; quelques-unes sont peut-être de Crussaire. En tout cas, celuici est l'initiateur de ce genre de dessin" (ibid.). Zumindest mit Blick auf Frankreich und auf die ‚klassische' Durcharbeitung des Motivs scheint Crussaire tatsächlich der Primat zuzustehen; der Erfinder der hier behandelten Figur-Grund-Umkehrung war er jedoch nicht. Der in Fig. 387 wiedergegebene Zustand mit Namensangabe, Bildtitel und Bildlegende stammt vermutlich aus der Zeit der Restauration, dürfte also nicht vor 1814 datieren. Die Collection Hennin kennt neben Crussaires mit Bildlegende versehenem Original zumindest eine Kopie. – Cf. [Bibliothèque Nationale, Département des estampes (Ed.)], Duplessis, Georges: *Inventaire de la collection d'estampes relatives à l'histoire de France léguée en 1863 à la Bibliothèque Nationale par M. Michel Hennin*, vol. 4, Paris 1882, Katalognr. 11974 und 11975 (148 f.); der Künstler wird dort und im Registerband (vol. 5, Paris 1884, 181) als „Gussaire" angegeben. Die Adresse von Crussaires Blatt in der Collection Hennin (Katalognr. 11974) lautet: „à Paris Chez JAGOT, Successeur de Pasquier, place de Cambray, N.[umer]o 4. Présentement A [?] Paris chez Lenoir et Pillot, rue S.[ain]t Jacques N.[umer]o 6" (der zweite Teil der Adresse ist auf dem Exemplar im Metropolitan Museum of Art, New York, Inventarnr. 56.558.56, noch nicht vorhanden, cf. Fig. 387). Zur Person Crussaires, über die nur wenige gesicherte Daten bekannt und entsprechend viele irreführende Annahmen in Umlauf sind, cf. Anm. 27.

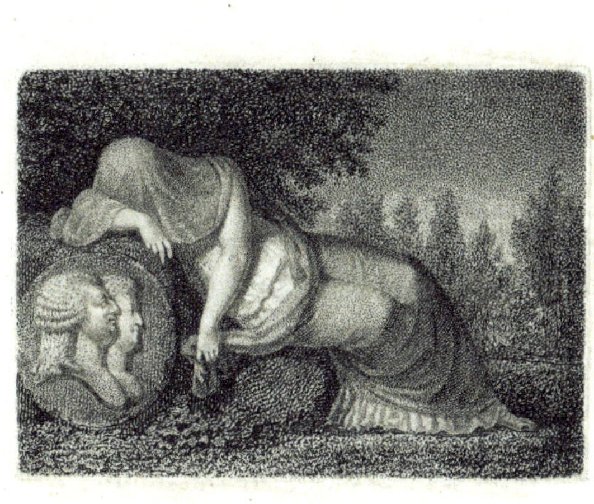

Anonym (Schule Francesco Bartolozzis, verlegt bei P. Molinari, London), *Mnemosina the Goddess of Memory […] London Pub.[lishe]d as the Act directs, October 30th 1793. by P. Molinari N.[umer]o 43. Rupert Street, Hay Market*, 1793, Punktierstich, 6.4 × 9.2 cm (Bild), 20.0 × 15.1 cm (Blatt), Bild und Text von verschiedenen Platten gedruckt. British Museum, inv. 2006,U.1817, London.

Fig. 389

dabei noch keinen Ansatz zu einer solchen emblematisch kanonisierten Darstellungsweise als Vexierbild [Fig. 389]. Die zugehörige Bildinschrift kann gleichwohl stellvertretend auch für die Darstellungen mit Urne und Trauerweide stehen:

> Mnemosina the Goddess of Memory | Weeping for the unfortunate Louis XVI King of France, | & Marie Antoinette Archdutchess of Austria his Spouse, | executed at Paris upon the Place Louis XV, | by Order of their own Subjects. | Louis XVI. the 21st of January, Marie Antoinette the 16th of October.[22]

Als Publikationsdatum ist der 30. Oktober 1793 angegeben. Das Blatt entstand also gerade einmal zwei Wochen nach der Hinrichtung Marie Antoinettes. Innerhalb weniger Monate, spätestens im Januar 1794, kam es dann zur Darstellung der königlichen Gesichtsprofile in Form der erwähnten Vexierbilder. Das British Museum verwahrt ein Londoner Blatt mit zwei derartigen Darstellungen [Fig. 391], dessen Inschrift lautet:

> A New Puzzle of Portraits, | Inv.[en]t[ed,] Pub.[lished] & Sold by Orme, | N.[umer]o 14. Old Bond S.[tree]t Jan.[uar]y 18. 1794. | Striking Likenesses | of the King & Queen of England, | and the late unfortunate King & Queen of France.[23]

Daniel Orme (1766–1837) war damit vielleicht der Erfinder dieses Typus einer Figur-Grund-Umkehrung. Dafür spricht auch die etwas ungelenke Form des Pokals, der noch nicht zu seiner ‚klassischen' Figurqualität gefunden hat.[24] Der Ursprung des

22
Cf. Fig. 389. Die Darstellung wurde parallel auch mit italienischem und mit französischem Text gedruckt (beide ebenfalls datiert London, 30. Oktober 1793).

23
Cf. Fig. 391.

24
Ob es dem ‚Rubinkelch' vergleichbare mehrdeutig lesbare Figur-Grund-Darstellungen beispielsweise schon auf griechischer Keramik gegeben hat, entzieht sich meiner Kenntnis. Für eine Erfindung durch Orme spricht weiterhin, dass der Pokal hier noch mit dem britischen Königspaar assoziiert ist, während die Silhouetten des französischen Königspaares aus zwei Schlangen gebildet werden. In späteren Drucken wurde der Pokal dann zur Urne und damit sinnfällig mit dem untergegangenen französischen Königspaar assoziiert. Es erscheint umso naheliegender, dass dieser Typus einer Figur-Grund-Umkehrung im Umfeld

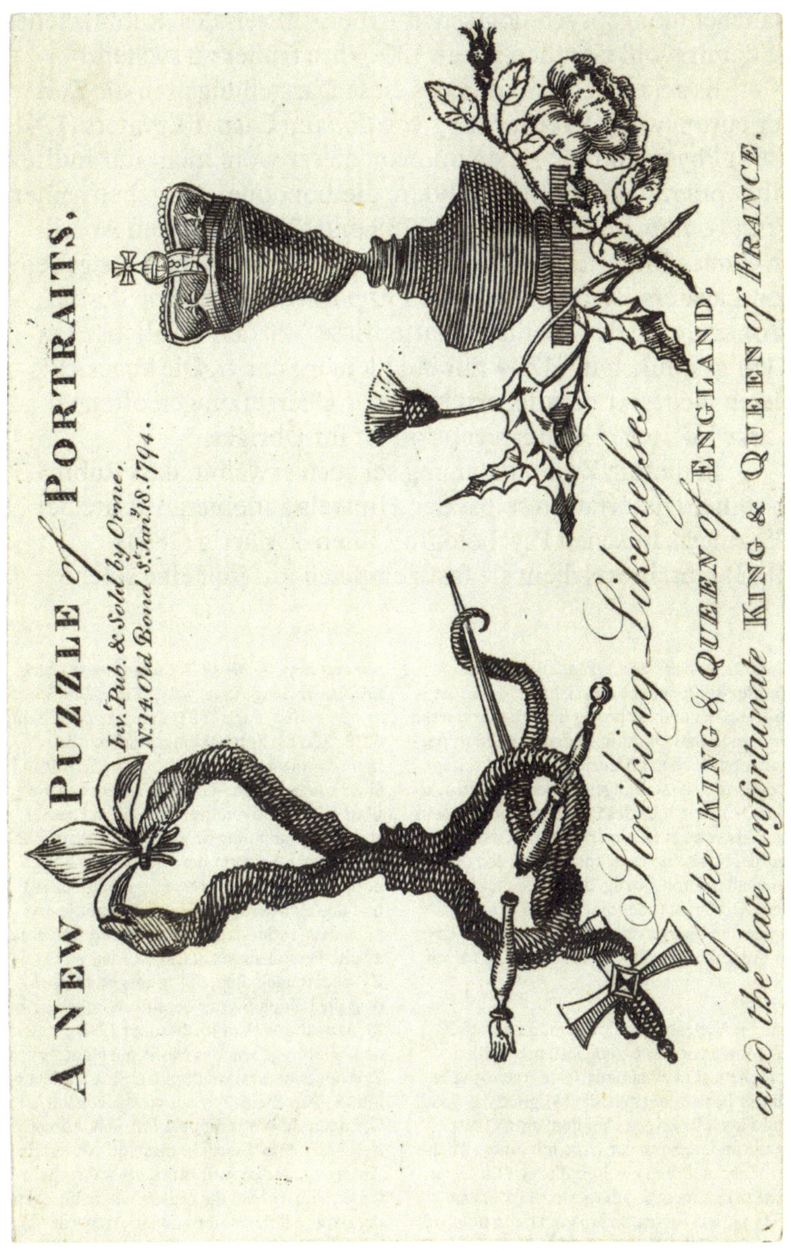

Daniel Orme, *A New Puzzle of Portraits,* | *Inv.[en]t[ed,] Pub.[lished] & Sold by Orme,* | *N.[umer]o 14. Old Bond S.[tree]t Jan.[uar]y 18. 1794.* | *Striking Likenesses* | *of the King & Queen of England,* | *and the late unfortunate King & Queen of France*, 1794, Radierung, 7.9 × 12.1 cm. British Museum, inv. J,11.126, London.

Fig. 391

wahrnehmungspsychologischen Arbeitsmittels des ‚Rubinkelches' ist damit wohl ziemlich genau 120 Jahre früher zu suchen.[25]

Es sei noch erwähnt, dass diese Darstellungen in die Zeit der europaweiten Verbreitung von Johann Caspar Lavaters (1741–1801) Physiognomik fallen und von dieser wohl nicht nur indirekt mitgeprägt wurden. Insbesondere die Londoner Ausgaben seiner *Essays on Physiognomy,* die ab 1789 erschienen, dürften Anteil an Ormes Bilderfindung haben.[26] Mit den zahlreichen Ausgaben von Lavaters *Physiognomischen Fragmenten* war es von dessen Propagierung des Profils (Schattenrisses) zu den royalistischen Kleingraphiken um 1794 nur ein kleiner Schritt. Die angesichts gleich mehrerer parallel erschienener Übersetzungen offenbar starke britische Lavaterrezeption tat ihr Übriges.

In diesem Zusammenhang sei auch erwähnt, dass Rubin in seiner Dissertation selbst den Hinweis auf einen Aufsatz der US-amerikanischen Psychologin Lillien J. Martin (1851–1943) gibt, in welchem sie fast zeitgleich mit ihm eine solche

einer Druckwerkstatt erfunden worden sein könnte, wenn man berücksichtigt, dass dort von der Originalzeichnung über das Gravieren der Druckplatte bis zum gedruckten Blatt permanent zwischen seitenrichtigen und seitenverkehrten Darstellungen gewechselt wird, so dass Orme die Idee des Pokals gekommen sein mag, als er zwei entgegengesetzte Gesichtsprofile, etwa eine Druckplatte und den davon gemachten Probeabzug, dicht nebeneinanderlegte. Ob Orme (oder einer seiner jüngeren Brüder) in die Herstellung der Londoner Lavater-Ausgaben involviert war, bleibt zu klären.

25
Aus der Vielzahl von Drucken, die um 1800 das Motiv von Urne und Gesichtsprofilen bemühen, sind zwei undatierte französische Blätter hervorzuheben, die lediglich das Profil Ludwigs XVI zeigen. Auf dem einen Blatt ist die andere Seite der Urne mit einem Tuch verhängt, auf dem zweiten Blatt ist die Urne nahezu symmetrisch dargestellt, indem sie offenbar auf *beiden* Seiten vom Gesichtsprofil Ludwigs XVI geformt wird (drei weitere Profile sind in den benachbarten Trauerweiden versteckt). – Cf. Bibliothèque Nationale, Département des estampes (Ed.), Aubert, Marcel/ Roux, Marcel: *Un siècle d'histoire de France par l'estampe 1770–1871. Collection de Vinck. Inventaire analytique*, vol. 3: *La législative et la convention*, Paris 1921, Katalognr. 5222 und 5219 (305 f.). Entwicklungsgeschichtlich hätte es eine gewisse Logik, wenn der Einfall einer solchen Figur-Grund-Umkehrung vom Blatt mit der linksseitig verhängten Urne stammte (Sammlung de Vinck, Katalognr. 5222), im nächsten Schritt eine symmetrische Verdoppelung erfahren hätte (Katalognr. 5219) und das eine der beiden Gesichtsprofile erst nach dem Tode Marie Antoinettes gegen eine zweite Person ausgetauscht worden wäre. Es scheint auch nicht völlig ausgeschlossen, dass die beiden Blätter bereits zwischen dem 21. Januar und dem 16. Oktober 1793 entstanden, allerdings war das Motiv auch noch zur Zeit der Restauration populär. Eine Datierung um 1815 erscheint mir aus verschiedenen Gründen (Motiv, Komposition, Stil, Adresse, Zeitgeschichte, Erscheinungsland), deren Erläuterung hier zu weit führt, als wahrscheinlicher, selbst wenn die Museumssammlungen derartige Blätter, sofern undatiert, gerne pauschal auf den Zeitraum zwischen 1793 und 1800 festlegen.

26
Cf. Anm. 14.

Darstellung der französischen Königsfamilie verwendet hatte. Die Veröffentlichung erfolgte allerdings erst kurz *nach* Rubins Wahrnehmungsexperimenten.[27] Wie populär derartige Vexierbilder

27 Die deutsche Fassung von Martins Aufsatz erschien im November 1914, die englischsprachige Originalfassung scheint unveröffentlicht geblieben zu sein. – Cf. Rubin, *Visuell wahrgenommene Figuren*, Anm. 1 auf 32, sowie Martin, Lillien J.: Über die Abhängigkeit visueller Vorstellungsbilder vom Denken. Eine experimentelle Untersuchung, in: *Zeitschrift für Psychologie* 70, 1914–1915 (3–4) (November 1914), 212–275: Taf. A auf 214. Als Abbildungsquelle gibt Martin lediglich an: „Porträts von König Ludwig XVI von Frankreich und seiner Familie (in einer Sammlung alter Kupferstiche, im Besitz von Prof. FRANK ANGELL, Stanford-University)." – Ibid., Anm. 3 auf 213. Über Müllers psychologisches Institut an der Universität Göttingen, an dem Martin sich von 1894 bis 1898 aufgehalten hatte, ist zudem eine mittelbare Verbindung zwischen Martin und Rubin gegeben. Der Psychologe Angell (1857–1939) wiederum hatte seinen Doktorgrad 1891 bei Wilhelm Wundt (1832–1920) in Leipzig erworben. 1892–1922 lehrte er in Stanford. Möglicherweise hatte Rubin die Idee zum ‚Rubinkelch', mit welchem er sich einen Platz im kollektiven Bildgedächtnis sicherte, trotzdem genau jenem Aufsatz Martins zu verdanken. Auf diesen Gedanken kann man kommen, wenn es heißt: „In fact, Rubin carried out almost all his experimental work with an alternating Maltese cross figure rather than the vase/faces motif with which he is most closely associated; the latter was presented at the conclusion of his thesis almost as an afterthought." – Piccolino, Marco/Wade, Nicholas J.: Flagging Early Examples of Ambiguity I. Guest Editorial Essay, in: *Perception* 35, 2006 (7), 861–864: 861. Tatsächlich habe ich in Rubins Dissertation keinen eindeutigen Hinweis darauf gefunden, dass er den dort als eine von mehreren Darstellungen zur Untersuchung des Figur-Grund-Phänomens abgebildeten ‚Rubinkelch' bereits während seiner zweijährigen Arbeit in Göttingen verwendete. Somit erscheint es möglich, dass Rubin diesen erst zwischen dem Erscheinen von Martins Aufsatz (November 1914) und dem Abschluss seines Manuskripts (Vorwort datiert Mai 1915) angefertigt und dann nachträglich einzelnen Versuchspersonen vorgelegt hat (cf. auch Anm. 5). Pind zeigt in seinem Buch zwar ein Foto des originalen ‚Rubinkelches', trägt zur Frage nach der Genealogie aber nichts Stichhaltiges bei. – Cf. Pind, *Edgar Rubin and Psychology in Denmark*, Fig. 7.6 auf 215. Bei der Abbildung in Martins Aufsatz handelt es sich offenbar um eine Umzeichnung des Blattes, das wohl als Vexierbild in der Kuriositätensammlung ihres Arbeitskollegen seinen Platz hatte. Die offenkundige Vorlage dieser (spiegelverkehrten) Darstellung ist beispielsweise reproduziert in Tapié, Alain/Zwingenberger, Jeanette (Ed.): *L'homme-paysage. Visions artistiques du paysage anthropomorphe entre le XVIe et le XXIe siècle* (Katalog zur Ausstellung im Palais des Beaux-Arts, Lille), Paris 2006, 24. Neben dieser ist eine einem gewissen Pierre Crussaire zugeschriebene, undatierte Variante der *Urne mystérieuse* (cf. Fig. 387) abgebildet (hier als *Saule pleureur*). Das *AKL* weiß zu François-Joseph Crussaire, den es mit Pierre Crussaire für identisch hält, zu berichten: „Während der Frz. Revolution als königstreu verfolgt (*L'Urne mystérieuse,* Rad.[ierung] mit royalist. Symbolik, sign., dat. 1794, Paris, BN, Dép. des Estampes, Coll. Hennin)." – T.[reydel], R.[enate]: Stichwort „Crussaire, François-Joseph", in: Meißner, Günter (Ed.): *Allgemeines Künstler-Lexikon. Die Bildenden Künstler aller Zeiten und Völker (AKL)*, vol. 22, München/Leipzig 1999, 481 f. In einem anderen biographischen Artikel, auf den sich das *AKL* bezieht, heißt es: „Il grava en différentes grandeurs le *Tableau des droits de l'homme* (1793), bien que de sentiments royalistes puisqu'il exécuta sous l'anonymat, à la même époque, *L'urne mystérieuse,* eau-forte séditieuse qui lui valut d'être recherché par le Comité de sûreté générale en 1795." – Jacquet, M.: Stichwort „Crussaire (François-Joseph)", in: d'Amat, Roman (Ed.): *Dictionnaire de biographie française*, vol. 9, Paris 1961, Sp. 1326. Dort wird auch sein älterer Bruder Martin-Pierre Crussaire (1755–1830), ein Anwalt und Schriftsteller, erwähnt. In einem vergleichsweise ausführlichen Aufsatz über François-Joseph Crussaire, der auch ein Werkverzeichnis enthält, heißt es im Abschnitt „L'affaire de l'urne mystérieuse": „Dans la séance du 18 Thermidor, An III (5 août 1793), tenue par

während mehrerer Jahrzehnte gewesen sein müssen, lässt sich unter anderem daran ermessen, dass nach dem Tode Napoleon Bonapartes (1769–1821) wiederum Darstellungen aufkamen, in welchen sein ‚Geist' in Ganzfigur zwischen den Stämmen zweier Trauerweiden an seinem Grab erscheint.[28]

Gestaltgesetze, Gestaltphänomene

Bevor ich exemplarisch darauf eingehen werde, wie sich das Thema ‚Figur und Grund' in der kunstwissenschaftlichen Literatur niedergeschlagen hat, möchte ich das Figur-Grund-Phänomen in das System der Gestaltpsychologie einordnen. Dafür greife ich auf die von David Katz[29] (1884–1953) vorgetragene Einteilung

la Convention, lecture est donnée d'une lettre émanant de la région lyonnaise et dénonçant une composition apparemment innocente mais dont le fond blanc sur lequel se détache un cénotaphe recouvert par les branches d'un arbrisseau, est dessiné de telle sorte qu'on y voit représentées les figures de la famille royale. [...] Saisi du document, le Comité de Sûreté générale alerta la police qui fut chargée de s'assurer de la réalité du fait par une visite domiciliaire chez Crussaire." – Marchal, Jean: Un graveur-dessinateur méconnu. François-Joseph Crussaire (1759–18...), in: *Études ardennaises* 44, 1966, 23–36: 25. Diese Information widerspricht meiner These bezüglich Ormes Primat nur scheinbar, da bei korrekter Umrechnung der Datumsangabe der 5. August 1795 gemeint ist. (Der französische Revolutionskalender war 1792–1805 in Kraft.) Zur in der Literatur durchaus ungewissen Datierung von Crussaires Todesjahr sei bemerkt, dass die *Biographie générale des Champenois célèbres, morts et vivants* ihn noch 1836 ausdrücklich als „Vivant." verzeichnet, während die Archives nationales einen *inventaire après décès* von 1831 verwahren. – Cf. Stichwort „Crussaire (François-Joseph)", in: [Letillois de Mézières]: *Biographie générale des Champenois célèbres, morts et vivants. Précédée des Illustres Champenois, poème lyrique, et enrichie de plusieurs tables chronologiques, très précieuses, pour l'intelligence de l'histoire artistique, littéraire et contemporaine de la Champagne*, Paris 1836, 44, und den Listeneintrag auf 222, sowie Godot, Ambroise Charles: *Inventaire après décès de François Joseph Crussaire, peintre, demeurant rue Servandoni, n° 10, décédé le 3 avril 1831*, 18. Mai 1831, Archives nationales, Paris, Signatur MC/RE/LXXXIV/14. Der allen Ungenauigkeiten zum Trotz stichhaltigste Beitrag über Crussaire, aus dem alle späteren ihre Informationen bezogen, ist der von Octave Guelliot verfasste (cf. Anm. 21).

28
Für drei Beispiele cf. Bibliothèque Nationale, Département des estampes (Ed.), Rosset, Anne-Marie: *Un siècle d'histoire de France par l'estampe 1770–1871. Collection de Vinck. Inventaire analytique*, vol. 5: *La Restauration et les Cent-Jours*, Paris 1938, Katalognr. 10381–10383 (451). Die Drucke tragen Titel wie *L'Ombre de Napoléon visitant son tombeau.* Zu diesem Genre unmittelbar passend die altgriechische Vorstellung der ψυχή (cf. Anm. 17), cf. insb. auch Katalognr. 10383.

29
Katz war von 1907 bis 1919, mit Unterbrechung durch den Kriegsdienst, Assistent bei Müller in Göttingen. 1919 wurde er nach Rostock berufen. „Hier entwickelte sich unter seiner Leitung eine der fruchtbarsten deutschen psychologischen Forschungsstätten. Durch seinen regen Austausch mit W.[illiam] Stern, Rubin und der Berliner Gestaltpsychologie schuf K.[atz] eine wissenschaftlich vielseitige, aufgeschlossene Arbeitsatmosphäre." – Arnold, Wilhelm: Stichwort „Katz, David", in: Historische Kommission bei der Bayerischen Akademie der Wissenschaften (Ed.): *Neue Deutsche Biographie*, vol. 11, Berlin 1977, 332 f.: 333.

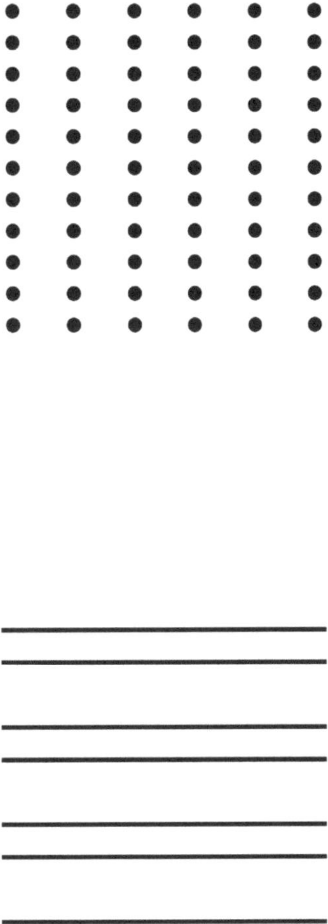

Gesetz der Nähe,
diese und die folgenden Zeichnungen: Tom Steinert.

Fig. 395

zurück.[30] Vorab sei bemerkt, dass die Gestaltpsychologie keineswegs auf die Wahrnehmungspsychologie und darin auf die visuelle Wahrnehmung beschränkt ist. Beispielsweise gibt schon Christian von Ehrenfels (1859–1932) 1890 den ‚klassischen' Beweis für das Vorhandensein von Gestaltqualitäten anhand der Klangwahrnehmung von Melodien.[31] Außer mit sinnlich wahrgenommenen Gestalten hat die Gestaltpsychologie sich auch mit sogenannten Denkgestalten, Handlungsgestalten und Gefühlsgestalten auseinandergesetzt.[32] Gleichwohl ist die visuelle Wahrnehmung ein Bereich, mit dem sich die Gestaltpsychologie in besonderem Umfang beschäftigt hat.[33]

Katz beschreibt Gestaltgesetze sowie Gestaltphänomene, welche auf den Gestaltgesetzen aufbauen. Ausgangspunkt für deren Erläuterung ist die Dingkonstitution, also die Frage, warum sich bestimmte Bereiche, die wir innerhalb des Gesichtsfeldes wahrnehmen, zu diskreten Einheiten zusammenschließen, die wir als eigenständige Objekte sehen. Warum zum Beispiel können wir im Wald einzelne Bäume erkennen und sehen nicht nur ein großes, zusammenhängendes Gebilde? Warum nehmen wir verstreute Papiere, die teilweise übereinanderliegen, nicht als eine kompliziert umrissene Fläche wahr, sondern jedes Blatt als regelmäßig geformte Einheit für sich, auch wenn es teilweise von einem anderen verdeckt wird?

Die Gestaltpsychologie hat festgestellt, dass bestimmte Faktoren dazu beitragen, dass einzelne Sinneseindrücke beispielsweise im Gesichtsfeld oder beim Hören sich in der Wahrnehmung zu einer Einheit zusammenschließen. Zumeist wurden diese

1933 emigrierte er dann zunächst nach Großbritannien. Katz zählte nicht zum Kern der Gestaltschule. Seine Position macht er 1944 im Vorwort zu *Gestaltpsychologie* deutlich: „Meine Beziehungen zur Gestaltpsychologie sind alt [...] So nahe ich auch in vielen Punkten, ja ich möchte sagen in den meisten den Gestaltpsychologen stehe, so stimme ich doch nicht in jeder Beziehung mit ihnen überein. Ich glaube nicht, daß sich alle psychischen Tatsachen der gestaltpsychologischen Betrachtungsweise fügen." – Katz, David: *Gestaltpsychologie*, Basel 1944, 7 f. Er darf damit als neutraler Beobachter und ohnehin als ausgezeichneter Kenner der Gestaltpsychologie gelten.

30 Cf. ibid., 30–37 und 46 f. Wiederaufgegriffen in Katz, David (Ed.): *Handbuch der Psychologie*, Basel 1951, 86–88, bzw. Katz, David und Rosa (Ed.): *Kleines Handbuch der Psychologie*, Basel/Stuttgart, ³1972, 94–97.

31 Cf. Ehrenfels, Ueber ‚Gestaltqualitäten', 258–260 und passim.

32 Cf. auch Katz, *Gestaltpsychologie*, 43 f.

33 Cf. ibid., 27 f.

Gestaltgesetze anhand einfacher, diagrammatischer Abbildungen demonstriert, was ich im Folgenden ebenfalls tun werde. Die sieben „wichtigsten Bedingungen für das Zustandekommen optischer Gestalten"[34] benennt Katz wie folgt:[35]

Das *Gesetz der Nähe* besagt, dass die „Zusammenfassung der Teile eines Reizganzen [...] unter sonst gleichen Umständen im Sinne des kleinsten Abstandes"[36] erfolgt. Dies lässt sich leicht anhand im Gesichtsfeld wahrgenommener Elemente demonstrieren. Entsprechend diesem Gesetz erkennt man in Fig. 395 oben leichter sechs vertikale Punktreihen als elf horizontale, obwohl letztere objektiv ebenfalls vorhanden sind. In der unteren Abbildung sehen die meisten Personen wahrscheinlich vier Linienpaare mit drei größeren Abstandsbereichen dazwischen und nicht zum Beispiel acht einzelne Linien. Es ist auch möglich, die Punktreihen horizontal und die Linien über den breiten Abstand hinweg zusammenzufassen, aber, wie Katz schreibt, „nur gegen einen deutlich gefühlten Widerstand".[37] Der willentliche oder spontane Wechsel von einer sich aufdrängenden Wahrnehmungsorganisation zu einer weniger naheliegenden spielt auch bei Vexierbildern, wie sie oben zu sehen waren, also für die Figur-Grund-Umkehrung, eine Rolle.

Das *Gesetz der Gleichheit* benennt die Tendenz, bei einer Anzahl verschiedenartiger Elemente diejenigen zusammenzufassen, welche zum Beispiel in Farbe oder Form gleichartig sind. In Fig. 398 oben sind die Abstände zwischen den einzelnen Punkten diesmal horizontal und vertikal gleich. Das Gesetz der Nähe kommt hier folglich nicht zum Tragen. Stattdessen führt das Aussehen der Punkte dazu, dass wir wahrscheinlich eher sechs homogene horizontale Punktlinien sehen als sechs alternierend gemusterte vertikale. In der unteren Abbildung dürften viele eher die beiden stärkeren Linien zusammenfassen als etwa eine stärkere mit einer benachbarten dünnen Linie, obwohl die beiden stärkeren Linicn weiter auseinanderliegen.

34
Ibid., 30.

35
Die folgenden Zeilen beruhen auf der Überblicksdarstellung, welche ich in meiner Dissertation gegeben habe. – Cf. Steinert, *Komplexe Wahrnehmung*, 200–205.

36
Katz, *Gestaltpsychologie*, 30.

37
Ibid., 32.

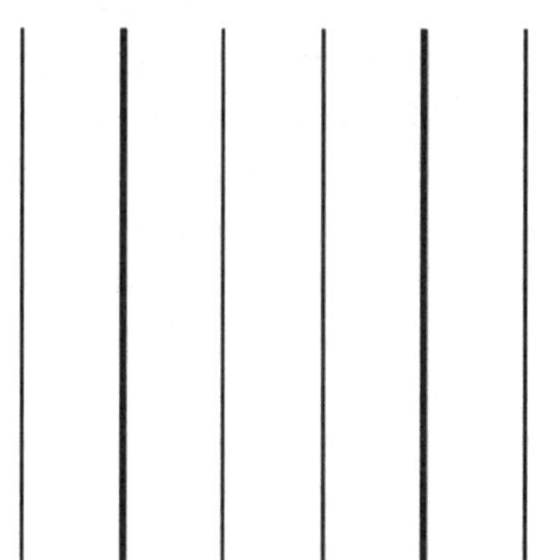

Gesetz der Gleichheit

Fig. 398

Gesetz der Geschlossenheit

Fig. 399

In Fig. 399 oben werden wir entsprechend dem Gesetz der Nähe wahrscheinlich die vier Linienpaare von Fig. 395 unten wiedererkennen. Diese Wahrnehmung ändert sich deutlich, sobald jeweils zwei weiter auseinanderliegende Linien durch Vertikallinien zu einem geschlossenen Kontur verbunden werden (unten). Bei ansonsten gleichartigen Bedingungen werden entsprechend dem *Gesetz der Geschlossenheit* folglich eher jene Linien als Einheit aufgefasst, die eine Fläche umschließen. Allerdings ist es mit einer gewissen Willensanstrengung auch weiterhin möglich, jeweils zwei näher beieinanderliegende Horizontallinien zusammen zu sehen. Wenn das gelingt, erscheinen die drei Rechtecke neu als eine Art Aussparung aus einer größeren Fläche, fast so, wie wenn man am Straßenrand in einen Regenablauf hineinschauen würde. In beiden Fällen sehen wir scheinbar zwei parallel hintereinandergestaffelte Ebenen: Entweder liegen die drei Rechtecke als Figur vorn oder das Gitter des Regenablaufs, durch welches man auf den dahinterliegenden Grund blickt. Das Gesetz der Geschlossenheit ist offensichtlich eine Grundlage des Figur-Grund-Phänomens. Es ist auch dann wirksam, wenn kein durchgehender Kontur vorhanden ist. Während wir in Fig. 401 oben eher vier einzelne Winkel sehen, stellt sich der Eindruck eines von ihnen umschlossenen Quadrats ein, sobald diese Winkel aufeinander bezogen sind (unten).

Das *Gesetz der guten Kurve oder des gemeinsamen Schicksals* bewirkt, dass diejenigen Elemente, die eine ‚gute Kurve' ergeben oder die ein ‚gemeinsames Schicksal' haben, eher zusammen gelesen werden. In Fig. 402 sind oben sechs lange Horizontallinien zu sehen, die von insgesamt vier kurzen schrägen Linien berührt werden. Die Lage der Schrägen zueinander führt dazu, dass wir eher keine H- oder Y-förmigen liegenden Gebilde erkennen, sondern eine durchgehende schräge Linie, welche scheinbar von drei darüberliegenden Horizontalstreifen teilweise verdeckt wird. Die Gesichtseindrücke der vier kurzen Schrägen werden in unserer Wahrnehmung einem einzigen ‚gesehenen' Objekt zugeordnet, auch wenn das Gesetz der Nähe hier bewusst ausgeschaltet wurde. In der unteren Darstellung ist ebenfalls das Gesetz der guten Kurve oder des gemeinsamen Schicksals wirksam, wenn wir wahrscheinlich eher zwei Halbkreise denn vier einzelne, gleichartige Kreissegmente oder möglicherweise kompliziertere Figuren erkennen.

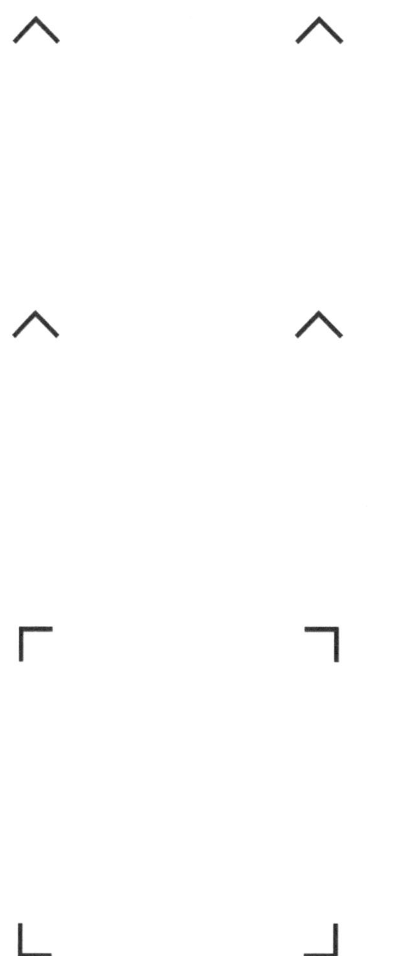

Gesetz der Geschlossenheit

Fig. 401

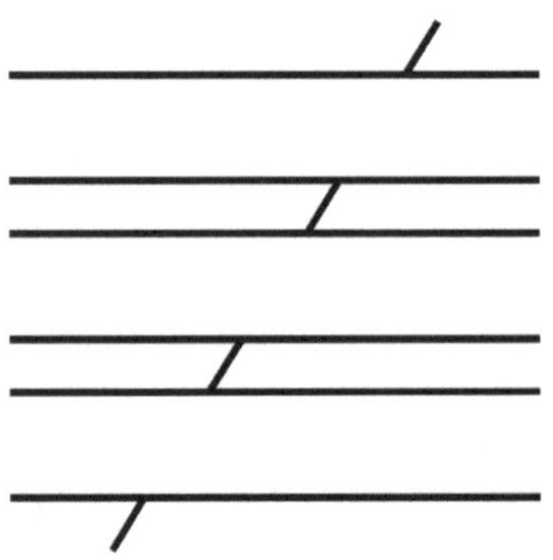

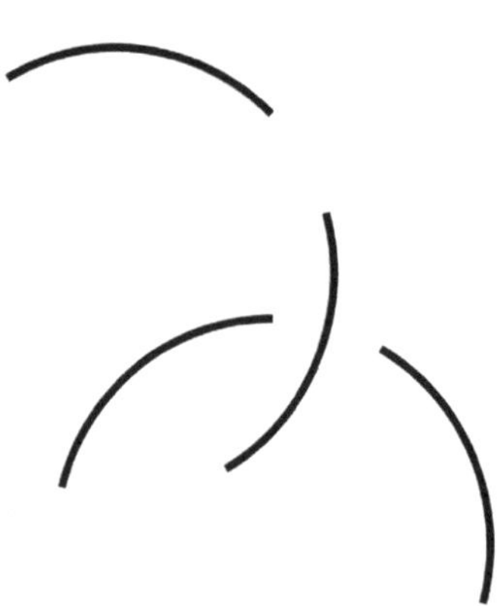

Gesetz der guten Kurve oder des gemeinsamen Schicksals

Fig. 402

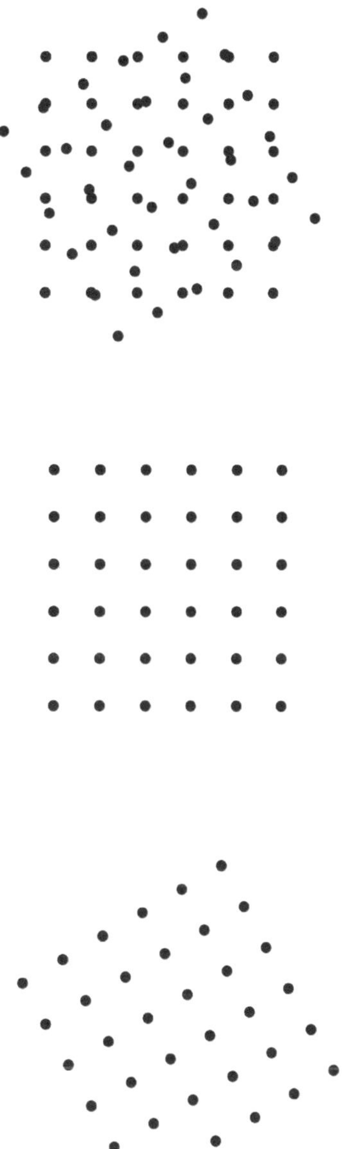

Gesetz der gemeinsamen Bewegung

Fig. 403

Das *Gesetz der gemeinsamen Bewegung* bewirkt, dass wir solche Reize oder Elemente zusammen sehen, die sich gemeinsam und auf ähnliche Weise bewegen. Das mag banal erscheinen, macht in der alltäglichen Wahrnehmung die Dingkonstitution aber sehr effektiv. Als experimentellen Nachweis dieses Gesetzes beschreibt Katz die Überlagerung zweier auf eine Fläche projizierten Punktstreuungen, die im Ruhezustand ein einziges Bild ergeben. Das Punktmuster in Fig. 403 oben nehmen wir wahrscheinlich als chaotisch oder vielleicht auch als ‚Kleeblatt', ‚Malteserkreuz', oder ‚Rotor' wahr. Verschiebt man nun einen der beiden Projektoren, wird man sofort die von ihm projizierten Punkte als eine Einheit auffassen, die unbewegten Punkte als eine andere. Im Beispiel würden bei einsetzender Bewegung dementsprechend zwei regelmäßige Punktraster erkennbar, wie sie in der Mitte und unten dargestellt sind.

Das *Gesetz der Prägnanz* besagt im Wesentlichen, dass wir tendenziell möglichst prägnante Gestalten wahrnehmen. Die visuellen Elemente werden zu solchen Gestalten zusammengefasst gesehen, die tendenziell größtmögliche Einfachheit, Regelmäßigkeit, Symmetrie, Geschlossenheit, Einheitlichkeit etc. besitzen. In Fig. 405 sehen wir dementsprechend zuerst vor allem den Kreis. Erst auf den zweiten Blick nehmen wir die Einzelformen genauer wahr, obwohl jede für sich ebenfalls große Prägnanz aufweist. Katz ergänzt: „Bietet man eine unregelmäßige Figur nur für kurze Zeit, etwa 1/10 sek dar, so sieht man sie meist regelmäßiger."[38] Und weiter: „Die Tendenz zur Prägnanz führt im Sinnlichen eher zu einer Falschnehmung als zu einer Wahrnehmung und nur dadurch, daß sie überwunden wird, kommen wir zu einer zutreffenderen Auffassung unserer Umgebung."[39] Das Gesetz der Prägnanz führt beispielsweise dazu, dass wir in Kasimir Malewitschs (1879–1935) *Schwarzem Quadrat* (ca. 1913–1915) auf den ersten Blick tatsächlich eine Art Quadrat sehen. Dass es sich um ein Viereck mit unterschiedlichen Winkeln und Kantenlängen handelt, wird erst bei genauerem Hinschauen deutlich.

Die Gestaltpsychologie vertritt aufgrund entsprechender Experimente die Auffassung, dass die bisher genannten

38 Ibid., 48.

39 Ibid., 49.

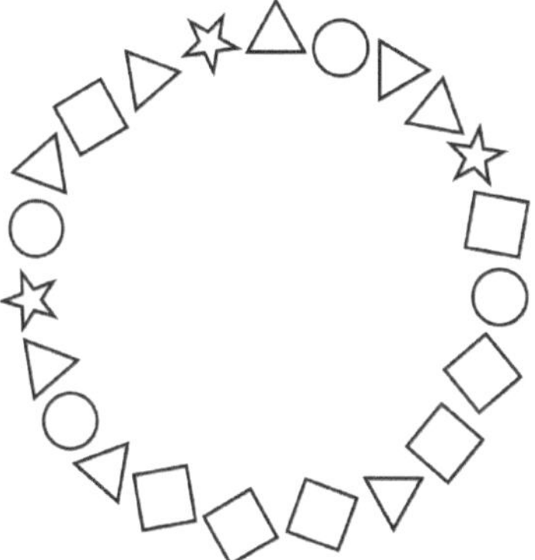

Gesetz der Prägnanz

Fig. 405

Tom Steinert

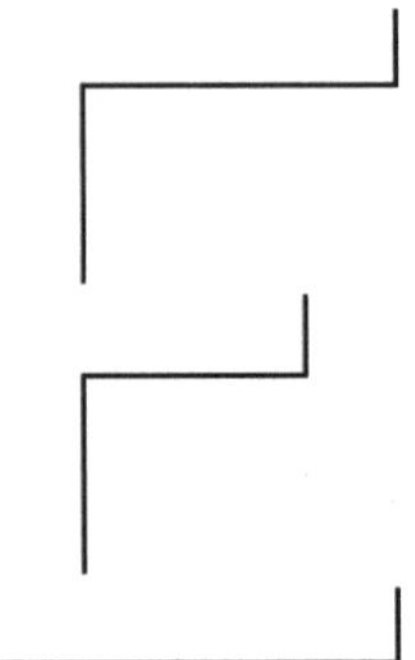

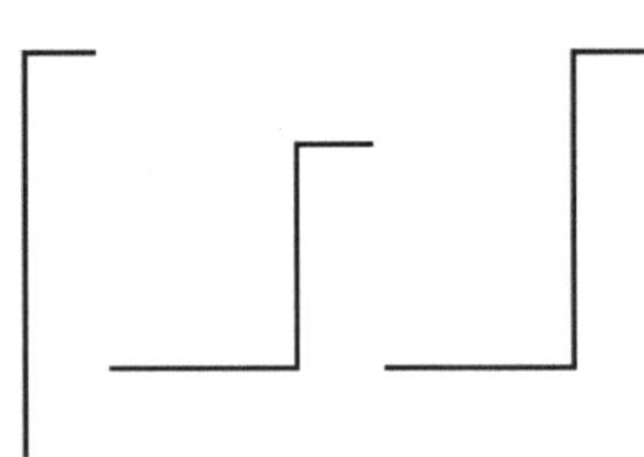

Gesetz der Erfahrung

Fig. 406

Gestaltgesetze unabhängig von einer früheren Wahrnehmung des Gesehenen wirksam sind. Zusätzlich zu diesen führt Katz das *Gesetz der Erfahrung* an, das ebenfalls zur Dingkonstitution beiträgt. Als Beispiel dient Fig. 406 oben. Wer in der Schule die römischen Versalien als Alphabet kennengelernt hat, wird in dieser Darstellung wohl eher ein ‚E' erkennen als drei separate Linienzüge, die nichts miteinander zu tun haben. Das ‚E' scheint sich mit einem leichten Schattenwurf geringfügig vom Hintergrund abzuheben. Dreht man diese Figur jedoch um 90°, ist es schon weniger selbstverständlich, das ‚E' zu sehen (unten). Zur Erfahrung der lateinischen Großbuchstaben, die wir in einer bestimmten Stellung zu sehen gewohnt sind, kommt die Erfahrung eines Lichteinfalls gewöhnlich von links oben hinzu, welche uns die schwarzen Linien in der oberen Zeichnung als Schattenwurf interpretieren lässt. Im Unterschied zu den übrigen Gestaltgesetzen ist die Erfahrung ein individueller Faktor der Gestaltwahrnehmung. Katz fügt hinzu:

> Überall, wo Linienzüge etwas symbolisieren (Wörter, schematische Zeichnungen, Diagramme), oder etwas zum Ausdruck bringen (Mimik), erweist sich die Gestaltauffassung von der Raumlage abhängig. Wenn man einen auf dem Kopf stehenden Text nur schwer lesen kann, so eine auf dem Kopf stehende unleserliche Handschrift überhaupt nicht. Man kann den Ausdruck einer auf dem Kopf stehenden Photographie einer Person nicht mehr erkennen.[40]

Die Abhängigkeit der Gestaltauffassung von der Raumlage lässt sich eindrücklich mit einer simplen Linienzeichnung demonstrieren, die ich Ernst Machs (1838–1916) *Beiträgen zur Analyse der Empfindungen* (1886) entnommen habe. Fig. 408 oben würde wohl jeder als Quadrat bezeichnen. Die untere Zeichnung hingegen würde mancher spontan vielleicht eher als Rhombus bezeichnen, obwohl beide Figuren, abgesehen von ihrer unterschiedlichen Lage, identisch sind. Mach schreibt dazu: „Zwei Gestalten

40
Ibid., 35.

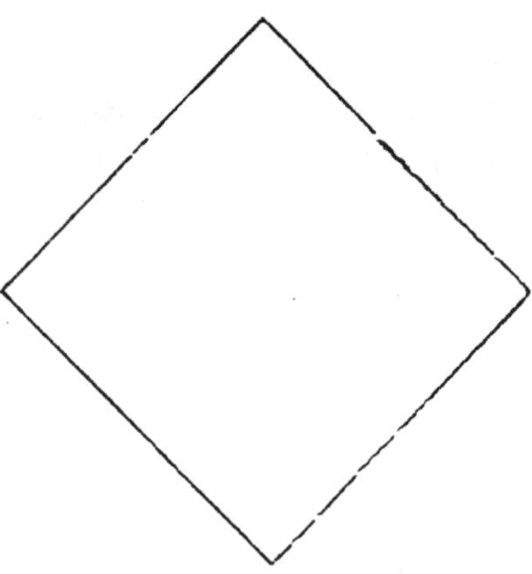

[Unterscheidung zwischen geometrischer und physiologischer (optischer) Ähnlichkeit], in: Ernst Mach, *Beiträge zur Analyse der Empfindungen*, Jena 1886, Fig. 3 auf 44.

Fig. 408

können geometrisch congruent, physiologisch aber ganz verschieden sein, wie dies die beiden [...] Quadrate veranschaulichen, welche ohne mechanische und intellectuelle Operationen niemals als gleich erkannt werden können."[41] „Optisch ähnlich werden die [geometrisch ähnlichen] Gebilde erst, wenn sie auch ähnlich liegen".[42] Aufgrund derartiger Untersuchungen gehört Mach zu den Vorläufern der Gestaltpsychologie im 19. Jahrhundert.

Die geschilderten Gesetze, die zur Wahrnehmung (visueller) Gestalten führen, wirken in der alltäglichen Wahrnehmung nicht isoliert, sondern selbstverständlich zusammen. Auf Grundlage dieser Gestaltgesetze kann eine Reihe von Gestaltphänomenen beobachtet werden. Am bekanntesten sind auch hier die sinnlich wahrgenommenen Gestalten und davon jene des Gesichtssinns. Als mit dem Gesichtssinn wahrgenommene Gestalten beschreibt Katz wiederum die Figurgestalten, die Farbgestalten und die Bewegungsgestalten.[43]

Die *Figur-Grund-Beziehung* zählt in den Bereich der Figurgestalten. Dieses Gestaltphänomen lässt sich eindrücklich anhand mehrdeutiger Darstellungen wie der oben gezeigten illustrieren. Katz führt aus, dass die Wirkung solcher Darstellungen durch eine ‚atomistische' Psychologie, welche die einzelnen Elemente getrennt betrachtet, nicht erklärbar sei, und schreibt:

> [...] man muß von der Täuschungsfigur als Ganzem ausgehen und nicht von ihren Elementen. Nur einer ganzheitlichen Betrachtung erschließen sich auch die doppeldeutigen Figuren. Diese sind nach Rubins grundlegenden Untersuchungen von größtem Interesse zur Illustrierung der Relation Figur–Hintergrund.[44]

41
Mach, *Beiträge zur Analyse der Empfindungen*, 44.

42
Ibid., 47. Zur Wirkungsgeschichte von Machs Zeichnung cf. den Hinweis in Steinert, *Komplexe Wahrnehmung*, Anm. 4.63 auf 365. Cf. ferner die analogen Ausführungen bei Rubin, *Visuell wahrgenommene Figuren*, 112.

43
Cf. Katz, *Gestaltpsychologie*, 36–39.

44
Ibid., 37.

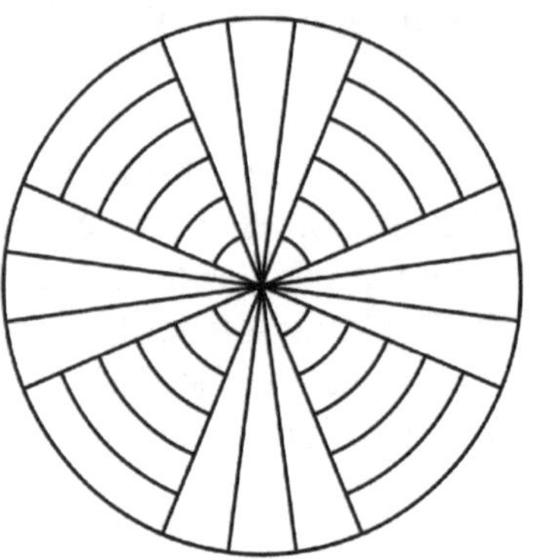

Diagramm zur Figur-Grund-Beziehung,
Zeichnung: Tom Steinert.

Fig. 410

Das gilt auch für Fig. 410, in der man zwischen der Wahrnehmung zweier verschiedener Kreuze hin und her wechseln kann. Entweder sieht man als Figur ein stehendes Kreuz vor einem aus konzentrischen Kreisen gebildeten Hintergrund oder ein liegendes Kreuz vor einem aus Kreisradien gebildeten Hintergrund. Figur und Grund befinden sich scheinbar auf zwei unterschiedlichen, hintereinanderliegenden Ebenen; in unserer Wahrnehmung wird der Grund partiell durch die Figur verdeckt.[45] Eine gleichzeitige Wahrnehmung der acht Sektoren als eine zusammengehörige, in einer einzigen Ebene liegende Figur ist eher schwer möglich – eine Folge des Gesetzes der Gleichheit.

Wie Katz weiter schreibt, ist die Figur-Grund-Beziehung in allen Bereichen sinnlicher Wahrnehmung nachzuweisen, besonders im akustischen.[46] Die Unterscheidung einer bedeutungsvollen Figur von einem mehr oder weniger indifferent wahrgenommenen Hintergrund ist eine der wichtigsten Voraussetzungen für die Orientierung in der Umwelt, sei es visuell oder akustisch. In Hinblick auf visuelle Figuren benennt Katz schließlich folgende Eigenschaften von Gestalten:

> Eine Gestalt ist [...] dadurch gekennzeichnet, daß sie abgesondert, abgehoben, geschlossen und gegliedert ist. Das figurale Gestalterlebnis stellt eine Einheit dar, die vom Erlebenden in der Regel nicht beliebig geändert werden kann. Je stärker die Gestalt, um so stärkeren Widerstand leistet sie äußeren Eingriffen. [...] Die Stücke eines Gestaltgefüges besitzen verschiedene Wertigkeit. Es gibt solche, die für die Erhaltung des Ganzen unentbehrlich sind, und daneben relativ entbehrliche Stücke.[47]

45
Cf. auch Rubins Beschreibung: „Wird zuerst das radiär und darauf das konzentrisch schraffierte Kreuz als Figur erlebt, so kann man einen eigentümlichen Unterschied an der konzentrischen Schraffierung bemerken, je nachdem sie der Figur oder dem Grund angehört. In letzterem Fall hat man eigentlich keinen Eindruck, daß die konzentrischen Kreisstücke unterbrochen seien; viel eher hat man den Eindruck, daß das Konzentrische unter der Figur weiterlaufe. Hiervon ist keine Spur zu merken, wenn die konzentrisch schraffierten Sektoren das ausmachen, was als Figur erlebt wird." – Rubin, *Visuell wahrgenommene Figuren*, 38.

46
Cf. Katz, *Gestaltpsychologie*, 37.

47
Ibid., 51 f.

Der Kontur wirkt bei der Wahrnehmung normalerweise nur nach *einer* Richtung. Das heißt, in der Regel nehmen wir den vom Kontur umschlossenen Bereich als Figur wahr, den übrigen Teil des Feldes als Grund. Katz schreibt: „Mit der einseitigen Funktion der Konturen hängt es zusammen, daß wir die *Dinge* sehen und nicht die Löcher dazwischen, selbst wenn es der Zufall will, daß die Grenzlinien eines Loches eine sinnvolle Figur ergeben."[48] Bei mehrdeutigen Darstellungen wie dem ‚Rubinkelch' sehen wir dementsprechend entweder den Kelch oder die Gesichtsprofile als Figur. Es dürfte aber nicht gelingen, beide im selben Augenblick deutlich als Figur zu erleben.[49]

Gestaltpsychologie in der Kunstwissenschaft

Im Tagungsaufruf zur Konferenz *Between Figure and Ground: Seeing in Premodernity* (2019) heißt es eingangs: „Die Begriffe ‚Figur' und ‚Grund' sind zentrale Begriffe der Kunstwissenschaft. Sie entstammen jedoch einer Kunstgeschichte der Moderne."[50] „Kunstgeschichte der Moderne" kann dabei auf zwei Arten verstanden werden: als Kunstgeschichte, die sich mit *Objekten* aus der Moderne befasst, oder als Kunstgeschichte, die auf modernen *Methoden* beruht. Im Folgenden will ich von der zweiten Auffassung ausgehen.

Worin die Modernität bestimmter kunstwissenschaftlicher Methoden bestehen könnte, hat etwa der Kunsthistoriker Günter Brucher (geb. 1941) in einem Aufsatz über „Gestalttheorie und Kunstwissenschaft" dargelegt. Zunächst postuliert er den Primat der „wahrnehmungsgestützte[n] Werkanalyse",[51] begleitet von

48
Ibid., 53.

49
Cf. ibid. Für eine weitere Vertiefung des Figur-Grund-Phänomens empfiehlt sich die im Vergleich zu Katz' *Gestaltpsychologie* wesentlich detailliertere, äußerst erhellende Diskussion in Koffka, K.[urt]: *Principles of Gestalt Psychology*, New York 1935, 177–210 (Kapitel 5, „The Environmental Field: Figure and Ground. The Framework"). Das bei Harcourt, Brace and Company erschienene Buch wurde auch mit lose überklebter Verlagsangabe „Routledge and Kegan Paul", London, ansonsten unverändert, verkauft. Die Londoner Ausgabe wiederum wurde ebenfalls in den USA gedruckt und erhielt eine doppelte Verlagsangabe: Koffka, K.[urt]: *Principles of Gestalt Psychology*, (Kegan Paul, Trench, Trubner & Co./Harcourt, Brace and Company) London/New York 1936.

50
Quené, Saskia C.: Call for Papers *Between Figure and Ground. Seeing in Premodernity (Basel, 4–6 Jun 20)*, 2. Dezember 2019, online unter: arthist.net/archive/22204, zuletzt aufgerufen am 15. Januar 2023.

der Forderung, „stets vom konkreten Werk auszugehen. Demgemäß definieren wir Kunstwissenschaft als eine primär durch die visuelle Wahrnehmung geprägte Disziplin", welche „von der ikonographisch-ikonologischen Methode" flankiert werde. Brucher gibt sich sodann unumwunden als Vertreter einer gestaltpsychologisch beeinflussten Kunstwissenschaft zu erkennen, wenn er schreibt, als Grundlage („Substrat") für eine „wissenschaftlich gesicherte Analysemethode" „dient dem Kunstwissenschaftler das methodologische Hilfsmittel der Gestalttheorie bzw. Wahrnehmungspsychologie, und erst danach wird er [...] andere Nachbarfächer [...] zu Rate ziehen." Von diesen Feststellungen leitet Brucher zu Rudolf Arnheim (1904–2007), einem Hauptvertreter gestaltpsychologisch geprägter Kunstwissenschaft im 20. Jahrhundert, über und konstatiert:

> Ohne Zweifel ist es ein Verdienst Rudolf Arnheims, die Gestalttheorie/Wahrnehmungspsychologie und deren Gestalt- bzw. Sehgesetze den Anforderungen der bildanalysierenden Kunstwissenschaft erstmalig dienstbar gemacht zu haben. Für ihn ist das Sehen „eine schöpferische Tätigkeit des menschlichen Geistes" und keinesfalls ein „nur mechanisches Aufzeichnen von Sinneseindrücken".[52]

Sieht man einmal von Bruchers Gleichsetzung von Wahrnehmungspsychologie, Gestaltpsychologie und Gestalttheorie ab, bleibt festzuhalten, dass hier ein ‚jüngerer' Vertreter der Kunstgeschichte der Gestaltpsychologie eine tragende Rolle konzediert und mit Arnheim zugleich auf eine Person verweist, die mit ihrem Standardwerk *Art and Visual Perception* (1954) maßgeblich an der Verbreitung einer gestaltpsychologisch fundierten Kunstbetrachtung beteiligt war. Allerdings ist zu ergänzen, dass mit Ernst H. Gombrich (1909–2001) ein Zeitgenosse existierte, der nicht minder einflussreich wahrnehmungs- und gestaltpsychologische

51 Hier und im Folgenden: Brucher, Günter: Gestalttheorie und Kunstwissenschaft. Am Beispiel der Stilllebenmalerei, in: Madersbacher, Lukas/Steppan, Thomas (Ed.): *De re artificiosa. Festschrift für Paul von Naredi-Rainer zu seinem 60. Geburtstag*, Regensburg 2010, 41–48: 41.

52 Ibid., 42.

Erkenntnisse verarbeitete und – im Unterschied zu Arnheim – ein originärer Kunsthistoriker war. Ein weiterer Kunsthistoriker, der aufgrund seiner Verstrickungen in der NS-Zeit etwas in Vergessenheit geratene, in letzter Zeit aber wieder stärker bearbeitete Hans Sedlmayr (1896–1984), hatte bereits ab 1925 versucht, Ideen der sich entwickelnden Gestaltpsychologie auf die Werkanalyse anzuwenden.[53] Damit relativiert sich Bruchers Einschätzung.

Arnheim ist in unserem Zusammenhang von besonderem Interesse, weil er nicht zu jenen Kunstwissenschaftlern zählt, welche die Ergebnisse der gestaltpsychologischen Forschung lediglich rezipierten. Vielmehr hatte er die Gestaltpsychologie in den 1920er Jahren, noch vor seiner Emigration – 1933 Italien, 1939 Großbritannien, 1940 USA –, als Doktorand am Psychologischen Institut der Berliner Universität aus erster Hand kennengelernt. Arnheim schreibt 1981 in einem *Lebenslauf:*

> An der Berliner Universität galt Psychologie damals noch als ein Teil der Philosophie, so dass man zwei Hauptfächer zu studieren hatte. […] Als Nebenfächer

53
Cf. Sedlmayr, Hans: Gestaltetes Sehen, in: *Belvedere. Kunst und künstlerische Kultur der Vergangenheit. Zeitschrift für Sammler und Kunstfreunde*, Heft 40 [Oktober oder November 1925] = vol. 8 (August–Dezember 1925), Heft 10, 65–73, 3 Fig. im Text sowie Fig. 1–4 auf Taf.; Fortsetzung: Sedlmayr, Hans: Zum Gestalteten Sehen, in: *Belvedere*, Heft 45 (März 1926) = vol. 9–10 (Januar–Dezember 1926), Heft 3, 57–62, Fig. 2–3 auf Taf. Es folgte eine Buchausgabe, in welcher Sedlmayr eingangs bemerkt: „Die vorliegende Arbeit wurde begonnen am 1. Januar 1925 und endgültig abgeschlossen im Mai 1929. Vorarbeiten gehen in das Jahr 1923 zurück" und anschließend auf die beiden Aufsätze von 1925 und 1926 verweist. – Sedlmayr, Hans: *Die Architektur Borrominis*, Berlin 1930, 5. Zu Sedlmayrs Rezeption der wahrnehmungs- und gestaltpsychologischen Literatur in den 1920er Jahren cf. detailliert Morgenthaler, Simon: *Formationen einer Kunstwissenschaft. Text- und Archivstudien zu Hans Sedlmayr*, Berlin/Boston 2020, 49–59 (Abschnitt „Ein bibliographisches Register als theoretisches Programm"). Morgenthaler stellt fest: „Neben der *Zeitschrift für Psychologie* […] kommt der ab 1922 von Kurt Koffka, Wolfgang Köhler, Max Wertheimer, Kurt Goldstein und Hans Walter Gruhle herausgegebenen Zeitschrift *Psychologische Forschung* besondere Bedeutung zu. Diese Zeitschrift, die sich im Laufe der 1920er Jahre als zentrales Publikationsorgan der Berliner Schule der Gestalttheorie etablieren sollte, hat Sedlmayr intensiv rezipiert". – Ibid., 52. Cf. ferner Bohde, Daniela: Gestalt, in: *kritische berichte* 35, 2007 (3), 67–72. Eine späte Fortsetzung von Sedlmayrs 1925 veröffentlichter gestaltpsychologisch inspirierten Analyse San Carlos alle Quattro Fontane in Rom findet sich bei [Arnheim, Rudolf]: Objective Percepts, Objective Values, in: Arnheim, Rudolf: *New Essays on the Psychology of Art*, Berkeley/Los Angeles/London 1986, 297–326: 301–309. Arnheim bezieht sich hier allerdings nicht direkt auf Sedlmayr, sondern auf Steinberg, Leo: *Borromini's San Carlo Alle Quattro Fontane. A Study in Multiple Form and Architectural Symbolism*, New York/London 1977. Es handelt sich um die überarbeitete Buchausgabe einer Dissertation von 1959. Steinberg gibt darin auch eine kritische Würdigung von Sedlmayrs Lesart San Carlos. – Cf. ibid., 30 f., 119 f. und passim.

> hatte ich Kunstgeschichte und Musikgeschichte. Vor allem aber verbrachte ich meine Zeit im kaiserlichen Schloss, das nach der Revolution leer stand und wo dem Psychologischen Institut zwei Stockwerke eingeräumt waren. Dort in den malerischen Räumen der Hofdamen wurden die für die Gestaltpsychologie grundlegenden Experimentalarbeiten gemacht. Wolfgang Köhler war der Direktor des Instituts, und neben ihm waren die bedeutendsten Dozenten Max Wertheimer und Kurt Lewin. Der Musikethnologe Erich Maria von Hornbostel und der Kunstpsychologe Johannes von Allesch gehörten ebenfalls zum Institut. Wir arbeiteten fast ausschließlich experimentell, und ich verbrachte viele Jahre mit meiner Dissertation unter Wertheimer, in der ich die Ausdruckswahrnehmung an Handschriften und Gesichtern untersuchte. Die Dissertation wurde im Jahre meiner Promotion, 1928, in unserer Zeitschrift *Psychologische Forschung* veröffentlicht.[54]

Damit konnte Arnheim bei der Anwendung der Gestaltpsychologie auf die Kunstbetrachtung auf einer substantiellen Kenntnis der psychologischen Fachliteratur aufbauen, wie schon ein oberflächlicher Blick in das Literaturverzeichnis von *Art and Visual Perception* beweist. Arnheim zählt zu jenen

54 Arnheim, Rudolf: Lebenslauf (1981), online unter: www.hhdiederichs.de/arnheim-forum/lebenslauf, zuletzt aufgerufen am 15. Januar 2023. Margarete Pratschke bezeichnet Arnheim als eine Art „gestaltpsychologischen Außenminister im zeitgenössischen Kunstbetrieb […]. Und noch mehr, er wechselte die Felder völlig von der Wahrnehmungspsychologie in die Kunst, von der akademischen Wissenschaft in die zeitgenössische Kunstkritik." – Pratschke, Margarete: *Gestaltexperimente unterm Bilderhimmel. Das Psychologische Institut im Berliner Stadtschloss und die Avantgarde*, Paderborn 2016, 145. Pratschke hält fest, „dass Arnheim dem [Psychologischen] Institut nach Abschluss der Promotion 1928 tatsächlich wohl den Rücken gekehrt hatte oder zumindest dem Institutsleben nicht mehr nahe genug stand, um am akademischen Tagesgeschäft der Psychologen teilzuhaben". – Ibid., 150. Gombrichs fast zur selben Zeit (1932) erfolgte Kontaktnahme mit der Gestaltpsychologie an der Berliner Universität wird von Pratschke auf 187–191 dargestellt. Nach ihrer Einschätzung „gerät der Besuch der Vorlesung des Gestaltpsychologen Köhler, der sich in seinem psychologischen Selbstverständnis den *Naturwissenschaften* verpflichtet sah, durch den Kunsthistoriker Gombrich, der sich durch und durch als *Geisteswissenschaftler* empfand, in mehrfacher Hinsicht zu einer Art Urszene: für das Verhältnis von Psychologie und Kunstgeschichte sowie – etwas allgemeiner gesprochen – von Geistes- und Naturwissenschaft." – Ibid., 189.

Persönlichkeiten, welche aufgrund ihrer Emigration den Ideentransfer von der deutschsprachigen Gestaltpsychologie in die angloamerikanische Wissenschaft und – dank Übersetzung der dort veröffentlichten Werke – zurück in den deutschsprachigen Raum vollzogen.[55]

Grundsätzlich kann man sagen, dass die Erarbeitung der wahrnehmungspsychologischen Grundlagen im Wesentlichen zwischen etwa 1900 und 1930 im deutschsprachigen Raum stattfand, während die Anwendung dieser Grundlagen auf die Kunstwissenschaft und die Kunstproduktion dann besonders im angloamerikanischen Raum erfolgte. Die Rezeption der Gestaltpsychologie im angloamerikanischen Raum begann allerdings nicht erst mit

55
Insofern trifft die Feststellung Jan C. Boumans von 1968, das Figur-Grund-Phänomen sei international nur sehr oberflächlich rezipiert worden, nur zur Hälfte zu. – Cf. Bouman, Jan C.: *The Figure-Ground Phenomenon in Experimental and Phenomenological Psychology* (= Diss. phil., Universität Stockholm), Stockholm 1968, 52. Zunächst hält Bouman in seiner Studie zum Figur-Grund-Phänomen zutreffend fest: „The figure-ground phenomenon is always associated with the name of the Danish psychologist Edgar Rubin. In 1915, he published, in the form of a doctor's thesis in the Danish language, his study ‚Synsoplevede Figurer'; this was followed, in 1921, by a German translation under the title ‚Visuell wahrgenommene Figuren'. By submitting the figure-ground phenomenon to a systematic scientific treatment, Rubin has gained a paramount place in the field of psychology. [...] However, when examining what has been achieved *since* Rubin's initial work, we are struck by how little has in actual fact been accomplished. [...] This is all the more amazing since, in the figure-ground phenomenon, we are confronted with an extremely important concept, as has been testified by several of the foremost psychologists." – Ibid., 51. Bouman fährt fort: „It is interesting to analyze the reasons why for more than fifty years [seit Rubins Dissertation 1915] the problem in question [das Figur-Grund-Phänomen] has not been discussed with greater profit by experimental psychologists." – Ibid., 52. Ähnlich heißt es 1936 bei Wolfgang Metzger: „Obgleich inzwischen fast ein halbes Jahrhundert verflossen ist [seit 1890], steckt die Lehre von den Gestalt-Qualitäten *noch ganz in den Anfängen.*" – Metzger, Wolfgang: *Gesetze des Sehens*, Frankfurt am Main 1936, XV. Hinsichtlich eines möglichen Ideentransfers äußert Bouman: „the fact that Rubin's book was written in German has much to do with the fact that his ideas, especially in the United States and England, were only disseminated in a general and decidedly superficial way." – Bouman, *The Figure-Ground Phenomenon*, 52. Und bekräftigend: „many important publications never come to the attention even of serious scientists because of lack of knowledge of foreign languages. Often, the rationalization is made, that if an article has not been translated into English, it cannot be important anyway. So either one has to depend on second-hand summaries or one neglects important publications." – Ibid., Anm. 48 auf 52 f. Im Unterschied zu dieser Auffassung suche ich im vorliegenden Essay zu zeigen, dass ein unmittelbarer und vielfältiger wissenschaftlicher Austausch beispielsweise zwischen Deutschland und den USA bestand und eine Reihe amerikanischer Wissenschaftler nicht nur ausgezeichnete sprachliche Fähigkeiten hatte, sondern ihre Karriere auch an den deutschen Hochschulen begann. Wie sehr um 1900 das Deutsche *eine* Lingua franca der Wissenschaft gewesen sein muss, können wir heute kaum mehr ermessen. – Cf. beispielsweise Ammon, Ulrich: *Die Stellung der deutschen Sprache in der Welt*, Berlin/München/Boston 2015, 519–539 (Kapitel „Von einer Weltwissenschafts- zu einer Nischensprache. Stationen und Ursachen").

der Immigration nach 1933, sondern bereits zuvor durch wissenschaftlichen Austausch in beide Richtungen.[56]

Infolge dieses Austauschs erschien beispielsweise 1938 in London ein *Source Book of Gestalt Psychology*, welches von Willis D. Ellis (1901–1942), zu jener Zeit Assistenzprofessor an der University of Arizona, in enger Zusammenarbeit mit dem in den USA wirkenden Gestaltpsychologen Kurt Koffka (1886–1941) herausgegeben wurde.[57] Mit dem *Source Book* wurde eine Reihe deutschsprachiger Gestaltaufsätze in ausführlichen Auszügen auf Englisch verfügbar gemacht. Ellis hatte sich von 1928 bis 1929[58] ebenfalls in Berlin aufgehalten. In seiner Dissertation bemerkt er 1930:

> The writer was privileged to hear the lectures of Professors Koffka, Köhler, Wertheimer and Lewin; to confer with them and with Dr. Metzger, upon occasion, and to participate frequently as Versuchsperson in experiments conducted at the *Psychologisches Institut* in Berlin.[59]

Rubins Forschungen zum Figur-Grund-Phänomen sind im *Source Book* nicht als eigenständiger Beitrag enthalten. Das mag auch darin begründet sein, dass seine Dissertation gerade nicht an der Berliner Universität, sondern in Göttingen entstanden war und der zu Rubins Zeit dort lehrende Müller später im Widerstreit, wohl auch im Wettstreit, mit den Gestaltpsychologen stand.[60]

56
„Already in 1922, at Robert Ogden's invitation, Koffka had published a full account of the Gestalt view on perception in *Psychological Bulletin*." – Wagemans et al., A Century of Gestalt Psychology, 1178. Cf. dazu auch die weiteren Hinweise ibid., 1177 f., sowie Koffka, Perception.

57
Ellis, Willis D. (Ed.): *A Source Book of Gestalt Psychology*, London [1938].

58
Cf. Stichwort „Ellis, Dr. Willis D(avis)", in: Cattell, J. McKeen/Cattell, Jacques (Ed.): *American Men of Science. A Biographical Directory*, New York [5]1933, 327.

59
Ellis, Willis Davis: *Gestalt Psychology and Meaning*, Berkeley 1930, VII. (Das Exemplar der Universitätsbibliothek Leipzig, ehemals in der Bibliothek des Instituts für Psychologie an der Universität Leipzig sowie mit dem Stempel „Krueger-Stiftung" versehen, enthält auf dem Titelblatt die handschriftliche Widmung „With the writer's | compliments | Willis D. Ellis." Es könnte ein Hinweis darauf sein, dass Ellis versucht haben könnte, an einer deutschen Hochschule Fuß zu fassen. Der Leipziger Professor Felix Krueger (1874–1948) war ein Vertreter der Ganzheitspsychologie.)

60 Cf. Müller, G.[eorg] E.[lias]: *Komplextheorie und Gestalttheorie. Ein Beitrag zur Wahrnehmungspsychologie*, Göttingen 1923. Zum einen nimmt Müller den Primat der „seit Dezennien von [ihm] vertretene[n] Komplextheorie" (ibid., 1) in Anspruch und betont, dass er anstelle des Begriffs „Gestalt" zuvor bereits den Begriff „Komplex" geprägt habe: „Köhler [...] bezeichnet als Gestalten ‚solche Gebilde, die als ganze spezifische Eigenschaften haben und deshalb mit gutem Recht als Einheiten aufzufassen sind'. Gelegentlich macht er auch von der Formulierung Gebrauch, nach welcher Gestalten diejenigen Zustände oder Vorgänge sind, deren charakteristische Eigenschaften und Wirkungen aus artgleichen Eigenschaften und Wirkungen ihrer sogenannten Teile nicht zusammensetzbar sind. Aus Vorstehendem ergibt sich, daß die Komplexe meiner Theorie Gestalten im Sinne von Köhler sind." – Ibid., 2. Müller konstatiert: „Die Gestalt ist bei mir eine Eigenschaft eines Komplexes." – Ibid. Dementsprechend heißt es abschließend: „Ich habe die Komplextheorie, allerdings nicht in der hier vorgelegten entwickelteren Form, schon zu einer Zeit vertreten, als noch keiner unsrer modernen Gestaltpsychologen die Schulreife besaß." – Ibid., 106. Zum anderen nimmt Müller eine Widerlegung der Gestalttheorie nach Wertheimer (1880–1943), Köhler und Koffka vor, insb. mit Hilfe physiologischer Argumente. – Cf. ibid., 88–106 (§ 15: „Die Wertheimersche Gestalttheorie"). Dazu erklärt er zunächst: „Auf die Wertheimersche Theorie der Bewegungsempfindung gehen wir hier nicht weiter ein. Wir haben es hier nur mit der Gestalttheorie Wertheimers zu tun. Man kann letztere Theorie verwerfen, ohne damit über die erstere etwas zu behaupten." – Ibid., Anm. 1 auf 88. Sein Zwischenfazit lautet: „Da [...] andere als die von Wertheimer und von Köhler gegebenen Fassungen der hier zu besprechenden Gestalttheorie, nach welcher ein einheitlicher Gestalteindruck durch eine Wechselwirkung der gegebenen Erregungen bedingt ist, zur Zeit nicht vorliegen, so könnten wir eigentlich diese Theorie als erledigt ansehen und unsere Besprechung derselben hier beenden. Um jedoch die Undurchdachtheit und Untauglichkeit dieser Theorie noch deutlicher hervortreten zu lassen, möchte ich im Nachstehenden noch in eine vergleichende Prüfung einerseits dieser Gestalttheorie [...] und anderseits der Komplextheorie [...] eintreten. Wir stellen also die Frage (die Grundfrage der Gestalttheorie): Wie kann ein Komplex (eine Gestalt) Eigenschaften oder Wirkungen besitzen, die aus den artgleichen Eigenschaften oder Wirkungen seiner Bestandteile nicht ableitbar sind?" – Ibid., 97. Es folgt eine weitere Widerlegung der Gestalttheorie, nun stärker auf der Ebene psychologischer Argumente. Ebenso deutlich fällt 1925 Wolfgang Köhlers Replik auf Müllers Schrift aus. Nachdem er die Grundzüge von Müllers Komplextheorie besprochen hat, stellt Köhler fest: „Von dieser Lehre als Operationsbasis hat *M.[üller]* heftige Angriffe gegen die Arbeits- und Denkweise unternommen, welche man als gestalttheoretisch bezeichnet. Im wesentlichen liege da nichts Neues vor, das übrige seien gänzlich unüberlegte und inkonsequente Auslassungen. Seine Polemik wird dadurch sehr vereinfacht, daß wesentliche Gedankengänge der Gegner nicht einmal Erwähnung finden, daß dafür Einzelannahmen gründlich mißdeutet, in dieser veränderten Form zu Hauptangriffsobjekten gemacht und nun als unhaltbar erwiesen werden. [...] Nichts Neues ist es nach *M.[üller]*, wenn jetzt gesagt wird, ‚die Gestalten seien in keiner Weise weniger unmittelbar als ihre Teile' *(Koffka)*, ein Komplex könne erfaßt werden, bevor seine Teile erfaßt werden u. dgl. Wenn *M.[üller]* jene Tatsache so gut bekannt ist und er *Koffka* gewissermaßen vorwirft, Selbstverständliches nachdrücklich zu wiederholen, wie kann er dann ein ganzes Buch Komplextheorie verfassen, in dem fortwährend das Gegenteil vorausgesetzt wird?" – Köhler, Wolfgang: Komplextheorie und Gestalttheorie. Antwort auf G. E. Müllers Schrift gleichen Namens, in: *Psychologische Forschung. Zeitschrift für Psychologie und ihre Grenzwissenschaften* 6, 1924–1925 (3–4) (April 1925), 358–416: 389. Köhler resümiert: „Die Komplexe seiner [Müllers] Theorie seien Gestalten im Sinne von Köhler, schreibt er einmal in Verwendung eines einleitenden Satzes der ‚Physischen Gestalten'. Dem Sinn, den dieser Satz durch alle folgenden Ausführungen meiner Schrift erhält, entspricht weder die Komplextheorie, die er selbst vertritt, noch das von ihm angegriffene Zerrbild einer ‚Gestalttheorie' im mindesten." – Ibid., 416. Im Übrigen war Köhler 1921 nach Müllers Emeritierung kurzzeitig Professor in Göttingen, bevor er 1922 an die Berliner Universität berufen wurde.

Dementsprechend ist es folgerichtig, wenn wir erfahren, dass Rubin sich selbst nie als Gestaltpsychologen verstanden habe, obwohl die Figur-Grund-Unterscheidung üblicherweise unter die Gestaltphänomene geordnet wird.[61]

Noch vor dem *Source Book* war 1935 *Gestalt Psychology. A Survey of Facts and Principles* erschienen, dessen Autor George W. Hartmann (1904–1955) auf dem Titelblatt als „Professor of Education" an der Columbia University und „sometime Social Science Research Council fellow at the University of Berlin" figuriert. Hartmanns Einlassungen können somit wohl ebenfalls als ‚first-hand' bezeichnet werden, wenngleich er kein Gestaltpsychologe war.[62] Im Sinne des Ideentransfers teilt er eingangs mit:

61
„Rubin has commonly been classified as a Gestalt psychologist in the psychological literature with his research often being silently incorporated into the findings and theories of Gestalt psychology. Thus, the distinguished perceptual psychologist Hochberg (1978) described five Gestalt laws of organization in his book *Perception.* The first of these concerns *area,* the smaller an enclosed area is, the more likely it is to be perceived as a figure. His fifth law is that of *symmetry,* the more symmetrical a closed region is, the more likely it is to be perceived as a figure. The first of these ‚laws' is of course Rubin's finding and the latter one that of his student Poul Bahnsen. In another publication, Hochberg counts figure and ground as one of the Gestalt phenomena [...]. Rubin was distinctly unhappy with being classified as a Gestalt psychologist. Kai von Fieandt recalled Rubin's disapproval of the attempts by the Gestalt psychologists to force all phenomena to yield to their Gestalt principles as a sort of ‚cure for all' [...]. This also held for their conception of figure and ground. As Rubin once wrote to professor Christian A. Ruckmick at the University of Iowa, ‚I am opposed to the extension of the use of the concepts ‚figure' and ‚ground' to other fields than the specifically visual,' adding also that ‚I am quite independent of the Gestalt psychologists, and I do not belong to any school' ([...] Rubin to Ruckmick, August 24, 1931)." – Pind, *Edgar Rubin and Psychology in Denmark,* 212. Auf einer Abgrenzung Rubins von der Gestaltpsychologie besteht auch Margarete Pratschke, während der von ihr erwähnte große Aufsatz anlässlich 100 Jahren Gestaltpsychologie die „figure-ground organization" ganz selbstverständlich als Teil der Gestaltpsychologie auffasst. – Cf. Pratschke, *Gestaltexperimente unterm Bilderhimmel,* Anm. 5 und 32 auf 195 f., sowie Wagemans et al., A Century of Gestalt Psychology. 2012 wurden übrigens parallel 100 Jahre Gestaltpsychologie und 100 Jahre Figur-Grund-Unterscheidung begangen: „In 1912, Max Wertheimer published his paper on phi motion, widely recognized as the start of Gestalt psychology." – Ibid., 1172. Demgegenüber datiert Pind anhand einer Briefstelle vom 15. Mai 1912 den Beginn von Rubins bahnbrechenden Figur-Grund-Untersuchungen. – Cf. Pind, Jörgen L.: Figure and Ground at 100, in: *the psychologist* 25, 2012 (1), 90 f.: 90. „Max Wertheimer, Wolfgang Köhler and Kurt Koffka, pioneers of the Gestalt movement [...] eagerly embraced Rubin's study, which came to feature prominently in Koffka's (1935) standard work, *Principles of Gestalt Psychology.*" – Ibid., 91.

62
Cf. dazu auch den Hinweis im Vorwort: „Essentially, I have aimed to give a sympathetic picture of the Gestalt system from the standpoint of a non-configurationist [i. e. eines Nicht-Gestaltpsychologen], although I must confess that an examination of the evidence has left me more favorably disposed toward the theory than I had originally anticipated." – Hartmann, George W.: *Gestalt Psychology. A Survey of Facts and Principles*, New York 1935, VI. Bezüglich seiner unmittelbaren

„Many passages derived from important scattered sources appear here in English for the first time".[63] Hartmann bespricht in seinem Buch selbstverständlich auch die Figur-Grund-Unterscheidung. Einen Abschnitt über *Rubin and Experimental Phenomenology* eröffnet er mit einer hellsichtigen Einordnung Rubins in den Gestaltdiskurs:

> But the one work outside their own circle which gave the initial Gestalt coterie more aid and comfort than any other was the product of the Danish psychologist Rubin, a protégé of Höffding [Høffding] at Copenhagen. Oddly enough, the study was performed at Göttingen where experimental phenomenology appears to have been well established about 1910 under the direction of G. E. Müller, one of the most ardent champions of the legitimacy of the sensory reduction of all mental processes. Since its findings have played such a prominent part in the development of *Gestalttheorie*, it will be rewarding to examine them in some detail.[64]

Weiterhin hielt sich mit dem bereits erwähnten Kurt Koffka ein Hauptvertreter der Gestaltpsychologie ab 1924 zunehmend in den USA auf, wo er lehrte und veröffentlichte.[65] Zeitgleich mit

Kenntnis der deutschsprachigen Gestaltpsychologie schreibt Hartmann: „I am indebted to the Social Science Research Council for the fellowship award which made it possible for me to spend the academic year 1930–1931 in the very citadel of Gestalt psychology, participating in characteristic investigations and profiting from the personal contacts and library facilities then available at the *Psychologisches Institut* of the University of Berlin." – Ibid., VII.

63
Ibid., VI.

64
Ibid., 23.

65
Über Koffka berichtet Wolfgang Metzger (1899–1979) in der *Neuen Deutschen Biographie (NDB)*, er sei 1910–1911 Assistent bei Friedrich Schumann in Frankfurt gewesen, „wo kurz nach ihm auch Wolfgang Köhler Assistent wurde und zu Beginn des Wintersemesters 1910 die Begegnung der beiden mit Max Wertheimer stattfand, aus der die lebenslange Zusammenarbeit am Aufbau der Gestalttheorie hervorging. 1911 wurde K.[offka] in Gießen mit der in Würzburg entstandenen Untersuchung ‚Zur Analyse der Vorstellungen und ihrer Gesetze' habilitiert. […] 1924/25 war er Gastprofessor an der Cornell University. […] 1926/27 lehrte er an der University of Wisconsin. 1927 beendete er seine Tätigkeit in Gießen und übernahm einen neu gegründeten Lehrstuhl am Smith College, den er bis zu seinem Tode innehatte. […] Große Verdienste hat sich K.[offka] durch seine umfassenden Darstellungen der Gestalttheorie erworben, deren erste, die ‚Grundlegung der Wahrnehmungslehre' [recte: *Zur Grundlegung der Wahrnehmungspsychologie*], 1915, die letzte, die ‚Principles of Gestalt Psychology', 1935

Hartmanns Buch brachte Koffka 1935 in New York und 1936 in London sein Standardwerk *Principles of Gestalt Psychology* heraus. ‚Figure and Ground' ist darin ein ganzes Kapitel gewidmet.[66]

Noch sechs Jahre früher war 1929 Wolfgang Köhlers (1887–1967) Buch *Gestalt Psychology* in New York, 1930 dann als ‚British Edition' in London erschienen; die deutsche Übersetzung *Psychologische Probleme* kam erst 1933 heraus.[67] In *Gestalt Psychology* suchte Köhler überhaupt erst einmal Verständnis für die neue Denkweise der Gestaltpsychologie zu wecken, in Abgrenzung von dem in der nordamerikanischen Psychologie dominierenden Behaviorismus.[68] Köhler, seit 1922 Professor und Direktor am Psychologischen Institut der Berliner Universität, emigrierte 1935 in die USA, nachdem er dort 1925/26 und 1934/35 bereits als Gastprofessor an der Clark University bzw. an der Harvard University gelehrt hatte.[69]

Damit sind einige der wichtigsten ‚Relaisstellen' des Ideentransfers von der deutschsprachigen Psychologie in die angloamerikanische Wissenschaft benannt.[70] Offensichtlich fand ein

erschienen ist." – Metzger, Wolfgang: Stichwort „Koffka, Kurt", in: Historische Kommission bei der Bayerischen Akademie der Wissenschaften (Ed.): *Neue Deutsche Biographie*, vol. 12, Berlin 1980, 417 f.

66
Wie Anm. 49.

67
Köhler, Wolfgang: *Gestalt Psychology*, New York 1929; id.: *Gestalt Psychology*, London 1930 („British Edition, reset from the 3rd American edition"); veränderte deutsche Übersetzung: id.: *Psychologische Probleme*, Berlin 1933.

68
Cf. insb. das Vorwort und das erste Kapitel, „The Viewpoint of Behaviorism", in: Köhler, *Gestalt Psychology*, 1929, VII–X und 3–34, bzw. verändert in der deutschsprachigen Ausgabe: Köhler, *Psychologische Probleme*, V–VII und 1–22. Noch 1980 schreibt Rudolf Bergius (1914–2004) im *NDB*-Artikel über Köhler: „Die gestaltpsychologische Schule überlebte nicht als solche, aber ihre wichtigsten Erkenntnisse sind Gesamtbesitz der modernen Psychologie [...]. K.[öhler]s Grundsatz, daß neurophysiologische Forschung von der unvoreingenommenen, genauen Beobachtung der Wahrnehmungserlebnisse geleitet werden müsse, wird wegen des immer noch vorhandenen behavioristischen Widerstandes nur selten befolgt." – Bergius, „Köhler, Wolfgang", 304.

69
Cf. ibid., 303. Zu Köhlers Engagement zugunsten des Psychologischen Instituts an der Berliner Universität zwischen 1933 und 1935 cf. Henle, Mary: One Man Against the Nazis. Wolfgang Köhler, in: *American Psychologist. Journal of the American Psychological Association* 33, 1978 (10), 939–944.

70
Weitere ließen sich anführen. Cf. in diesem Zusammenhang auch die Forschungen zur Emigration von Wissenschaftlern und Kunsthistorikern, unter anderem: vorbereitend Dilly, Heinrich: *Deutsche Kunsthistoriker 1933–1945*, München/Berlin 1988; sodann Hassler, Marianne/Wertheimer, Jürgen (Ed.): *Der Exodus aus Nazideutschland und die Folgen. Jüdische Wissenschaftler im Exil*, Tübingen 1997; Michels, Karen: *Transplantierte Kunstwissenschaft. Deutschsprachige Kunstgeschichte im amerikanischen Exil*, Berlin 1999; Wendland, Ulrike: *Biographisches Handbuch deutschsprachiger Kunsthistoriker*

umfangreicher Austausch statt, der nicht nur mit Hilfe von Übersetzungen erfolgte, sondern insbesondere auch durch Aufenthalte von Gastwissenschaftlern in Berlin und durch die Vertreter der Gestaltpsychologie selbst, spätestens nach ihrer erzwungenen Emigration.[71]

Figur/Grund in der kunstwissenschaftlichen Literatur

1944 erschien in Chicago György Kepes' (1906–2001) Buch *language of vision*. Das reich illustrierte Werk ist eher in die Rubrik ‚visuelle Kommunikation' als unter ‚Kunstwissenschaft' einzuordnen.[72] Bedeutung hat es als vergleichsweise frühes Beispiel für den Ideentransfer aus der Wahrnehmungs- und Gestaltpsychologie – wenn man von den Einflüssen während der Bauhauszeit einmal absieht.[73] Gleich das erste Kapitel, „Plastic Organization",

im Exil. Leben und Werk der unter dem Nationalsozialismus verfolgten und vertriebenen Wissenschaftler, 2 vol., München 1999.

Michels und Wendland zählen Arnheim übrigens zu den Kunsthistorikern, während (ausgerechnet) das von ehemaligen Angehörigen der Humboldt-Universität Berlin herausgegebene *Metzler Kunsthistoriker Lexikon* auch in seiner zweiten Auflage auf einen entsprechenden Eintrag verzichtet. – Cf. Betthausen, Peter/Feist, Peter H./Fork, Christiane: *Metzler Kunsthistoriker Lexikon. Zweihundert Porträts deutschsprachiger Autoren aus vier Jahrhunderten*, Stuttgart/Weimar 1999, ²2007.

71
Zur Wiederbegegnung der Emigranten in den USA cf. exemplarisch Arnheim, Lebenslauf. Zu den seltenen Fällen, in denen ein Vertreter der Gestaltpsychologie sich selbst im kunstwissenschaftlichen Kontext äußerte, zählt Koffkas 1940 veröffentlichter Beitrag zu einer Vorlesungsreihe am Bryn Mawr College: Koffka, K.[urt]: Problems in the Psychology of Art, in: Bernheimer, Richard/Carpenter, Rhys/Koffka, K.[urt]/Nahm, Milton C.: *Art. A Bryn Mawr Symposium*, Bryn Mawr, PA, 1940, 179–273. Es handelt sich um grundsätzliche Betrachtungen mehr erkenntnistheoretischer denn wahrnehmungspsychologischer Natur. Zu Beginn legt Koffka die bereits erwähnte Unterscheidung zwischen Verhaltens- und Wahrnehmungspsychologie (bzw. Behaviorismus und Gestaltpsychologie) dar (cf. ibid., 180–182), um anschließend festzustellen: „I had never written on psychological problems of art, nor had I given them much systematic thought, when I received the invitation to give two lectures in the Bryn Mawr Symposium on Art" (182). Auf die Wahrnehmungspsychologie, die uns hier interessiert, geht er erst zum Ende hin ein (cf. 256–262) und stellt fest: „it is obvious that the psychology of perception will be of very great importance for the psychology of art; for not only does it investigate the establishment of the art-objects in the spectators [...] but [...] perception of his own work guides the artist throughout his act of creation" (259). „Figure and background" werden lediglich erwähnt (cf. 260).

72
Kepes, Gyorgy: *language of vision*, Chicago 1944 (mit Vorworten von S.[igfried] Giedion und S.[amuel] I.[chiye] Hayakawa). Drei Jahre später wurde im selben Verlag (Paul Theobald) Moholy-Nagys *vision in motion* veröffentlicht: Moholy-Nagy, L.[ászló]: *vision in motion*, Chicago 1947.

73
Ich denke hier beispielsweise an Josef Albers und Paul Klee. Zum bereits vor der Bauhauszeit einsetzenden Ideentransfer cf. unter anderem Teuber, Marianne L.: Zwei frühe Quellen zu Paul Klees Theorie der Form. Eine Dokumentation, in: Zweite, Armin (Ed.): *Paul Klee. Das Frühwerk 1883–1922* (Katalog zur

beschreibt die visuelle Wahrnehmung mit Sätzen, die ebenso gut von einem Wahrnehmungspsychologen stammen könnten – wenngleich von Kepes mit deutlich mehr Verve vorgetragen: „We live in the midst of a whirlwind of light qualities. From this whirling confusion we build unified entities, those forms of experience called visual images."[74]

Die ‚unified entities' entsprechen den ‚Ganzheiten' bzw. ‚Gestalten' der Psychologie. Zwei Seiten darauf zitiert Kepes bereits Wolfgang Köhler, auch wenn er die Zusammenhänge stark vereinfacht.[75] Dementsprechend erklärt er zu Beginn des Buches: „all terms used are arbitrary, and are not to be considered as scientifically established."[76] Was das bedeutet, sehen wir beispielsweise, wenn er mit wechselnden *termini technici* die Gestaltgesetze wiedergibt. So heißt es unter der Überschrift „Nearness": „Proximity is the simplest condition of organization."[77] Kepes ist um Verständlichkeit bemüht, nicht um Konsistenz. Offensichtlich beschreibt er hier aber das Gesetz der Nähe. Bei den zugehörigen Bildbeispielen bezieht er sich auf Koffka. Hinter den darauffolgenden Überschriften „Similarity or Equality", „Continuance" und „Closure"[78] verbergen sich weitere Gestaltgesetze (Gesetz der Gleichheit, Gesetz der guten Kurve oder des gemeinsamen Schicksals, Gesetz der Geschlossenheit).

Die Figur-Grund-Unterscheidung erläutert Kepes zwar auf einfache und einleuchtende Weise,[79] dennoch dürften die

Ausstellung vom 12. Dezember 1979 bis zum 2. März 1980 in der Städtischen Galerie im Lenbachhaus, München), [München] [1979], 261–296; ead.: *Blue Night* by Paul Klee, in: Henle, Mary (Ed.): *Vision and Artifact*, New York 1976 (mit einem Vorwort von Rudolf Arnheim), 131–151.

74
Kepes, *language of vision*, 15.

75
Cf. ibid., 17. Kepes' unklare Quellenangabe „W. Kohler, Physikal Gestalten 1920" bezieht sich übrigens auf den englischsprachigen Auszug aus einer deutschsprachigen Veröffentlichung Köhlers im *Source Book*, was die weite Rezeption des später auch in mehreren Neuauflagen verbreiteten *Source Book* unterstreicht. – Cf. Köhler, Wolfgang: Physical Gestalten, in: Ellis, *A Source Book of Gestalt Psychology*, 17–54: 20. Für die deutsche Originalfassung cf. id.: *Die physischen Gestalten in Ruhe und im stationären Zustand. Eine naturphilosophische Untersuchung*, Braunschweig 1920, XVIII.

76
Kepes, *language of vision*, 15.

77
Ibid., 46.

78
Cf. ibid., 47–51.

79
„We cannot bear chaos – the disturbance of equilibrium in the field of experience. Consequently, we must immediately form light-impacts into shapes and figures. Exposed to

Gestaltpsychologen nicht damit einverstanden gewesen sein, wenn er den Vorgang der visuellen Wahrnehmung im Grunde ‚atomistisch' erklärt: „This organization of figures and backgrounds is repeated progressively until the whole visual field is perceived as a formed, ordered unity".[80] Demgegenüber weist beispielsweise Katz auf „die Unmittelbarkeit, mit der die Gestalt sich einstellt",[81] hin.

Kepes machte die Ideen der Wahrnehmungs- und Gestaltpsychologie populär, auch wenn er sie dabei vereinfachte und offenkundig auch nicht immer bis in die Details durchdrang. Seine Leistung ist, dass er die wissenschaftlichen Erkenntnisse mit zeitgenössischen Illustrationen auf überzeugende Weise anschaulich machte und somit in den Alltag und in die gestalterische Anwendung holte, was bei den Gestaltpsychologen abstrakt wirkende diagrammatische Darstellungen geblieben waren.[82]

a visual field that in its light-quality is to the slightest degree heterogeneous, one organizes that field at once into two opposing elements; into a figure against a background. […] Every image is based upon this dynamic dualism, the unity of opposites. Certain impulses are tied together in a stable visual whole, while other impulses are left in their unorganized fluid state and serve only as a background and are perceived as intervals." – Ibid., 31.

80
Ibid.

81
Katz, *Gestaltpsychologie*, 45; cf. auch die Ausführungen auf 44 f. Dass das wahrgenommene Ganze nicht das Resultat einer fortschreitenden Addition von Einzeleindrücken ist, betonen beispielsweise auch Wagemans et al.: „Wertheimer claimed that functional relations determine what will appear as the whole and what will appear as parts (i.e., reciprocal dependency). Often the whole is grasped even before the individual parts enter consciousness. The contents of our awareness are by and large not additive but possess a characteristic coherence. They are structures that are segregated from the background, often with an inner center, to which the other parts are related hierarchically. Such structures or Gestalten are *different from* the sum of the parts. They arise from continuous global processes in the brain, rather than combinations of elementary excitations." – Wagemans et al., A Century of Gestalt Psychology, 1175.

82
Paradox erscheint, dass Kepes sich für das Vorwort neben Samuel Ichiye Hayakawa (1906–1992) vom Illinois Institute of Technology ausgerechnet Sigfried Giedion (1888–1968) suchte. Giedions Tragik besteht darin, dass er die Gestaltpsychologie nicht als prägende Kraft von Kepes' Buch zu erkennen scheint (während dieser seine Danksagung mit den Worten beginnt: „First of all the author wishes to acknowledge his indebtedness to the Gestalt psychologists." – Kepes, *language of vision*, 4). Wenn Giedion von der „optical revolution – around 1910 –" (hier und im Folgenden: ibid., 7) spricht, denkt er eben *nicht* an die sich damals formierende Gestaltpsychologie, sondern ausschließlich an die moderne Kunst – „from cubism to surrealism" –, um sogleich auf sein eigenes Großthema zu verweisen: „a new spatial conception". – Cf. hierzu Giedion, Sigfried: *Space, Time and Architecture. the growth of a new tradition*, Cambridge, MA/London ²1941, insb. 355 ff. Bedenkt man den verwandten, vielleicht journalistisch zu nennenden Schreibstil Kepes' und Giedions, ist es freilich naheliegend, dass Giedion ein Vorwort zu Kepes' Buch beitrug.

Für einen präziseren Umgang mit der Gestaltpsychologie fehlte Kepes möglicherweise der unmittelbare Zugang, wie Arnheim ihn hatte.[83] Von diesem stammt das zweite Buch, das hier – noch einmal – erwähnt werden soll, das 1954 erschienene *Art and Visual Perception. A Psychology of the Creative Eye.*[84] Die Anfänge des Buches reichen bis in die erste Hälfte der 1940er Jahre zurück. 1981 teilt Arnheim über die erste Zeit nach seiner Ankunft 1940 in den USA Folgendes mit:

> Die Rockefeller Foundation gab mir ein Stipendium und verschaffte mir Forschungsarbeit am Office of Radio Research der Columbia University. [...] Ein Jahr später erhielt ich ein weiteres Stipendium, von der Guggenheim Foundation, diesmal für Anwendung der Gestaltpsychologie auf die Kunst. Mit dieser Arbeit legte ich die Grundlage für mein späteres Buch, *Kunst und Sehen*, das erst 1954 erschien.[85]

Arnheims Buch wurde offensichtlich von Anfang an als Medium eines avant la lettre transdisziplinären Ideentransfers konzipiert. Dementsprechend schreibt er in der Einleitung: „From its beginnings and throughout its development during the last half century, gestalt psychology has shown a kinship to art. The writings of Max Wertheimer, Wolfgang Köhler, Kurt Koffka are pervaded by it"[86] – um zu dem Schluss zu gelangen, dass die Denkweise der

83
Kepes lernte Arnheim bereits um 1930, vor ihrer Zeit in Amerika, kennen. Letzterer erinnert sich wie folgt: „Mein Buch *Film als Kunst* war gerade noch im Herbst (?) 1932 bei Rowohlt erschienen (auf dem Schutzumschlag mit einem Photogramm von Gyorgy Kepes, einem Schüler von Moholy-Nagy und später in Amerika ein guter Freund), hatte dann aber natürlich keine weitere Verbreitung in Deutschland." – Arnheim, Lebenslauf. Und Kepes wiederum: „For more than sixty years Rudi Arnheim has been one of my closest friends. Our first contact was in Berlin in the early 1930s, when I was asked by the publisher Rowo[h]lt Verlag to design a jacket for a book, *Film als Kunst,* by Rudolf Arnheim. We met several times in Berlin, and then we did not see each other again until the early 1940s when we came across each other by chance in New York." – Kepes, Gyorgy: July 20, 1996 – Wellfleet, Massachusetts, in: Kleinman, Kent/Van Duzer, Leslie (Ed.): *Rudolf Arnheim. Revealing Vision,* Ann Arbor 1997, 16 f.: 16.

84
Arnheim, Rudolf: *Art and Visual Perception. A Psychology of the Creative Eye,* Berkeley/Los Angeles/London 1954; dt. Erstausgabe: *Kunst und Sehen. Eine Psychologie des schöpferischen Auges,* Berlin 1965.

85
Arnheim, Lebenslauf. 1943 hatte er dem Thema bereits einen kleinen Aufsatz gewidmet: id.: Gestalt and Art, in: *The Journal of Aesthetics and Art Criticism* 2, 1942–1943 (8) (Herbst 1943), 71–75.

Gestaltpsychologie gewissermaßen Voraussetzung jedes künstlerischen Schaffens sei. In Arnheims Worten:

> [...] the spirit underlying the reasoning of these men [– Wertheimer, Köhler, Koffka –] makes the artist feel at home. [...] The realization that a whole cannot be attained by adding up isolated parts was not new to the artist. For many centuries scientists had been able to say valuable things about reality without going beyond the relatively simple level of reasoning that excludes the complexities of organization and interaction. But at no time could a work of art have been made or understood by a mind unable to conceive the integrated structure of a whole.[87]

Wie erwähnt, offenbart schon das umfangreiche Literaturverzeichnis von Arnheims Buch die Prägung des Autors durch die wahrnehmungs- und gestaltpsychologische Fachliteratur. Anstelle des Begriffs ‚Gestalt', wie in der deutschen Ausgabe (1965), verwendet Arnheim in der amerikanischen Originalausgabe 1954 übrigens das Wort ‚Shape'.[88] Dem Thema ‚Figure and Ground' ist ein ganzer Abschnitt im Kapitel „Space" gewidmet,[89] unmittelbar nachdem er das Thema des Konturs dargelegt hat. Den Abschnitt beginnt Arnheim mit einem Hinweis auf Rubin, so dass der Leser sich via Literaturverzeichnis direkt in die wahrnehmungspsychologische Originalliteratur vertiefen kann. Das Thema Figur/Grund bespricht er dann zunächst anhand einiger typischer Gestaltdiagramme, versucht sich gleich darauf aber auch an der Übertragung auf die Kunst.

Arnheim erläutert in Anlehnung an Rubin verschiedene Bedingungen des Figur-Grund-Phänomens, etwa dass eine umschlossene Fläche eher als Figur, die umschließende eher als Grund wahrgenommen wird; dass die kleinere zweier Flächen

86 Arnheim, *Art and Visual Perception*, VII.

87 Ibid.

88 Cf. die Überschrift von Kapitel 2 sowie die Formulierungen innerhalb des Kapitels: „What is Shape?" (Arnheim 1954, 32) – „Was ist eine Gestalt?" (Arnheim 1965, 34); „Seeing Shape" (Arnheim 1954, 34) – „Gestaltsehen" (Arnheim 1965, 36) und passim.

89 Hier und im Folgenden: Arnheim, *Art and Visual Perception*, 182–185.

eher als Figur erlebt wird; dass konvexe Formen eher als Figur aufgefasst werden, während die ihnen komplementären konkaven Formen eher zu einer Wahrnehmung als Grund tendieren. Aufgrund seiner Lehrjahre am Psychologischen Institut der Berliner Universität kann man davon ausgehen, dass Arnheim zu den wahrnehmungspsychologisch bestinformierten Autoren gehört, die über Kunst geschrieben haben.

In Gombrichs *Art and Illusion. A Study in the Psychology of Pictorial Representation* (1960)[90] ist Figur/Grund anders als bei Arnheim kein explizites Thema.[91] Stattdessen verwendet er die Begriffe beiläufig im Text, kaum wahrnehmbar in die Argumentation eingewoben. Ebenso deutlich, wie Arnheim als Wahrnehmungspsychologe geprägt wurde, war Gombrich Kunsthistoriker. Dass das Register der deutschen Erstausgabe (1967)[92] ‚Figur und Grund' als eigenes Stichwort aufführt, ist einer der wenigen expliziten Hinweise auf den Einfluss der Wahrnehmungspsychologie. In der englischsprachigen Erstausgabe 1960 wurde ‚figure/ground' noch nicht lemmatisiert. Im Unterschied zu Kepes und Arnheim stand Gombrich die gesamte Kunstgeschichte als Material zur Verfügung. Die Bibliographie verzeichnet aber auch eine

90
Gombrich, E.[rnst] H.: *Art and Illusion. A Study in the Psychology of Pictorial Representation*, New York 1960 (The A.W. Mellon Lectures in the Fine Arts, delivered at the National Gallery of Art, Washington, 1956); britische Parallelausgabe: London/New York 1960.

91
Cf. indes beispielsweise seinen Aufsatz „Illusion and Visual Deadlock", in: Gombrich, E.[rnst] H.: *Meditations on a Hobby Horse and Other Essays on the Theory of Art*, London 1963, 151–159 und 173 (Anm.), Fig. 126–135. Gombrich gelangt in diesem 1961 ursprünglich als Zeitschriftenbeitrag veröffentlichten Text von der Figur-Grund-Umkehrbarkeit von Vexierbildern (‚puzzle pictures'; als Beispiel zeigt er das royalistische Urnenmotiv, cf. in Anm. 27 den Hinweis auf die Abbildung in *L'homme-paysage*) über Maurits Cornelis Eschers (1898–1972) Werke und den Kubismus hin zur mehrdeutigen Lesbarkeit der Zeichnungen Josef Albers' und bemerkt abschließend: „It was by exploring these paradoxes [of Cubism] that artists wanted to discover new modes of organization. It is not only Escher who shows us their success. Even abstract art owes some of its most interesting possibilities to the fascination of unresolved ambiguities as in many of the ingenious designs by Albers." – Ibid., 159. Über das Blatt mit dem royalistischen Urnenmotiv schreibt Gombrich: „It was circulated during the French Revolution as a clandestine tribute to the royal family." – Ibid., 153. Ganz so heimlich können diese Darstellungen kaum gewesen sein, wenn man bedenkt, dass selbst die französischen Blätter wenigstens später mit Legende versehen wurden und die britischen Vexierbilder von Anfang an explizit auf die versteckten Gesichtsprofile hinwiesen. Zu Fig. 391 und drei weiteren, dazugehörigen Blättern ist sogar eine Lesehilfe (Textblatt mit Umzeichnung) erschienen: *A Key to Orme's New Puzzles of Portraits*, British Museum, inv. Nr. J,11.127 bzw. 1983,U.897.

92
Gombrich, E.[rnst] H.: *Kunst und Illusion. Zur Psychologie der bildlichen Darstellung*, Köln 1967.

Reihe wahrnehmungspsychologischer Werke, darunter als einschlägig gestaltpsychologisches Buch Wolfgang Metzgers *Gesetze des Sehens* in der zweiten, erweiterten Auflage (1953). In der Einleitung zitiert Gombrich an einer Stelle Wolfgang Köhler, den er als „one of the greatest pioneers in the field of perceptual psychology“[93] bezeichnet, um dann vielsagend fortzufahren:

> At least one of Köhler's followers [...] has ventured from psychology into the field of art. Rudolf Arnheim's book *Art and Visual Perception* deals with the visual image from the point of view of Gestalt psychology. I have read it with much profit. His chapter on growth, which deals with child art, seems to me so instructive that I was relieved to be able to exclude this much-discussed example from the field of my inquiry. For the historian and his problems of style, on the other hand, the book yields less.[94]

Arnheim reagierte mit einer ausführlichen Rezension von Gombrichs Buch, deren nicht minder süffisanter Schlussabsatz wie folgt lautet:

> In offering the foregoing critique this reviewer is fully aware that progress in any field of knowledge tends to come from one-sided theses. Gombrich has made the strongest possible case for his position. He has also revealed with admirable clarity its weaknesses, at which the counterthrust must aim. In his Preface, Gombrich assures his readers that he will not play safe. He has kept his promise.[95]

93 Id., *Art and Illusion*, 26.

94 Ibid., 26 f.

95 Arnheim, Rudolf: Rezension von E.[rnst] H. Gombrich, *Art and Illusion*, New York 1960, in: *The Art Bulletin* 44, 1962 (1), 75–79: 79. Zuvor fällt das Verdikt: „In accordance with his own views of human behavior, Gombrich has taken from psychology what he came to find in it“ (ibid., 78), nachdem eine persönliche Fehde pariert worden ist (ibid., 77), welche an die oben zitierte Passage über Arnheim anschließt.

Ideengeschichte als vielschichtiger Komplex

Die Geschichte der menschlichen Kultur ist ein eng verwobenes Beziehungsgeflecht, das hier naturgemäß nur ganz punktuell angehoben und zur Sichtbarkeit gebracht wurde. Der Text rückt einige Interdependenzen in den Vordergrund, stellt sie in eine chronologische Abfolge, während andere vernachlässigt werden oder unerwähnt bleiben. Zu berichten ist nicht nur das Was, das bloße Faktum. Oft sind das Wie und der Zusammenhang, in welchen das Was eingebettet ist, von durchaus größerer Bedeutung und Wirkmacht. Die Vielschichtigkeit der Beziehungen wird als *condicio sine qua non* nicht zuletzt dann deutlich, wenn man die in bestimmtem Zusammenhang erwähnten Personen in der den Beitrag beschließenden Liste der Lebensdaten in anderer, bisweilen überraschender Nachbarschaft wiederfindet.

So vielfältig und verzweigt die Beziehungen zwischen Kunst und Wahrnehmungspsychologie bzw. zwischen Gestaltpsychologie und Kunstwissenschaft mitunter sind, wurde längst nicht alles Wissenswerte über die wechselseitigen Beziehungen – etwa auch zwischen bestimmten Protagonisten – berichtet. Das bestätigen zwei abschließende ‚Tiefenbohrungen‘, die mit einem Blick in das Weimar der frühen Goethezeit und anderthalb Jahrhunderte später in das Weimar der Bauhauszeit weitere Details der Ideengeschichte von ‚Figur und Grund‘ zutage fördern.

Exkurs 1:
Zu Lavaters Wechselwirkung mit dem Weimar der Goethezeit

Im Subskribentenverzeichnis bereits des ersten Bandes von Lavaters publizistischem Großprojekt zur Physiognomik sind auch „die Herzoginn von Weimar“ (Anna Amalia, 1739–1807) und „der Erbprinz Carl August von Weimar“ (1757–1828) aufgeführt.[96] Zu den drei in Band 1 genannten Londoner Subskribenten zählt mit gleich drei Exemplaren der Übersetzer Johann Friedrich Schiller (1737–1814), ein Verwandter Friedrich Schillers

96
Cf. Lavater, Johann Caspar: *Physiognomische Fragmente, zur Beförderung der Menschenkenntniß und Menschenliebe. Erster Versuch*, Leipzig/Winterthur 1775, [277].

(1759–1805).[97] In Band 2 figuriert dann auch „Herr Hofrath Wieland in Weimar" (1733–1813) als Subskribent.[98] In Band 4 kann Lavater schließlich „Ihro Majestät die Königinn von Engelland" zu seinen Subskribenten zählen.[99] Zu Schiller und dem Verlag der deutschen Erstausgabe, Weidmanns Erben und Reich, heißt es in der Forschungsliteratur:

> Der bedeutendste Importeur englischen Schrifttums des 18. Jahrhunderts war [...] die Leipziger Firma Weidmann und Reich. Der Sortimenthandel mit ausländischen Büchern hatte im Hause Weidmann Tradition. [...] Unter Philipp Erasmus Reich stieg das Haus Weidmanns Erben und Reich (seit 1762) nicht nur zum ersten Verlag Deutschlands, sondern auch zum führenden Importeur englischsprachigen Schrifttums auf. [...] Reich beschäftigte in London eigene Agenten und Korrespondenten, wie Johann Friedrich Schiller, [...] der zwischen 1776 und 1784 dort für Reich tätig war. In eben diesem Zeitraum boten Weidmann und Reich den Großteil ihrer englischen Buchimporte auf den Messen an. Es ist vorstellbar, dass Schiller diese Bücher vor Ort angekauft und vielleicht sogar den Hauptteil der Titel selbst ausgewählt hatte.[100]

Mit der Verlagswahl für die deutsche Originalausgabe der *Physiognomischen Fragmente* und Schillers Tätigkeit als Verlagsagent in London erklärt sich folglich wohl auch die oben erwähnte rasche internationale Verbreitung von Lavaters Werk, gerade auch in Großbritannien.[101]

97
Cf. ibid., [279].

98
Cf. id.: *Physiognomische Fragmente, zur Beförderung der Menschenkenntniß und Menschenliebe. Zweyter Versuch*, Leipzig/Winterthur 1776, [300].

99
Cf. id.: *Physiognomische Fragmente, zur Beförderung der Menschenkenntniß und Menschenliebe. Vierter Versuch*, Leipzig/Winterthur 1778, [500].

100
Willenberg, Jennifer: *Distribution und Übersetzung englischen Schrifttums im Deutschland des 18. Jahrhunderts*, München 2008, 113; cf. auch 203–205 und passim.

101
Schiller war allerdings 1783 nach 22 Jahren Aufenthalts in London nach Württemberg zurückgekehrt. – Cf. Börckel, Alfred: Der Buchdrucker und Sprachmeister Johann Friedrich Schiller. Nach archivalischen Quellen dargestellt, in: *Zeitschrift für Bücherfreunde*.

1775 ist nicht nur der Erscheinungsbeginn von Lavaters *Physiognomischen Fragmenten,* sondern auch das Jahr, in dem Johann Wolfgang Goethe (1749–1832) auf Einladung des soeben volljährigen Herzogs Carl August nach Weimar kam, wo bald darauf, zwischen 1775 und 1780, eine Silhouette von jenem angefertigt wurde. Zu der noch vor Weimar etablierten persönlichen Beziehung zwischen Goethe und Lavater gibt uns der Kommentar zur Goethe-Briefausgabe genaueren Aufschluss:

> Auf Goethe, der 1772 den 3. Band der ‚Aussichten in die Ewigkeit' [von Lavater] kritisch rezensiert hatte, war Lavater durch dessen zu Beginn des Jahres 1773 anonym erschienenen ‚Brief des Pastors zu *** an den neuen Pastor zu ***' aufmerksam geworden. Im 14. Buch von ‚Dichtung und Wahrheit' erinnert sich Goethe: (...) *so kam ich auch mit Lavatern in Verbindung* [...] Im Frühjahr 1773 hatte er [Lavater] seinen Frankfurter Kommissionär [...] nach dem Verfasser gefragt [...]. [Am 14. August 1773] wandte sich Lavater [...] mit einem [...] Brief an Goethe [...]. Dies ist der erste überlieferte Brief der beiderseitigen Korrespondenz. Goethes Antworten auf Lavaters erste Briefe sind nicht oder nur fragmentarisch überliefert; doch es ging, und zwar von Anfang an kontrovers, um religiöse Fragen [...]. Ein zweites Thema des frühen Briefwechsels [...] war die Physiognomik: Goethe förderte die Veröffentlichung von Lavaters ‚Physiognomischen Fragmenten', die von 1775 an bei Reich in Leipzig erschienen. Goethe vermittelte nicht nur das Manuskript an den Verleger, nachdem er es redigiert und

Monatshefte für Bibliophilie und verwandte Interessen 8, 1904–1905 (2) (Mai 1904), 58–71: 64. Zu Schillers Londoner Tätigkeit für den Leipziger Verlag Weidmanns Erben und Reich cf. auch die erst kürzlich im Druck erschienene Berliner Diplomarbeit Mark Lehmstedts aus dem Jahr 1987. – Lehmstedt, Mark: *„Uebersetzungsmanufactur" und „proletarische Scribenten". Buchmarkt und Übersetzungswesen im 18. Jahrhundert*, Leipzig 2023, 54 und passim. Warum die ersten Übersetzungen ausgerechnet in Amsterdam und La Haye erschienen, erhellt aus 27 f. In seiner Dissertation bezeichnet Lehmstedt Schiller als „Reichs bedeutendste[n] ‚literarische[n] Agent[en]'". – Id.: *Struktur und Arbeitsweise eines Verlages der deutschen Aufklärung. Die Weidmannsche Buchhandlung in Leipzig unter der Leitung von Philipp Erasmus Reich zwischen 1745 und 1787* (= Diss. phil., Universität Leipzig), [Leipzig] [1990], 130.

> korrigiert hatte, sondern er war auch bei der Besorgung und Herstellung von Abbildungen, Zeichnungen und Silhouetten behilflich und lieferte eigene Beiträge [...]. Zur persönlichen Bekanntschaft kam es im Juni 1774, als Lavater Frankfurt besuchte.[102]

Goethe als Lavaters Lektor und Literaturagent! Die Weimarer Situation, in der Lavaters Physiognomik im Folgenden so dankbar aufgenommen wurde, fasst Gudrun Körner, Ernst Biesalski zitierend, so zusammen:

> In Deutschland begann man etwa ab 1750 zu silhouettieren, ein Kunsthandwerk, das [...] in den siebziger und achtziger Jahren zur wahren Sucht wurde. [...] In Weimar wurden Scherenschnitt und Physiognomik zu einer wichtigen Begleiterscheinung des gesellschaftlichen Lebens. „Vielleicht das größte, sicher aber das anziehendste und abwechslungsreichste Zentrum der Schattenkunst ist das Weimar zu Zeiten der Herzoginmutter Amalia, Karl Augusts und Goethes ..."[103]

Die Passage stammt aus dem Katalogtext zu dem erwähnten frühen Scherenschnitt-Profil Goethes, das wie folgt beschrieben wird: „Anonym, *Johann Wolfgang Goethe. Lebensgroßer geschnittener Schattenriß*, um 1775–80 [...] Aus weißem Papier ausgeschnitten [= Grund], schwarz unterlegt [= Figur]".[104] Herstellungstechnisch handelt es sich mithin um eine Figur-Grund-Umkehrung: Der schwarz unterlegte Grund wird zur

102
Kurscheidt, Georg/Richter, Elke (Ed.), Goethe, Johann Wolfgang: *Briefe*, vol. 2 · II: *Anfang 1773–Ende Oktober 1775. Kommentar*, Berlin 2009, 140 f.

103
Körner, Gudrun: Über die Schwierigkeiten der Porträtkunst. Goethes Verhältnis zu Bildnissen, in: Schulze, Sabine (Ed.): *Goethe und die Kunst* (Katalog zur Ausstellung in der Schirn Kunsthalle, Frankfurt am Main, vom 21. Mai bis zum 7. August 1994 sowie in den Kunstsammlungen zu Weimar vom 1. September bis zum 30. Oktober 1994), Stuttgart 1994, 150–158 und 159–191 (Katalog): 161. Zur Beziehung Goethe–Lavater cf. ferner im selben Katalog: Barta Fliedl, Ilsebill: Lavater, Goethe und der Versuch einer Physiognomik als Wissenschaft, in: Schulze (Ed.), *Goethe und die Kunst*, 192–203 und 204–217 (Katalog). Cf. ferner Biesalski, Ernst: *Scherenschnitt und Schattenrisse. Kleine Geschichte der Silhouettenkunst*, München 1964, 27.

104
Körner, Über die Schwierigkeiten der Porträtkunst, 161.

Figur, das weiße Blatt, aus dem die Silhouette ausgeschnitten wurde, zum Grund.

Die Schattenrisse der Goethezeit wirkten bis in die Zeit von Rubins Wahrnehmungsexperimenten fort. So war 1911, unmittelbar zu Beginn von Rubins Aufenthalt 1911–1913 in Göttingen, ein Band erschienen,[105] welcher neben einer Einleitung mit einer kleinen Geschichte des Silhouettierens eine Vielzahl teils aufwendiger Schattenbildnisse aus dem ‚Kosmos Weimar' enthielt.[106] Die Omnipräsenz der Silhouetten zur Goethezeit wird hier folgendermaßen beschrieben:

> An praktischer und künstlerischer Bedeutung gewann die Silhouette in dem Augenblick, als man anfing, die lebensgroßen Schattenrisse mit dem als ‚Storchschnabel' [Pantograph] [...] bekannten Verjüngungszirkel zu verkleinern. Die Prägnanz im Ausdruck nahm zu [...] gleichviel, ob man die im Innern schwarz ausgetuschten Konturen auf weißem Grunde stehen ließ oder ob man sie mit der Schere sorgfältig ausschnitt und sie dann auf helles Papier aufklebte. [...] Bücher wurden angelegt, in denen man die sorgfältig ausgeschnittenen Profile aufklebte. [...] In jenen Tagen spielte die Silhouette eine ähnliche Rolle wie heute die Photographie. „Kein Fremder zog vorüber, den man nicht abends an die Wand geschrieben hätte: die Storchschnäbel durften nicht rasten", berichtet Goethe. Freunde tauschten miteinander ihre Schattenrisse; getuschte wie geschnittene Exemplare fügte man mit Vorliebe in Briefen bei. So bittet Lavater Goethen am 15. Mai 1780 [...] um ganzfigurige Silhouetten vom Herzog Carl August, der Herzogin u. a. m.[107]

105
Kroeber, Hans Timotheus (Ed.): *Die Goethezeit in Silhouetten. 74 Silhouetten in ganzer Figur vornehmlich aus Weimar und Umgebung*, Weimar 1911.

106
Keines davon jedoch ein Vexierbild, selbst dort nicht, wo eine dem ‚Rubinkelch' entsprechende Figur-Grund-Umkehrung ohne weiteres möglich gewesen wäre, cf. die Büsten auf Taf. 34, 52 und 55 a–c sowie ferner Taf. 65.

107
Ibid., 11. Zum Goethezitat, das der *Campagne in Frankreich 1792* entstammt, cf. Goethe, [Johann Wolfgang von]: *Aus meinem Leben. Zweyter Abtheilung Fünfter Theil*, Stuttgard/Tübingen 1822, 323.

Exkurs 2: Interdependenzen im Weimar der Bauhauszeit

Erhellend ist auch ein Blick in das persönliche Umfeld Wolfgang Köhlers. Dessen Bruder Wilhelm (1884–1959) war Kunsthistoriker, sein Schwager Adhémar Gelb (1887–1936) ebenfalls Psychologe.[108] Gelb hatte sich frühzeitig mit dem Gestaltbegriff befasst. Seine Dissertation ist eine kritische Auseinandersetzung auf dem Stand von 1910, also in dem Augenblick, in dem die eigentliche Gestaltpsychologie gerade erst begründet wurde.[109] Er war 1909–1912 Volontärassistent am Psychologischen Institut der Universität Berlin und 1912–1914 Assistent am Psychologischen Institut der Akademie für Sozial- und Handelswissenschaften in Frankfurt am Main (ab 1914 Teil der neugegründeten Universität), wo sich 1910 bei Friedrich Schumann die Begründer der Gestaltpsychologie Wertheimer, Köhler und Koffka kennengelernt hatten.[110] 1919 Habilitation an der Universität Frankfurt, 1924 ao., 1929 o. Professor sowie Direktor (gemeinsam mit Wertheimer) des Psychologischen Instituts in Frankfurt, ab 1931 o. Professor in Halle, 1933 aus dem Dienst entlassen.[111]

Wilhelm Köhler wiederum wurde im Juni 1918, noch während des Ersten Weltkrieges, als Direktor der beiden großherzoglichen Kunstmuseen in Weimar berufen, mit Dienstantritt im Februar 1919. Nach der 1920 erfolgten Gründung des Landes Thüringen mit Weimar als Landeshauptstadt überführte er die Weimarer Museen und Kunstbestände in die Staatlichen Kunstsammlungen.[112]

108
Cf. Bergius, „Köhler, Wolfgang“, 302 f.

109
Am 14. Juli 1910 wurde Gelb in Berlin von Alois Riehl (1844–1924) und Carl Stumpf (1848–1936) promoviert (Gelb, Theoretisches über ‚Gestaltqualitäten‘).

110
Cf. Anm. 65.

111
Cf. Bergius, Rudolf: Stichwort „Gelb, Adhémar Maximilian Maurice“, in: Historische Kommission bei der Bayerischen Akademie der Wissenschaften (Ed.): *Neue Deutsche Biographie*, vol. 6, Berlin 1964, 168 f.

112
Cf. Stichwort „Köhler, Wilhelm, R., W.“, in: [Volz, Robert (Redaktion)]: *Reichshandbuch der deutschen Gesellschaft. Das Handbuch der Persönlichkeiten in Wort und Bild*, vol. 1, Berlin [1930], 980, sowie Siebenbrodt, Michael: Wilhelm Köhler und das Bauhaus in Weimar, in: Ulferts, Gert-Dieter/Föhl, Thomas (Ed.): *Von Berlin nach Weimar*, vol. 2: *Von der Kunstkammer zum Neuen Museum. 300 Jahre Sammlungen und Museen in Weimar. Kolloquium zu Ehren von Rolf Bothe*, München/Berlin 2003, 174–183: 175, sowie Wahl, Volker (Ed.): *Das Staatliche Bauhaus in Weimar. Dokumente zur Geschichte des Instituts 1919–1926* (= Veröffentlichungen der Historischen

„Die schon in [Wilhelm Köhlers] Wiener Zeit angeknüpften Verbindungen mit zeitgenössischen Künstlern wurden in Weimar durch Beziehungen zum Bauhaus vertieft, wo er Klee und Feininger besonders nahestand."[113] Wilhelm Köhler war damit – als Bruder des Psychologen Wolfgang Köhler – möglicherweise eine jener Personen, die zwischen der sich entwickelnden Wahrnehmungs-/Gestaltpsychologie und den Bauhausmeistern vermittelte. Marianne L. Teuber kommt indes zu folgender Einschätzung:

> Es ist ab und zu vermutet worden, daß Klees Werk etwas mit der Gestaltpsychologie zu tun habe, die in den [19]20er Jahren bekannt wurde. Aber es stellt sich jetzt heraus, daß es eher die Vorläufer der Gestalttheoretiker waren, vor allem die Vertreter der phänomenologischen Richtung [...]. [...] Klee steht den qualitativen Beobachtungen der phänomenologischen Schule, die bis ungefähr 1920 vorherrschte, viel näher als den späteren objektiven Organisationsprinzipien der Gestaltschule. [...] Statt vom Primat des Ganzen der Gestalttheoretiker ging Klee von den Elementen aus [...]. Erst während der Bauhausjahre machen sich einige Aspekte der Gestaltpsychologie in Klees Werk und Unterricht bemerkbar, vor allem in Dessau (1925–1930), und auch in seinem Spätstil der dreißiger Jahre in Bern. [...]
> Am Bauhaus selber wurde die Gestaltpsychologie erst von 1929 an bekannt, als Hannes Meyer [...] Gestaltpsychologen zu Vorlesungen ans Bauhaus einlud.[114]

So stichhaltig Teubers Argumentation bezüglich der Vorläufer der Gestaltpsychologie ist, scheint die Frage, ob Wilhelm Köhler nicht vielleicht schon deutlich *vor* 1929 als Ideenvermittler zwischen Gestaltpsychologie und Bauhaus – bzw. zwischen

Kommission für Thüringen, Große Reihe 15), Begleitband, Köln/Weimar/Wien 2009, 253 und 256. Cf. ferner Köhler, [Wilhelm]: Zur Eröffnung des Landesmuseums am Museumsplatz in Weimar, in: *Allgemeine Thüringische Landeszeitung Deutschland*, Montag, 13. November 1922, [5] f.

113 Mütherich, Florentine: Stichwort „Köhler, Wilhelm", in: Historische Kommission bei der Bayerischen Akademie der Wissenschaften (Ed.): *Neue Deutsche Biographie*, vol. 12, Berlin 1980, 301 f.: 302.

114 Teuber, Zwei frühe Quellen, 262.

Wolfgang Köhler und beispielsweise Klee – gewirkt haben könnte, noch nicht ernsthaft untersucht worden zu sein. Die bisherige Forschungsliteratur beschränkt sich im Wesentlichen auf die Historie von Wilhelm Köhlers Beziehungen zum Bauhaus und seine Förderung desselben; sein Bruder Wolfgang und die Gestaltpsychologie werden allenfalls erwähnt. Tilmann Buddensieg, der die familiäre Verwandtschaft anspricht (wenngleich er Wolfgang Köhler nicht in Berlin, sondern in Leipzig lokalisiert), konstatiert lediglich: „Die beiden Brüder standen sich sehr nahe."[115] Demgegenüber wurde die enge Verbundenheit Wilhelm Köhlers mit Klee, Lyonel Feininger (1871–1956) und dem Bauhaus – 1920 heiratete er mit Margarete Bittkow (1887–1964) eine Bauhausschülerin, 1925 regte er die Übernahme des „Bauhaus-Archivs" und weiterer Objekte in den Bestand der Staatlichen Kunstsammlungen zu Weimar an – in der Forschung wiederholt erörtert.[116] So schreibt Buddensieg über die Phase nach der Ernennung zum Weimarer Museumsdirektor:

> Wilhelm Koehler nahm sofort die Verbindung mit dem Bauhaus in Weimar auf, schloss Freundschaft mit Paul Klee und Lyonel Feininger und entfaltete [...] eine reiche Ausstellungstätigkeit im Bereich der Moderne. [...] Neuere Arbeiten [...] haben erstmals [...] seine „rückhaltlose Zuwendung zur zeitgenössischen Kunst" als Weimarer Museumsdirektor aus der Vergessenheit gezogen. [...] [Die reiche Ausstellungstätigkeit] war bestimmt von Solidarität mit den Künstlern am Bauhaus, vor allem mit Paul Klee und Lyonel Feininger. [...] 1920 bemühte er sich, die erste große Klee-Ausstellung der Münchner Galerie Hans Goltz nach Weimar zu bringen.[117]

115
Cf. Buddensieg, Tilmann: Die karolingischen Maler in Tours und die Bauhausmaler in Weimar. Wilhelm Koehler und Paul Klee, in: *Zeitschrift für Kunstgeschichte* 73, 2010 (1), 1–18: 5.

116
Cf. beispielsweise Siebenbrodt, Wilhelm Köhler und das Bauhaus in Weimar; cf. zuletzt Wendermann, Gerda: Wilhelm Köhler als Direktor der Staatlichen Kunstsammlungen Weimar und seine frühen Ausstellungen des Weimarer Bauhauses, in: Seemann, Hellmut Th./Valk, Thorsten (Ed.): *Entwürfe der Moderne. Bauhaus-Ausstellungen 1923–2019*, Göttingen 2019, 51–71 (mit Hinweisen auf die weiterführende Literatur).

117
Buddensieg, Die karolingischen Maler, 2 f.

Buddensieg verunklart hier die Chronologie der Ereignisse. Das Bauhaus wurde erst im April 1919 gegründet, Klee erst im Oktober 1920 als Bauhausmeister berufen – wozu Köhler möglicherweise selbst beigetragen hatte.[118]

Die Frage, wo seine große Wertschätzung für Klee, Feininger und die Moderne herrührte, wird stets nur allgemein mit einem studentischen Atelierbesuch bei Auguste Rodin (1840–1917) bzw. der Aufgeschlossenheit von Köhlers Wiener Kunsthistorikerkreisen gegenüber der zeitgenössischen Kunst beantwortet.[119] Offen bleibt, ob dafür nicht auch – oder vor allem – die Beschäftigung seines Bruders mit der Wahrnehmungs- und Gestaltpsychologie eine Rolle gespielt haben könnte. Vielleicht erkannte Wilhelm Köhler in Klees naiv anmutenden Arbeiten unvermittelt die künstlerisch verarbeiteten Grundelemente wieder, die er in der wahrnehmungspsychologischen Literatur seines Bruders in Gestalt abstrakter Diagramme kennengelernt hatte?

Hier sollte weitergeforscht werden. Um den entscheidenden Querbezügen auf die Spur zu kommen, müssen wir bereit sein, immer wieder neu unsere disziplinären Grenzen zu überwinden. Dann aber offenbart sich die Existenz präzise benennbarer historischer Schnittstellen. Das Begriffspaar ‚Figur und Grund'

118
Cf. dazu auch Bothe, Rolf: Paul Klee und Lyonel Feininger in den Ausstellungen der Weimarer Kunstsammlungen von 1920 bis 1930, in: id./ Föhl, Thomas (Ed.): *Aufstieg und Fall der Moderne* (Katalog zur Ausstellung der Kunstsammlungen zu Weimar und der Weimar 1999 – Kulturstadt Europas GmbH), Ostfildern-Ruit [1999], 274–281: 274 f. Klees Dienstvertrag mit dem Staatlichen Bauhaus Weimar datiert vom 26. November 1920, mit Wirkung zum 1. Dezember 1920. Cf. Wahl, *Das Staatliche Bauhaus in Weimar*, Begleitband, 177 f. Zur Chronologie cf. ferner den Brief Walter Gropius' (1883–1969) in Berlin an Hugo Freiherr von Fritsch (1869–1945) in Weimar vom 31. Januar 1919: „Noch unter der alten Regierung hat seit Jahren das Ministerium in Weimar mit mir Verhandlungen angeknüpft für eine eventuelle Übersiedlung meinerseits nach Weimar als Nachfolger Professor [Henry] van de Veldes. Nach einer Audienz beim Großherzog und Besprechungen im Ministerium durfte ich aus verschiedenen Schreiben entnehmen, daß die entscheidenden Stellen einer auf mich fallenden Wahl sympathisch gegenüberstehen würden. In neuerer Zeit hat sich dann Herr Dr. [Wilhelm] Köhler in gleicher Weise für mich eingesetzt." – Wahl, Volker (Ed.): *Das Staatliche Bauhaus in Weimar. Dokumente zur Geschichte des Instituts 1919–1926* (= Veröffentlichungen der Historischen Kommission für Thüringen, Große Reihe 15), Hauptband, Köln/Weimar/ Wien 2009, 57 f.: 57.

119
Cf. beispielsweise Wright, David H.: Wilhelm Koehler and the Original Plan for Research at Dumbarton Oaks, in: Barker, John W. (Ed.): *Pioneers of Byzantine Studies in America* (= *Byzantinische Forschungen. Internationale Zeitschrift für Byzantinistik* 27, 2002), Amsterdam 2002, 134–175: 136, bzw. Wendermann, Gerda: Förderer und Freund der modernen Kunst. Wilhelm Köhler als Direktor der Staatlichen Kunstsammlungen Weimar, in: Bothe/Föhl (Ed.): *Aufstieg und Fall der Moderne*, 308–324: 308 f.

bringt zu heller Sichtbarkeit, wie fruchtbar eine Verschränkung der disziplinengeschichtlichen Forschungen zu Kunstgeschichte und -wissenschaft, Wahrnehmungs- und Gestaltpsychologie für die Selbstvergewisserung über die eigenen fachlichen Grundlagen sein kann. Doch zuallererst sind es die konkreten persönlichen Interessen, Begegnungen und Schicksale, welche den Gang der Ideengeschichte bestimmen.

Lebensdaten im Überblick

384 – 322	Aristoteles
23/24 – 79	Plinius der Ältere
1606 – 1688	Joachim von Sandrart der Ältere
1728 – 1815	Francesco Bartolozzi
1729 – 1796	Katharina die Große
1733 – 1813	Christoph Martin Wieland
1737 – 1814	Johann Friedrich Schiller
1739 – 1807	Anna Amalia
1741 – 1801	Johann Caspar Lavater
1749 – 1832	Johann Wolfgang von Goethe
1754 – 1793	Ludwig XVI
1755 – 1793	Marie Antoinette
1757 – 1828	Carl August
1759 – 1831	François-Joseph Crussaire
1766 – 1837	Daniel Orme
1768 – 1835	Franz II Joseph Karl
1769 – 1821	Napoleon Bonaparte
fl. 1775 – 1804	John Eginton
fl. 1791 – 1805	P. Molinari
fl. 1792 – 1799	Edward Jee
1805 – 1883	Wilhelm Eduard Daege
1832 – 1920	Wilhelm Wundt
1838 – 1916	Ernst Mach
1840 – 1917	Auguste Rodin
1844 – 1924	Alois Riehl
1847 – 1921	Adolf von Hildebrand
1848 – 1936	Carl Stumpf
1850 – 1934	Georg Elias Müller
1851 – 1943	Lillien J. Martin
1857 – 1939	Frank Angell
1858 – 1905	Alois Riegl

1859 – 1932	Christian von Ehrenfels
1863 – 1940	Friedrich Schumann
1871 – 1956	Lyonel Feininger
1879 – 1935	Kasimir Malewitsch
1879 – 1940	Paul Klee
1880 – 1943	Max Wertheimer
1884 – 1953	David Katz
1884 – 1959	Wilhelm Köhler
1886 – 1941	Kurt Koffka
1886 – 1951	Edgar Rubin
1887 – 1967	Wolfgang Köhler
1887 – 1964	Margarete Bittkow
1887 – 1936	Adhémar Gelb
1888 – 1976	Josef Albers
1888 – 1968	Sigfried Giedion
1895 – 1946	László Moholy-Nagy
1896 – 1984	Hans Sedlmayr
1898 – 1972	Maurits Cornelis Escher
1899 – 1979	Wolfgang Metzger
1901 – 1942	Willis D. Ellis
1904 – 1955	George W. Hartmann
1904 – 2007	Rudolf Arnheim
1906 – 1992	Samuel Ichiye Hayakawa
1906 – 2001	György Kepes
1908 – 1961	Maurice Merleau-Ponty
1909 – 2001	Ernst H. Gombrich
1914 – 2004	Rudolf Bergius
1925 – 1995	Gilles Deleuze
1926 – 1999	Hans Wille
geb. 1931	Bridget Riley
geb. 1941	Günter Brucher

Part 4
Navigating Dichotomies

Das Verhältnis von Bild und Bildmedium, wie es in verschiedenen Bildtheorien und Bildbegriffen eine zentrale Rolle spielt,[1] ist mit dem Verhältnis von Figur und Grund nicht deckungsgleich, steht aber in engem Kontakt zu ihm. Dieser Kontakt ist dabei keineswegs ohne Spannung, aber gerade deshalb ist er produktiv für eine Befragung des Figur/Grund-Verhältnisses.[2] Im Vorliegenden möchte ich dieses Verhältnis vor dem Hintergrund zweier dreistelliger Bildbegriffe beleuchten, die ich – rein heuristisch – als ‚vormoderne' und ‚moderne' Fassung des Bildbegriffs bezeichnen werde.[3] Diese beiden Bildbegriffe formulieren, wie ich zeigen möchte, eine je spezifische *Meta-Physik*. Sie besteht, kurz gesagt, darin, dass beide Begriffe auf diametral entgegengesetzte Weise einen Bereich auszeichnen, der dem Physischen enthoben, also buchstäblich meta-physisch ist. Meine These lautet dabei, dass diese Bildbegriffe und ihre Meta-Physiken mittels einer spezifischen Transponierung zum Bildraum und zu darin formulierten Figur/Grund-Konstellationen in einem aufschlussreichen Verhältnis stehen. Diese These impliziert, dass auf diese Weise auch ein reflektierter Umgang mit der Materialität und der Medialität des Bildträgers mit in den Blick rückt.

Im ersten Teil des Beitrags werde ich die zwei genannten Bildbegriffe sowie ihre Meta-Physiken skizzieren und sie mit den Begriffen von Figur und Grund engführen. Im zweiten Schritt werde ich diese Konstellation dann an einem ersten Bildvergleich, zwischen der Apotheose Ottos III. im Aachener Liuthar-Evangeliar aus der Aachener Domschatzkammer und Raffaels *Disputa del Sacramento* in der *Stanza della Segnatura* im Vatikan,

1
„Bildtheorien" begreife ich im vorliegenden Kontext in einem weiten Sinne. Dies schließt also auch jene teils expliziten, teils aber auch implizit vorliegenden theoretischen Behandlungen des Bildbegriffs in der Vormoderne mit ein. Vgl. für diese Sichtweise exemplarisch Alloa, Emmanuel: Bildwissenschaft in Byzanz. Ein *iconic turn* avant la lettre?, in: *Studia philosophica* 69, 2010, 11–35.

2
Mit „Figur/Grund-Verhältnis" sei hier vorerst das *begriffliche* Verhältnis *als solches*, nicht eine spezifische historische Ausprägung desselben gemeint. Dies orientiert sich an den weiter unten gegebenen heuristischen Definitionen von Figur und Grund.

3
Eventuell wäre auch von „neuzeitlicher" und „vorneuzeitlicher" Fassung zu sprechen – je nachdem, wo man jeweils den Beginn der Neuzeit bzw. der Moderne lokalisiert (was zusätzlich dadurch verkompliziert wird, dass das deutsche „modern" und das englische „modern" inhaltlich nicht deckungsgleich sind).

exemplarisch erproben. Im dritten Schritt werde ich abschließend ein weiteres Beispiel, eine Illumination aus dem ältesten erhaltenen Manuskript der *Topographia Christiana*, hinzuziehen. Meine Herangehensweise ist dabei insbesondere im ersten Schritt begrifflich-philosophischer Natur. Gleichwohl werde ich versuchen, diese abstrakteren Überlegungen im zweiten und dritten Teil des Beitrags mit einem ‚close reading' konkreter Bilder zu verschränken.

Zwei dreistellige Bildbegriffe – Zwei Meta-Physiken

Unter einem *zweistelligen* Bildbegriff verstehe ich einen Bildbegriff, der einzig den außerbildlichen Bezugspunkt und das Bild selbst unterscheidet, also etwa ein Haus und ein Gemälde dieses Hauses. Den Bezugspunkt des Bildes bezeichne ich im Folgenden als *Referent*, wobei der ontologische Status dieses Bezugspunktes vorerst bewusst unbestimmt bleibt und nicht auf raumzeitliche, visuell wahrnehmbare Gegenstände restringiert ist. Unter einem *dreistelligen* Bildbegriff verstehe ich in der Folge einen Bildbegriff, der nicht nur Bild und Referent als Momente beinhaltet, sondern aufseiten des Bildes genauer zwischen *Bild* und *Bildmedium* unterscheidet. Das Bildmedium umfasst hierbei all jenes, *in dem* das Bild realisiert ist.[4] Bezogen auf das vorangegangene Haus-Beispiel umfasst dies also alle materiellen Elemente des Haus-Gemäldes, etwa die Leinwand und die Farben. Besonders mit Blick auf das Verhältnis von Figur und Grund ist hierbei zu beachten, dass die Unterscheidung von Bild und Bildmedium nicht mit der Unterscheidung etwa von Malgrund und Leinwand einerseits sowie Motiv und Farben andererseits koinzidiert. Vielmehr ist *alles* Materielle Teil des Bildmediums. Innerhalb des Bildmediums unterscheide ich deshalb weiterhin *Bildträger* und

4 Wolfram Pichler und Ralph Ubl haben zu Recht darauf hingewiesen, dass die – in bildtheoretischen Kontexten gängige – Bezeichnung „Bildträger" für das, was im Vorliegenden „Bildmedium" heißt, aus kunsthistorischer Perspektive ungenau und missverständlich ist, da kunsthistorisch mit dem Bildträger seit langem speziell jener materielle Teilaspekt gemeint ist, welcher der Malschicht als Trägersubstrat dient (nachfolgend als „Bildträger" bezeichnet); vgl. Pichler, Wolfram/Ubl, Ralph: *Bildtheorie zur Einführung*, Hamburg 2014, 22–23. Der stattdessen von ihnen eingeführte Terminus „Bildvehikel" scheint mir jedoch wenig intuitiv, weshalb ich im Vorliegenden auf den Ausdruck „Bildmedium" zurückgreife, der mir jenen Teil, *in dem* das Bild realisiert ist, gut zu treffen scheint.

Bildschicht, Letztere als eigentlich bildgebender Teil des Mediums (etwa die aufgetragene Farbschicht), Ersteren als tragendes Substrat der Bildschicht (etwa Leinwand und Keilrahmen). Innerhalb des Bildes differenziere ich zwischen *Bildraum* und *Bildgegenstand*, wobei der Bildraum die je spezifische Raumauffassung innerhalb jenes imaginären Bereichs meint, der das Bild selbst ist, während mit dem Bildgegenstand (bzw. den Bildgegenständen) einzelne, definierte Elemente und Entitäten innerhalb dieses Bildraumes gemeint sind.

Die Gründe für die Einführung eines dreistelligen Bildbegriffs liegen vor allem darin, sinnvoll wahrheitsfähige Aussagen zum materiellen Bildmedium und zum imaginären Bereich des Bildes unterscheiden zu können. Beispielsweise wäre es unter der Annahme, dass das Bildmedium aus Altersgründen Schimmel angesetzt hat, wenig sinnvoll, davon zu sprechen, dass das Haus im Bild selbst schimmelig ist, wenngleich der Schimmel sich über jene materiellen Partien des Bildmediums erstreckt, in denen die Hauswand realisiert ist. Auch in die Gegenrichtung wäre es – zum Beispiel unter der Annahme, dass das Haus im Bild brennend dargestellt ist – unsinnig, Aussagen über den Bildgegenstand auf das Bildmedium zu übertragen: Schließlich brennt nur das Haus im Bild, nicht aber das Bildmedium.[5] Dem Bild kommt also eine eigentümliche eigene Seinsweise, eine eigene Realität zu, über die sich wahrheitsfähige Aussagen treffen lassen, die nicht *per se* gleichermaßen auf das Bildmedium zutreffen. Soweit eine bekannte dreistellige Unterscheidung in der Bildtheorie, die von verschiedenen Positionen zwar mit unterschiedlichen Ausdrücken formuliert wurde,[6] die aber *grosso modo* sachlich deckungsgleich sind.

Für die vorliegende Frage nach Figur und Grund in der Vormoderne ist diese Unterscheidung nun vor allem deshalb

5
Für weitere, analog gelagerte und sehr anschauliche Beispiele vgl. Wiesing, Lambert: *Artifizielle Präsenz. Studien zur Philosophie des Bildes*, Frankfurt/M. 2005, 28.

6
So findet sich die Konstellation Referent, Bild und Bildmedium etwa als Trias von „Bildsujet", „Bildobjekt" und „Bildträger" (Edmund Husserl) oder „das Dargestellte", „die Darstellung" und „das Darstellende" (Hans Jonas). Vgl. hierfür Wiesing, *Artifizielle Präsenz*, 26–36 (auf die weiterführende Differenzierung, etwa zwischen einer phänomenologischen oder einer semiotischen Fassung der fraglichen Trias, sei im Vorliegenden verzichtet – sie ist für das folgende Argument von nachrangiger Bedeutung; für eine umfassende Ausarbeitung des zeichentheoretischen Bildbegriffs vgl. grundlegend Scholz, Oliver: *Bild, Darstellung, Zeichen. Philosophische Theorien bildlicher Darstellung*, Frankfurt/M. ^{3}2009).

aufschlussreich, weil es historisch gesehen zwei Grundfassungen des dreistelligen Bildbegriffs gibt, die ich, wie eingangs erwähnt, heuristisch als ‚moderne' und ‚vormoderne' Fassung dieses Bildbegriffs fassen möchte. Diese beiden Fassungen bilden, wie ich im Folgenden ausführen werde, zwei spezifische *Meta-Physiken* des Bildes aus.

Doch was ist mit der Meta-Physik der Bilder im Rahmen dreistelliger Bildbegriffe gemeint? Gemeint ist ein je spezifischer Entzug des Bildes aus dem Physischen, wobei die moderne und die vormoderne Fassung diesen Entzug diametral entgegengesetzt konzipieren. Entscheidend ist nämlich, dass der dreistellige Bildbegriff kein Produkt der Moderne oder der modernen Bildtheorie darstellt, sondern bereits vorher eindeutig greifbar ist. Und zwar findet er sich paradigmatisch bereits in Platons Dialog *Timaios*.[7] Dort heißt es, dass es „einem Bild – da genau dasjenige, auf das hin es entstanden ist, nicht bei ihm selbst liegt, sondern es immer die Erscheinung eines anderen an sich trägt – deshalb zukommt, in etwas anderem zu entstehen."[8] Platon unterscheidet an dieser Stelle eindeutig zwischen Referent, Bild und Medium. Er kennt also genau jene drei Elemente, die auch die modernen dreistelligen Bildbegriffe aufweisen. Entscheidend ist dabei jedoch, dass bei Platon das Bild mit dem Physischen selbst zusammenfällt, während der Referent – die berüchtigten platonischen Ideen – und das Medium – die nicht minder berüchtigte ‚Raummaterie' χώρα – beide gerade *nicht* in den Bereich des Physischen fallen.[9]

7
Vgl. zum Nachfolgenden ausführlicher Poetsch, Christoph: *Platons Philosophie des Bildes. Systematische Untersuchungen zur platonischen Metaphysik*, Frankfurt/M. 2019, 210–222.

8
ὡς εἰκόνι μέν, ἐπείπερ οὐδ᾽ αὐτὸ τοῦτο ἐφ᾽ ᾧ γέγονεν ἑαυτῆς ἐστιν, ἑτέρου δέ τινος ἀεὶ φέρεται φάντασμα, διὰ ταῦτα ἐν ἑτέρῳ προσήκει τινὶ γίγνεσθαι, οὐσίας ἁμωσγέπως ἀντεχομένην, ἢ μηδὲν τὸ παράπαν αὐτὴν εἶναι (Tim. 52c2–5; Übers. CP) Ich erlaube mir, Platons Bildbegriff hier typologisch als den vormodernen Bildbegriff anzusetzen. Damit sei keineswegs behauptet, dass er der einzige ausgearbeitete vormoderne Bildbegriff ist.

9
Auf eine genauere Analyse der χώρα sei im Vorliegenden verzichtet. Vgl. hierzu grundlegend Happ, Heinz: *Hyle. Studien zum aristotelischen Materie-Begriff*, Berlin 1971 sowie Miller, Dana R.: *The third kind in Plato's Timaeus*, Göttingen 2003. Letztlich fungiert die χώρα raum- und bildtheoretisch als dreidimensionaler Projektionsschirm; vgl. hierzu im Detail Poetsch, *Platons Philosophie des Bildes*, 223–248. Für den systematischen Zusammenhang der χώρα mit den *verae icones* vgl. Poetsch, Christoph: Chôra und Vera Icon. Über die Bildräumlichkeit des ‚wahren Christusbildes' vor dem Hintergrund des platonischen Raumbegriffes, in: Delarue, Dominic/Kaffenberger, Thomas/Nille, Christian (Ed.): *Raumbilder / Bildräume. Studien aus dem Grenzbereich von Raum und Bild*, Regensburg 2017, 43–66.

Beide, der vormoderne wie der moderne Bildbegriff,[10] kennen also einen buchstäblichen Bereich des Meta-Physischen, der über das Physische hinausgeht bzw. von ihm abgetrennt ist.[11] Im Falle des modernen Begriffs ist es das Bild als „stoffloses Gebilde",[12] das mitsamt seinem Inhalt dem „Kausalverkehr der Dinge"[13] und damit dem Physischen entzogen ist. Im modernen Begriff ist das Bild demnach etwas, das *innerhalb* des Physischen einen eigenen, nicht-physischen Bereich für sich reklamiert und offenhält. Das Bild ist eine eigene, imaginäre Realität, die von der des Bildmediums zwar durchaus abhängig ist, aber nicht auf diese reduzierbar ist.[14] Der vormoderne Begriff setzt hingegen das Physische *insgesamt* an die Stelle des Bildes und kennt so entsprechend zwei Bereiche des Meta-Physischen: den Referenten

10
Aus Gründen der besseren Lesbarkeit verzichte ich ab hier auf die Qualifikation „dreistellig". Solange vom „Bildbegriff" ohne weiteren Zusatz gesprochen wird, ist im Folgenden durchgängig ein dreistelliger Begriff gemeint.

11
Um das vorliegende Begriffspaar – neben den bereits in den Anmerkungen genannten Arbeiten – in den bestehenden Klassifizierungen und Topographien der zeitgenössischen Bildtheorie noch etwas genauer zu verorten: Innerhalb der von Scholz, *Bild, Darstellung, Zeichen*, 5–13 vorgeschlagenen Einteilung weist der vorliegende ontologische Bildbegriff einige Schnittmengen mit (B 4), der „metaphysische[n] oder auch typologische[n] Verwendung" (ibid., 11) des Bildterminus, auf, obwohl es im Vorliegenden weniger um das bei Scholz für diesen Bildtyp primär hervorgehobene Verhältnis der Dependenz geht – wenngleich es weiterhin zu einem gewissen Grade impliziert ist. Insofern die nachfolgenden Fallbeispiele ein ums andere Mal auf die Referenten der Bilder zu sprechen kommen, finden sich auch Anknüpfungspunkte an Scholz' eigenen, zeichentheoretischen Ansatz – freilich auch hier mit dem Unterschied, dass im Vorliegenden dem ontologischen Status der Referenten ein besonderes Augenmerk gilt.

12
Fiedler, Konrad: Vom Ursprung der künstlerischen Tätigkeit [1887], in: Id: *Schriften zur Kunst*, hg. v. Gottfried Boehm, vol. 1, München 1991, 40.

13
Jonas, Hans: Homo Pictor und die Differentia des Menschen, in: *Zeitschrift für philosophische Forschung* 15, 1961, 161–176: 166.

14
Durch seine – unten noch weiter auszuführende – Verwiesenheit auf ein Subjekt weist ein derartiges Bild in seiner imaginären Realität eine gewisse Nähe zu mentalen Bildern auf (zum Bildtyp der mentalen Bilder vgl. u. a. Scholz, Oliver R.: Artikel ‚Bild', in: Barck, Karlheinz et al. (Ed.): *Ästhetische Grundbegriffe*, vol. 1. Stuttgart 2010, 618–669: 621–622); jedoch mit dem Unterschied, dass mentale Bilder ihren Sitz eindeutig und ausschließlich in der menschlichen Imagination haben, während es im vorliegenden Vorschlag eine Relation zwischen der mentalen Imagination des Subjekts und dem vorliegenden Bildartefakt ist. Vgl. in diesem Kontext auch die – v. a. im englischen Sprachraum virulente – Differenzierung von ‚image' und ‚picture', etwa bei Mitchell, W. J. T.: Vier Grundbegriffe der Bildwissenschaft, in: Sachs-Hombach, Klaus (Ed.): *Bildtheorien. Anthropologische und kulturelle Grundlagen des Visualistic Turn*, Frankfurt/M. 2009, 319–327: 322–324. Vgl. speziell zum materiellen Bild auch die Ausführungen von Seel, Martin: *Ästhetik des Erscheinens*, Frankfurt/M. 2003, 255–294.

und das Medium. Für diesen Bildbegriff ist alles Sinnlich-Körperliche insgesamt Bild und das Bild selbst infolgedessen nicht Abbildung des ebenfalls Sichtbaren, sondern allererst die Sichtbarwerdung dessen, was selbst nicht sinnlich ist.[15] Dies bedeutet wohlgemerkt nicht, dass im Rahmen dieser Konzeption nicht auch sinnvoll innerhalb des Physischen zwischen bildlichen Artefakten, physischen Entitäten als deren Referenten sowie einem Bildmedium unterschieden werden könnte. Dies ist vielmehr zweifelsohne der Fall – nur hat, zumindest soweit ich sehen kann, vormodern niemand diese Option explizit in der Theorie ergriffen und den vormodernen dreistelligen Bildbegriff in der Weise invertiert, wie dies im modernen Bildbegriff geschieht.[16]

Eine ‚invertierende Umstülpung' beschreibt das Verhältnis der beiden Bildbegriffe zueinander am besten: Der vormoderne Bildbegriff hat das als Bild verstandene Physische zum innersten, abgeleiteten Element der Trias, während der moderne Bildbegriff wiederum das Physische zuäußerst kehrt und das Bild zu einem Residuum des Imaginären innerhalb des Physischen macht. Im zweiten Fall ist das Physische die Realität, innerhalb derer Imaginäres seinen Platz haben kann, im ersten Fall wird das Physische selbst als imaginär begriffen und seinerseits in eine weiter gefasste, umfassendere Realität eingebettet.

Nimmt man beide Bildbegriffe als bildtheoretische Optionen systematisch ernst, so lassen sich gegenüber beiden Auffassungen zweifelsohne Einwände formulieren – wobei wohl nicht selten die grundsätzliche ontologische Position für die jeweilige Präferenz (mit) ausschlaggebend sein dürfte. So ließe sich gegenüber der vormodernen Fassung eine starke ontologische

15
Diese Fassung des Bildbegriffs, also die Versinnlichung des Unsichtbaren, ist historisch beinahe als die gängige zu bezeichnen. Er findet sich in Ägypten (Assmann, Jan: Altägyptische Bildpraxen und ihre impliziten Theorien, in: Sachs-Hombach (Ed.): *Bildtheorien*, 74–104), in Mesopotamien (Berlejung, Angelika: *Die Theologie der Bilder. Herstellung und Einweihung von Kultbildern in Mesopotamien und die alttestamentliche Bilderpolemik*, Fribourg/Göttingen 1998) und möglicherweise auch in Indien (Smith, Brian K.: *Reflections on Resemblance, Ritual, and Religion*, New York et al. 1989, 76–77).

16
Besonders augenscheinlich wird dies an der konzisen Übersichtsdarstellung verschiedener spätantiker und mittelalterlicher Bildbegriffe von Wirth, Jean: Soll man Bilder anbeten? Theorien zum Bilderkult bis zum Konzil von Trient, in: Dupeux, Cécile/Jezler, Peter/Wirth, Jean (Ed.): *Bildersturm. Wahnsinn oder Gottes Wille?*, Zürich 2000, 28–37 – durchgängig bleibt der Zug in die Transzendenz, über das Bild hinaus; das immanent Imaginäre des modernen Bildbegriffs ist in diesem Denken offenkundig keine Option.

Hypothek angesichts der Stellung des Physischen als Einwand formulieren: Sie verlangt nicht nur, dass es neben der physischen Wirklichkeit noch anderes Wirkliches gibt, sondern auch, dass diese physische Wirklichkeit nur einen abgeleiteten und untergeordneten Status hat. Auch wäre zu fragen, ob die so vorgestellte Bildbeziehung über die Grenze der Sichtbarkeit hinweg überhaupt adäquat mit Abbildbeziehungen innerhalb des Sichtbaren – also mit dem, was wir zunächst und zumeist als Bildbeziehungen verstehen – in Einklang zu bringen ist und somit diesem Bildbegriff mehr als nur Homonymie zugrunde liegt. Im Gegenzug wäre jedoch beispielsweise zu überlegen, ob ein solcher Bildbegriff nicht geeigneter ist, um bildliche Bezüge zu Abstraktem und Unanschaulichem, nicht nur, aber auch im Bereich der Allegorie etwa, zu erfassen.

Aber auch gegen die moderne Fassung lassen sich grundlegende Einwände erheben, die ebenfalls auf implizite ontologische Grundannahmen zuführen. Und zwar ließe sich einwenden, dass die moderne Fassung des Bildbegriffs die ihr eigentümliche metaphysische Seinsweise des Bildes überhaupt nur dann sinnvoll als solche ansetzen kann, wenn sie ein spezifisch geartetes *Subjekt* präsupponiert, das in der Lage ist, das Bild als ebensolches zu imaginieren. In einer durchgängig materialistisch konzipierten Welt scheint dies jedoch schwer möglich. Das heißt: Die moderne Fassung des Begriffs kann den bildlichen Bereich des Imaginären im Grunde nur dann adäquat als solchen auszeichnen, wenn sie an anderer Stelle, beim betrachtenden Subjekt, eine ontologische Differenzierung einführt. Dieses Subjekt muss einen immateriellen, mentalen Anteil aufweisen, da erst über diesen zuallererst sichergestellt wird, dass die Ebene des Bildes überhaupt *als solche* existiert.[17] Nur in der Perspektive eines solchen Subjekts trennen sich überhaupt Bild und Bildmedium. Andernfalls verbleibt das Bildmedium in seiner Materialität nur und ausschließlich das, was es ist. Der moderne Begriff muss also die ontologische Differenzierung an anderer Stelle investieren, um die entscheidende Trennung von Bild und Bildmedium in seinem Sinne leisten zu

17
Dieser Gedanke taucht in der Moderne prominent bei Edmund Husserl im Begriff des „Bildbewusstseins“ auf; vgl. auch Pichler/Ubl, *Bildtheorie*, 58–59.

können. Ansonsten wäre nicht zu erklären, warum zwar ich als Betrachter angesichts eines Gemäldegegenstandes sinnvoll zwischen Bild und Bildmedium unterscheiden und dem Bild die ihm eigene, vom Bildmedium unterschiedene Seinsweise zuschreiben kann – während der Gemäldegegenstand dies mir gegenüber jedoch gerade nicht vermag und als rein physischer Gegenstand an mir eben nicht Bild und Bildmedium unterscheiden kann.[18] Im Gegenzug ließe sich wiederum zugunsten des modernen Bildbegriffs ins Feld führen, dass er zweifelsohne weniger voraussetzungsreich ist und auf die an Bildern zunächst und zumeist verhandelte Abbildungsbeziehung einen direkteren Zugriff hat.

Unabhängig davon jedoch, welchem Bildbegriff man theoretisch aus welchen Gründen schlussendlich den Vorzug geben mag, ist doch zweifelsohne der vormoderne Begriff dort in Rechnung zu stellen, wo Bilder unter seinem – impliziten oder expliziten – Verständnis entstehen und wo somit die entstandenen Artefakte nur unter Einbezug dieses Bildbegriffs adäquat zu fassen sind. Schließlich ist der vormoderne Begriff besonders dort von Interesse, wo der intendierte Referent selbst ganz oder partiell jenseits des Physischen liegt. Denn hier stellt sich mit besonderer Dringlichkeit die Frage, wie diese Referenz in der Bildräumlichkeit und durch die in ihr etablierten Figur/Grund-Verhältnisse künstlerisch konkret umgesetzt wird.

Zu bedenken ist angesichts all dessen weiterhin, dass vor allem mit Blick auf (annähernd)[19] zweidimensionale Bildmedien durch die Trennung von Bild und Bildmedium die Möglichkeit besteht, dass die imaginäre Räumlichkeit des Bildes und die Räumlichkeit des Bildmediums auseinandertreten.[20] Dies wird insbesondere dann offensichtlich, wenn auf unterschiedliche Weise der Bildraum als jener dreidimensionale physische Raum ausgewiesen

18
Und das selbst dann nicht, wenn etwas an mir grundsätzlich dazu Anlass gäbe, z. B. wenn ich gerade als Schauspieler den Mephistopheles aus Goethes *Faust* verkörperte oder meine momentan eingenommene Körperhaltung an ein Pferd, oder allgemeiner: ein vierfüßiges Tier, erinnerte.

19
„Annähernd", da strikte Zweidimensionalität im dreidimensionalen physischen Raum natürlich ausgeschlossen ist: Noch die dünnste Bildschicht ist im Prinzip dreidimensional.

20
Vgl. hierzu auch – exemplarisch anhand der Werke Lucio Fontanas; und stärker im Hinblick auf das Verhältnis Bild und Skulptur – die aufschlussreichen Überlegungen von Seel, *Ästhetik des Erscheinens*, 258–260.

wird, der uns in der sinnlichen Wahrnehmung begegnet und der entsprechend von der (annähernden) Zweidimensionalität des Bildmediums bzw. der Bildschicht divergiert. Hier, in diesem Fall, können wir uns in der Folge imaginativ innerhalb dieses drei- oder sogar vierdimensionalen Bildraumes bewegen, folgen bestimmten impliziten Vorannahmen und können entsprechende wahrheitsfähige Aussagen treffen, die abermals nur mit Bezug auf das Bild, nicht aber mit Bezug auf das Medium korrekt sind. So können wir uns etwa imaginativ um das Haus aus dem eingangs erwähnten Beispiel herumbewegen oder uns gedanklich in es hineinbegeben. Ebenso nehmen wir wie selbstverständlich an, dass das Haus über eine Rückseite verfügt, obwohl dem in der Bildschicht keinerlei Information entspricht. Ebenso folgen wir in den allermeisten Fällen der Vorannahme der Objektkonsistenz: So würden wir etwa, wenn die Hauswand unseres Hauses partiell durch einen Baum verdeckt würde, ohne Zweifel voraussetzen, dass die Hauswand hinter dem Baum weitergeht, ohne dass dem notwendigerweise irgendeine Information im Bildmedium entsprechen müsste.[21] In der Bildschicht des Mediums kann an der entsprechenden Stelle nur die Information ‚Baum' gegeben sein und dennoch tun wir so, als wäre dahinter – der Ausdruck ergibt nur mit Blick auf Bild und Bildraum, nicht aber mit Blick auf das Bildmedium den intendierten Sinn[22] – auch noch die Information ‚Hauswand' gegeben. Und im gleichen Sinne ist die Aussage ‚Vor dem Haus befindet sich ein Baum' nur mit Blick auf das Bild, nicht aber hinsichtlich des Bildmediums korrekt.

Diese Unterscheidung der Räumlichkeit von Bild und Medium ist nun aus mindestens zwei Gründen für das Verhältnis von Figur und Grund in der Vormoderne aufschlussreich und relevant. Und zwar zum einen in solchen Fällen, in denen der Referent des Bildes entscheidend über jene physische Räumlichkeit hinausreicht, welche die moderne Fassung des Bildbegriffs gleichsam als den äußersten und umfassendsten Bereich ansetzt.

21 Ich schreibe „notwendigerweise", weil dies bei Übermalungen, also mehreren Ebenen in der Bildschicht, durchaus der Fall sein *kann*. In diesem Fall würde auch der verdeckten Hauswand eine Information in der Bildschicht entsprechen.

22 Der Ausdruck ergibt wohlgemerkt auch für das Bildmedium Sinn, freilich einen anderen: Hier meint ‚hinter' der Bildschicht z. B. den Bildträger, also etwa die Leinwand oder – noch weiter ‚dahinter' – den Keilrahmen usw.

Zum anderen wird die Frage der Räumlichkeit von Bild und Bildmedium dort relevant, wo beide dergestalt in einem Figur/Grund-Verhältnis zueinander stehen, dass im Bild wie in der Bildschicht gewisse ‚Nullstellen' an Information gegeben sind, die auf spezifische Weise einen Einbezug des Bildträgers und des Bildmediums im Ganzen ermöglichen. Denn wo das Bildmedium einen Raum aufspannt, der in der Bildschicht selbst nicht durchgängig mit materieller Information erfüllt ist, ergeben sich, wie wir später an Beispielen sehen werden, gerade durch dieses Figur/Grund-Verhältnis weitreichende Möglichkeiten zu genuinen Bildaussagen.

Bevor diese rein begrifflichen Überlegungen an konkreten Artefakten hinsichtlich des Figur/Grund-Verhältnisses erprobt werden können, sind zuletzt auch Figur und Grund selbst noch heuristisch zu definieren. Als *Figur* begreife ich im Vorliegenden jenen relationalen Teil eines asymmetrischen Differenzgeschehens im Bild, der sich *prima facie* als ein bestimmtes, formiertes Etwas und als das Eigentliche abhebt.[23] Als *Grund* begreife ich entsprechend jenen relational hierauf bezogenen anderen Teil dieses Differenzgeschehens, der *prima facie* vor allem *ex negativo* an der Erscheinung des anderen Relats mitwirkt.[24] Dabei ist es zumeist der Fall, dass der als Grund gefasste Teil das Relat der Figur ganz oder partiell umschließt, wobei sich die vorliegenden Definitionen auf zweidimensionale Bildmedien beschränken.

Zu diesem heuristischen Definitionspaar sind mehrere Punkte anzumerken. Besonders wichtig ist, erstens, dass es auf den intuitiven, ersten Zugriff abhebt. Das heißt: Diese Definitionen wollen gar nicht bestreiten, dass man sich auch dem Grund im Sinne eines an sich bestimmten Etwas zuwenden kann und ihn entsprechend als das Eigentliche oder zumindest als gleichberechtigtes

23
Vgl. hierzu grundlegend Gottfried Boehms Begriff der „ikonischen Differenz". Etwa Boehm, Gottfried: Ikonische Differenz, in: *Rheinsprung 11 – Zeitschrift für Bildkritik* 1, 2011, 170–176. Siehe für eine englische Übersetzung 169–178 in diesem Band.

24
Unbenommen sei bei der vorliegenden heuristischen Definition von Figur und Grund, dass ihr Verhältnis hier im Sinne begrifflicher Analysewerkzeuge dichotomischer gedacht wird, als dies im konkreten, speziellen Einzelfall des künstlerischen Artefakts der Fall sein mag. Zu bedenken ist weiterhin auch die fundamentale Dichotomie von Linie und Farbe; vgl. hierzu grundlegend Benjamin, Walter: Über die Malerei oder Zeichen und Mal [1917], in: Id.: *Gesammelte Schriften* II/2, hg. v. Rolf Tiedemann und Hermann Schweppenhäuser, Frankfurt/M. 1989, 603–607, sowie die erhellende Kommentierung hierzu in Hildebrandt, Toni: *Entwurf und Entgrenzung: Kontradispositive der Zeichnung 1955–1975*. München 2017, 88–93.

Moment begreifen kann, es mithin also so etwas wie ein ‚Eigenrecht des Grundes' – oder auch: Hintergrundes – gibt. Entscheidend ist vielmehr, dass wir in asymmetrischen Konstellationen intuitiv meist sehr gut unterscheiden können, welchem Element hierin der Primat zukommt, und dass diese Zuschreibung durchaus Sinn ergibt bzw. ergeben kann. Dies schließt, zweitens, natürlich keineswegs aus, dass es Bilder gibt, die im Sinne von ‚Kippbildern' spezifisch mit der genannten Unterscheidung spielen oder sie gezielt unterlaufen.[25] Meine Definitionen implizieren weiterhin, dass es Bilder gibt, in denen ein Figur/Grund-Verhältnis nicht adäquat feststellbar ist, entweder weil – wie zum Beispiel bei strikten Monochromen – kein Differenzgeschehen vorliegt oder weil – wie etwa bei strikt symmetrischen zweifarbigen Bildern – keine Asymmetrie vorliegt.[26] Viertens und letztens ist der Status von Figur und Grund nur je relativ zu verstehen und infolgedessen iterierbar: Was im einen Verhältnis Figur ist, kann in einem anderen Verhältnis desselben Bildes die Funktion des Grundes einnehmen. Man denke etwa an ein Haus, das sich als Figur vor einem Himmelsgrund abhebt, während die Hauswand ihrerseits als Grund für ein darauf befindliches Objekt, etwa ein Efeugewächs oder ein Plakat, fungiert.

Soweit die rein begrifflichen Überlegungen. Im Folgenden sollen nun die beiden skizzierten dreistelligen Bildbegriffe und mit ihnen die Figur/Grund-Relation mit konkreten historischen Artefakten in Beziehung gesetzt werden.

Liuthar und Raffael

Für all jene schon angedeuteten Fälle, in denen der Referent umfassender ist als der physische Raum, mag eine exemplarische Gegenüberstellung der Apotheose Ottos III.[27] im Aachener

25
Hier bietet etwa das Œuvre René Magrittes eine Vielzahl an Beispielen.

26
Asymmetrie ist wiederum nicht *per se* mit der Figur/Grund-Relation identisch: Ich kann mir z. B. ein queroblonges Bild vorstellen, das zu zwei Dritteln grün und zu einem Drittel rot ist – ein solches Bild weist eine Asymmetrie, aber keine Figur/Grund-Relation auf.

27
Es ist für die vorliegende Argumentation nicht von Belang, ob – wie vielfach diskutiert – in der Apotheose letztlich Otto II. oder Otto III. zur Darstellung kommt. Gleiches gilt für die damit verbundene Frage der genauen Datierung.

Liuthar-Evangeliar [Fig. 454] mit Raffaels *Disputa del Sacramento* [Fig. 455] in den vatikanischen Stanzen aufschlussreich sein. Beide Darstellungen kommen darin überein, dass ihr Referent entscheidend über das Physische hinausreicht. Beide stellen, im unteren Bereich, die physische Welt und, im darüber liegenden Bereich, eine immateriell-transzendente Himmelswelt dar.[28] In beiden Fällen wird die Schwelle zwischen diesen beiden Bereichen als eigener Bildgegenstand einbezogen, einmal, im Falle der ottonischen Darstellung, als Tuch[29] und einmal, in Raffaels Fresko, in Form des unteren Wolkenbandes. Und in beiden Fällen ist diesen beiden Bereichen Gottvater als dritte und höchste Ebene übergeordnet: Im Liuthar-Evangeliar ist er durch die in einer violetten Kreisform abgesetzte *dextera Dei* angedeutet,[30] im Falle des vatikanischen Freskos ist er durch eine (partiell verdeckte) Ganzkörperfigur präsent, die einerseits durch ein weiteres Wolkenband vom himmlischen Bereich abgegrenzt ist und andererseits vor einem – allerdings figurativ gestalteten – goldenen Grund erscheint. Dass das Verhältnis der materiellen zur immateriellen Welt eine zentrale Rolle spielt, wird in der *Disputa* zudem u. a. durch die Gesten der beiden älteren Männer links und rechts des Altars unterstrichen.[31] Auch die Position der Monstranz mit der Hostie als bleibende Instanz der Inkarnation spielt auf den Übergang der immateriellen in die materielle Welt an. In beiden Fällen ist der Referent damit die Gesamtwirklichkeit, bestehend aus materieller und immaterieller Welt, sowie ihre Abhängigkeit von Gottvater als Urgrund der Gesamtwirklichkeit und oberster, dritter Ebene der Hierarchie.

Bezogen auf die Divergenz der Bildräumlichkeit sowie das Figur/Grund-Verhältnis ergeben sich hieraus nun mehrere

28
Ich folge hier Kantorowicz, Ernst H.: *Die zwei Körper des Königs. Eine Studie zur politischen Theologie des Mittelalters*, München 1990, 81–95.

29
Dass dieses Tuch dabei von den Symbolen der vier kanonischen Evangelisten gehalten wird, dürfte wohl (auch) so zu verstehen sein, dass der Übergang Christi vom himmlischen in den irdischen Bereich in den Evangelien selbst beschrieben wird. Durchaus bemerkenswert ist, dass an analoger Stelle in der *Disputa* die vier Evangelien links und rechts des Heiligen Geistes zu stehen kommen.

30
Anders als Kantorowicz, *Zwei Körper des Königs*, 97 (mit Anm. 85) dies erwägt, glaube ich nicht, dass dies die Hand des Sohnes ist.

31
Ihnen korrespondieren, in der *Stanza della Segnatura* gegenüberliegend, die Gesten von Platon und Aristoteles in der *Scuola di Atene*.

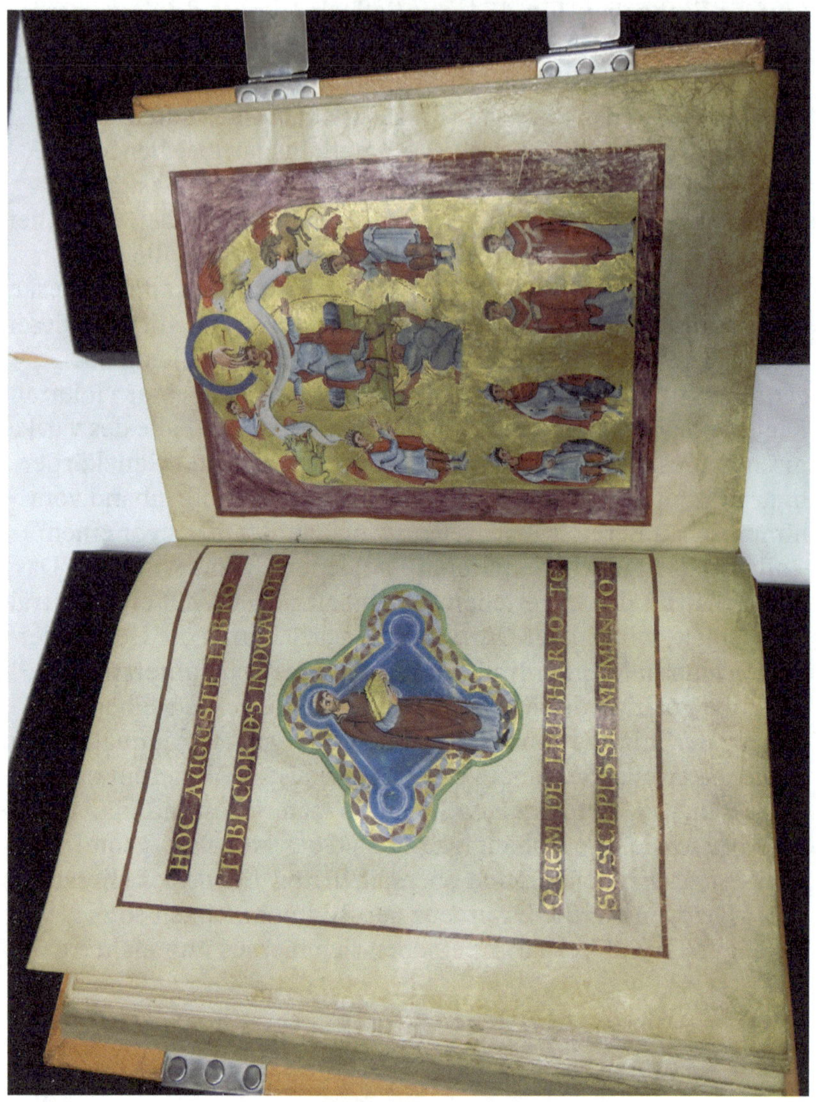

Liuthar-Evangeliar, ca. 975–1000, Reichenau.
Aachen, Aachener Domschatzkammer, fol. 16r.

Fig. 454

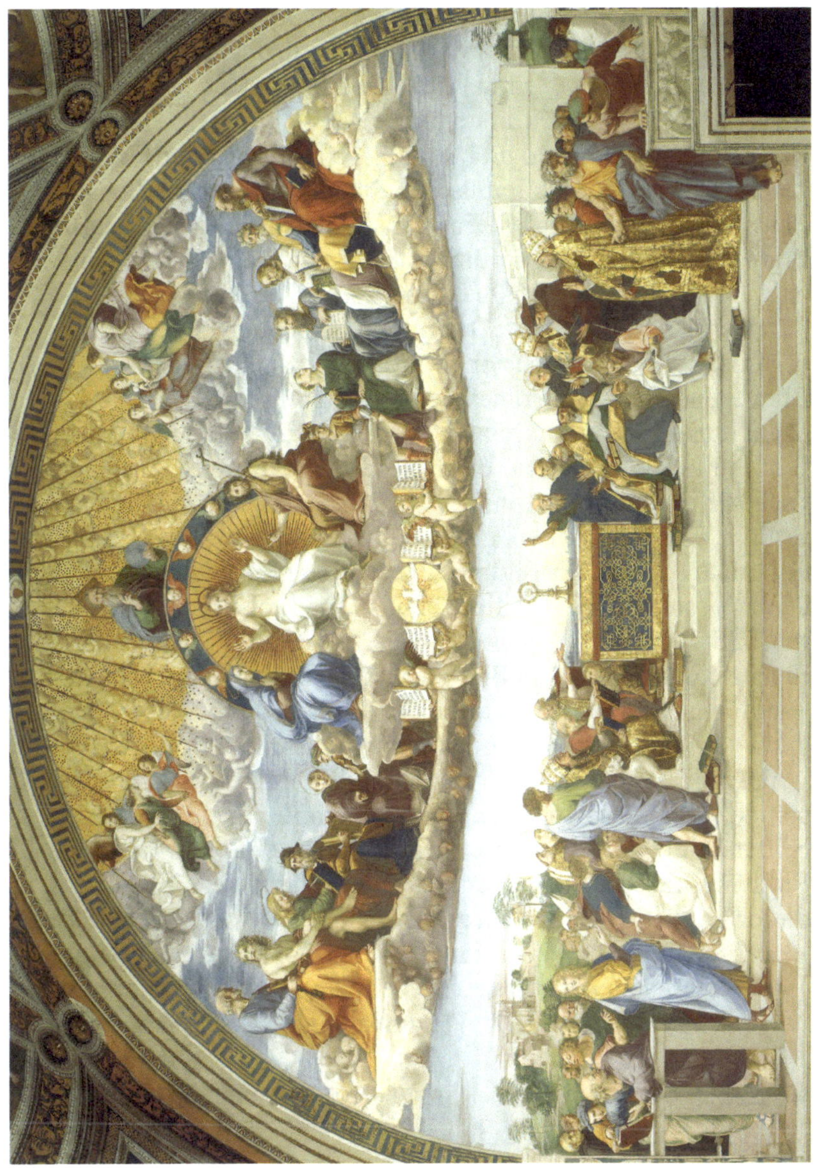

Raffael, *Disputa del Sacramento*, 1509–1510, Fresco, ca. 500 × 770 cm.
Vatikanische Museen, Vatikan.

Fig. 455

Beobachtungen und Konsequenzen.[32] Zuvorderst ist zu bemerken, dass in Raffaels Darstellung der himmlische und der irdische Bereich beide in *einen* einheitlichen Bildraum eingeholt werden, während in Liuthars[33] Darstellung diese beiden Bereiche von Blattgold umgeben sind. Bei Raffael ist der Grund der Figurationen im irdischen und himmlischen Raum damit der Bereich des Physischen, ganz wie dies – in Transponierung[34] – im modernen Bildbegriff nahegelegt wird: Der umfassendste, äußerste Bereich ist das Physische, innerhalb dessen sich der Bereich des Imaginären eröffnet. Das heißt: Der Bildraum ist ein perspektivisch organisierter, dreidimensional-physischer Raum, in dem sich jene Bildgegenstände versammeln, deren Referenten materiell wie auch immateriell sind. Dabei ist besonders zu betonen, dass diese Beziehung zwischen dem Bildbegriff einerseits und der spezifischen Konfiguration von Bildraum und Bildgegenständen andererseits, wie geschrieben, in einer *Transponierung* besteht. Es ist also nicht so, dass der Bildbegriff und diese Konfiguration einfach deckungsgleich sind – alleine schon deshalb nicht, weil das Bild mit Bildraum und Bildgegenständen ja nur ein *Teil* der konzeptuellen Konstellation im Bildbegriff ist. Wohl aber ist es möglich – und in meinen Augen entscheidend –, dass der bei der Anfertigung des Werkes implizit oder explizit präsente Bildbegriff Auswirkungen darauf hat, *wie genau* im Bild Bildraum und Bildgegenstände organisiert sind. In *dieser* Transponierung können die beiden Bildbegriffe und ihre Meta-Physiken eine entscheidende Rolle im Bild spielen. Im Umkehrschluss kann der Einbezug dieser Bildbegriffe dazu beitragen, in der Analyse die spezifische Verfasstheit und Organisation des Bildes adäquat zu adressieren.

Während bei Raffael der gemeinsame Grund des himmlischen und des irdischen Bereichs als Raum der physischen Anschauung

32
Ich spare im Folgenden den gesamten Komplex der Christomimesis durch den Kaiser aus, dass also Otto III. im Evangeliar eine systematische Stellung einnimmt, der in der *Disputa* recht genau Christus und die Hostie entsprechen.

33
Ich nutze hier und im Folgenden der Einfachheit halber ausschließlich ‚Liuthar' als Autorenname, wenngleich der Aachener Evangeliar das Werk einer Gruppe ist.

34
Unter „Transponierung" verstehe ich hier eine analoge Übertragung von Verhältnissen innerhalb des Bildes auf Verhältnisse innerhalb des Bildbegriffs. Dabei ist es entscheidend, das konkrete Artefakt und den Bildbegriff weiterhin getrennt zu halten; nur dann ist auszumachen, wie ein (auch nur implizit vorliegender) Bildbegriff – möglicherweise – auf das Bild und den Bildraum selbst zurückwirken kann.

erkennbar ist, ist dieser gemeinsame Grund im ottonischen Evangeliar aus mehrerlei Gründen schwieriger zu bestimmen. Zum einen ist in Rechnung zu stellen, dass auch die ottonische Buchillumination einen dreidimensionalen Bildraum kennt, der allerdings anders kodiert ist als bei Raffael – insofern etwa ein Übereinander der Figuren ein Hintereinander kodieren kann.[35] Zum anderen ist auffällig, dass das Blattgold auch den Bereich markiert, in dem die Hand Gottvaters erscheint, was wiederum einen gemeinsamen Grund aller drei Bereiche nahelegen würde. Vor allem aber ist, drittens, die Figur/Grund-Konstellation in der ottonischen Darstellung dadurch entscheidend intrikater, dass der den Bereichen gemeinsame Grund seinerseits von einem purpur-rotvioletten Grund umfangen wird, welcher abermals gegenüber dem Grund der Folioseite durch eine dunklere Rahmung abgegrenzt ist. Die Stellung des rotvioletten Grundes, auf und in dem der gemeinsame Grund der irdischen und der himmlischen Welt erscheint, ist damit sachlich – also in seinem Referenten – nicht ohne Weiteres zu fassen, zumal die Grenze zwischen Gold und Rotviolett durch die Flügel der vier Evangelistensymbole markant überspielt wird. Unter Berücksichtigung des vormodernen dreistelligen Bildbegriffs wäre so an eine explizite Einholung der Materie, also des Bildmediums in diesem Bildbegriff zu denken. Auch hier wäre dann, wie bei Raffael, der Bildbegriff in der Bildkonfiguration selbst wirksam.

Auch wenn somit dic Situation der Figur/Grund-Konstellationen bei Liuthar komplexer und die Rolle des Goldes ambivalenter ist, als dies auf den ersten Blick erscheinen mag,[36] so lässt

35
Dies ist etwa im Münchner Evangeliar Ottos III. bei der Darstellung von Jesu Einzug in Jerusalem (fol. 236v) gut zu erkennen.

36
Somit ist die einfache Gleichsetzung des Goldgrundes mit einem immateriell-transzendenten Raum ebenso inadäquat wie die schlichte Identifikation des perspektivischen Raumes mit dem physischen Raum. Vgl. zu Ersterem auch Beer, Ellen, J.: Marginalien zum Thema Goldgrund, in: *Zeitschrift für Kunstgeschichte* 46/3, 1983, 271–286, bes. 272–273, 276. Angesichts der Schwierigkeit und Komplexität der Thematik sei zudem bemerkt, dass das vorliegende Argument weder voraussetzt, dass es die *eine* Perspektive gibt, noch, dass Bilder notwendigerweise vollständig und ungebrochen diesem Paradigma unterliegen können bzw. müssen. Ebenso wenig gehe ich davon aus, dass Perspektivkonstruktionen einen wie auch immer gearteten Fortschritt im schlichten Sinne darstellen. Vorausgesetzt ist einzig, dass Raffaels Darstellung im komparativen Sinne deutlich stärker als Liuthar einer perspektivischen Darstellungs- und Funktionsweise folgt. Dass Goldgrund und Perspektive kein einfaches, dichotomisches Gegeneinander bilden, sondern sich vielmehr verschränken können, zeigt ausführlich am Werk Fra Angelicos Quené, Saskia: *Goldgrund und Perspektive. Fra Angelico im Glanz des Quattrocento*, Berlin/Boston 2022.

sich doch insgesamt festhalten, dass Raffael hinsichtlich der Denkart, die seiner Darstellung zugrunde liegt, dem modernen, Liuthar dagegen dem vormodernen Bildbegriff folgt, zumal bei Liuthar die Erde – als *pars pro toto* des Physischen? – durch eine Personifikation unterhalb des Thrones eingeholt ist. Somit dürfte insgesamt die Vermutung ebenso naheliegend wie berechtigt sein, dass Liuthar die Entscheidung Raffaels bzgl. des Bildraums mit Blick auf den himmlischen und irdischen Bereich als Referenten durchaus problematisch erschienen wäre, wenngleich die beiden Künstler möglicherweise in ihrer Konzeption weniger weit voneinander entfernt sind, als dies auf den ersten Blick den Anschein hatte. Schließlich liegt – wenn der Goldgrund im Evangeliar potentiell auch als dreidimensionaler Bildraum fungieren kann – in beiden Fällen ein beide Welten umfassender Bildraum vor; der in beiden Fällen allerdings unterschiedlich kodiert ist. Die Ausweitung des Gemeinten über den Bereich der Sinnlichkeit – die in beiden Fällen insofern präsent ist, als die Referenten nicht ausschließlich physisch sind – wäre also eine Frage nicht des grundsätzlich unterschiedlichen Bildraumes, sondern der *Darstellung und Kodierung* dieses Bildraumes: Raffael folgt einer geometrisch-idealisierten Fassung unseres optischen Seheindrucks zur Vermittlung des dreidimensionalen Bildraumes, während sich Liuthars Fassung des Bildraumes auf formfunktionale und materielle Prämissen stützt.

Die beiden Darstellungen entsprechen sich ferner nicht nur bzgl. des himmlischen und des irdischen Bereichs als Referent, sondern kommen auch darin überein, dass sie die Domäne Gottvaters, also der ersten Person der Trinität, miteinbeziehen. Bei Raffael ist dies, wie beschrieben, der oberste, goldene Bereich, der durch ein zweites Wolkenband abgesetzt ist. Bei Liuthar bildet ein kreisförmiger, blauviolett umrandeter Bereich mit Kreuzsymbol und der *dextera Dei* in der oberen Bildmitte die Domäne Gottvaters. Diese ist wiederum markant durch die Mandorla der Kaiserfigur überschnitten, womit der Kaiser im Moment der Salbung und Krönung selbst *innerhalb* des obersten Bereiches der insgesamt dreigliedrigen Hierarchie präsent ist. Bei beiden Darstellungen sind mit Blick auf die vorliegende Frage mehrere Beobachtungen festzuhalten.

Zum Aachener Evangeliar ist erstens zu bemerken, dass Gottvater als erste trinitarische Person durch seine rechte Hand nur angedeutet, nicht aber ganzfigurig eingeholt wird. Dies entspricht der – letztlich latent subordinationistisch gefassten – Trinitätsvorstellung, wonach Gottvater als erste Person der Fassbarkeit in besonderer Weise entzogen ist und ein Zugang zu ihm nur vermittelt durch den Sohn als zweite und eminent fassbare Person möglich ist.[37] Aufschlussreicher noch als diese trinitätstheologische Überlegung ist für die vorliegende Fragestellung zum Verhältnis von Figur und Grund jedoch, *wie* die Domäne Gottvaters im Bild konkret umgesetzt wird. Denn zum einen ist bemerkenswert, dass die bereits zuvor angesprochene Konfiguration von Gold- und Rotviolettgrund in bzw. hinter dem gottväterlichen Bereich zusammenzulaufen scheint. Hier schließen sich – wie immer man das Verhältnis von Gold und Rotviolett in seiner Referenz genauer fassen mag – diese beiden Gründe gleichsam in der obersten Instanz als deren Fluchtpunkt zusammen.

Vor allem ist aber, zweitens, hervorzuheben, dass der kreisförmige Bereich Gottvaters *über* den Rotviolettgrund und dessen Umrandung noch hinausreicht und in das unmarkierte Pergament der Buchseite selbst hineinragt. Dieses scheint, durch eine ganz spezifische Figur/Grund-Konstellation, die Enthobenheit der obersten göttlichen Instanz umzusetzen. Denn die Domäne Gottvaters findet sich partiell in einem Bereich der Bildschicht, in der keine Differenz zwischen zwei markierten Flächen eine potentielle Figur/Grund-Beziehung ermöglicht, sondern in der ein markierter Bereich an einen unmarkierten Bereich angrenzt – nämlich den Bildträger selbst, der hier in seiner Materialität und Eigenfarbigkeit zugleich Teil und Nullstelle innerhalb der Bildschicht ist. Dies ist eine bildtechnische Umsetzung der Absolutheit der obersten göttlichen Instanz, die zugleich einen reflektierten Umgang mit der Medialität des Bildträgers belegt, insofern dieser kongenial in die Bildaufgabe einbezogen wird. Die Instanz Gottvaters reicht in einen Bereich, in dem sie selbst das Einzige und losgelöst, buchstäblich das Absolute ist; das heißt: in einen Bereich, in dem sie sich selbst nicht mehr in Abgrenzung gegen anderes, je für sich Bestimmtes, definiert, sondern in dem (sie) einzig sie selbst ist. Bildimmanent ist dies freilich abermals nur durch eine Figur/

37
Vgl. etwa die klassischen Stellen im Johannes-Evangelium dazu: Joh 1,18; Joh 14,6.

Grund-Relation zu realisieren, die sich jedoch, wie gesagt, nicht durch ein Differenzgeschehen zwischen zwei Markierungen, sondern, innerhalb der Bildschicht, zwischen Markierung und Nicht-Markierung abspielt. Bei aller theologischen Komplexität, die sich hinter der vorliegenden Darstellung verbergen mag, ist die spezifische bildliche Umsetzung, gerade in Bezug auf die konkrete Rolle des Bildträgers, deshalb miteinzubeziehen. Das Verhältnis Gottvaters zum Foliogrund wird damit gleichsam zu einem Figur/Grund-Verhältnis zweiter Ordnung, das sich markant gegenüber den Figur/Grund-Verhältnissen innerhalb der Bildschicht absetzt.

In Raffaels *Disputa* ist der Bereich Gottvaters auch durch Gold ausgezeichnet, dessen gelber Grund von Putti durchzogen ist [Fig. 461]. Insofern dieser Grund die Domäne von Gottvater vom physischen Bildraum der beiden darunterliegenden Bereiche ausgrenzt, steht Raffael mit seiner Bildauffassung gleichsam an der Schwelle zum modernen Bildbegriff – wobei wir gleich sehen werden, dass diese Schwelle in letzter Instanz doch überschritten ist. Dass Gottvater als zentrale und einzige Figur des oberen Bereichs nicht symbolisch angedeutet, sondern von Raffael als (partiell verdeckte) Ganzkörperfigur vollständig in den Bereich der Sichtbarkeit eingeholt wird, dürfte, wie schon bei der Fassung des Bildraumes für den himmlischen und irdischen Bereich, aus Liuthars Perspektive wohl fragwürdig erschienen sein. Schließlich ist die anschauliche Darstellung des himmlischen Bereichs auf die rein geistige Denkbarkeit hin zu übersetzen, womit die Enthebung Gottvaters aus dem Bereich des Sichtbaren zuletzt wohl für dessen Transzendenz über die reine Denkbarkeit zu verstehen ist. Dennoch bildet in der Konstellation der *Disputa* Gottvater als erste trinitarische Person *nicht* den höchsten Punkt. Denn die Domäne Gottvaters ist von einem radialen Strahlenkranz durchzogen,[38]

38
Ein vom höchsten Prinzip auf die Engelshierarchien ausgehender Strahlenkranz ist auch in Bergognones *Krönung der Jungfrau Maria* (San Simpliciano, Mailand, um 1500) in Andeutung zu sehen. Ich danke Raphael Rosenberg für den Hinweis auf dieses Fresko. Sicherlich durchziehen die Strahlen nur die ersten Hierarchieebenen – und natürlich ist der höchste Punkt hier Gottvater selbst –, dennoch ist auch hier ein Durchziehen der Engelshierarchien durch Strahlen festzustellen. Als Beispiel aus der Tafelmalerei wäre exemplarisch Stefan Lochners *Darstellung im Tempel* (1447) zu nennen; auch hier trägt ein von Gottvater ausgehender Strahlenkranz eine Vielzahl an Engeln. Siehe ferner Hecht, Christian: *Die Glorie. Begriff, Thema, Bildelement in der europäischen Sakralkunst vom Mittelalter bis zum Ausgang des Barock*, Regensburg 2003.

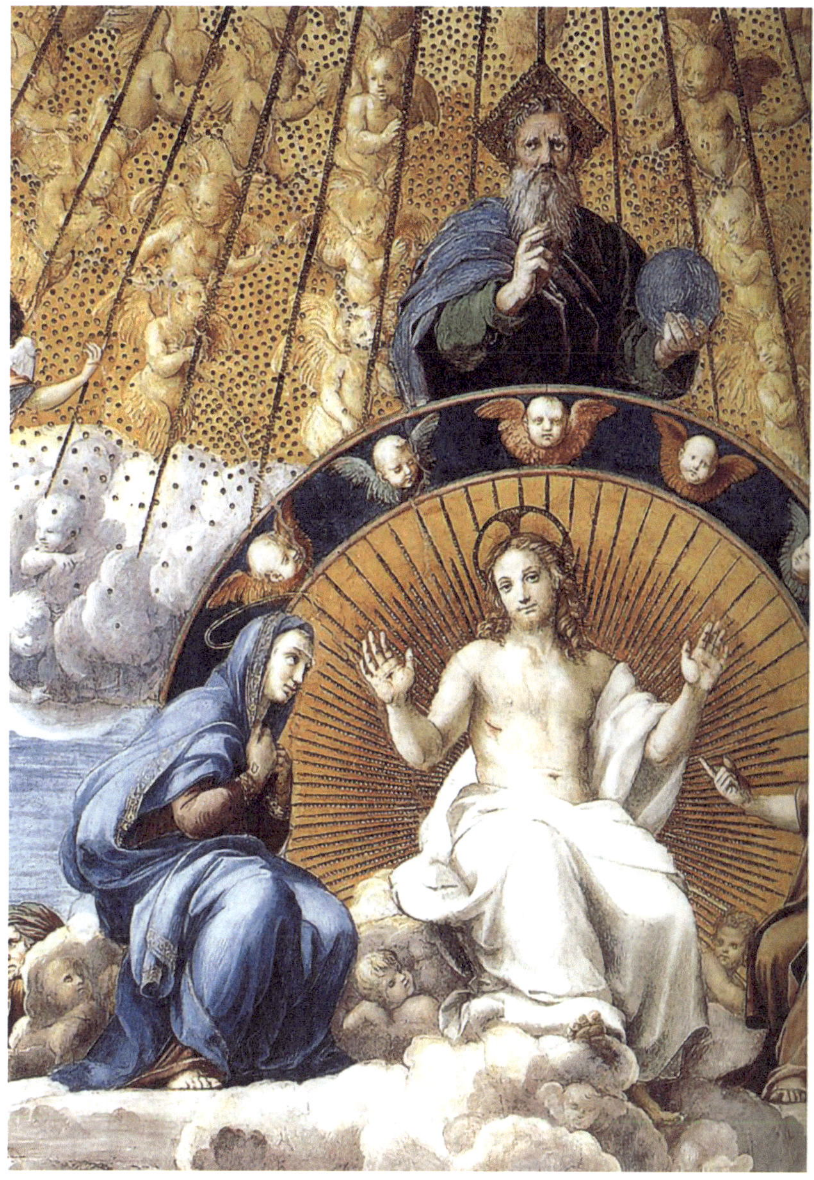

Detail Fig. 455.

Fig. 461

dessen Ursprung und Schnittpunkt selbst nicht sichtbar ist, sondern weit oberhalb, hinter dem illusionistisch gemalten, umfassenden Halbrundbogen verborgen bleibt.[39] Konsequent gedacht würde dies als höchste Instanz eine Gottheit jenseits des trinitarischen Gottes nahelegen,[40] wie sie in den vor allem vom paganen Platonismus inspirierten Theologien, etwa bei Dionysios Areopagita oder Meister Eckhart, zu finden ist. Wenn dem so wäre, dann wäre auch bei Raffael die höchste Instanz der Sichtbarkeit – und in der Übersetzung: der Denkbarkeit – im negativ-theologischen Sinne entzogen.

Jenseits dieser theologischen Fragen ist jedoch abermals entscheidend, *wie genau* Raffael diesen Entzug der höchsten Instanz bildimmanent fasst. Denn obwohl die Domäne Gottvaters durch das Gold vom umfassenden dreidimensionalen Bildraum im ersten Moment ausgenommen zu sein scheint, wird der Entzug der höchsten göttlichen Instanz maßgeblich doch durch eben diesen Bildraum inszeniert. Letztlich ist es nämlich der Rundbogen, welcher die Sicht auf den Ursprung der Strahlen verwehrt. Dieser Bogen umfasst somit, in der Bildschicht, einerseits die gottväterliche Domäne und verpflichtet diese damit, insofern er sie umfängt, auf den dreidimensionalen Bildraum.[41] Andererseits

39
Da die Strahllinien nach oben hin keinerlei Konvergenz zeitigen, scheint es mir schwer möglich, diese Linien als Andeutung einer (Apsis)kuppel zu verstehen. Letztlich macht auch der Ausgang der Strahlen nach unten, in das erste Wolkenband, eine solche Deutung unmöglich: Die Strahlen liegen nicht hinter, sondern vor dem Wolkenband und haben noch dazu – typisch für Strahlen, untypisch für Gewölbegrate – klar erkennbar unterschiedliche Längen. Ich kann auch in den Studien und Vorzeichnungen zur *Disputa* (vgl. Fischel, Oskar (Ed.): *Raphaels Zeichnungen*, vol. 6: *Die Disputa*, Berlin 1925; Digitalisat/DOI: 10.11588/diglit.11122) kein Indiz dafür finden, dass hier eine Kuppel angedeutet werden soll.

40
Ein winziges Detail stützt diese Beobachtung: Der rechte, rot und blau gewandete Engel in der Engelsgruppe links von Gottvater, vor dem oberen Wolkenband, deutet mit seiner Linken nach oben, exakt auf den Ursprung der Strahlen, nicht jedoch auf Gottvater. Die Geste – welche zudem die Geste der Figur in der untersten Bildebene rechts neben der Monstranz aufnimmt – ist so eng mit den Strahlen verbunden, dass der Zeigefinger des Engels direkt auf einem der Strahlen liegt.

41
Dies gilt auch insofern, als in der Domäne Gottvaters die Putti selbst einer dreidimensionalen Bildraumauffassung verpflichtet sind: In Schatten- und Volumenbildung sind sie deutlich als dreidimensionale Körper aufgefasst, was sich auch im Vergleich mit den Putti in den beiden Wolkenbändern sowie dem Befund bestätigt, dass der goldene Engel oberhalb des Kreuzes von Johannes dem Täufer sich geradezu auf dem oberen Wolkenband abzustützen scheint.

unterstützt der Bogen, mit Blick auf den Bildraum, entscheidend die räumliche Tiefenwirkung, und der Ursprung der Strahlen bleibt so in der imaginären Bewegung durch den Bildraum im Prinzip erreichbar. Ebenso können wir in der Vorstellung durch den Bogen bis zu den Stufen vor dem Altar hindurchgehen, um nach oben, zum Ursprung der Strahlen aufzublicken. Der illusionistische Rundbogen, der bei Raffael die äußerste bildliche Instanz ist, verpflichtet damit das gesamte Bild letztlich auf einen einheitlichen dreidimensionalen Bildraum im Sinne des hier rekonstruierten modernen Bildbegriffs. Der letzte Grund, auf dem sich die Bildfiguration im Ganzen abzeichnet, bleibt damit der physische Raum – was seinerseits, in der Transponierung, der Konstellation des modernen Bildbegriffs entspricht.

Kosmas und die *Topographia Christiana*

Im abschließenden dritten Schritt möchte ich eine Darstellung aus dem 9. Jahrhundert hinzuziehen, die einerseits zeitlich den beiden vorherigen Bildbeispielen vorangeht, andererseits eine Auffassung der Bildräumlichkeit und des Figur/Grund-Verhältnisses aufweist, welche zeigt, dass auch das vormoderne Figur/Grund-Verhältnis von *beiden* Bildbegriffen profitieren kann. Es handelt sich um eine Illumination des *Codex Vaticanus graecus* 699, der ältesten erhaltenen Abschrift der *Topographia Christiana*, deren Autor unter dem Namen Kosmas Indikopleustes bekannt ist [Fig. 464]. Das Werk selbst stammt aus der Mitte des 6. Jh. n. Chr. und beinhaltet neben Reiseberichten insbesondere die Darlegung einer christlichen Kosmologie, der zufolge die Gesamtwirklichkeit einem riesigen, zweigeschossigen Tabernakel gleicht, auf dessen Boden sich die Erde in programmatisch flacher und nicht sphärischer Form befindet.[42]

Die Darstellung auf fol. 43r ist im vorliegenden Kontext insbesondere deshalb bemerkenswert, weil sie sich mit den vorangegangenen Beispielen in mehrfacher Hinsicht in Beziehung

42
Vgl. zu diesen frühchristlichen Kosmographien im Detail Gleede, Benjamin: *Antiochenische Kosmographie? Zur Begründung und Verbreitung nichtsphärischer Weltkonzeptionen in der antiken Christenheit*, Berlin/Boston 2021.

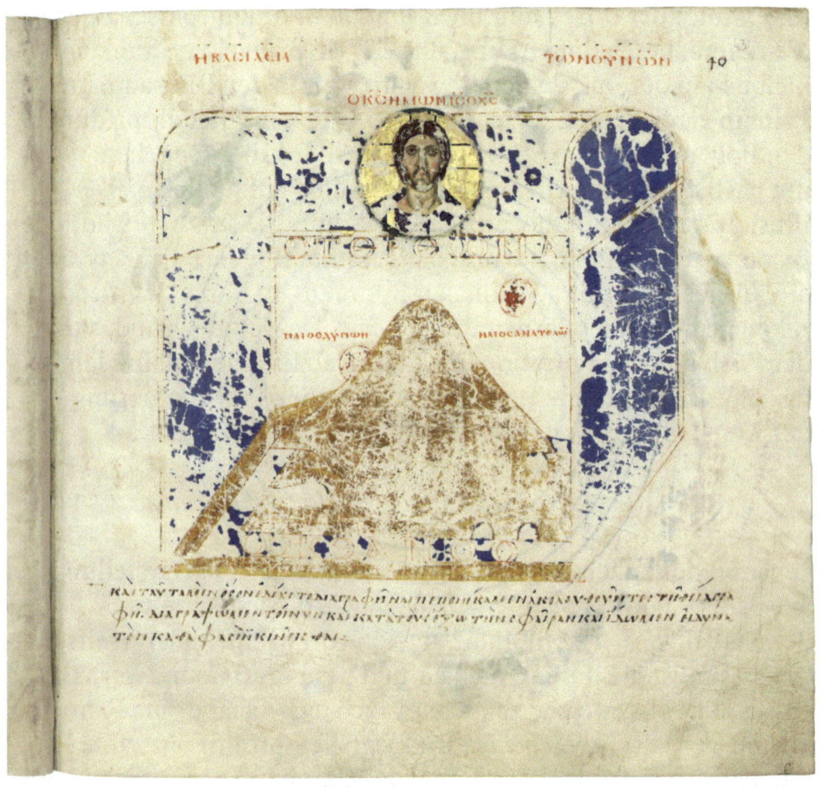

Topographia Christiana, 9. Jahrhundert,
Vatikan, Bibliotheca Apostolica Vaticana, Codex Vat. gr. 699, fol. 43r.

Fig. 464

setzen lässt. Diese Beziehungen betreffen zum einen die spezifische Fassung der Bildräumlichkeit und zum anderen ein Detail einer Figur/Grund-Konstellation, das wie schon im Liuthar-Evangeliar einen sehr reflektieren Umgang mit der Medialität des Bildträgers nahelegt.

Für Kosmas – und für seinen Illuminator – besteht die Wirklichkeit grundsätzlich aus zwei Ebenen, dem immateriell-himmlischen und dem materiell-irdischen Bereich, also jenen zwei Bereichen, die uns bereits im Liuthar-Evangeliar und bei Raffael begegnet sind und die Kosmas programmatisch in Gen 1,1 – „Im Anfang schuf Gott Himmel und Erde" – angesprochen findet.[43] Auffällig ist nun, dass der Kosmas-Illuminator diese zwei Ebenen der Wirklichkeit durch eine gemeinsame dreidimensionale Bildräumlichkeit fasst. Wenn man etwa auf die Linien des Halbzylinders blickt, welcher als Truhendeckel den oberen, den (ersten) himmlischen Bereich fasst,[44] so spricht die geometrische Darstellung des Objektes dafür, dass dem Illustrator an einer Fassung des Bildraumes gelegen war, die dem dreidimensionalen Raum unserer sinnlichen Anschauung entspricht [Fig. 466]. Damit sind in dieser Fassung der materielle wie der immaterielle Bereich der Wirklichkeit im Bild letztlich in einem gemeinsamen, physisch kodierten Raum eingefasst. Kosmas' Illuminator ist folglich, in der Transponierung, näher am modernen Bildbegriff.

Besonders bemerkenswert ist nun aber, dass diese Bildraumauffassung eine markante und entscheidende Brechung erfährt, welche die Darstellung zuletzt doch, insbesondere mit Blick auf die Figur/Grund-Verhältnisse, stärker an die vormoderne Fassung des Bildbegriffs bindet. Und zwar findet sich in der Wölbung des Truhendeckels eine Christusdarstellung, welche – hierauf hat auch Herbert L. Kessler hingewiesen[45] – dem Typus des wahren

43
Top. Christ. 4.186–187. Vgl. auch Gleede, *Antiochenische Kosmographie*, 49–50.

44
Vgl. diesbezüglich auch das in die Berührungsebene zwischen Truhen- und Deckelraum eingefügte CTEPEΩMA, das nach Gen 1,6–8 die Trennfläche zwischen dem irdischen und dem (ersten) himmlischen Bereich bildet. Interessant ist auch der Vergleich der Darstellung fol. 43r mit der Darstellung fol. 39v. Hier ist das CTEPEΩMA in der Mitte des Truhenraums angesetzt; entsprechend ist auch die Christusdarstellung nach unten transponiert – was in jedem Fall ein Indiz dafür ist, dass die Platzierung des Christusbildes (in beiden Darstellungen) genau durchdacht ist.

45
Vgl. Kessler, Herbert L.: Il mandylion, in: Morello, Giovanni/Wolf, Gerhard (Ed.): *Il volto di Cristo*, Mailand 2000, 67–76: 74.

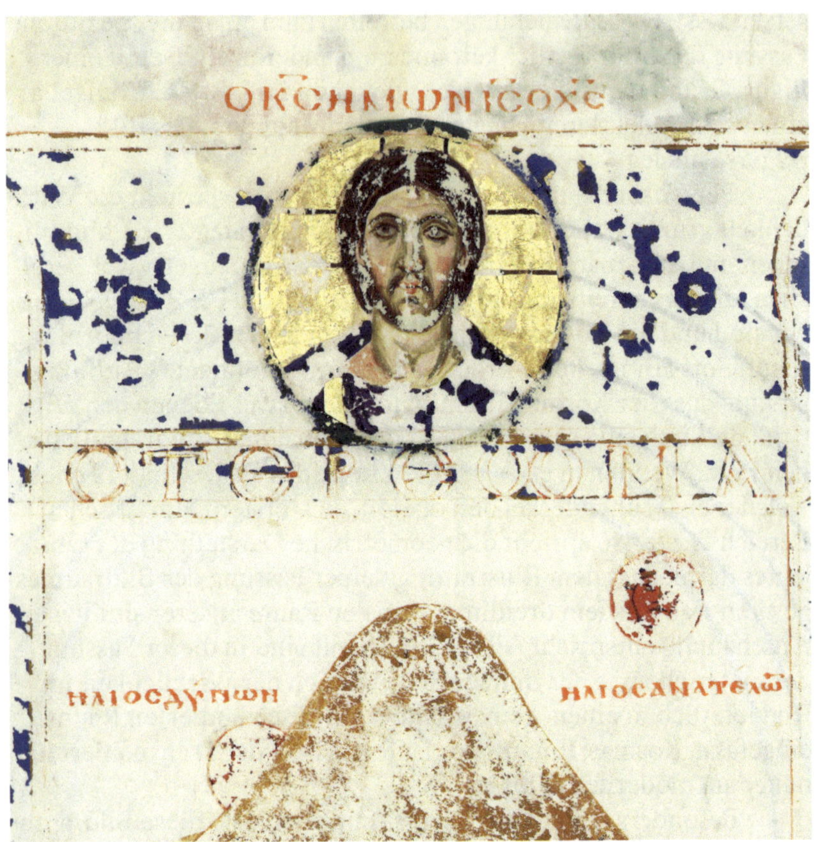

Detail Fig. 464.

Fig. 466

Christusbildes folgt. Am obersten Punkt der räumlichen Hierarchie findet sich damit – wenn man sie anachronistisch so nennen darf – eine *vera icon* in die Gesamtdarstellung mit einbezogen. Dieser Bildgegenstand ist nun, im sachlichen Vergleich mit Raffael und Liuthar, aus drei Gründen aufschlussreich.

Erstens nimmt der Kosmas-Illuminator in der bildtheologischen Frage bzgl. der Stellung und Darstellbarkeit Gottvaters die äußerste Position ein: Gottvater ist kein eigener Bildgegenstand, auch nicht in symbolischer Andeutung wie bei Liuthar. Vielmehr ist erst Christus, als zweite göttliche Person und Erscheinung der ersten Person im Bereich des Intelligiblen, überhaupt fass- und damit darstellbar. Dies entspricht – ohne dies hier weiter auszuführen – der an Philon von Alexandria anschließenden und etwa bei Origenes greifbaren Logos-Theologie, der zufolge überhaupt erst in der zweiten trinitarischen Hypostase, im Logos, eine erste Form der rein geistigen Fassbarkeit und folglich eine (annähernde) Darstellbarkeit gegeben ist.[46] Gottvater verbleibt in dieser Auffassung in absoluter Transzendenz, was in der Kosmas-Illustration entsprechend konsequent umgesetzt ist.

Wichtiger für die vorliegenden Überlegungen ist jedoch, zweitens, dass die Christusdarstellung der Deckelkrümmung, und damit dem dreidimensionalen Bildraum, gerade *nicht* folgt. Dies ist dabei wohlgemerkt nicht dem Unvermögen des Illuminators zuzuschreiben. Während für die kosmische Truhe als solche das Pergament letztlich lediglich den materiellen Bildträger bereitstellt, dessen es notgedrungen bedarf, um die Bildschicht zu fixieren, ist dies für das Christusbild anders. Für das Christusbild, das mit seiner exakten Kreisform einer gänzlich anderen Auffassung des Bildraumes wie auch des Figur/Grund-Verhältnisses folgt, ist der materielle Bildträger als Grund entscheidend mehr: Er spielt genau jene Rolle, welche sonst das Tuch in den *verae icones* spielt. Auch dies darf, ähnlich wie im Liuthar-Evangeliar,

Zu bedenken ist allerdings, dass der Truhendeckel, auf und in dem das Christusbild erscheint, nicht das Firmament ist – Letzteres fällt mit dem στερέωμα, also dem Übergang vom Deckel- zum Truhenraum, zusammen.

46 Vgl. hierzu Bruns, Christoph: Christologischer Universalismus. Der Johannesprolog in der Wirklichkeitsdeutung des Origenes, in: Enders, Markus/Kühn, Rolf (Ed.): *„Im Anfang war der Logos…". Studien zur Rezeptionsgeschichte des Johannesprologs von der Antike bis zur Gegenwart*, Freiburg/Basel/Wien 2011, 7–46.

als ein reflektierter Umgang mit der materialen Medialität des Bildträgers selbst verstanden werden. Insgesamt bedeutet dies, dass die Darstellung den Bildträger und damit auch den Bildgrund in zwei Hinsichten zugleich beansprucht: einmal als rein notwendiges Substrat für die dreidimensionale Bildräumlichkeit und einmal gleichsam als latenten Bildgegenstand, insofern das Pergament die Rolle des Tuches für das Christusbild übernimmt und folglich diese Darstellung auch der grundsätzlich anders gelagerten Auffassung des Bildraumes in der *vera icon* folgt.[47]

Zuletzt findet sich hier nämlich, drittens, jene präzise gesetzte Überschneidung, die in ähnlicher Form schon im Liuthar-Evangeliar zu beobachten war: Auch in der Kosmas-Illumination ragt der Kreis des Christusbildes markant über den himmlischen Bereich hinaus. Hier sogar zweifach, nämlich sowohl in den irdischen Bereich wie auch in den Bereich jenseits des Himmels. Ersteres dürfte als Formulierung der Inkarnation Christi zu lesen sein, Letzteres verknüpft Christus mit jenem Bereich jenseits des Himmels, der die genuine Domäne Gottvaters ist. Den obigen Überlegungen zur ersten trinitarischen Person folgend, hätte dieses Hineinragen der Christusfigur in den Grund jenseits der Truhe eine ganz entscheidende, weitere Pointe: Es würde dann genau diesen Grund nicht nur als Quasi-Tuch, sondern auch als – buchstäblich negativ bestimmten – eigenen Bildgegenstand einholen, der im Fehlen jeglicher positiver Markierung die adäquate Fassung der nur negativ fassbaren ersten innertrinitarischen Person wäre. Der Pergamentgrund würde sich so gleichsam als die eigentliche Domäne des Absoluten entpuppen.

Darüber hinaus ist bemerkenswert, wie die Christusdarstellung in ihrem Übertritt in die Bereiche diesseits und jenseits des Himmlischen die Darstellung, welche dem dreidimensionalen Bildraum folgt, *als solche* zu überspielen scheint. Letztendlich bilden so jene Bildgegenstände, die in diesen Bildraum eingebettet sind (am prominentesten: die Truhe im Ganzen), ihrerseits den Grund, auf dem sich die Christusdarstellung mit ihrer eigenen Raumauffassung als Figur abhebt. So bilden die beiden Bildauffassungen, die in der Kosmas-Illumination überblendet sind, ihrerseits eine Figur/Grund-Konstellation. Und zwar – als Grund –

47 Vgl. Poetsch, Chôra und vera icon, 57–62.

die dreidimensionale Bildräumlichkeit, wie sie sich auch im modernen Bildbegriff findet, und – als Figur – die genuine Zweidimensionalität des Trägers. Auf diese Weise bietet die Illumination bei Kosmas folglich – spannungsreicher noch als bei Liuthar und Raffael – eine intrikate *Überblendung* zweier Figur/Grund-Auffassungen, die sich markant in der Auffassung der Bildräumlichkeit manifestieren. Und diese sind, wie ich versucht habe zu zeigen, letztlich in die beiden dreistelligen Bildbegriffe mit ihren inversen Meta-Physiken transponierbar. In diesem Sinne eröffnen diese beiden Bildbegriffe einen Möglichkeitsraum spezifischer Darstellungsweisen, die mit ihnen, wie exemplarisch angeführt, auf mehrfache Weise verschränkt sind.

Part 4
Navigating Dichotomies

Raphael's paintings have been described by art historians as being composed of simple geometric shapes. Heinrich Wölfflin, for example, writes of the *Madonna del Cardellino*: "Es ist eine Komposition nach dem Schema des gleichseitigen Dreieckes. … Warum fällt der Rock Mariä an der Schulter herunter? Es soll das Ausspringen der Silhouette beim Buche vorbereitet werden, so dass die Linie in gleichmäßigem Rhythmus herunterzugleiten scheint."[1] While Wölfflin sees an equilateral triangle, i.e., a two-dimensional shape, other authors describe a three-dimensional pyramid.[2]

Did Raphael use geometric shapes like triangles or pyramids to design his paintings? To answer this question, we could look for sketches with composition lines. I did that for thirty years but could not find a single drawing with compositional lines by Raphael or by any other sixteenth-century artist. None of the colleagues with whom I have discussed the subject have been able to point to examples, either on paper or in the underdrawings of easel paintings and frescoes.[3] Another possibility is to search for texts that mention triangles, pyramids, or other geometric shapes in relation to the composition of paintings or sculptures. I did this as well, with just as few results, the oldest of which dates from 1584.[4]

I would like to thank Zoya Dare and Jozsef Arato for their great help in completing this paper. Together with Rosa Sancarlo, Zoya was also involved in collecting and analyzing the data for the *Last Supper* study, and Jozsef designed the algorithms and performed the statistical analyses. Saskia Quené, Gerd Blum, and an anonymous reviewer provided very helpful critical feedback on the manuscript. I would also like to thank Sandra Hindriks for her comments.

1
Heinrich Wölfflin, *Die klassische Kunst: Eine Einführung in die italienische Renaissance* (Munich: F. Bruckmann, 1899), p. 82.

2
See, for example, Jacob Burckhardt, *Der Cicerone: Eine Anleitung Zum Genuss Der Kunstwerke Italiens* (Basel: Schweighauser, 1855), p. 895 and John Pope-Hennessy, "Beccafumi in the Victoria and Albert Museum," *The Burlington Magazine for Connoisseurs* 76, no. 445 (1940), p. 110. See also "Madonna del Cardellino" *Wikipedia*, last modified January 23, 2024, https://en.wikipedia.org/wiki/Madonna_del_Cardellino.

3
Raphael Rosenberg, *Turner – Hugo – Moreau: Entdeckung der Abstraktion* (Munich: Hirmer, 2007), pp. 33–42.

4
Giovanni Paolo Lomazzo, *Trattato dell'arte de la pittura* (Milan: Paolo Gottardo Pontio, 1584), p. 23, famously writes: "dovesse sempre fare la figura piramidale, serpentinata." Throughout the seventeenth century there are only a few other examples and most of them explicitly refer to Lomazzo. Mentioning the geometry of figures seems thus restrained to the reception of his treatise. It is only from the eighteenth century on that it became common to write about the design of figures with geometric terms: Raphael Rosenberg, "'Une ligne horizontale interrompue par une ligne

Geometry was an essential part of any school education, and since Leon Battista Alberti's *Della Pittura* (1435), painters used geometry to depict spatial distances between objects and figures. Geometric perspectival constructions were systematically used to design the lines of buildings, the size of figures and objects, and their foreshortening. Geometry was thus common knowledge, but not a single sentence was written about geometric forms as a basis for pictorial composition—not during Raphael's lifetime, not in Vasari's *Vite*, not in the 1550 edition, not in the 1568 one. If Raphael and his contemporaries used triangles and pyramids to compose a Madonna, they certainly did not write about it.

The modern concept of pictorial composition as a formal relationship between the elements within a picture emerged in the seventeenth century[5] and is often linked to statements about the movement of the viewer's eye.[6] In 1668, for example, André Félibien wrote: "Que la disposition des figures ..., doit être composée de parties, de groupes et de contrastes. Les parties partagent la vue, les groupes l'arrêtent et lient le sujet."[7] Since then, theories of pictorial composition have increasingly gained ground. In the twentieth century, the concept of composition played a central role in abstract art. "Composition" is still very important in art-historical education and discourse; however, central questions remain unanswered: 1) Is pictorial composition an objective

diagonale': De la géométrie dans la description d'œuvres d'art," in *La description de l'oeuvre d'art: Du modèle classique aux variations contemporaines*, Olivier Bonfait, ed. (Paris: Somogy, 2004), pp. 55–74.

5
Jeroen Stumpel, "On Grounds and Backgrounds: Some Remarks about Composition in Renaissance Painting," *Simiolus* 18 (1988): 219–243; Thomas Puttfarken, *The Discovery of Pictorial Composition: Theories of Visual Order in Painting 1400–1800* (New Haven: Yale University Press, 2000); Frank Fehrenbach, "Komposition," in *Metzler Lexikon Kunstwissenschaft*, Ulrich Pfisterer, ed. (Stuttgart: J. B. Metzler, 2003), pp. 178–183; Andreas Meyer and Steffan Egle, "Komposition," in *Enzyklopädie der Neuzeit* (Stuttgart: J. B. Metzler, 2015).

6
Raphael Rosenberg and Rudolf Groner, "Eye Tracking and Visual Arts: Introduction to the Special Thematic Issue," *Journal of Eye Movement Research* 13, no. 2 (2022): pp. 1–10.

7
André Félibien, ed., *Conférences de l'Académie Royale de Peinture et de Sculpture pendant l'année 1667* (Paris: Frederic Leonard, 1668), p. 79. I suppose that this idea and the wording are more by Félibien than Lebrun (cf. Raphael Rosenberg, "André Félibien et la Description de Tableaux: Naissance d'un Genre et Professionalisation d'un Discours," *Revue d'esthétique* 31/32, (1997): pp. 156–158).

property of images? 2) Does pictorial composition physically guide the viewer's eyes? 3) Is pictorial composition a property of surfaces and/or depicted spaces? And last but not least, is it possible to answer these fundamental questions? This paper will show that experimental methods can provide new insights into these questions. I will present the results of a study conducted in my Laboratory for Cognitive Research in Art History (CReA) at the Department of Art History at the University of Vienna.[8]

The *Last Supper* Study

Some recent papers examined the relationship between image composition and eye movements but considered pictorial composition as a given. They did not ask what exactly "composition" is and whether it objectively exists.[9] In contrast, we developed a novel experiment and studied how different viewers move their eyes while seeing images and asked them to sketch the composition of the images they viewed. To determine whether composition is an objective property of images (Question 1), we measured the similarity between the composition sketches of our participants. To determine whether their eyes followed the composition (Question 2), we measured the deviation between the eye movements and the composition sketches. Finally, comparing the composition sketches with the eye movement patterns helps to determine whether the eye movements and/or the participants'

8
Rosa Sancarlo, Zoya Dare, Jozsef Arato, and Raphael Rosenberg, "Does Pictorial Composition Guide the Eye? Investigating Four Centuries of Last Supper Pictures," *Journal of Eye Movement Research* 13, no. 2 (2020): pp. 1–13. Whereas this publication contains comprehensive details on the study, the present paper expands the art-historical discussion.

9
Raphael Rosenberg, "Dem Auge auf der Spur: Blickbewegungen beim Betrachten von Gemälden – historisch und empirisch," in *Jahrbuch der Heidelberger Akademie der Wissenschaften für 2010* (2011), pp. 78–91; Michael Garbutt and Branka Spehar, "The Wanton Chase: Using Eye Tracking to Test Theories of Pictorial Composition in Landscape Painting," in *Researching the Visual. Demystifying "The Picture That's Worth a Thousand Words,"* Arianne Rourke and Vaughan Rees, eds. (Champaign, IL: Common Ground, 2014), pp. 32–56; Raphael Rosenberg and Christoph Klein, The Moving Eye of the Beholder: Eye-Tracking and the Perception of Paintings," in *Art, Aesthetics and the Brain,* Joseph P. Huston et al., eds. (Oxford: Oxford University Press, 2015), pp. 79–108; Clare Kirtley, "How Images Draw the Eye: An Eye-Tracking Study of Composition," *Empirical Studies of the Arts* 36, no. 1 (2018): pp. 41–70; Tanya Beelders and Luna Bergh, "The Role that Composition Plays in Determining How a Viewer Looks at Landscape Art," *Journal of Eye Movement Research* 13, no. 2 (2020): pp. 1–23.

sketches were guided by shapes perceived on the picture plane and/or by the depicted pictorial space (Question 3).

To conduct our study, we used images that are comparable as well as sufficiently different and selected fourteen depictions of the Last Supper from the late twelfth to the early seventeenth centuries.[10] They all showed the same iconography and a similar number of figures, but different compositions. To reduce the variables that could influence the results, we decided to focus on participants with similar interests and knowledge of art. We recruited art history students at the University of Vienna by advertizing in courses and offering a financial incentive (of ten euros). We assumed that they were used to looking at artworks and were familiar with the iconography of the Last Supper and the modern concept of composition. We excluded male participants to eliminate possible gender effects. None of the participants were informed about the purpose of the study. We explained that it was about art perception and did not mention eye movements. We recruited forty participants but had to exclude eight data sets due to insufficient recording quality. The analysis is hence based on thirty-two participants.

The study was conducted in an office-like room at the Department of Art History at the University of Vienna. We used a state-of-the-art eye tracker (SR Research, EyeLink 1000 Plus) that recorded eye movements with digital IR cameras at a rate of 1,000 frames per second without physically interacting with the participant. The Last Supper images were displayed on a high-resolution monitor as high-resolution digital copies

10
Nicholas de Verdun, *The Last Supper*, 1181, enamel, Leopold Chapel of the Monastery of Klosterneuburg; Giotto, *The Last Supper*, 1306, fresco, Scrovegni Chapel, Padua; Pietro Lorenzetti, *The Last Supper*, 1320, fresco, S. Francesco, Lower Church, Assisi; Andrea del Castagno, *The Last Supper*, 1445–1450, fresco, S. Apollonia, Florence; Dieric Bouts, *The Last Supper* from the Altarpiece of the Holy Sacrament 1465, oil on panel, St. Pieterskerk, Louvain, Belgium; Domenico Ghirlandaio, *The Last Supper*, 1480, fresco, Ognissanti Monastery Refectory, Florence; Luca Signorelli, *The Last Supper*, 1512, oil on panel, Diocesan Museum, Cortona; Unknown Netherlandish Painter, *The Last Supper*, Central Panel of a triptych, 1515–1520, oil on wood, The Metropolitan Museum of Art, New York; Lucas Cranach the Elder, *The Last Supper* from the *Reformation Altarpiece*, 1547, St. Mary, Wittenberg; Juan de Juanes, *The Last Supper*, 1555–1562, oil on panel, Prado Museum, Madrid; Jacopo Tintoretto, *The Last Supper*, 1578, oil on canvas, Scuola Grande di San Rocco, Venice; Paolo Veronese, *The Last Supper*, 1585, oil on canvas, Pinacoteca di Brera, Milan; Jacopo Tintoretto, *The Last Supper*, 1592, oil on canvas, Basilica of San Giorgio Maggiore, Venice; Federico Barocci, *The Last Supper*, 1608, oil on canvas, Cathedral of Urbino.

[fig. 477].[11] Participants first viewed the fourteen images in a randomized order while their eye movements were recorded. Each image was displayed for sixty seconds. They were then asked to sketch the composition of each image using a maximum of five lines drawn with a finger on a tablet on the images.[12]

Drawing Composition: Figure, Ground, or Perspective

As a first example to discuss the composition drawings made during the study, we can take Nicholas of Verdun's Last Supper from the 1181 altar at Klosterneuburg [fig. 478a]. I initially chose it because I was struck by the composition, which forms a cross, an unusual way of referring to Christ's Passion in Last Supper scenes. Many participants did indeed draw a cross—with the vertical bar as the central line, running from Judah's leg through his, John's, and Christ's faces, and an upper horizontal line running through the faces of the other apostles [figs. 478b and 478c]. Some participants added more horizontal lines, such as along the table. Other participants drew one or more diagonal lines, such as the one from the fish Judah is hiding behind his back to Christ's right hand that gives him the food [figs. 478c and 478d]. While expecting the cross, I did not notice the diagonals until I saw them in the drawings.

The variety of the drawings makes it clear that composition is not a purely objective property [figs. 478b–f]. On the other hand, there are strong similarities between the participants' lines. When we superimpose them, we see that many drew similar lines [fig. 479b]. Participants emphasized the course of limbs and gestures, prominent elements such as the table, and connections between elements, especially between heads. The same is true for

11
"BENQ LCD 30," 3,840 × 2,160 pixels, using a maximum width of 2,880 pixels to minimize the distance between the participants and the monitor to 70 centimeters.

12
The instruction was: "Art Historians tend to define composition as the most important lines for the structure of the painting. Please draw the lines that, in your opinion, are the most important for the composition of the following paintings." There was a third task, aiming to judge the degree of three-dimensional space. Participants were given prints of the fourteen pictures and asked to put them in order according to the depth perceived in the images. The instruction was: "You will now be given the reproductions of all the paintings you have seen. Please order them on the table according to the amount of depth represented: from the most flat to the one with the most depth." For a discussion of the results of this task, please refer to Sancarlo et al., "Does Pictorial Composition," p. 9.

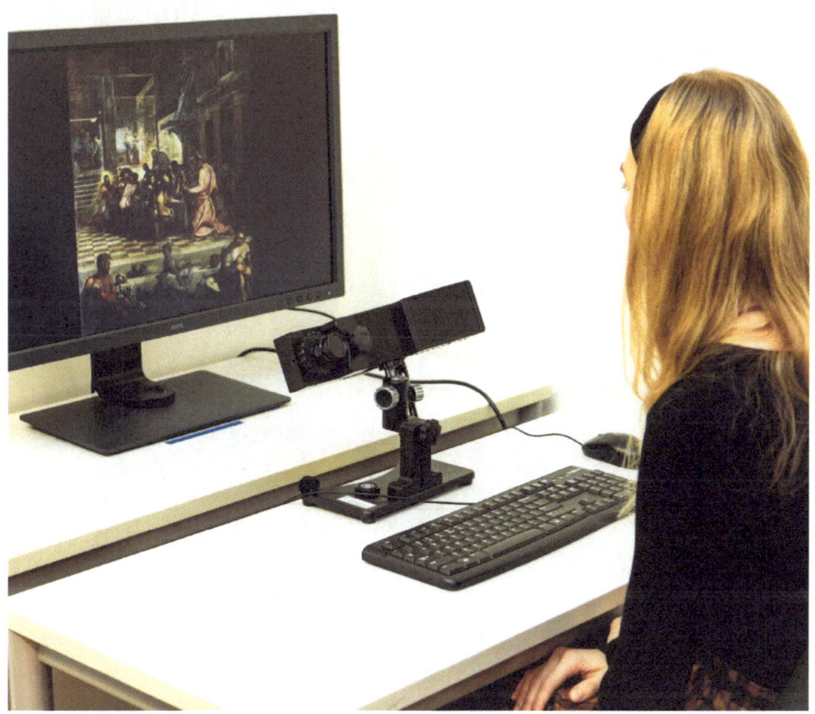

Setup of the eye-tracking experiment.

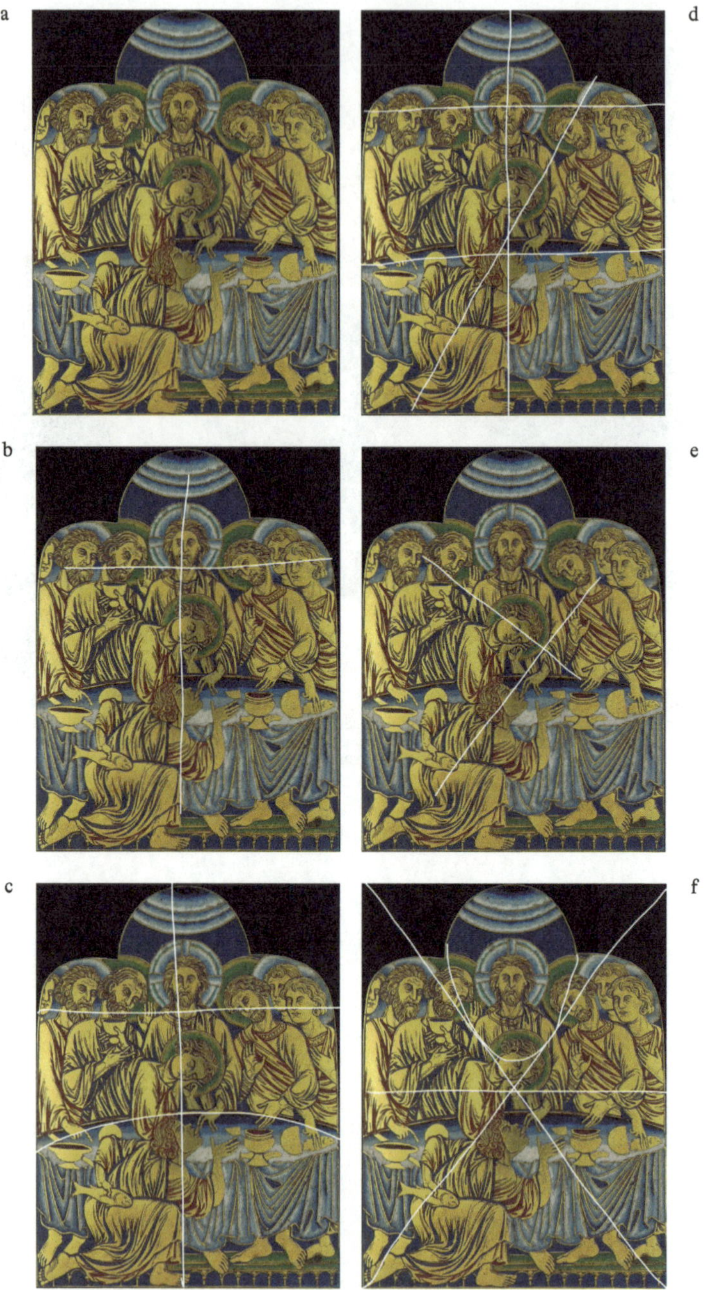

Nicholas of Verdun, *The Last Supper* (detail from the Verdun Altar), ca. 1181, champleve enamelwork on wood panel, 20.5 × 16.5 cm. Stift Klosterneuburg.

Fig. 478

a

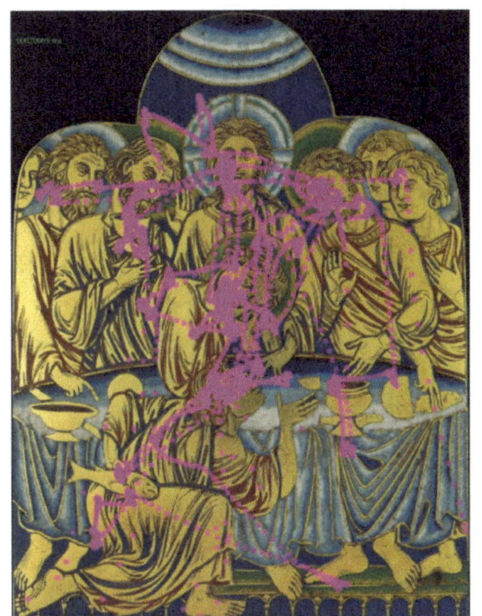

Eye movements recording (gaze points at 1,000 Hz) of one participant during the first twenty seconds of viewing *The Last Supper* by Nicholas of Verdun.

b

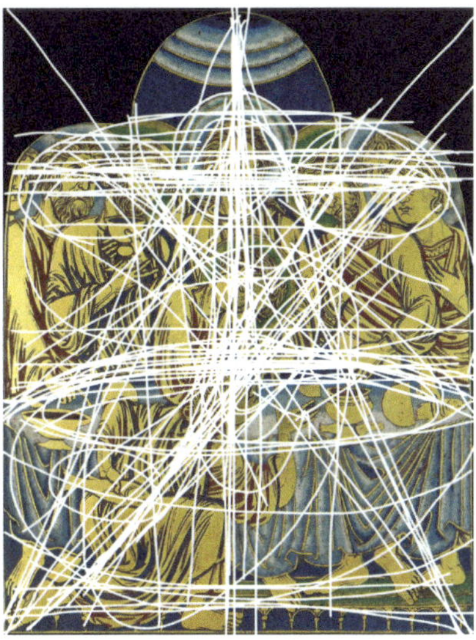

Cumulative compositional drawings of thirty-two participants

c

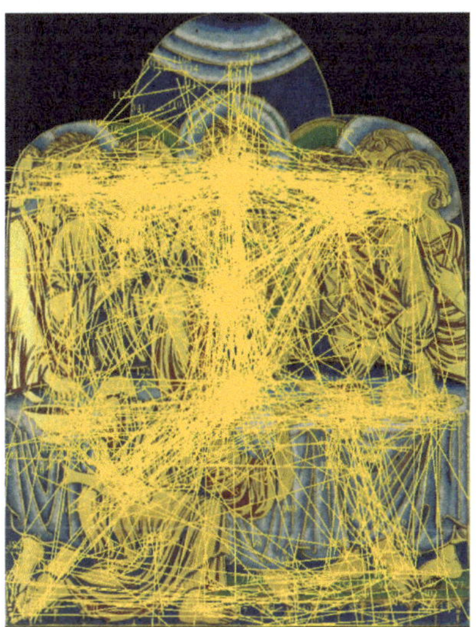

Saccades of thirty-two participants (sixty seconds each)

Fig. 479

most other images used in the study.[13] For example, most participants drew horizontal lines across Castagno's *Last Supper* [fig. 481a]—through the heads of the apostles, along the table and the depicted architecture, parallel to the border of the image [fig. 481b]. This mid-fifteenth-century fresco in the refectory of the former Benedictine convent of Sant'Apollonia in Florence, is one of many depictions of the Last Supper with Christ seated at the center behind a broad table surrounded by apostles lined up parallel to the picture plane—a simple structure, emphasized by most participants' drawings. The highly dynamic composition of Paolo Veronese's *Last Supper* [fig. 482a], painted more than a century later, contrasts with Castagno's simple uniformity. The compositional lines drawn on top of the image are correspondingly more complex [fig. 482b]. They follow the figures' various and often diagonal postures and architectural elements like columns.

The lines described so far point to what is depicted in the pictorial space of the images. They abstract the objects in the picture and their linear relations. Referring to the title of this book, we can say that they are concerned with the *composition of figures*, using the term "figure" in its broad sense to refer to anything depicted in the picture: people, animals, inanimate objects, and architecture. Other lines, however, testify to a different understanding of composition, one that refers not to the representation, but to the picture plane—not to the figures or the background but to the *planimetry of the pictorial ground*. For example, in the Verdun Altar case, a participant drew the two large diagonals and a central horizontal line, even though these do not seem to relate to any figure the artist depicted [fig. 478f]. Most of the composition lines drawn on Federico Barocci's *Last Supper* [fig. 483a] refer to the pictorial ground: two main diagonals and several horizontal and vertical axes [fig. 483b]. Accordingly, on Dieric Bouts' *Last Supper* [fig. 484a], many drawn lines also refer to the pictorial ground and not, or at best only secondarily, to the figures and architecture represented: participants emphasized the central vertical line, the central horizontal line, several other

13
Some participants sketched curved lines and circled salient areas (as Christ's head), counteracting our expectations. For an overview of the drawn composition sketches, see the supplementary materials in Sancarlo et al., "Does Pictorial Composition."

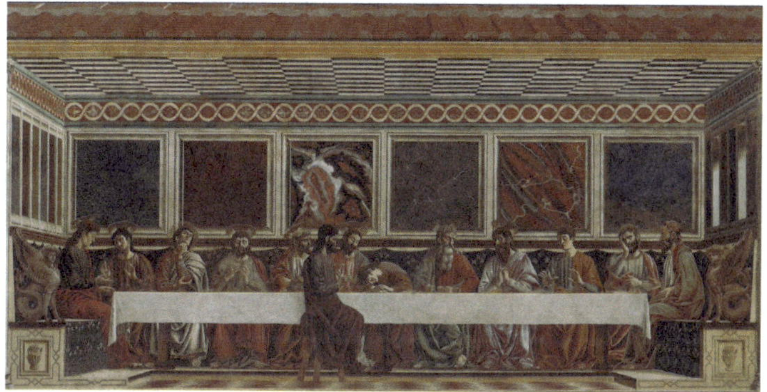

a

Andrea del Castagno, *The Last Supper*, 1447, fresco, 470 × 975 cm.
Sant'Apollonia, Florence.

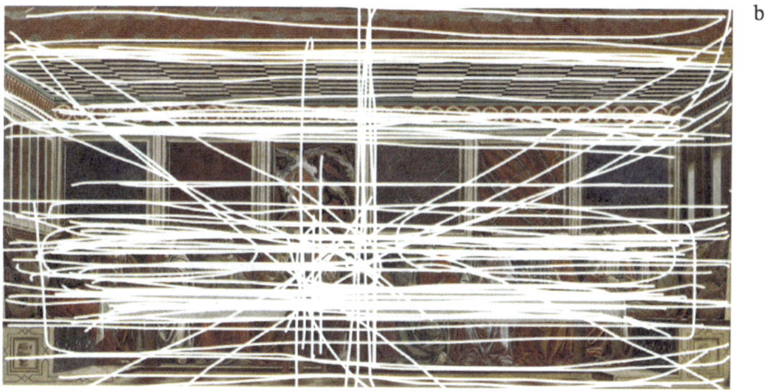

b

Cumulative compositional drawings of thirty-two participants

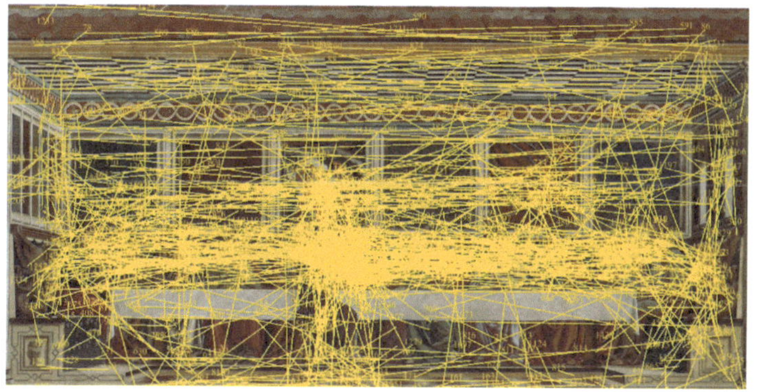

c

Saccades of thirty-two participants (sixty seconds each)

Fig. 481

a

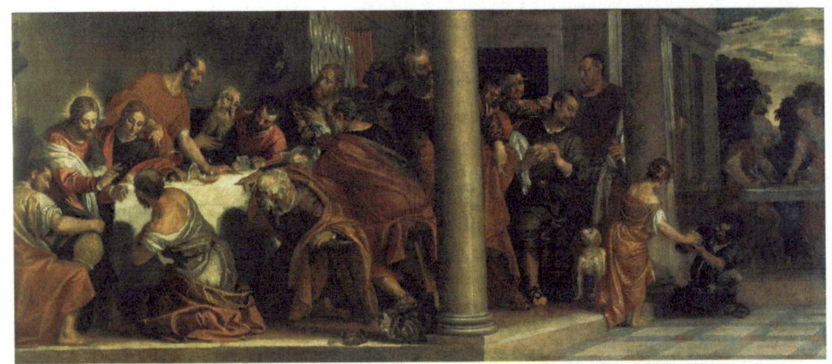

Paolo Veronese, *The Last Supper*, 1585, oil on canvas, 220 × 523 cm.
Pinacoteca di Brera, Milan.

b

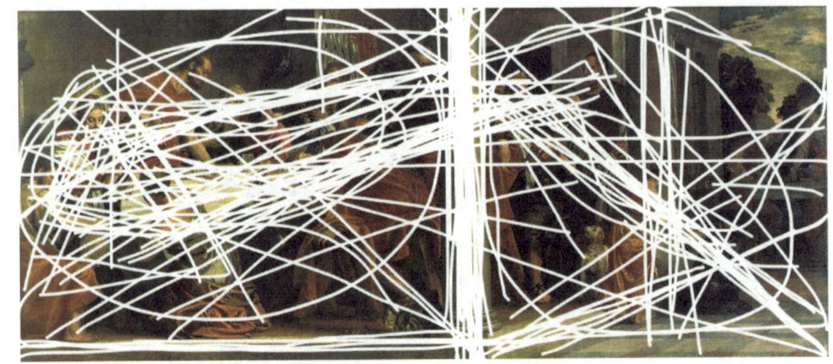

Cumulative compositional drawings of thirty-two participants

c

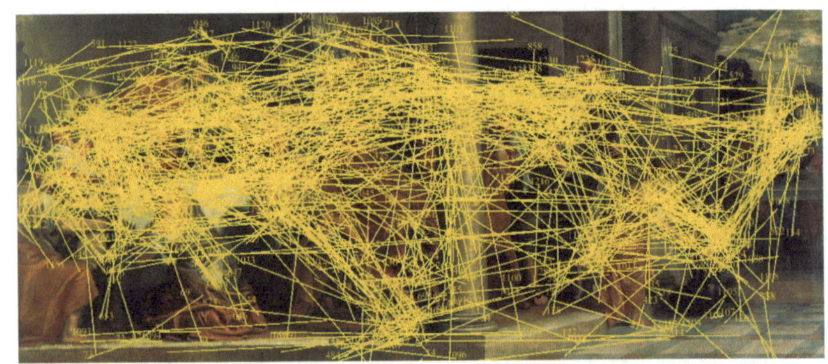

Saccades of thirty-two participants (sixty seconds each)

Fig. 482

a

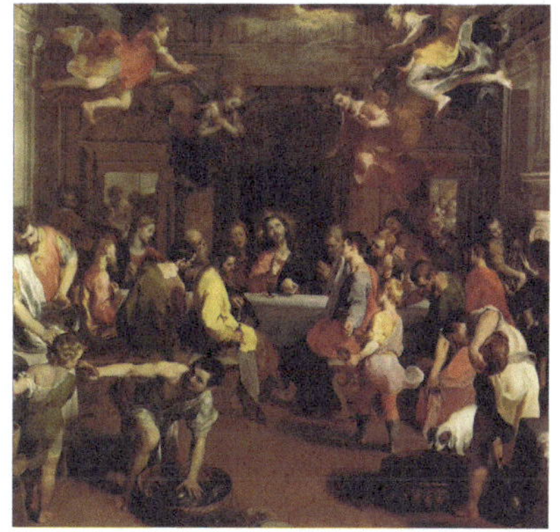

Federico Barocci, *The Last Supper*, 1612, oil on canvas, 299 × 322 cm. Urbino Cathedral, Urbino.

b

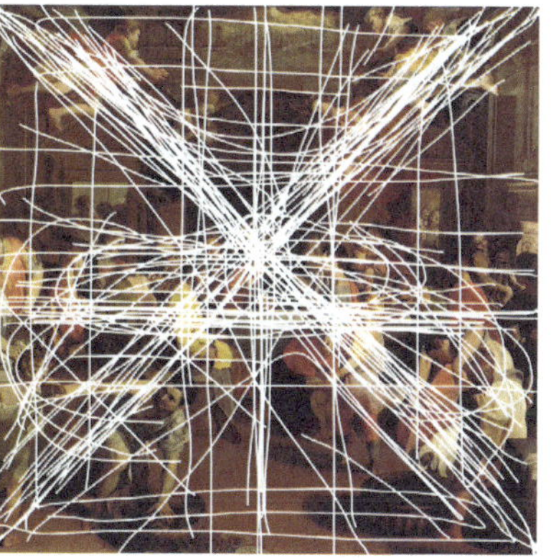

Cumulative compositional drawings of thirty-two participants

c

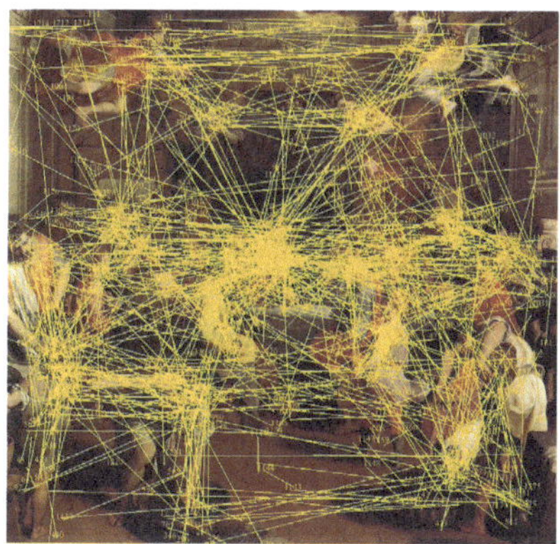

Saccades of thirty-two participants (sixty seconds each)

Fig. 483

a

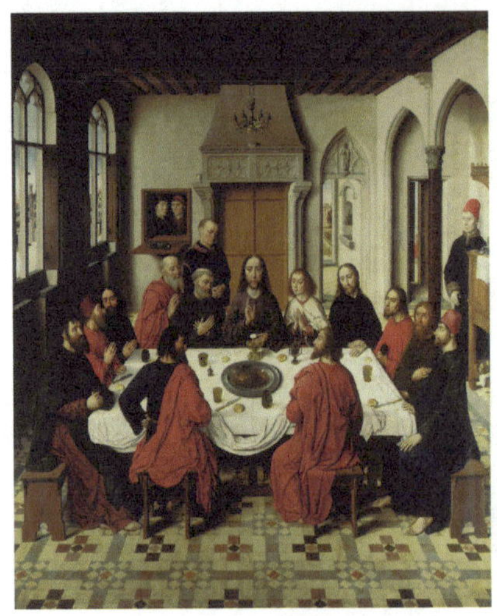

Dieric Bouts, *The Last Supper* from the Altarpiece of the Holy Sacrament, 1465, oil on panel, 180 × 151 cm. St. Peter's Church, Leuven.

b

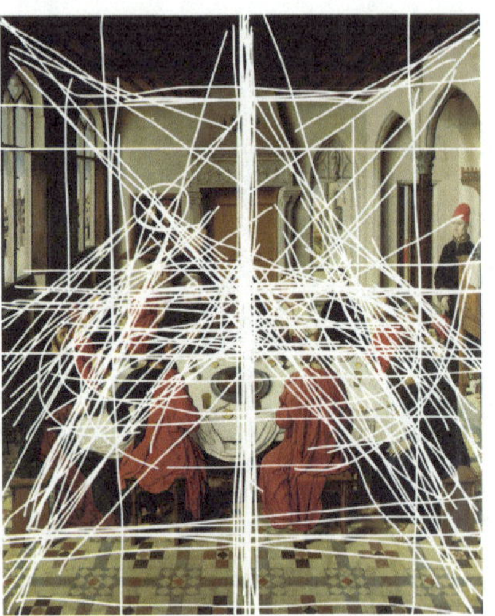

Cumulative compositional drawings of thirty-two participants

c

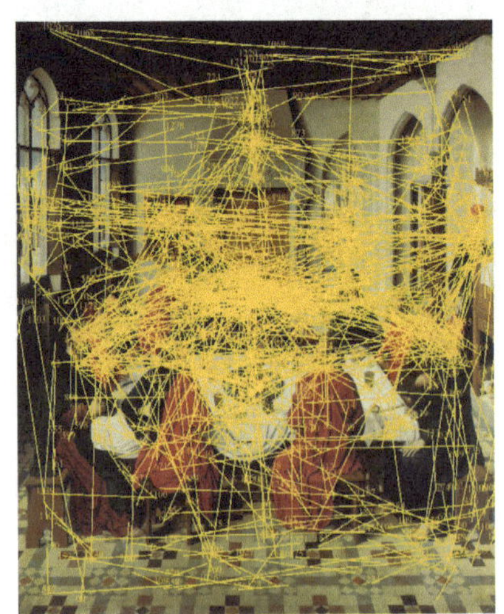

Saccades of thirty-two participants (sixty seconds each)

Fig. 484

horizontal and vertical lines, the main diagonals, and lines running from the bottom edges to the top center [fig. 484b].

However, participants also used a third type of line: diagonals that converge toward assumed vanishing points, tracing single-point perspectival constructions. These occur most frequently in the drawings made over Tintoretto's *Last Supper*, painted in 1592 for San Giorgio Maggiore [fig. 486a]. The Venetian painter demonstratively departed from the traditional table placed parallel to the picture plane, as in Castagno. Accordingly, most subjects drew diagonal lines toward the vanishing point at the far right [fig. 486b]. We also find perspectival diagonals in the drawings made over the works discussed earlier. For example, the lines tracing the architecture in Bouts's *Last Supper* [fig. 484b], one of the first Flemish paintings in which the architecture (but not the objects and figures) was drawn using linear perspective.[14]

Quantifying Agreement: The Similarity Coefficient

Comparing the superimpositions of the composition drawings, it becomes clear that the participants largely agreed with each other, albeit with individual variations. To quantify similarities and differences, we developed a *similarity coefficient*, a mathematical measure of the degree of agreement between subjects. First, we mapped a grid onto each composition drawing, dividing it into rectangular cells. An algorithm then counted the number of lines crossing each cell and determined how many lines were parallel within each cell, calculating a coefficient between 0 and 1. If all thirty-two composition drawings were identical, each cell would have either no lines or sets of thirty-two parallel lines; the similarity coefficient would be 1. If the drawings were completely different, no lines would be parallel in any cell, the similarity coefficient would be 0. We defined a tolerance of up to five degrees of deviation as parallel.[15]

The similarity coefficient is not absolute because it depends on variable parameters—the grid size and the maximum degree of

14
Peter Carpreau, "Bouts and Perspective," in Peter Carpreau, ed., *Dieric Bouts: Creator of Images* (Munich: Prestel, 2024), pp. 157–160.

15
We made and considered tests with fifteen different grid sizes (Sancarlo et al., "Does Pictorial Composition," pp. 7–8). The three graphs reprinted here are based on 9 × 9 grids.

a

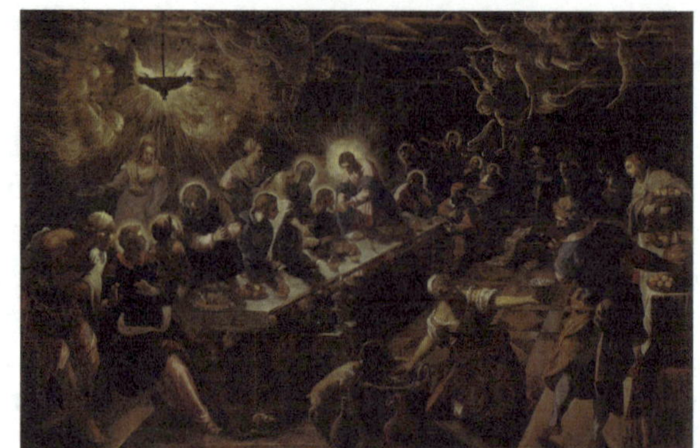

Jacopo Tintoretto, *The Last Supper*, 1592, oil on canvas, 365 × 568 cm.
Basilica di San Giorgio Maggiore, Venice.

b

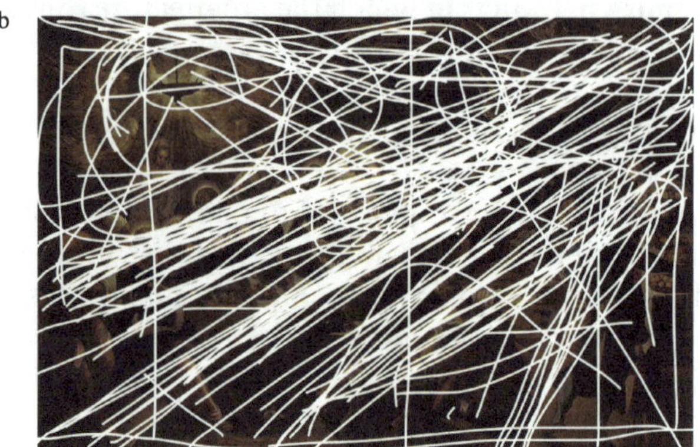

Cumulative compositional drawings of thirty-two participants

c

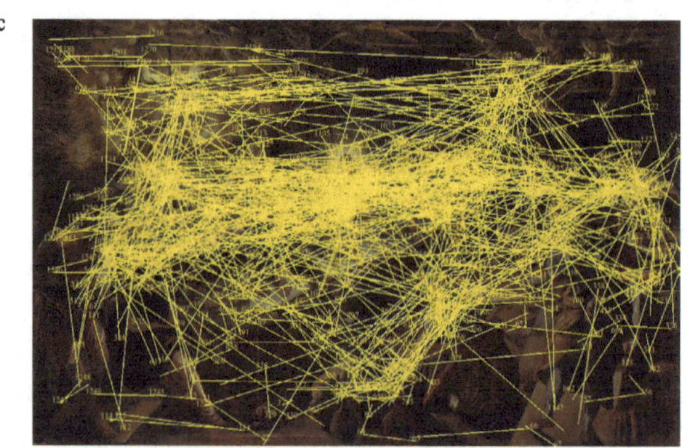

Saccades of thrity-two participants (sixty seconds each)

Fig. 486

deviation. However, it is possible to compare cumulative drawings using the same parameters. We performed the analysis and visualized the results in a graph [fig. 488]. The green dots mark the coefficients for each painting, while the red bars form a baseline that can be seen as chance: the similarity of the composition drawings made on this image compared to those made on the other paintings in the experiment. The graph shows that the green dots are consistently above the red bars. This means that the composition lines drawn on the same painting were consistently more similar than those on any other painting. This may sound trivial, but it is scientific proof that although people perceive images differently, they agree in principle about compositional structures. This is a statistically robust finding.[16]

We can, therefore, conclude that composition is not an absolute, objective quality of paintings but a category that can be defined with a high degree of intersubjective agreement. Notably, the degree of agreement is sometimes higher and sometimes lower [fig. 488]: higher for Castagno [fig. 481b] and the 1592 Tintoretto I will discuss below [fig. 486b], lower for Nicholas [fig. 479b], and lower again for, among others, Veronese [fig. 482b] and Bouts [fig. 484b]. Such differences suggest that "composition" is not equally important for all paintings. To fully understand this claim, we would need more and more diverse examples. For the images included in this study, I see two factors that led to a lower level of similarity: visual complexity and the significance of composition.

To begin with complexity, it is interesting to compare Castagno's *Last Supper* with the visually more complex depiction by Veronese, who painted not only Christ and the twelve apostles, but also servants, a beggar, a dog, and a secondary scene in the background on the right.[17] All the figures in Castagno's fresco have a similar posture. Except for John, the Lord's favorite disciple, they are seated upright and appear calm, their hands and heads only slightly turned. In contrast, Veronese painted quite

16
Sancarlo et al., "Does Pictorial Composition," pp. 7–8.

17
For a further discussion of the dimensions of complexity in early modern painting, see Laura Commare, Raphael Rosenberg, and Helmut Leder, "More Than the Sum of Its Parts: Perceiving Complexity in Painting," *Psychology of Aesthetics, Creativity, and the Arts* 12, no. 4 (2018): pp. 380–391.

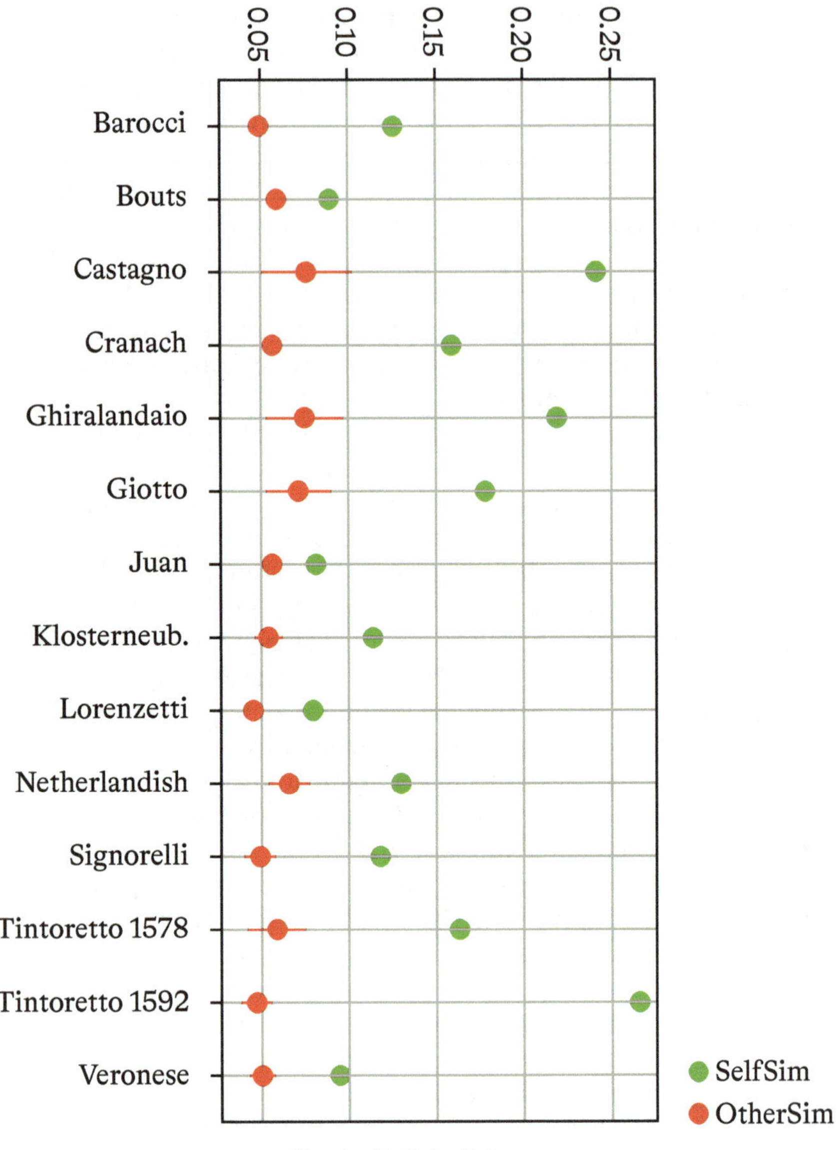

Drawing Similarity Ration:
Variability of the composition drawings.

Fig. 488

different attitudes. As they were given a maximum of five lines, drawing the composition of his *Last Supper* must have been challenging. It is not surprising that each participant made rather diverse choices, especially compared to the lines drawn on the image by Castagno.

The second reason for greater deviation is historical: pictorial composition as a concept was developed with reference to Italian Renaissance art. While it seems easy to discuss composition in relation to paintings from that place and period, we have seen that this already becomes harder for Early Netherlandish paintings. Bouts brilliantly depicted an abundance of realistic details—several objects on the table, two portraits in the background at the left, and intricately illustrated landscapes through the narrow windows [fig. 484a]. Overarching "compositional" lines play a lesser role; accordingly, our subjects drew them less [fig. 484b]. Instead, they focused on the pictorial ground and perspectival lines. This led to greater diversity, thus to a lower similarity coefficient.

Tracking Saccades: Do Eyes Follow Composition?

Eyes are constantly moving. We know that, but we do not realize how fast and erratic these movements are. The saccadic nature of eye movements was discovered in the late nineteenth century: eyes do not move smoothly and continuously, but rapidly and jerkily.[18] We typically make three fixations and quick jumps (saccades) per second. We look in zigzags, and at first glance, the gaze paths appear random [fig. 479a]. Every single path is diverse. However, when we superimpose the saccades of thirty-two subjects, patterns emerge: the saccades repeat similar paths over and over again [fig. 479c].[19]

The algorithm that calculates the similarity coefficient between the participants' drawings in our experiment can also

18
Nicholas J. Wade and Benjamin W. Tatler, *The Moving Tablet of the Eye: The Origins of Modern Eye Movement Research* (Oxford: Oxford University Press, 2005).

19
Visualizing all saccades of all participants produces overcrowded images. We, therefore, automatically skipped every second and third saccade. For alternative ways of visualizing often repeated saccades, see Thomas Kübler et al., "Novel Methods for Analysis and Visualization of Saccade Trajectories," in *Computer Vision – ECCV 2016 Workshops*, Proceedings, Part I, Gang Hua and Hervé Jégou, eds. (Cham: Springer, 2016), pp. 783–797.

measure if saccades resemble each other and whether and to what extent the saccades of different viewers looking at the same image repeat patterns. Using the same grid as before, we calculated the similarity coefficients of all viewers' saccades for each image [fig. 491]. The baseline (red bars) marks the coefficient comparing these saccades with those made by the same viewers while looking at other images. The results are similar to the composition drawings: saccades vary between participants, but similarities are strong. The similarity coefficient (green dots) is always higher than the baseline, and again, the similarity is statistically significant.[20]

This brings us to the crucial question: Do eye movements follow composition lines? Do saccade paths correlate with composition lines? Comparing the superposition of the composition lines [fig. 479b] and the cumulated saccades [fig. 479c], similarities are obvious. We can quantify these similarities using the similarity coefficient: the algorithm counts how many drawn lines and saccades crossing the cells of a grid are parallel. The results are visualized as green dots in fig. 492. The baseline (red bars) is calculated by comparing the saccades recorded while looking at one image to the lines drawn on the other ones. The calculation confirms the similarity for eleven of fourteen pictures, which is a statistically significant result.[21] However, in the case of a *Last Supper* by Juan de Juanes [figs. 493a–c], the comparison is inconclusive; for Barocci [figs. 483a–c] and Bouts [figs. 484a–c], the coefficient is even below chance. This allows us to conclude that eye movements often follow composition lines. But how can we explain that this is not always the case? Why do saccades and compositional drawings not match in some cases?

We must return to the distinction between the three types of composition lines drawn in our experiment. The first one, the arrangement of figures, is matched by eye movements. See, for instance, Castagno's *Last Supper* [figs. 481a–c] where most saccades are as much horizontal as the drawn lines indicate. This similarity can also be observed if we compare the drawn lines and saccades on Nicholas de Verdun [figs. 479a–c] and Veronese

20 Sancarlo et al., "Does Pictorial Composition," pp. 7–8.

21 Ibid. It is noteworthy that we found an even higher similarity on the individual level of every participant.

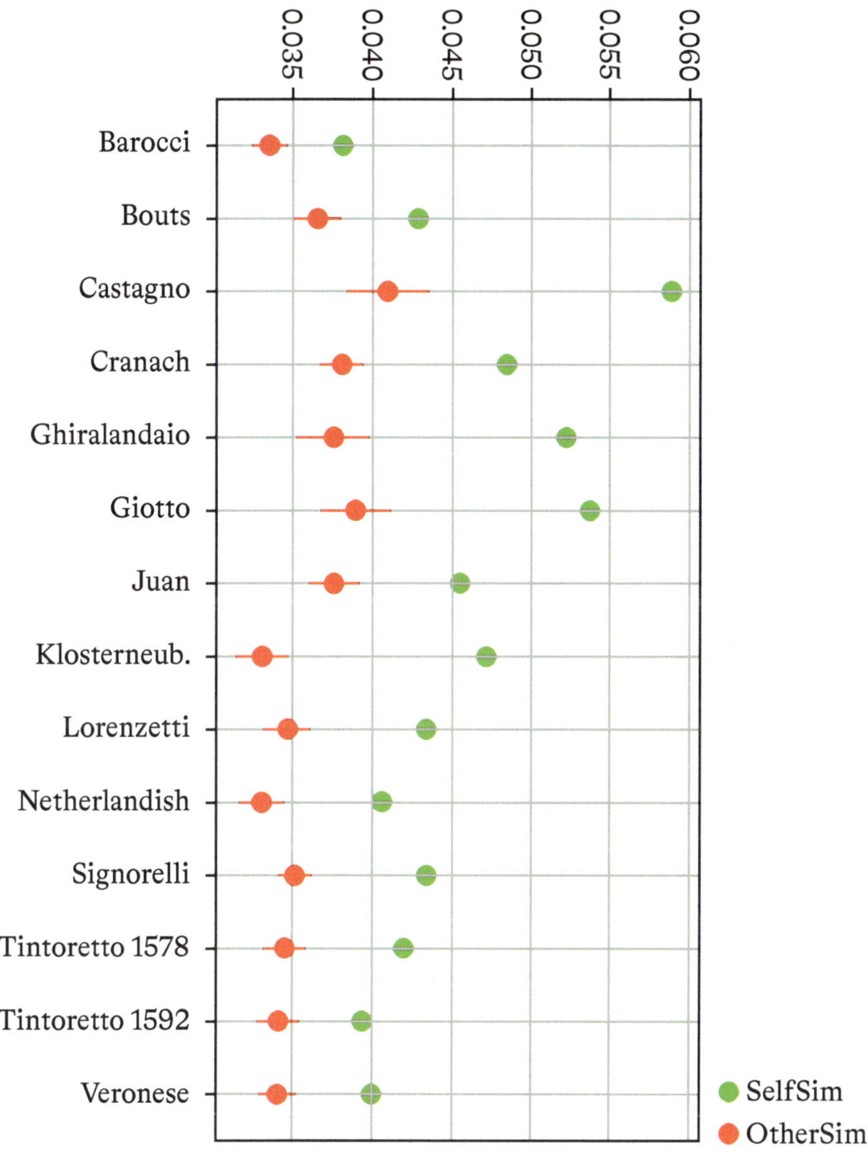

Saccade Similarity Ratio:
Variability of saccade patterns.

Fig. 491

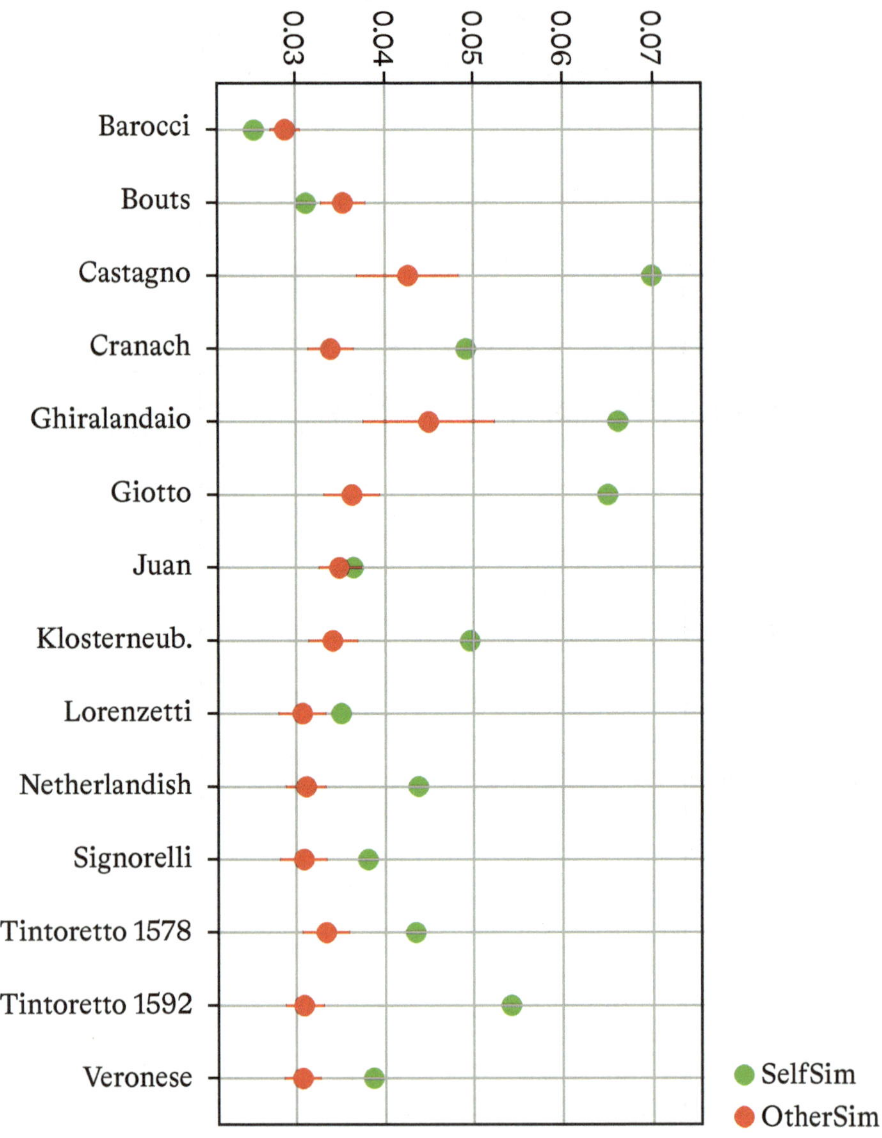

Saccade Drawing Similarity Ratio:
Similarity of saccades to drawn compositional lines for each painting.

Fig. 492

a

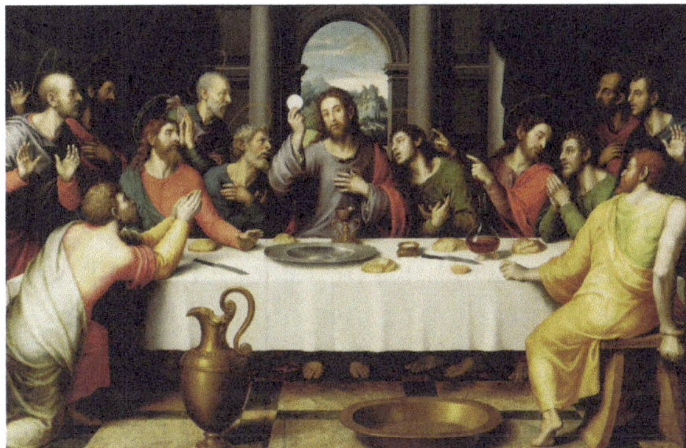

Juan de Juanes, *The Last Supper*, 1562, oil on panel, 116 × 191 cm.
Museo del Prado, Madrid.

b

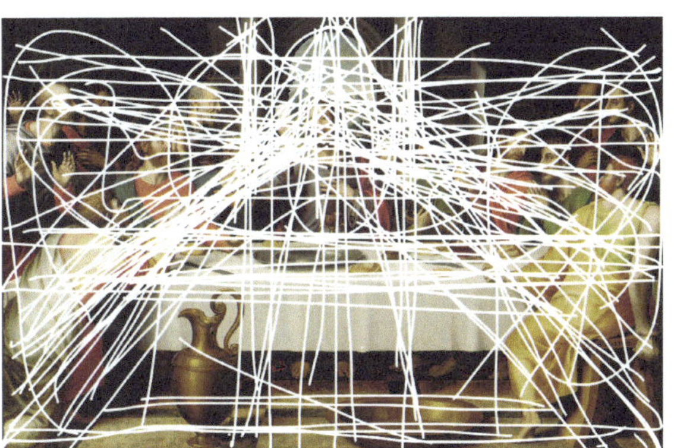

Cumulative compositional drawings of thirty-two participants

c

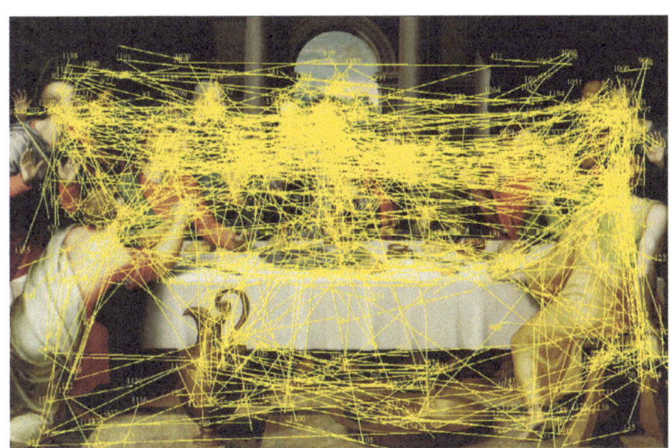

Saccades of thirty-two participants (sixty seconds each)

Fig. 493

[figs. 482a–c]. By contrast, we do not find saccades running along the two other types of "composition": lines structuring the pictorial ground or perspectival construction lines. While looking at Barocci's *Last Supper* [figs. 483a–c] no saccades followed the main diagonals that many participants underlined in their drawings. Moreover, when looking at Nicholas's image, the saccades did not follow the central vertical lines in the lower and upper part of the image, the main diagonals, or those running from the lower edges to the upper center [figs. 479a–c]. The same applies to Bouts: saccades did not follow drawn perspectival lines [figs. 484a–c]. Even when foreshortening was seen as decisive for the composition, as in Tintoretto's *Last Supper* in San Giorgio Maggiore, it did not trigger gaze movements [figs. 486a–c]. Whereas most drawn lines are diagonal, most saccades in the center of the picture are horizontal.[22] Astonishingly, the foreshortening diagonal along the platform on the bottom right in Veronese's painting was often drawn but does not appear in the recorded saccades [figs. 482a–c].[23]

Leonardo and many others depicted the apostles' surprise when Christ prophesied that one of them would betray him. Juan de Juanes did it in an impressive manner: the disciples' bodies, heads, and arms are captured in strong movements and seized in different directions [fig. 493a]. Juan depicts noisy confusion by avoiding overarching lines. Accordingly, it was challenging for our subjects to draw composition lines [fig. 493b]. Different horizontals, diagonals, and verticals appear with little consistency, which explains the low similarity coefficient [fig. 488]. The saccades, in contrast, are more uniform, sweeping from one figure's head to the next; some gazes moved downwards to Judah's right hand, to the jug and the bowl at the bottom of the picture [fig. 493c].

22
Accordingly, the similarity coefficient for this image falls above average if the tolerance is set to two instead of five degrees (however, the similarity between saccades and composition lines remains significantly above chance). Regardless of the task, saccades run preferentially horizontally and more often vertically than diagonally. Future studies could investigate the extent to which this natural preference affects the perception of images.

23
These results confirm the findings of Arthur Crucq, "Viewing Patterns and Perspectival Paintings: An Eye-Tracking Study on the Effect of the Vanishing Point," *Journal of Eye Movement Research* 13, no. 2 (2021): pp. 1–21.

Conclusion

Can the *Last Supper* experiment answer our initial questions? First, it shows that composition is not an objective property of images. Our participants drew "composition" quite differently—future studies could examine whether the differences diminish among experts. However, what we perceive as an image's composition is not entirely subjective either. On the one hand, differences can be attributed to different understandings of what composition relates to: the figures, i.e., the elements (re)presented in the picture, the planimetry of the picture plane, or the perspectival construction. On the other hand, we must remember that the concept of composition was developed in a specific art-historical and scholarly context. Transferring it to pictures made in other places and times defeats the purpose and can be compared to exploring an area with a map of a different country.

Second, we found statistically significant similarities between drawn composition lines and frequently repeated saccades. Composition thus guides the gaze. However, this is only true in relation to "figures," i.e., elements represented in the pictures, and not for the planimetry of the picture, the pictorial ground, or the perspectival construction. We should therefore distinguish between a *natural level* of composition—the organization of the objects (re)presented in the picture—and at least two *theoretical levels*—the geometry of the picture's ground and the perspectival construction. Both may be important in producing art but do not directly affect the viewer's eye. Future studies could investigate whether and how the correlation between composition and eye movement patterns holds for images without figures and faces, like landscapes, still lives, or abstract art.[24]

The third question was whether composition is a property of the surface, or the three-dimensional space depicted. Since the experiment was not designed to answer this question, we did not choose images that would clearly show differences—Raphael's

24
This is the topic of an ongoing master's thesis by Sophia Kury. Moreover, one could look at differences stemming from sizes and framings or from the difference between original works of art and reproductions.

Madonna or isolated geometric shapes like triangles versus pyramids. However, it became clear that although participants often drew diagonal perspectival lines referring to the depth of the spaces represented, their eyes had not followed these lines. While viewing the images, our participants were not exploring the three-dimensional spaces depicted through one-point perspectival methods. The question arises if this could be historically determined. Would it be possible that modern eye movements differ from those of premodern artists and viewers, who might have been more triggered by the then new cultural technique of linear perspective?[25] Future projects will hopefully investigate in more detail what factors affect eye movements and, more generally, perception. They would help to further clarify the relationship between figure, ground, perspective, and eye movement and enhance discourses on the role of geometry in art.

25
Sigrid Weigel, "Die Richtung des Bildes: Zum Links-Rechts von Bilderzählungen und Bildbeschreibungen in kultur- und mediengeschichtlicher Perspektive," *Zeitschrift für Kunstgeschichte* 64 (2001): pp. 449–474, made insightful suggestions for a historical shift from a rather space oriented gaze in premodern to more surface oriented perception of images in modern times. For the history of the idea of a history of seeing in art history, see Raphael Rosenberg, "Vom technischen Fortschritt zur Geschichte des Sehens: Entwicklung als Paradigma der Kunsthistoriografie," in *Umgang mit der Temporalität in den Sozial- und Geisteswissenschaften*, Thomas Maissen et al., eds. (Bochum: Winkler, 2019), pp. 175–196. For an experiment testing the influence of cultural influences on the perception of art see also Hanna Brinkmann et al., "Cultural Diversity in Oculometric Parameters When Viewing Art and Non-art," *Psychology of Aesthetics, Creativity, and the Arts* 17, no. 4 (2023): pp. 398–411.

Part 5
Transgressing Depth

According to a long tradition, the art of painting arose at the meeting of light, figure, and ground. Writing in the first century CE, Pliny the Elder explained:

> De pictura initiis incerta ... aegyptii sex milibus annorum aput ipsos inventam, priusquam in graeciam transiret, adfirmant, vana praedicatione, ut palam est; graeci autem alii sicyone, alii aput corinthios repertam, omnes umbra hominis lineis circumdata.[1]

The "human shadow" that figures in the competing origin stories rehearsed by Pliny is a *cast* shadow. It was this kind of shadow, produced by a light source falling upon a figure and projected from that figure over and upon an adjacent surface or ground, that ancient painting took as its point of departure, that painters in the Middle Ages forgot or could not manage, and that the Renaissance rediscovered. Or so we are told.

The cast shadow has continued to play an important role in histories of painting since Pliny. Masaccio's famous painting of the miraculous healings worked by St. Peter's shadow (Acts 5:15), is a case in point [fig. 499].[2] Painted on one wall of the Brancacci

I am deeply grateful to Saskia C. Quené for including me in this volume, and for her generous editorial patience and encouragement during the preparation of this chapter. My thanks also go to Matteo Burioni and Saskia Quené for inviting me to contribute to the "Between Figure and Ground" conference at the eikones – Zentrum für die Theorie und Geschichte des Bildes in 2022, and to the colleagues whose papers and comments at the conference were truly inspiring. My research assistants, Vanessa Gonzalvez and Julia Karrer, tirelessly tracked down bibliography as well as images and image rights needed for this chapter and I thank them for their excellent work. So, too, am I grateful to the anonymous colleague who undertook the peer review for this text and whose critical comments I found valuable. Finally, conversations with Gregory Bryda, Ingrid Greenfield, Masha Goldin, Christopher Lakey, and last, but not least, Martin Schwarz shaped and sharpened my thinking as I worked on this essay: I thank each of them.

1
Pliny the Elder, *Naturalis Historia*, Bk. 35, ch. 5, Karl Friedrich Theodor Mayhoff, ed. (Leipzig: Teubner, 1906), as republished online by the Perseus Digital Library, Gregory R. Crane, ed., http://data.perseus.org/citations/urn:cts:latinLit:phi0978.phi001.perseus-lat1:35.5. Translation: "We have no certain knowledge as to the commencement of the art of painting, nor does this enquiry fall under our consideration. The Egyptians assert that it was invented among themselves, six thousand years before it passed into Greece; a vain boast, it is very evident. As to the Greeks, some say that it was invented at Sicyon, others at Corinth; but they all agree that it originated in tracing lines round the human shadow." Pliny the Elder, *The Natural History*, trans. John Bostock (London: Taylor and Francis, 1855), as republished online by the Perseus Digital Library, Gregory R. Crane, ed., http://data.perseus.org/citations/urn:cts:latinLit:phi0978.phi001.perseus-eng1:35.5.

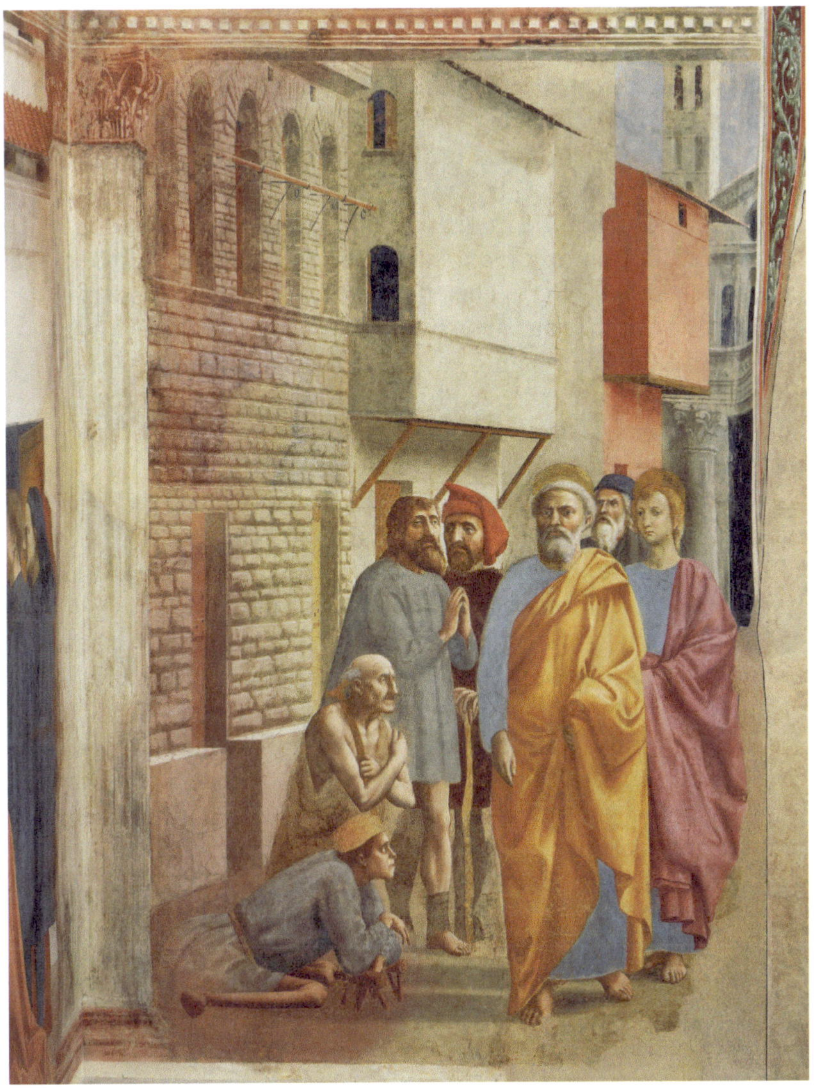

Masaccio, St. Peter's shadow healing the sick, ca. 1425, fresco.
Brancacci Chapel in Santa Maria del Carmine, Florence.

Fig. 499

Chapel within Santa Maria del Carmine in Florence in ca. 1425, Masaccio's work has acted as a landmark in the history of the shadow in art, clearly demarcating the Renaissance from the medieval period.

Picturing the thaumaturgical miracle in resolutely sober terms, Masaccio depicts Peter's cast shadow, together with the shadow of John behind him, as a consequence of a strong light source that falls upon the apostles from the right side of the scene (as the beholder sees it).[3] The effect of Peter's cast shadow can be discerned in the four male figures to the left of the Apostles, who form a tableau ranging from prone disability in the foreground to upright health. A white-bearded onlooker, glimpsed between Peter and John's heads, acts as a stunned witness to the thaumaturgic power of Peter's shadow.

A charismatic exploration of sunlight and shade, as well as the simulation of pictorial depth, Masaccio's wall painting both conceals and conveys the miraculous in the guise of the mundane. Its naturalistic choreography of the play of light and shadow upon figures and ground has been celebrated in many art-historical accounts as an epistemic and artistic turning point: the end of the Middle Ages and the start of the Renaissance.

By contrast, Giovanni di Paolo's equally wonderful and equally weird exploration of a cast shadow, painted within a year, possibly in the same year as Masaccio's St. Peter, has not been granted the same periodizing force by art historians [fig. 501].[4]

2
For further analysis, with additional bibliography, see Luba Freedman, "Masaccio's *St. Peter Healing with his Shadow*: a Study in Iconography," *Notizie Da Palazzo Albani* 19 (1990), pp. 13–30; Victor Stoichiţă, *A Short History of the Shadow* (London: Reaktion Books, 1999), pp. 54–60; Gerd Mathias Micheluzzi, "'Apostolorum Gloriosissimus Princeps': Saint Peter Healing the Sick with His Shadow in the Late Medieval Painting between the Acts and the Golden Legend," in *Mary, the Apostles, and the Last Judgment: Apocryphal Representations from Late Antiquity to the Middle Ages*, Stanislava Kuzmová and Andrea-Bianka Znorovszky, eds. (Budapest: Trivent, 2020), pp. 187–220.

3
Like all of the wall paintings Masaccio executed in the chapel, the lighting of the scene of St. Peter's shadow healing the sick is coordinated with the chapel's sole window, in the rear wall directly above the altar and to the right of the depiction of Peter's shadow: Koichi Toyama, "The Headless Cast Shadow: Cast Shadows in 15th-Century Sienese Painting and the Case of Sassetta's 'Stigmatization of St. Francis,'" in *Zeitschrift für Kunstgeschichte* 69 (2006): pp. 531–540 at 531.

4
Usually dated 1426, this painting on panel was once part of a predella in the Malavolti family chapel within the church of San Domenico in Siena; today the painting is in the Walters Art Museum, Baltimore (acc. no. 37.489D).

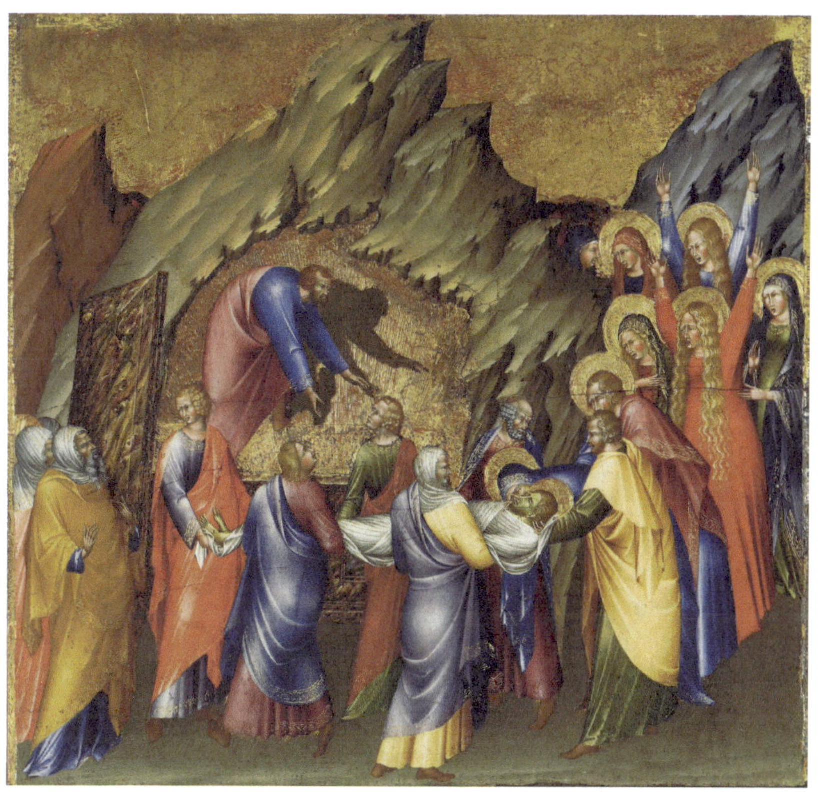

Giovanni di Paolo, Entombment, from the predella in the chapel of the Malavolti family in San Domenico, Siena, 1426, tempera and gold leaf on panel, 40.4 × 43.8 cm. Walters Art Museum, inv. nr. 37.489 D, Baltimore.

Fig. 501

It is always hazardous to make arguments *ex silentio*, but I suspect that Giovanni di Paolo's panel has not served the periodizing function of Masaccio's wall painting because its dramatic cast shadow does not conform to what many art historians recognize as a "Renaissance" cast shadow.[5] To put this differently and in positive terms: the central cast shadow in di Paolo's Entombment plays a different, medieval game.

The shadow doubles the energetic figure of a man, perhaps Nicodemus, who reaches out with both arms to help place Christ's corpse into a sarcophagus situated within a cave. The space of the cave is filled with gold leaf upon which the artist incised a series of fine lines. The pictorial effect is striking. Flooded from within by rays of light, the cave's interior is at once full and flat: a space of paradox. In the convergence of the figure's left hand and its shadow double, and in the distance between the extended right arm and its cast shadow, the painter insinuates a depth at once pictorial and poignant. Reaching to receive Christ's body, the man and his shadow measure the space of the cave-tomb, the width of the sarcophagus straddled by the straining figure, and the pain of the Triduum, the three days that stretch from Christ's death on the cross to his resurrection.

The light that falls upon the man's form, so that it is redoubled as a figure of darkness within the cave-tomb, is singular and singularly mysterious. It seems to touch him and him alone; the grieving figures in the foreground of the painting do not cast shadows. And so, too, the rays of light within the cave defy the laws of nature: touched by shadow, they do not catalyze shadows in turn. In Giovanni di Paolo's Entombment, painted shadow flaunts the laws of the natural world and defies art-historical expectations for Renaissance naturalism, alike.

For further discussion of the painting, see Millard Meiss, "Some Remarkable Early Shadows in a Rare Type of Threnos," in *Festschrift Ulrich Middeldorf* 1, Antje Kosegarten and Peter Tigler, eds. (Berlin: De Gruyter, 1968), pp. 112–118.

5
In contrast to this relative neglect, the shadows cast by middle-ground figures in Giovanni di Paolo's *Flight into Egypt* (1436) have attracted considerable commentary precisely because of their seemingly paradoxical contrast with the shadowless foreground figures. See, with citations of antecedent literature, Koichi Toyama, "'La Fuga in Egitto' di Giovanni di Paolo riesaminata: luce, ombre portate," in *Bullettino senese di storia patria* 103 (1996), pp. 477–490; Stoichiță, *A Short History of the Shadow*, pp. 45–48.

The non-naturalism of the dramatic cast shadow in Giovanni di Paolo's painting is deliberate and more than a merely dramatic pictorial gambit. Doubling the flesh-and-blood figure of the straining man, whose curved back and splayed arms distantly echo the disposition of Christ's body brought down from the cross in deposition scenes, the cast shadow introduces an immaterial figure at the center of the composition. The parallelism and coordination of the shadow figure and the corporeal form within the luminous cave, surrounded by other bodies that cast no shadows, is marked; I would suggest it is a hermeneutically potent species of visual prolepsis. In the conjunction of figure and shadow against a luminous ground, Giovanni di Paolo visually foreshadows Christ's Resurrection, a soteriological event beyond the laws of nature that confirms the supernatural truth of Christ's hypostasis, the union of man and God in his being. The aberration of the cast shadow at the center of the painting is not a tentative or faltering step in the direction of Renaissance naturalism, but rather a deft contribution to a long medieval tradition of hermeneutically charged shadow painting.[6]

It is, however, an art-historical *dictum* that cast shadows cannot be found in medieval paintings. In works dedicated to the shadow's presence in art, both Ernst Gombrich and Victor Stoichiță omit the Middle Ages, leaping, as it were, from Pliny's origin story to the shadow of Masaccio's Peter, as if cast shadows were banished from medieval European paintings either by blinding

6
If, to some readers, the shadow play staged by Giovanni di Paolo may call to mind the famous allegory of the cave in Book 7 of Plato's *Republic*, it is worth noting that the *Republic* was not available in a Latin translation during the Middle Ages. Despite some Patristic-era references, the allegory seems to have been little known to medieval Europeans. In Gregory the Great's "prison analogy" (in Book 4, ch. 1 of his *Dialogi*), a child born within a dark prison cell, who has no first-hand knowledge of the world beyond the cell's walls, serves as a figure for carnal men unable to apprehend the invisible, immaterial, and immortal aspects of God's creation; the analogy notably dispenses with the shadow play so crucial to Plato's allegory of the cave. For further discussion, see Anthony Meredith, "Plato's 'Cave' (*Republic*, vii 514a–517e) in Origen, Plotinus, and Gregory of Nyssa," in *Studia Patristica* 27 (1993): pp. 49–61; Adalbert de Vogüé, "Un avatar du mythe de la caverne dans les Dialogues de Grégoire le Grand," in *Homenaje Justo Pérez de Urbel, O.S.B.* 2 (Silos: Abadía de Silos, 1977), pp. 19–24; Meinolf Schumacher, "Noch ein Höhlengleichnis: zu einem metaphorischen Argument bei Gregor dem Grossen," in *Literaturwissenschaftliches Jahrbuch* 31 (1990), pp. 53–68. For further philosophical reflection on the metaphoric complex, see Hans Blumenberg, *Höhlenausgänge* (Frankfurt am Main: Suhrkamp, 1989). I thank the anonymous peer reviewer for prompting me to address this point and for directing me to Blumenberg's book.

metaphysical light or uniform "non-naturalistic" gloom.[7] As Stoichiță has succinctly observed:

> Although those who studied medieval optics were very interested in attending to the projection of the shadow, it was virtually ignored by artists of the period. This can be attributed to the (onto-)logical status of the medieval image, since it was an entity that, in principle, did not wish to become a physical reality. This notion lasted, *grosso modo*, as late as Giotto, but it was not until the discovery of perspective that the shadow finally became an object of serious study for painters.[8]

Setting aside the untenable claim that the existential and logical status of "the image" in the Middle Ages was somehow antithetical to its participation in "physical reality," Stoichiță's assertion that the projected (i.e., cast) shadow was "virtually ignored" by medieval artists warrants further scrutiny.

It is true that the inclusion of cast shadows in paintings was not a reflex or routinized practice in medieval Europe until the fifteenth century. Nonetheless, in the first decades of the fourteenth century, certain Italian artists—e.g., Giotto, Taddeo Gaddi, and Pietro Lorenzetti—depicted shadows cast by figures and objects upon grounds in a studiously selective fashion.[9] So, too, to remain with the terms of Stoichiță's stock-taking, the cast shadows that proliferated in fifteenth-century painting north of the

7
Ernst H. Gombrich, *Shadows: The Depiction of Cast Shadows in Western Art* (New Haven, CT: National Gallery Publications and Yale University Press, 1995); Stoichiță: *A Short History of the Shadow*; exh. cat. *La sombra*, ed. Victor I. Stoichiță, Museo Thyssen-Bornemisza (Madrid, Museo Thyssen-Bornemisza, 2009). Casati and Cavanagh follow suit: Roberto Casati and Patrick Cavanagh, *The Visual World of Shadows* (Cambridge, MA: MIT Press, 2019). In *Shadows and Englightenment*, Michael Baxandall dives deeply into historically contingent thinking about and picturing of shadows. Despite a substantial appendix dedicated to Renaissance-era theory in which both Giotto and Masaccio are discussed, and Leonardo plays a major role, medieval picturing and thinking about shadows are utterly absent from Baxandall's analysis: Michael Baxandall, *Shadows and Enlightenment* (New Haven, CT: Yale University Press, 1995). That Leonardo's exploration of and writing about shadows was indebted to a fourteenth-century scholastic source that, in turn, depended upon an earlier Arabic text concerning the "science of shadows" (*'ilm al-aẓāl*) is demonstrated by Dominique Raynaud, "A Hitherto Unknown Treatise on Shadows Referred to by Leonardo da Vinci," in *Perspective as Practice: Renaissance Cultures of Optics*, Sven Dupré, ed. (Turnhout: Brepols, 2015), pp. 259–277. I am grateful to Saskia Quené for bringing Raynaud's essay to my attention.

8
Stoichiță, *A Short History of the Shadow*, p. 44.

Alps did so in the absence of unified, geometrical perspectival constructions.[10] Nor was the presence of cast shadows in paintings an exclusively late medieval phenomenon: as I discuss below, cast shadows appear in painting in the early eighth century (if not before).

In this essay, I aim to make a case for the necessity and the rewards of examining the meeting of figure, ground, and light in medieval painting from perceptual and conceptual angles other than those that have long framed our perspective upon European medieval painting. From start to finish, this chapter considers the interaction of figure and ground as it was registered—or rather simulated—in painted cast shadows, but the reader will be forgiven if they do not instantly see cast shadows in the first works to be discussed. The painted cast shadows I examine in this essay were projected according to logics that included but were not limited to the physics of light and phenomenological experience; few of them conform to art-historical expectations.

Many medieval cast shadows are hiding in plain sight, obscured not from what we can see in works of art, but rather by what we expect to see in medieval works of art. To perceive the shadows cast by medieval painters, we must relax the grip of inherited art-historiographical notions of what a cast shadow is and how cast shadows look when they are painted. This, of course, involves critically questioning what we expect to see when figure, ground, and light meet in "premodern" works of art.[11]

9
See Gerd Mathias Micheluzzi, "Der Schlagschatten im Trecento am Beispiel von Taddeo Gaddis Verkündigung an die Hirten," in *Zeitschrift für Literaturwissenschaft und Linguistik* 45 (2015): pp. 98–120.

10
For further discussion, see Lukas Madersbacher, "Der lange Schatten des Jan van Eyck: Zur Wirkungsgeschichte eines hintergründigen Motivs," in *Original – Kopie – Zitat: Kunstwerke des Mittelalters und der frühen Neuzeit Wege der Aneignung – Formen der Überlieferung*, Veröffentlichungen des Zentralinstituts für Kunstgeschichte in München 26, Wolfgang Augustyn and Ulrich Söding, eds. (Passau: D. Klinger Verlag, 2010), pp. 185–205; Stephan Kemperdick, "Heilige mit Schatten: Konrad Witz und die niederländische Malerei," in *Konrad Witz: Katalog zur Ausstellung "Konrad Witz" im Kunstmuseum Basel, 6. März – 3. Juli 2011* (Ostfildern: Hatje Cantz, 2011), pp. 32–45. Konrad Witz's complex painted shadows merit (and require) extended consideration; I plan to consider them at length in a future study.

11
What follows reflects the results of a process of discovering cast shadows in medieval painting that was, at first, aleatory and became a preoccupation; it makes no claims to comprehensiveness. It is my hope that this essay will encourage others to join the hunt for cast shadows in medieval works of art and the project of learning from them.

In principio: Light and Darkness Before the Ground

In the twelfth-century Stammheim Missal, God's creation of light appears within one of a series of framed circular fields that together compose a synopsis of the Book of Genesis's accounts of the work of the first six days, dominated by the creation of Eve at its center [fig. 507].[12] Although the inscription encircling the medallion depicting the work of the first day quotes Genesis 1:3—*Fiat lux et facta est lux* ("And God said: Be light made. And light was made")—within the painted field both light and darkness are present [fig. 508].[13] Primordial darkness is rendered as a loamy brown zone traversed by pale blue-gray lines that extend from a central node to six circular forms. These luminous linear elements echo the blue radial lines and circles painted against the bright white half of the circular field. The painted roundel goes beyond the moment of God's *fiat* to give us a vision of the sentences that follow: "And God saw the light that it was good; and he divided the light from the darkness. And he called the light Day, and the darkness Night; and there was evening and morning, one day" (Gen. 1:4). On this account, *lux* is created by divine *fiat*, but darkness (*tenebrae*) is created by an act of division and distinction.

Despite the luminous clarity of the Stammheim Missal's rendering of the first six days of creation, the account of how the cosmos is called into existence by God in Genesis is obscure. How can there be days and nights before the sun and moon are created on the fourth day? What is light if it is not sunlight? What is darkness or shadows—the Latin word *tenebrae* can mean either—if both the sun and the night do not yet exist? In his

12
Los Angeles, J. Paul Getty Museum, MS 64, fol. 10v. The manuscript is thought to have been produced in the scriptorium of St. Michael's, Hildesheim, ca. 1160–1170. For further discussion, see Beate Fricke, "Wisdom's Creation: A Double Beginning in the Stammheim Missal (1160–1170)," in *Codex Aquilarensis* 37 (2021), pp. 357–376; Elizabeth C. Teviotdale, "The Pictorial Program of the Stammheim Missal," in *Objects, Images, and the Word: Art in the Service of the Liturgy*, Colum P. Hourihane, ed. (Princeton, NJ: 2003), pp. 79–93; Elizabeth C. Teviotdale, *The Stammheim Missal*, Getty Museum Studies on Art (Los Angeles: J. Paul Getty Museum, 2001); Elizabeth C. Teviotdale, et al., *Das Stammheimer Missale / The Stammheim Missal: Die schönste Bilderhandschrift der deutschen Romanik* (Luzern: Quarternio Verlag, 2020). For digital images of the manuscript and extensive further bibliography see the Getty website, https://www.getty.edu/art/collection/object/107TJA.

13
All English translations of scripture are quoted from the Douay-Rheims translation.

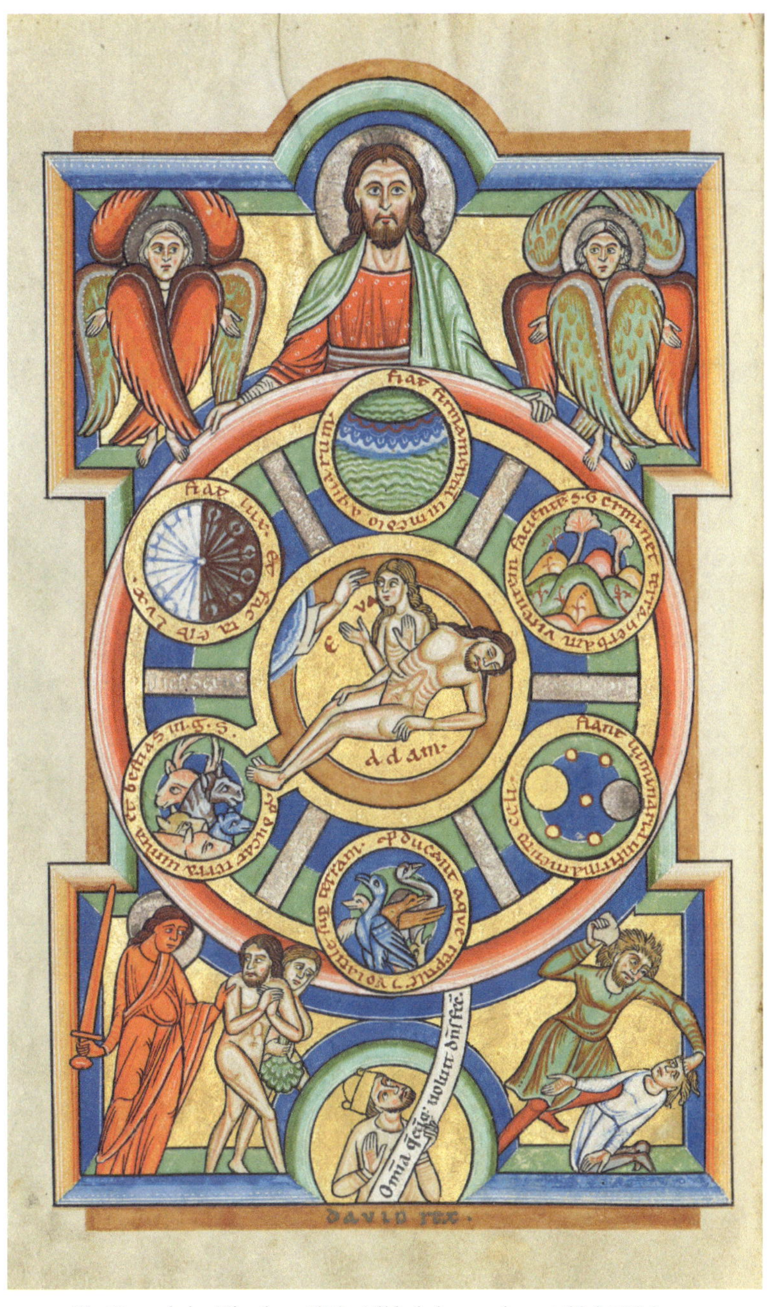

The Stammheim Missal, ca. 1070s, Hildesheim, parchment, 28.2 × 18.9 cm.
Los Angeles, J. Paul Getty Museum, MS 64 (97.MG.21), fol. 10v.

Fig. 507

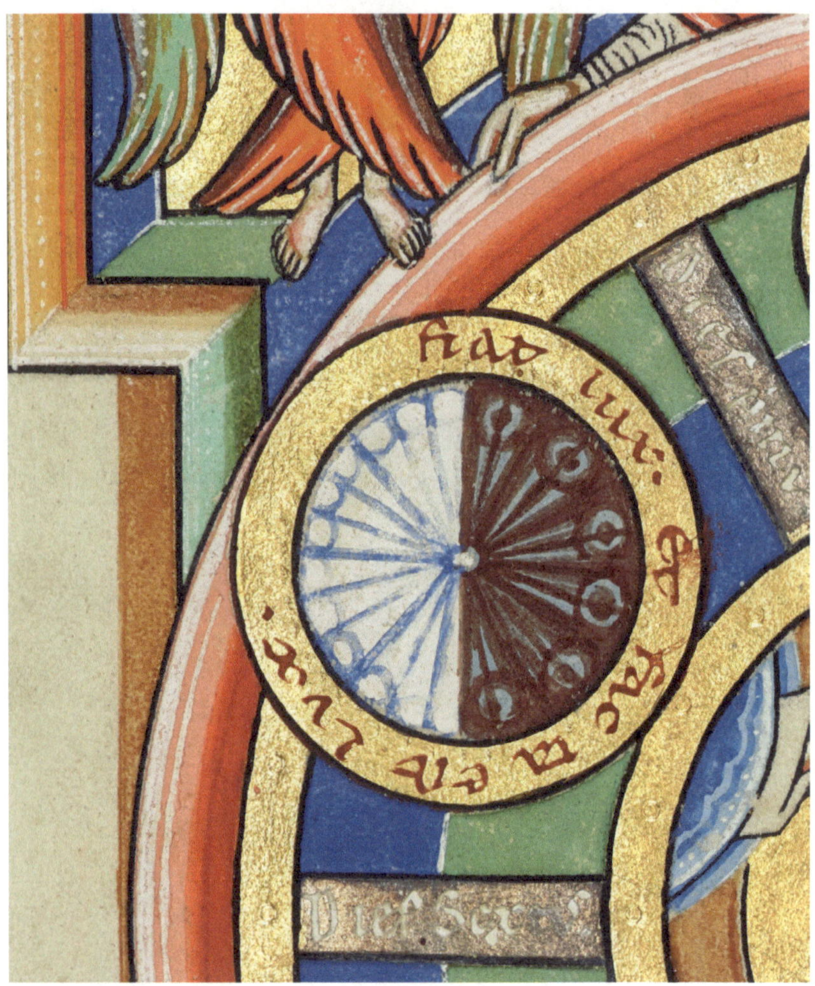

Detail of Fig. 507.

Fig. 508

first attempt at a literal commentary on the book of Genesis, the so-called *liber imperfectus*, Augustine took up these questions:

> divisisse Deum inter lucem et tenebras, eo ipso quo lux facta est, oportet accipi, quod aliud est lux, aliud illae privationes lucis, quas in contrariis tenebris ordinavit Deus. Non enim Deum fecisse tenebras dictum est: quoniam species ipsas Deus fecit, non privationes quae ad nihilum pertinent, unde ab artifice Deo facta sunt omnia; quas tamen ab eo ordinatas intellegimus, cum dicitur: *Et divisit Deus inter lucem et tenebras,* ne vel ipsae privationes non haberent ordinem suum, Deo cuncta regente atque administrante. Sicut in cantando interpositiones silentiorum certis moderatisque intervallis, quamvis vocum privationes sint, bene tamen ordinantur ab iis qui cantare sciunt, et suavitati universae cantilenae aliquid conferunt. Et umbrae in picturis eminentiora quaeque distinguunt, ac non specie, sed ordine placent.[14]

Through a comparison to the pauses or moments of silence that are integral to the ordered structure of sung melody and the shadows that structure a visual composition through contrast with highlights, Augustine identifies darkness as an ordered and ordering presence in the cosmos as soon as light was created.[15]

14
Aurelius Augustinus, "De Genesi ad litteram imperfectus liber," in *Opera Omnia. 3*, PL 34, Migne 1845, cols. 219–246, at col. 229 (c. 5, 25). Translation (by author): "It should be accepted that God distinguished light from darkness by the very act of creating light, since light is one thing and privations of light, which God ordered as contrary/opposite to darkness, quite another. Nor is it said that God created the darkness: forasmuch as God created those very *species*, he did not create privations, which pertain to the nothingness from whence all things were made by the divine artist. Which [privations], we understand nevertheless to be ordered by him, when it is said: 'God separated the light from the darkness'; with God governing and managing all things, even those privations are not deprived of his order. Just as in singing, there are silent pauses at certain measured intervals; although they are privations of voices/sounds, when they are well ordered by those who know how to sing, they add something to the charm/sweetness of the whole song. And so shadows in paintings/pictures, which distinguish the highlights/highpoints, not because of what they are *(ac non specie)*, but by their order." My understanding of Augustine's treatment of the participation of darkness in divine order and ordering is indebted to Marcia Lillian Colish, "The Carolingian Debates over 'Nihil' and 'Tenebrae': A Study in Theological Method," *Speculum* 59 (1984), pp. 757–795, esp. p. 773.

Darkness, according to Augustine, is *not* nothing, but nor is it an autonomous existent: its being is relational, it exists as a privation of light. Although the darkness of the first day is not a shadow in the way we usually think of shadows—recall the sun has not been created yet according to Genesis—Augustine's imperfect analogy to painted shadows suggests that the first darkness's existence is already an epiphenomenon of light. As with the production of quotidian, sublunary shadows, light is darkness's *sine qua non*.

In the Stammheim Missal's medallion for the work of the first day the distinction of darkness and light is also figured as a relation. Darkness, divided from light, is painted as light's opposed, symmetrical double. Darkness's relational derivation from light is figured by the ghostly luminous rays that extend over the dark half of the circular field, reiterating with a difference the blue radial lines and circles in light's complementary side of the medallion.

By contrast, in the roundel for the work of the fourth day, God's creation of the sun and moon to "rule the day and night, and to divide the light and darkness" (Gen. 1:18) results in discrete bounded round forms within a bounded round field. Positioned in diametric opposition, the sun and moon were executed in gold and silver leaf, respectively.[16] These metallic disks sparkle. They catch light on their surfaces and scatter it. Luminous clarity is the order of the fourth day of creation, according to the Stammheim Missal.

The positioning of the forms of sun and moon in diametric opposition with an intervening form between them was a well-known schema in the Middle Ages, not least thanks to a long tradition of astronomical diagrams. A lunar eclipse diagram in

15
See also Augustine's differently oriented analogy concerning the color black in pictures (sometimes construed as a reference to painted shadows) in Augustine, *The City of God Against the Pagans* (vol. III: Books 8–11), trans. David S. Wiesen, Loeb Classical Library 413 (Cambridge, MA: Harvard University Press, 1968), pp. 516–517, http://www.loebclassics.com/view/augustine-city_god_pagans/1957/work.xml (Bk. 11, c. 23: 3). For further discussion of this passage see Micheluzzi, "Der Schlagschatten," p. 115.

16
For detailed analysis of materials and technique, see Nancy Turner's contribution in Teviotdale, et al., *Das Stammheimer Missale*, pp. 103–105 and pp. 285–295.

a fifteenth-century Austrian manuscript of Konrad of Megenberg's translation of Johannes de Sacro Bosco's *Sphaera mundi* (*On the Sphere of the World*) presents the form of the earth interposed between a golden sun and the darker metallic form of the moon [fig. 512].[17] Extending from the earth to the moon, the earth's shadow is rendered as a modulated gray zone; within it, darker striations echo the linear rays of sunlight that touch the other side of the earth [fig. 513]. An inscription makes the astronomical situation clear: "*die figur der umschattung des mones*" (the figure of the overshadowing of the moon").

The earth's cast shadow and the astronomical contingency of all shadows on earth were phenomena of interest throughout the medieval period. Like the behavior of natural light on earth, shadows were understood to be produced by, and thus to reveal the interaction of celestial bodies, their sizes, and their distance from earth. Indeed, for medieval *perspectiva*, the natural philosophical and theological study of optics, shadows were phenomena inseparable from their astronomical causes.[18] Drawing upon observation and mathematical reasoning, medieval perspectivists primarily understood shadows as revelatory consequences. As Roger Bacon (ca. 1220–ca. 1292), explained:

> umbra non est activa, nec sui similis generativa, sed generatur umbra per aliud et requirit illud aliud, scilicet corpus obiectum, preter medium in quo fit.[19]

Bacon's *umbra* is passive: it is generated, not generating. Its being derives from the action of the species of light (*lumen*), multiplying through a medium—that is, an interval that is not empty, but

17
New York, The Morgan Library & Museum, MS M.722, fol. 16v. For further information and bibliography, see the PML's online cataloging, https://www.themorgan.org/manuscript/128487.

18
On this topic, see the stimulating discussion in Lukáš Lička, "Shadows in Medieval Optics, Practical Geometry, and Astronomy: On a *Perspectiva* Ascribed to Thomas Bradwardine," *Early Science and Medicine* 27 (2022), pp. 179–223.

19
Roger Bacon, *De Multiplicatione specierum*, Pars III, c. 1, ll. 117–120 in *Roger Bacon's Philosophy of Nature: A Critical Edition*, David C. Lindberg, ed. (Oxford: Clarendon Press/Oxford University Press, 1983), p. 184. Translation: "shadow is not active, nor able to generate its like, but is generated by something else and requires that other thing, namely the umbrageous body, in addition to the medium in which it comes into being." Lindberg, *Roger Bacon's Philosophy*, p. 185.

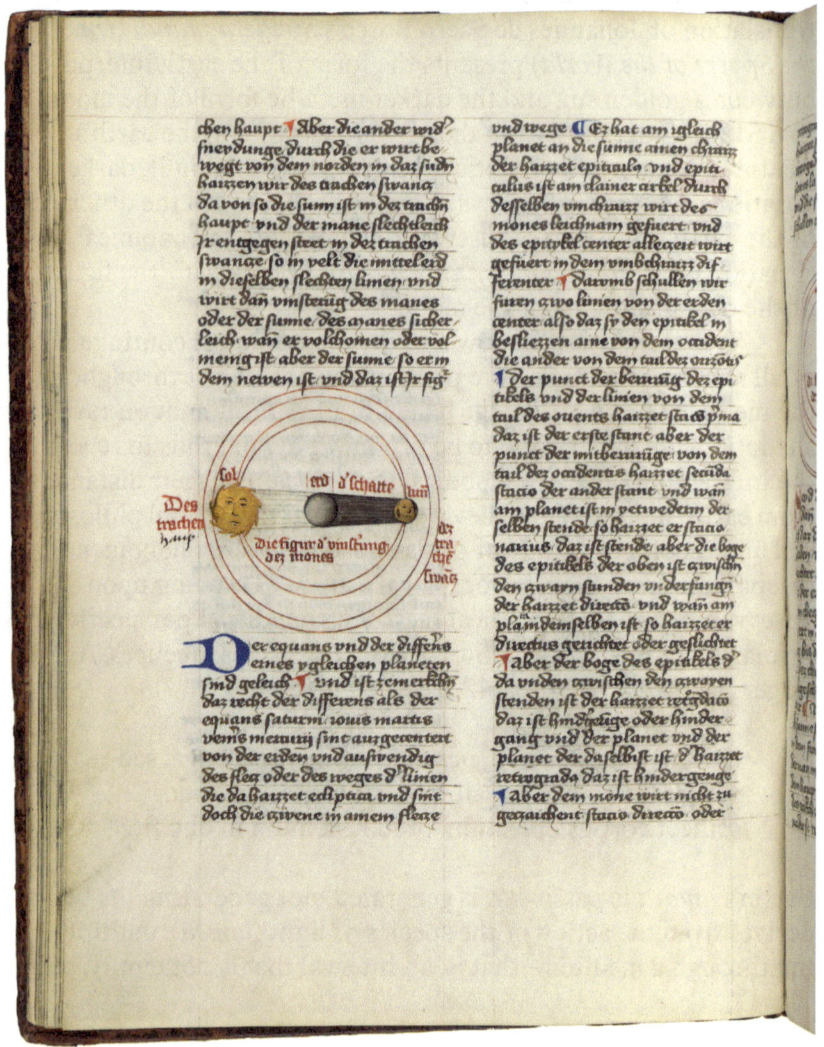

Johannes de Sacro Bosco, Sphaera mundi, in the German translation of Konrad von Megenberg, ca. 1425, Austria. New York, The Morgan Library & Museum, MS M.722, fol. 16v.

Fig. 512

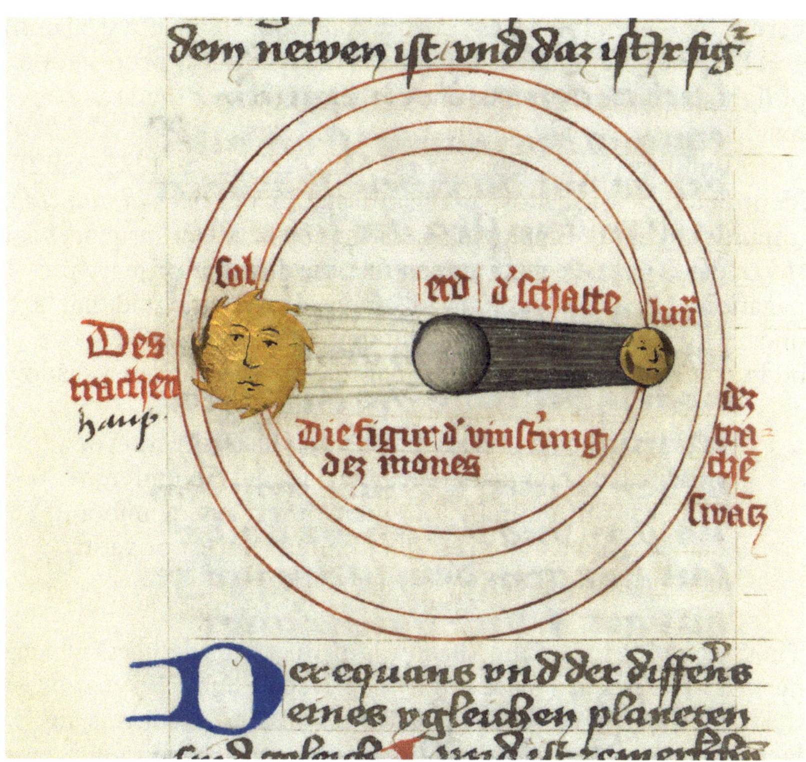

Detail of Fig. 512.

Fig. 513

permeable—until it reaches a *corpus obiectum*.[20] That physical entity, as it becomes illuminated, also affects the rectilinear propagation of light, with varied results: one of them is the cast shadow, a dependent, passive *similis* of the *corpus obiectum*.

Building upon Bacon's work, John Pecham (ca. 1235–1292) identified the cast shadow as a manifestation of *lumen diminutum* (diminished light). Employing a distinction between "primary" and "secondary" light, Pecham agreed that the direct or primary propagation of light is blocked by an opaque body, but noted that "secondary light," propagating circumferentially around the opaque body, continues past it in the form of that obstruction's cast shadow:

> quamvis opacum impediat transitum lucis directum et principalem, non tamen secundarium qui circumferencialiter se diffundit. In hoc autem differt autem umbra a tenebra, quia umbra est lux diminuta ubi est privatio lucis primarie et derivatio secundarie.[21]

Thus, according to Pecham, shadow is distinct from darkness which, he writes, "exists in a place totally deprived of light."[22] What the human eye perceives as the darkness of a cast shadow is, in fact, a manifestation of light slipping over and around the contours of objects or figures and continuing to propagate or

20
David Lindberg translates this last element as "an umbrageous body," but it should be noted that a *corpus obiectum* is, quite literally, a physical entity "thrown in the way" and, more specifically in this context, a physical entity thrown in the way of *lumen*, the species of solar light in the air, which, according to Bacon, propagates or multiplies itself in a medium thanks to its active virtue (in distinction to shadow). Roger Bacon, *De Multiplicatione specierum*, Pars III, c. 1, ll. 105–117: Lindberg, *Roger Bacon's Philosophy*, p. 184.

21
John Pecham [Peckham], *Perpsectiva communis*, I.25; quoted from David C. Lindberg, ed., *John Pecham and the Science of Optics: Perspectiva communis*, University of Wisconsin publications in medieval science (Madison, WI: University of Wisconsin Press, 1970), p. 102. I am grateful to Gottfried Boehm for his suggestion that I should revisit Pecham's *Perspectiva communis* with cast shadows in mind. Translation: "[A]lthough an opaque object impedes the direct and principal propagation of light, it does not impede the secondary propagation, which proceeds circumferentially. However, shadows differ from darkness in that shadows are diminished light, [produced] whenever there is a privation of primary light together with a derivation of secondary light." Lindberg, *John Pecham*, p. 103. For further discussion of Pecham's theorization of shadows in relation to other medieval perspectivist positions, see Lička, "Shadows in Medieval Optics"; Raynaud, "A Hitherto Unknown Treatise."

22
"Tenebra vero est si tamen alicubi est ubi nichil est de lumine," *Perspectiva communis*, I.25: Latin and English translation quoted from Lindberg, *John Pecham*, pp. 102–103.

self-project behind those figures in a diminished fashion. On this account, the cast shadow is nothing other than a different intensity of light.

Bacon, Pecham, and other medieval perspectivists sought to understand the behavior of light in the world and how it was perceived and apperceived by human eyes and minds, both accurately and erroneously. Within this larger intellectual project, the investigation of visual error was a major preoccupation.[23] According to medieval *perspectiva*, the interaction of the physics of light, environmental factors, the structure of the eye, and the internal faculties could and did induce people to perceive counterfactually. Doubled reflections, afterimages, optical color blending, and the perceived distortion of forms induced by refraction were among the perceptual errors that perspectivists investigated in pursuit of a rigorous understanding of human perception and apperception. The perspectivist project thus ambitiously aimed to investigate and elucidate not only how things really were, but also how the appearance of things might conceal both empirical and super-empirical truths.[24] Not all medieval shadows, however, submitted to this regime of aggressive interrogation and reasoned elucidation.

23
On perspectivist discussions of visual error, see Dallas G. Denery, *Seeing and Being Seen in the Later Medieval World: Optics, Theology and Religious Life* (Cambridge, UK: Cambridge University Press, 2005); Dallas G. Denery, "Vision and Visual Error in Later Middle Ages," in *Arabic and Latin Theory of Perspective*, Micrologus 29, Agostino Paravicini Bagliani, ed. (Florence: SISMEL, 2021), pp. 203–218; Lička, "Shadows in Medieval Optics"; Juhana Toivanen, "Perceptual Experience: Assembling a Medieval Puzzle," in *Philosophy of Mind in the Early and High Middle Ages*, The History of the Philosophy of Mind 2, Margaret Cameron, ed. (New York: Routledge, 2018), pp. 134–156; José Filipe Silva and Juhana Toivanen, "Perceptual Errors in Late Medieval Philosophy," in *The Senses and the History of Philosophy*, Rewriting the History of Philosophy, Brian Glenney, Brian and José Filipe Silva, eds. (New York: Routledge, 2019), pp. 106–130; Dominik Perler, "Can We Trust our Senses? Fourteenth-Century Debates on Sensory Illusions," in *Uncertain Knowledge: Scepticism, Relativism, and Doubt in the MiddleAges*, Disputatio 14, Dallas G. Denery, Kantik Ghosh, and Nicolette Zeeman, eds. (Turnhout: Brepols, 2014), pp. 63–90.

24
Although much recent scholarship has focused on perspectivist interest in perceptual deception, medieval Christian *perspectiva* was also deeply interested in how the study of optics could yield moral-theological and metaphysical fruit; this aspect of the perspectivist project was pursued both in intellectual/academic circles and in preaching and preaching aids, most notably in Peter of Limoges's *De oculi morali*. For further discussion, see Peter of Limoges, *The Moral Treatise on the Eye*, trans. Richard Newhauser, Mediaeval Sources in Translation 51 (Toronto: Pontifical Institute of Mediaeval Studies, 2012); David L. Clark, "Optics for Preachers: the *De oculi morali* by Peter of Limoges," in *The Michigan Academician* (1977), pp. 329–343; Richard Newhauser, "Nature's Moral Eye: Peter of Limoges' *Tractatus Moralis De Oculo*," in *Man and Nature in the Middle Ages*, Sewanee Mediaeval Studies 6, Robert G. Benson and Susan Ridyard, eds. (Sewanee, TN: The Press of

Overshadowing

Many Christians in the Middle Ages would have contested Bacon's claim that shadows were intrinsically passive. The Bible told them this was not true.[25] The verb *obumbrare* ("to overshadow") occurs repeatedly in Jerome's Vulgate translation of the Hebrew Bible, always as an evocation of God's protective, sheltering presence. In the Vulgate New Testament, active forms of the verb are used to describe a series of transformative supernatural events. The healing action of Peter's shadow, depicted by Masaccio, was described in the Acts of the Apostles (5:15) as an "overshadowing." When the apostles Peter, James, and John witnessed Christ's Transfiguration, they were "overshadowed" by a cloud (Mt. 17:5; Mk. 9:6; Lk. 9:34). And according to the Gospel of Luke (Lk. 1:35), the angel Gabriel told Mary that "the power of the most High shall overshadow" her.[26] It is to this overshadowing that Mary assented, becoming the mother of God.

the University of the South, 1995), pp. 125–136; Richard Newhauser, "Inter scientiam et populam: Roger Bacon, Peter of Limoges, and the 'Tractatus moralis de oculo,'" in *Nach der Verurteilung von 1277: Philosophie und Theologie an der Universität von Paris im letzten Viertel des 13. Jahrhunderts: Studien und Texte; After the Condemnation of 1277: Philosophy and Theology at the University of Paris in the Last Quarter of the Thirteenth Century: Studies and Texts*, Miscellanea mediaevalia 28, Jan Aertsen, Kent Emery, and Andreas Speer, eds. (Berlin: De Gruyter, 2001), pp. 682–703; Richard Newhauser, "Educating the Senses on Love or Lust: Richard de Fournival and Peter of Limoges," in *Public Declamations: Essays on Medieval Rhetoric, Education, and Letters in Honour of Martin Camargo*, Disputatio 27, Georgiana Donavin, ed. (Turnhout: Brepols, 2015), pp. 213–230; Denery, *Seeing and Being Seen*; Katherine H. Tachau, *Vision and Certitude in the Age of Ockham: Optics, Epistemology, and the Foundations of Semantics, 1250–1345*, Studien und Texte zur Geistesgeschichte des Mittelalters 22 (Leiden: Brill, 1988); Klaus Bergdolt, *Das Auge und die Theologie: Naturwissenschaften und "Perspectiva" an der päpstlichen Kurie in Viterbo (ca. 1260–1285)*, Vorträge / Nordrhein-Westfälische Akademie der Wissenschaften. Geisteswissenschaften Vorträge G 413 (Paderborn: Schöningh, 2007).

25
Although I cannot address the rich lexical and semantic range of scriptural references to shadows here, I am grateful to Gunnar Mikosch for sharing his stimulating thoughts on this point (personal communication, March 24, 2023). For further discussion of shadows in the Hebrew Bible, New Testament, and the medieval exegetical-literary tradition, see Mira Mocan, "'Lucem demonstrat umbra': ombra e immagine fra letteratura e arte nel Medioevo," in *Manipolare la luce in epoca premoderna*, Daniela Mondini and Vladimir Ivanovici, eds. (Mendrisio: Mendrisio Academy Press/ Silvana Editorale, 2014), pp. 185–199; Anja Becker, "Der Schatten des Heiligen Geistes: Metaphorologische Erkundungsgänge durch mittelalterliche Textwelten," *Zeitschrift für Literaturwissenschaft und Linguistik* 45 (2015): pp. 121–146; Max Milner, *L'envers du visible: essai sur l'ombre* (Paris: Ed. du Seuil, 2005), pp. 37–63.

26
"Spiritus Sanctus superveniet in te, et virtus Altissimi obumbrabit tibi. Ideoque et quod nascetur ex te sanctum, vocabitur Filius Dei." ("The Holy Ghost shall come upon thee, and the power of the most High shall overshadow thee. And therefore also the Holy which shall be born of thee shall be called the Son of God.")

The outpouring of divine shadow upon Mary is the central drama of the Hitda Codex's painting of the Annunciation [fig. 518].[27] Pushed back by Gabriel's advance, a torrent of white pigment describes the rippling edge of the space around the Virgin.[28] Filled with modulated rosy-red painting, the upper limit of this space is designated by a dark undulating line that swells and narrows, crowned by a segment of golden zig-zag. In the upper-right corner of the miniature, we see the rooftops and upper stories of Nazareth. We can only guess how these buildings meet the ground; our view of the city is blocked by the divine shadow that pours down on the Virgin from above, flooding pictorial space. What, at first glance, might seem like an inert painted ground behind the figure of Mary is anything but. The dusky purple color that surrounds Mary is a divine *plenum:* a soft opaque fullness invested with optical and epiphanic salience by the painter. Momentarily obscuring the recessive forms of Nazareth's cityscape, this divine shadow also imposes itself upon the striated bands of color behind Gabriel's figure. Where the divine shadow's bright, rippling contour pools before the Virgin's feet, golden plants sprout: it is an active, animating presence that resists conventional distinctions of light from darkness. Calling into question the subordination of painted ground to painted figure, and defying the logic of Bacon's perspectivist shadow, in the painting Mary's *corpus* and the shadow of the Almighty interact and collaborate in the Incarnation of Christ, the *lux vera* ("true light"; Jn 1:9).

27
Darmstadt, Universitäts- und Landesbibliothek, Hs 1640, fol. 20r. Produced in Cologne, ca. 1020, the Evangeliary is available in a facsimile, with commentary, *Der Darmstaedter Hitda-Codex: Bilder und Zierseiten aus der Handschrift 1640 der hessischen Landes- und Hochschulbibliothek*, Propyläen Faksimilie (Berlin: Propyläen Verlag, 1968). From an extensive literature dedicated to the manuscript, see also Klaus Gereon Beuckers, ed., *Äbtissin Hitda und der Hitda-Codex (Universitäts- und Landesbibliothek Darmstadt, Hs. 1640); Forschungen zu einem Hauptwerk der ottonischen Kölner Buchmalerei* (Darmstadt: Wissenschaftliche Buchgesellschaft, 2013); Rainer Warland, "Himmlischer Lichtglanz im Evangeliar: Zum ästhetischen Konzept des Hitda-Codex," in *Otium: Festschrift für Volker Michael Strocka*, Thomas Ganschow and Matthias Steinert, eds. (Remshalden: B.A. Greiner, 2005), pp. 433–436; Christoph Winterer, *Das Evangeliar der Äbtissin Hitda: Eine ottonische Prachthandschrift aus Köln* (Darmstadt: Wissenschaftliche Buchgesellschaft, 2010). I regret that I was not able to consult Jeremia Kraus, "Worauf gründet unser Glaube?: Jesus von Nazaret im Spiegel des Hitda-Evangeliars," Freiburger theologische Studien 168 (Freiburg im Breisgau: Herder, 2005).

28
In seeing Gabriel's form as pushing back the rippling white edge, my account echoes Winterer, *Das Evangeliar der Äbtissin Hitda*, p. 49. See also Herbert Leon Kessler, "Sacred Light from Shadowy Things," in *Codex Aquilarensis* 32 (2016), pp. 237–270, at pp. 263–264.

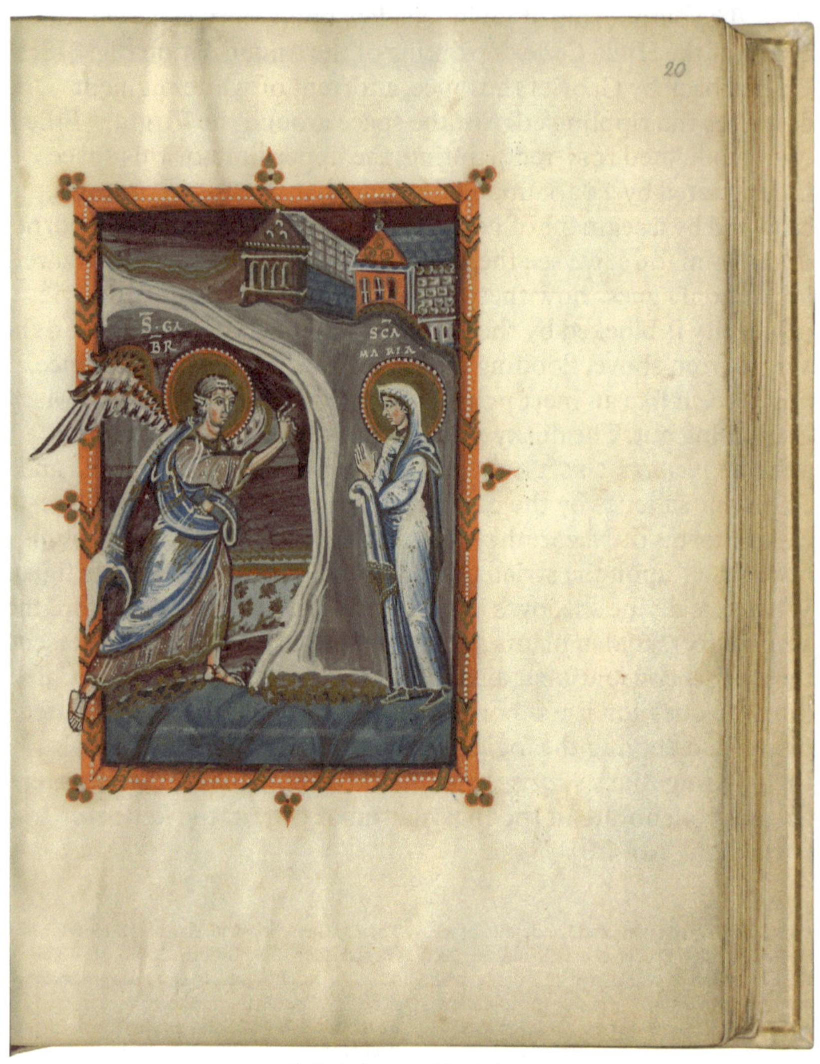

Hitda Codex, ca. 1020, Cologne.
Darmstadt, Universitäts- und Landesbibliothek, Hs. 1640, fol. 20r.

Fig. 518

Foreshadowing: The Painted Cast Shadow as Typological *Figura*

The Annunciation is represented in the Hitda Codex as a dramatic epiphany in which the shadow of God, projected forward to engulf Mary, plays a leading role. The role of the cast shadow as a figure for divine presence, pregnant with soteriological significance, in medieval paintings is notable: it forms a delicate red thread linking quite different works of art over the medieval *longue durée.* In contrast to the drama of the Hitda Codex's Annunciation, however, soteriologically-charged cast shadows are often subtle elements in medieval paintings. Easily overlooked, they nonetheless make important contributions to the images in which they appear.

Consider, for example, the famous portrait of Ezra in the Codex Amiatinus, the earliest surviving pandect or complete bible, finished in or by 716 CE at the double monastery of Wearmouth–Jarrow in Northumbria [fig. 520].[29] An inscription above the framed image glosses the fervent scribal labor depicted below: "Codicibus sacris hostili clade perustis / Esdra Deo feruens hoc reparauit opus."[30] Like the inscription, the image celebrates Ezra as the heroic restorer of scripture after it had been reduced to ashes in the Chaldean invasion, a feat reported in the apocryphal 4 Esdras (also known as the Apocalypse of Erza) and discussed by Christian exegetes.[31]

29
Florence, Biblioteca Medicea Laurenziana, MS Amiat. 1, fol. 4/Vr. The dating of the Codex Amiatinus has long been debated. Offering a comprehensive critical review of antecedent scholarship, as well as meticulous analysis of internal and contextual evidence, Ceila Chazelle's recent *opus magnus* makes a compelling and judicious case for a likely production of the codex's "biblical manuscript" (i.e., ff. 9–1030 in the current binding) by ca. 703, followed by the completion and addition of its "preliminary gathering" (i.e., ff. 1/I–8/VIII), including the image of Ezra discussed here, as early as 710 and certainly by June 716 when Ceolfrith left Wearmouth–Jarrow for Rome, bringing the pandect as a gift for the shrine of St. Peter: Celia Martin Chazelle, *The Codex Amiatinus and Its "Sister" Bibles: Scripture, Liturgy, and Art in the Milieu of the Venerable Bede*, Commentaria: sacred texts and their commentaries: Jewish, Christian and Islamic 10 (Leiden: Brill, 2019).

30
Transcription and English translation quoted from Chazelle, *The Codex Amiatinus,* p. 320. For further discussion of the inscription and the painting, with consideration of prior scholarship, see Chazelle, *The Codex Amiatinus*, pp. 320–336, 402–413, 446–447. Translation: "After the sacred codices were incinerated in the enemy devastation, Esdra, burning for (or with) God, repaired this work."

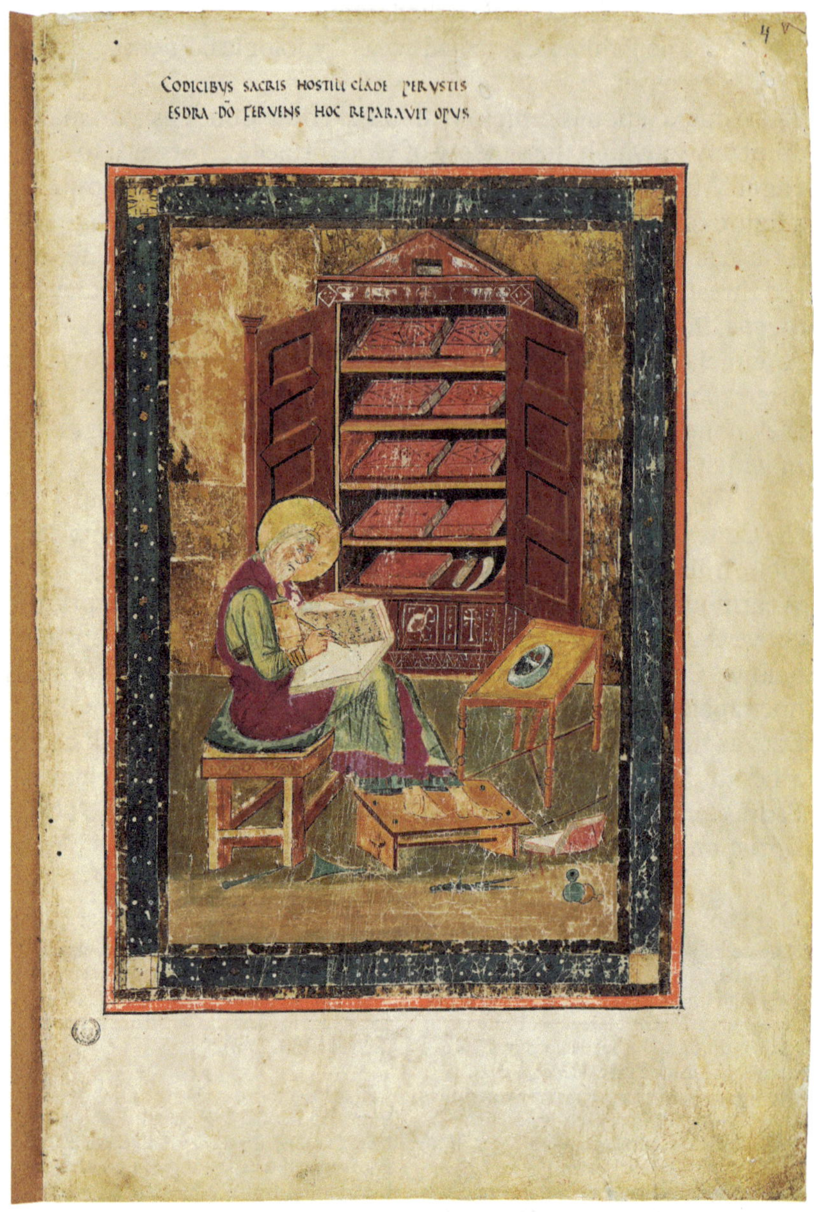

Codex Amiatinus, Ezra Writing, ca. 688–713, Wearmouth-Jarrow, England.
Florence, Biblioteca Medicea Laurenziana, MS Amiat. 1, fol. 4/Vr.

Fig. 520

As the prophet-scribe is depicted at work in the foreground of the image, the results of his labor are visible in nine bound codices placed within the imposing *armarium* (book cupboard) set against the gold rear wall of his scriptorium.[32] Golden letters on the spines of these volumes once spelled out their contents [fig. 522]. Although they are difficult to read today, these highly abbreviated "titles" were once legible. In left to right order, working downwards from the uppermost shelf, they have been reconstructed as:

OCT. LIB. LEG	REG. PAR. L. VI
HIST. LIB. VIII	PSAL. LIB. I
SAL. LIB. V	PROP. L. XVI
EVANGL. L. IIII	EPIST. AP. XXI
ACT. AP. APOC. IS[33]	

("Eight books of the law [i.e., the Octateuch]	Kings and Paralipomenon six books
Histories eight books	Psalms one book
Solomon five books	Prophets sixteen books
Gospels four books	Letters of the Apostles twenty-one

Acts of the Apostles [and] Apocalypse")[34]

31
As Chazelle notes (p. 333), the use of the word "*reparavit*" in the inscription suggests that its author knew Isidore of Seville's comment that Ezra "[b]ibliothecam Veteris Testamenti ... reparavit" in his *Etymologies* (Bk. 6, c. 3.2), but the textual source that seems to most closely resonate with numerous specific aspects of the inscription and the depiction of Ezra in the Codex Amiatinus is Bede's *In Regum librum*; see Chazelle, *The Codex Amiatinus,* pp. 332–336. Christian exegetes, including Bede, interpreted the report of 4 Esdras as indicating that Ezra, inspired by God, with the assistance of other scribes, restored all of the Jewish scriptures included in the Bible, but there were yet other destroyed texts from the Temple that remained lost: Chazelle, *The Codex Amiatinus,* pp. 333–334.

32
On the gold leaf surface of this rear wall, which doubles as a kind of pictorial ground, see Chazelle, *The Codex Amiatinus,* p. 321. For closer analysis of the depicted *armarium*, see Janina Ramirez, "*Sub culmine gazas*: The Iconography of the Armarium on the Ezra Page of the Codex Amiatinus," *Gesta* 48 (2009): pp. 1–18.

33
Different reconstructive readings of these texts have been proposed; here I follow Richard Marsden's convincing argument (itself validating the first of Rupert L. S. Bruce-Mitford's reconstructions): Richard Marsden, "Job in His Place: The Ezra Miniature in the Codex Amiatinus," *Scriptorium* 49 (1995): pp. 3–15.

34
English translation quoted from Chazelle, *The Codex Amiatinus,* p. 323.

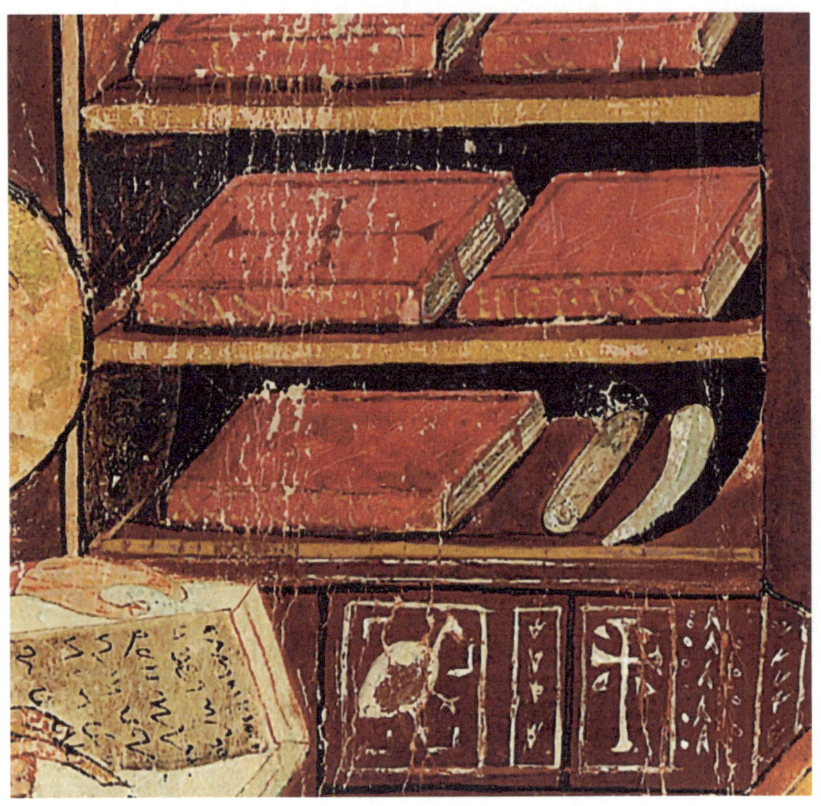

Detail of Fig. 520.

Fig. 522

The glittering titles indicate that the cupboard contains a complete scriptural *bibliotheca*: all of the canonical books of the Hebrew Bible and the New Testament are present, distributed among the nine bound volumes within the cupboard. The painting thus significantly deviates from accounts of the historical event of Ezra's restoration of Jewish scripture. The codices depicted within the *armarium* contain not only the texts destroyed by the Chaldeans, but also, anachronistically, the books of the Christian New Testament.[35] In a further seeming paradox, the image presents Ezra writing in a tenth bound book, with yet another unidentified volume splayed on the floor before him. In this fashion, the image presents Erza's work as simultaneously in progress and already completed in the forms of the bound codices arrayed within the *armarium*.

The juxtaposition of scribal labor underway and completed within a single painted scene is not the only paradox to be found in the painting. Among the tools of scribal labor scattered at Ezra's feet, only one object casts a shadow: the small blue-green ink pot prominently depicted in the lower right foreground [fig. 524]. The shadow thrown by the little vessel is no darker reiteration of its form, but rather a golden-brown double whose projection upon the tawny ground defies lived experience of cast shadows.[36] Some interpreters of the image have treated the luminous shadow cast by the ink pot as a symptom of earnest, yet inept classicism. On this account, the golden cast shadow in the foreground of the image reveals how the naturalism of a putative late antique model was misunderstood by an early medieval painter.[37] What has, to the best

35
The organization of the bible into nine volumes, coupled with the presence of the tenth book on the floor before the figure of Ezra, lends support to the view that the image-model employed in the making of this painting was a depiction of Cassiodorus working on the Codex Grandior, with the Codex Minor at his feet, and his *novem codices* displayed in a book cupboard; for further discussion of this line of argumentation, and its broader stakes in relation to the making of the Codex Amiatinus as a whole, see Chazelle, *The Codex Amiatinus*, pp. 324–326 passim.

36
On the various tools depicted within the image, see especially J. Merten, "Die Esra–Miniatur des Codex Amiatinus: Zu Autorenbild und Schreibgerät," in *Trierer Zeitschrift für Geschichte und Kunst des Trierer Landes und seinger Nachbargebiete* 50 (1987): pp. 301–320. Chazelle tentatively suggests that certain of the tools may perhaps have evoked the art of painting, rather than writing: Chazelle, *The Codex Amiatinus*, pp. 321, 325, 408.

37
For example, Merten opines: "Hier hat aber der Illuminator des Codex Amiatinus nicht den in seiner Vorlage dargestellten Schlagschatten abbilden wollen; vielmehr hat er den Schatten des Tintenfläschchens mißverstanden und zu einem weiteren, braun gemalten Gefäß umgedeutet:" Merten, "Die Esra-Miniatur," p. 313.

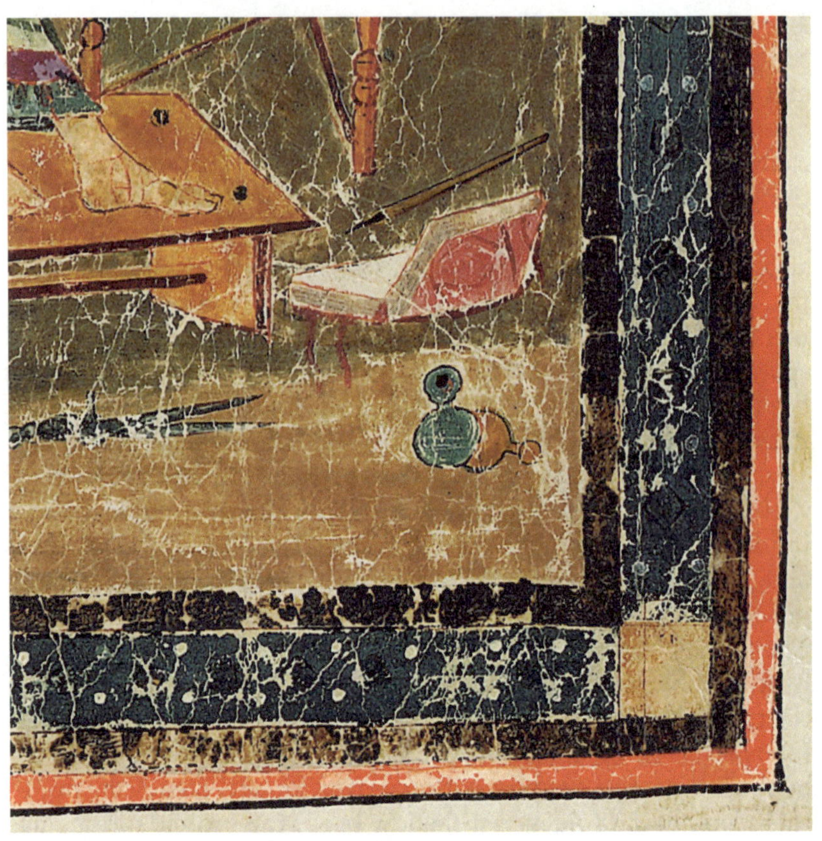

Detail of Fig. 520.

Fig. 524

of my knowledge, gone unremarked is the presence of yet other cast shadows within the painting, whose depiction suggests that the medieval painter of the image made selective, deliberate use of this pictorial device to *super*-naturalistic ends.

Tucked away within the bottom shelf of the imposing *armarium*, two black shadows are thrown by an inkhorn on the right and by another object—likely a pencase—to its left [fig. 522].[38] Harder to see today, the nine bound volumes of scripture within the bookcase also cast discrete shadows: these dark bounded forms must have once strongly contrasted with the golden, glittering titles spelled out on their spines.

By contrast, no shadow doubles the figure of Ezra at work; nor does the volume splayed on the floor of his scriptorium, the bench upon which he sits, or the table placed adjacent to him project shadows upon the canted ground plane [fig. 520]. Within the image, the cast shadow was reserved for the finished physical manifestation of God's word and some of the tools employed its material (re)creation. Like the presence of the books of the Christian New Testament among the codices in the depicted *armarium*, the selective granting of cast shadows to the completed volumes of Holy Writ and to certain of the scribe's tools was a hermeneutic gesture. The shadows cast within the cupboard, like the golden shadow cast by the inkpot in the foreground of painting, do not pictorially render the effect of a simulated natural light source playing over figures and grounds. They are instead produced by the strong raking light of Christian typology directed upon Jewish history and sacred scripture.[39]

For discussion of evidence that an earlier image of Mediterranean provenance, likely a portrait of Cassiodorus, served as a model for the Ezra painting in Amiatinus (with citations of previous scholarship), see Chazelle, *The Codex Amiatinus*, pp. 323–324.

38
Merten hesitated to identify the right-hand object as an inkhorn, noting that it does not correspond to the form of late antique ink containers (actual and depicted): Merten, "Die Esra-Miniatur," pp. 314–315. Nonetheless, I see no difficulty in identifying this depicted object as an inkhorn, and perhaps (as Merten mooted) the earliest known depiction of an animal horn adapted to serve as a vessel for ink (in keeping with numerous early medieval Evangelist and scribal portraits); Chazelle also sees the right-hand object as an inkhorn, and notes that the object to its left "may be a scraper or a case of writing utensils": Chazelle, *The Codex Amiatinus*, p. 322.

39
This typological *hermeneusis* is also evident in the use of light-reflecting gold in the painting, not only to cover the back wall/ground in the image, but also in the titles inscribed on the codices in the *armarium*, as well as in the rendering of the pen held by Ezra, his halo, and his sandals; for further discussion, with

Although a non-naturalistic, metaphysical form of light has often been imputed to medieval images, numerous medieval paintings feature cast shadows that cannot be attributed to the workings of divine light or supernatural darkness, even when the ostensible occasion for their representation is overtly religious. A marginal image in a late eleventh-century manuscript of John Climacus's *Heavenly Ladder* is a case in point [fig. 527].[40] The small scene in the margin responds to a passage that treats dreams experienced by novice monks. John warns his monastic readers that "he who believes in dreams is like a person running after his own shadow and trying to catch it."[41] Although the text emphasizes the illusory nature of dreams and their tempting danger to the would-be monk, the marginal painting does not present a scene of futile pursuit, nor of shadowy menace, but rather of mutual longing. The hard-edged gray-green rectangular shape upon which the figure dressed in blue stands is also the ground upon which his shadow appears. The shadow does not, however, spread immaterially over that painted ground, like an intangible projection of the privation of light. Its dark unmodelled form has an uncanny volume, even plasticity. Construed in relation to the text it accompanies, one is tempted to identify a dream logic instantiated, and thereby reflexively thematized, in the configuration of figure, shadow, and

a complimentary emphasis on the literal and exegetical dynamics of golden illumination within the image, see Chazelle, *The Codex Amiatinus,* pp. 403–404.

40
A full digital surrogate is freely available online: https://digi.vatlib.it/view/MSS_Vat.gr.394. For further discussion of this manuscript, see John Rupert Martin, *The Illustration of the "Heavenly Ladder" of John Climacus,* Studies in Manuscript Illumination 5 (Princeton, NJ: Princeton University Press, 1954), pp. 47–88; Kathleen Corrigan, "Constantine's Problems: The Making of the Heavenly Ladder of John Climacus, Vat. gr. 394," *Word & Image* 12 (1996): pp. 61–93; Maria Evangelatou, "The Heavenly Ladder," in *A Companion to Byzantine Illustrated Manuscripts,* Brill's Companions to the Byzantine World 2, Vasiliki Tsamakda, ed. (Leiden: Brill, 2017), pp. 407–417, at pp. 416–417; Nancy Patterson Sevcenko, "Monastic Challenges: Some Illustrated Manuscripts of the 'Heavenly Ladder,'" in *Byzantine Art: Recent Studies: Essays in Honor of Lois Drewer,* Medieval and Renaissance Texts and Studies 378/Arizona Studies in the Middle Ages and Renaissance 33, Colum P. Hourihane, ed. (Princeton, NJ/Tempe, AZ/Turnhout: Index of Christian Art/ACMRS/Brepols, 2009), pp. 39–62.

41
English translation quoted from Saint John Climacus, *The Ladder of Divine Ascent* (Boston: Holy Transfiguration Monastery, 2012), p. 67 (Step. 3:27).

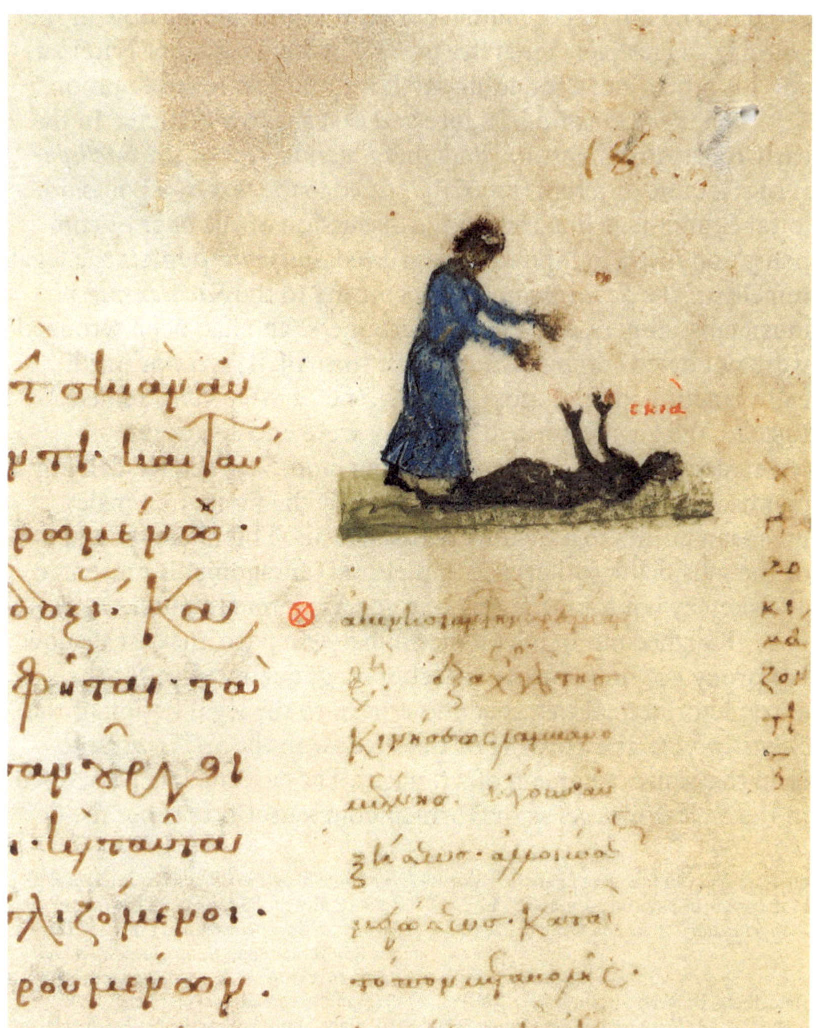

John of Climacus, The Heavenly Ladder, late eleventh century, Constantinople.
Vatican, Biblioteca Apostolica Vaticana, Vat. Gr. 394, detail of fol. 18r.

Fig. 527

ground. The mirrored, mutual desire of figure and shadow in the painting suggestively reiterates the fatal mutual regard of Narcissus and his reflection: a founding myth for mimetic representation.[42]

The relationship of figure and cast shadow depicted in the early fourteenth-century Heidelberg manuscript of the *Sachsen-spiegel* is quite different [fig. 529].[43] Cued to the text by a Lombardic letter S, an image illustrating the discussion of the *buze* or compensation owed to injured or aggrieved *Spielleute* depicts the legal remedy of the *Schattenbuße*.[44] According to the *Sachsenspiegel*, musicians, singers, and other entertainers who had been wronged were not owed compensation in the form of *Wergeld* or juridically sanctioned retaliatory violence (i.e., a *ius talionis* remedy). Instead, the law prescribed that they were entitled to the wrongdoer's cast shadow and nothing more.[45] In the Heidelberg manuscript's image of this *Schattenbuße*, the figure of a male musician points to a shadow that is not his. This shadow-image of the musician's (otherwise unpictured) antagonist is presented as a sketchy contour drawing of a generic human figure.

Roughed out in ink on the animal-skin page, the cast shadow is a proxy not only for the unseen wrongdoer, but also for the extrapictorial, real cast shadows crucial to the legal fiction of the *Schattenbuße*: the drawing of the shadow in the *Sachsenspiegel* is, in this sense, a figment of a figment. The cast shadow prescribed in the *Sachsenspiegel* as the form of compensation proper to

42
On Narcissus as a founding figure for accounts of the origin of painting, see Stoichiță: *A Short History of the Shadow*, pp. 31–41.

43
Heidelberg, Universitätsbibilothek, Cod. Pal. germ. 164, fol. 20r. A catalog description, bibliography and digital facsimile of the manuscript is available from the Heidelberg University Library, https://digi.ub.uniheidelberg.de/diglit/cpg164.

44
"Spilluten unde allen den, de sich ze eigene geben, den gibit man ze buze den schaten eines mannes": Eike (von Repgow), *Sachsenspiegel*, III, 45 § 9, quoted from Friedrich Ebel, ed., *Sachsenspiegel: Landrecht und Lehnrecht* (Stuttgart: Reclam, 1993), p. 141. On legal conceptions and juridical treatments of *Spielleute* see Harald Lacina, *Die Spielleute nach spätmittelalterlichen deutschen Rechtsquellen* (Kiel: Solivagus Verlag, 2010). For further discussion of *Schattenbuße* and other *Scheinbuße*, see Rolf Stratmann, *Die Scheinbussen im mittelalterlichen Recht*, Rechtshistorische Reihe 5 (Frankfurt am Main: Peter Lang, 1978); Dietlinde Munzel, "Schattenbuße, Scheinbuße," in *Handwörterbuch zur deutschen Rechtsgeschichte* 4, Adalbert Erler and Ekkehard Kaufmann, eds. (Berlin: Schmidt, 1990), pp. 1358–1360.

45
Whereas the *Sachsenspiegel* prescribes that the wrongdoer's shadow should be "given" (*geben*) as a penalty or compensation (*buze*), the *Schwabenspiegel* envisions permitting the *Spilman* to inflict whatever injury he received upon the wrongdoer's shadow. For further discussion, see Lacina, *Die Spielleute*, pp. 83–89.

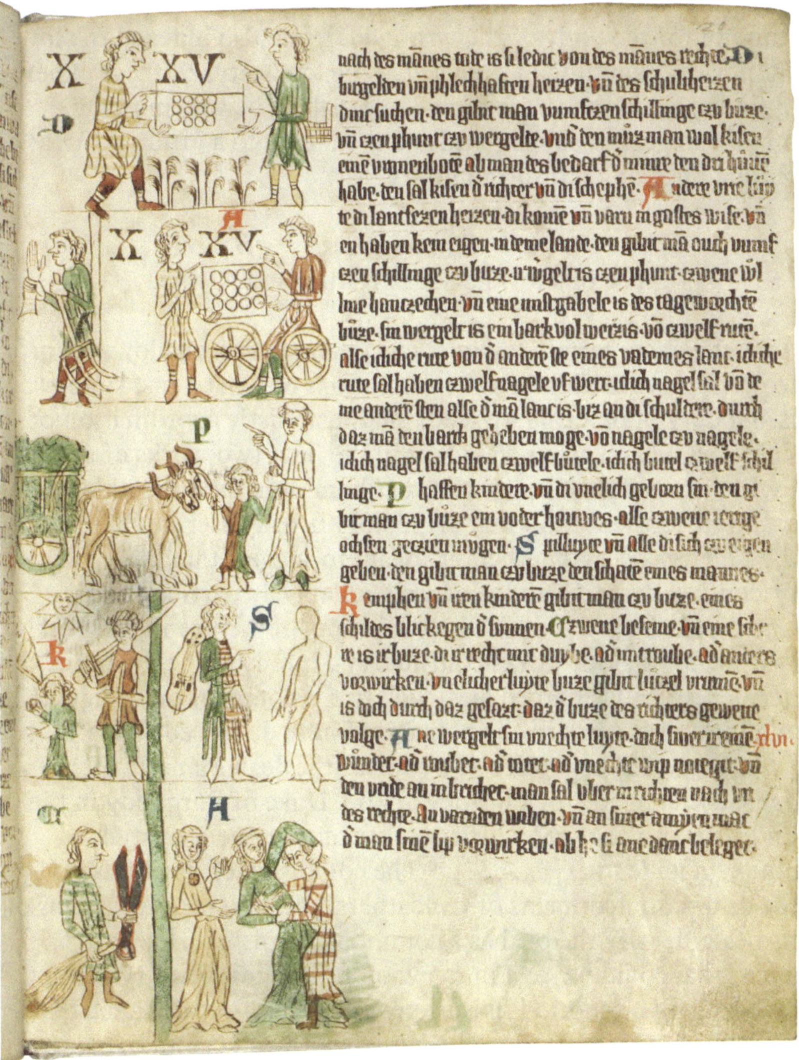

The Heidelberg Sachsenspiegel, early 14th century, east central Germany (Thuringia?). Heidelberg, Universitätsbibliothek, Cod. Pal. germ. 164, fol. 20r.

Spielleute, was, of course, a denigrating legal device that not only stood in for the body of the wrongdoer, but also indexed the low, "honorless" standing of *Spielleute*. The low status of these experts in fiction-making—professional tale-tellers, players in pantomimes, singers of songs—entitled them only to a juridical *Schattenspiel* that added insult to injury.

Counterfacts: The Shadow between Nature and Artifice

At first glance, certain late medieval painted cast shadows seem to conform to art-historical expectations of what a cast shadow is and does in painting. Indeed, the illusionistic coordination of light, figure, and ground evident in the final two works of art I will discuss could be construed as heralding the epistemic and aesthetic reorientation that art history usually ascribes to the Renaissance. Nonetheless, I want to suggest that these two fifteenth-century works of art self-reflexively participate in a medieval tradition of shadow painting. In their renderings of cast shadows, both works continue and intensify the inventive, hermeneutically charged approach to the conjunction of figure and ground at work in the paintings I have discussed above.

In the lower border of a copy of the Jean Mansel's *Fleur des histoires*, made for Philippe le Bon, Duke of Burgundy in the mid-fifteenth century, a bird perches on a segment of stylized blue vegetal tendril [fig. 531].[46] The coloration of its plumage, the differentiated forms of its feathers, and the shape and color of its beak identify the bird as a common Kingfisher (*Alcedo atthis*), a bird that could be seen in the wild in fifteenth-century Europe and can still be spotted in Europe today. Carefully depicted in the margin of the manuscript, the Kingfisher would seem to confirm the new interest in the direct study of nature and the rise of artistic naturalism that art history credits with inaugurating, or else announcing the Renaissance.

46
The manuscript is the second volume of a two-volume copy of the text (the first volume is Paris, Bibliothèque de l'Arsenal, MS 5087). A colophon in MS 5088 (fol. 345r) indicates that the "*les hystores romaines*" were "*abregies et achevees*" in Hesdin on November 19, 1454. The illuminator Loyset Liédet was paid for the illumination of the manuscript (the second volume of the two-volume copy of the work) in 1460, but other illuminators were certainly

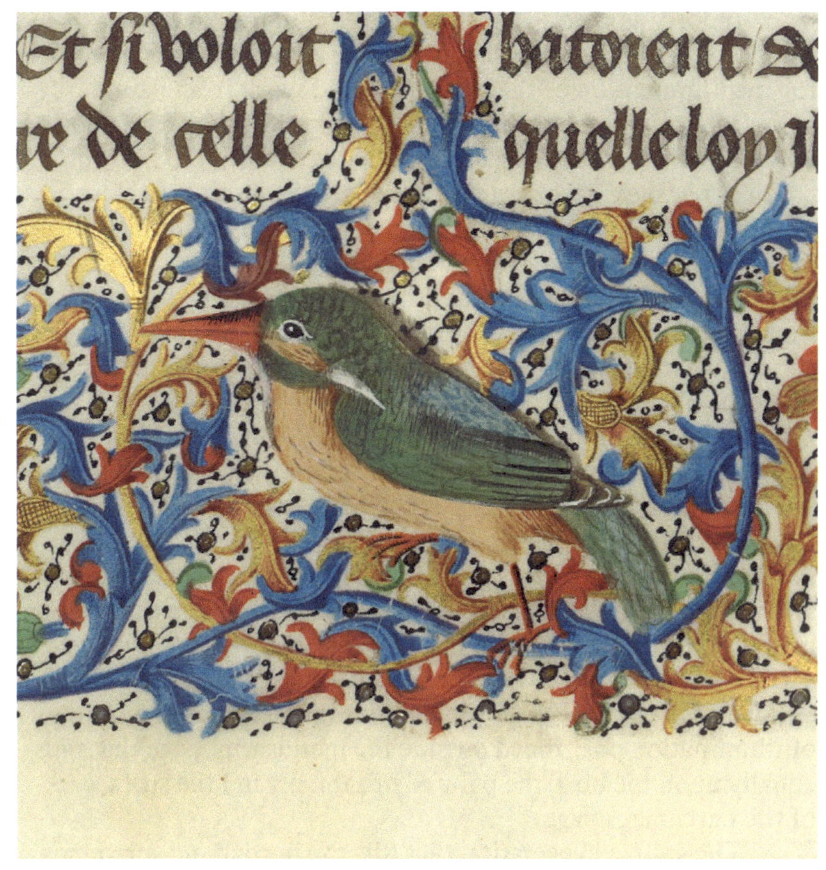

Detail of Fig. 534.

Indeed, as Otto Pächt showed, the illuminator Simon Marmion (ca. 1425–1489), a collaborator with the artist responsible for the illumination of the Kingfisher, did work from nature, at least in its stilled, taxidermical state [fig. 533].[47] A meticulous study of a Hoopoe bearing an inscribed attribution to Marmion credibly testifies, Pächt argued, to the artist's interest in close observation of *realia*, even as the majority of his paintings perpetuated a medieval tradition depicting supernatural subjects. The meticulous, naturalistic approach to depiction evident in Marmion's rendering of the Hoopoe's feathers and coloration is further corroborated by the specular reflection of a light source upon the bird's eyeball.

Like Marmion's Hoopoe, the painted Kingfisher's eye also reflects a light source, seemingly situated in the beholder's space outside the painting [fig. 534].[48] The little Kingfisher, however, has something that the depicted Hoopoe does not: namely, a subtle shadow that it casts upon the stylized painted vegetation and the parchment surface that surround it. Doubling the curved profile of the bird's back and the descent of its tail feathers, the shadow is coordinated with the specular light reflection upon the surface of the bird's eye. It, too, implies the presence of a source of illumination positioned outside the manuscript page that falls equally upon the bird, the painted ornament, and the surface of the parchment page.

The stylized vegetation that fills the border and surrounds the Kingfisher is quite conventional for high-quality manuscripts produced within the Burgundian lands in the first-half of the fifteenth-century. Densely filled with exuberant vegetal tendrils painted in gold, blue, red, and green, this illuminated bower is filled with fantastic flora cultivated in the illuminator's hot house.

involved, including the Rambures Master. Nicole Reynaud identified a single hand in all of the manuscript's illuminated borders, an artist also responsible for the borders painted in Rouen, Bibliothèque municipal, MS I, 2 (927): François Avril and Nicole Reynaud, *Les manuscrits à peintures en France: 1440–1520* (Paris: Flammarion/Bibliothèque nationale, 1993), pp. 93–94 (cat. no. 44). For further discussion of the manuscript see Otto Pächt, "Simon Mormion myt der handt," *Revue de l'Art* 46 (1979), pp. 7–15 at p. 12. For the BnF's online catalog entry (with further bibliography) and a full digital surrogate of MSS 5087-5088, see https://archivesetmanuscrits.bnf.fr/ark:/12148/cc85294t.

47
Pächt, "Simon Mormion myt der handt."

48
As observed in Pächt, "Simon Mormion myt der handt," p. 12.

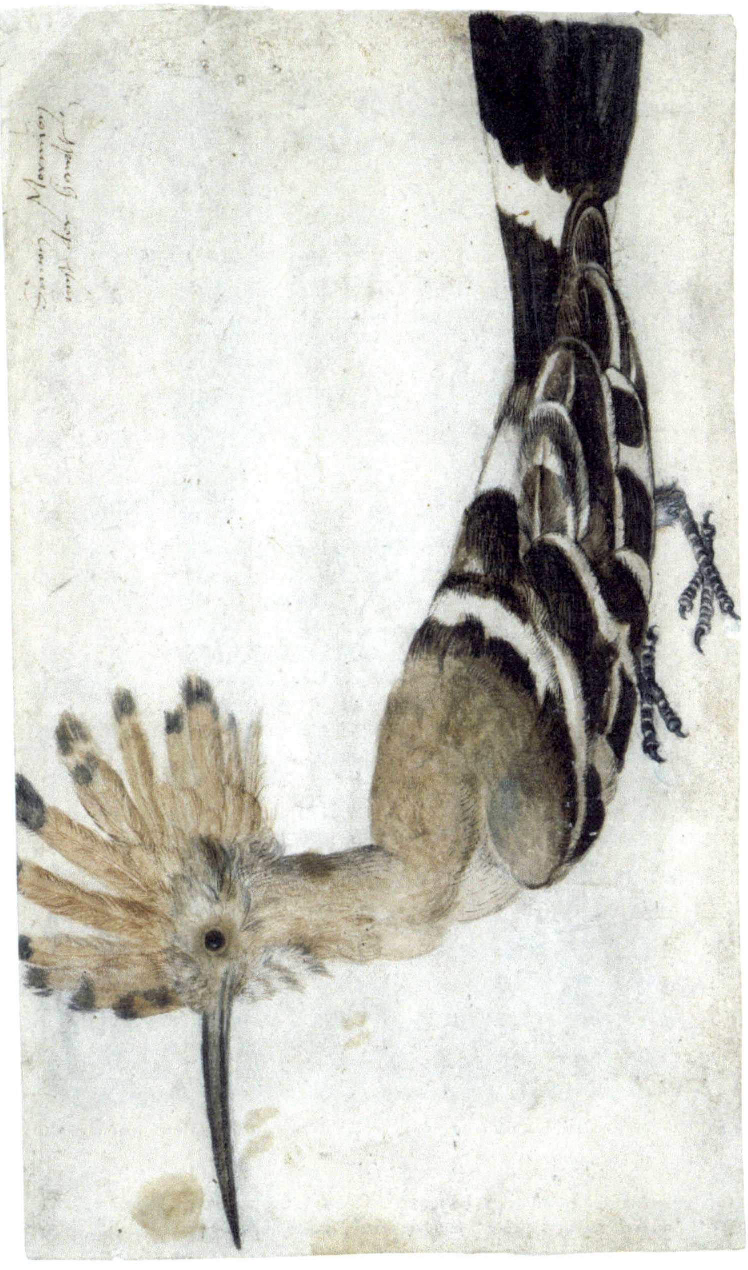

Simon Marmion, Study of a Hoopoe, fifteenth century.
Vienna, Österreichische Nationalbibliothek, Cod. Min. 42, fol. 55r.

Fig. 533

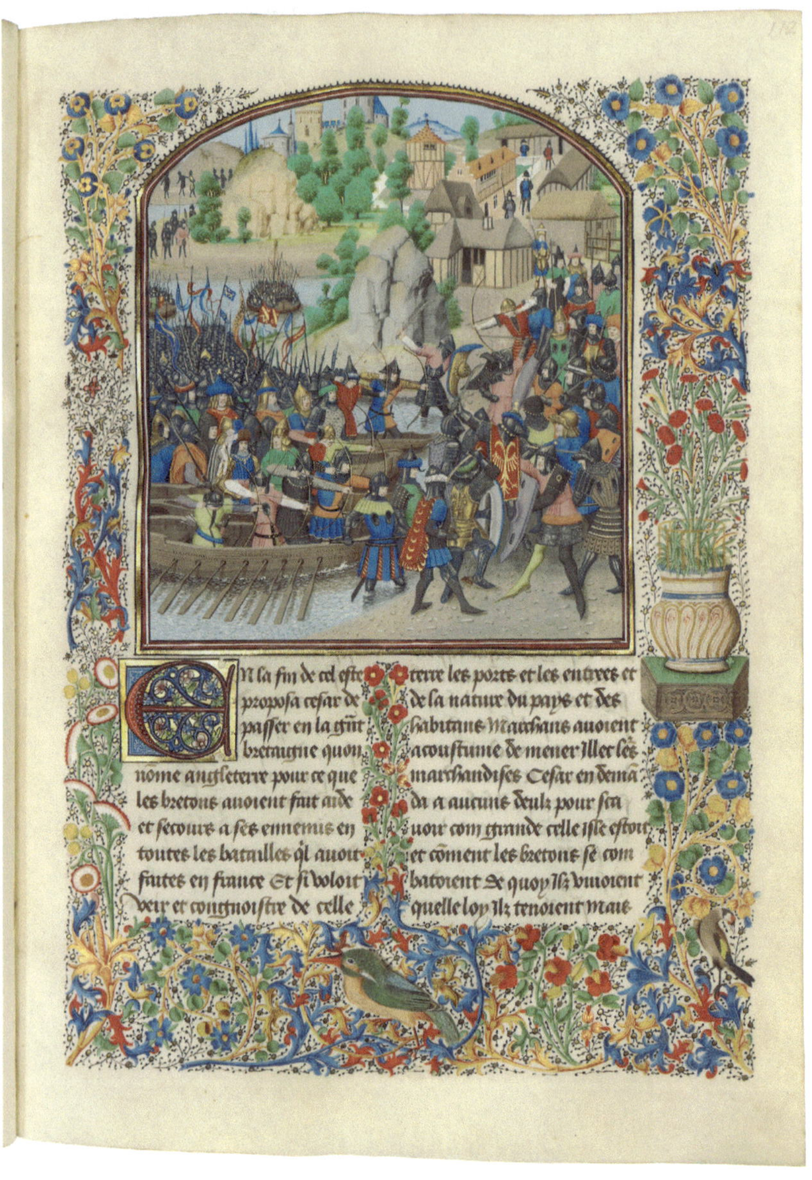

Jean Mansel, La Fleur des histoires, ca. 1454–1456, made for Philippe le Bon.
Paris, Bibliothèque de l'Arsenal, MS 5088, fol. 112r.

Fig. 534

The non- or anti-naturalistic character of the painted vegetation is further heightened by small golden circles, outlined in black and sprouting short wriggling lines, that punctuate the border.

The insistently naturalistic painting of both the Kingfisher and its discrete cast shadow works a queer magic upon this exuberantly stylized vegetation. Collaborating with the bright painted reflection upon the bird's eyeball and with the naturalistic rendering of its feathers and beak, the bird's shadow subtly, yet effectively defamiliarizes the ornamental reflexes of fifteenth-century northern European illumination. The modest cast shadow invites us to perceive a slight interval of space between the form of the bird and the ground upon which its shadow falls. In that interval, the shadow optically and conceptually spans a shift from the volumetric to the planar. In that transitional space, measured by the shadow, the illuminator slyly insinuates an ontological distinction between the small bird lit by extra-pictorial light and the vivid pigments, gold leaf, and ink lines of the vegetal ornament painted upon the flat surface of the parchment. The bird's form interrupts our view of the ornamental bower it occupies; the reach of its shadow dims the vibrant hues of painted ornament and the bright creamy-white surface of the page.

Nonetheless, the longer one looks, the more one perceives how the implied space between figure and ground is too slight to accommodate the volumetric form of the bird. Heightening this paradoxical perceptual situation, the aniconic gold disks outlined in black that surround the bird's figure possess an optical salience: they press forward, as if through the shadow, closing the gap between nature and artifice. If we perceptually assent to the cast shadow's proposal, we must conclude that the bird is a paradoxical creature. Invested with volume and casting a shadow upon the parallel plane of the parchment page and its painted ornament, the Kingfisher also, somehow, perches upon a segment of blue ornamental vegetation.

We might conclude that the Kingfisher's cast shadow "does not work"; that is, that it fails the test of convincing naturalism or illusionism. But, of course, it does work. With it, the illuminator invites us to an artful perceptual game that subverts the physics and ecology of a real Kingfisher perched in the natural world. The painted Kingfisher's cast shadow is a deft artistic gambit that playfully calls into question the relation of figure to ground, and with it the putative boundary between the artificial and the natural, between the world made by painting and the world in which we see painting on the page and, perhaps, actual birds and their ephemeral shadows.

Of course, the stylized vegetal ornament painted in the manuscript is just as real as the painted Kingfisher and a real bird in the real world. Indeed, the fantastic vegetation, painted with the same pigments as the fictive bird, belongs to a counterfactual space carved out within the real world. This point comes home, when we consider the larger habitat of the bird and the vegetation [fig. 534]. Seeing the painted Kingfisher in the full context of the manuscript page puts its cast shadow into perspective. The bird and its shadow are nested within a larger, quite complex composition of visual representation and words. They are rendered at a scale that diverges from the heroic action of the framed miniature, with its scene of an army disembarking from ships. And the Kingfisher and its shadow are also depicted out of proportion to the other fictive birds and objects represented in the border. No attempt at unified space and light obtains within the page as a whole. The coordinates of the mise-en-page are fundamentally planar and the artists responsible for the miniature and the painted border worked both with and against the grain of this insistent planarity. The naturalistic Kingfisher standing on a segment of resolutely artificial blue rinceau is a chimera in this flat world of artifice. Its shadow subtly effects a paradoxical coincidence of volume and plane, of nature and art, in the interval between figure and ground that it spans.

Whereas the cast shadow of the painted Kingfisher revels in painting's counterfactual powers—its ability to simulate the volumetric on and within a plane—only to call into question the painted bird's illusory existence between three and two dimensions, in the final work I will discuss a painted cast shadow is deftly deployed upon the surface of sculptural figure as if it were no painting at all.

Counterfacts: The Shadow's Reach

In a polychrome wood sculpture of John the Baptist in the collection of the Augustinermuseum in Freiburg, one can see a shadow cast in circa 1470–1480 [fig. 538].[49] Projected upon the surface of the figure's golden mantle, the shadow seems to register the blocking of light by the Baptist's upraised right forearm and hand. In an evenly lit photograph this shadow is exceedingly difficult to see [fig. 539]. Enclosed within a vitrine and lit from above by artificial lights in the museum, the shadow initially appears to be a real cast shadow produced by gallery lighting interacting with the plastic form of the figure's right forearm and hand. This appearance is, however, deceptive.

At some point in its history, the fingers of sculpture's right hand were lost. In the shadow seemingly cast upon the golden outer surface of figure's mantel, however, the extended index and middle finger of the Baptist's right hand are still visible [fig. 538]. Registering the original, undamaged state of the sculpture, the shadow is, in fact, a *painting* of a cast shadow.

When the sculpture was cleaned and treated in 2009, the conservator, Susanne Fenkes (Augustinermuseum und Museum für Neue Kunst, Freiburg), made a careful report of her findings concerning the condition of the sculpture.[50] As one would expect, she found considerable overpainting in several areas of the sculpture; the golden outer surface of the mantle with its painted cast shadow is not among them.[51]

49
Augustiner Museum, Freiburg, inv. nr. S 53/1; likely made in Straßbourg, ca. 1470–1480. Although the Augustiner Museum and Roland Recht attribute the sculpture to Niclaus Hagenauer, in her recent study of Hagenauer's oeuvre, Berenike Berentzen rejects this attribution; see Berenike Berentzen, *Patientia und passions: Studien zum bildhauerischen Werk des Niclaus Hagenower* (Petersberg: Michael Imhof Verlag, 2014), pp. 288–289, cat. no. VII.1. See further Detlef Zinke, *Bildwerke des Mittelalters und der Renaissance, 1100–1530: Auswahlkatalog* (Munich: Hirmer, 1995), pp. 64–67, cat. no. 27; Roland Recht, *Nicolas de Leyde et la sculpture à Strasbourg (1460–1525)* (Strasbourg: Presses Universitaires de Strasbourg, 1987), pp. 276–277, p. 361, cat. no. V.13.

50
I owe great thanks to Sabrina Kunz, restorer at the Städtische Museen Freiburg, for kindly providing me with a copy of Susanne Fenkes's 2009 conservation and restoration report. As Fenkes notes, her findings were based on unassisted and stereomicroscopic observation of the sculpture: Susanne Fenkes, "Konservierungs- und Restaurierungsbericht," unpublished report, dated June 2009, p. 2.

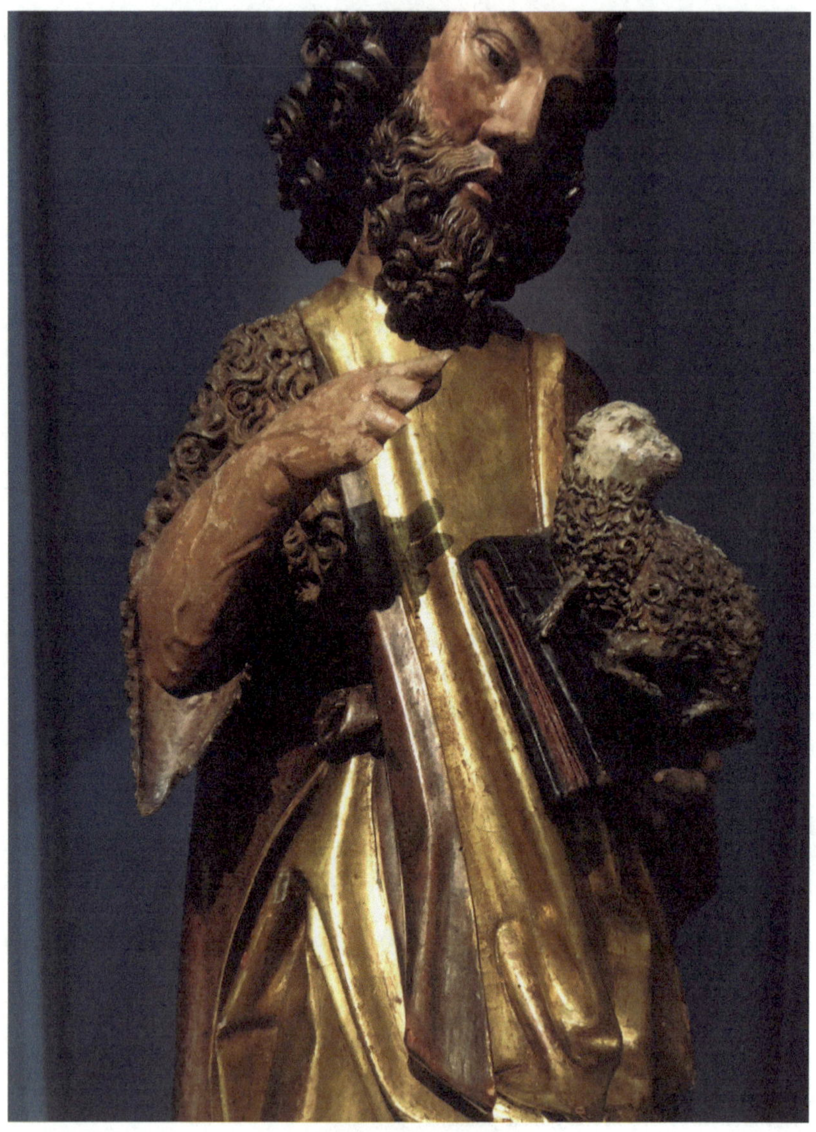

Detail of Fig. 539.

Fig. 538

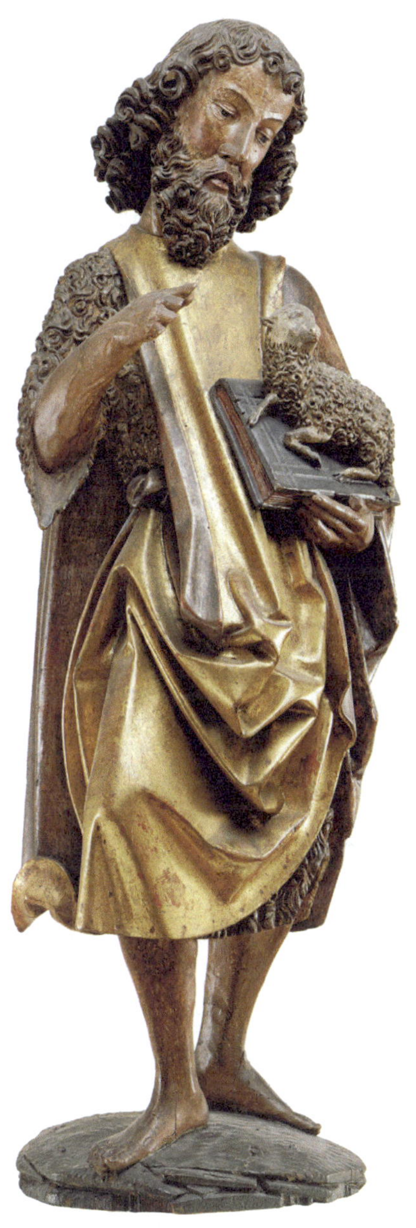

Niclaus Hagenauer (?), St. John the Baptist, ca. 1480, carved limewood with medieval and post-medieval polychromy. Augustinermuseum, inv. nr. S 53/001, Freiburg im Breisgau.

Fig. 539

The cast shadow of the Baptist's right hand was painted in a layer (or layers) of green glaze upon the gilt surface of the drapery.[52] The glazing of metal foils applied to wood sculpture was a widespread practice, already attested in the Romanesque period.[53] Such glazes were applied to manipulate the hue, as well as the reflective and refractive qualities of foils.[54] So, too, glazes were applied to the concavities of drapery folds in order to enhance both the plastic articulation of recessive depth and as a further aid in the differentiated simulation of materials and their surface qualities (e.g., applied embroideries, lampases, damask silks, pile-on-pile velvets etc.).[55]

51
Indeed, the golden outer surface of the mantle (with the exception of its lower hem) is the only area of the sculpture that the 2009 report identifies as being "in einem guten Zustand": Fenkes, "Konservierungs- und Restaurierungsbericht," p. 4. By contrast, the report inventories multiple layers of overpainting and/or the loss of original paint layers, as well as ground, in the inner surface of the mantle, the camelhair tunic, the skin, the plinth, the lamb, and the book held by the figure. It should be noted that the depicted shadow cast by the figure's right hand is not mentioned in the report.

52
The 2009 report identifies the golden outer surface of the mantle as composed of three layers: a ground, a red poliment layer, and gold leaf; no mention of glazing is made: Fenkes, "Konservierungs- und Restaurierungsbericht," p. 7. On medieval polychrome wood sculpture see Michele D. Marincola and Lucretia Kargère, *The Conservation of Medieval Polychrome Wood Sculpture: History, Theory, Practice* (Los Angeles: The Getty Conservation Institute, 2020); Kaja Kollandsrud, *Evoking the Divine: The Visual Vocabulary of Sacred Polychrome Wooden Sculpture in Norway between 1100 and 1350*, PhD diss. (University of Oslo, 2017); Johannes Taubert, *Polychrome Sculpture: Meaning, Form, Conservation*, Michele D. Marincola, ed., trans. Carola Kleinstück-Schulman (Los Angeles: The Getty Conservation Institute, 2015).

53
For further discussion of the use of metal foils and the application of varnishes, glazes, and/or egg white or glue wash upon such foils, see especially Kollandsrud, *Evoking the Divine*, pp. 146–161 passim; Marincola and Kargère, *The Conservation of Medieval Polychrome Wood Sculpture*, pp. 42–51; Renate Woudhuysen-Keller, "Aspects of Painting Technique in the Use of Verdigris and Copper Resinate," in *Historical Painting Techniques, Materials, and Studio Practice: Preprints of a Symposium, University of Leiden, the Netherlands, 26–29 June, 1995*, Arie Wallert, Emma Hermens, Marja Peek, eds. (Los Angeles: The Getty Conservation Institute, 1995), pp. 65–69; Kaja Kollandsrud and Unn Plahter, "Twelfth and Early Thirteenth Century Polychromy at the Northernmost Edge of Europe: Past Analyses and Future Research," *Medievalista Online* 26 (2019), http://journals.openedition.org/medievalista/2303; Unn Plahter, "Norwegian Art Technology in the Twelfth and Thirteenth Centuries: Materials and Techniques in a European Context," *Zeitschrift für Kunsttechnologie und Konservierung* 28 (2014): pp. 298–332; Unn Plahter, "Medieval Painting Materials and Techniques in Norway: To What Extent Did the Painters Atempt to Simulate Goldsmith's Work?" *Zeitschrift für Konservierung* 24 (2010): pp. 160–168.

54
Kollandsrud and Plahter, "Twelfth and Early Thirteenth Century," pp. 27–29; Kollandsrud, *Evoking the Divine*, pp. 135–167 et passim; Kristin Kausland, "Setting the Stage, Framing the Picture; the Gilding and Polychromy of Late Medieval Altarpiece Structures in the North," *CLARA* 5 (2020): pp. 1–21.

The cast shadow painted on the Freiburg sculpture is another thing entirely. The painted cast shadow activates the negative space separating the sculpture's raised right forearm and hand from its torso as the space of the medium, understood in perspectivist terms. Across this interval, the figure's shadow reaches, unseen, until it appears as a ghostly second hand upon the golden folds of the Baptist's mantle. In this fashion, the feigned shadow simulates the blocking of light upon the reflective surface of the Baptist's golden mantle. It transforms the surface of the figure into a ground upon which the figure's own shadow seems to be projected.

Implying the existence of a luminous cause external to the sculpture—that is, a strong light source located above the figure on its right side—the painted cast shadow registers the sculpture's spatial relation to that feigned, illusory light source and qualifies that light as falling upon the sculpture at a certain angle of incidence, with a certain intensity. Within this counterfactual situation the painted shadow proposes that the Baptist's carved right forearm and hand act like the gnomon of a sundial.[56] Yet, unlike the moving shadow cast by a gnomon over the surface of a sundial, the shadow cast upon the surface of the Baptist's golden mantle does not lengthen, shorten, or change position. Frozen in painting, its immutability implies an equally unchanging light source. This fictive light source is not the even glow of luminous

55
The John the Baptist sculpture discussed here seems to preserve painted "attached" or "primary" shadows in the recesses of the outer surface of its golden mantle. I make this observation tentatively; both the vitrine and strong reflections from the gallery lighting make visual inspection of passages of the outer surface of the mantle cast into strong (real, not painted) shadow difficult. The 2009 conservation and restoration report does not identify any painted shadows (be they modeling shadows or cast shadows) in the sculpture's polychromy. On the simulation of luxury textiles in polychrome sculpture, see Ingrid Geelen and Delphine Steyaert, *Imitation and Illusion: Applied Brocade in the Art of the Low Countries in the Fifteenth and Sixteenth Centuries*, Scientia Artis 6 (Brussels: Koninklijk Instituut voor het Kunstpatrimonium, 2011); Ariane Pinto and Florian Bouquet, "Imiter des tissus de prestige par une technique prestigieuse : les 'brocarts appliqués,'" *E-Phaïstos*, X–2 (2022), https://doi.org/10.4000/ephaistos.10599, http://journals.openedition.org/ephaistos/10599; Laurence Rivière Civaldini, ed., "Imiter le textile en polychromie à la fin du Moyen Âge: Le cas du brocart appliqué," *CeROArt*, hors-série (2021), https://doi.org/10.4000/ceroart.6943, https://journals.openedition.org/ceroart/6943.

56
Visual examination revealed no painting of highlights upon the surface of the figure corresponding to this fictive light source: the feigning of its existence seems to be accomplished entirely through the simulated effect of its obstruction (the cast shadow) by the figure's right forearm and hand.

eternity, the putative "metaphysical light" that art historians have often attributed to medieval painting. Painted as if it were struck by a strong directed light, the sculptural form produces not *a* shadow, but *this* shadow.

Internal and integral to the sculpture, the painted cast shadow resolutely asserts the figure's place and participation in the phenomenal world; a sublunary world in which light interacts with real *corpora objecta,* be they living bodies or carved figures. In the Freiburg sculpture, the phenomenological dynamics of light are also dramatically activated by the golden mantle worn by the Baptist, whose polished metallic surface reflects light back to the beholder. Before it lost its gleam, the original silver surface of *agnus dei* perched upon the book held by the Baptist also caught and reflected light falling upon its form.

The illusionistic choreography of real reflected light and subtle, simulated cast shadow in the Freiburg sculpture is as hermeneutically charged as the selective cast shadows painted in the Codex Amiatinus's depiction of Ezra writing or the outpouring of divine shadow upon Mary's figure in the Hitda Codex's painting of the Annunciation. In medieval Christian typological exegesis, the "old dispensation" of the Mosaic law was often characterized as a shadowy regime, whose rites and prophecies obscurely contained and concealed the luminous revelation of Christ's future Incarnation, Passion, and messianic sacrifice.[57] Accordingly, the "era of Grace" was understood as a period of decisive salvific enlightenment; according to the Gospel of John (8:12), Christ himself taught: *Ego sum lux mundi: qui sequitur me, non ambulat in tenebris, sed habebit lumen vitae* ("I am the light of the world:

57
In this connection, Hebrews 10:1 ("For the law having a shadow of the good things to come, not the very image of the things") served as a major touchstone for Patristic and medieval Christian thinkers; for further discussion of the trope of the shadow/shadowy in medieval typology, see Erich Auerbach, "Figura," in *Scenes From the Drama of European Literature,* Theory and History of Literature 9, Erich Auerbach (Minneapolis, MN: University of Minnesota Press, 1984), pp. 11–76; Herbert L. Kessler, "'Thou Shalt Not Paint the Likeness of Christ Himself': The Mosaic Prohibition as Provocation for Christian Images," in *Spiritual Seeing: Picturing God's Invisibility in Medieval Art,* Herbert Kessler (Philadelphia: University of Pennsylvania Press, 2000), pp. 29–52; Sophie Schweinfurth, "When Writing Prefigures Painting : Some Remarks on 'Typology' within the Conception of the Byzantine Icon," in *Writing As Intermediary: Text-Image Relations in Early Modern Islamic Cultures,* Bamberger Orientstudien 16, Lorenz Korn and Berenike Metzler, eds. (Bamberg: University of Bamberg Press, 2022), pp. 45–64, https://fis.uni-bamberg.de/handle/uniba/57632.

he that followeth me, walketh not in darkness, but shall have the light of life").

The Precursor who foretold Christ's redemptive sacrifice as the *agnus dei*, John the Baptist was, according to Christian teaching, the last of the Jewish Prophets and a witness to Christ's two natures. As Jacobus de Voragine explained in his *Legenda Aurea:*

> John the Baptist has many titles. He is called prophet, friend of the bridegroom, lamp, angel, voice, Elijah, baptizer of the Savior, herald of the judge, and forerunner of the King. Each of these titles denotes a particular prerogative of John: the title of prophet, his prerogative of foreknowledge; the title of friend of the bridegroom, his prerogative of loving and being loved; burning light, his prerogative of sanctity; angel, his prerogative of virginity; voice, his prerogative of humility; Elijah, his prerogative of fervor; baptizer, the wonderful honor of baptizing the Lord; herald, the prerogative of preaching; and forerunner, the prerogative of preparation.[58]

For medieval Christians, John the Baptist was thus a "burning light" poised at the soteriological threshold between obscurity and illumination, announcing Christ's luminous *adventus* in the shadowy language of prophecy.[59]

In the Freiburg sculpture, John the Baptist's role in salvation history is conveyed through the iconographic conventions of

58 Jacobus de Voragine, *The Golden Legend: Readings on the Saints* 1, trans. William Granger Ryan (Princeton, NJ: Princeton University Press, 1993), p. 328.

59 The trope of John as an ardent source of illumination in the late Middle Ages is examined further in James Marrow, "John the Baptist, Lantern for the Lord: New Attributes for the Baptist from the Northern Netherlands," *Oud Holland* 83 (1968): pp. 3–12; James Marrow, "John the Baptist, Lantern for the Lord: A Supplement," *Oud Holland* 85 (1970): pp. 188–193. See also Kathleen Corrigan, "The Witness of John the Baptist on an Early Byzantine Icon in Kiev," *Dumbarton Oaks Papers* 42 (1988), pp. 1–11; Michael Alan Anderson, "The One Who Comes After Me: John the Baptist, Christian Time, and Symbolic Musical Techniques," *Journal of the American Musicological Society* 66 (2013): pp. 639–708; Jane Hawkes, Éamonn Ó Carragáin, Ross Trench-Jellicoe, "John the Baptist and the *Agnus Dei*: Ruthwell (and Bewcastle) Revisited," *The Antiquaries Journal* 81 (2001): pp. 131–153.

the *agnus dei*, the prophetic book upon which the lamb rests, and the figure's right hand raised in a gesture of prophetic blessing. Far more remarkable is how the Baptist's special status is artfully enacted in the choreography of light and cast shadow within and upon the carved and polychromed figure. The Freiburg figure's metallic gold mantle both reflects the light of the (real) world back to the beholder and serves as the ground for the arresting painted shadow cast by his gesture of prophetic blessing: together, reflected light and painted shadow situate the figure in a world determined by physics and metaphysics in equal measure.

At the meeting of figure and ground, medieval shadows took many forms. And many of these forms have little to do with what art history customarily wants from painted cast shadows. Although it is often assumed that cast shadows disappeared from the European artistic scene in the medieval period—as if the art of medieval Europe was flooded with impossibly even, ubiquitous, blinding light—the works of art I have discussed show that this is not true. Nor is it true that cast shadows first reappear in the late medieval European paintings only as precocious harbingers of a new regime of artistic naturalism or illusionism. The medieval painted cast shadows that I have examined tell a different story.

In the vast majority of medieval paintings, shadows do not appear at the meeting of light, figure, and ground. Never routinized or systematized, the painting of cast shadows in medieval Europe was always a choice, a deliberate pictorial deviation from established artistic conventions. The works I have discussed suggest, at least in a preliminary fashion, that painted cast shadows were highly motivated elements employed to meaningful ends in medieval images. In other words, the cast shadow was a rare, but potent hermeneutic device in medieval painting, whose presence invites the beholder to question and reflect upon what painting gives them to see and to understand. If many medieval shadows fail the test of naturalism, this is because they were devised to fulfill other aims, to serve as figures and grounds for other forms of pictorial truth.

Part 5
Transgressing Depth

David Bailly's *Portrait of a Painter with Vanity Symbols*, dated 1651 and signed, has provided us with a rich history of interpretation [fig. 547]. Despite many differences in approach and theory, it is generally understood as a painted autobiography in which there has been sustained reflection on the relationship between visibility and invisibility, between figure and ground. David Bailly's biography is known primarily from an entry in Jan Jansz. Orlers's *Beschrijvinge der stad Leyden* (*Description of the Town of Leiden*) from 1641, aside from a brief mention in Arnoldus Buchelius's *Res Pictorae* (between 1619 and 1639). Orlers tells of Bailly's living situation, of his encouragement by his father, who was a calligrapher and fencing master with close ties to the university, also of Bailly's training, first under the painter and engraver Jacques de Gheyn II (1565–1629) in Leiden and then under Adriaen Verburch (active in Amsterdam between 1587 and 1598), who had mainly made a name for himself as a surgeon but was also a successful painter.[1] In 1601, Bailly's family moved to Amsterdam for a few years. The family was originally from Antwerp but had left that city for religious reasons. In Amsterdam David Bailly trained further under the Antwerp portrait painter Cornelis van der Voort (1576–1624), who at precisely this time moved to Sint Anthoniespoort, more specifically into the house that Rembrandt would later purchase. Orlers also tells of Bailly's journeyman years, which in 1608 led him to Hamburg, Frankfurt, Nuremberg, Augsburg, and on to Venice and Rome. In 1613, David Bailly was back in Leiden devoting himself to portrait painting, then ten years later he exchanged his "clever brush," it is said, "for a sharp pen," and produced portrait drawings on parchment, mainly of Leiden university professors.[2]

1
Jan Jansz. Orlers, *Beschrijvinge der Stad Leyden* (Leiden, 1641), pp. 371–372.

2
See Arnold Houbraken, *De groote schouburgh der Nederlantsche konstschilders en schilderessen* (Amsterdam: B.M. Israël, 1976), pp. 118–119: "In dit zelve jaar is binnen de Stad Leiden geboren DAVID BAILII, Zoon van Pieter Bailii, die in zyn tyd een Konstig Schilder is geweest. Zyn Vader ziende in hem van der jeugt aan een natuurlyke drift tot de Konst doorsteken, liet hem eenigen tyd by zig zelven zoo wat teekenen naar prenten. By toeval gekomen op den winkel van Jaques de Geyn, kreeg hy genegenheid om het graafyzer te leeren behandelen, 't geen hy oeffende een jaar lang, en daar in wel toenam. Dog hebbende meerder zugt tot de Schilderkonst, besteeden hem zyn Vader by Adriaan Verburg om in de Konst onderwezen te worden, alhoewel hy zig in dien tyd geneerde met de geneeskonst te oeffenen, en bleef daar eenigen tyd, tot hy in den jare 1601 naar Amsterdam vertrok om

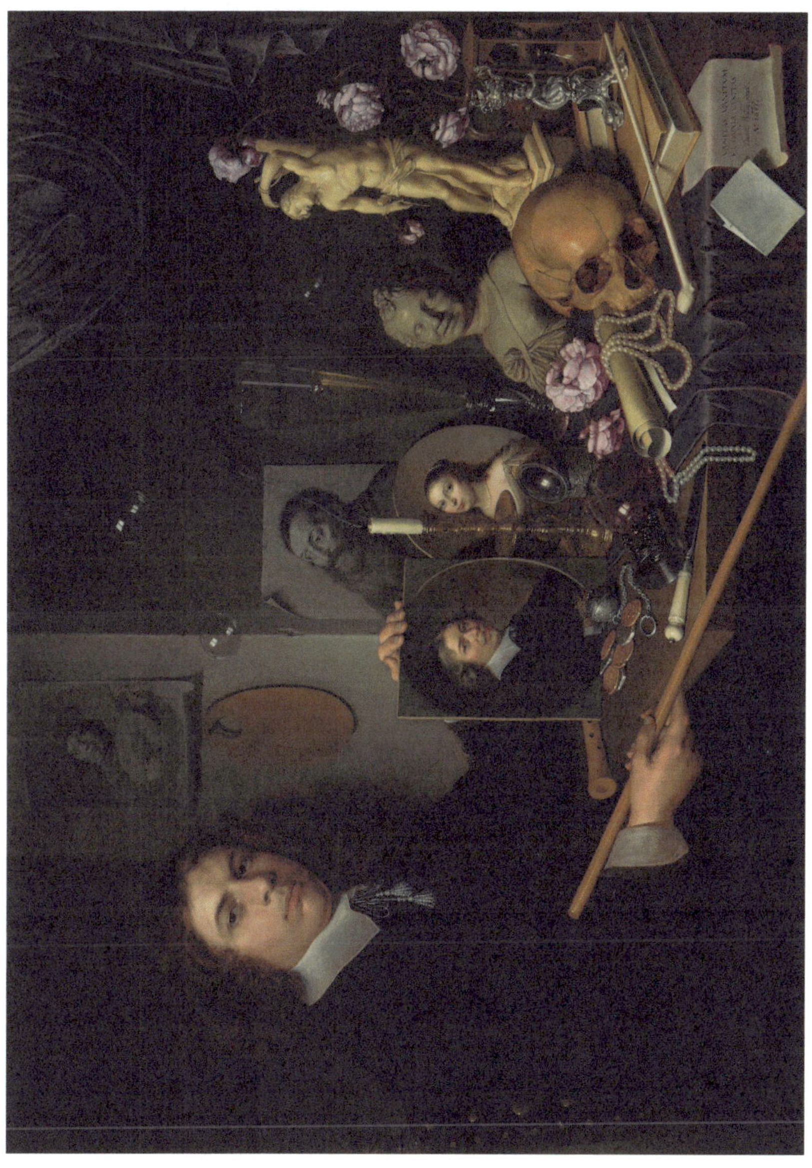

David Bailly, *Vanitas Still Life with Portrait of a Young Painter*, 1651, oil on panel, 89.5 × 122 cm. Museum De Lakenhal, inv. nr. S 1351, Leiden.

Fig. 547

Bailly's early reception history was first summarized by Josua Bruyn in 1951, and it was also Bruyn who pointed out the source published by Paul Mantz in 1860 that describes the unusual Bailly painting that will occupy us here.[3] Mantz had discussed the famous painting collection of Alexandre Dumont in Cambrai for the *Gazette des Beaux-Arts* and paid particular attention to the *Portrait of a Painter with Vanity Symbols* by David Bailly. According to Mantz it was a work of unique preciousness and rarity. Particularly unusual was its combination of portrait, on the one hand, and still life on the other, owing to which the composition as a whole was not altogether successful. Mantz describes it as follows: on one side of the canvas, almost in a corner, a young man is pictured seated at a table and holding a maulstick in his hand. He is dressed all in black with the exception of his white collar; his head is bare, his face brightly illuminated, his lips red and supple, his eyes filled with thoughts. This young dreamer, Mantz continues, is thus pictured next to a table on which David Bailly placed various objects that seemed to him best suited for expressing the brevity of human life: a piece of paper on the corner of

de Konst voort te zetten onder 't onderwys van Kornelis vander Voort, toen geagt den besten Pourtret Schilder, waar by hy omtrent zes jaren bleef. En alzoo dezelve veele konstige Schilderyen van andere meesters hadde, vond hy gelegenheid om 'er nu en dan een na te schildern, onder deeze was een Tempel van Steenwyk, dien hy zoo konstig naargebootst had, dat de gemelde Steenwyk bezwaahet een stuk van het andere konde onderkennen. Van Amsterdam weder tot Leiden gekomen, maalde hem de reislust in' hoofd. Dus vertrok hy in den Wintertyd 1608, naar Hamborg; daar van daan naar Duitschland, tot Frankfoort, Noremborg, Augsborg, en verscheide andere Steden; door Tirol naar Venetien, en van daar tot Romen, om de behandelinge der Italiaansche Konstschilders, waar 't mogelyk, af te zien, en een lange wyl verblyf te nemen; maar zeker toeval deed hem, als hy daar niet lang geweest was, van voornemen veranderen en weder naar Venetien keeren; daar hy maar vyf maanden bleef, en van daar genoegzaam weder langs den zelven weg dien hy van te vooren gereist had, naar zyn Vaderland keerde; dit was in 't jaar 1610. Door Duitschland naar beneden komende heeft hy verscheiden Hoven aangedaan, daar hy een staal van zy Konst tot gedagtenis liet, inzonderheid aan 't Hof van Brunswyk, daar hem de Hertog een jaarlykse wedde wilde toeleggen, zoo hy zig voor eenige jaren tot zyn dienst wilde verbinden, 't welk hy afsloeg. Endelyk wars van 't reizen, is hy in den jare 1613 weder tot Leiden gekomen, om, als hy uitgerust zoude hebben, zyn Konst in stilheid te oeffenen. De menschen (zeit het spreekwoord) leven by veranderinge: dit is aan onzen David Bailii, ook gebleken, want in den jare 1623, verwisselde hy zyn kloek penceel, voor de fyn versnede Pen; en teekend veele Pourtretten uitvoerig, met inkt, (die hy dan met het penceel voort opmaakte) op parkement, daar de lief hebbeers van de Konst groot genoegen in hadden."

3

Josua Bruyn, "David Bailly: 'Fort bon peintre en pourtraicts et en vie coye,'" in *Oud Holland* *66* (1951), pp. 148–164.

the table bears in very clear letters the melancholy formula: *Vanitas vanit[at]um et omnia vanitas*. The young philosopher's hand rests on a portrait of David Bailly himself, recognizable from his Louis XIII beard and gray hair. Next to this in another oval picture the figure of a young woman is portrayed, the embodiment of beauty as a transient quality. Nearby are a clock that tells how swiftly time passes, a few gold coins, a candlestick with a candle that has just been snuffed out, a tumbler that has tipped over, roses, a skull, a book, an hourglass, an ivory statuette, a female bust, a half-full champagne flute through which the image of voluptuousness becomes visible, and a few soap bubbles on which a ray of light plays and whose fragile structure will dissolve into mist—all of them ultimately symbols that indicate that a man lives but for a day and that his pursuits are but phantoms, mere chimeras.

According to Mantz, the flaw in this painting, which basically presents us with two paintings in one—portrait and still life—is its lack of subordination, the inordinate importance accorded to the objects placed on the table next to the painter dressed in black. David Bailly has namely painted the face of the earnest young man with the same passion as the "philosophical rummage" arrayed before him to illustrate the futility of all human effort. It is for that reason, so that the face of the young thinker does not disappear among the thousand details that surround him, that it is executed with such brightness and animation. The contrast between his alert eyes, the slightly parted lips, and the lively hair and the inanimate things is necessary in terms of picture structure. In this early analysis, therefore, Mantz recognized a great deal, and with his emphasis on the hybrid picture structure, expressing in its content a tension between animate and inanimate life, between vitality and stasis, he gave us a first interpretation. Mantz also identified the self-portrait of Bailly in the small oval picture, and dismissed the young painter into anonymity. But what is most astonishing is how Mantz saw the apparitional female figure rising up behind the half-filled champagne flute as unsurprising, and in a brief comment characterized the chimera as a vaguely recognizable image of voluptuousness.[4]

4
Paul Mantz, "Collections d'amateurs I. Le Cabinet de M. A. Dumont, a Cambrai," in *Gazette des Beaux-Arts* 8 (1896), p. 306.

The specter must have made an impression, for in an exhibition review from 1874 Alfred Darcel would once again go into the picture's hybrid nature. He thus repeated Mantz's assessment, but also included an illustration that quite clearly shows the ominous female portrait that Mantz mentions only peripherally [fig. 551].[5] To be sure, a wood engraving is not an ideal medium in which to capture the nebulous and ephemeral. All the more interesting, therefore, is the differentiation and separation of the woman's head from the ground, so that the specter becomes a clearly outlined figure [fig. 552]. This shows us that in the nineteenth century it was clearly visible and understood to be an integral part of the composition.

Chasing the Specter

But how has scholarship since then perceived Bailly's mysterious woman's head and interpreted it? Astonishingly, despite having been written about and exhibited in the nineteenth century, over the following hundred years the specter would lead—literally—only a shadowy existence. Kjell Boström, who in 1949 worked on a comprehensive study of Dutch still life painting and tried to gather together the few surviving still lifes by David Bailly, says not a word about the specter in his otherwise pathbreaking essay on Bailly's vanitas picture.[6] Likewise Ingvar Bergström, on whom Boström draws quite heavily, and who had previously discovered a Bailly drawing with vanitas motifs produced in 1624 for the *album amicorum* of Cornelis de Glarges (1599–1683), then Dutch ambassador to Calais.[7] Also Josua Bruyn, in the aforementioned article in *Oud Holland* from 1951, appears to have either failed to notice the specter or at least had no interest in it. Yet, Bruyn found an astonishing similarity between Bailly's self-portrait in the Rijksprentenkabinet and a portrait with vanitas motifs by Thomas de Keyser (1596–1667) that in its arrangement shows

5
Alfred Darcel, "Exposition de Lille," in *Gazette des Beaux-Arts* (1874), pp. 481–492.

6
Kjell Boström, "David Baillys stilleben," in *Konsthistorisk Tidstrif* 18 (1949), pp. 99–110.

7
Ingvar Bergström, *Studier i Holländskt Stillebenmåleri under 1600-talet*, PhD diss. (University of Gothenburg, 1947), p. XX.

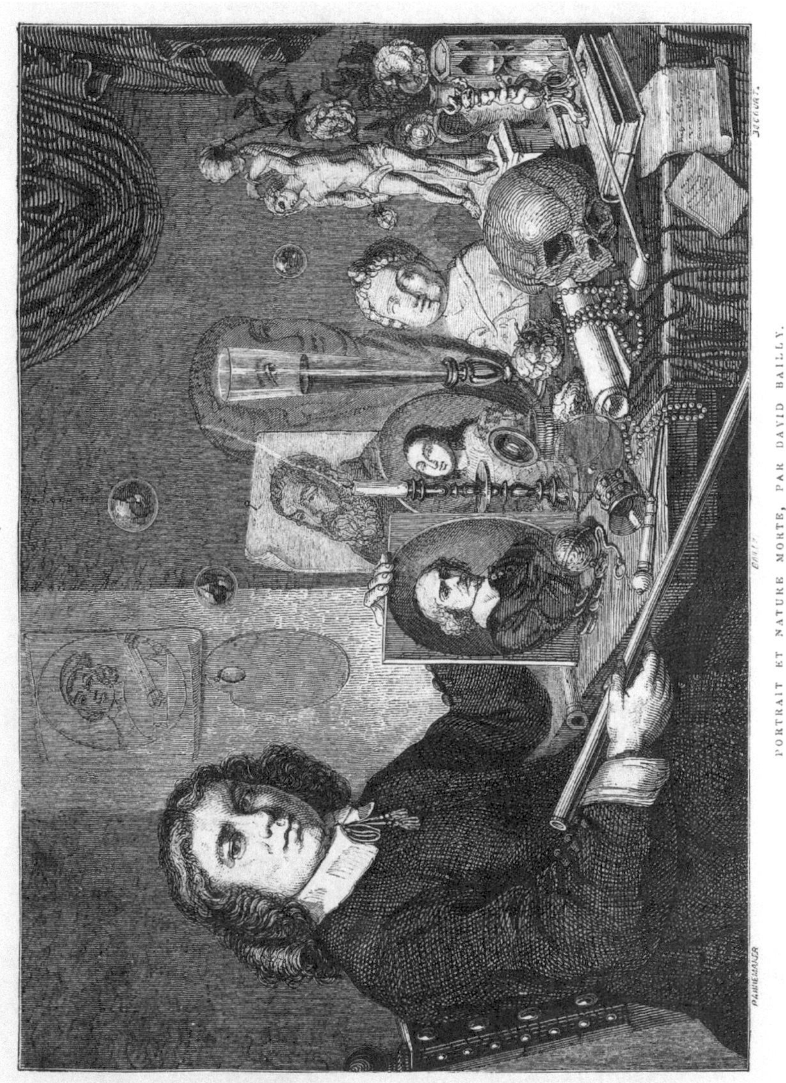

M. Pannemaker, *Portrait et Nature Morte, par David Bailly*, wood engraving from Alfred Darcel, "Exposition de Lille," in Gazette des Beaux-Arts (1874), p. 485.

Fig. 551

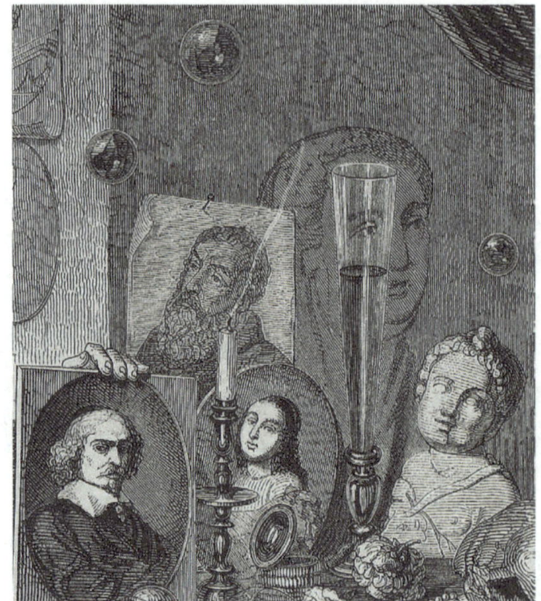

Detail of Fig. 551.

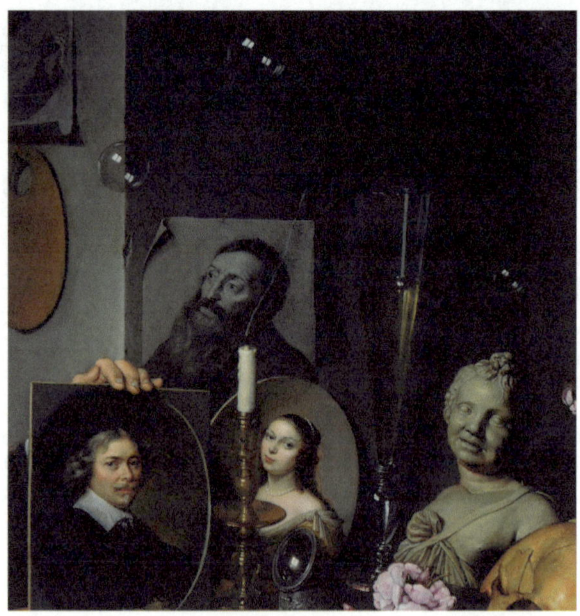

Detail of Fig. 547.

Fig. 552

clear parallels with the famous depiction of Constantijn Huygens (1596–1687) in the National Gallery, London [figs. 554 and 555]. In fact, the reference to Bailly is unmistakable, the Bailly portrait had obviously been patterned after the Amsterdam drawing, and there are a few objects in the picture—like the roll of paper next to the skull, for example—that are virtual trademarks of Bailly's. Bruyn therefore even assumed that De Keyser was responsible for the portrait of Bailly, while the still life in the picture had to be the work of Bailly himself. This attribution is questionable, but more important is Bruyn's observation that the female portrait in the open book that lies prominently on the table and functions almost like a second portrait is similar to the female portrait in the vanitas picture and depicts Bailly's wife Agneta. He shares this observation with the reader only in a footnote, to be sure, but it has been taken up by scholars and heatedly debated.

For example, in her comprehensive study of Bailly's vanitas painting from 1973, Naomi Popper-Voskuil once again confirmed the connection between the De Keyser painting and Bailly's vanitas picture and commented as follows: "Many of the objects recur on the painting of 1651: the skull and the parchment already mentioned, the female portrait showing a bust of a young woman, with a deep décolleté, while the small statue on the table and the lute on the wall have been transformed on the later painting into a standing statue and a lute-player respectively."[8] Unlike Bruyn, Popper-Voskuil makes no conjectures about the identity of the woman depicted in De Keyser's painting; however, she is also certain that the oval portrait in the Leiden vanitas picture represents Bailly's wife Agneta. As a comparison she refers to a double portrait of Bailly and his wife produced in the year of their marriage in 1642 [figs. 556 and 557]. Bailly had married very late; he was at that point already fifty-eight years old.

However, whereas Bailly's self-portrait in the Leiden vanitas picture is an exact copy of that image, the female portrait must be based on an earlier likeness. For Popper-Voskuil there is nevertheless no doubt about her identity, and she gives good reasons

8
Naomi Popper-Voskuil, "Selfportraiture and Vanitas Still-life Painting in 17th-Century Holland in Reference to David Bailly's Vanitas Oeuvre," *Pantheon* 31 (1973): pp. 58–74, here p. 58.

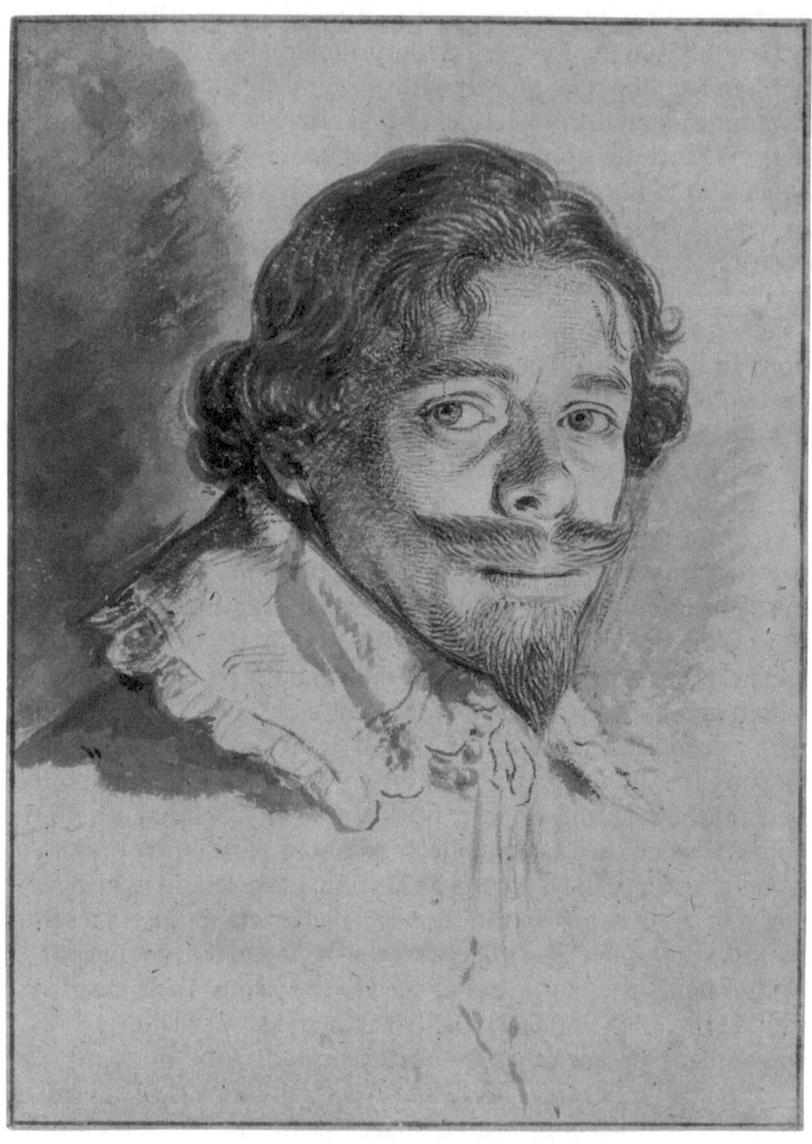

David Bailly, *Self-Portrait*, ca. 1625–1626, brush and black and gray ink, heightened with white body color, 164 × 122 mm. Rijksmuseum, inv. nr. RP-T-1913-11, Amsterdam.

Fig. 554

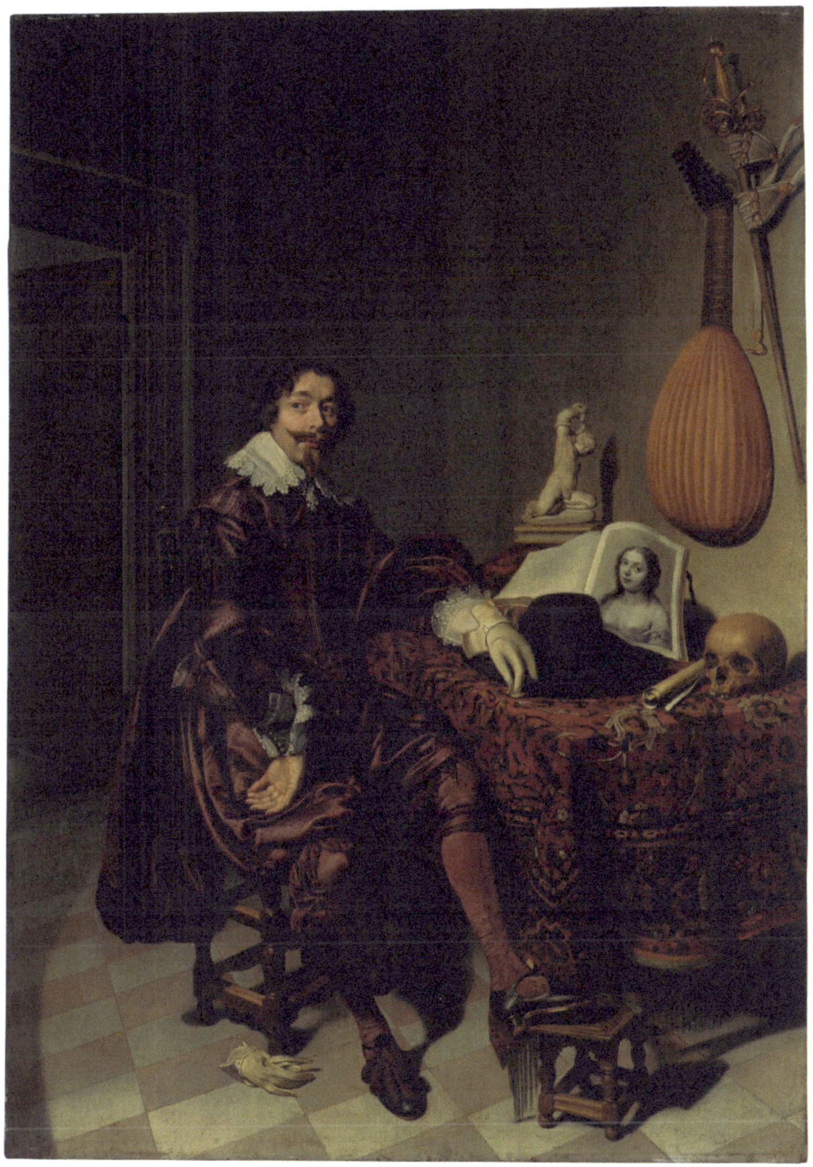

Thomas de Keyser, *Portrait of David Bailly with Vanitas Still Life*, ca. 1625–1630, oil on panel, 73.5 × 53.7 cm. Private collection, long-term loan to the Rijksmuseum, Amsterdam.

Fig. 555

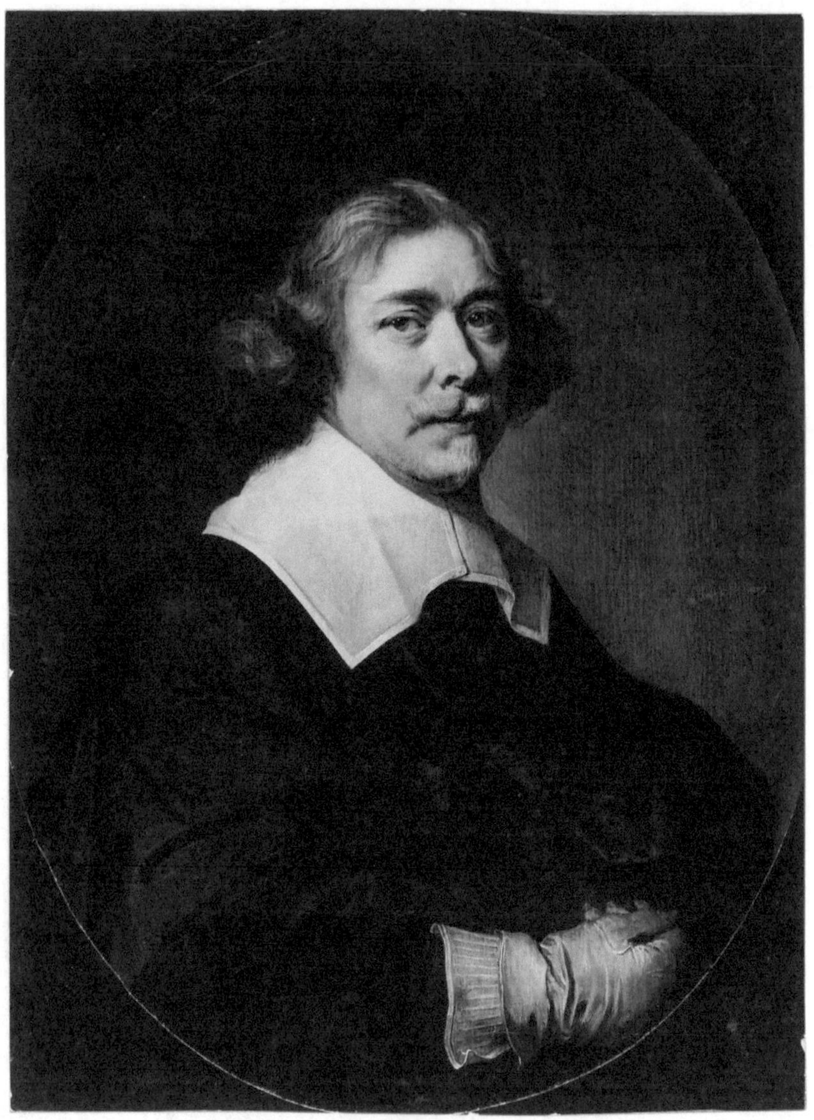

David Bailly, *Self-Portrait*, ca. 1642, oil on panel, 37 × 29 cm (oval). Location unknown.

Fig. 556

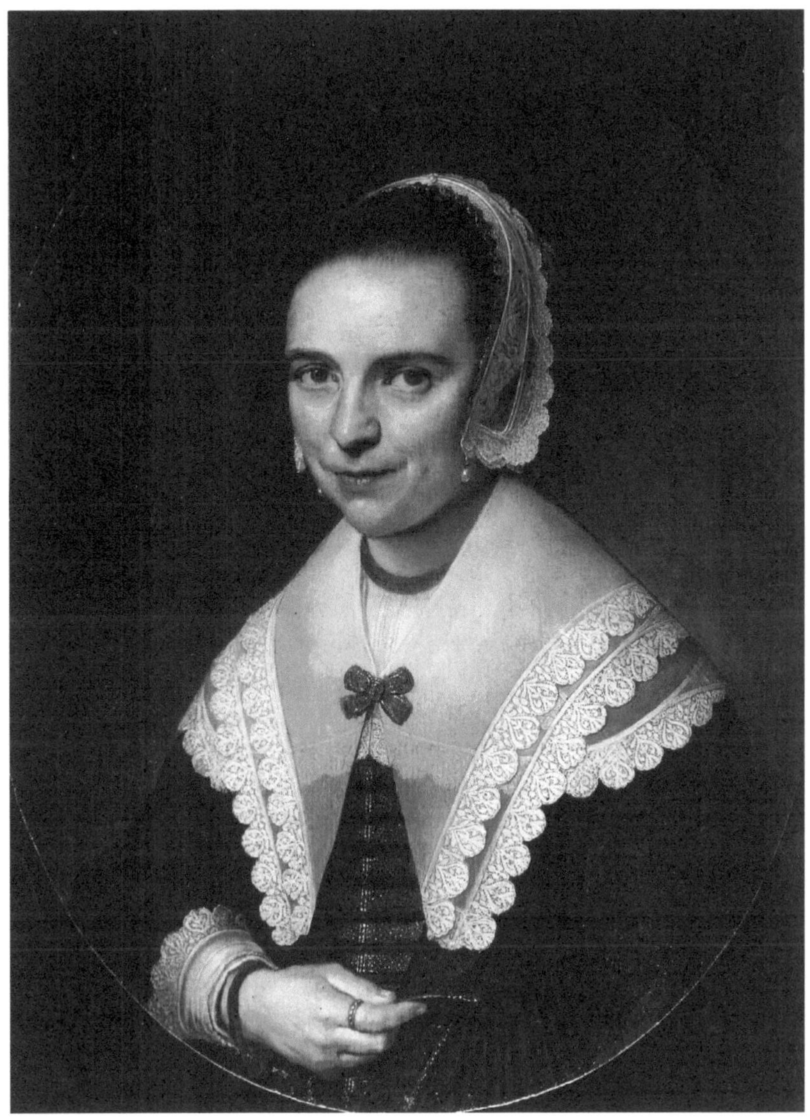

David Bailly, *Portrait of Agneta van Swanenburg*, ca. 1642, oil on panel, 37 × 29 cm (oval). Location unknown.

Fig. 557

for this that lead us into the picture structure itself. According to her, the composition is permeated with doublings that complicate the picture's sense of time; past, present, and future are equally evoked and intriguingly intertwined:

> The young man in a chair to the left is a representation of the artist in his atelier, which is clear from the requisites accompanying him: his palette on the wall and the maulstick in his right hand. His left hand resting on the self-portrait indicates that he is the owner and the master of this work of art. That this young painter is also representative of Bailly himself—though depicted as a retrospective, idealized image—is obvious from the similarity in both portraits of features, posture and details of the garments. Thus, this painting is also a double self-portrait of the artist.[9]

For Popper-Voskuil the figures' identities are so obvious that she is even able to relate the chimerical female figure in the background to them:

> The living image of the young painter forms a pair in contrast with the hazy image of a woman's head in the background behind the flute glass which, unlike the other portrayed figures, is represented neither as a living image nor as an art-object. This portrait hidden in the background is probably a personification of a prospective image of Bailly's young wife and is intended to be a pendant to the retrospective representation of her aged husband in the foreground. Here then the material concreteness of the past is shown opposite a spiritualized irreality of the future.[10]

In 1644, Bailly and his wife had drawn up a will, after which Agneta had been beset with a serious illness. Popper-Voskuil has related this event to Bailly's production of still lifes, which, as far as we know, began only in the 1640s and from the beginning

9
Ibid., p. 63.

10
Ibid., p. 67.

presents obvious vanitas motifs; before this he had mainly worked as a portraitist. According to her, the subject of the Leiden painting was

> the artist reproducing his own image in two different stages of his life in one and the same composition.... His double self-portrait represented as a juxtaposition of youth and old age inherently carries the idea of Vanitas.... Behind him stands his own youth, next to him his companion of life, in front of him death (in the form of the skull). His worldly achievements and his wealth are symbolized by the objects scattered on the table, whereas at the far end of it, as a summary of a life's experience, a parchment facing the beholder reads the moral: "Vanitas Vanitum et Omnia Vanitas, David Bailly pinxit Ao 1651." However, this clearly stated moral message about the futility of worldly vanities seems to contrast with the obvious desire of the painter to perpetuate his existence and to conform to the idealized image in which he chose to appear before posterity.[11]

For even the medallion that the young painter cannily displays does not present, as we know, a current portrait of the then sixty-seven-year-old, but one from nearly ten years earlier, at the time of his marriage. With this the time levels of the vanitas painting become increasingly blurred.

We also have Popper-Voskuil to thank for the fact that we now know of another Bailly still life with vanitas motifs found in a French private collection, one that she was able to study only in a poorly focused photograph: "No further information is available," she writes. "But it may be considered Bailly's most important Vanitas sill life in relation to the Leyden Vanitas"[12] [fig. 560]. In fact, the similarity of the utensils employed is astonishing, also the way the painting is unusual in its composition and perspective. It is a night piece, which in its dramatic view from above and resulting proportional distortion—a piece of experimental bravura—and in its lighting is unusual for Bailly. A burning candle casts its glow on

11 Ibid., p. 65.

12 Ibid., p. 72, note 8.

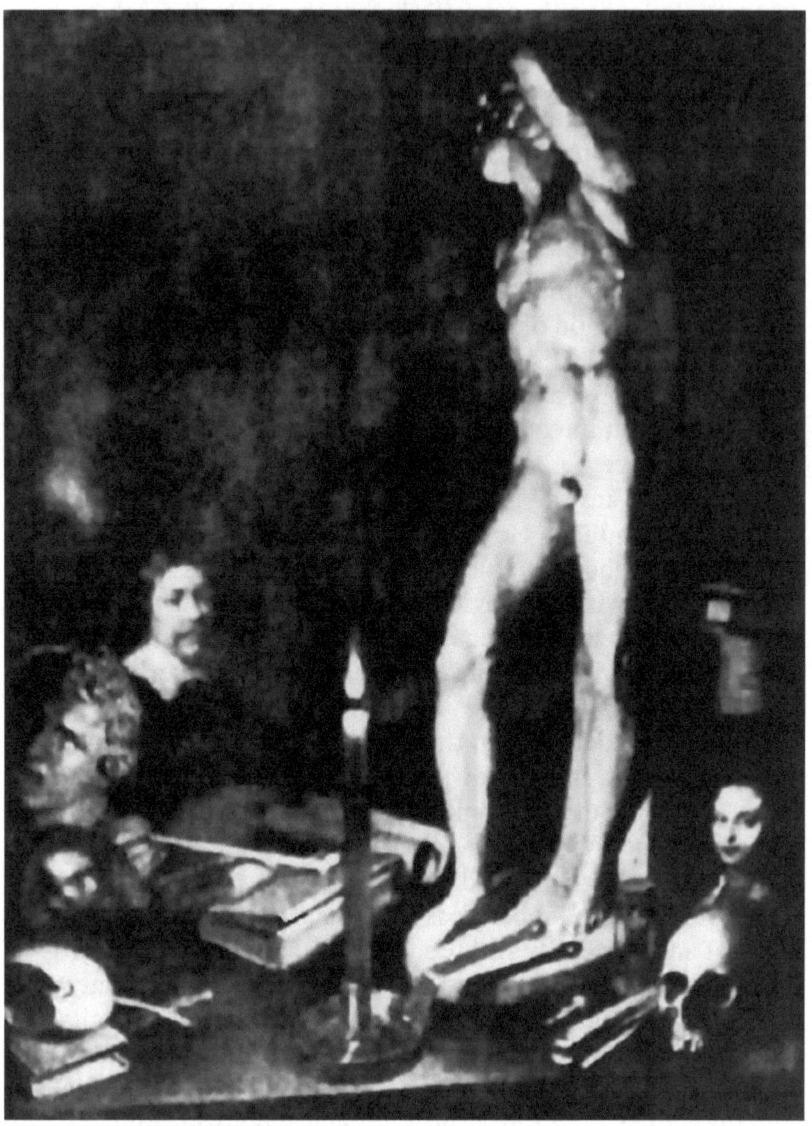

David Bailly, *Vanitas Still Life with Self-Portrait of the Painter*, ca. 1642–1645.
Measurements and location unknown.

Fig. 560

a few highly symbolic objects collected on a table. The skull and roll of parchment are already familiar to us as Bailly's signum; however, the candlelight also illuminates a few books and a pair of crossed clay pipes, a nautilus shell, and the copy of an antique bust that also appears in a third Bailly still life also in a private collection. Most prominent are the wonderfully formed, convulsively writhing figure of a Saint Sebastian, a female portrait that addresses the viewer with an intense gaze, and the already familiar self-portrait of David Bailly. There appears to be a secret connection between the self-portrait and the female portrait, one intersected in the picture's structure by the towering figure of Sebastian and the candle. In our Leiden still life the candle has been snuffed out, and only a wisp of smoke rises as a trace up through the picture. But the arrangement of both paintings is comparable, in as much as the polarity between self-portrait and female portrait forms the basis for every other relationship of the pictured objects. These lie around the dual core as a second layer, commenting on it or varying it.

Pairs and Pairings

No one has better described the dual, perhaps even dualistic picture structure on which the composition is based than Maarten Wurfbain, a description with which he comes to wholly different conclusions than Bruyn or Popper-Voskuil [fig. 562]: "Close examination reveals that most of the objects and pictures fall logically into pairs," Wurfbain writes:

> First is the background: A1 to the left, and A2 to the right. Then we have the purple drapery top right (B1) and the purple velvet (?) tablecloth (B2). (The lively young man (C1) is matched by the shadowy woman on the same scale behind the flute-glass (C2). Bailly's small self-portrait (D1) is clearly paired with that of the young woman with the low neckline (D2) whom we would like to ... identify as the personification of Vanitas. The oval drawing after Frans Hals' Luteplayer (E1) forms a pair with the gloomy, bearded man on the other drawing (E2).... Next we have two pieces of

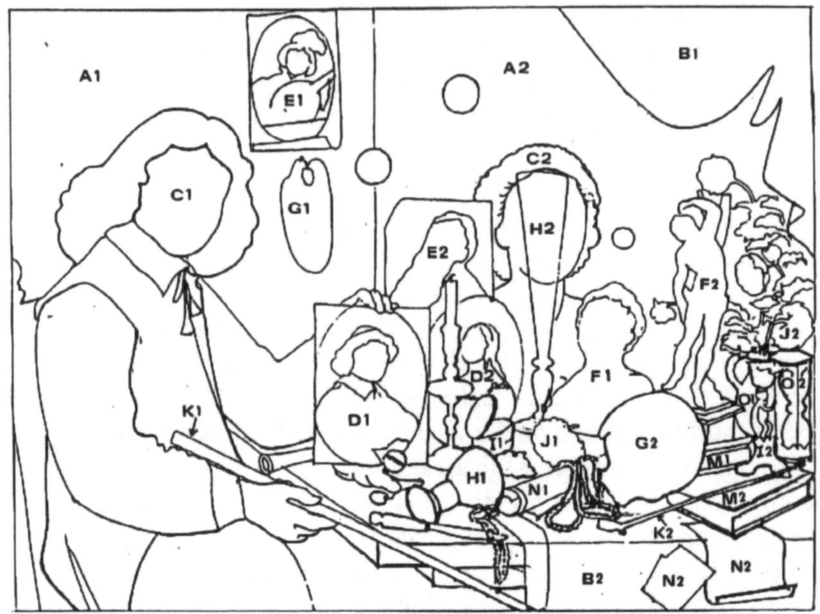

M. L. Wurfbain, “David Bailly’s Vanitas of 1651,” in: R. E. Fleischer and S. S. Munshower, eds., *The Age of Rembrandt. Studies in Seventeenth-Century Dutch Painting* (1988).

Fig. 562

> sculpture: the young Bacchante, after Lucas Faydherbe (F1) and the St. Sebastian (F2). Through their brownish color and oval shapes, the palette (G1) and the skull (G2) are probably also companions; the first meaning the beginning and the second the end of things. Then we have two glasses: the rummer-glass ("roemer") lying on the table (H1) and the flute-glass (H2).… There are also two pieces of silver: the oval vanity box (I1) exactly underneath Mistress Vanity herself, and the rummer-holder ("*bekerschroef*") of the young boy seated on a dolphin (I2). There are two groups of roses, one consisting of only two flowers lying on the table (J1) and another of at least five grouped in an earthenware vase (J2), subtly echoing Sebastian's drooping body. These last flowers could possibly be peonies. By their juxtaposition, the maulstick (K1) and the pipe (K2) seem to form a pair.… Then there are two books (M1 and M2) and two rolled-up sheets of paper (N1 and N2).[13]

The doubling of motifs makes it possible, Wurfbain asserts, to negotiate between the poles of past and future, youth and age or life and death, living flesh and *nature morte*, etc., which despite their temporal differences are evoked simultaneously in the medium of the picture. It appears to be a matter of balancing vitality and stasis, physical presence and pictorial representation, or of, even better, establishing a transitory relationship between them. For that reason, the portrait and still life are necessarily intertwined, and produce the hybrid nature of the composition that already occupied Mantz and Darcel. And for that reason, the painting's division into light and shadow proves just as necessary as the two-fold division into figure and objects; hence it is obvious to Wurfbain that there must be a correlation between the young painter and the shadowy female figure. The painting is based on the dialectic of becoming and passing away, just as

13
Maarten Wurfbain, "David Bailly's Vanitas of 1651," in *The Age of Rembrandt: Studies in Seventeenth-century Dutch Painting*, Roland Fleischer and Susan S. Munshower, eds. (University Park, PA: Penn State University Press, 1988), pp. 49–80, here pp. 51–53.

the prominently placed blank palette stands for the beginning of the imaginary animation of the picture, which continues across the reduced coloring of the drawings on the wall and ends in the mimetic oval portraits and busts that imitate the human form. Wurfbain categorically excludes a possible relationship between the painter and the subject of the portrait; however, he does not see it as a double portrait of Bailly as a younger and older man. In this he follows Paul Mantz:

> The sole indisputable identification is that of Bailly's oval self-portrait (D1), held upright on the table by the young artist. The two men bear some relationship to each other.... The young man on the left, the only figure clearly rendered as a living person, has generally been—and wisely so!—referred to as an unknown, young painter.[14]

Wurfbain then turns to the identity of the female portrait, which to his eyes has just as little to do with Bailly's biography as the portrait of the young painter itself:

> As we see in the painting of about 1627 by de Keyser and Bailly, and in the candlelight piece, as well as in the 1651 Vanitas, Bailly delighted in contrasting himself with a young woman. Since in 1627 (the approximate date of the portrait by de Keyser) his marriage was still fifteen years in the future, the woman in that painting is unlikely to be Agneta van Swanenburgh.... Bearing that in mind, we realize that it is quite appropriate and consistent that in the 1651 Vanitas, Bailly did not represent the woman whom he had married nine years earlier, and who was to outlive him by thirteen years.[15]

At this point scholarship becomes confused, for Bruyn had maintained that Agneta had already died at the time the painting was done, an assertion that some interpreters have followed, especially

14
Ibid., p. 53.

15
Wurfbain, "David Bailly's Vanitas of 1651," pp. 51–52.

since "the painting incorporates a number of references to her illness: the ball and chain is a *bezoir* (a seventeenth-century medical device for steeping medicine), the flute is a glass used at funerals."[16] The statue of St. Sebastian, in turn, could point to both: to a major illness that had caused Agneta to draw up her will in 1644 or to a recovery or the hope for it. In any case, Wurfbain had taken the repeated motif in Bailly's oeuvre of the juxtaposition of man and woman as a reason for advancing a bold thesis—one promptly rejected in scholarship as being out of the question: according to him the young man in the picture is Frans Mieris, who was just then making a name for himself in Leiden, while the small oval portrait pictures the universal scholar Anna Maria van Schuurman, and the puzzling specter on the wall is a portrait of Anna Roemers Visscher, the famous poet.

Svetlana Alpers has also taken on the painting, and interestingly, in her interpretation she first follows Wurfbain, and identifies only the oval portrait, but not the young painter, with Bailly himself. What then follows is a continuation of Wurfbain's argument, though Alpers focuses less on the polar relationship of man and woman or of death and life than on the competitive relationship between art and nature. The artistic, transformative power of craftsmanship, namely, functions as a mediator between art and nature, that is to say that it is precisely technical ability that transforms transient nature into eternal art, even at the price of the mortification of the subject. Accordingly, human life can be represented in all possible materials and mediums, indeed, it is precisely the depiction of the most varied materials that can be formed by the artist that makes Bailly's vanitas picture

> an exemplary work made in mid-century Leiden that provides extraordinary testimony to the Dutch painters' embrace of craft. A young artist, identified as such by the maulstick resting in his hand, sits beside a table on which is strewn a crowded offering of objects. We can

16 Wayne M. Martin, "Bubbles and Skulls: The Phenomenological Structure of Self-Consciousness in 17th Century Dutch Still Life Painting," in *A Companion to Phenomenology and Existentialism*, Hubert L. Dreyfus, Hubert and Mark A. Wrathall, eds. (Oxford: Wiley-Blackwell, 2006), pp. 559–584, here p. 581, note 27.

> call it an assemblage of materials made by nature and worked by man. It is a catalogue: wood, paper, glass, metals, stone, plaster, clay, bone, hide, earthenware, pearls, petals, water, smoke, and paint. What is more, these are materials worked to reveal or ... to betray their nature: wood is shaped, paper curled, stone is carved, pearls polished and strung, cloth is draped, hides (as vellum) are treated to provide smooth covers for a book. Several materials betray their multiple natures: glass is solid and shaped, as in the overturned goblet, but it can contain liquid or sand and it reflects light even as it offers us a view through its transparent surface; metal is imprinted in coins, fashioned into links of chain, sharpened to form a knife blade, turned to a candlestick, or molded into the sprightly putto supporting the glass holder at the far right.[17]

Alpers goes on to read the juxtaposition of the many materials and mediums in Bailly's painting as an homage to the transformative power of art, which is capable of bringing out the living presence and "living flesh" of nature step by step, i.e., gradually, and preserving it.

> Art does not simply imitate nature, nor is it a play of the imagination, but rather it is the techne or craft that enables us, through constraint, to grasp nature.... In a subtle yet powerful instrumental manner, art can lead to a new kind of knowledge of the world.... Bailly's pictorial assemblage resists summation or closure. Crafted objects themselves are subject to replication: the string of pearls discarded on the table reappears around the painted woman's neck; the gathered drapery of her painted dress is sculpted in stone at the breast of the bust beside her and also hangs over head in a swatch that frames our view; the leaves and petals of the roses

17
Svetlana Alpers, *The Art of Describing: Dutch Art in the Seventeenth Century* (Chicago: University of Chicago Press, 1983), p. 103.

> are wrought in the metal of the tiny box. Such transformations also work through corresponding shapes: the painted lute is hung above an empty palette whose oval shape mimics it only to be repeated in the pair of portraits on the table and the cover of the small box. Colors also correspond: a subtle gradation of tans relates the sculpted body of Sebastian, the skull, and the vellum of the book; the youthful bust is gray as is the female face faintly visible on the wall, and both are played off against the ruddy flesh tones of the young artist and the portrait. Set off against bodies of plaster, stone, and metal, the bony skull, and the images in paint, Bailly (for the man in the oval portrait is the painter himself) and the attendant youth appear as living flesh. But as we withdraw from this painted world we must acknowledge that the youth, though realer again than the portraits, is himself an image fashioned out of paint.[18]

Thus Alpers suspects that Bailly's painting represents a parable on painting's ability to visualize its subject, bring it to life: starting from the empty palette and onward in the shadowy woman's head on the wall the human body gradually takes on form in the two sketches on the wall (still in grisaille), then in the medium of the painted picture (in color), in the sculptures (again monochrome), to finally culminate in the flesh tone of the young man. But precisely because this progression of animation started from the empty palette, Alpers writes, even the painter cannot deny being ultimately made only of pigment. To continue this line of thinking, this is where the true vanity of Bailly's painting lies—just as life passes away, the actuality of the portrayed subject is ultimately reduced to mere pigment, and thus dissolves into nothingness. In any case, according to this theory the shadowy woman's head is crucial, inasmuch as it symbolizes, emerging as it does from the ground, the incarnate power of painting, and Alpers wonders: "Is this perhaps a reference to one version of the origin of painting as found in Pliny?"[19]

18 Alpers, *The Art of Describing*, pp. 10–141.

19 Ibid.

All the more astonishing is it that none of the writers introduced so far, not even Alpers, has thought about whether the shadowy woman's head is a deliberate invention of Bailly's or perhaps an "accident," more precisely: a (rejected) part of the work that has bled through the overpainting. This was already suspected by Bruyn, though he failed to mention this in his influential article. However, he once said as much in discussion with Wurfbain who summarizes the dispute as follows:

> It has been debated whether this female face was intended to be visible or not in the finished painting. I have always taken for granted that it was Bailly's intention to depict the bust in such a way, that it appears as a shadow. Bruyn, however, thought that this portrait had been Bailly's initial idea, but had then been overpainted with the flute-glass by the artist himself, with the intent of masking.[20]

In Bruyn's opinion what we see of the face now, and what was already visible in 1874, judging by the illustration published by Darcel, is due to the fact that this portrait contained a considerable quantity of lead-white, which surfaced only at a relatively recent date, through the layer of paint covering it. "The fact that the drawing of the man with the beard, the flute-glass, and the oval vanity portrait are all painted over part of her face, suggests that this might indeed be the case. But it is a moot point that could possibly be cleared up by analysis of the paint layers in that area of the picture."[21] In fact, there is an X-ray photograph that reveals that in this spot Bailly first placed a large, oval-framed female portrait [fig. 569]. These art-technological findings have barely been registered in the scholarship. Or to be fair, one of the few to mention them is Svetlana Alpers, but only very casually, and with no wish to really evaluate and consider them. This seems

20
Bruyn in oral communication with Wurfbain in 1967, cf. Wurfbain, "David Bailly's Vanitas of 1651," p. 55.

21
Ibid.

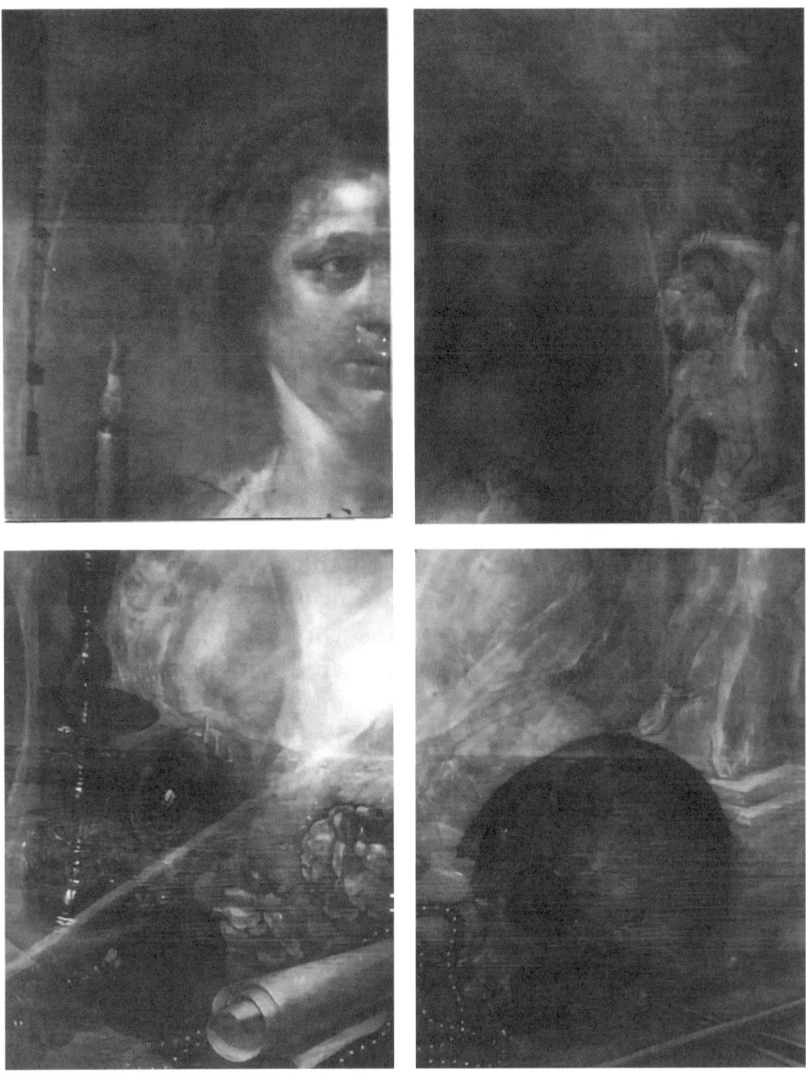

X-ray images, taken ca. 1970 of Bailly's *Vanitas Still Life with Portrait of a Young Painter*.
Museum De Lakenhal, Leiden.

Fig. 569

inexcusable, precisely in view of the specter's central role in her theory of the origin of painting:

> X-rays reveal that in this picture Bailly laid painted forms upon completed ones beneath: the shadow visage on the wall and the portraits placed before it were in turn fully executed before further objects were placed over them. The layered design of the picture thus expresses or mimics the manner of its execution or craft. Bailly shows us art emerging into crafted objects from the shadowy female face against the wall.[22]

Several authors writing on self-portraiture or on Netherlandish still life painting in the 1980s and 1990s took up this interpretation but did not mention the ghostly female head at all—though they all emphasize the various degrees of reality and illusion in Bailly's painting. So how to explain the recurring scholarly disagreement and uncertainty regarding this ominous part of the picture? To put it bluntly: Is the shadowy female head utterly meaningless or, on the contrary, a rather sensational pictorial invention? Why is it completely overlooked on the one hand, and wholly exaggerated on the other? Has it simply been overlooked by many writers, or is it in fact meaningless (because unintended by the painter and only revealed over time)? Or, conversely, is it the most significant element in the whole composition, the reflection of a theory of art or of the specific medium, i.e., painting?

All these assumptions can be found in past interpretations. The real problem was put in a nutshell by Julian Kliemann in 1996. He, too, notes the obvious reserve on the part of scholars regarding the apparitional female head. He writes: "Hitherto the literature has only briefly mentioned the remarkable appearance of this portrait without including it in an interpretation of the picture,"[23] which leads him to ask: "Is the spectral face only visible

22
Alpers, *The Art of Describing*, pp. 104–105.

23
Julian Kliemann, "Überlegungen vor David Baillys 'Porträt eines Malers mit Vanitassymbolen,'" in *Ars naturam adiuvans: Festschrift für Matthias Winner*, Victoria von Flemming and Sebastian Schütze, eds. (Mainz: P. von Zabern, 1996), pp. 430–452, here p. 440.

now owing to some chemical process? Was it wholly hidden from the contemporary viewer?" For

> all deliberations linked to this face have to be of interest if we are to understand the genesis of Bailly's picture; however, in an explanation of the picture itself the face need not be considered. Or is it possible that Bailly rejected his original composition, to be sure, but deliberately painted over the face to the extent that even in his own time it appeared in the form we see it today?[24]

Despite his thorough study, Kliemann leaves it at this, without wishing to take one side or the other, and especially fails to pursue the second possibility. Alpers is, therefore, virtually the only writer to take up this aspect, using it as the basis for her theory of the painting's inception, on the one hand, and of its vitality on the other—an approach represented by Gregor J. M. Weber in his *Praise of Painting Topos,* but has not been further touched upon in scholarship.[25] Celeste Brusati took up this interpretation in her 1990 essay,[26] but did not mention the ghostly female head. Likewise, Eric Jan Sluijter emphasized the various degrees of reality and illusion in Bailly's painting in his essay "Painting as Mirror of Nature" from 1988 but failed to mention the female head. The same is true of Hans-Joachim Raupp in his much-quoted study from 1984, *Künstlerbildnis und Künstlerdarstellung in den Niederlanden im 17. Jahrhundert,* although he believes—following the conclusions of Popper-Voskuil—that Bailly's vanitas painting was definitely a response to some experience in the painter's life.[27]

24
Ibid.

25
Gregor J. M. Weber, *Der Lobtopos des „lebenden" Bildes: Jan Vos und sein „Zeege der Schilderkunst" von 1654* (Hildesheim: Georg Olms Verlag, 1991).

26
Celeste Brusati, "Self-Portraiture and Self-Reflection in Seventeenth-Century Netherlandish Still-Life Painting," *Simiolus* 20 (1990–1991): pp. 168–182, here p. 180: "It is not simply the presence of all these emblems but their status as crafted representations which is significant here."

27
Eric Jan Sluijter, "'Een volmaekte schildery is als een spiegel van de natuer': Spiegel en spiegelbeeld in de Nederlandse schilderkunst van de 17de eeuw," in *Oog in oog met de spiegel,* Nico J. Brederoo, ed. (Amsterdam: Aramith, 1988), pp. 146–163; Hans-Joachim Raupp, *Untersuchungen zu Künstlerbildnis und Künstlerdarstellung in den Niederlanden im 17. Jahrhundert,* PhD diss. (University of Hildesheim, 1984).

Even in the 1994 essay on "Painting as the Subject of Painting" by Hermann Asemissen and Gunter Schweikart it is touched upon only briefly, though it would have been only logical to make use of the self-referential potential of the shadowy woman's head.[28]

Whereas Kliemann is undecided relative to the work's original state, Martin's phenomenological interpretation and Alpers's theory of an "art of describing" rely on the present-day pictorial evidence and thus the significance of the ephemeral female head. Yet, they too do so without wishing to determine the actual genesis of the picture—almost as if they had no interest in toppling the tempting theory of a "painted theory of art" in Bailly's painting in favor of a material accident. And is there not in this a healthy skepticism vis-à-vis the findings of scientific material analysis, which themselves require interpretation? How, for example, do the findings from art-technological study affect the plausibility of the picture structure itself, that is in view of what I have just referred to as "pictorial evidence"? As Wurfbain noted quite parenthetically, he had "always taken for granted that it was Bailly's intention to depict the bust in such a way, that it appears as a shadow."[29]

But what are the possible explanations proposed by the writers mentioned?[30] Bruyn apparently considered it possible that the "portrait contained a considerable quantity of lead-white, which surfaced only at a relatively recent date, through the layer of paint covering it." He was doubtless referring to the lead white employed in the flesh tone, which would mean that the white of the woman's complexion had bled through the layer of gray pigment on top of it and lightened the painting's surface in those spots. Yet such an explanation is more than improbable, not least because a bleeding of lead-white soaps, produced from a chemical reaction between the pigment and the oil, onto the surface of the picture is possible, to be sure, but would at most result in deposits of transparent granules giving it a noticeably rough

28
Hermann Ulrich Asemissen and Gunter Schweikhart, *Malerei als Thema der Malerei* (Berlin: Akademie Verlag, 1994), pp. 162–171.

29
Wurfbain, "David Bailly's Vanitas of 1651," p. 55.

30
I would like to take this opportunity to thank Tilly Laaser, Cologne Institute of Conservation Sciences, TH Cologne, for her expertise and the joint discussion of the X-ray.

texture (which has not happened in our case). Another conceivable possibility—namely that the lead white of the portrait could have darkened through contact with pollutants in the air—is also hardly supported by critical examination. It is true that lead white can form a black lead sulfide, but this almost never occurs in paints bound with oil, for the overpainting prevents contact with the air, and the underpainting is encapsulated as though in a sealed tin. So, both explanations that assume the overpainted portrait has migrated evenly onto the surface from the picture ground, or a lower layer, can be rejected as implausible. If one reads him carefully, Kliemann suggests another alternative: according to him it is conceivable that the specter is a preliminary draft of the portrait in grisaille, which owing to the lead white in the gray pigment has "bled" through the overpainting. Kliemann does not say so, but what he means is probably the process known as "saponification," in which the lead white in the gray overpainting becomes transparent, allowing the first draft of the female portrait executed in chiaroscuro to show through. In the case of saponification, it would be the chemical process taking place in the upper paint layer that is revealing, not a process of the lower paint layer's bleeding through, as proposed by Bruyn. Since Kliemann in fact draws on Bruyn in his considerations, one sees that he had not truly understood the latter's argument. According to Kliemann, if the spectral head was not an intentional element of the picture—here, as suggested, he is indecisive—it is the monochrome underpainting for a portrait that has come to light thanks to the increasing transparency of the overpainting.

However, with respect to this thesis one has to ask whether it would have been typical of Bailly's painting technique for him to first create a portrait in grisaille and apply the flesh tone only in a second step. This also seems unlikely, just as one can hardly imagine that the female portrait can have worked its way through the gray paint layer uniformly, so as to present itself to our eyes perfectly intact. Kliemann places an X-ray photograph next to these considerations, but it is mistakenly inverted. Yet, he is the only writer who even takes the trouble to refer to them, and if one views such illustrations in the correct orientation, something becomes clearer: for then it is apparent that Bailly actually executed the woman's head and body with care, modeling them in the most nuanced detail, and in fact as a full bust, including the onset of her breast and arms as well as a portion of fabric. The format of the portrait also becomes clearly recognizable; it is visibly framed with an oval line. But most of all the flesh tone with its component of lead white stands out distinctly in the X-ray photograph. It extends fully formed beneath the smaller portrait in the foreground, so that one has to treat the thesis repeatedly expressed in the literature that the large oval portrait and the two smaller ones were executed simultaneously with skepticism. Alpers, for one, made much of this; however, a glance at the X-ray photo shows that this can by no means be so readily assumed.

Smoke and Mirrors?

It is possible to make out relevant changes to the composition. For example, a string of pearls is woven into the beautiful woman's hair, and her face has remarkably individualized features. But, and this is of particular importance, in an earlier version the candle was not extinguished but was rather topped by a flickering flame: a candle that is first seen burning, then suddenly extinguished [fig. 575]. It is difficult to resist relating this detail to the picture's two versions; the burning or extinguished candle on the one hand and the portrait or specter on the other would appear to be closely connected. As already mentioned, the graceful wisp of smoke from the candle closely hugs the outline of the female head, and even appears to possibly form it, as if it too were composed of smoke. Kliemann felt that the specter seemed like the reflection of a picture with a dark ground painted on wood and heavily varnished, as if the subject were standing before the painting and seeing herself reflected in it, and referred to the glaze invented by Apelles (*altramentum*) and the Narcissus myth in support of his thesis. But it is much more plausible, precisely on the basis of the depiction of the candle in the two versions, to establish a connection between the female specter and smoke or fumes in both a literal and a figurative sense. That way the hypothesis of an intentional incorporation of the ominous female head in the final version of the painting is strengthened.

To bring greater clarity to the situation, however, it would be necessary to resolve the different superimposed paint layers

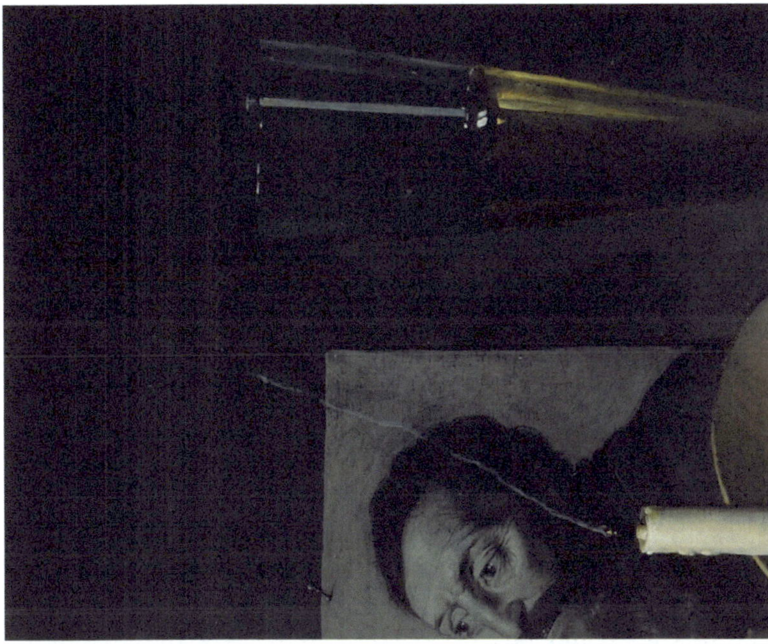

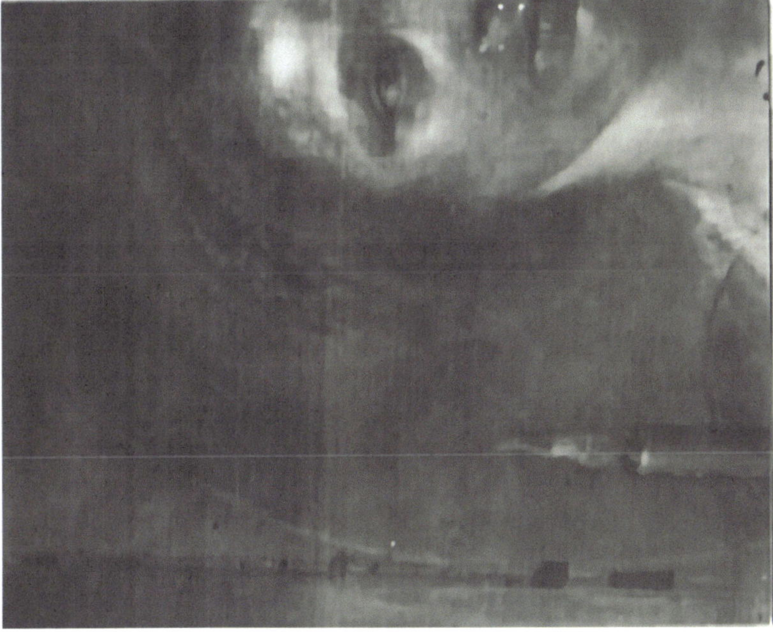

Details of Figs. 547 and 569.

Fig. 575

into a chronological view. The 1970s X-radiographs of the central area have already shown that a large oval portrait was planned in the original composition, and that this portrait was almost finished before it was covered with gray pigment. It would now have to be determined whether the painter again modeled the picture's top layer in chiaroscuro. "Is the mysterious phantom image of a woman behind the flute glass a deliberate addition, or an overpainted portrait that has reemerged over the course of time? To what extent is the vanitas still life on the table a personal reference to the transience of the life of the painter himself?"[31]
It is no surprise that these questions, which have been pondered for so many years, have prompted the Museum De Lakenhal to subject the vanitas still life to further technical examination when it was on loan to the Rijksmuseum from 2016 to 2019.[32] The results were recently presented in an exhibition organized on the artist's life and work.[33] Noninvasive imaging techniques, such as Macro X-Ray Fluorescence scanning (MA-XRF) and Infrared Reflectography (IRR) were applied, "unveiling changes that were so far unknown and have the potential to reshape the current interpretations of Bailly's intriguing composition."[34] For instance, another small female portrait to the left of Bailly's self-portrait became visible that was also probably fully executed in color. Bailly replaced her with a larger, oval version, just as he placed a portrait or *tronie* of a young man at the upper-right corner of the wall only to paint it out again quite early in the development of the composition. This portrait is particularly interesting because it resembles a small painting that is now in the Louvre and is sometimes treated as a self-portrait of the young Bailly [fig. 577].

31
Cf. Janneke Van Asperen, Rudi Ekkart, and Christiaan Vogelaar, "Introduction," in *David Bailly: Time, Death, and Vanity*, exh. cat. Museum De Lakenhal, Leiden (Zwolle: Waanders, 2023), p. 17.

32
Ibid. The Museum De Lakenhal was closed for renovation and the building of an extension during that time. Erma Hermens, who was then Rijksmuseum professor of studio practice and technical art history at the University of Amsterdam, performed the technical examination of the panel.

33
David Bailly – Tijd, Dood, en Ijdelheid, Museum De Lakenhal, Leiden, March 10–July 23, 2023. For a short summary of this article, see the contribution to the catalogue by Karin Leonhard, "'Cherchez la femme!' The Reception History of David Bailly's *Vanitas Still Life With Portrait of a Young Painter*," in Van Asperen et al., eds., *David Bailly*, pp. 93–102.

34
Erma Hermens and Nathan Daly, "Phantoms, Portraits, Pigments," in Van Asperen et al., eds. *David Bailly*, p. 105.

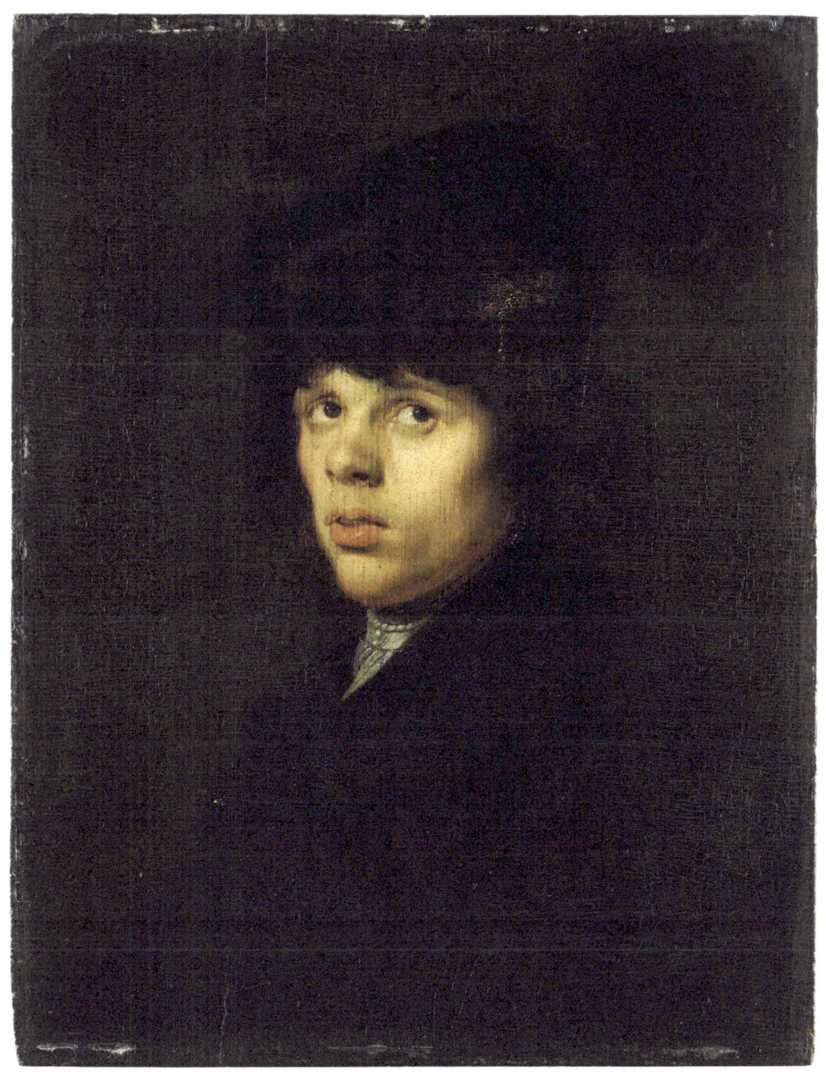

David Bailly, *Young Man with a Black Beret*, 1637, oil on panel, 30 × 23.8 cm.
Musée du Louvre, inv. nr. RF 792, Paris.

Fig. 577

Accordingly, the curtain was drawn lower at a later stage because it would otherwise have obscured the male portrait. Bailly arranged and rearranged the many pictures and utensils almost like the director of a play for which the wall and table form a stage and the curtain has been drawn aside to reveal different scenes of his artistic and private life.

Did Bailly use the motif of "picture-within-picture" as an opportunity to insert biographical references into his vanitas painting? Or is the contrapposto doubling of motifs, as we determined earlier, not rather a negotiation between two poles—i.e., past and future, youth and age, or living flesh and *nature morte*, etc.—that, despite their opposition, can appear simultaneously in the medium of the picture? It is necessarily an open question whether the seamless transition between invisibility and visibility results in a triumph of painting—one that rises above the transience of the earthly world—or conversely, whether the achievements of painting ultimately have to be subjected to the principle of ephemerality; the reciprocal relationship is, it seems, dialectical. In such an interpretation Bailly's spectral female head plays a significant role in the picture's structure—marking nothing less than the beginning and end of what art can make visible, represent, or bring to life. But we can also approach the painting differently, namely by focusing on the relationship between figure and ground, which interests us in the present volume. For if we understand the depth of the stage not spatially, but temporally, i.e., if we consider the various paint layers in their chronological order, then this results in a time travel into the past of the image's creation, which fills its space with a more intimate meaning. Then it seems as if the painter had deposited the objects in these material depths of the picture as in a chest of memory. At least this is how Gaston Bachelard would probably have seen it and would not have understood the many objects as "philosophical rummage" that is arrayed before and on the wall of the painter's studio to illustrate the futility of all human effort. Rather, they would be embedded in a hidden, mysterious inner space—in the pictorial ground as a hiding place. Bachelard sees "a homology between the geometry of the small box and the psychology of secrecy."[35] This also applies to the deep inside of the casket that the philosopher associates above all with memory: "The casket contains the things that

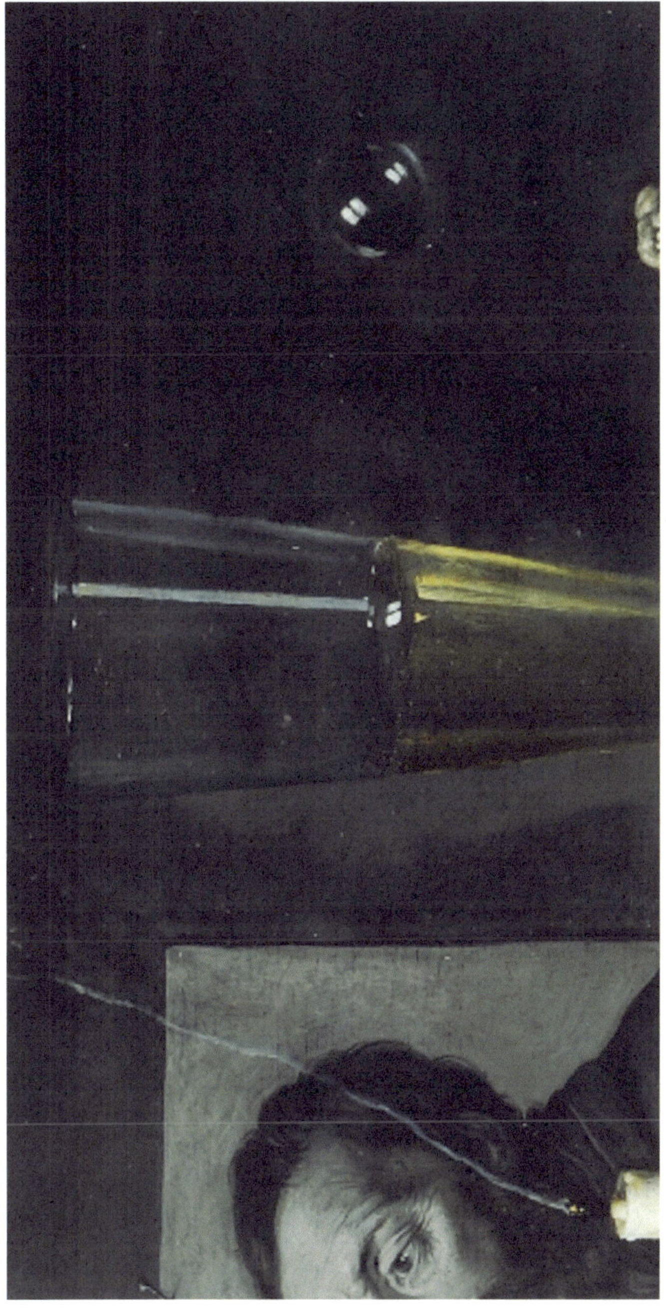

Detail of Fig. 547.

Fig. 579

are unforgettable, unforgettable for us, but also unforgettable for those to whom we are going to give our treasures. Here the past, the present, and a future are condensed.... The outside has no more meaning. And quite paradoxically, even cubic dimensions have no more meaning, for the reason that a new dimension—the dimension of intimacy—has opened up."[36] If we take these observations seriously, then there would be not only one pictorial ground from which the figures stand out clearly, but several grounds or rather a bottomless "*fond*," into which they have sunk and which now allows them to stay in the picture on different levels of time and (in)visibility. And indeed, even now, despite the added clarity that recent technical analysis has provided, only contradictory impressions and statements can be recorded. For example: look at the eye that came to lie directly behind the flute glass [fig. 579]. It is most carefully executed and appears to be gazing at us through the curved glass as though through a thick lens. The pupil is most clearly rendered, but a bright reflection has also been placed on the eyeball and iris. This can no longer be explained as a chemical reaction, but only as a later addition on the part of the painter. However, the map of the Pb-M-X-ray line that presents the distribution of lead in the upper paint layers, thus the last to be applied, does not show the portrait.[37] So, do all interpretations of the mysterious female specter continue to be smoke and mirrors? If we think of the classic technique in magical illusions that makes an entity appear to hover in empty space, then this description would be very appropriate. For even after the detailed technical examinations, vagueness remains, so that the chimera—unlike in the wood engraving of 1874—reveals itself precisely only when the duality of figure and ground dissolves in our perception.

35
He also writes: "With the theme of drawers, chest, locks and wardrobes, we shall resume contact with the unfathomable store of daydreams of intimacy. Wardrobes with their shelves, desks with their drawers and chests with their false bottoms are veritable organs of the secret psychological life." Gaston Bachelard, *The Poetics of Space* (Boston: Beacon Press, 1994), p. 78.

36
Ibid., pp. 84–85.

37
Hermens and Daly, "Phantoms, Portraits, Pigments," p. 112.

Part 5
Transgressing Depth

As has been amply noted, new forms of spatial representation in fourteenth- and fifteenth-century European painting involved a series of practical and theoretical negotiations between virtual space, surface, and ground.[1] Max Imdahl argued that around 1300, in Giotto's frescoes in the Arena Chapel, Padua, the painting's surface retained some of its physical flatness. At the same time, it had to be transformed into a simulated field that served as the ground of the image, emphasizing a new cohesion in spatiality.[2] In most cases, this meant creating a primary pictorial space with a fictive ground to accommodate figures.

In early Renaissance painting, the depiction of virtual space relied on the painter's ability to represent the ground, setting, and figures in foreshortening. In *The Science of Art*, Martin Kemp convincingly highlighted the connection between optical theory and the visual arts in Europe, a connection recently reaffirmed by Sven Dupré and Dominique Raynaud, among others.[3] This affinity does not imply a strict hierarchy where visual solutions derive directly from theoretical concerns or vice versa. Rather, it denotes a mutually inspiring dialogue between the sciences and the arts. I propose to examine an overlooked aspect of this exchange: the construction of secondary pictorial space in Cosimo Rosselli's *Last Supper* (ca. 1481–1482, part of the New Testament cycle in the Sistine Chapel) and Andrea Mantegna's *Picture-Bearers* (ca. 1486–1506, part of the *Triumphs of Caesar* series).

Secondary pictorial space refers to a phenomenon where independent orders of representation are embedded within the primary spatial order of a painting. Its most common form is images-within-images, where the embedded images have their

1
Matteo Burioni, "'Grund un Campo': Die Metaphorik des Bildgrundes in der frühen Neuzeit oder: Paolo Uccellos Schlacht von San Romano," in *Der Grund: Das Feld des Sichtbaren*, Gottfried Boehm and Matteo Burioni, eds. (Munich: Fink, 2012), pp. 95–139; David Young Kim, *Groundwork: A History of the Renaissance Picture* (Princeton, NJ: Princeton University Press, 2022), pp. 1–21; Saskia Quené, *Goldgrund und Perspektive: Fra Angelico im Glanz des Quattrocento* (Berlin/Boston: Deutscher Kunstverlag, 2022).

2
Max Imdahl, *Giotto Arenafresken: Ikonographie, Ikonologie, Ikonik* (Munich: W. Fink, 1988).

3
Martin Kemp, *The Science of Art: Optical Themes in Western Art from Brunelleschi to Seurat* (New Haven, CT: Yale University Press, 1990), pp. 7–52; Dominique Raynaud, *Studies on Binocular Vision: Optics, Vision and Perspective from the Thirteenth to the Seventeenth Centuries* (Cham: Springer, 2016), pp. 1–67; Sven Dupré, ed., *Perspective as Practice: Renaissance Cultures of Optics* (Turnhout: Brepols, 2019).

own system of representation, often differing from the spatial structure of the principal work.[4]

Whereas the development of the primary virtual space of the image has been extensively traced, the secondary perspective of images-within-images has received only scant attention. By the beginning of the seventeenth century, twofold composite systems had become widespread in gallery and cabinet paintings. The first theoretical description of images-within-images dates to the first half of the seventeenth century. The Florentine statesman Pietro Accolti dedicated his work on perspective, *Lo Inganno de gl'Occhi* (1625), to Cardinal Carlo de' Medici.[5] In his book, he called attention to an unusual pictorial practice.[6] The caption of chapter XXXIV introduces the issue: "How should the painter confine himself if he happens to show a painting [*Pittura*] in painting [*Pittura*]." Accolti writes:

> We judge that it goes quite well with our present treatise on Perspective to demonstrate another singular exercise. No one, who had written about this material, observed or considered this exercise. It can happen to a painter that he must paint [*dipingere*] and represent [*figurare*] the view [*veduta*] of a Painting [*Pittura*], or any other image in a framed picture [*immagine in quadro*], within his own real framed picture [*quadro*]. Their surfaces [*superficie*] should not be parallel to each other, since in this case the inner space [*dintorni*] of one painting would coincide with the inner space of the other, with proportionate foreshortening

4
For a general introduction on images-within-images see André Chastel, "Picture-within-Picture," in *Renaissance Metapainting*, Péter Bokody and Alexander Nagel, eds. (London: Harvey Miller, 2020), pp. 295–322; and Péter Bokody, *Images-within-Images in Italian Painting: Reality and Reflexivity* (Burlington, VT: Ashgate, 2015), pp. 1–10.

5
Pietro Accolti, *Lo inganno degl'occhi, prospettiva pratica* (Florence: Appresso Pietro Cecconcelli, 1625), pp. 45–46. See also: Adonella Barbara Parenti, *Pietro Accolti e Lo inganno de gl'occhi:tradizione e rinnovamento nella letteratura prospettica di primo Seicento* (Montevarchi: Accademia Valdarnese del Poggio, 2011).

6
Emmanuelle Hénin, "Parrhasios and the Stage Curtain: Theatre, Metapainting and the Idea of Representation in the Seventeenth Century," *Art History* 33 (2010): 248–261, here 256.

> [*diminuzione*] of the distances from their surfaces. And I have regularly seen painters of great fame not knowing how to paint one or the other. If not, finally, in the same manner and with similar inner spaces, and consequently, the figures in one were conceived as surfaces, and as bodies in the other. To get a Painting, the different inner spaces must be sorted from each other.[7]

By integrating an image in the space of another, the painter encounters a series of pictorial choices and challenges. If a three-dimensional painting is depicted obliquely to the principal plane, the painter will have to harmonize two or more orders of representation. Accolti provides detailed geometric steps to avoid confusion in this process. In the passage, he claims originality for his approach in describing and resolving the issue. The discussion focuses on framed canvases (*quadro*), and therefore the newly emerging medium of painting as a portable commodity. The hesitant terminology of "*pittura*" for paintings and "*immagine in quadro*" for images in framed pictures reflects the unsettled state of the theoretical language.

Pietro Accolti did not address a purely hypothetical possibility, as the context of his example presupposes the existence of cabinet and gallery paintings that became widespread in Antwerp at the beginning of the seventeenth century.[8] These intertextual machines often assembled dozens of paintings within the single space of a gallery. For example, in the allegory of *Sight* (1617), a collaborative work by Peter Paul Rubens and Jan Brueghel the Elder, several paintings are arranged, with many positioned obliquely to the principal plane. A similarly collaborative piece, this time by Brueghel the Elder and Hieronymus Francken II, commemorates the visit of Archdukes Albert and Isabella to the collection of Pierre Roose (ca. 1621–1623) [fig. 585]. Although the setting is more of a cabinet of curiosities than a formal art

7
Accolti, *Lo inganno degl'occhi*, p. 45. Translation P. B.

8
Zirka Zaremba Filipczak, *Picturing Art in Antwerp* (Princeton, NJ: Princeton University Press, 1987); and Alexander Marr, "The Flemish 'Pictures of Collections' Genre: An Overview," *Intellectual History Review* 20 (2010): 5–25.

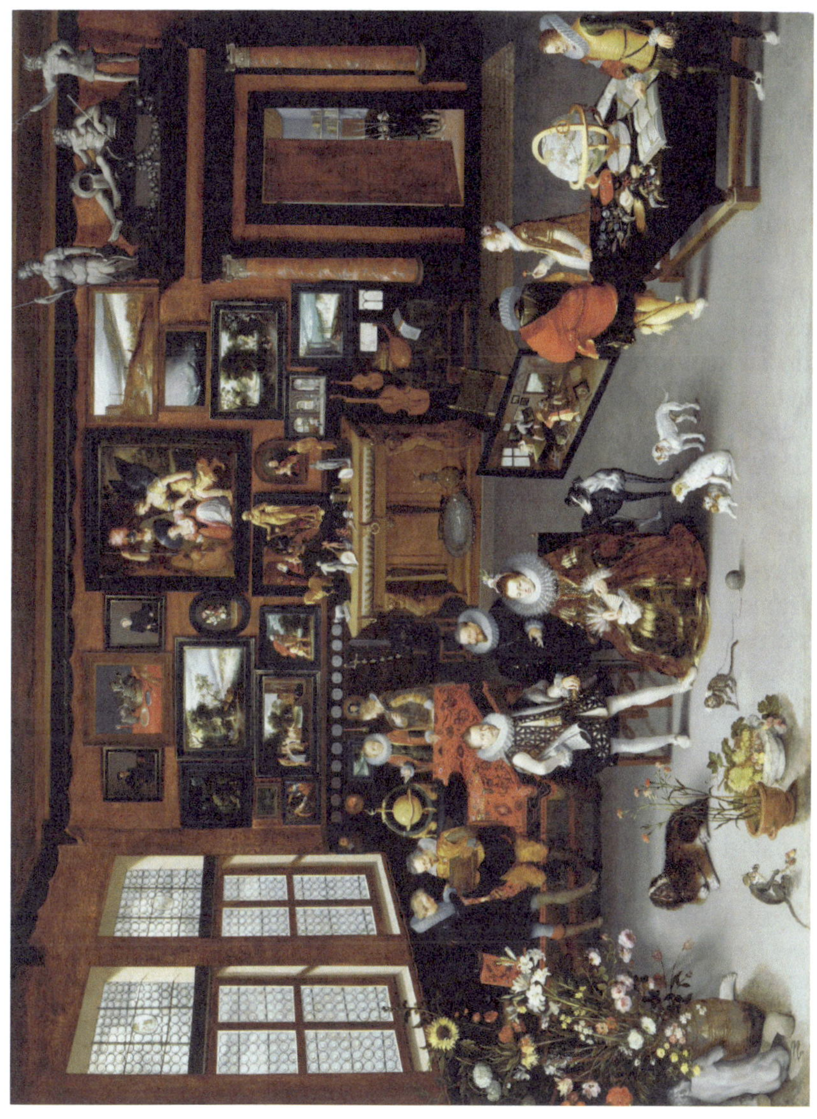

Jan Brueghel the Elder and Hieronymus Francken II, *The Archdukes Albert and Isabella Visiting a Collector's Cabinet*, 1621–1623, oil on panel, 94 × 123.3 cm. The Walters Art Museum, inv. nr. 37.2010, Baltimore.

Fig. 585

collection, and most paintings hang parallel to the picture plane on the back wall, there is one centrally placed at an angle. This work depicts the vandalism of iconoclast donkeys—a common theme of the period—and its strong linearity demonstrates full mastery of the pictorial challenge.

The entanglement of multiple systems of representation within the same work have been noted by Victor I. Stoichiță and Ian Verstegen for early modern painting, and has been discussed by Beate Fricke and others for the medieval period.[9] The first examples of panels depicted within panels appeared in the traditional iconography of St. Luke painting the Virgin, gradually evolving into studio paintings by the end of the fifteenth century. Verstegen noted that around 1500, the portrait of the Virgin and Child is sometimes depicted with coherent foreshortening, treating the embedded image and its content as an object. In other cases, the Virgin disregards the constraints of the panel, turns toward the viewer, and appears more lifelike.[10] He defines this rift as "head-frame disjunction" and convincingly connects it to the changing status of cult images even before the Reformation. Stoichiță observed comparable tendencies in early modern portraiture.[11] Furthermore, Isaac van Aelst engraved an elaborate frontispiece featuring the personifications of Painting and Geometry beneath the monument of Vitruvius for the 1629 (or 1638?) edition of *Perspective* by Samuel Maroloys in Amsterdam.[12] Painting holds a palette, a maulstick, and brushes in her left hand, while leaning on a panel. The panel shows the geometrically exact construction of a corridor in foreshortening. As it is set parallel to the plane, the opposition between the two perspectival systems is negligible. Nevertheless, the vanishing point clearly differs from that of

9
Beate Fricke, "Horizont und Panorama – Darstellungsmodi und Bildraum im 15. Jahrhundert am Beispiel der Scherzliger Passionswand," in *Jerusalem am Thunersee – Das Scherzliger Passionspanorama neu gedeutet*, Katharina Heyden and Maria Lissek, eds. (Basel: Schwabe, 2021), pp. 75–107.

10
Ian Verstegen, "Between Presence and Perspective: The Portrait-in-a-Picture in Early Modern Painting," *Zeitschrift für Kunstgeschichte* 71 (2008): 513–526.

11
Victor I. Stoichiță, *The Self-Aware Image: An Insight into Early Modern Metapainting*, trans. Lorenzo Pericolo (Chicago: Harvey Miller, 2015), pp. 89–99.

12
Stoichiță, *The Self-Aware Image*, pp. 87–89.

the overall monument, and similar divergences are evident in the two framed shallow reliefs on the base, which depict preliminary phases of a pavement and a house.

However, as mentioned earlier, the phenomenon did not begin in the seventeenth century; it emerged as early as 1300, possibly linked to increased naturalistic tendencies.[13] However, it appears that the combination of primary and secondary virtual spaces was avoided in early Renaissance painting. This raises the question of whether the embedded painting should be perceived as two- or three-dimensional. The former simplifies the painting process but limits the composition and depth of the image-within-image. Mainstream practice typically referenced images-within-images as objects without depth, such as statues, wood and stone carvings, or mosaics and panels. An unequivocal example from the fourteenth century shows the virtual space of a painting included within another. In 1372, Niccolò di Tommaso depicted a fresco-within-fresco in the Church of Tau in Pistoia [fig. 588].[14] Here, the image of St. Anthony Abbot is shown above a wooden chest. The figure is placed in the fictive, secondary space of the embedded fresco. Despite its limited depth, the work indicates awareness of and engagement with multiple orders of spatial representation.[15]

Examples from the fifteenth century are scarce as well. While one might wish to avoid reductive explanations, it is difficult to dismiss Pietro Accolti's observation in the previously quoted passage. As he establishes a distinction between the surface (*superficie*) and the inner space (*dintorni*) of an embedded image, he also emphasizes that the surface is relatively easy and straightforward to depict, whereas fictive space poses a challenge and requires a systematic approach. I will contextualize this seventeenth-century

13
Bokody, *Images-within-Images in Italian Painting*, pp. 59–88.

14
Ugo Feraci and Laura Fenelli, "Gli affreschi di Niccolò di Tommaso nella chiesa del Tau: una rilettura iconografica," in *Il museo e la città: vicende artistiche pistoiesi del Trecento*, Damien Cerutti, ed. (Pistoia: Gli Ori, 2012), pp. 81–119, here pp. 81–83.

15
See also the chapter "Zwei Meta-Physiken des Bildes? Zur Figur/Grund-Relation in der Vormoderne aus der Perspektive dreistelliger Bildbegriffe" by Christoph Poetsch in this volume.

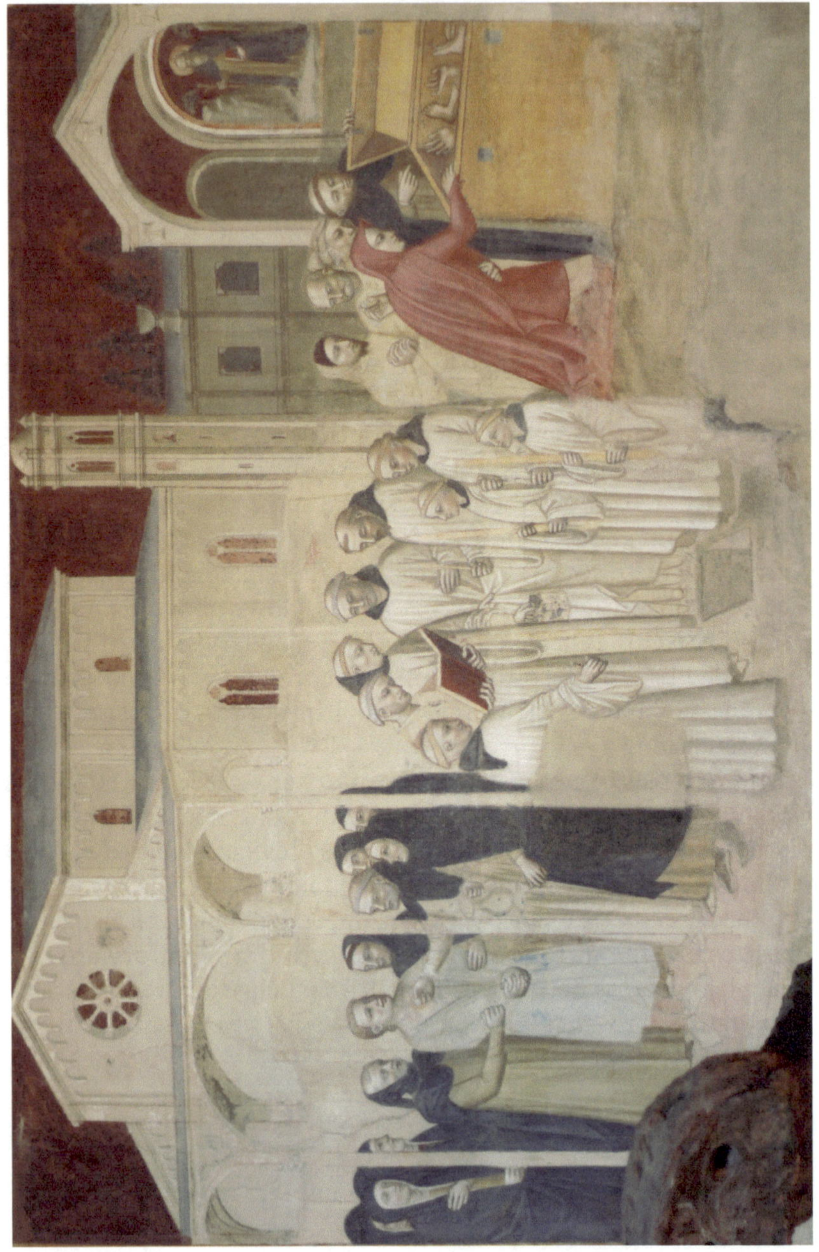

Niccolò di Tommaso, *Three Scenes from the Everyday Life of a Preceptory*, 1372, fresco. Palazzo del Tau, Pistoia.

Fig. 588

primary source by tracing the dichotomy of surface and depth in fifteenth-century treatises on painting, particularly in the writings of Leon Battista Alberti and Leonardo da Vinci. I argue that the possibility of combining different orders of virtual space was not recognized in these theoretical texts. However, the lack of geometric engagement did not entirely preclude the possibility of actual pictorial execution; it merely made such experiments less straightforward. It is perhaps not surprising, therefore, that the sporadic examples emerged in response to iconographic and narrative needs. Andrea Mantegna and Cosimo Rosselli both employed secondary fictive spaces in their works. Comparing these examples highlights the potential of this experimental pictorial practice before 1500, especially in terms of how new perspectival forms can present and question themselves.[16]

Surface and Depth in Theory

Since Erwin Panofsky's seminal study on perspective as "symbolic form" from 1927, a key question has revolved around the notion of a preexistent, homogenous, and infinite space.[17] Panofsky insisted on an art historical narrative in which the representation of three-dimensional figures evolved into the representation of space itself. For him, this transition also meant the gradual emancipation of painting from sculpture and its tangible spatiality. The mathematical model that regulated and facilitated the creation of this independent space played a key role in his evolutionary scheme.[18] Subsequent critics rightly pointed out that foreshortening was neither exclusive to painting nor necessarily indicative of the construction of such Euclidean space. Christopher Lakey's work demonstrated the use of pictorial illusionism in medieval relief sculpture.[19] Similarly, James Elkins argued that Renaissance

16
For a plural history of perspective see Hubert Damisch, *The Origin of Perspective*, trans. John Goodman, (Cambridge, MA: MIT Press, 1994), pp. 1–55.

17
Erwin Panofsky, *Perspective as Symbolic Form*, trans. Christopher Wood (Brooklyn: Zone Books, 1991), p. 27.

18
John White, *The Birth and Rebirth of Pictorial Space* (London: Faber and Faber, 1967), pp. 19–56 and 113–134.

19
Christopher R. Lakey, *Sculptural Seeing: Relief, Optics, and the Rise of Perspective in Medieval Italy* (New Haven, CT: Yale University Press, 2018), pp. 39–120.

theoretical writings and the actual works focused more on the accurate depiction of objects rather than on the depiction of space.[20]

Leon Battista Alberti's *De Pictura* (1435) has been at the forefront of these discussion.[21] Importantly, he approaches pictorial practice through the concept of surface rather than depth. In the oft-quoted instruction for painters, he states:

> Therefore, all other things about it left aside, I will say what I myself do when I paint. First, I trace as large a quadrangle as I wish, with right angles, on the surface (*superficie*) to be painted; in this place, it certainly functions for me as an open window through which the *historia* is observed.[22]

In this statement, painting becomes the protocol for creating virtual locations, which in turn serve as the necessary setting for a story. The term "space," in the sense of the depth of a painting, is not mentioned in this passage; instead, the "open window" serves as a metaphor for a fictive three-dimensional reality. Alberti uses the term "surface" (*superficie*) to describe the inherent tension between the physical reality of the object and the virtual reality of the painting. It is telling that the object is not defined; therefore, the surface can be understood as paper (for drawing), wood (for panel painting), or the wall itself (for mural painting). At one point, he refers generally to "either of a panel (*tavola*) or of a wall (*muro*)."[23] Alberti's profession and the architectural reference to the window certainly favors the wall, but there is no conclusive evidence in the text for the primacy of the fresco, the most versatile medium of the early Renaissance.

20
James Elkins, "Renaissance Perspectives," *Journal of the History of Ideas* 53 (1992): 209–230, here 209–10.

21
Charles H. Carman, "Meanings of Perspective in the Renaissance: Tensions and Resolutions," in *Renaissance Theories of Vision*, John Shannon Hendrix, Charles H. Carman, and Allison Levy, eds. (Burlington, VT: Ashgate, 2010), pp. 39–50, here pp. 39–44.

22
Leon Battista Alberti, *On Painting*, trans. and ed. Rocco Sinisgalli (Cambridge, UK: Cambridge University Press, 2011), p. 35.

23
Alberti, *On Painting*, p. 32.

Whereas "window" is mentioned only once in *De Pictura*, the term "surface" occurs over a hundred times, and it is a constitutive part of the argument.[24] It is not limited to the surface of the painting; it can describe the exteriors of all manner of things waiting to be depicted. At the beginning of Book One, Alberti defines surface as "the extreme part of a body, which is not recognizable through a certain depth (*profondità alcuna*) but only by length (*longitudine*) and width (*latitudine*)."[25] The formulation possibly harks back to Campanus of Novara's presentation of Euclid's *Elements*, where bodies are described by their three dimensions: length (*longitudine*), width (*latitudine*), and height (*altitudine*). Piero della Francesca would later fully adhere to this terminology in his monumental work *On Perspective for Painting*.[26] Alberti's Italian is more complex here, as he describes surfaces as units without depth rather than applying Euclid's clear geometric division of length, width, and height to bodies. This choice is plausible because surfaces in three-dimensional space can have length and width, length and height, or width and height, and still be considered two-dimensional entities. However, Alberti introduces a new term, *profondità alcuna*, which is linked to the empirical experience of spatiality rather than to its geometric notation. Similar to the window, *profondità alcuna* is mentioned only once in the work.

For Alberti, therefore, the surface is devoid of depth and lacks the spatial complexity of a body. Its simplicity allows it to become the fundamental building block of painting, even more essential than points or lines. The subsequent pages of the book provide a rich taxonomy of surfaces based on their limits and shapes and describe vision as the interaction between these surfaces and the eye (and the visual pyramid) through extreme, median, and centric rays.[27] His geometrical system for depicting distances relies on the consistency of surfaces, as they are the primary facets of objects and figures that the painter maps and reproduces. This emphasis on the surface will be reiterated in Alberti's synthesis on the *historia*, where he explains the connection between body, member,

24
See on this aspect in Alberti's passage: Quené, *Goldgrund und Perspektive*, pp. 117–152.

25
Alberti, *On Painting*, p. 25.

26
Piero della Francesca, *De Prospectiva Pigendi*, Gizzi, Chiara, ed. (Venice: Ca' Foscari, 2016), pp. 139 and 419.

27
Alberti, *On Painting*, pp. 25–29.

and surface: "the first parts of a work [are], therefore, the surfaces, because from these are formed the members, from the members the bodies, [and] from the bodies the *historia* from which surely one obtains that outstanding and perfect work of the painter."[28]

The pervasiveness of this definition can be measured by the fact that the preference for the surface informs Leonardo da Vinci's notes: "For painting does not, as a matter of fact, extend beyond the surface; and it is by its surface that the body of any visible thing is represented."[29] Alberti's axiom, the distinction between surface and depth, appears logical and intuitive: things (bodies) are three-dimensional, therefore they have depth, but their appearance can be reduced to surfaces without volume. Leonardo, again, subscribes to this without hesitation: "A surface is an extension made by the transversal movement of a line, and its extremities are lines. A surface has breadth (*larghezza*) and length (*lunghezza*), but no depth (*profondità*). A body is a quantity formed by the lateral movement of a surface and its boundaries are surfaces. A body is a length, and it has breadth with depth formed by the lateral movement of its surface."[30] Leonardo's focus remains the simulation of plasticity on a surface.[31]

If compared to Pietro Accolti's treatise, it is indicative that these sections consistently ignore the possibility of a surface that may have depth without becoming a body. The option of inner space, or *dintorno* in Accolti's words, which does not lead to volume or spatial extension, is missing from the discussion. This, however, can be nothing other than the depiction of a plane within a three-dimensional fictive depth: a painting. While mapping the theoretical and practical ways of representing bodies and things in space, fifteenth-century authors exclude the scenario in which this virtual space itself could become the subject of representation. I doubt that this dismissal follows a decision, but I believe that it

28
Alberti, On Painting, p. 44.

29
Leonardo da Vinci, *Notebooks*, Irma A. Richter and Thereza Wells, eds. (Oxford: Oxford University Press, 2008), p. 39.

30
Leonardo da Vinci, *Notebooks*, p. 39.

31
Martin Kemp, *Leonardo da Vinci: The Marvellous Works of Nature and Man* (London: J. M. Dent, 1981), pp. 247–255; and Martin Kemp, *Leonardo da Vinci: Experience, Experiment and Design* (London: V&A Publications, 2006), pp. 109–114.

is nevertheless symptomatic of a historical situation when painting was challenged to establish itself as simulating the natural world and its spatial aspects. The discursive field protects the straightforwardness of the pictorial practice by separating representations from the objects of representation. The inclusion of additional virtual spaces into the virtual space of the painting would have led to severe complications. The theoretical discourse does not encourage or even consider the depiction of paintings within paintings.

The Last Supper Fresco in the Sistine Chapel

Cosimo Rosselli and possibly Biagio d'Antonio encountered this pictorial challenge while working in the Sistine Chapel in Rome. The architectural setting of the Last Supper fresco includes three images behind the protagonists: the Agony in the Garden, the Taking of Christ, and the Crucifixion [fig. 594]. The embedded images have their own spatial order, different from the depicted virtual space in the fresco. I suggest that the hesitant execution of the imagery betrays the pioneering nature of the details. They were included to complement the iconography of the entire New Testament cycle.

The Last Supper fresco in the Sistine Chapel was part of the initial typological program comparing the life of Moses to the life of Christ, with special emphasis on Peter, the head of the apostles. The renovation of the *capella magna* of the Vatican palace started after the election of the Franciscan friar Francesco della Rovere to Pope Sixtus IV in 1471.[32] Even before its extensive fresco decoration, the chapel played a significant role in the institutional life of the papacy and the religious routine of the *curia*. On October 27, 1481, Cosimo Rosselli, together with Perugino, Botticelli, and Ghirlandaio, signed a contract to complete ten frescoes with depictions from the Old and New Testaments by March 15, 1482.[33] The document allowed the use of assistants (*familiares*).[34] The

32
Ulrich Pfisterer, *The Sistine Chapel: Paradise in Rome*, trans. David Dollenmayer (Los Angeles: The Getty Research Institute, 2018), pp. 2–8.

33
Edith Gabrielli, *Cosimo Rosselli: Catalogo Ragionato* (Turin: Umberto Allemandi, 2007), p. 275.

34
Virginia Budny and Frank Dabell, "Hard at Work 'di notte chome di dì:' A Close Reading of Cosimo Rosselli's Career, with Some New Documents," in *Cosimo Rosselli: Painter of the Sistine Chapel*, Arthur R. Blumenthal, ed. (Winter Park: George D. and Harriet W. Cornell Fine Arts Museum, 2001), pp. 23–43, 34–35.

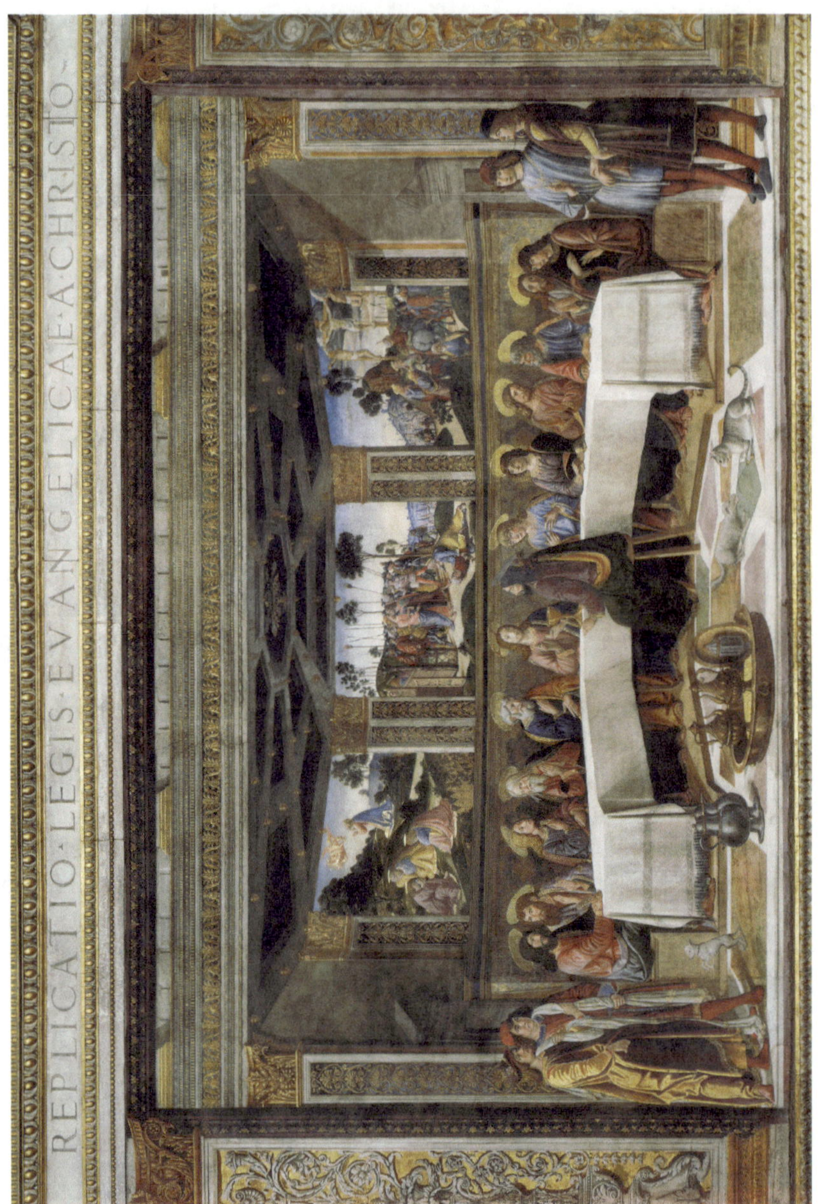

Cosimo Rosselli, *The Last Supper*, 1481–1482, fresco.
Sistine Chapel, Vatican.

Fig. 594

hiring of three painters from Florence and another with ties to the city must have been the result of a conscious cultural policy, and it may have marked a deliberate gesture of reconciliation between the pope and Lorenzo Medici, who suspected papal endorsement of the Pazzi conspiracy in 1478.[35] Altogether, sixteen scenes were painted, of which twelve survive. The attribution of the *Last Supper* to Cosimo Rosselli is generally accepted, though the three images-within-images are assigned to other contributors.[36] Before examining these metapictorial aspects, it is relevant to discuss their iconographies. I believe that their subject matter promoted their integration, which may explain their visual inconsistencies.

The Last Supper scene has strong eucharistic references: Christ holds a piece of bread and blesses the chalice in front of him.[37] Judas sits on the other side of the table, in line with the contemporary Florentine iconography of the scene, such as Ghirlandaio's work for the refectory of the Ognissanti (1480).[38] A devil on his back and the dark halo underline his perdition. The scene also references the betrayal of Christ, who is about to hand over the dipped bread to Judas. The composition follows the Gospel of John (John 13:21–30), with the important omission of the beloved disciple leaning on Christ's bosom. The reason for this shift was to increase the prominence of Peter, who is now facing Judas on Christ's right. This focus on Peter appears to extend to the three scenes on the rear wall: the Agony in the Garden, the Taking of Christ, and the Crucifixion [fig. 596–598]. The inclusion of these narratives must have meant to remedy the absence of the key moments of the Passion from the overall iconography of the Sistine Chapel. The typological comparison of Moses and Christ, which consolidated the role of Peter as leader of the Church, had difficulties accommodating his repeated

35
Michelle O'Malley, "Finding Fame: Painting and the Making of Careers in Renaissance Italy," in *Renaissance Studies* 24 (2010): 9–32, 26–32; Pfisterer, *The Sistine Chapel*, pp. 28–33.

36
Pfisterer, *The Sistine Chapel*, p. 18; Paula Nuttal, "The Life and Times of Cosimo Rosselli," in *Cosimo Rosselli: Painter of the Sistine Chapel*, Arthur R. Blumenthal, ed. (Winter Park: George D. and Harriet W. Cornell Fine Arts Museum, 2001), pp. 11–21, here p. 15; Gabrielli, *Cosimo Rosselli*, pp. 168–176.

37
Leo Steinberg, *Leonardo's Incessant Last Supper* (New York: Zone Books, 2001), pp. 31–53.

38
Joseph Polzer, "Reflections on Leonardo's Last Supper," *Artibus et Historiae* 32 (2011): 9–37.

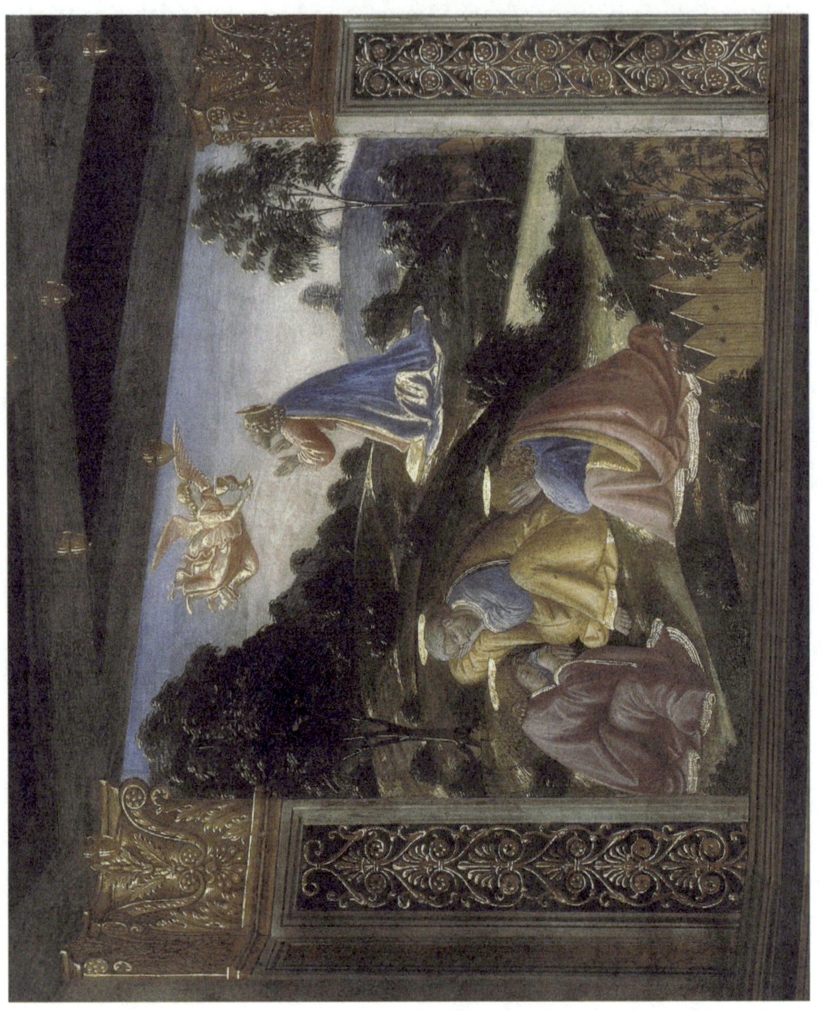

Biagio d'Antonio (?), *Agony in the Garden*, detail of Cosimo Rosselli, *The Last Supper*, 1481–1482, fresco. Sistine Chapel, Vatican.

Fig. 596

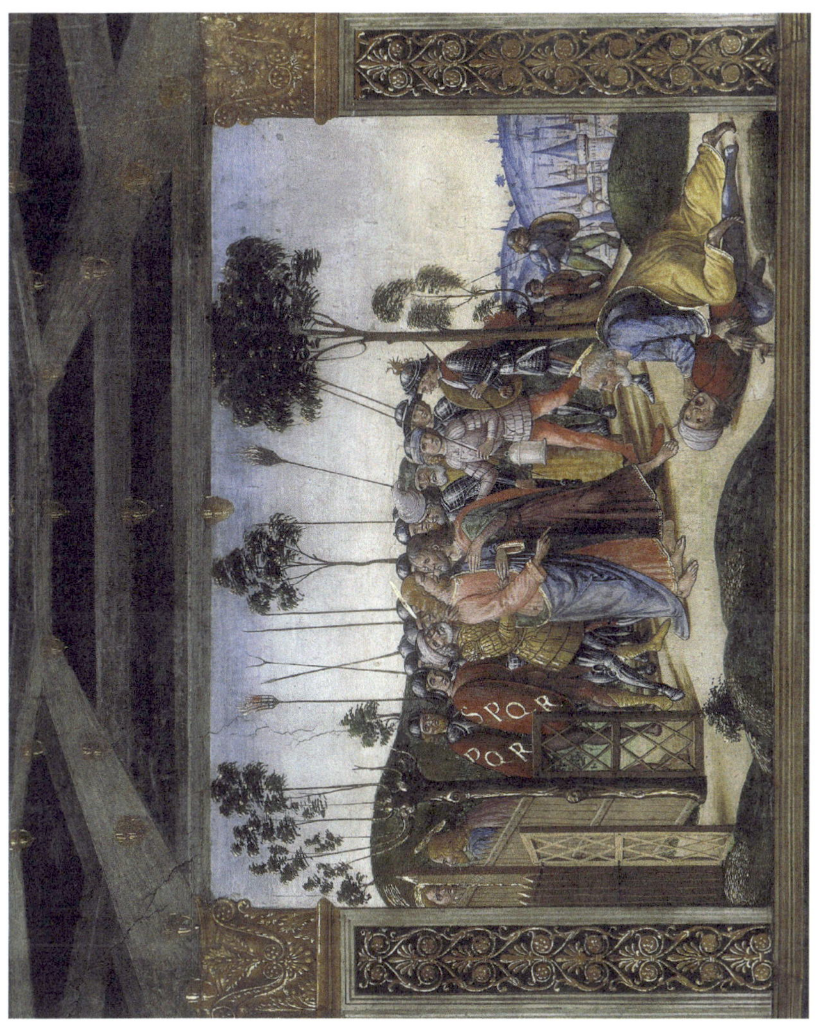

Biagio d'Antonio (?), *Taking of Christ*, detail of Cosimo Rosselli, *The Last Supper*, 1481–1482, fresco. Sistine Chapel, Vatican.

Fig. 597

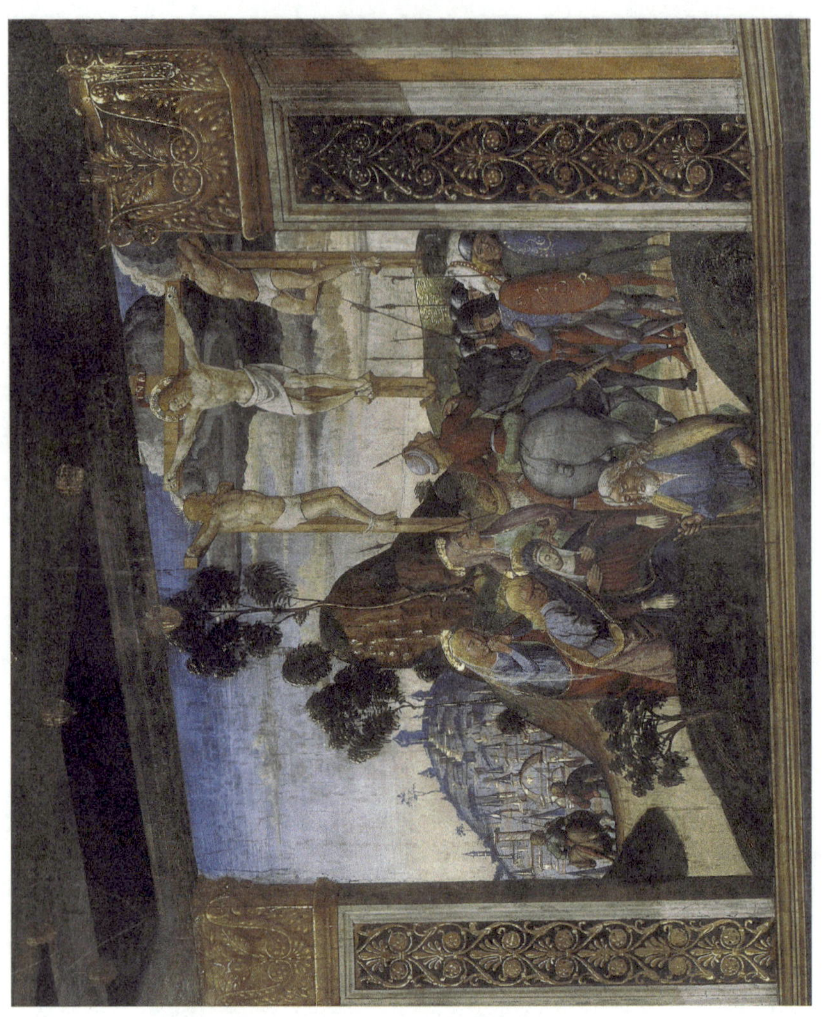

Biagio d'Antonio (?), *Crucifixion*, detail of Cosimo Rosselli, *The Last Supper*, 1481–1482, fresco. Sistine Chapel, Vatican.

Fig. 598

denunciations; therefore, these passages were not included in the full-scale program. However, they could not be completely left out either. Their reduced versions as part of the *Last Supper* were an acceptable compromise.

Timothy Verdun has convincingly argued that the scenes link back to the presentation of the Eucharist in the foreground.[39] This correspondence was widely established for the Crucifixion [fig. 598]. In the Garden, Christ prays for the chalice to be removed from him (Matthew 26:39, Mark 14:36, Luke 22:42) [fig. 596]. Therefore, the angel presents to chalice to him in the embedded image. Similarly, during the Taking, Christ scolds Peter for cutting Malchus's ear off and tells him that he must drink from the chalice (John 18:10–11) [fig. 597]. In the embedded image, Christ embraced by Judas gestures towards Peter. I would, therefore, propose that in addition to the emphasis on the Eucharist the choice of the scenes relates to the papacy's self-representation. Peter was a key protagonist in the Garden and Taking of Christ scenes, being the confidant and protector of the Savior. In this context, it is in fact only his absence during the Crucifixion that is challenging. Here, the composition is split between the enigmatic half-length figure of an old man in the foreground and the traditional iconography in the background with John and Evangelist and the three Marys. The man has white beard and long white hair, wears a blue robe and a yellow cloak, and holds a clutch. All these features link him to the presentation of Peter across the entire cycle, with the exception of the missing tonsure and halo. If the figure is indeed Peter, his presence may allude to Luke 23:49, where Christ's acquaintances follow his Passion from afar. This would suggest that he witnessed his death.

In any case, from these iconographic considerations it is clear that the inclusion of the three narrative scenes in the background had some bearing on the principal subject matter. In other words, they were not incidental embellishments. The split execution of the fresco makes this issue even more intriguing. Rosselli's authorship of the inserted scenes have been questioned from the

39 Timothy Verdon, "L'Ultima Cena della Sistina: Appunti d'Iconologia," in *Cosimo Rosselli – Tre Restauri*, Cristina Acidini and Niccolò Rosselli Del Turco, eds. (Florence: Polistampa, 2018), pp. 129–138.

late-nineteenth century. One possible candidate is Biagio d'Antonio, who may have been responsible for painting the Crossing of the Red Sea in the same cycle.[40] However, there are notable deviations between the depiction of the Agony in the Garden on the one hand and the Taking of Christ and the Crucifixion on the other, which may allow assigning them to different workshop assistants.[41]

Regardless of the identification, the embedded images and their hybrid systems of foreshortening are the works of different painters. The images-within-images form three sides of an octagon that follows the similarly polygonal shape of the table, the walls, and the ceiling. Consequently, the two images on the flanks are depicted in a forty-five-degree angle to the plane of the fresco. Already Giorgio Vasari noted this unusual construct in the first and second edition of the *Lives* (1550 and 1568) on Cosimo Rosselli, focusing on the ceiling and the table:

> Being afterwards summoned, with other painters, to execute the work that Pope Sixtus IV had undertaken in the Chapel of the Palace ... he painted three scenes with his own hand, wherein he depicted the Submersion of the Pharaoh in the Red Sea, the Preaching of Christ to the people on the shore of the Sea of Tiberias, and the Last Supper of the Apostles with the Savior. In the last scene he made an octagonal table drawn in perspective (*tirate in prospettiva*), with the ceiling above it likewise octagonal, the eight angles of which he foreshortened (*scortando*) so well as to show that he had as good a knowledge of this art as any of the others.[42]

Vasari did not comment on the embedded images, which can be read either as an indication of their insignificance or a testament

40
Roberta Bartoli, *Biagio d'Antonio* (Milan: Motta, 1999), pp. 201–202.

41
Gabrielli, *Cosimo Rosselli*, p. 174.

42
Giorgio Vasari, *Le vite dei piú eccellenti architetti, pittori, et scultori italiani*, Luciano Bellosi and Aldo Rossi, eds. (Turin: Einaudi, 1986), pp. 448–449; Giorgio Vasari, *Le vite de' piv eccellenti pittori, scvltori, et architettori* (Florence: Giunti, 1568), p. 438; and Giorgio Vasari, *Lives of the Most Eminent Painters, Sculptors, and Architects* 3, trans. Gaston du C. De Vere (London: Macmillan and The Medici Society, 1912), p. 188.

to their relatively seamless execution. The depiction of various episodes of the same story was used extensively in the Sistine Chapel, Sandro Botticelli's *Trials of Moses* being a prime example. Here, the episodes are distributed within the landscape, confirming what Wolfgang Kemp called the "narrativization of depth" and the "chronotopos of the road."[43] On Rosselli's fresco their medium is more ambiguous. One can read them as windows through which the spectator observes a narrative space. However, they are also plausible as images. Their architectural framing repeats the decorative pattern of the fictive colonnade of the entire cycle [fig. 594]. Moreover, their ontological status intentionally copies the ontological status of the principal images, and in this sense, they are frescoes-within-frescoes. The repetition of the fictive architectural pattern turns this element of the *Last Supper* into a self-reflexive visual commentary on mural painting.

It is possible that Cosimo Rosselli created the basic architectural context for these images through the design of the setting, and Biagio d'Antonio was left to accommodate the three narratives within these constraints, which required him to innovate to some extent. It is without doubt that he confronted the pictorial challenge of depicting the virtual spaces of the three embedded images: deep landscapes characterize the compositions. In the first instance, this meant adhering to the general viewpoint of the cycle required by the elevated placement of the frescoes, and showing the events from below. In this sense, the painter followed the established pattern of foreshortening. For the Taking of Christ no further readjustment was needed, since it runs parallel to the plane of the main scene. The handling of the Garden scene and the Crucifixion are more complex. Their vanishing points diverge from the principal perspective of the fresco. However, to highlight their different status, Biagio d'Antonio also shifted the center of the compositions to the left and the right and created a relatively empty space on the side that flanks the Taking of Christ. The intention in all probability was to underline the oblique angle of the embedded images. However, the alteration gives the impression that the frame

43
Wolfgang Kemp, *Die Räume der Maler: Zur Bilderzählung seit Giotto* (Munich: C. H. Beck, 1996), pp. 109–119 and 159–198.

of the scene is lagging behind its subject matter. These aspects indicate yet again that the oblique inclusion of images-within-images was imposed on the painter rather than organically emerging from the pictorial practice.

Andrea Mantegna and the *Picture-Bearers*

Contemporary of Cosimo Rosselli, Andrea Mantegna faced a similar problem when depicting the Picture-Bearers as part of *The Triumphs of Caesar* series [fig. 603]. However, unlike his Florentine colleague, Mantegna demonstrates a full mastery of the secondary pictorial space, creating what Stephen J. Campbell calls a "striking metapictorial device."[44] In Mantegna's case, the narrative context of the work prompted the inclusion of details, but it did not determine their exact content. This relative freedom allowed more coherent pictorial experiments.

Andrea Mantegna is documented as working on *The Triumphs of Caesar* on August 26, 1486, when Guidobaldo da Montefeltro, the young Duke of Urbino, visited Mantua and had the opportunity to see some of the paintings.[45] Although the marquess Federico I Gonzaga might have initiated the project, it was Francesco II Gonzaga who financed the majority, if not the entirety, of the work, which may have lasted until the artist's death in 1506.[46] Its original location is unknown, the order of the execution of the paintings is debated, and it cannot be conclusively established that the surviving nine canvases present the intended complete work. The patron(s), the contemporaries, and subsequent generations of painters and owners recognized the significance of the undertaking, and several copies of the series survive.[47]

44
Stephen J. Campbell, *Andrea Mantegna: Humanist Aesthetics, Faith, and the Force of Images* (London: Harvey Miller, 2020), p. 257.

45
Andrew Martindale, *The Triumphs of Caesar by Andrea Mantegna in the Collection of Her Majesty the Queen at Hampton Court* (London: Harvey Miller, 1979), p. 31.

46
Caroline Elam, "Les Triomphes de Mantegna: la Forme et la Vie," in *Mantegna, 1431–1506*, Giovanni Agosti, Giovanni and Dominique Thiébaut, eds. (Paris: Hazan, 2008), pp. 363–372, here p. 363; Andrea Campbell, *Mantegna*, pp. 257–260.

47
Elam, "Les Triomphes de Mantegna," pp. 367–371; and Martindale, *The Triumphs of Caesar*, pp. 97–108.

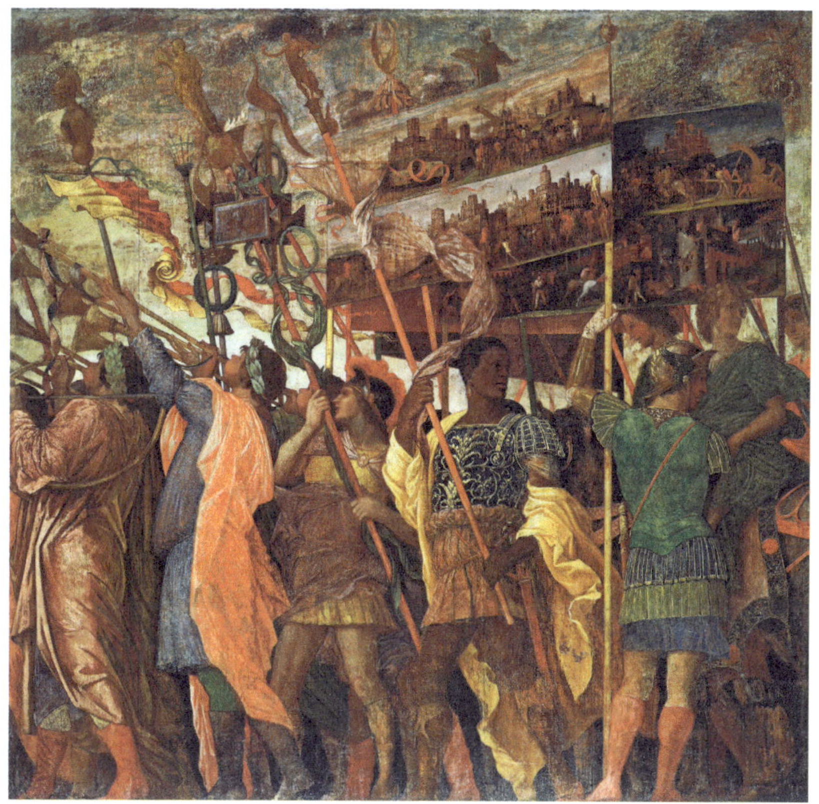

Andrea Mantegna, *The Picture-Bearers*, ca. 1486–1506, tempera on canvas, 270.3 × 280.7 cm. Hampton Court Palace, The Royal Collection, inv. nr. RCIN 403958, London.

Fig. 603

The series depicts Julius Caesar's triumphal procession, likely following the Gallic Wars. Mantegna relied either directly on ancient sources ranging from Plutarch to Appian or on their compilation, such as the one compiled by his friend Giovanni Marcanova, which unfortunately no longer survives. Contemporary treatises on Roman triumphal processions, like Roberto Valturio's *De re militari* (1472) or Flavio Biondo's *Roma triumphans* (1472) must have been available to him as well.[48] While painting the series, he also traveled to Rome between 1488 and 1490, obtaining further archaeological input for the recreation of the material culture of antiquity.[49] The basic structure is a sequence of several categories of military spoils from siege engines to captives, and it concludes with the figure of Julius Caesar on his chariot.

The first image in the narrative order shows the picture-bearers. The composition consists of three main parts: the group of the trumpeters on the left, the standard-bearers in the center, and the picture-bearers on the right. The scene is painted from below conforming to the general vantage point used throughout the entire series. As Andrew Martindale noted in his seminal monograph on the cycle, their condition deteriorated following the arrival of the paintings in England (before 1649), leading to several rather questionable restoration attempts, notably by Louis Laguerre in 1701–1702 and, specifically in the case of *The Picture-Bearers*, by Roger Fry in the 1910s.[50] Coincidentally, the upper part of the canvas showing the images on banners are the few remaining areas that can be assigned to Mantegna. Two subsequent copies—the engravings by Andrea Andreani (1595–1599) and a set of grisaille aquarelles now in Vienna (1590/1620, Kunsthistorisches Museum)—confirm the original composition. It is likely that the aquarelles are the work of Bernardino Malpizzi, who provided these models for Andreani's engravings [figs. 606–607].[51]

48
For an overview of the written sources see Anthony Halliday, "The Literary Sources of Mantegna's 'Triumphs of Caesar,'" in *Annali della Scuola Normale Superiore di Pisa: Classe di Lettere e Filosofia* III/24 (1994), pp. 337–396.

49
Sarah Vowles and Caroline Campbell, "Mantegna, Bellini and Antiquity," in *Mantegna and Bellini*, Caroline Campbell, Dagmar Korbacher, Neville Rowley, and Sarah Vowles, eds. (London: National Gallery, 2018), pp. 232–248, here p. 242.

50
Martindale, *The Triumphs of Caesar*, pp. 115–118 and pp. 133–134.

The pretext or reason for depicting the picture-bearers can be found in historical sources. Plutarch recorded the triumph celebrating the Third Macedonian War (171–168 BCE) in his *Life of Aemilius* and noted that the first day "barely sufficed for the exhibition of the captured statues, paintings (*tabulisque*), and colossal figures, which were carried on two hundred and fifty chariots."[52] The Greek passage was available in a Latin translation by Bruni from ca. 1470, and Flavio Biondo also repeats the sentence.[53] It suggests that the images were spoils of war, piled up together with other artifacts. On the other hand, Appian of Alexandria wrote in Book VIII of the *Roman History* about images that commemorated the military exploits during Scipio Africanus's triumph after the Second Punic War (218–201). This Greek passage was available in a Latin translation by Piero Candido Decembrio from ca. 1477: "Wooden towers were brought along showing the likeness (*simulacra*) of captured cities. Then writings (*scripturae*) and images (*imagines*) of what they managed."[54] Here, the images had an ostensive function since their narrative content on the war was made for and tailored to the triumph.

It is symptomatic that Flavio Biondo cited the sentence about the wooden towers but omitted the reference to the images.[55] Regarding the triumph of Pompey after the Third Mithridatic War (73–63), Appian writes about excessive and detailed imagery:

> There were carried in the procession images of those who were not present, of Tigranes and of Mithridates, representing (*simulacbra annotata erat*) them as fighting, as vanquished, and as fleeing. Even the besieging of Mithridates and his silent flight by night were represented. Finally, it was shown how he died, and the

51
Agosti and Thiébaut, eds., *Mantegna, 1431 1506*, pp. 397–399.

52
Plutarch, *Plutarch's Lives* 6, trans. Bernadotte Perrin (Cambridge, MA: Harvard University Press, 1954), p. 441; Martindale, *The Triumphs of Caesar*, pp. 136–137 and p. 178.

53
Flavio Biondo, *De Roma triumphante libri decem diligentissime castigati* (Brescia, 1503), CLXXIIv.

54
Appian, *Appian's Roman History* 1, trans. Horace White (Cambridge, MA: Harvard University Press, 1972), p. 507. Martindale, *The Triumphs of Caesar*, pp. 136–137 and p. 178.

55
Biondo, *De Roma triumphante*, CLXXIr.

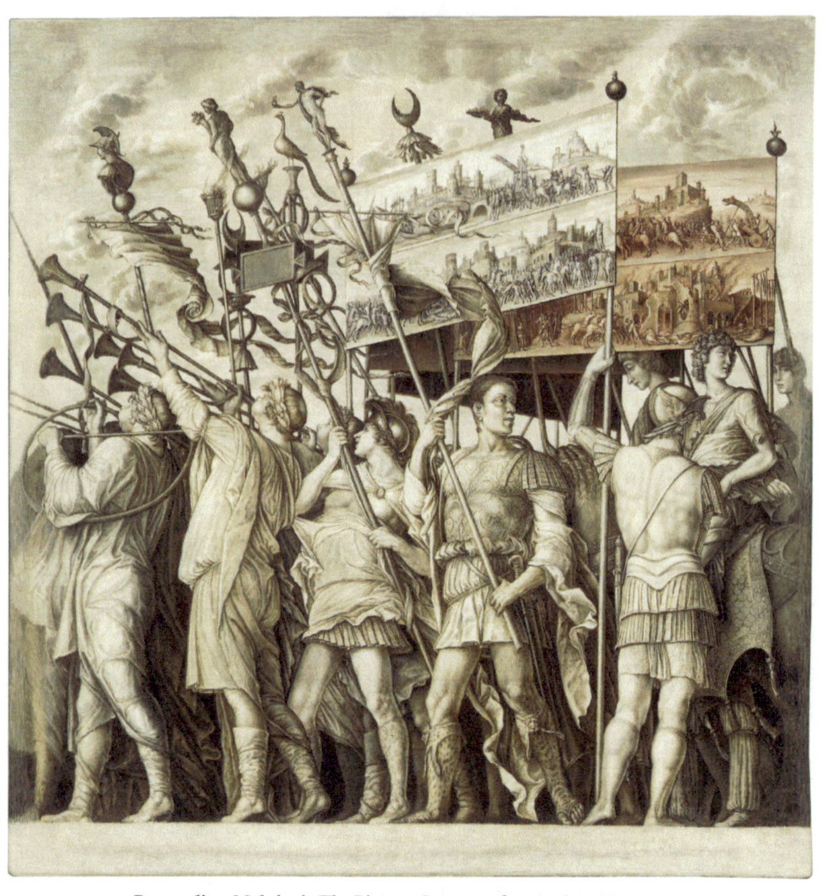

Bernardino Malpizzi, *The Picture-Bearers*, after Andrea Mantegna, ca. 1590, pigment on paper, 38 × 38 cm. Kunsthistorisches Museum, inv. nr. Gemäldegalerie, 297, Vienna.

Fig. 606

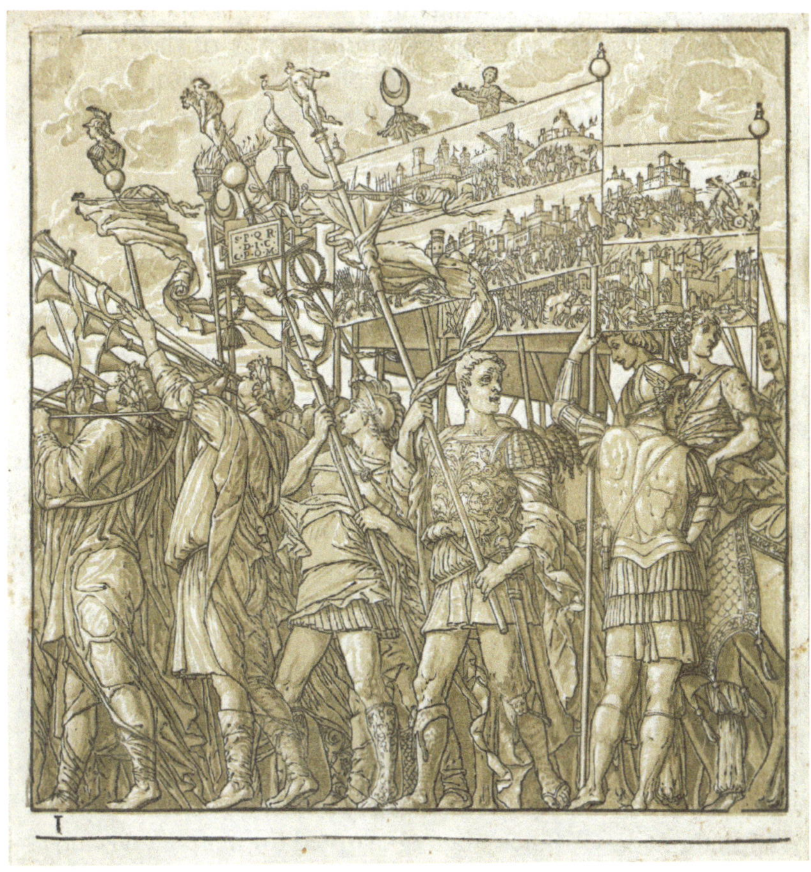

Andrea Andreani, *The Picture-Bearers*, after Bernardino Malpizzi,
1595–1599, engraving, 40 × 39 cm.
The Metropolitan Museum of Art, inv. nr. 22.73.3-89, New York City.

Fig. 607

> daughters who perished with him were depicted (*depicte*) also, and there were figures (*similitudines*) of the sons and daughters who died before him, and images (*imagines*) of the barbarian gods decked out in the fashion of their countries.[56]

In this case the content is further specified, and the passage differentiates between the images of gods, relatives, and narrative paintings about military events. These specifications are missing in Flavio Biondo's account on Pompey.[57] Roberto Valturio did not repeat the descriptions of these triumphs, but addressed various forms of remembrance systematically in Book XI, such as obelisks and pyramids.[58] He concludes with Aemilius Paulus and Scipio, who used paintings (*tabula pictum*) to commemorate publicly their deeds and victories.[59] None of these passages account for the exact content of Mantegna's *Picture-Bearers*, but they nevertheless indicate an intellectual milieu where narrative paintings are considered integral parts of military triumphs.[60]

Mantegna depicts four paintings on banners [fig. 609]. Two appear to be without visual content, and they are mostly covered. Horizontal lanes divide the other two, resulting in four elongated rectangular images. The thickness of the right side of the first banner suggests that they are painted on panel instead of fabric, which would have been the customary choice for medieval processional imagery.[61] Since Mantegna opted for tempera on canvas for the *Triumphs of Caesar*, the reference to wood in the images-within-images introduces a material distinction between the primary and secondary medium.

The actual subject matter of the four images cannot be identified with certainty, and the compositions are partially

56
Appian, *Appian's Roman History* 2, pp. 467–469.

57
Biondo, *De Roma triumphante*, CLXXIIIrv.

58
Roberto Valturio, *De Re Militari* (Verona, 1472), pp. 487–493.

59
Valturio, *De Re Militari*, p. 493.

60
Keith Christiansen, *The Genius of Andrea Mantegna* (New York: The Metropolitan Museum of Art, 2010), pp. 38–41.

61
Jessica N.Richardson, "The Brotherhood of Saint Leonard and Saint Francis: Banners, Sacred Topography and Confraternal Identity in Assisi," *Art History* 34 (2011): 884–913, here 886.

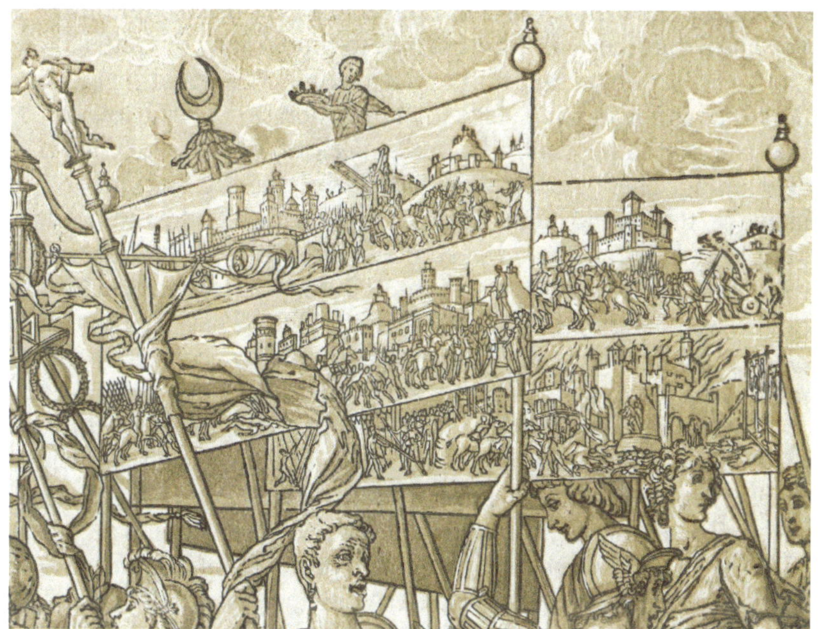

Detail of Fig. 607.

Fig. 609

obscured. The visible content relates to sieges of strongholds and cities, but they cannot be linked to topography of Gallia, Caesar's most important military campaign. The upper image on the first banner shows a siege tower in operation. In the lower one, a leader addresses his troops (*adlocutio*) while a skirmish is developing. These scenes take place during the day. The upper image on the second banner depicts the towing of a dragon-headed catapult, while the lower image shows a devastated city burning, with its inhabitants being slaughtered. Emphatically, dead bodies can be seen hanging from gallows on the right. These scenes take place at night. The imagery exposes the gruesome reality of war, thereby further emphasizing the power of the military leader.

The virtual space of these embedded images is carefully constructed. Both banners are positioned obliquely to the principal plane, requiring Mantegna to harmonize distinct spatial realms. This remains true even if the image-pairs on the banners align with each other, since the superimposition of the banners generates additional tension between the two depicted systems. The contrast between the lighter tonality of daytime and the darker tone of the night sky reinforces this distinction. The spatial structures on all four images rely on fortifications set obliquely to the plane of the banner, creating a strong sense of recession. Therefore, the various military confrontations develop within this deep space. All in all, Mantegna not only uses the triumphal context to display images-within-images but also takes advantage of the embedded banners to seamlessly combine and contrast different perspectives. The crowded composition of the principal images, with bodies lined up in the foreground, further underscores this difference.

There is yet another piece of visual evidence regarding the genesis of the *Picture-Bearers*. The drawing currently in the Louvre was either a preparatory sketch by Mantegna himself or by a workshop assistant after Mantegna's original, due to some inconsistencies in the anatomy of the human figures [fig. 611].[62] Its significance

62
Agosti and Thiébaut, eds., *Mantegna*, pp. 382–383; and Sarah Vowles, "New Light on Mantegna's 'Triumphs of Caesar,'" *Master Drawings* 57 (2019): 33–46, here pp. 39–40. For other preparatory drawings and readjustments in the *Triumphs* see Richard Cocke, "The Changing Face of the Temple of Janus in Mantegna's 'The Prisoners:' Politics and the Patronage of the 'Triumphs of Caesar,'" *Zeitschrift für Kunstgeschichte* 55 (1992): 268–274.

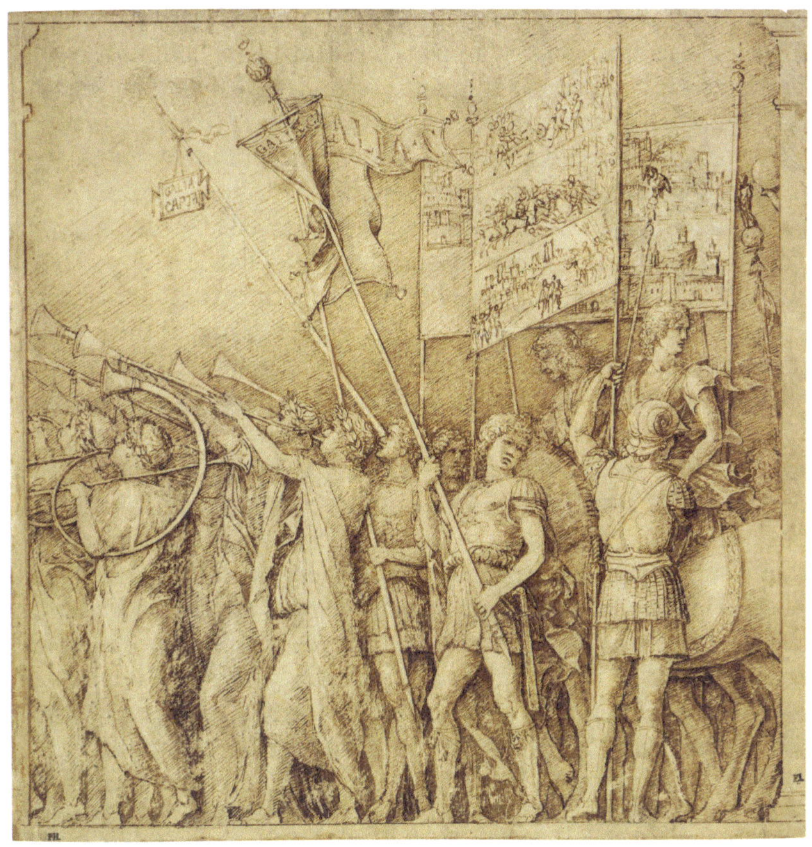

Andrea Mantegna (?), *The Picture-Bearers*, ca. 1486–1490, pen-and-ink drawing, 27 × 27 cm. Musée du Louvre, inv. nr. 775 DR/ Recto, Paris.

for the overall series is generally acknowledged.[63] It depicts the intended architectural framing of the scenes with columns, and the three inscriptions on the standards (GALIA CAPTA) specifically link the work to the Gallic War, a detail missing from the final paintings. The embedded images show different understandings of virtual space on this preparatory sketch.[64] There are only two banners [fig. 613]. The first banner is placed at an angle to the plane and comprises three images that depict battle scenes. Although the lowest image also features a fortification in the background, the virtual space overall has limited depth, as the composition is confined to the scenes in the foreground. The second banner parallels the plane, it consists of two images, which depict fortifications. These fortifications align horizontally with the virtual plane of the banner and thus with the actual plane of the drawing. The complex union of oblique banners with dominant oblique buildings is missing. Consequently, the entanglement of multiple perspectival systems is less evident here. It appears that by multiplying, rotating, and redesigning the embedded images in the final painting, Mantegna aimed to create a more pronounced contrast between the primary and secondary perspectives.

Even if Mantegna saw Cosimo Rosselli's *Last Supper* fresco during his sojourn in Rome between 1488 and 1490, the *Picture-Bearers* does not directly respond to it. Painted presumably within a decade, the two works show experiments with secondary pictorial space in different media, resulting in markedly different outcomes. However, since these are among the few surviving images from the period depicting images-within-images, any conclusions must be drawn with caution.[65] Rosselli's *Last Supper* is indebted to the rich iconography of the New Testament and a narrative practice that incorporates multiple episodes within the same

63
Sandrina Bandera, Howard Burns, and Vincenzo Farinella, eds., *Andrea Mantegna: rivivere l'antico, costruire il modern* (Venice: Marsilio, 2019), pp. 163–164.

64
Martindale remarked this difference but linked it to the iconography of the banners. Martindale, *The Triumphs of Caesar*, pp. 137–138 and p. 163.

65
For instance, Giovanni Bellini's Pesaro Altarpiece (Civic Museum, Pesaro) dated to the 1470s is an intriguing parallel, with its ambiguous landscape in an architectural frame.

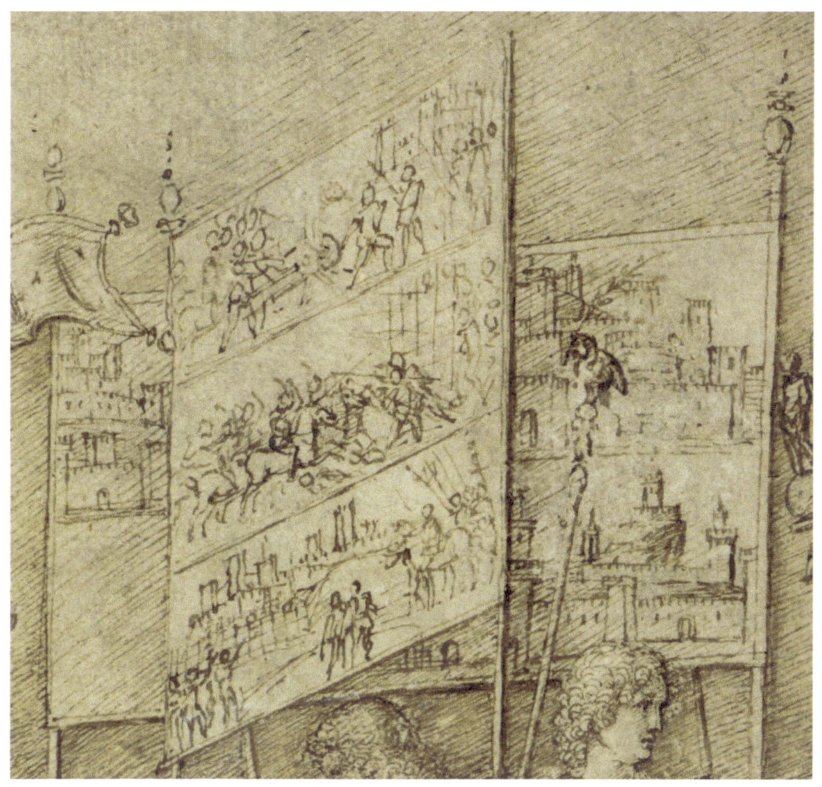

Detail of Fig. 611.

Fig. 613

work. His images-within-images address and resolve the demands of the subject matter. In this process, the pictorial execution adapts to these demands, but some details, such as the handling of secondary spatial systems, may be less coherent. Mantegna's *Picture-Bearers* are the result of an archaeology of Antiquity. Although they respond to the iconography of Roman triumphs, the indeterminate subject, combined with the desire to recreate a bygone material culture, results in a nuanced composition in terms of primary and secondary spaces. Judged by the surviving drawing, Mantegna sought to expose his mastery of spatial orders.

All in all, the two works point toward a moment in European art in which perspectival systems are challenged. Without doubt, the hierarchy of primary and secondary perspective is maintained (as it would be in gallery and cabinet paintings), but the images-within-images introduce a plurality to the prevailing system of foreshortening. Images-within-images have been interpreted as an afterthought to composite medieval image-fields, but in this case, they have a bearing on the construction of virtual space itself. Viewers are once again invited to abandon their prescribed point of view and explore the multiplicity of virtual spaces. In this process, the painting's ground becomes destabilized. The physical surface of the image does not transform into a single fictive surface but offers a plurality of virtual grounds. Therefore, Rosselli's and Mantegna's experiments stand at the beginning of a metapictorial process that will ultimately question any notion of painting being a standalone and self-sufficient virtual projection of reality. The multiplicity of embedded spaces and their virtual grounds signal immanently the possibility of adding a further layer to any visual construct. This does not necessarily result in the infinite regression implied by *mise en abyme* or, subsequently, the Droste effect. However, it does demonstrate that the ground is not a fixed boundary but rather a frontier for innovation.

Part 5
Transgressing Depth

I

Pieter Bruegels d. Ä. Tafel *Die Elster auf dem Galgen* aus dem Hessischen Landesmuseum Darmstadt stellt eine gelungene Verbindung aus Landschafts- und Genremalerei dar [Fig. 617].[1] Während im linken Vordergrund Bauern ausgelassen tanzen und feiern, eröffnet das Bild zugleich ein grandioses Panorama. Aus leicht erhöhter Position blicken wir zwischen zwei Bergzügen hindurch auf eine Flusslandschaft, die sich bis an den Horizont erstreckt. Die in das Jahr 1568 datierte Tafel misst gerade einmal 46 × 51 cm und weist damit eine nahezu quadratische Form auf. Bei dem in Öl und Tempera auf Holz gemalten Bild handelt es sich um ein Kabinettformat, das der Künstler auch für andere Werke genutzt hat. Man könnte es problemlos in die Hände nehmen, um es aus großer Nähe zu studieren.[2] Wie auch bei der Grisaille vom *Marientod,* dem *Gähnenden* und den *Affen* aus Berlin haben wir es mit einem Bild zu tun, dessen rätselhafter Gehalt sich geradezu umgekehrt proportional zu seiner überschaubaren Größe verhält. Der Künstler hat zahlreiche Szenen und Details miniaturhaft in der Landschaft verborgen.[3] Menschen sind unterwegs, Tiere befinden sich auf der Weide, Schiffe ankern am Ufer oder befahren den Fluss in Richtung Horizont. Gemächlich ziehen die Wolken dahin. Es ist ein träger Sommertag, der uns

1
Zur bisherigen Forschung sei verwiesen auf: Gibson, Walter S.: *Bruegel*, London 1977, 193–195; Genaille, Robert: La pie sur le gibet, in: Sulzberger, Suzanne (Ed.): *Relations artistiques entre les Pays-Bas et l'Italie à la Renaissance*, Brüssel 1980, 143–152; Marijnissen, Roger H.: *Bruegel. Tout l'œvre paint et dessiné*, Antwerpen 1988, 370–375; Simonson, Anne: Pieter Bruegel's Magpie on the Gallows, in: *Konsthistorik Tidskrift* 67, 1998, 71–92; Kavaler, Ethan Matt: *Pieter Bruegel. Parabels of Order and Enterprise*, Cambridge 1999, 217–233; Roberts-Jones, Philippe/Roberts-Jones, François: *Pieter Bruegel*, New York 2002, 177–179; Ludwig, Heidrun: Pieter Bruegels Elster auf dem Galgen. Forschungsgeschichte und Bibliographie, in: *Kunst in Hessen und am Mittelrhein* 7, 2012, 49–65; Levesque, Catherine: Truth in Painting – Comedic Resolution in Bruegel's Landscape with the Magpie on the Gallows, in: Smith, David R. (Ed.): *Parody and festivity in early modern art. Essays on comedy as social vision*, Farnham 2012, 63–83. Außerdem: Müller, Jürgen/Schauerte, Thomas: *Pieter Bruegel. Das vollständige Werk*, Köln 2018, 169 und 299, Nr. 37.

2
Vgl. hierzu: Müller, Jürgen: Vorsicht ansteckend! Pieter Bruegel d. Ä. „Der gähnende Mann". (K)eine Bagatelle, in: Ruhkamp, Uta (Ed.): *In aller Munde. Das Orale in der Kunst und Kultur* (Ausst.-Kat. Kunstmuseum Wolfsburg, Wolfsburg), Berlin 2020, 112–117.

3
Die interessanteste Deutung der flämisch-niederländischen Landschaftsmalerei des 16. Jahrhunderts verdanken wir Falkenburg, Reindert L.: *Joachim Patinir. Landscape as an image of the pilgrimage of life*, übers. v. Michael Hoyle, Amsterdam/Philadelphia 1988.

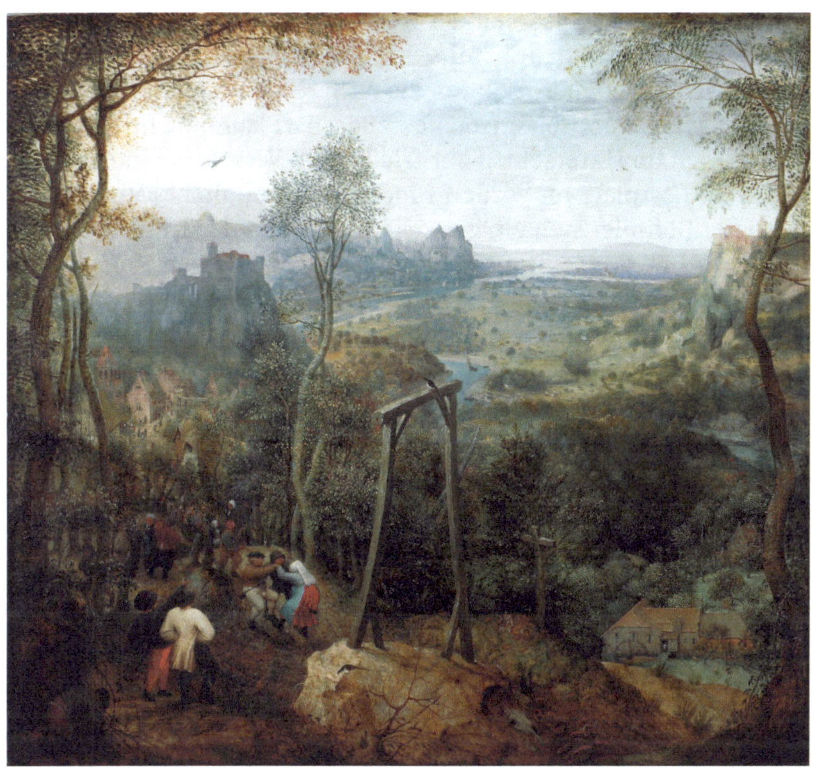

Pieter Bruegel d. Ä., *Die Elster auf dem Galgen*, 1568, Öl und Tempera auf Holz, 45.9 × 50.8 cm. Hessisches Landesmuseum, inv. Nr. GK 165, Darmstadt.

Fig. 617

in dieser Überschau geboten wird. Gleichwohl ist die Sonne im Bild nicht zu sehen. Sie steht bereits tief und muss sich links oberhalb des Platzes befinden, was durch die nach rechts fallenden Schatten deutlich wird. Poetischer ist eine Landschaft kaum mehr denkbar.[4]

Doch im Unterschied zur friedlichen Welt des Hintergrunds geht vom Festplatz im Vordergrund eine unheimliche Wirkung aus. Hier befindet sich ein großer Galgen, den der Künstler auf merkwürdige Weise dargestellt hat. Während dessen Pfosten parallel zueinander stehen, scheint der Querbalken von vorn nach schräg hinten zu führen und nimmt einen anderen Verlauf, als es die darunter befindliche Konstruktion erlauben würde. Der Maler hat ein optisches Paradox realisiert, durch das unsere Bildwahrnehmung verunsichert wird. Unterhalb des auffällig inszenierten Hinrichtungsinstruments befindet sich ein Kreuz, um das herum zahlreiche rote Backsteine angeordnet sind, für die es bisher keine rechte Erklärung gibt. Noch weiter unten entdecken wir eine Wassermühle, deren weiß gekleideter Müller gerade über eine kleine Brücke ins Innere des Gebäudes schreitet. Gut sichtbar hat Bruegel das große Wasserrad dargestellt, dessen Radnabe auf einer Mauer aufliegt.

Der Künstler hat für seine Erzählung eine proleptische Zeitkonstruktion gewählt. Sind bisher auch nur wenige Personen auf der Anhöhe eingetroffen, wird sich dies bald ändern. Eine Gruppe von zwei Männern und einer Frau hat bereits zu tanzen begonnen und der hinzugeeilte Dudelsackpfeifer spielt munter auf. Und schaut man auf den Weg links in die Ortschaft hinab, so hat sich eine größere Gruppe von Menschen auf den Weg gemacht. Entsprechend wird der Platz rund um den Galgen schon bald voller Menschen sein. Die Ausgelassenheit der Tanzenden wird dazu führen, dass weder der Galgen noch der erhabene Ausblick in die Landschaft für die Festgemeinschaft von Bedeutung sein wird. Nicht der Schrecken des finsteren Mordinstruments,

4
Zu Poetik und Ikonographie der Jahreszeitenfolge bei Bruegel vgl. Kaschek, Bertram: *Weltzeit und Endzeit. Die „Monatsbilder" Pieter Bruegels d. Ä.*, München 2012. Außerdem: Müller Hofstede, Justus: Zur Interpretation von Pieter Bruegels Landschaft. Ästhetischer Landschaftsbegriff und Stoische Weltbetrachtung, in: Simson, Otto von/Winner, Matthias (Ed.): *Pieter Bruegel und seine Welt*, Berlin 1979, 73–142, Abb. Tafel 44–51; Michalsky, Tanja: Imitation und Imagination. Die Landschaft Pieter Bruegels d. Ä. im Blick der Humanisten, in: Laufhütte, Hartmut (Ed.): *Künste und Natur in Diskursen der Frühen Neuzeit*, vol. 1, Wiesbaden 2000, 383–405.

sondern vielmehr die hereinbrechende Dunkelheit wird dem Fest ein Ende bereiten. Den ausgelassenen Menschen bleiben die dräuenden Zeichen verborgen.

In der linken unteren Ecke scheinen zwei Männer die übrige Festgemeinschaft willkommen zu heißen. Einer der beiden hat die Hände in die Hüften gestemmt, als würde er selbst zu tanzen beginnen, während der andere mit seinem rechten Arm in Richtung Elster und Galgen weist. Bruegel hat die beiden als Rückenfiguren dargestellt, als wären sie aus einer anderen Richtung gekommen als die hinaufstrebende Dorfbevölkerung. Links unten hat der Künstler einen defäkierenden Bauern versteckt. Solche sogenannten „Kacker" sind Bestandteile der deutschen wie auch der niederländischen Malerei, wie uns ein Blick auf die *Ruhe auf der Flucht* von Joachim Patinir zeigen kann [Fig. 620].[5] In diesem Zusammenhang wurde in der Forschung auf das Sprichwort vom „auf den Galgen scheißen" hingewiesen, wie es Bruegel in seinem Berliner Sprichwörter-Bild genutzt hat [Fig. 621]. In Wirklichkeit scheißt der Bauer im Darmstädter Bild aber nicht wirklich auf den Galgen, sondern hat sein Hinterteil sichtbar für den Betrachter positioniert. Auch die sprichwörtliche Redensart vom „sich an den Galgen tanzen" ist in diesem Zusammenhang angeführt worden. Gleichwohl bleiben solche Hinweise auf Sprichwörter oder Redensarten unscharf, da sie kein komplexes Verständnis des Bildes ermöglichen.

Stephanie Porras ist in ihrem Aufsatz „Resisting the Allegorical" sogar so weit gegangen, die Deutbarkeit des kleinen Bildes überhaupt in Frage zu stellen.[6] Ihres Erachtens habe der Künstler gar keine Botschaft mitteilen wollen. Dies erscheint insofern problematisch, als Porras den existierenden Interpretationen keine

5
Büttner, Nils: Cacatum est pictum. Überlegungen zu einem übersehenen Thema der frühneuzeitlichen Kunst, in: *Niederdeutsche Beiträge zur Kunstgeschichte*, Ser. NF II, 2016, 157–174. Zu den theologischen Implikationen vgl. Müller, Jürgen/Schmidt Frank: Blumenfürze und Schmeißfliegen. Zwei neuentdeckte Luther-Satiren, in: Israel, Uwe/Müller, Jürgen (Ed.): *Körper-Kränkungen. Der menschliche Leib als Medium der Herabsetzung*, Frankfurt a. M./New York 2021, 259–295.

6
Porras, Stephanie: Resisting the Allegorical. Pieter Bruegel's Magpie on the Gallows, in: *Rebus* 1, Spring 2008, 86–100; id.: *Pieter Bruegel's historical imagination*, University Park 2016, 149–150; id.: Gossiping Tongues and Piles of Bricks. Pieter Bruegel, Iconoclasm and Revolt, in: Arciniega García, Luis/Serra Desfilis, Amadeo (Ed.): *Imágenes y espacios en conflicto. Las Germanías de Valencia y otras revueltas en la Europa del Renacimiento*, Valencia 2021, 437–453.

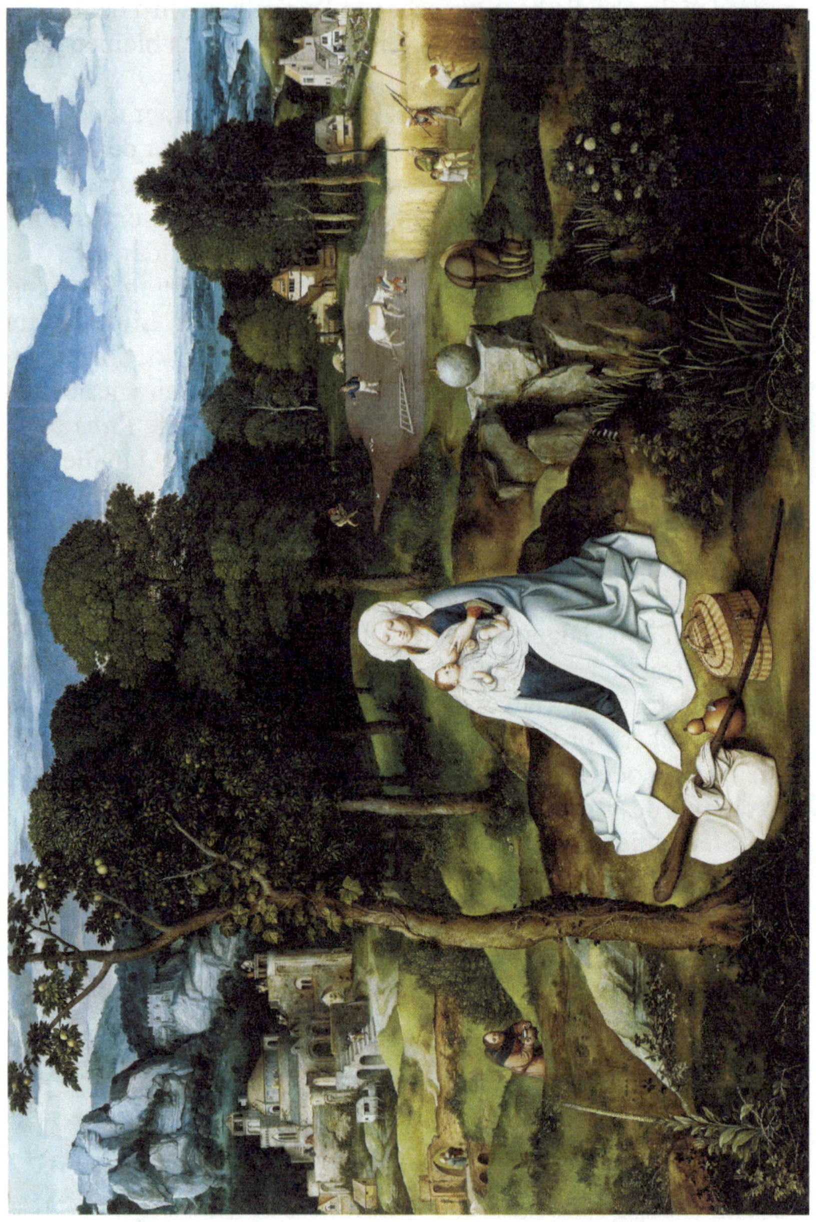

Joachim Patinir, *Landschaft mit der Ruhe auf der Flucht nach Ägypten*, 1518–1520, Öl auf Holz, 121 × 177 cm. Museo Nacional del Prado, inv. Nr. P001611, Madrid.

Fig. 620

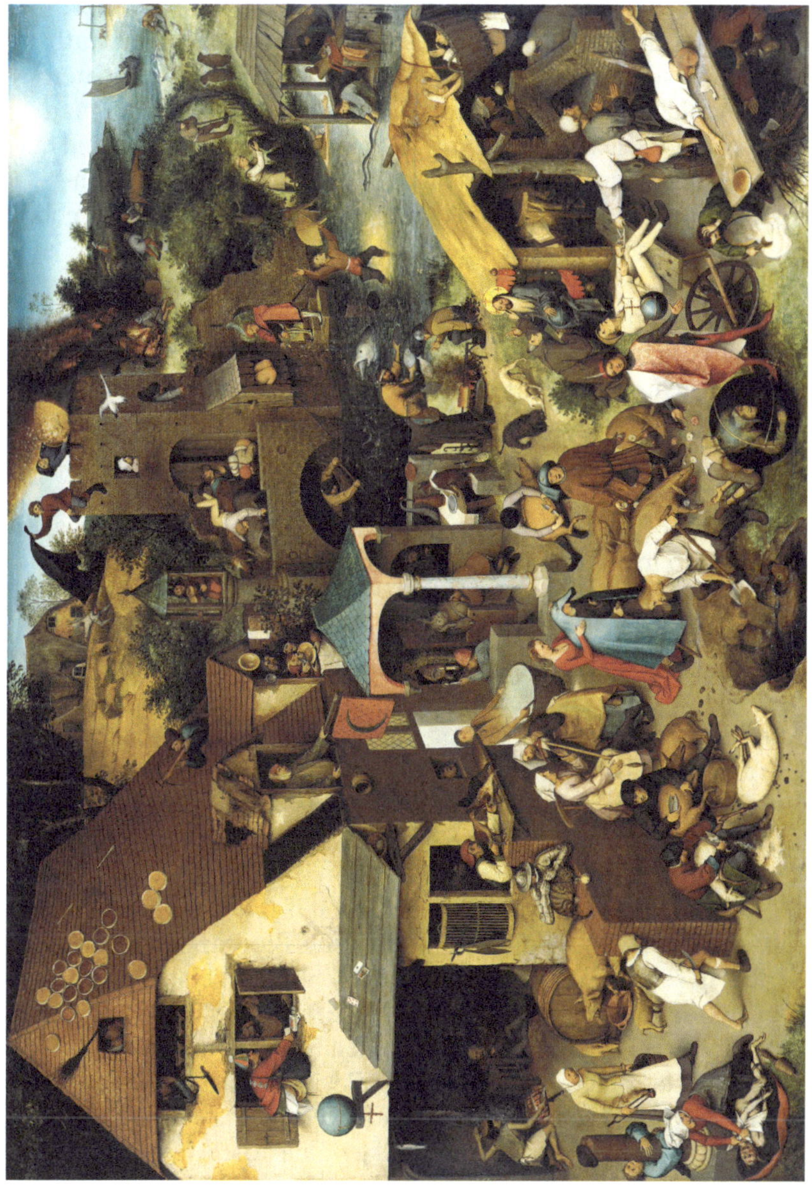

Pieter Bruegel d. Ä., *Die niederländischen Sprichwörter*, 1559, Öl auf Holz, 117 × 163.5 cm.
Gemäldegalerie, inv. Nr. 1720, Berlin.

Fig. 621

einzige Quelle oder Beobachtung hinzufügt. Sie kommentiert, nutzt und verwirft bestehende Deutungen, um am Ende Deutbarkeit als Illusion zu erweisen. Wenn der Künstler ihres Erachtens keine Absicht bei der Erstellung des Bildes verfolgte, kann man eine solche freilich auch nicht wiederfinden und entsprechend enthält sie sich eigener ideengeschichtlicher oder religiöser Kontextualisierung. Eine solche Position ist unangreifbar, aber auch unbefriedigend, weil jede Plausibilisierungsmöglichkeit von Deutung außer Acht gelassen wird. Um diese Einbahnstraße zu verlassen, sei im Folgenden eine bildtheologische Deutung angestrebt, die im Rätsel des vor- und zurückspringenden Galgens ihren Ausgangspunkt nimmt. Es versteht sich von selbst, dass dabei keine endgültige Lösung zur Erklärung des Bildes geliefert werden kann, aber immerhin eine Deutung, die im Sinne des Zusammengehens von Form und Inhalt hoffentlich eine höhere Plausibilität für sich beanspruchen kann als die bisherigen. Dabei bemühe ich mich, meine kunsthistorische Deutung durch kulturhistorische Überlegungen zu Bruegels Bildbegriff zu ergänzen.

Porras' Skepsis in Bezug auf zahlreiche Ausdeutungen ist ohne Zweifel zuzustimmen; der Hinweis auf das ein oder andere Sprichwort ist nicht mit einer wirklichen Analyse zu verwechseln. Aber ihr ist entschieden zu widersprechen, wenn sie Deutbarkeit als Illusion erweisen und in ein paradiesisches Reich sinnlicher Unmittelbarkeit zurückkehren will, wie es die Interpreten des frühen zwanzigsten Jahrhunderts glaubten in Bruegels Kunst erkennen zu dürfen.[7]

Zwei Elstern haben der Tafel ihren Namen verliehen. So schreibt Karel van Mander als wichtigster Biograph des Künstlers bereits in seinem *Schilder-Boeck* von 1604, Bruegel habe seiner Frau auf dem Sterbebett dieses Werk vermacht und damit sagen wollen, dass er die Klatschbasen an den Galgen wünsche. So vertreten zahlreiche Interpreten die Position, dass es in der Zeit der Habsburger Fremdherrschaft nahegelegen haben muss, die beiden Vögel auf Denunzianten zu beziehen, die Andersgläubige an die katholische Inquisition verraten.[8] Eine solche Auslegung

7
Porras, Resisting the Allegorical, 87. Zu Bruegel in volkstümlicher Deutung und als Maler von „Sittenbildern" vgl. Glück, Gustav: *Bruegels Gemälde*, Wien 1932, 22.

8
Zur Gefahr häretischer Aussagen von Bildern in Bezug auf die Inquisition, vgl. Müller, Jürgen: Von Kirchen, Ketzern und anderen Blindenführern. Pieter Bruegels d. Ä.

korrespondiert mit dem Umstand, dass die Elster auf dem Galgen besonders hervorgehoben wird und sich nahezu im absoluten Bildzentrum befindet. Ein zweite sitzt unmittelbar vor dem linken Pfosten des Hinrichtungsinstruments.

Das Elster-Bild, wie ich es der Einfachheit willen im Folgenden nennen möchte, war häufig Gegenstand der Forschung. Dabei lassen sich im Wesentlichen zwei Interpretationsansätze unterscheiden. Entweder hat man im Sinne der Mitteilung van Manders eine politische Deutung angestrebt oder dem Bild lediglich einen diffusen, volkstümlichen Inhalt im Sinne eines Sprichwortes zugewiesen. Die Beschreibung des Biographen macht aber vor allem deutlich, dass sich das Bild über den Tod des Malers hinaus im Besitz der Familie befunden hat.[9] Indes wissen wir weder, ob es einen Auftraggeber oder einen Adressaten gab, für den es als Freundschaftsgabe gedacht war, noch, ob es der Künstler für sich selbst geschaffen hat. Für die These einer persönlichen Zueignung spräche sowohl das Kabinettformat wie auch die intellektuelle Dichte der Ikonographie. Im Falle von Bruegels Verbundenheit mit dem Kartographen Abraham Ortelius ist überliefert, dass sich in dessen Besitz die Grisaille des *Marientodes* befand, nach deren Vorbild er sogar einen Kupferstich hat anfertigen lassen.[10]

Meine Beschreibung der Tafel macht deutlich, dass unsere Wahrnehmung des Bildes durch zahlreiche Gegensätze bestimmt wird. Dem Hinrichtungsinstrument steht im Mittelgrund ein großes Kreuz gegenüber und der selbstvergessenen Festgesellschaft die beobachtenden Männer vorne links; das gewaltige erhabene Panorama kontrastiert in der Dunkelheit des Waldes der Bauer, der seine Hose heruntergelassen hat und im Begriff ist, seine Notdurft zu verrichten. Vulgäres und Erhabenes finden in ein und demselben Bild statt. Dem bewegten Hier und Jetzt des Vordergrundes steht

„Blindensturz" und die Ästhetik der Subversion, in: Schwerhoff, Gerd/Piltz, Eric (Ed.): *Gottlosigkeit und Eigensinn. Religiöse Devianz im konfessionellen Zeitalter* (Zeitschrift für Historische Forschung, Beiheft 51), Berlin 2015, 493–530.

9
Zu van Manders Bruegel-Vita vgl. Müller, Jürgen: „Pieter der Drollige" oder der Mythos vom Bauern-Bruegel, in: Ertz, Klaus (Ed.): *Pieter Breughel der Jüngere, Jan Brueghel der Ältere. Flämische Malerei um 1600. Tradition und Fortschritt* (Ausst.-Kat. Villa Hügel, Essen, Kunsthistorisches Museum, Wien, Koninklijk Museum voor Schone Kunsten, Antwerpen), Lingen 1997, 42–53.

10
Das Freundschaftsalbum des Kartographen gibt eine Vorstellung von der intellektuellen Exzellenz des Freundeskreises, vgl. Puraye, Jean (Ed.): *Abraham Ortelius. Album Amicorum*, Amsterdam 1969.

der zeitlose Raum des Horizonts gegenüber – wäre da nicht der Galgen, der uns daran hindert, die erhabene Schönheit der Landschaft zu genießen und mit unseren Augen imaginär zu erwandern.

In der Forschung wurde dem optischen Paradox des Galgens wenig Aufmerksamkeit geschenkt. Im Unterschied zu Anamorphosen oder anthropomorphen Formen in Wolken oder Gesteinsformationen bildet eine solche Kippfigur einen Spezialfall visueller Wahrnehmung und kommt auf Tafeln und Gemälden des 16. Jahrhunderts insofern nicht zur Anwendung, als mit einer solchen Störung ein extremer Fiktionsbruch einhergeht, der die räumliche Kontinuitätsbehauptung des Bildes empfindlich stört.[11] Denn obwohl sich mit jeder neuen Wahrnehmung die Entstehung einer vollständigen Gestalt ankündigt, springt sie immer weiter um. Es handelt sich um eine paradoxe Figur, die sich aufgrund ihrer widersprüchlichen räumlichen Konfiguration nicht im dargestellten Raum verorten lässt, obwohl sie doch auf dem Festplatz zu stehen scheint. Sie entzieht sich dem Betrachter auch in dem Sinne, als sich jedes Stillstellen als unmöglich erweist.

Der Galgen stellt einen Stolperstein dar, dem zunächst einmal die Aufgabe des *attentum parare* zukommt.[12] Er erweist sich als diabolisches Detail und hält uns in Schach, ohne dass wir dessen Umschlagen anhalten könnten. Ja es ist, als würde uns der Galgen verhöhnen. Schlimmer noch, als würde mit seinem Umspringen die Gegenwart enteilen, sich permanent verschieben, ohne dass wir sie je erreichen könnten. Er wird zur tickenden Uhr, die uns an das Verrinnen der Zeit gemahnt.

Kann man für die widersprüchliche Darstellung des Galgens auch kein direktes Vorbild benennen, so lassen sich immerhin zahlreiche philosophische Paradoxien der Antike anführen, die auch heute noch verblüffend anmuten.[13] Xenons Erzählung vom Wettlauf zwischen Achilles und der Schildkröte kommt in den

11
Vgl. Villers, Jürgen: *Das Paradigma des Alphabets. Platon und die Schriftbedingtheit der Philosophie*, Würzburg 2005, 242.

12
Ueding, Gert/Steinbrink, Bernd: *Grundriß der Rhetorik. Geschichte, Technik, Methode*, Stuttgart 1986, 241. Marcus Fabius Quintilianus: *Ausbildung des Redners. Zwölf Bücher*, hg. u. übers. v. Helmut Rahn, 2 vols., Darmstadt [3]1995, vol. 1, IV, 1, 33 (416–419), IV, 1, 48 (422–425), V, 14, 30 (662 f.).

13
Vgl. Colie, Rosalie Littell: *Paradoxia Epidemica. The Renaissance Tradition of Paradox*, Princeton 1966.

Sinn, aber auch dessen ebenso einfache wie hinterhältige Frage, worin sich der Raum denn befände, wenn er ausgedehnt wäre.[14] Paradoxe Fragen und Erzählungen muten zunächst sinnvoll an, um dann unweigerlich in einen logischen Regress zu führen. Bruegels Kunst sind solche Denkfiguren nicht unvertraut. Auch in seinem Gemälde *Der Misanthrop* von 1568 aus dem Neapler Museo di Capodimonte spielt er mit der Tradition des Paradox, wenn er auf den Kreter Epimenides Bezug nimmt, der behauptete, alle Kreter würden lügen.[15] Darüber hinaus ist zur Erklärung seiner Kunst wiederholt auf Sebastian Francks Schrift *Paradoxa* aus dem Jahre 1534 zurückgegriffen worden, in der Verse aus der Bibel so miteinander verbunden werden, dass sie einen unaufhebbaren Widerspruch bilden.[16] Paradoxe sind schillernde Figuren des Undenkbaren. Wer sich ihrer bedient, will verblüffen oder beunruhigen.

Der Galgen befindet sich in einem widersprüchlichen Raum, der sich als Zeitschleife realisiert und *en permanence* die Unsichtbarkeit der Zeit in die Sichtbarkeit einer räumlichen Erscheinung überführt. Das Elster-Bild offenbart sich als irritierendes visuelles Experiment, das die Instabilität des Raums und die Zeit als vierte Dimension erweist. Bekanntlich stellen Raum und Zeit Anschauungsformen dar und sind für jede empirische Erkenntnis vorauszusetzen. Aber während sich der Raum des Bildes als Staffelung von vorn nach hinten und als Kontinuum offenbart, bleibt die Zeitlichkeit des Wahrnehmungsaktes als solche unsichtbar und ist nur indirekt als unaufhaltsamer Gestaltwandel zu erleben.[17] Ganz

14
Siehe dazu: Ferber, Rafael: *Zenons Paradoxien der Bewegung und die Struktur von Raum und Zeit*, Stuttgart 1995.

15
Vgl. Müller, Jürgen: Tous les Cretois mentent. *Le Misanthrope* de Pieter Bruegel: une nouvelle interprétation, in: *Die Bibel in der Kunst* 5, 2021, 2–19.

16
Hendrik Bonger und Arie-Jan Gelderblom weisen auf, dass zwischen 1558 und 1621 Übersetzungen von siebzehn größeren und kleineren Schriften des Theologen vorlagen und damit sogar mehr als von Luther oder Calvin. Francks spiritualistisches Denken übte immensen Einfluss in den Niederlanden aus. Vgl. hierzu Bonger, Hendrik/Gelderblom, Arie-Jan: Coornhert en Sebastian Franck, in: *De Zeventiende Eeuw* 12, 1996, 321–336: bes. 323. Sein Erfolg war sogar so groß, dass Johannes Calvin 1562 eine Schrift gegen den bereits 1542 verstorbenen deutschen Theologen veröffentlichte, die den Titel „Response à un certain Holondois" trägt und zeigt, dass man ihn als Niederländer erachtete. Vgl. mit weiterführender Literatur Kaschek, *Weltzeit und Endzeit*, 307–308.

17
Vgl. hierzu meinen früheren Versuch in Bezug auf das *Bauernhochzeitsmahl*, Müller, Jürgen: Bild und Zeit. Überlegungen zur Zeitgestalt von Pieter Bruegels „Bauernhochzeitsmahl", in: Pochat, Götz/Werner, Brigitte (Ed.):

so als würde das Voranschreiten der Zeit den Raum nicht zur Ruhe kommen lassen und seine Identität bestreiten. Mit dieser irritierenden Erfahrung geht aber auch ein Misstrauen gegenüber dem Bild selbst einher, das nur solange begreiflich bleibt, bis wir das verwirrende Detail erblicken. Und verführt uns die Räumlichkeit des Bildes auch zunächst zur Annahme der Gleichzeitigkeit des Bildgeschehens, kann sich der Galgen nicht im selben Zeit-Raum befinden wie die laufenden und tanzenden Bauern. Wir haben es mit einer Art von Gleichzeitigkeit des Ungleichzeitigen zu tun.

II

Wer das Verhältnis von Figur und Grund in frühneuzeitlicher Malerei zu bestimmen sucht, denkt über räumliche Verhältnisse und solche der Fläche zugleich nach: Was ist oben oder unten, was links oder rechts im Bild? Aber auch: Was befindet sich im Vorder-, Mittel- oder Hintergrund? Mit dem Problem von Figur und Grund ist also immer ein doppeltes Erkenntnisinteresse formuliert. Sowohl das eine wie das andere dient der Orientierung. Die Fläche betrifft das Bild als Träger, Unter- oder Malgrund, der im Bild illusionierte Raum hingegen das Davor und Dahinter. Mit der Bestimmung des Letzteren haben wir allerdings das räumliche Orientierungswissen des Rezipienten vorauszusetzen. Es dient der Selbstvergewisserung, mit der man sich immer auch selbst als räumliches Wesen definiert. Wir erkennen und erfahren Raum als ein für-mich, als Begeh- und Erreichbarkeit. Dies geschieht vorbewusst und stellt einen Automatismus dar.

Gottfried Boehm hat in einem instruktiven Aufsatz zur Figur-Grund-Problematik auf die Vielstimmigkeit des Begriffes Grund verwiesen.[18] Gleichwohl wird einem in deutscher Sprache zuallererst das Begründen in den Sinn kommen. Der Begriff offenbart seine metaphorische Qualität, wenn er Halt verspricht oder aber in übertragenem Sinne Kausalität zum Ausdruck bringt.[19]

Erzählte Zeit und Gedächtnis. Narrative Strukturen und das Problem der Sinnstiftung im Denkmal, Graz 2005, 72–81.

18
Vgl. Boehm, Gottfried: Der Grund. Über das ikonische Kontinuum, in: Id./Burioni, Matteo (Ed.): *Der Grund. Das Feld des Sichtbaren*, München/Paderborn 2012, 28–92.

19
Ibid., 30–31.

Dabei stellt sich die Frage, ob in historischer Perspektive das Reden von Figur und Grund nicht unter der Bedingung entstanden ist, den zeitlichen Umstand der Bildwahrnehmung außer Acht zu lassen. Blicken wir nämlich auf die Vorgeschichte des Problems, geht in Bezug auf die Begriffsgeschichte des Bildes unausgesprochen die Festlegung der Zeit als Augenblick und die Stillstellung des Auges einher. Führt man sich in diesem Zusammenhang Leon Battista Albertis *De pictura* aus dem Jahre 1435 vor Augen, erkennt man darin zunächst die Verbindung humanistischer wie auch mathematisch-geometrischer Überlegungen. Frank Zöllner hat Albertis Traktat mit den rhetorischen Konventionen jener Zeit in Verbindung gebracht.[20] Dieser soliden Herleitung ist nichts hinzuzufügen. Allerdings bleibt in seiner Auseinandersetzung die Frage nach der Abfolge der drei Bücher unberücksichtigt. Wenn wir es in *De pictura* lediglich mit dem Aufweis rhetorischer Kategorien für die Malerei zu tun haben, warum thematisiert der Humanist dann eingangs nicht den Maler als *vir bonus*, um stattdessen Perspektivlehre und geometrische Definitionen von Punkt, Linie und Fläche zu erörtern?

Dies wird erst begreiflich, wenn man sich vor Augen führt, dass Albertis Traktat einen Gegner hat, den es zu widerlegen gilt. Kein Geringerer als Platon hat in seinem Dialog *Der Staat* den mimetischen Künsten eine Absage erteilt, ist doch im zehnten Buch von der Unzulänglichkeit des Sehsinns die Rede. Vor dem Hintergrund seiner Ideenlehre wirft der Philosoph der Malerei vor, lediglich Abbilder von Abbildern zu produzieren, und spricht ihr jegliche Dignität ab. Dabei nimmt er die Relativität der Größenwahrnehmung zum Anlass, auf die Unzulänglichkeit des Sehens zu schließen. Gegenstände, die aus der Nähe groß, würden in der Ferne klein erscheinen. Auf diese Schwäche unserer Natur, so führt Sokrates aus, haben es die „perspektivischen Maler" abgesehen, die kein Mittel der Täuschung unversucht lassen und deren Werke dem Philosophen als Blendwerk gelten. Es wundert daher nicht, dass der Philosoph die Maler nur wenig später als „Gaukler" bezeichnet, die lediglich „Kinder und Toren" zu täuschen

20 Vgl. Zöllner, Frank: Leon Battista Albertis „De pictura". Die kunsttheoretische und literarische Legitimierung von Affektübertragung und Kunstgenuß, in: *Georges-Bloch-Jahrbuch des Kunsthistorischen Seminars der Universität Zürich* 4, 1997, 23–39.

vermögen. Schließlich wird die Malerei vollends vernichtet, wenn Sokrates dekretiert, Nachahmungskunst sei unedel, verkehre mit Unedlem und erzeuge bloß Unedles.[21]

Erst vor dem Hintergrund des Topos von der Malerei als Lügnerin erkennt man das eigentliche Interesse Albertis. Wir haben es bei seinem Traktat nicht bloß mit einer Aufwertung der Malerei in den Rang einer freien Kunst zu tun, sondern mit dem ambitionierten Versuch, die Wahrheitsfähigkeit der Bilder in Bezug auf die Darstellung der äußeren Wirklichkeit zu erweisen.[22] Der italienische Humanist beabsichtigt, die Vorurteile des antiken Philosophen zu widerlegen. Er zeigt, dass der Abstand der Gegenstände zum Auge durch die Zentralperspektive berechenbar und darstellerisch zu bewältigen ist.[23] Größenwahrnehmung ist keinesfalls relativ und trügerisch, sondern rational zu erklären. Mehr noch, mit der Perspektivlehre vermag es der Humanist, die Zweidimensionalität der Bildoberfläche mit der Dreidimensionalität des projektierten Raumes in überzeugender Weise zu vermitteln. Denn wenn dreidimensionale Körper aus Linien und Flächen zusammengesetzt sind, so bilden diese gleichermaßen die Grundlage für deren Darstellung auf einer Oberfläche. Alberti liefert nichts weniger als eine begründete Definition der Malerei als eines zur Wahrheit fähigen Mediums. Dies funktioniert allerdings unter der Prämisse, dass man das zeitliche Kontinuum der Realität auf einen Punkt hin festlegt und räumlicher Darstellung unterordnet. Das Bild ist zeitlos. Es wird zum *momentum*.

Bruegel meldet gegenüber dieser Konstruktion Zweifel an, realisiert sich der Galgen im Elster-Bild doch als Zeitgestalt. Mehr noch, bereits die Organisation seiner Tafel vollzieht sich als eine absichtsvolle Zweiteilung des Raumes. Während der Blick in die ferne Landschaft die Zeit als unermessliche Dauer offenbart, bringt das wuselige Geschehen des Vordergrunds die Zeit als unablässige Veränderung zum Ausdruck. Schon bald wird sich alles verändert haben: Die Dorfbewohner werden die Anhöhe

21
Platon: *Der Staat. Über das Gerechte*, übers. u. erläutert v. Otto Apelt, Hamburg 1989, 598d.

22
Vgl. Panofsky, Erwin: *Idea. Ein Beitrag zur Begriffsgeschichte der älteren Kunsttheorie*, Berlin 1924, 3.

23
Alberti, Leon Battista: Della pittura, in: Id., *Kleinere kunsttheoretische Schriften*, hg. v. Hubert Janitschek, Wien 1877.

hinaufgelaufen sein, die ersten Paare haben zu tanzen begonnen und der Galgen tanzt mit. Selbst wenn es nicht Bruegels Absicht war, macht er gleichwohl deutlich, dass sich das Wirkliche in der Zeit und sogar in unterschiedlicher Geschwindigkeit ereignet. Blicken wir in die Ferne, scheint sich alles zu verlangsamen, blicken wir aber auf den Vordergrund, ist es in permanenter Veränderung begriffen.

Im Unterschied zu Alberti bringt sein Galgen-Paradox zum Ausdruck, dass in unserer Wahrnehmung die Zeit dem Raum vorgeordnet ist. So springt der gemalte Galgen auch nicht von sich aus um, vielmehr wird er durch unser Auge in Bewegung versetzt. Diese Behauptung bedarf weiterer Erläuterung. Dass sich für Bruegel das Sehen in der Zeit ereignet und unsere Wirklichkeit als Zeitgeschehen zu begreifen ist, macht er in zahlreichen Tafeln und Kupferstichen zum Thema.[24] Zeit und Zeitlichkeit sind dabei sowohl dem zu Sehenden wie auch dem Sehenden selbst eigen. Das fließende Bier im *Bauernhochzeitsmahl* zeigt die Flüssigkeit auf eine derartige Weise, als würde sie immer weiterfließen und nie versiegen. Eine vergleichbare Irritation findet sich in der New Yorker *Kornernte* [Fig. 630]. Im Bildmittelgrund sind Frauen dargestellt, die Äpfel vom Boden auflesen, deren rote Farbe sie auffällig hervorhebt. Doch hat man den Mann im Baum entdeckt, der durch Schaukelbewegungen die Äpfel zum Fallen bringt, wird deutlich, dass einige Äpfel, von denen man zunächst dächte, sie lägen auf dem Boden, in Wirklichkeit im Begriff sind herabzufallen. In zahlreichen Tafeln inszeniert der Flame solche Irritationen der Wahrnehmung und zeigt, dass im Sehen das folgende oder bevorstehende Ereignis antizipiert wird. Die noch ausstehende Zukunft verändert kurioserweise die Wahrnehmung der Gegenwart.

Die gezeigten Beispiele erweisen das Phänomen der Darstellung und Wahrnehmung von Bewegung als ambivalentes Geschehen. Bewegung vermittelt die Größen Raum und Zeit, deren Wahrnehmung sich durch die den Gegenständen eigene Geschwindigkeit als trügerisch erweisen kann. Bei gleichem Tempo wirkt eine laufende Figur aus der Ferne langsam, während sie

24
Zum Kupferstich *Der Triumph der Zeit* und der darin enthaltenen Auseinandersetzung mit Augustinus vgl. Müller, Jürgen: *Das Paradox als Bildform. Studien zur Ikonologie Pieter Bruegels d.Ä.*, München 1999, 172–178.

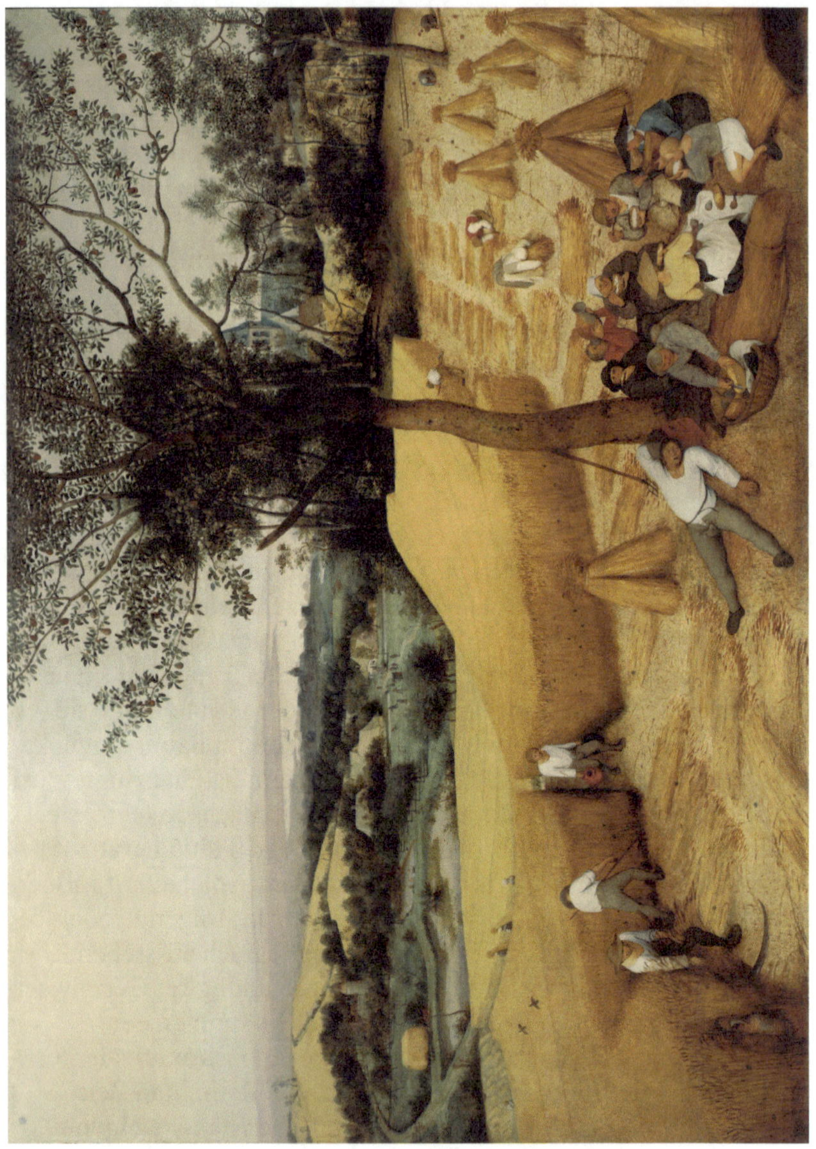

Pieter Bruegel d. Ä., *Die Kornernte*, um 1565, Öl auf Leinwand, 118 × 163 cm. Metropolitan Museum of Art, inv. Nr. 19.164, New York.

Fig. 630

aus der Nähe betrachtet schnell erscheinen kann. Meines Wissens enthält kein frühneuzeitlicher Kunsttraktat Hinweise auf das Phänomen der Geschwindigkeit oder gar auf Beschleunigung und Verlangsamung. Indes werden solche Besonderheiten der Wahrnehmung durch Nicolaus von Cues im *Gespräch über das Seinkönnen* erörtert, wenn er im Rahmen eines theologischen Lehrgesprächs auf den Kreisel zu sprechen kommt.[25] Dieser würde nämlich, je stärker er gedreht worden sei, desto unbeweglicher erscheinen. Bei schneller Drehung mute er sogar stillstehend an. Hohes Tempo erwecke den Eindruck von Stillstand.[26] Die Beschreibung dieser Wahrnehmungsirritation erfährt im genannten Dialog eine Fortsetzung. Bei jäher Geschwindigkeit sei keine Aufeinanderfolge der Bewegung mehr sichtbar, weshalb man „wegen des Ausbleibens der Aufeinanderfolge" keinerlei Bewegung mehr wahrnehme. Die Überlegungen des Theologen finden ihren Höhepunkt jedoch erst in der Feststellung, dass man die größte Bewegung als die kleinste oder gar als Stillstand wahrnehme.[27] Die Beobachtung rasenden Stillstands gerät dem Kardinal zum Anlass, den Zusammenfall der Gegensätze im Sinne der *coincidentia oppositorum* anzudeuten.

Durch die Inszenierung unterschiedlicher Modi der Zeitlichkeit ist das Problem von Figur und Grund im Fortgang meiner Überlegungen unversehens zur Frage nach der zeitlichen Verfasstheit von Bruegels Bild geraten. Aber selbst diese Entdeckung reicht zum tieferen Verständnis seiner Tafel nicht aus, denn das Elster-Bild bleibt solange unverstanden, wie man nicht ein weiteres Problem entdeckt. So spielt der Künstler nicht allein auf den komplexen Zusammenhang von Raum und Zeit, sondern auch auf jenen der Quadratur des Kreises an. Bei der Lösung des mathematischen Problems der Quadratur des Kreises muss ein durch eine bestimmte Fläche definierter Kreis in endlich vielen Schritten in ein Quadrat desselben Ausmaßes überführt werden. Dass diese mathematische Aufgabe auch eine symbolische Dimension aufweist, machen

25
Vgl. Nicolaus von Cues: *Gespräch über das Seinkönnen*, Übersetzung, Nachwort u. Anmerkungen v. Hans Rupprich, Stuttgart 2000, 16.

26
„Je mächtiger die Kraft des Armes ist, desto rascher dreht sich der Kreisel herum, so zwar, daß er bei stärkerer Bewegung zu stehen und zu ruhen scheint." Ibid., 17.

27
„Die größte Bewegung wäre zugleich die kleinste und gar keine." Ibid.

bereits die geometrischen Elementarformen deutlich. Kreis und Quadrat repräsentieren den Gegensatz von Transzendenz und Immanenz oder Gott und Welt. Mit einer möglichen Übereinstimmung dieser gegensätzlichen Größen und Formen wäre der Beweis erbracht, dass durch eine ideale Harmonie die Gegensätze überwunden sind und der Mensch eine solche herstellen kann. Bekanntlich hat sich nicht erst der flämische Maler dem Problem einer möglichen Überwindung der Gegensätze gewidmet. Zentral sind in diesem Zusammenhang die Überlegungen des Nicolaus von Cues, der bereits in seiner Schrift *De docta ignorantia* auf das Quadratur-Problem zurückgekommen ist und ihm sogar eigene Untersuchungen gewidmet hat, um das Verhältnis von Transzendenz und Immanenz besser bestimmen zu können.[28]

In künstlerischer Hinsicht ist Leonardo da Vincis sogenannter vitruvianischer Mensch sicherlich das prominenteste Beispiel, um sich die Anstrengung einer mathematisch-geometrischen Konstruktion idealer Schönheit vor Augen zu führen. Nach den Vorgaben Vitruvs konstruiert der Künstler einen „wohlgeformten Menschen" [Fig. 634].[29] Seiner Zeichnung einer männlichen Gestalt sind nicht nur die Formen von Quadrat und Kreis eingeschrieben, sondern deren Proportionen folgen auch dem Anspruch harmonischer Darstellung, wenn sich die Seitenlänge des Quadrats zum Radius des Kreises im Verhältnis des goldenen Schnitts befindet. Auch Albrecht Dürer adressiert mit Bezug auf Vitruv in seinem 1525 erschienenen Traktat *Von der Unterweisung der Messung mit dem Zirkel und Richtscheit* das mathematische Problem, wenn er das Schema illustriert und darlegt: „Von nöten wer zuwisen *quadratura circuli*, das ist die vergleychnus eines cirkels vnnd eines quadrates, also das eins als vil inhielt als daz ander. Aber soliches ist noch nit von den gelerten demonstrirt."[30]

28
Vgl. Nagel, Fritz: *Nicolaus Cusanus – mathematicus theologus. Unendlichkeitsdenken und Infinitesimalmathematik* (Trier Cusanus Lecture vol. 13), Trier 2007, 10.

29
Bredekamp, Horst: Störung als Maßnahme. Leonardos Vitruvmann und die Quadratur des Kreises, in: Renn, Jürgen/Valleriani, Matteo/Hoffmann, Sabine/Becchi, Antonio (Ed.): *Leonardos intellektueller Kosmos*, Florenz/Mailand 2021, 263–266; Vitruv: *Zehn Bücher über Architektur*, Lateinisch u. Deutsch, übers. u. mit Anm. v. Curt Fensterbusch, Darmstadt [7]2013, I, 1–9, 136–143.

30
Und weiter heißt es: „Mechanice, aber das ist beyleyfig, also das es im werck nit oder gar ein kleyns felt, mag dise vergleychnuß also gemacht werden. Reyß ein fierung vnd teyl den ortstrich in zehen teyl, vnd reys darnach ein

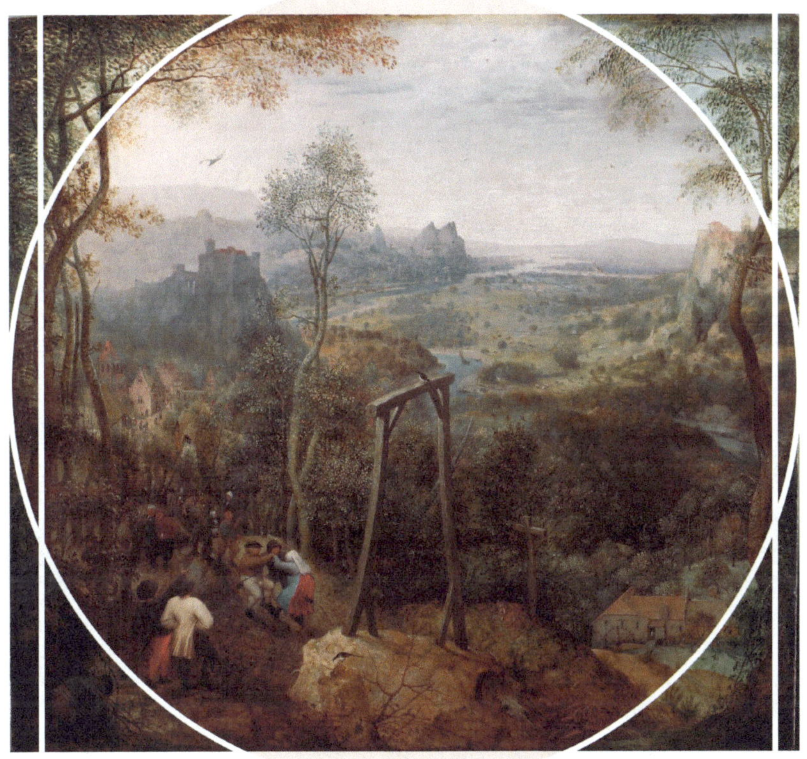

Schema zur Quadratur des Kreises von Pieter Bruegel d. Ä., *Die Elster auf dem Galgen*, 1568, Öl und Tempera auf Holz, 45.9 × 50.8 cm.
Hessisches Landesmuseum, inv. Nr. GK 165, Darmstadt.

Fig. 633

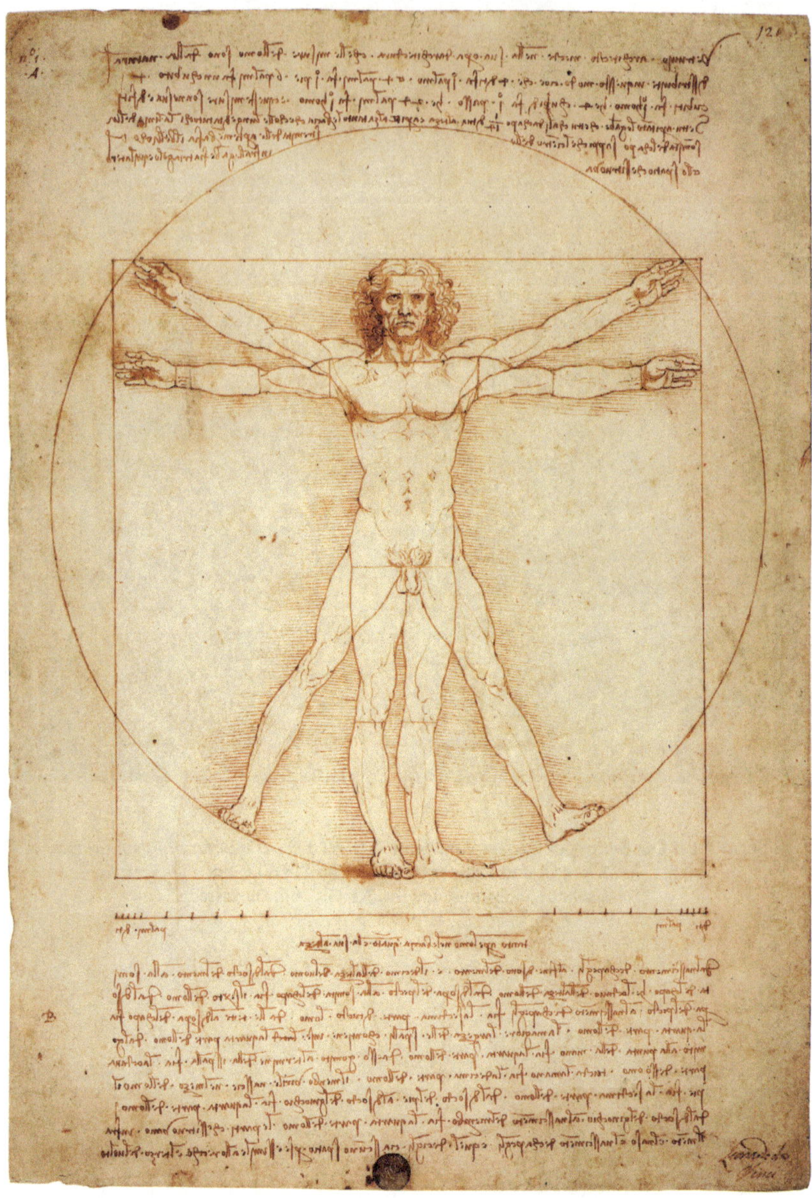

Leonardo da Vinci, Proportionsstudie nach Vitruv, sogenannter „Vitruvianischer Mensch“, 1492, Feder und braune Tinte, 34.5 × 24.5 cm. Galleria dell’Accademia, inv. Nr. 228, Venedig.

Fig. 634

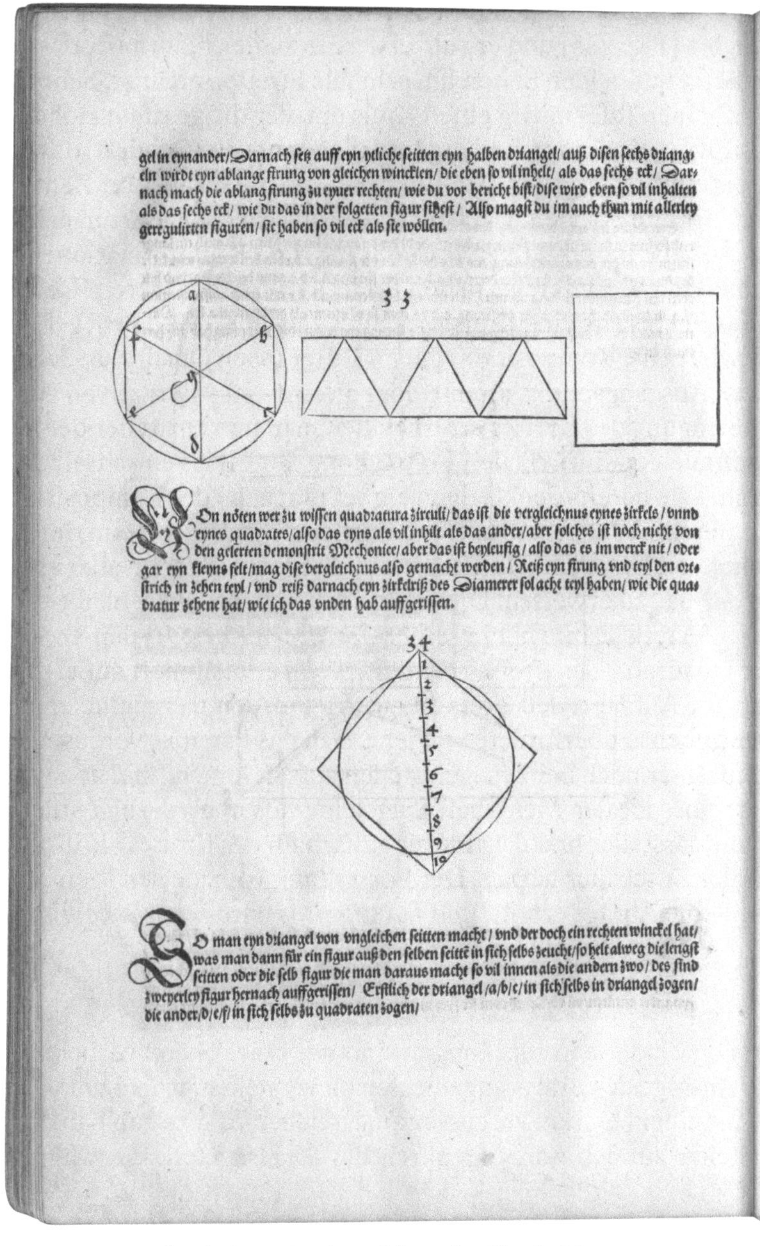

gel in eynander/Darnach setz auff eyn ytliche seitten eyn halben driangel/ auß disen sechs driangeln wirdt eyn ablange fırung von gleichen wincklen/ die eben so vil inhelt/ als das sechs eck/ Darnach mach die ablang fırung zu eyner rechten/ wie du vor bericht bist/dise wird eben so vil inhalten als das sechs eck/ wie du das in der folgetten figur sihest/ Also magst du im auch thun mit allerley geregulirten figuren/ sie haben so vil eck als sie wöllen.

Von nöten wer zu wissen quadratura zirculi/ das ist die vergleichnus eynes zirkels / vnnd eynes quadrates/also das eyns als vil inhilt als das ander/aber solches ist nöch nicht von den gelerten demonstrit Mechonice/ aber das ist beyleufig / also das es im werck nit / oder gar eyn kleyns felt/mag dise vergleichnus also gemacht werden / Reiß eyn fırung vnd teyl den ortstrich in zehen teyl / vnd reiß darnach eyn zirkelriß des Diamerer sol acht teyl haben/ wie die quadratur zehene hat/ wie ich das vnden hab auffgerissen.

So man eyn driangel von vngleichen seitten macht / vnd der doch ein rechten winckel hat/ was man dann für ein figur auß den selben seittē in sich selbs zeucht/so helt alweg die lengst seitten oder die selb figur die man daraus macht so vil innen als die andern zwo / des sind zweyerley figur hernach auffgerissen/ Erstlich der driangel /a/b/c/ in sich selbs in driangel zogen/ die ander/d/e/f/ in sich selbs zu quadraten zogen/

Albrecht Dürer, Quadratur-Schema, in: Albrecht Dürer,
Von der Unterweisung der Messung mit dem Zirkel und Richtscheit, 1525,
Holzschnitt und Typendruck, Nürnberg 1538, 74, Fig. 34.
Biblioteka Książąt Czartoryskich – The Princes Czartoryski Library, Sig. 2349 III Cim, Krakau.

Fig. 635

Bruegels Komposition orientiert sich an Dürers Quadratur-Schema [Fig. 635] und er subvertiert es zugleich, wenn er das Quadrat auf beiden Seiten um schmale Streifen ergänzt. Schreibt man seiner Tafel mittig einen Kreis ein, der die gesamte Höhe des Bildes einnimmt, und ergänzt diesen um ein Quadrat, das den Kreis einfasst, ergeben sich links und rechts jeweils fünf Zentimeter breite Streifen. Dass der Maler eine solche Lesart nahelegt, machen die innerbildlichen, durch Ast- und Baumformationen gebildeten Viertelkreise in den Bildecken deutlich, deren Zusammenspiel bereits eine Kreisform andeutet [Fig. 633]. Bruegel entwirft eine Komposition, die im Dürer'schen Quadratur-Schema ihren Ausgangspunkt nimmt, aber gleichwohl Alternativen zur Anbringung des Kreises eröffnet, den man nun entweder der horizontalen oder vertikalen Erstreckung des Bildes einschreiben kann. Wie bereits dem Galgen eignet nun auch der Komposition ein innerer Widerspruch. Der Künstler stellt die Übereinstimmung von Kreis und Quadrat in Aussicht, um sie dann aber als unerreichbar zu erweisen. Die *coincidentia oppositorum* bleibt aus.

Bereits Dante hat in seiner *Göttlichen Komödie* den Topos der Quadratur des Kreises genutzt, wenn er resigniert äußert, dass die Aufgabe, den Kreis zu quadrieren, den menschlichen Geist ebenso überfordere wie jene, sich das Paradies vorzustellen. Schlimmer noch bei Bruegel, stellen sich in seiner Tafel doch statt eines idealen Menschen Galgen und Elster als die eigentlichen Hauptdarsteller und der Kacker außerhalb des Kreises als ihr idealer Zuschauer heraus. Der Vorstellung vom idealen Menschen wird eine Absage erteilt, und aus *dignitas* wird *miseria hominis*.

III

Erst durch diese Entdeckungen sind wir hinreichend vorbereitet, die Aussage des Bildes angemessen zu verstehen, wobei wir es mit einem extrem voraussetzungsreichen Bild zu tun haben. In Bezug auf den Adressatenkreis der Bilder bietet die erwähnte

cirkelris, des diameter sol acht teyl haben, wie die quadratur zecchne hat, wie ich das vnden hab aufgerissen." Dürer, Albrecht: *Schriftlicher Nachlass*, hg. v. Hans Rupprich, 3 vols., Berlin 1969, vol. 3: Die Lehre von menschlicher Proportion: Entwürfe zur Vermessungsart der Exempeda und zur Bewegungslehre; Reinschriftszyklen; Der Ästhetische Exkurs / Die Unterweisung der Messung / Befestigungslehre / Verschiedenes, 307–367: 325.

Freundschaft zwischen Bruegel und Ortelius der Forschung einen wichtigen Anknüpfungspunkt, da wir durch das *Album amicorum* des Kartographen zuverlässige Informationen über das Netzwerk des Künstlers besitzen. Ortelius widmet dem früh verstorbenen Freund sogar ein literarisches Epitaph.[31] Darüber hinaus belegt ihre zweijährige Reise durch Italien in den Jahren von 1552 bis 1554, wie nah sich die beiden standen.[32] Der um den Antwerpener Kartographen verbundene Freundeskreis bildet den notwendigen Ausgangspunkt jeder weiterführenden Deutung. Die hier vertretenen Maler, Literaten und Gelehrten gehörten unterschiedlichen Konfessionen an und zeichneten sich durch irenische Überzeugungen aus. Zahlreiche von ihnen sahen sich gezwungen, *religionis causa* zu emigrieren. Ortelius als Zentrum dieser Freundesgruppe offenbart seine religiöse Überzeugung in zwei Briefen an seinen Neffen Ortelianus.[33] Er stellt sich als Anhänger des deutschen Theologen Sebastian Franck dar, dessen Schriften bereits um die Mitte des 16. Jahrhunderts ins Niederländische übersetzt wurden.[34] In der Nachfolge Erasmus von Rotterdams müssen wir den deutschen Theologen als einen radikalen Kritiker der Institution Kirche erachten, vertritt er doch eine der Mystik und *devotio moderna* nahestehende Position.

Dieser historische Kontext sei vorausgesetzt, wenn es nun gilt, die verborgene theologische Aussage des Bildes genauer zu bestimmen. Verborgen ist Bruegels Bildaussage insofern, als sich der Künstler einer elliptischen Argumentation bedient. Ellipsen stellen Auslassungen dar. Der Redner verkürzt seine Aussage der Prägnanz willen.[35] Quintilian unterscheidet Wortfiguren, die sich entweder durch Hinzufügung oder Auslassung realisieren ließen. Ellipsen zeichnen sich dadurch aus, dass die ausgelassenen Wörter

31
Das *Album* bietet nicht nur den wichtigsten Anhaltspunkt in Bezug auf das intellektuelle Milieu, in dem sich der Maler bewegte, sondern auch den einzig überprüfbaren.

32
Vgl. Büttner, Nils: „Quid siculas sequeris per mille pericauls terras?“. Ein Beitrag zur Biographie Pieter Bruegels d. Ä. und zur Kulturgeschichte der niederländischen Italienreise, in: *Marburger Jahrbuch für Kunstwissenschaft* 27, 2000, 209–242.

33
Kaschek, *Weltzeit und Endzeit*, 34–38.

34
Vgl. Müller, *Das Paradox als Bildform*, 95–120.

35
Vgl. Quintilian, *Ausbildung des Redners*, vol. 2, IX, 3, 58, 342–343.

durch die verbleibenden ergänzt und vervollständigt werden können.[36] Sie gestalten sich als Teil-Ganze-Beziehungen und vermögen zu überraschen, indem sie Bekanntes auf neue und unerwartete Weise erscheinen lassen. Quintilian weist darauf hin, dass mit dieser rhetorischen Figur das Risiko des Missverstehens einhergeht. Wenn man es aber darauf anlegt, einen kritischen Inhalt zu tarnen, bieten Ellipsen ungeahnte Möglichkeiten. Sie ermöglichen, die *clavis interpretandi* zu verbergen. Hat man diese jedoch entdeckt, provoziert sie eine semantische Horizontverschiebung.

Deshalb sei noch einmal nach der Elster als dem zentralen Sinnbild der Tafel gefragt. Anders als in der Sekundärliteratur zumeist geschrieben und von Porras behauptet, gibt es für Bruegels Inszenierung der diebischen Elster einen Text, der mir als Quelle plausibler als jedes Sprichwort erscheint. Denn Sebastian Brants *Narrenschiff* in der flämischen Ausgabe von 1548 kann als das vom Maler am häufigsten verwendete Vorbild gelten. Der Kupferstich des *Alchemisten*, der Nesträuber aus *Der Bauer und der Vogeldieb*, *Die klugen und törichten Jungfrauen*, aber auch der *Blindensturz* seien erwähnt, um nur wenige Beispiele für die Vertrautheit des Flamen mit der christlichen Weisheitslehre des Straßburger Humanisten zu erweisen. Im neunzehnten Kapitel des „*Sotten Schip*" jedenfalls ist von der Elster als unvorsichtigem und geschwätzigem Wesen schon im Titelvers die Rede, wenn es heißt:

> *Als dexter schatert so wroechse haer jonghen*
> *Die sot wroeg het met sijnder tonghen.*[37]

Verse und Paarreim seien in freier Übersetzung folgendermaßen wiedergeben:

> (Wenn) krächzend die Elster verrät ihre Jungen,
> Der Narr verrät es mit seiner Zunge(n).

36
Ibid.

37
Brant, Sebastian: *Der Sotten Schip* [Antwerpen 1548], hg. v. Loek Geeraedts, Middelburg 1981, fol. g ij.

Der geschwätzige Vogel verrät sich und seine gesamte Brut und wird zum Sinnbild des unvorsichtigen Menschen. Die Interpretation eines bevorstehenden Verrats findet im einsam aufsteigenden Kranich eine Fortsetzung, der in zahlreichen Emblembüchern jener Zeit als Symbol der Wachsamkeit und Schweigsamkeit genannt wird.[38] Es scheint mir kein Zufall, dass die zwei Elstern in den beiden Männern unten links eine Entsprechung haben, die trotz aller Leutseligkeit als katholische Spitzel offenbar werden.[39] Für diese Deutung spricht der Umstand, dass bei der rechten Person durch das Zurückstreifen des hellen Rocks ein Dolch zum Vorschein kommt, der einem Bauern nicht geziemen würde. Darüber hinaus werden die Männer von einem Hund begleitet, der sich rechts von ihnen befindet und sein Haupt gesenkt hat, als würde er eine Fährte aufnehmen. Der Galgen, auf dem die Elster sitzt, macht zudem auf die tödlichen Konsequenzen des Verrats für Andersgläubige aufmerksam. Besonders auch deshalb, weil sich das Hinrichtungsinstrument als instabile Figur zu erkennen gibt. Sogar der defäkierende Bauer, der sich außerhalb des innerbildlichen Kreises befindet, erhält nun eine neue Bedeutung und wird zum Sinnbild. Denn bereits die Kirchenväter mutmaßten, dass die Ausscheidungen des Menschen die Konsequenz seiner Vertreibung aus dem Paradies bedeuten, was übrigens noch Luther wiederholt.[40] Der Bauer repräsentiert so die unter der Erbsünde lebende Menschheit. Aber erst der neben dem Galgen befindliche und im Halbschatten liegende Pferdeschädel stellt die *clavis interpretandi* dar. Mit ihm geht ein Hinweis auf Golgatha als Ort der Kreuzigung einher, wie wir ihn auch aus dem Wiener *Aufstieg zum Kalvarienberg* aus dem Jahre 1564 kennen. Er kennzeichnet den Ort als Schädelstätte und parallelisiert das Fest auf der

38
Zum Kranich vgl. Henkel, Arthur/Schöne, Albrecht (Ed.): *Emblemata: Handbuch zur Sinnbildkunst des XVI. und XVII. Jahrhunderts*, Stuttgart 1967, Sp. 818.

39
Bereits Louis Maeterlinck hat vermutet, dass es in der Tafel um die Denunziation und Verfolgung Andersgläubiger durch die katholische Inquisition geht. Vgl. Maeterlinck, Louis: *Le genre satirique dans la peinture flamande*, Gent 1903, 274–275.

40
Martin Luthers Werke. Kritische Gesamtausgabe, 120 Bände, Weimar 1883–2009, Text der Genesisvorlesung, hg. v. G. Rossmane und D. Reichert, vol. 42, Weimar 1911, 84; Ropper, Lyndal: *Der feiste Doktor. Luther, sein Körper und seine Biographen*, übers. v. Karin Wördemann, Göttingen 2012, 57.

Anhöhe mit der Passion Christi. Wie das Wiener Bild zeigt, ist mit dessen Verrat und bevorstehendem Tod die Passion keineswegs beendet, vielmehr dauert sie an und wiederholt sich bis auf den heutigen Tag.[41] Darüber hinaus verweist der Galgen auf das Schicksal von Judas, der mit seinem Verrat erst die Kreuzigung und damit den Opfertod Christi ermöglichte. Und ist es nicht aufschlussreich und gleichsam ein Wink, dass der Galgen, neben dem der Schädel liegt, in einem übertragenen Sinne zu einer Art neuem Kreuz wird, während rund um das darunter befindliche Kreuz die roten Backsteine liegen? Dass es mit dem Galgen eine besondere Bewandtnis hat, macht auch der Untergrund deutlich, auf dem er steht. Die konvexe Steinformation erinnert an einen Totenkopf, von dem lediglich die Schädelkalotte aus dem Boden ragt und dessen rechte Augenhöhle man glaubt erkennen zu dürfen. Der lateinische Ausdruck für eine solche Kalotte lautet *calvaria*, womit ein weiterer Hinweis auf das Passionsgeschehen gegeben wäre. Seine Grundlage hat dieses ikonographische Spiel in klassischen Kreuzigungsdarstellungen, die zu Füßen des Kruzifixes Adams Schädel zeigen und auf das Grab des Erzvaters verweisen. Mit diesem Detail wird zum Ausdruck gebracht, dass die gesamte Menschheit, so wie sie durch eine einzige Person in den Stand der Erbsünde geriet, durch die Heilstat Christi von einem einzigen Menschen davon erlöst wird.[42]

Erst wenn wir das vielfältige Spiel mit der Golgatha-Metaphorik entdeckt haben, ergibt sich eine semantische Horizontverschiebung, die alle Bildelemente in anderem Licht erscheinen lässt und zu einem Vergleich der Tafel mit der Wiener *Kreuztragung* anregt. Mehr noch, in strukturell-argumentativer Hinsicht stimmen *Der Aufstieg zum Kalvarienberg* und *Die Elster auf dem Galgen* überein. Wie bereits in der Wiener Tafel [Fig. 642] mit ihrer unübersehbaren, auf einem steilen Felsen stehenden Windmühle bildet auch im Elster-Bild die Welt des Menschen das Korn, welches

41
Mt. 23.

42
„Das Motiv des Schädels [...] findet sich in der christlichen Kunst zunächst in Kreuzigungsdarstellungen als Zeichen für das Grab Adams auf dem Hügel Golgotha unter dem Kreuz. [...] Der Todesverfallenheit und Erlösungsbedürftigkeit des alten Adam, wie sie im Schädel sichtbar wird, entspricht die erlösende Kraft des am Kreuz vergossenen Blutes des neuen Adam Christus." Hamm, Berndt: *Religiosität im späten Mittelalter*, Tübingen 2011, 216.

durch die Wassermühle gemahlen wird.[43] Der Künstler modifiziert das Konzept der mystischen oder Hostienmühle, mit dem sowohl die Konzeption der Eucharistie, aber auch des Widerstreits von wahrer und falscher Kirche im Sinne von Ecclesia und Synagoge einhergehen können. Zur wahren Kirche gehören für Bruegel im Anschluss an Franck nur jene als Ketzer verachteten und leidenden Christen, die sich der falschen Glaubenspraxis entziehen.

Schaut man auf das Werk des Flamen im Ganzen, so fällt auf, dass er keinen Altar gestaltet hat. Vielmehr war es sein Ansinnen, in extremer Form die historischen Erzählungen der Evangelien auf seine eigene Zeit hin zu aktualisieren. Nicht das historische Ereignis biblischer Erzählung, sondern ihre aktuelle Geltung wird durch ihn inszeniert. Im *Aufstieg zum Kalvarienberg* etwa transponiert der Maler das Geschehen der Kreuzigung in seine eigene Gegenwart, indem er die durch einen Mönch begleiteten Ketzer mit dem bevorstehenden Tod Christi am Kreuz parallelisiert. Auch im Elster-Bild verkennen die Menschen die wahre Bedeutung des Geschehens und lassen es zum Volksfest werden. Aus dem Kreuz wird ein Galgen, dessen geheimnisvolle Instabilität im Wasserrad seinen Ursprung hat und dessen Bewegung nicht zu beenden ist. Wie das Mühlrad dreht sich der Galgen um seine eigene Achse und wird zur dämonischen Gestalt. Selbst die Bauern tanzen im Kreis. Ja sogar die Stämme der Bäume wachsen nicht gerade, sondern spiralförmig in die Höhe. Alles dreht sich und beginnt wieder von vorn. Das Passionsgeschehen erweist sich als andauerndes und unaufhaltbares Ereignis.

Doch während die Windmühle im Wiener Bild das offensichtliche Zentrum der Kreisbewegungen darstellt, bleibt die Macht der Wassermühle in der Darmstädter Tafel verborgen. Gleichwohl ist sie es, die den Galgen ohne Unterlass umspringen lässt. Darüber hinaus besteht zwischen dem Hausierer im Wiener und dem defäkierenden Bauern im Darmstädter Bild eine strukturelle Übereinstimmung. Während der Erste im *Aufstieg zum Kalvarienberg* dem Ereignis gleichmütig zuschaut, ist der Zweite derart mit sich selbst beschäftigt, dass er dem Geschehen keine Beachtung schenkt.

43 Vgl. Art. „Die mystische Mühle“, in: Kirschbaum, Engelbert u. a. (Ed.): *Lexikon der christlichen Ikonografie [LCI]*, 8 vols., Sonderausgabe, Freiburg 1990, vol. III, Sp. 297–299.

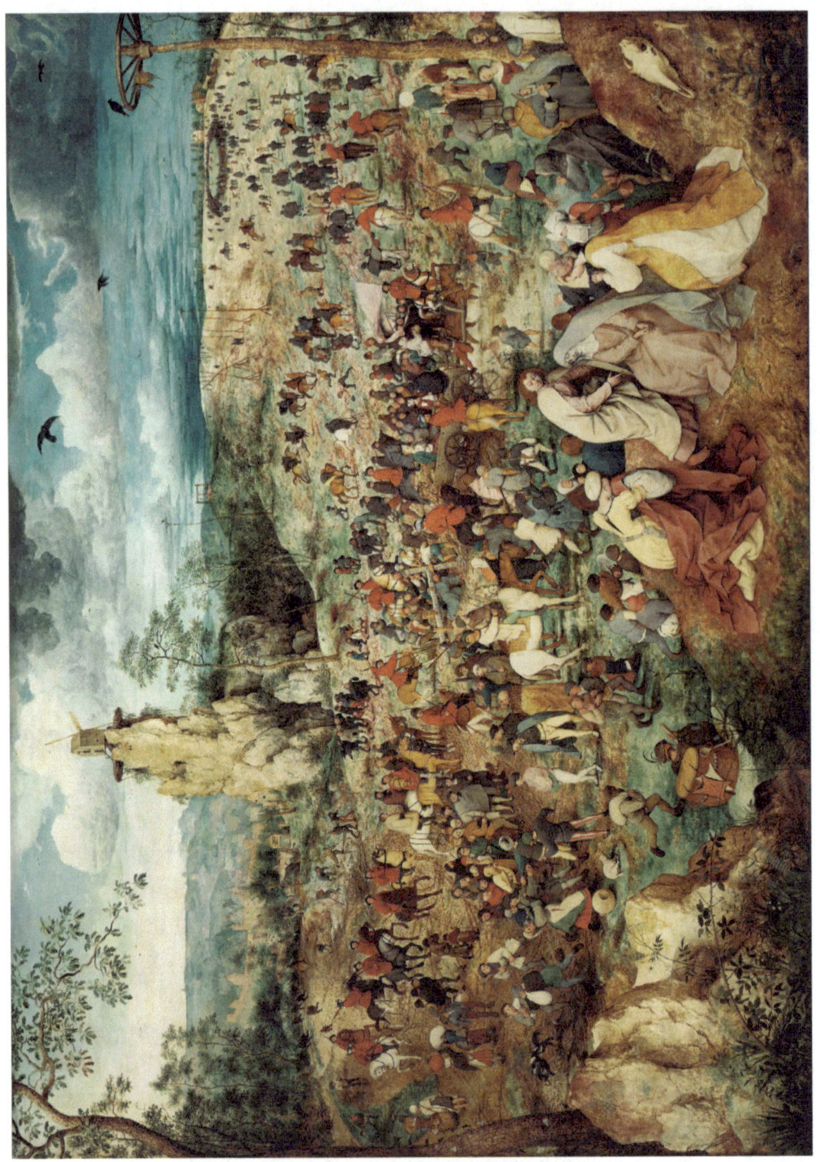

Pieter Bruegel d. Ä., *Kreuztragung Christi (Aufstieg zum Kalvarienberg)*, 1564, Öl auf Eichenholz, 124 × 170 cm. Kunsthistorisches Museum, inv. Nr. Gemäldegalerie 1025, Wien.

Fig. 642

Das ikonographische Programm des Elster-Bildes ist noch weitaus rätselhafter als die Wiener Tafel und schwieriger zu durchschauen, weshalb wir uns einem weiteren Detail zuwenden müssen.

Mit dem christlichen Symbol des Kreuzes ist in der Regel die Hoffnung auf Auferstehung verbunden, aber im Darmstädter Bild wird dies konterkariert. Bereits der Umstand, dass das Kreuz aus dem gleichen Holz besteht wie der Galgen, stellt einen verborgenen und kritischen Hinweis dar. Mit der formalen Gleichstellung geht eine Abwertung des unterhalb des Galgens befindlichen Kreuzes einher, wird es doch Teil der profanen Welt. Zudem hat der Künstler mit den zahlreichen roten Backsteinen, die verstreut um das Kreuz herumliegen, einen weiteren Kommentar verborgen. Wie lässt sich die Anwesenheit der Steine erklären? Weit und breit ist kein Gebäude zu erkennen, zu dessen Errichtung oder Reparatur die Steine benötigt würden. Naheliegender als eine solche praktische Erklärung erscheint mir der Hinweis auf die Tempelzerstörung und Bedrängnis der Christen in der Endzeit, wie sie im Matthäusevangelium beschworen wird. „Wahrlich, ich sage euch", beginnt der zweite Vers des 24. Kapitels, „Hier wird nicht ein Stein auf dem anderen gelassen werden, der nicht abgebrochen wird."[44] Das Kreuz wird in der Darmstädter Tafel zum negativen Symbol der Kirche als Institution, wie es auch in anderen Bildern des Künstlers geschieht.[45]

In meiner Interpretation habe ich die Instabilität der Figur des Galgens mit der Frage nach der Zeitlichkeit des Bildes in Zusammenhang gebracht. Auf untrennbare Weise werden Raum und Zeit in einer nie endenden Bewegung verschränkt. Meine Deutung hat die Skepsis des Malers zu Tage gefördert. Im Zentrum stand dabei die Erkenntnis intellektueller Endlichkeit des Menschen, seine Unfähigkeit, das Absolute erkennen und darstellen zu können. In Bruegels Tafel verrätselt die Zeit den Raum. Sie bedingt die Relativität der Raumwahrnehmung und hebt das kausale Bedingungsverhältnis des modernen Figur-Grund-Gefüges auf. Gleichwohl ist in Bruegels Tafel Zeit nicht nur Geschehens- oder Handlungszeit, sondern auch Welt- und Endzeit. Der Künstler entwirft eine Allegorie, welche die Heilsvergessenheit

44 Mt. 24,2.

45 Vgl. Müller, Von Kirchen, Ketzern und anderen Blindenführern.

der Menschheit zentral stellt. Mit Bruegel haben wir zu lernen, dass der Mensch das unsichtbare Gefängnis der Zeit nicht verlassen kann, was nicht erst Husserl und Heidegger, sondern bereits Augustinus in seinen *Bekenntnissen* schreibt.[46] Der Kirchenvater analysiert im elften Buch die Zeit als einen paradoxen Umstand der Gleichzeitigkeit von Vergehen und Dauer. Der Mensch kann das Jetzt der Gegenwart nie erreichen, der ihm eigene Zeitmodus ist das Futur II. Wir werden gewesen sein, Teilnehmer einer paradoxen Zeitreise. Keiner hat diesen Gedanken besser zum Ausdruck gebracht als Sebastian Franck im 106. Paradoxon seiner gleichnamigen Schrift, in welcher der Gedanke einer ewigen Wiederkehr unter christlichen Vorzeichen ausgedrückt wird:

> Es treibt ein Tag den anderen, die Welt ist sinnvoll und gehen alle Dinge in einem Zirkel wie die Sonne, nichts Bleibendes oder Stetes ist auf Erden. [...]. Darum muss die ganze Bibel für und für wiederholt [...] gehen: [...]. Welt ist allweg Welt und muss sich die Kugel der Welt immerzu herumwälzen, damit was heut' gewesen ist, morgen nimmer sei und wiederkomme.[47]

IV

In meinem Beitrag bin ich der Figur-Grund-Problematik in exemplarischer Weise nachgegangen. Ich habe das neuzeitliche Denken von Figur und Grund in einem historischen Sinn als Teil eines sich zunehmend etablierenden Rationalisierungsprozesses verstehen wollen und dessen Relevanz für Bruegels Kunst zu erörtern versucht. Ohne dies weiter ausführen und diskutieren zu können, sei behauptet, dass sich in der Wissenschaftsgeschichte der Frühen Neuzeit der Anspruch der Beherrschbarkeit des Raumes und der Effizienz als einer der Kausalität gemäßen Form der Leistung beobachten lassen. Die Welt wird zum Bild, und es ist

46
Augustinus: *Bekenntnisse*, Lateinisch u. Deutsch, eingeleitet, übers. u. erläutert v. Joseph Bernhart, mit einem Vorwort v. Ernst Ludwig Grasmück, Frankfurt a. M. 1987, XI, 602–671; vgl. Flasch, Kurt: *Was ist Zeit? Augustinus von Hippo, das XI. Buch der Confessiones, historisch-philosophische Studie, Text, Übersetzung, Kommentar*, Frankfurt a. M. 2004.

47
Franck, Sebastian: *Paradoxa*, hg. v. Siegfried Wollgast, Berlin ²1995, 171.

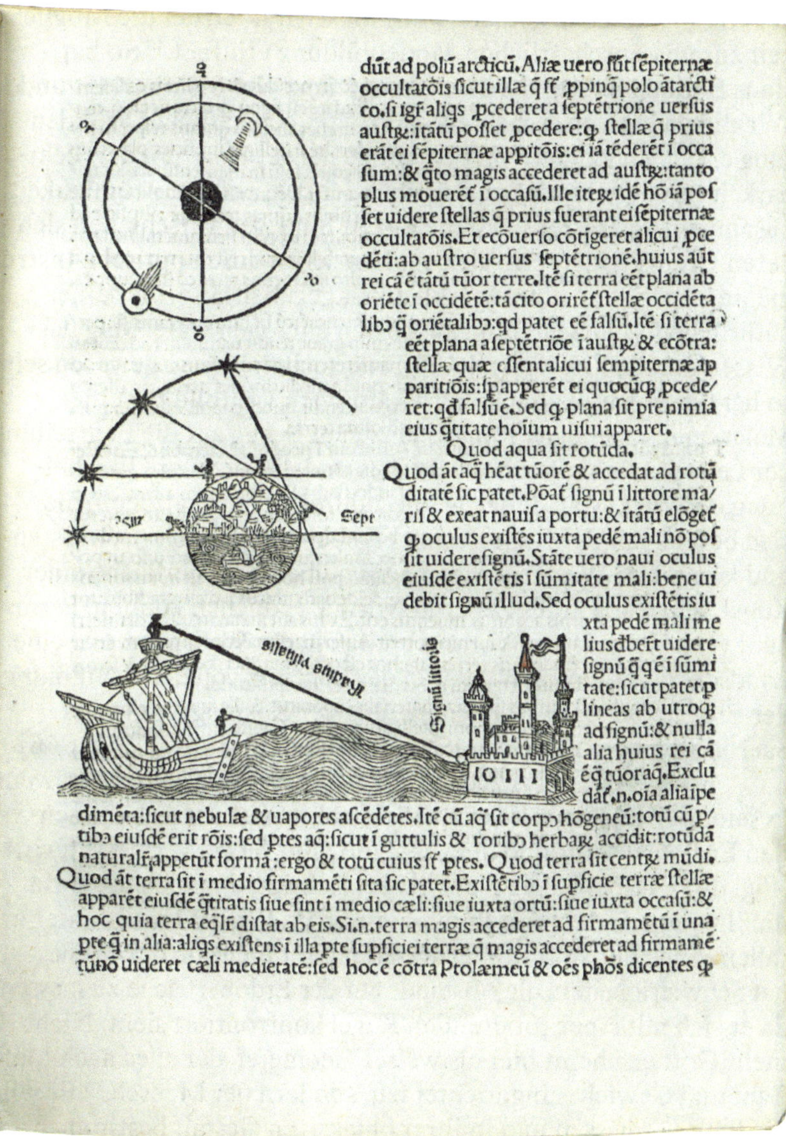

dūt ad polū arcticū. Aliæ uero ſūt ſēpiternæ occultatōis ſicut illæ q̄ ſt̄ ꝓpinq̄ polo ātarcti co. ſi igr̄ aliqs ꝓcederet a ſeptētrione uerſus auſtꝝ: ītātū poſſet ꝓcedere: ꝙ ſtellæ q̄ prius erāt ei ſēpiternæ appitōis: ei iā tēderēt ī occaſum: & q̄to magis accederet ad auſtꝝ: tanto plus mouerēt ī occaſū. Ille iteꝝ idē hō iā poſſet uidere ſtellas q̄ prius fuerant ei ſēpiternæ occultatōis. Et ecōuerſo cōtigeret alicui ꝓcedēti: ab auſtro uerſus ſeptētrionē. huius aūt rei cā ē tātū tūor terre. Itē ſi terra eēt plana ab oriētē ī occidētē: tā cito orirēt ſtellæ occidētalibꝫ q̄ oriētalibꝫ: qd patet eē falſū. Itē ſi terra eēt plana a ſeptētriōe ī auſtꝝ & ecōtra: ſtellæ quæ eēnt alicui ſempiternæ apparitiōis: ſp apperēt ei quocūqꝫ ꝓcederet: qđ falſū ē. Sed ꝙ plana ſit pre nimia eius q̄titate hoīum uiſui apparet.

Quod aqua ſit rotūda.

Quod āt aq̄ hēat tūorē & accedat ad rotūditatē ſic patet. Pōat ſignū ī littore mariſ & exeat nauiſ a portu: & ītātū elōget ꝙ oculus exiſtēs iuxta pedē mali nō poſſit uidere ſignū. Stāte uero naui oculus eiuſdē exiſtētis ī ſūmitate mali: bene uidebit ſignū illud. Sed oculus exiſtētis iuxta pedē mali melius dƀeřt uidere ſignū q̄ q ē ī ſūmitate: ſicut patet ꝑ lineas ab utroqꝫ ad ſignū: & nulla alia huius rei cā ē q̄ tūor aq̄. Excludat̄. n. oīa alia īpedimēta: ſicut nebulæ & uapores aſcēdētes. Itē cū aq̄ ſit corpꝫ hōgeneū: totū cū ꝑtibꝫ eiuſdē erit rōis: ſed ptes aq̄: ſicut ī guttulis & roribꝫ herbaꝝ accidit: rotūdā naturalr̄ appetūt formā: ergo & totū cuius ſt̄ ptes. Quod terra ſit centꝝ mūdi.

Quod āt terra ſit ī medio firmamēti ſita ſic patet. Exiſtētibꝫ ī ſupficie terræ ſtellæ apparēt eiuſdē q̄titatis ſiue ſint ī medio cæli: ſiue iuxta ortū: ſiue iuxta occaſū: & hoc quia terra eq̄lr̄ diſtat ab eis. Si. n. terra magis accederet ad firmamētū ī una pte q̄ in alia: aliqs exiſtens ī illa pte ſupficiei terræ q̄ magis accederet ad firmamētū nō uideret cæli medietatē: ſed hoc ē cōtra Ptolæmeū & oēs phōs dicentes ꝙ

Johannes de Sacrobosco, *De Sphaera mundi*, Venedig 1490,
Holzschnitt und Typendruck, 48 unfolierte Blätter.
München, Bayerische Staatsbibliothek, Sig. 4 Inc.c.a. 785, fol. 8r.

Fig. 645

der von Platon noch getadelte Fiktionscharakter, der die Möglichkeit zur wissenschaftlichen Modellbildung eröffnet.[48] So hat Hans Blumenberg in der Nichtkongruenz von Sichtbarkeit und Wirklichkeit ein entscheidendes Prinzip neuzeitlicher Weltdeutung erkennen wollen.[49] In der Antike fiel der Horizont der Sichtbarkeit mit dem Horizont der Wirklichkeit und der Möglichkeit zusammen. Spätestens in der Neuzeit hingegen verschieben sich deren Grenzen insofern, als dem Menschen durch optische Instrumente Zugänge zu einer Wirklichkeit gegeben sind, die seiner natürlichen Wahrnehmung ansonsten entzogen wäre. Mag das Wissen um die Kugelgestalt der Erde auch nicht neu gewesen sein, so hat der Wechsel zum kopernikanischen Weltbild für einen Maler doch erhebliche Konsequenzen in Bezug auf die Beurteilung der Leistungsfähigkeit des Sehsinns und die sichtbare Erscheinung der Welt. Man denke an die zahlreichen Irritationen, die sich bereits mit der Kugelgestalt ergeben: Man segelt nach Osten und kommt im Westen an. Wir laufen über die Oberfläche einer Kugel, deren absolutes Zentrum wir nie erreichen können. Permanent verschiebt sich im Voranschreiten in der Wahrnehmung einer Landschaft der Horizont, woran der Lehrsatz von der Krümmung der Erde, *quod terra sit rotunda*, aus der Kosmographie des Sacrobosco vom Ende des 15. Jahrhunderts erinnert [Fig. 645]

Bruegel erlaubt sich dazu einen ironischen Kommentar, wenn in seinem *Temperantia*-Stich ein Astrologe auf der sich drehenden Erdkugel steht und den Abstand zum Mond vermessen will [Fig. 647]. Dabei hat er nicht berücksichtigt, dass sich die Erde um ihre eigene Achse dreht und er nun im Begriff ist, hinunterzufallen. Auch der ambitionierte Geometer unterhalb der Szene hat Schwierigkeiten, die Abstände auf der Erdoberfläche zu messen, da er sich mit einer rotierenden Kugel konfrontiert sieht. Nicht mehr Gott erscheint hier als weiser Geometer, der alles nach Maß, Zahl und Gewicht eingerichtet hat, sondern der Mensch.[50] Er will die Welt vermessen und in ihrer objektiven Gestalt bestimmen –

48
Vgl. Heidegger, Martin: Die Zeit des Weltbildes, in: Id.: *Gesamtausgabe*. vol. 5: *Holzwege*, Frankfurt a. M. 1977, 87–88.

49
Vgl. Bruno, Giordano: *Das Aschermittwochsmahl*, übers. v. Ferdinand Fellmann, mit einer Einleitung v. Hans Blumenberg, Frankfurt a. M. 1981, 53–54.

50
Weish 11,20.

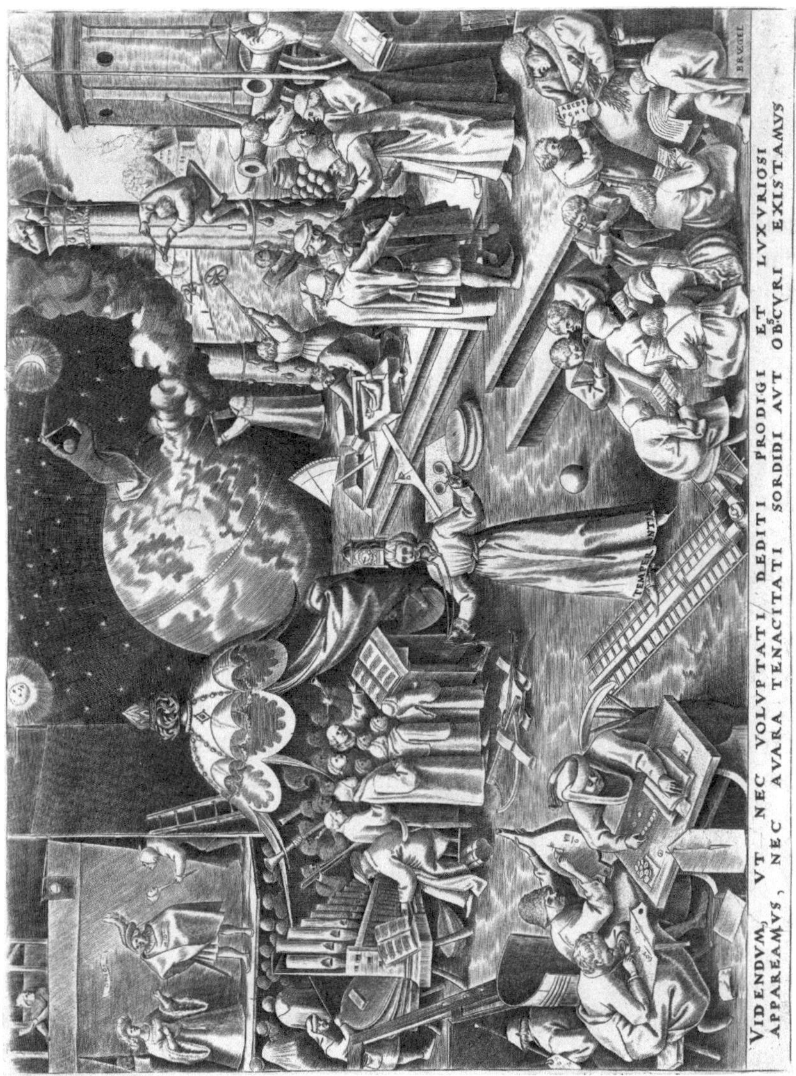

Philips Galle (nach Pieter Bruegel, d. Ä.), *Temperantia* aus der Serie *Die Sieben Tugenden*, 1560–1562, Kupferstich, 224 × 296 mm.
Rijksmuseum, inv. Nr. RP-P-OB-7376, Amsterdam.

Fig. 647

was sich aber durch die Tücke des Objekts in Form eines sich drehenden Planeten als problematisch erweist. Diese ironische Volte erhält durchaus einen ernsten Hintergrund, wenn man sich fragt, welche Konsequenzen der Umstand eines sich um seine eigene Achse drehenden Planeten für den Maler gehabt haben könnte. Dass wir über eine konvexe Oberfläche laufen, die wir nicht als solche erkennen können, stellt dabei noch die einfachste Irritation dar.[51] Beunruhigender ist, dass wir in unserer alltäglichen Wahrnehmung glauben, es mit einer stillstehenden Erde zu tun zu haben, während wir Sonne und Mond als beweglich erachten, deren Voranschreiten am Firmament den Ablauf der Tageszeiten bedeutet. Alles ist anders, als uns die natürliche Weltwahrnehmung Glauben macht. Die Bewegung einer sich drehenden Erde bleibt unsichtbar. In unserer Anschauung erleben wir die Auswirkungen der Planetenbewegungen, ohne deren Ursachen sehen zu können. Sehen und Erkennen sind nicht mehr ein und dasselbe. Wir dürfen unserer Alltagswahrnehmung nicht mehr trauen: Man läuft über eine Kugel, die sich bewegt, ohne es zu merken. Wir sehen die Sonne auf- und untergehen, was nichts mit dem astronomischen Sachverhalt zu tun hat. Gleichwohl erweisen sich perspektivische Darstellungsmodi als Instrumente der Welterkenntnis. Vermessen, Erfassen und Objektivieren werden zu den bestimmenden Aufgaben und die Erde zum Gegenstand. Von nun an stellt sie ein Modell dar, das man von außen betrachten kann. Es ist offensichtlich, dass Bruegel mit dem Rätsel-Galgen und den beiden ‚Forschern' im *Temperantia*-Stich Skepsis formuliert. So wie sich der springende Galgen im Elster-Bild als unbeherrschbar erweist, so gestaltet sich das Vermessen im *Temperantia*-Stich als undurchführbar. Wenn man eine solche, sich der christlichen Überlieferung verdankende Wissens- und Wissenschaftsskepsis für den Maler in Betracht zieht, dann hätte Bruegel an jenes *noli altum sapere* des Paulus aus dem Römerbrief erinnert und dem Wissen, Forschen und Erkennen von Gott gewollte Grenzen aufgezeigt.[52]

51
So beschreibt Nicolaus von Cues in seinem Dialog *Vom Globusspiel*, dass man die Kugelgestalt der Erde nicht sehen könne: Nicolaus von Cues, *Vom Globusspiel (De ludo globi)*, übers. u. mit Einführung u. Anm. v. Gerda von Bredow, Hamburg 1978, 11–12.

52
Vgl. Ginzburg, Carlo: High and Low: The Theme of Forbidden Knowledge in the Sixteenth and Seventeenth centuries, in: *Past & Present* 73, Nov. 1976, 28–41.

Image Credits

Sharing Ground: An Introduction in Conversation with David Young Kim Saskia C. Quené

Fig. 15, 16: © The J. Paul Getty Museum, Los Angeles **Fig. 18:** Staatliche Museen zu Berlin, Gemäldegalerie / Christoph Schmidt; Public Domain Mark 1.0 **Fig. 19, 20:** © Gabinetto Fotografico, Gallerie degli Uffizi **Fig. 21:** © National Gallery Picture Library

In the Round: Master WA's Figureless Prints and Fifteenth-Century Painted Grounds Noa Turel

Fig. 51: Photo: Dominique Provost, Collection KMSKA – Flemish Community, Public Domain **Fig. 54, 62:** © Staatliche Museen zu Berlin, Kupferstichkabinett / Dietmar Katz **Fig. 55, 69, 71, 78:** © The Trustees of the British Museum **Fig. 56:** © Rijksmuseum, Amsterdam **Fig. 59:** © KBR – Prints and Drawings Cabinet **Fig. 61:** © Art Institute Chicago (CC0) **Fig. 67:** © Metropolitan Museum of Art (OA) **Fig. 74:** © Benjamin Gavaudo / Centre des monuments nationaux **Fig. 75:** RKDimages (CC0) **Fig. 76, 79:** © INHA **Fig. 82:** © Photo: Simon Knott

Tableau-Vivant Curtains as Mediators between Figure and Ground: Petrus Christus, the Salzburg Master, and Jean Fouquet Claudia Blümle

Fig. 88: Birmingham Museums Trust, licensed under CC0 **Fig. 91:** © Sammlung Oskar Reinhart "Am Römerholz", Winterthur **Fig. 94:** © RMN-Grand Palais (Musée du Louvre) / Tony Querrec **Fig. 101, 103, 106, 107, 108, 109, 111, 112, 113, 124:** © Staatliche Museen zu Berlin, Kupferstichkabinett / Dietmar Katz

Miracles of Mediation: Staging the Sacred in the Annunciation by Pedro da Córdoba Beate Fricke

Fig. 133, 134, 136, 141: Wikimedia Commons **Fig. 137:** © RMN-Grand Palais. Paris, Musée de Cluny – Musée national du Moyen Âge / Foto: Jean-Gilles Berizzi **Fig. 138, 140:** CC BY-SA 4.0 **Fig. 142:** © Ken Welsh / Alamy Stock Foto **Fig. 150:** meemoo, Flemish Institute for Archives, Public Domain **Fig. 151:** © National Gallery Picture Library **Fig. 153:** © RMN-Grand Palais. Musée du Louvre / Foto: Angèle Dequier **Fig. 154:** Foto: Joanbanjo, Wikimedia Commons, edited by Gregor von Kerssenbrock-Krosigk **Fig. 155, 157, 158:** © Archivio de la Mezquita-Catedral de Córdoba **Fig. 159:** Photo: author **Fig. 161:** © Alamy Stock Foto **Fig. 162:** CC BY SA 2.0 **Fig. 163:** PDM 1.0

Campus as *Locus* and Narrative Stained Glass Bruno Haas

Fig. 191: Wikimedia Commons, edited by Gregor von Kerssenbrock-Krosigk **Fig. 193, 194, 195:** © Photo: Denis Krieger **Fig. 196:** Staatliche Museen zu Berlin, Kunstgewerbemuseum / Jürgen Liepe **Fig. 197:** © Rheinisches Bildarchiv Köln, rba_c019827 **Fig. 198:** Photo: Corpus Vitrearum Medii Aevi, Freiburg **Fig. 200:** Photo: Rüdiger Tonojan, CVMA Freiburg, CC BY-NC 4.0 **Fig. 201:** Wikimedia Commons **Fig. 202:** Public Domain **Fig. 204, 205, 207, 209, 212, 214, 216, 217, 218:** © C.I.V./ Chartres, photo: H. Gaud

Lineage of a Paradigm: "Figure and Ground" in Encyclopedic Sources
Veronica Peselmann

Fig. 229: Photo: Kunstmuseum Basel, Sammlung Online, Public Domain **Fig. 236:** The Internet Archive **Fig. 246, 247:** © Photo: Staatliche Museen zu Berlin, Gemäldegalerie, Christoph Schmidt

A Foray of Stained Glass: Color, Grisaille, Transparency
Marion Gartenmeister

Fig. 259, 260: © Vitrocentre Romont im Auftrag der Berner Münster-Stiftung, Bern (Foto: Sophie Wolf) **Fig. 263, 265:** © Etat du Valais / SIP / Photo Bernard Dubuis et Michel Martinez **Fig. 268:** Foto: Christoph Gysin, icona Basel **Fig. 272, 276, 278, 286:** © Vitrocentre Romont **Fig. 274:** © Historisches Museum Basel, Maurice Babey **Fig. 279:** Staatliche Museen zu Berlin, Kunstbibliothek / Dietmar Katz, Public Domain Mark 1.0 **Fig. 281:** Bernisches Historisches Museum, Bern. Foto Stefan Rebsamen **Fig. 282:** Bernisches Historisches Museum, Bern. Foto Yvonne Hurni. Depositum der Schweizerischen Eidgenossenschaft, Bundesamt für Kultur, Bern **Fig. 284:** Bernisches Historisches Museum, Bern. Foto: Yvonne Hurni **Fig. 287:** © Vitrocentre Romont (Foto: Yves Eigenmann) **Fig. 289:** © Vitrocentre Romont (Foto: author)

Between Figure and Ground: Lorenzetti's Gold
Christopher Lakey & Saskia Quené

Fig. 293: Su concessione del Ministero della Cultura Pinacoteca Nazionale di Siena. Foto archivio Pinacoteca Nazionale di Siena **Fig. 295, 299, 313:** Photo: Saskia Quené **Fig. 301, 303:** Getty (Public Domain) **Fig. 304:** © 2024. Photo Scala, Fondazione Magnani Rocca **Fig. 307:** Metropolitan Museum of Art (Public Domain) **Fig. 308, 316:** © Gabinetto Fotografico, Gallerie degli Uffizi **Fig. 310:** © Photo: Andrea Lensini **Fig. 311, 318:** © Bridgeman Images **Fig. 319:** Photo: Gregor von Kerssenbrock-Krosigk **Fig. 321:** © Staatliche Museen zu Berlin, Gemäldegalerie / Jörg P. Anders

Leonardos Untergrund: Zur Gedächtniskunst des Pausens
Nicola Suthor

Fig. 327, 328, 336, 354, 368: Royal Collection Trust / © His Majesty King Charles III **Fig. 345, 346, 353:** Photo (C) RMN-Grand Palais (musée du Louvre) / Michel Urtado **Fig. 348:** © Photo: Ghigo G. Roli **Fig. 357, 360, 362, 365:** © The Trustees of the British Museum / Art Resource, NY **Fig. 358:** © Gemäldegalerie, SMB / Christoph Schmidt

Zwischen Gestaltpsychologie und Kunstwissenschaft: Zur Ideen- und Begriffsgeschichte von ‚Figur und Grund'
Tom Steinert

Fig. 378: Staatliche Museen zu Berlin, Nationalgalerie / Andres Kilger (CC BY-NC-SA 4.0) **Fig. 380, 408:** Scan from original publication: author **Fig. 385, 389, 391:** © The Trustees of the British Museum **Fig. 387:** Metropolitan Museum of Art, Public Domain **Fig. 395, 398, 399, 401, 402, 403, 405, 406, 410:** © author

Zwei Meta-Physiken des Bildes? Zur Figur/Grund-Relation in der Vormoderne aus der Perspektive dreistelliger Bildbegriffe
Christoph Poetsch

Fig. 454: © Domkapitel Aachen, Photo: Pit Siebigs **Fig. 455, 561:** Wikimedia Commons (https://commons.wikimedia.org/wiki/File:Disputa_del_Sacramento_(Rafael).jpg) **Fig. 464, 466:** © 2024. Biblioteca Apostolica Vaticana. Reproduced by permission of Biblioteca Apostolica Vaticana, with all rights reserved.

What Guides the Beholder's Eye: Figures, Ground, or Perspective?
Raphael Rosenberg

Fig. 477, 478b–f, 479a–c, 481b–c, 482b–c, 483b–c, 484b–c, 486b–c, 493b–c: © CReA, University of Vienna **Fig. 478a:** © Foto: Erich Lessing **Fig. 481a, 482a, 484a, 486a, 493a:** Wikimedia Commons **Fig. 483a:** © Richard Stracke, https://www.christianiconography.info/Edited%20in%202013/Italy/lastSupperBarocci.html

Painting Shadows in the Middle Ages
Aden Kumler

Fig. 499: Photo Scala, Florence / Fondo Edifici di Culto – Min. dell'Interno **Fig. 501:** Photo: The Walters Art Museum, CC0 **Fig. 507, 508:** courtesy of Getty's Open Content Program **Fig. 512, 513:** The Morgan Library & Museum Fig. 518: Photo: Universitäts- und Landesbibliothek, Darmstadt **Fig. 520, 522, 524:** Reproduced with permission of the Biblioteca Medicea Laurenziana **Fig. 527:** © Bibliotheca Apostolica Vaticana, Vatikan **Fig. 529:** Universitätsbibliothek Heidelberg **Fig. 531:** Photo: BnF / Gallica **Fig. 533, 534:** ÖNB **Fig. 538:** Photo: author. **Fig. 539:** Augustinermuseum Freiburg

Smoke and Mirrors? The (In)visible Worlds of David Bailly
Karin Leonhard

Figs. 547, 552, 575, 579: Museum De Lakenhal, Leiden – René Gerritsen fotografie **Fig. 551, 552:** Alfred Darcel: 'Exposition de Lille', in: Gazette des Beaux-Arts 1874, p. 485. **Fig. 554:** © Rijksmuseum, Amsterdam **Fig. 555:** Private Collection, long-term loan to the Rijksmuseum, 2023 / Photo: Carola van Wijk **Fig. 556, 557, 560:** RKD (Netherland Institute for Art History) **Fig. 562:** Scan from original publication: Author **Figs. 569,:** Erma Hermens / Museum De Lakenhal, Leiden **Fig. 577:** © RMN-Grand Palais (musée du Louvre) / Tony Querrec

Embedded Space in Early Renaissance Painting
Péter Bokody

Fig. 585: © Creative Commons License **Fig. 588:** © Photo: Giacomo Guazzini **Fig. 594, 596, 597, 598:** © Photo Scala, Florence **Fig. 603:** © His Majesty King Charles III 2023 **Fig. 606:** © KHM-Museumsverband **Fig. 607, 609** © Metropolitan Museum of Art, Public Domain **Fig. 611, 613:** © RMN-Grand Palais (musée du Louvre) / Michèle Bellot

Zeit als Figur ohne Grund
Jürgen Müller

Fig. 617, 620, 621, 634, 635, 642: Wikimedia Commons **Fig. 630:** Metropolitan Museum of Art, Public Domain **Fig. 633:** Wikimedia Commons, edited by Jürgen Müller **Fig. 645:** © Bayerische Staatsbibliothek, München, CC BY-NC-SA 4.0 **Fig. 647:** Rijksmuseum, Amsterdam, Public Domain